Collaborative Computing: Networking and Applications

Collaborative Computing: Networking and Applications

Edited by Leland Morrow

CLANRYE
INTERNATIONAL
www.clanryeinternational.com

Clanrye International,
750 Third Avenue, 9ᵗʰ Floor,
New York, NY 10017, USA

ISBN: 978-1-63240-590-6

Cataloging-in-Publication Data

Collaborative computing : networking and applications / edited by Leland Morrow.
   p. cm.
Includes bibliographical references and index.
ISBN 978-1-63240-590-6
1. Computer networks. 2. Electronic data processing--Distributed processing. 3. Multimedia systems.
4. Online social networks. 5. Web co-browsing. I. Morrow, Leland.
TK5105.5 .C65 2017
004.6--dc23

For information on all Clanrye International publications
visit our website at www.clanryeinternational.com

Printed in the United States of America.

Contents

Preface

Over the recent decade, advancements and applications have progressed exponentially. This has led to the increased interest in this field and projects are being conducted to enhance knowledge. The main objective of this book is to present some of the critical challenges and provide insights into possible solutions. This book will answer the varied questions that arise in the field and also provide an increased scope for furthering studies.

Collaborative computing is the practice of involving multiple parties located at different regions to contribute ideas and suggestions to a common project or undertaking. This book on collaborative computing deals with the various applications that are available for editing and enhancing documents and media. Topics in this book seek to contribute to the simple and effective manner of collecting and verifying information that is followed by collaborative computing. From theories to research to practical applications, case studies related to all contemporary topics of relevance to this field have been included in this book. As this field is emerging at a rapid pace, the contents of this book will help the readers understand the modern concepts and applications of the subject. It will be of great help to students and researchers in the fields of software engineering, telecommunications and wireless networking.

I hope that this book, with its visionary approach, will be a valuable addition and will promote interest among readers. Each of the authors has provided their extraordinary competence in their specific fields by providing different perspectives as they come from diverse nations and regions. I thank them for their contributions.

Editor

Is Email Business Dying?: A Study on Evolution of Email Spam Over Fifteen Years[*]

De Wang[1,†], Danesh Irani[1,*], and Calton Pu[1,†]

[1]College of Computing, Georgia Institute of Technology, Atlanta, Georgia 30332-0765

Abstract

With the increasing dedication and sophistication of spammers, email spam is a persistent problem even today. Popular social network sites such as Facebook, Twitter, and Google+ are not exempt from email spam as they all interface with email systems. While some report predicts that email spam business is dying due to the decreasing volume of email spam. Whether email spam business is really dying is an interesting question. In this paper, we analyze email spam trends on Spam Archive dataset, which contains 5.5 million spam emails over 15 years (1998 – 2013). We statistically analyze emails contents including header information (e.g. content type) and embedded items (e.g. URL links). Also, we investigate topic drift using topic modeling technique. Moreover, we perform network analysis on sender-to-receiver IP routing networks. Our study shows the dynamic nature of email spam over one and a half decades and demonstrate that the email spam business is not dying but more capricious.

Keywords: email, spam, evolution

1. Introduction

As a method to communicate both for individuals and businesses everyday, email is also used as an information management tool [1]. What started primarily as a person-to-person communication medium has spread widely to one-to-many (e.g. mailing-lists) and many-to-one (e.g. forwarded traffic) communication medium [2]. As social media has grown dramatically, email also enhances the functionality provided by them. For instance, users are sometimes given pseudo-email addresses which can be used to receive emails on the social networks as well as email can sometimes be used to interact with the social networks using specially crafted email addresses.

Due to the convenience and popularity of email system, malicious users also take it as a major target to launch Denial of Information (DoI) attacks [3].

Spam pollution is one kind of DoI attacks, which prevents users from finding non-spam content. Spam is unsolicited and unrelated content sent to users, which most commonly is associated with email, but also applies to several different domains including instant messaging, websites, and Internet Telephony [4–8]. Spam degrades a user's experience as, by definition, it is an annoyance and gets in the way of users consuming non-spam content.

In August 1998, Cranor et al. [9] described the rapidly growing onslaught of unwanted email and since then the volume of spam has grown even more as the amount of all email sent has grown exponentially. Constituting an annoyance, email spam has increased to as much as 90% today [10] from approximately 10% of overall mail volume in 1998, which results in an enormous burden on the thousands of email service providers (ESPs) and millions of end users on the Internet [11].

In addition to being on the receiving side of spam, ESPs need to invest in developing filters to combat the spammers and likewise spammers evolve to avoid spam filters. The co-evolution nature of spammers and spam filters is an "arms-race", which has resulted in numerous publications employing

---

[*]Extended version of conference paper at CollaborateCom 2013.

[*]The work done on the paper was during Danesh Irani's PhD at Georgia Institute of Technology. He is software engineer at Google now.

[†]Corresponding authors. Email: wang6@gatech.edu, calton.pu@cc.gatech.edu

adversarial strategies to tackle the spam problem [12–14]. Pu et al. [15] and Fawcett [16] developed techniques for characterization and measurement of email spam trends and researchers have also examined other types of spam including phishing [17] and Web spam [18]. In addition, Guerra et al. [19] compared the effectiveness of old and recent filters over old and recent spam to obtain spam trends on email spam dataset.

In this paper, we investigate the trends of email spam in terms of content, topics, and sender-receiver network over 15 years by performing an evolutionary study on the Spam Archive dataset [20]. We aim to answer the question of whether the email spam business is dying (also, as identified by our title). More concretely, we make the following contributions:

- We perform a long-term evolutionary study on a large email spam dataset, which includes statistical analysis, topic modeling and network analysis.

- We demonstrate the changes of email spam over time with respect to contents and spammer behaviors.

- We prove that email spam business is not dying but is becoming sophisticated by the evolutionary study on large scale real data.

The remainder of the paper is organized as follows. We motivate the problem further in Section 2. Section 4 introduces the Spam Archive dataset used in our study. Section 5 presents the analysis performed on the dataset and findings derived from the results. Section 6 discusses the future of email spam business and the limitations of our study. We talk about related work in Section 3 and conclude the paper in Section 7.

2. Motivation

The paper is inspired by an article by Kaspersky labs [21] named "The dying business of email spam" [22], which stated that "Spam email is on the wane. And no one on God's green Earth is going to miss it". The conclusions were based on their annual report [23] citing that the share of spam in email traffic decreased steadily throughout 2012 to hit a five year low.

We are excited by the decline in the volume of email spam but it also raises the question as to whether the email spam business is dying and will continue to decline. Besides the volume change, we also consider the quality of email spam and the impact, which may be constituting a new trend of email spam business. For instance, spammers may post email spam in a more complicated way using spoofed email addresses and changing email relay servers. Those kind of email spam may slip away under the inspection of spam filters.

Thus, it motivated us to investigate the evolution of email spam using advanced techniques such as topic modeling and network analysis. We try to find out the real trend of email spam business through email content, meta information such as headers, and sender-to-receiver network over a long period of time.

3. Related Work

3.1. Email Spam Detection

Email spam detection has been studied by lots of researchers in different directions. For instance, Carreras et al. [24] applied boosting trees to filter out email spam. Wang et al. [25] used heuristic feature selection techniques to improve the performance of email spam filtering. Chan et al. [26] co-trained with a single natural feature set in email classification. Liu et al. [27] adopted multi-field learning for email spam classification. Sculley et al. [28] used relaxed online SVMs for email spam filtering. Besides those machine learning techniques, more researchers tried other kinds of detection methods. Attenberg et al. [29] introduced collaborative email spam filtering with the hashing trick. Balakumar et al. [30] offered ontology based classification of email. Dasgupta et al. [31] combined similarity graphs to enhance email spam filtering. Jung et al. [32] used DNS black lists and spam traffic to detect email spam. Ramachandran et al. [33] filtered email spam with behavioral blacklisting. Clayton et al. applied extrusion detection in stopping email spam by observing distinctive email traffic patterns. Xie et al. [34] provided an effective defense approach against email spam laundering. Additionally, researchers also have used email spam to help detecting other types of spam. For instance, Zhuang et al. [35] developed an approach to map botnet membership using traces of spam email. Webb et al. [36] identified an interesting link between email spam and Web spam and used it to extract large Web spam samples from the Web. Wang et al. [37] demonstrated the relationship among different formats of social spam including user profile spam, message spam and Web spam, in which message spam contain email spam.

3.2. Information Retrieval on Email Data

Another focus of researchers is information retrieval on email data. Bird et al. [38] constructed social networks of email correspondents to address some interesting questions such as the social status of different types of participants and the relationship of email activity and other activities. McCallum et al. [39] illustrated experimental study on Enron and academic email to discover topic and role in social networks from emails, in which the model builds on Latent Dirichlet Allocation (LDA) and the Author-Topic (AT) model.

Culotta et al. [40] presented an end-to-end system that extracts a user's social network and its members' contact information given the user's email inbox.

3.3. Evolutionary Study of Spam

Research work on evolutionary study of spam is close to this paper [41, 42]. Pu et al. [15] presented a study on dataset collected from Spam Archive and focused on two evolutionary trends: extinction and existence. Irani et al. [17] studied the evolution of phishing email messages and classified them into two groups: flash attacks and non-flash attacks. Wang et al. [18, 43] compared two large Web spam corpus: Webb spam corpus 2006 and Webb spam corpus 2011 and shown the trending of Web spam. Chung et al. [44] and Fetterly et al. [45] also have done intensive study on evolution of web spam. Guerra et al. [19] investigated how the popularity of spam construction techniques changes when filters start to detect them and determined automatically techniques that seemed more resistant than others. The evolution of spamming techniques shows the increasing sophistication of spammers. Our work focuses on tactics changes of email spam over time and inspires more researchers to work on email spam detection collaboratively.

4. Data Collection

In this section, we introduce the Spam Archive dataset and show the overview of the dataset used in our study.

Spam Archive dataset [20] is collected by Bruce Guenter since early 1998 using honey-pot addresses. The project is still ongoing with monthly releases of new email spam. Since it provides a continuous long-term email spam data source from a consistent source, it is an excellent dataset for our investigation into spam trends. The volume of email messages received over the 15 years is shown in Fig. 1, with the date on the x-axis and log-scale volume of email messages received per month on the y-axis. From the figure we see that email spam volume grows steadily over time. For the spike of email spam during 2006, Bruce Guenter has attributed this to one of the spam traps having a wild-card address which received increasingly large amounts of spam which was subsequently disabled after 2006, since most of the spam was duplicates of other spam received.

Besides showing the trend of overall volume of email spam, we also present the volume changes monthly for different years in Fig. 2, with the month of the year on the x-axis and the log-scale volume of spam messages per month on the y-axis. It shows volume trends over the previous 15 years. The volume of email spam is not always increasing over time such as the email spam volume changes during 1999. Some years' volumes also shows fluctuations over time. For instance,

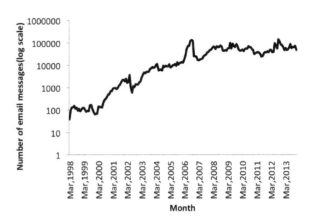

Figure 1. Number of email messages (per month) over time

during 2002, the volume first went up in May and decreased dramatically afterward until July. Several factors may have contributed to this change such as new strategies used by spammers (e.g. image spam is introduced in emails), improved spam filters (e.g. URL analysis tool is adopted) and even political influence from governments (e.g. Electronic Communications and Transactions Act, 2002 [46]). We investigate the details and potential reasons of these changes in more detail in the following sections.

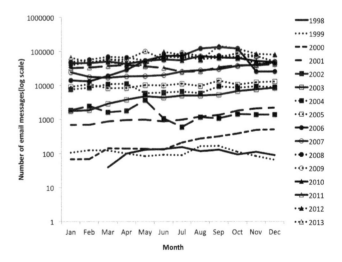

Figure 2. Number of email messages in month order for different years

5. Data Analysis

In this section, we start with content analysis of Spam Archive dataset, followed by topic modeling and network analysis.

5.1. Content Analysis

The two main types of email message content are "Text" and "Multipart". Messages in type "Text" are simple text messages while messages in type "Multipart" have parts arranged in a tree structure where the leaf nodes are any non-multipart content type and the non-leaf nodes are any of a variety of multipart types [47]. To have a better sense of the distribution of main types in email spam, we show the main type distribution in different years in Fig. 3.

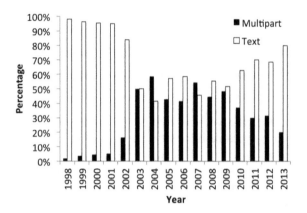

Figure 3. The distribution of main types of message content

Fig. 3 demonstrates that the distribution of two main types in our dataset changed over time. For instance, before 2003, more email spam had the message format in the main type "Text". After that, the two main types almost occupied the same percentage until 2010. The new trend is that email spam is using more messages in main type "Text" (e.g. the percentage of email spam in main type "Text" is about 80% for the year of 2013).

Next thing we are interested in is the embedded items in email spam such as HTML web page, images, and URL links. After scanning all email spam in our dataset, we present the distribution of embedded items in email spam over time in Fig. 4.

Fig. 4 shows that low percentage of email spam, which was always less than 5% in our dataset, contained image attachments. On the contrary, more email spam had embedded HTML web pages and URL links. But the percentages of email spam containing HTML web pages and URL links changed dramatically over time. Several peaks and valleys appeared over 15 years in the Fig. 4. For instance, HTML pages had peaks in 2003, 2007, and 2009 and valleys in 2006 and 2008. While for URL links, peaks appeared in 2004, 2008 and 2012 and valleys appeared in 2006 and 2011. Since HTML page normally carries URL links, they should have similar fluctuations along the time. However, we observe that an exception occurred after 2011. The percentage of email spam containing HTML web pages decreased suddenly after 2009. While the percentage

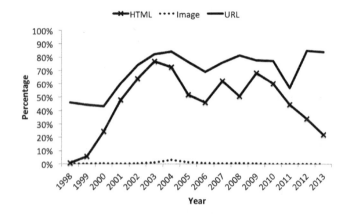

Figure 4. The distribution of embedded items in email spam over time

of email spam containing URL links dropped down along with HTML web pages until 2011 and it increased sharply afterwards. One possible reason is that more URL camouflage techniques, which are quite efficient in avoiding spam filters, appeared such as shortened URLs and hidden URLs in recent years. To investigate further the trend of URL links, we aggregate all URL links on a yearly basis for email spam that contain URL links and show the cumulative distribution of URL links in email spam in Fig. 5 (1998 – 2013).

Fig. 5 shows the number of URL links for the majority of email spam is below 10. Only a small portion of email spam have more than 1,000 URL links which may be embedded in different depths of email messages. Even though the densities of URL links in email spam changed variously, email spam contained more and more URL links over time.

Through the analysis, we obtain the following observation (**Observation I**):

- In terms of percentage, very few image embedded items appear in the email spam. One possible reason is that email system, such as the Gmail system, adopts new policy to automatically hide the images in emails unless user chooses to display them.

- Email spam contains more text and more URL links in recent years. Many URL links are legitimate URL links such as Facebook or Google official website. Spammers use legitimate URL attack to avoid detection and increase the cost of filtering at least since the spam filter needs to go through all the URL links in email to distinguish the message from legitimate ones.

In addition to looking into embedded items, we also investigate the top *n*-grams in email spam over time. The tool we used for obtaining n-grams of email spam is

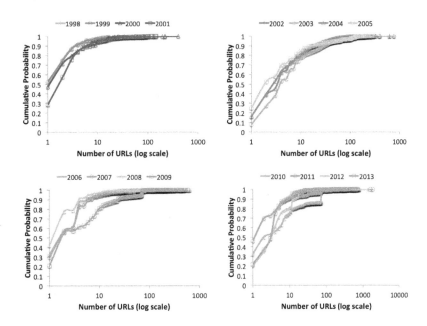

Figure 5. Cumulative distribution of URL links in different years

Perl's module Text::Ngrams [48]. First, we need to clean our dataset by filtering out stop words and striping out HTML tags. And then we calculate top-10 n-grams (n ranges from 1 to 3) on a monthly basis over 15 years. Due to space limit, we only list the top-10 n-grams starting from June 1998 to June 2013, which is shown in Table 1.

In Table 1, $\langle N \rangle$ denotes any number sequence. Top-10 n-grams set contained different words or word sequences along the time, showing different topics as well. For instance, the n-grams set in June 1998 tells us that the email spam was advertising fake dental services using attractive words such as "free", "nationwide near", and "month save average". The n-grams set in June 2003 was about marketing and market leaders leading people to click external URL links. The n-grams set in June 2008 was about DASS (Defensive Aids Sub System) [49] which is a fighter system from European countries. After checking the original email, it is a trap news or game to attract the email receivers to enter into. The n-grams set in June 2013 was more related to new media announcement and membership registration. Thus, we have the observation (**Observation II**):

- The content of N-gram sets changed over time. Spammers try to obtain users' interests by keeping the content up-to-date and attractive. Also, frequent changes of contents make email spam hard to be detected by spam filters based on content analysis.

Moreover, the differences indicate the topic drift in email spam over time (e.g. from fake advertising to fake registration services). To learn more about the topic

drift of email spam, we will apply topic modeling on the dataset next.

5.2. Topic Modeling

Topic modeling is defined as a technique that looks for patterns in the use of words and it is an attempt to inject semantic meaning into vocabulary, in which a "topic" consists of a cluster of words that frequently occur together [50]. The tool we used in our topic modeling is a machine learning toolkit for language named "MALLET" [50]. It provides an efficient way to build up topic models based on Latent Dirichlet Allocation model (LDA) [51].

To simplify the illustration, we set up the number of topics to 10 in the data processing. After the calculation, we obtain the word (also called term) lists associated with topics and topic composition for different months over time, which is shown in Table 2 and Fig. 6.

In Table 2, it shows the topic name and the samples of the most related terms. After the topic modeling, we only have the word or term clusters for each topic which has not been labeled. Based on associated terms with each topic and experience with email spam, we label the topics as "Account Information", "Order Information", "Business News", "Sales News", "Adult Product", "Software Product", "Official News", "Free Product", "Medical Product", and "Newsletter" separately. Due to the space limit, we just list sample of most related terms for each topic in Table 2.

Fig. 6 shows the topic drift in our dataset. We observe that the popular topics drifted along the time. Before 2004, the topic "Business News" was the most popular topic in email spam. After that, the most popular

Table 1. List of top-10 n-grams every 5 years on a monthly basis (n ranges from 1 to 3)

June, 1998	June, 2003	June, 2008	June, 2013
dental	$\langle N \rangle$	$\langle N \rangle$	$\langle N \rangle$
free	click	euro	important
plan	email	dass	garden
$\langle N \rangle$	information	online	class
details	bait	http	email
call	mail	mail	media
please	free	original	screen
doctor	message	super	dark
dentistry	work	time	right
procedures	please	active	registration
plan free	$\langle N \rangle \langle N \rangle$	$\langle N \rangle \langle N \rangle$	$\langle N \rangle \langle N \rangle$
teeth whitening	email bait	euro euro	garden $\langle N \rangle$
nationwide near	august $\langle N \rangle$	super active	$\langle N \rangle$ garden
waiting periods	market information	active euro	media screen
root canals	world leader	tabs doses	important media
details june	auction records	kinder dass	important important
dental procedures	remove email	autopilot dass	dark skin
canals crowns	reply message	original stress	screen class
doctor locator	link work	stress angst	class important
polishing fillings	leader market	angst dass	rights reserved
sealants prevent cavities	$\langle N \rangle \langle N \rangle \langle N \rangle$	$\langle N \rangle \langle N \rangle \langle N \rangle$	garden $\langle N \rangle$ garden
doctor locator number	world leader market	euro euro euro	$\langle N \rangle$ garden $\langle N \rangle$
crowns dentures braces	leader market information	active euro euro	$\langle N \rangle \langle N \rangle \langle N \rangle$
problems qualify waiting	case link work	super active euro	important media screen
month save average	demander plus figurer	dass kinder dass	media screen class
receive optical plan	allow mail removed	dass autopilot dass	important important media
call $\langle N \rangle$ please	removed thank operation	dass dass kinder	class important media
canals crowns dentures	modifier sera effective	autopilot dass dass	screen class important
optical plan free	message modifier sera	original stress angst	limited become member
plan receive optical	effective coop demander	kinder dass super	become member soon

Table 2. List of topics and associated terms

Topic Name	Samples of Most Related Terms
Account Information	email important pass check account address information
Order Information	click message privacy online policy information address view order receive required
Business News	click information price free professional time link business work
Sales News	price life money make time today offer year online real world women retail deal credit
Adult Product	world price penis back people product degree patch life make great experience enlarge
Software Product	price professional click software company copy softwares read suite online site office
Official News	united states world state national city government international people
Free Product	online pills price click quality save products email item prices service offer free
Medical Product	generic save price time products medications order pharmacy home service product
Newsletter	mail click email privacy newsletter message receive view offers link subscribed

topic changed more frequently than before. First, the most popular topic changed to "Software Product" for around a year. And then it changed back to the topic "Business News" again. And later on, the most popular topic changes happened in the following order: "Adult Product", "Free Product", "Sales News", "Free Product", "Newsletter", "Official News", "Order Information", "Medical Product", and "Account Information". For each topic, it contains certain features that are attractive to certain group of users. For instance, topic "Free Product" is more attractive to users who like free stuff. Topic "Medical Product" is more attractive to users

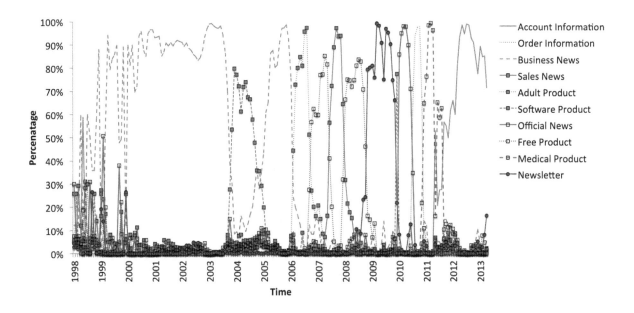

Figure 6. Topic drift in time order (time unit: month)

who need medical service or special medical products. Topic "Sales News" and "Order Information" are more attractive to users who like shopping. Meanwhile, as social media have interfaces with email systems normally and gain increasing popularity, email spam which have the content related to social media are growing rapidly. For instance, by investigating the content of email messages which belonging to the recent most popular topic "Account Information", we observe that a lot of email spam have associations with social media. One example is that social media account registration email spam which contains spam URLs that camouflaged as confirmation URL links. Another example is social media account notifications. For example, it informs you that your account has been changed by someone and needs immediate action to reset the password, followed by the spam URL links. Thus, one possible reason why the topic "Account information" becomes popular is that a lot of spammers try to impersonate the support team of social media to steal sensitive information, such as credential and credit information, or lead users to spam or phishing web pages for further actions. Thus, we conclude our observation as follows (**Observation III**):

- The topic "Business News" dominated in earlier years while the topic "Account Information" dominates recently. Topic drift happened frequently between 2004 and 2011. Meanwhile, lots of social engineering attacks are launched in later email spam.

5.3. Network Analysis

Besides content analysis and topic modeling, we also try to find out the sending behavior changes of spammers over time through analyzing the routing network between sender and receiver. Before entering into the detail of network analysis, we will talk about data processing and some findings during the process.

For the data processing, we need to process the headers of email message to obtain the information about routing between sender and receiver. The headers which are related to the routing info are "From", "To", "CC", "BCC" and "Received". The header "From" and "To" provide the sender and receiver email addresses. The header "CC" and "BCC" show the recipient lists in carbon copy and blind carbon copy mode. The header "Received" contains routing information from sender and receiver. First, we look into the headers "From" and "To" and intend to use them to extract the sender-to-receiver network. However, the fact is that we cannot use them in our study since most of the messages in the dataset contain forged "From" headers in one form or another, which is also mentioned in the Spam Archive dataset homepage. Although "From" header should not be trusted, we still extract top-10 domains from the "From" header to find out what are those popular domains used by spammers to set up social engineering traps for users. It is hard for users to recognize fake senders based on senders' email address especially when the email address is belonging to the domains they trust. The list of top-10 domains is shown in Table 3.

Table 3. List of top-10 domains

1998	1999	2000	2001
hotmail.com	yahoo.com	yahoo.com	hotmail.com
yahoo.com	hotmail.com	hotmail.com	yahoo.com
msn.com	aol.com	earthlink.net	excite.com
usa.net	usa.net	aol.com	msn.com
earthlink.net	ibm.net	usa.net	aol.com
att.net	msn.com	excite.com	btamail.net.cn
aol.com	iname.com	mail.com	earthlink.net
mailexcite.com	hotbot.com	bigfoot.com	mail.com
juno.com	bigfoot.com	email.com	pacbell.net
prodigy.com	mailcity.com	postmark.net	mail.ru

2002	2003	2004	2005
yahoo.com	yahoo.com	yahoo.com	yahoo.com
hotmail.com	hotmail.com	hotmail.com	hotmail.com
aol.com	aol.com	msn.com	msn.com
msn.com	msn.com	yahoo.co.kr	yahoo.co.kr
excite.com	artauction.net	aol.com	gmail.com
link2buy.com	earthlink.net	attbi.com	yahoo.co.jp
eudoramail.com	excite.com	yahoo.co.jp	163.com
flashmail.com	artaddiction.com	excite.com	msa.hinet.net
netscape.net	juno.com	seznam.cz	mail.com
btamail.net.cn	artists-server.com	netscape.net	126.com

2006	2007	2008	2009
yahoo.co.jp	yahoo.com	dyndns.org	dyndns.org
hotmail.com	dyndns.org	yahoo.com	homeip.net
mail.ru	hotmail.com	adelphia.com	untroubled.org
0451.com	yahoo.co.jp	hotmail.com	gmail.com
em.ca	paran.com	gmail.com	hotmail.com
yahoo.com	gmail.com	wikipedia.org	yahoo.com
0733.com	163.com	earthlink.net	untroubled.org
aol.com	msn.com	att.net	ezmlm.org
infoseek.jp	msa.hinet.net	163.com	em.ca
msn.com	so-net.ne.jp	cox.net	mail.ru

2010	2011	2012	2013
dyndns.org	yahoo.com	yahoo.com	yahoo.co.jp
yahoo.com	dyndns.org	garden.md	li-brooz.jp
homeip.net	ymail.com	yahoo.co.jp	yahoo.com
untroubled.org	gmail.com	ageha.cc	mixi1mega.biz
untroubled.org	mail.ru	peach.6060.jp	netstar-inc.co.uk
ezmlm.org	msn.com	ts5558.com	garden.md
em.ca	bk.ru	momoiro.cc	for-dear-2013.mobi
comcast.net	qip.ru	koikoilkoii.com	wakuwaku06.info
gmail.com	list.ru	wakuwaku-happy.net	greemmix.info
pfizer.com	aol.com	get-c.com	docomo.ne.jp

From Table 3, we observe that several popular email domains are used by spammers such as "yahoo.com", "hotmail.com", "msn.com", and "gmail.com". Also some top domains are related to receiver domains such as "untroubled.org" and "dyndns.org". It reveals that spammers were camouflaging themselves coming from the same domains as the users' domains. In addition, some domains in the top-10 list are from countries outside US such as "163.com" which is the largest email service domain in China. In 2013, the top domains list contains more special domains such as ".biz" which is intended for registration of domains to be used by businesses and ".mobi" which is used by mobile devices for accessing Internet resources via the Mobile Web. It indicates that spammers were spoofing the sender addresses targeting business and mobile users.

Meanwhile, it proves that spammers recognize the trend of information flow in the Internet and evolve to take advantage of the trending.

Next, we investigate the header "CC" and "BCC" in email message to know whether spammers use those functions to spread email spam. The trends of "CC" and "BCC" are shown in Fig. 7.

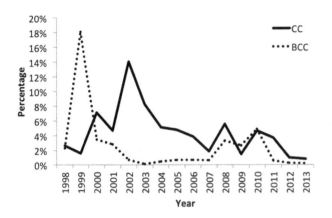

Figure 7. Cc and Bcc trends

Fig. 7 shows that spammers used more "CC" and "BCC" in the early years (1999-2004) and less in the recent years (2011-2013). One possible reason is that most spam filters have taken the number of "CC" and "BCC" as important features to detect spam [52]. Meanwhile, people become alert to email message which contains a long recipient list in the header "CC" and "BCC" so that this type of email spam lost markets gradually.

Thus, we conclude the observation as follows (**Observation IV**):

- Fields "FROM" and "TO" cannot be trusted. Meanwhile, they are used in social engineering attacks to camouflage email spam as emails from legitimate domains.

- Spammers use less CC and BCC now. Besides, they are also easy to be forged. So, they cannot be used in our network analysis.

Based on observations above, we realize that the header "From", "To", "CC", and "BCC" are not helpful in extracting routing network from email spam. To have a better understanding of the changes in terms of spammers' behaviors, we still need to find a way to extract the real sender and the routing information.

The header "RECEIVED" provides us the routing information such as hops' IP addresses between sender and receiver. Here is one example "RECEIVED" field in email header shown in Figure 8:

Due to that the "RECEIVED" field is hard to be forged, we will use it to extract sender-to-receiver IP

```
Return-path: <sender@senderdomain.tld>
Delivery-date: Wed, 13 Apr 2011 00:31:13
+0200
(3) Received: from mailexchanger.recipient
domain.tld([ccc.ccc.ccc.ccc]) by mailserver.
recipientdomain.tld running ExIM with
esmtp id xxxxxx-xxxxxx-xxx; Wed, 13
Apr 2011 01:39:23 +0200
(2) Received: from mailserver.senderdomain.
tld ([bbb.bbb.bbb.bbb] by mailexchanger.
recipientdomain.tld with esmtp id xxxxxx-
xxxxxx-xx for recipient@recipientdomain.tld;
Wed, 13 Apr 2011 01:39:23 +0200
(1) Received: from senderhostname [aaa.
aaa.aaa.aaa]} by mailserver.senderdomain.tld
 with esmtpa (Exim x.xx) (envelope-from
<sender@senderdomain.tld) id xxxxx-
xxxxxx-xxxx for recipient@recipientdomain.tld;
Tue, 12 Apr 2011 20:36:08 -0100
Message-ID: <xxxxxxxx.xxxxxxxx@senderdomain.
tld>
Date: Tue, 12 Apr 2011 20:36:01 -0100
X-Mailer: Mail Client
From: Sender Name <sender@senderdomain.tld>
To: Recipient Name <recipient@recipientdomain.tld>
Subject: Message Subject
```

Figure 8. Example of "RECEIVED" field in email header

routing information and construct routing network. The tool we used in extraction is the email module in Python [53] and the network analysis tool is the open source network visualization software Gephi [54].

During the process of extracting networks, we also collect two extra features: average hops between sender and receiver and the Geolocation distribution of sender IP addresses. The list of average hops and the Geolocation distribution of sender IP addresses over time are shown in Fig. 9 and Fig. 10 respectively.

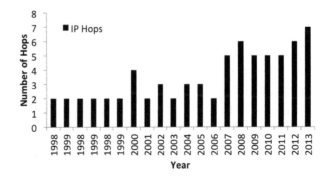

Figure 9. Average hops between sender and receiver

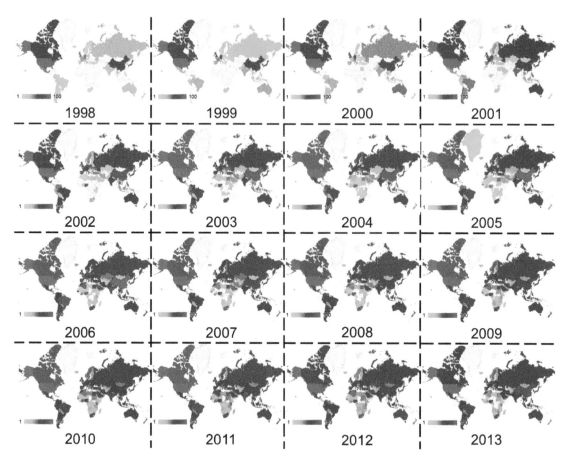

Figure 10. Geolocation distribution of senders' IP addresses (in log scale and normalized)

Fig. 9 presents the trend of average hops between sender and receiver. We observe that the number of hops was increasing over time. For instance, the average hops for 1998 was only two while it became almost eight in 2013. One possible reason is that it increased the cost for spam filters to detect or trace back the senders of email spam as spammers used more hops through intermediate proxies. It also indicates that the sender-to-receiver network becomes more complicated.

The study of header "Received" finds out the following observations (**Observation V**):

- "RECEIVED" header is hard to be forged since it is updated along the path from the sender to the receiver.

- Spammers use more mail exchange services to avoid detection.

Fig. 10 shows the Geolocation distribution of senders' IP addresses over time. Due to space limit, we only present the Geolocation maps every two years based on the normalized number of IP addresses coming from different countries. We use the GeoIP service provided by MaxMind [55] to do the mapping between IP address and Geolocation. Also, we employ Google Geo Chart APIs [56] to implement the map drawing.

The number of IP addresses from different countries has been put into log scale and then normalized into the same range from 1 to 100. Also we use green color to label countries who had the fewest sender IP address and red color to label countries who had the more sender IP addresses. White color means that no sender IP address came from the country. Observing the maps, we have the following findings in our dataset: 1) the sender IP addresses almost come from all over the world; 2) United States has the largest number of sender IP addresses along the past fifteen years; 3) Besides United States, the distribution of sender IP addresses shows dynamic changes over time. For instance, the number of sender IP addresses coming from China kept increasing until 2007 and grew again in 2013. Also, some countries had sudden increase of sender IP addresses in particular years. For example, Canada and France had sudden increase in 2003. India had sudden increase in 2011. And Japan had sudden increase in 2013. It indicates that spammers used global email service servers and also kept changing the traffic from different countries. Thus, we obtain the following observation (**Observation VI**):

- The sender IP addresses come from all over the world. United States has the largest number of

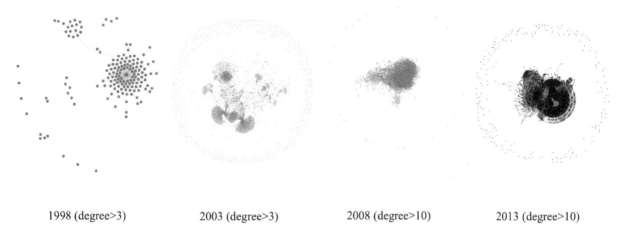

1998 (degree>3)   2003 (degree>3)   2008 (degree>10)   2013 (degree>10)

Figure 11. Sender-to-receiver routing networks every five years from 1998 to 2013

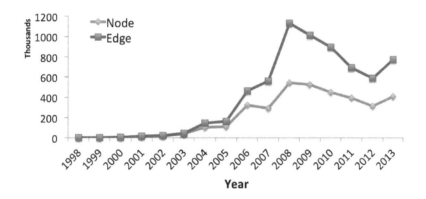

Figure 12. The trends of nodes and edges from 1998 to 2013

sender IP addressees. Generally, the distribution of IP addresses changes over time.

For the purpose of better visualization, we remove those nodes whose degree is lower than certain threshold. And also due to the space limit, we only present the network graph every five years (1998, 2003, 2008, and 2013) in Fig. 11. For 1998 and 2003, we keep the nodes whose degree is greater than 3. While for 2008 and 2013, we keep the nodes whose degree is greater than 10. The reason is that too many node overlaps occur if we choose the threshold 3 for 2008 and 2013.

Fig. 11 shows the sender-to-receiver routing network based on the IP addresses extracted from email header "Received". We observe that the complexity of graph increases explicitly along the time. For 2013, the routing network has shown much more complicated than the routing network in 2008. We also draw the trends of nodes and edges from 1998 to 2013 shown in Figure 12. In 2008, the number of nodes and edges reached the peak and later on they were decreasing to

the valley in 2012. But the number of nodes and edges increased a lot in 2013. We summarize the observation as follows (**Observation VII**):

- Connection network is changing over time. Networks in recent years are more complicated than networks in earlier years.

- The number of nodes and edges have a peak value in 2008 and a valley value in 2012. The new trend is that they are both increasing.

Next, we extract the networks from our dataset for each year and use three major metrics to measure the complexity of them. The three metrics are network diameter (the longest of all the calculated shortest paths in a network), average degree (average number of edges connected to or from one node), and average clustering coefficient (a measure of degree to which nodes in a network tend to cluster together). We use those metrics to show the trend of complexity of email sender-to-receiver connection network. if the values of those metrics are large, it indicates that the complexity of

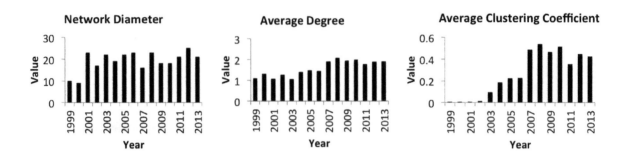

Figure 13. The comparison of three metrics from 1999 to 2013

connection network is high. The result of measurement is shown in Fig. 13.

Fig. 13 shows the three metrics comparison from 1999 to 2012. The values of them have the increasing trend overall but fluctuations existed along the time. Network diameter became more stable after 2007 and it is the same for the metrics average degree and average clustering coefficient. Those metrics kept staying at high value in terms of complexity of network. Thus, we have the following observation (**Observation VIII**):

- The complexity of networks is staying at high level and has no sign of decrease.

6. Discussion

Our large-scale evolutionary study on email spam dataset in a long period of time shows the trend of email spam business. Although the volume of email spam had a slight drop in recent years, we cannot conclude that email spam business is dying and email spam filters have won the battle against spammers. Through intensive analysis including content analysis, topic modeling and network analysis, we demonstrated that the battle is still ongoing and even worse since spammers become more sophisticated and capricious. Moreover, our study still have the following limitations and future work to do.

The dataset we used does not cover all the email spam over the fifteen years, which may influence the accuracy of our results, especially for the portion in the early years such as 1998-2000 that contains small number of email spam. Also, the bait email addresses used in data collection may cause some biases in the dataset. For example, the domain of the email address may result in that spammers forge their email addresses to the same domain.

Besides the limitation on dataset, we also have limitation on our analysis. In the topic modeling analysis, we set up the number of topics to 10 that may influence the result of topic modeling . If we change the number of topics to larger value, the result may be more accurate and fine-grained. But it should

not conflict with our conclusion that the topic drift occurs frequently over time. We will take the fine-grained analysis as future work. Additionally, in the network analysis, we used the study of the header "Received" to extract sender-to-receiver network. But we cannot guarantee that no forged information exists in the header "Received". Spammers also have some techniques to spoof the header "Received" but the portion of forged headers is low since it costs spammers a lot and has certain strict requirements to meet. We will also look into the further validation work in the future.

7. Conclusions

Spam Archive dataset, which contains over 5.5 million email messages from 1998 to 2013, provides research opportunity for us to explore the real trend of email spam. In this paper, we performed a long-term (over 15 years) evolutionary study on this large scale email spam corpus. Content analysis of email spam including n-grams analysis shows the change of email content and new attacks from spammers such as legitimate URL attack and short URL camouflage. It inspires us to investigate the topic change and complexity of spamming activities. Thus, we adopted topic modeling and network analysis techniques to study topic drift and complexity of sending behaviors of spammers.

For topic modeling on email spam, we clustered the dataset based on LDA model and categorized them into ten topics: "Account Information", "Order Information", "Business News", "Sales News", "Adult Product", "Software Product", "Official News", "Free Product", "Medical Product", and "Newsletter" based on the most related terms associated. The result shows spammers changed topics over time and those topics are very attractive to users. We also found out two dominant topics, "Business News" and "Account Information", in earlier years and recent years separately. The examples we gave show that many social engineering attacks have been launched from spammers. For network analysis on complexity of spamming activities, we presented social engineering attacks from spammers by observing senders' domains. After studying the header "Received", we extracted sender IP addresses and the sender-to-receiver routing networks from the dataset. The Geolocation distribution of senders' IP addresses shows that spammers employed the servers all over the world and dynamically switched locations among different countries. Moreover, we chose three metrics: network diameter, average degree, and average clustering coefficient to measure the complexity of routing networks, showing that the sending behaviors of spammers are becoming more complicated and harder to track.

To sum up, we have obtained many new observations (Observation I-VIII). Those observations show that email spam business is becoming more sophisticated along the time and the spammers behind it evolve into more capricious in the ongoing battle with spam filters.

Acknowledgement. This research has been partially funded by National Science Foundation by CNS/SAVI (1250260), IUCRC/FRP (1127904) , CISE/CNS (1138666), RAPID (1138666), CISE/CRI (0855180), NetSE (0905493) programs, and gifts, grants, or contracts from DARPA/I2O, Singapore Government, Fujitsu Labs, and Georgia Tech Foundation through the John P. Imlay, Jr. Chair endowment. Any opinions, findings, and conclusions or recommendations expressed in this material are those of the author(s) and do not necessarily reflect the views of the National Science Foundation or other funding agencies and companies mentioned above.

References

[1] S. Whittaker, V. Bellotti, and J. Gwizdka, "Email in personal information management," *ACM Communications*, vol. 49, pp. 68–73, Jan. 2006.

[2] R. Clayton, "Email traffic: a quantitative snapshot," in *the 4th Conference on Email and Anti-Spam (CEAS 2007)*, (Mountain View, CA, USA), July 2007.

[3] "DoI: Denial of Information." http://www.cc.gatech.edu/projects/doi/, 2014.

[4] M. Sahami, S. Dumais, D. Heckerman, and E. Horvitz, "A bayesian approach to filtering junk e-mail," in *Learning for text categorization: papers from the 1998 workshop*, 1998.

[5] A. Cournane and R. Hunt, "An analysis of the tools used for the generation and prevention of spam," *Computers & Security*, vol. 23, no. 2, pp. 154 – 166, 2004.

[6] Z. Gyongyi and H. Garcia-Molina, "Web spam taxonomy," Technical Report 2004-25, Stanford InfoLab, March 2004.

[7] S. Y. Park, J.-T. Kim, and S.-G. Kang, "Analysis of applicability of traditional spam regulations to voip spam," in *Advanced Communication Technology, 2006. ICACT 2006. The 8th International Conference*, vol. 2, pp. 3 pp.–1217, 2006.

[8] P. Hayati, V. Potdar, A. Talevski, N. Firoozeh, S. Sarenche, and E. Yeganeh, "Definition of spam 2.0: New spamming boom," in *Proceedings of the 4th IEEE International Conference on Digital Ecosystems and Technologies (DEST)*, pp. 580–584, 2010.

[9] L. F. Cranor and B. A. LaMacchia, "Spam!," *ACM Communications*, vol. 41, pp. 74–83, Aug. 1998.

[10] MAAWG, "Email Metrics Report 2011," tech. rep., November 2011.

[11] J. Goodman, G. V. Cormack, and D. Heckerman, "Spam and the ongoing battle for the inbox," *ACM Communications*, vol. 50, pp. 24–33, Feb. 2007.

[12] N. Dalvi, P. Domingos, Mausam, S. Sanghai, and D. Verma, "Adversarial classification," in *Proceedings of the tenth ACM SIGKDD international conference on Knowledge discovery and data mining*, KDD '04, (New York, NY, USA), pp. 99–108, ACM, 2004.

[13] D. Chinavle, P. Kolari, T. Oates, and T. Finin, "Ensembles in adversarial classification for spam," in *Proceedings of the 18th ACM conference on Information and knowledge management*, CIKM '09, (New York, NY, USA), pp. 2015–2018, ACM, 2009.

[14] B. Biggio, G. Fumera, and F. Roli, "Evade hard multiple classifier systems," in *Applications of Supervised and Unsupervised Ensemble Methods* (O. Okun and G. Valentini, eds.), vol. 245 of *Studies in Computational Intelligence*, pp. 15–38, Springer Berlin Heidelberg, 2009.

[15] C. Pu and S. Webb, "Observed trends in spam construction techniques: A case study of spam evolution," in *Proceedings of the Third Conference on Email and Anti-Spam (CEAS 2006)*, (Mountain View, CA, USA), July 2006.

[16] T. Fawcett, ""in vivo" spam filtering: a challenge problem for kdd," *SIGKDD Explor. Newsl.*, vol. 5, pp. 140–148, Dec. 2003.

[17] D. Irani, S. Webb, J. Giffin, and C. Pu, "Evolutionary study of phishing," *eCrime Researchers Summit, 2008*, pp. 1–10, 2008.

[18] D. Wang, D. Irani, and C. Pu, "Evolutionary study of web spam: Webb spam corpus 2011 versus webb spam corpus 2006," in *Proceedings of the 8th International Conference on Collaborative Computing: Networking, Applications and Work-sharing (CollaborateCom)*, (Pittsburgh, PA, USA), pp. 40–49, October 2012.

[19] P. Guerra and D. Guedes, "Exploring the spam arms race to characterize spam evolution," in *Proceedings of the 8th Annual Collaboration, Electronic messaging, Anti-Abuse and Spam Conference (CEAS 2010)*, (Redmond, Washington USA), July 2010.

[20] "Untroubled dataset website." http://untroubled.org/spam/, 2014.

[21] "Kaspersky lab." http://usa.kaspersky.com/, 2013.

[22] K. Rapoza, "The dying business of email spam." http://usa.kaspersky.com/about-us/press-center/in-the-news/dying-business-email-spam, 2012.

[23] D. Gudkova, "Kaspersky security bulletin: Spam evolution 2012." http://www.securelist.com/en/analysis/204792276/Kaspersky_Security_Bulletin_Spam_Evolution_2012, 2012.

[24] X. Carreras and L. Marquez, "Boosting trees for anti-spam email filtering," *arXiv preprint cs/0109015*, 2001.

[25] R. Wang, A. Youssef, and A. Elhakeem, "On Improving the Performance of Spam Filters Using Heuristic Feature Selection Techniques," in *Proceedings of 23rd Biennial Symposium on Communications, 2006*, pp. 227–230, Ieee, 2006.

[26] J. Chan, I. Koprinska, and J. Poon, "Co-training with a Single Natural Feature Set Applied to Email Classification," in *Proceedings of IEEE/WIC/ACM International Conference on Web Intelligence (WI'04)*, pp. 586–589, Ieee, 2004.

[27] W. Liu and T. Wang, "Multi-field learning for email spam filtering," in *Proceeding of the 33rd international ACM SIGIR conference on Research and development in information retrieval*, (New York, NY, USA), p. 745, ACM Press, 2010.

[28] D. Sculley and G. Wachman, "Relaxed online SVMs for spam filtering," in *Proceedings of the 30th annual international ACM SIGIR conference on Research and development in information retrieval*, pp. 415–422, April 2007.

[29] J. Attenberg, K. Weinberger, and A. Dasgupta, "Collaborative Email-Spam Filtering with the Hashing Trick," in *CEAS*, pp. 1–4, 2009.

[30] M. Balakumar and V. Vaidehi, "Ontology based classification and categorization of email," in *Proceedings of Signal Processing, Communications and Networking*, pp. 199–202, 2008.

[31] A. Dasgupta, M. Gurevich, and K. Punera, "Enhanced email spam filtering through combining similarity graphs," in *Proceedings of the fourth ACM international conference on Web search and data mining*, (New York, NY, USA), p. 785, ACM Press, 2011.

[32] J. Jung and E. Sit, "An empirical study of spam traffic and the use of DNS black lists," in *Proceedings of the 4th ACM SIGCOMM conference on Internet measurement*, (New York, NY, USA), p. 370, ACM Press, 2004.

[33] A. Ramachandran, N. Feamster, and S. Vempala, "Filtering spam with behavioral blacklisting," in *Proceedings of the 14th ACM conference on Computer and communications security*, (New York, NY, USA), p. 342, ACM Press, 2007.

[34] M. Xie, H. Yin, and H. Wang, "An effective defense against email spam laundering," in *Proceedings of the 13th ACM conference on Computer and communications security*, (New York, NY, USA), p. 179, ACM Press, 2006.

[35] L. Zhuang, J. Dunagan, D. Simon, and H. Wang, "Characterizing Botnets from Email Spam Records.," in *Proceedings of the first USENIX workshop on large-scale exploits and emergent threats (LEET 08)*, 2008.

[36] S. Webb, J. Caverlee, and C. Pu, "Introducing the webb spam corpus: Using email spam to identify web spam automatically," in *Proceedings of the Third Conference on Email and Anti-Spam (CEAS 2006)*, (Mountain View, CA, USA), July 2006.

[37] D. Wang, D. Irani, and C. Pu, "A social-spam detection framework," in *Proceedings of the 8th Annual Collaboration, Electronic messaging, Anti-Abuse and Spam Conference (CEAS 2011)*, (Perth, Australia), pp. 46–54, September 2011.

[38] C. Bird, A. Gourley, and P. Devanbu, "Mining email social networks," in *the 2006 international workshop on Mining software repositories*, pp. 137–143, 2006.

[39] A. McCallum, X. Wang, and A. Corrada-Emmanuel, "Topic and role discovery in social networks with experiments on enron and academic email.," *J. Artif. Intell. Res.(JAIR)*, vol. 30, pp. 249–272, 2007.

[40] A. Culotta, R. Bekkerman, and A. McCallum, "Extracting social networks and contact information from email and the web," in *Proceedings of the First Conference on Email and Anti-Spam (CEAS 2004)*, 2004.

[41] D. Wang, D. Irani, and C. Pu, "A study on evolution of email spam over fifteen years," in *Collaborative Computing: Networking, Applications and Worksharing (Collaboratecom), 2013 9th International Conference Conference on*, pp. 1–10, Oct 2013.

[42] D. Wang, "Analysis and detection of low quality information in social networks," in *Proceedings of Ph.D. Symposium at 30th IEEE International Conference on Data Engineering (ICDE 2014)*, (Chicago, IL, United States), 2014.

[43] D. Wang, D. Irani, and C. Pu, "A perspective of evolution after five years: A large-scale study of web spam evolution," *Int. J. Cooperative Inf. Syst.*, vol. 23, no. 2, 2014.

[44] Y. Chung, *A Study on the Evolution and Emergence of Web Spam*. PhD thesis, Univ. of Tokyo, Tokyo, Japan, 2011.

[45] D. Fetterly, M. Manasse, M. Najork, and J. Wiener, "A large-scale study of the evolution of web pages," in *Proceedings of the 12th international conference on World Wide Web*, WWW '03, (New York, NY, USA), pp. 669–678, 2003.

[46] "Electronic communications and transactions act, 2002." http://www.internet.org.za/ect_act.html, 2002.

[47] "Multipurpose internet mail extensions (MIME) part one: Format of internet message bodies." http://tools.ietf.org/html/rfc2045, 1996.

[48] "Text::Ngrams - flexible ngram analysis (for characters, words, and more)." http://search.cpan.org/dist/Text-Ngrams/Ngrams.pm, 2014.

[49] "Defensive aids sub system (DASS)." http://www.eurofighter.com/capabilities/technology/sensor-fusion/defensive-aids-sub-system.html, 2014.

[50] A. K. McCallum, "MALLET: A machine learning for language toolkit." http://mallet.cs.umass.edu, 2002.

[51] D. M. Blei, A. Ng, and M. Jordan, "Latent dirichlet allocation," *JMLR*, vol. 3, pp. 993–1022, 2003.

[52] S. Hao, N. A. Syed, N. Feamster, A. G. Gray, and S. Krasser, "Detecting spammers with snare: Spatio-temporal network-level automatic reputation engine," in *Proceedings of the 18th Conference on USENIX Security Symposium*, SSYM'09, pp. 101–118, 2009.

[53] "Python: email – an email and MIME handling package." http://docs.python.org/2/library/email, 2014.

[54] "Gephi: an open source graph visualization and manipulation software." http://gephi.org, 2014.

[55] "MaxMind – IP geolocation and online fraud prevention." http://www.maxmind.com/en/home, 2014.

[56] "Visualization: Geochart – Google charts – Google developers." https://developers.google.com/chart/interactive/docs/gallery/geochart, 2014.

Tracing Coordination and Cooperation Structures via Semantic Burst Detection

Yu-Ru Lin[1,*], Drew Margolin[2], David Lazer[3]

[1]School of Information Sciences, University of Pittsburgh, Pittsburgh, PA 15260, USA
[2]Department of Communication, Cornell University, Ithaca, NY 14850, USA
[3]Political Science Department, Northeastern University, Boston, MA 02115, USA

Abstract

Developing technologies that support collaboration requires understanding how knowledge and expertise are shared and distributed among community members. We explore two forms of knowledge distribution structures, coordination and cooperation, that are central to successful collaboration. We propose a novel method for detecting the coordination of strategic communication among members of political communities. Our method identifies a "rapid semantic convergence," a sudden burst in the use linguistic constructions by multiple individuals within a short time, as a signature of coordination. We apply our method to the public statements of U.S. Senators in the 112th U.S. Congress and construct coordination and cooperation networks among these individuals. We then compare aspects of these networks to other known properties of the Senators. Results indicate that the detected networks reflect underlying tendencies in the social relationships among Senators and reveal interesting differences in how the different parties coordinate communication.

Keywords: semantic burst, semantic convergence, burst detection, coordination, cooperation, social networks, public statement, political network, strategic communications

1. Introduction

Developing technologies that support collaboration requires an understanding of how knowledge and expertise are shared and distributed among individuals in both formal organizations or more informal social groups. However, knowledge distribution structures vary greatly with the culture and inner workings of different groups. These endogenous structures implicitly influence how group members interact with each other and perform as a whole. Hence, capturing the knowledge distribution structures specific to individual groups has been an intriguing problem in studying human collaborations. In this article, we explore two forms of knowledge distribution structures, coordination and cooperation, that are central to successful collaboration, among members in political communities.

According to Engesröm, coordination and cooperation are two of the fundamental forms in human interaction[1] [1]. At the level of coordination, each actors work independently without explicit communicating with each other, while in cooperation, actors try to find mutually acceptable ways to solve a shared problem [1]. In this article, we propose a novel method for detecting the structures of coordination and cooperation from communication data automatically.

An obvious challenge in this research is the difficulty of obtaining data and assessing the results. The recent increase in the availability of enormous digital archives of communication behavior offers a novel opportunity to address this issue [2]. Here, we utilize the public statements by U.S. Senators in our research. While publicly available data do not directly reveal coordination and cooperation structures, patterns in these trace data can suggest when coordination by some mechanism appears to be operating [3, 4]. By identifying these cases, analysis can then be tuned more finely to examine the potential causes of and processes involved in this coordination.

In the context of politics, communicating effectively through public statements is important for politicians. Through effective strategic communication, politicians can influence both media and voters, promoting attention to favored positions as well as favorable interpretations for their own policies and unfavorable interpretations of opponents and their views [5–7].

Despite the recognition that strategic communication is important to a politician's ability to gain power

---

Corresponding author. Email: yurulin@pitt.edu
*[1]The third form is reflective communication.

and win elections, little research has considered the social processes that influence politicians' communication strategies. Outside of the study of politicians and those in power, a variety of research suggests that coordination and cooperation in strategic communication are critical to the success and failure of political and social movements [8, 9]. While it is possible that the achievement of formally elected positions of power reduces or obviates the need for strategic communication coordination, there is also reason to expect this would not be the case. At the very least, political parties appear to be highly influential in the persuasion of audiences [10, 11]. Furthermore, many of the arguments for the advantages that elected politicians possess in strategic communication, such as the ability to provide information subsidies to media outlets, suggest that pooling and coordinating resources across individuals would also have benefits [12, 13].

In this study we focus on one such pattern of traces: rapid semantic convergence, which we defined as sudden bursts in the frequency with which particular phrases, measured as trigrams, are used in the public statements of U.S. Senators. The basic logic of this approach is that rapid semantic convergence indicates a coordinating mechanism – a causal process that brings senators' together linguistically.

We articulate four broad candidates for these coordinating processes: emergent contexts and events, shared persuasive interests, rhetorical innovation, and collaboration. For each of these categories we describe the extent to which the process that leads to convergence is a matter of individual and/or collective choices on the part of the individuals. If the behavioral structural signatures, in the form of shared language, can be identified, the incidence of these signatures may provide substantial insight into how politicians coordinate their activities and influence on another.

The article is structured as follows. Followed by a review of related work, we provide the theoretical and empirical foundations for our approach. We illustrate these theoretical processes with examples detected by our method from the public statements of U.S. Senators. We then articulate our approach for detecting rapid semantic convergence using two methods – a burst detection algorithm as well as a means for detecting joint authorship of public statements. Using these methods, we generate three networks built from the tendency for pairs of senators to suddenly deploy similar language. We compare the structures of these networks and explore their relationship to covariates, such as shared committee membership networks and party leadership structure.

2. Related Work

There are several ways to measure the underlying construct of "rapid semantic convergence." We briefly review three principle methods for doing so and describe their strengths and weaknesses in capturing the phenomenon of interest.

Correlations in Semantic Frequency. A fundamental question in semantic analysis is semantic representation and extraction. Semantic representation deals with the problem concerning the relationship between "concepts" and "word meanings." Popular approaches include semantic networks and co-occurrence models. Semantic networks is a network based representation that represents the meaning of each word by its relation of other words. For example, in WordNet [14], words are represented as nodes and semantic relationship are labelled connections between them. It is based on holistic views [15] which assumes a non-decomposable, one-to-one mapping between the lexical representation (the word) and conceptual representations of things, events, etc. In such representation, the connections between words are constructed based on prior knowledge.

A different approach based on co-occurrence analysis seeks to learn the representations of words in terms of their relationship to other words, automatically from corpora of texts. It is based on the assumption that similar words tend to appear in similar contexts. The approach can be found in widely-adopted vector space models such as Latent Semantic Analysis (LSA) [16] and probabilistic models such as Probabilistic Latent Semantic Analysis (pLSA) [17] and Latent Dirichlet Allocation (LDA) [18].

In Latent Semantic Analysis (LSA) [16], a document is represented as a vector where each dimension corresponds to a separate feature (a term) from the document. The entire corpus is represented as a term-document matrix and the values are commonly determined by the tf-idf weighting scheme [19]. The idea of LSA is to project the documents and their term features into a lower-dimensional latent concept space in order to represent a relation between the terms and some concepts, and a relation between those concepts and the documents. The low-dimension semantic latent space is obtained by decomposing the term-document matrix using Singular Value Decomposition. Despite its success for modeling implicit semantic structures between documents and words, one issue with this approach is that the resulting dimensions might be difficult to interpret, for example, the LSA approximation of the term-document matrix may contain negative values.

The Probabilistic Latent Semantic Analysis (pLSA, or the aspect model) [17] was introduced to overcome the weakness of LSA. It is based on a generative model that associates a latent variable with each occurrence of a word in a document. The Latent Dirichlet Allocation (LDA) [18] further improves the pLSA by introducing a Dirichlet prior on document-topic distribution. LDA represent documents as mixtures of topics (like "concepts" in LSA or "aspects" in pLSA), where a topic is a probabilistic distribution over words. Compared to the LSA model, the probabilistic models provide ways of interpreting the relationships between document-topic and topic-word in terms of probability weights.

Such topic mixing representation effectively is compact (the number of topics is significantly fewer than the number of terms) while still preserving salient statistical relationships. However, the resulting topics are synthetic and do not explicitly correspond to the prior knowledge of document topics. Furthermore, the meaning of words are determined without considering its specific contextual use in the documents, which makes it difficult to inform a potential social process corresponding to the particular use of words.

Burst Detection. In time series data, the presence of a burst suggests that the occurrence of a data feature or value is unexpectedly frequent in a short period. This unexpected occurrence is often associated with an unusual event. Intuitively, burst detection can be achieved by identifying a burst region where the data value exceeds certain threshold. The threshold can be determined based on heuristics [20], different data distribution assumptions [21] or statistical tests [22]. The Cumulative Sum (CUSUM) method [23] is one of the most popular statistical approach for change point detection. However, threshold-based methods lack flexibility to recognize bursts with various lengths, for example, a longer burst may be identified as several short bursts. Kleinberg [24] proposed a state-based model using Hidden Markov Model (HMM), which extends the threshold-based method with a more relaxed threshold. The idea behind this method is that it models the state transitions as low-probability events, and a cost function is assigned such that a smooth state tends to be more persistent than transitions. Mane and Böner [25] used this method to track the temporal evolution of major topics in scientific publication. In their study, the potential topic words are pre-specified according to Biologists' domain knowledge. [2]. Although the state-based burst detection method has the ability to identify longer bursts with noises, it remains a challenge to deal with emergent topics or ambiguous signals – the variable notion of threshold makes it difficult to recognize whether there is a drift in the meaning of a given term.

As described above, previous work has focused on identifying the meaning of terms and expressions observed in semantic trace data and grouping documents and individuals based on these shared meanings. In these contexts, rapid semantic convergence would represent shared understandings and intentions among group members [26, 27]. Yet another way to conceive of rapid semantic convergence is as the residue of a group process that imposes itself on individual behavior independent of textual meaning. More precisely, when individuals converge in their public use of language it might be because, as typical models assume, they have reached a consensual agreement regarding a shared set of ideas, with their words reflecting this unified psychological state. However, their convergent semantic behavior may also reflect the fact that the group, or incentives within the group, has the power to encourage them to issue statements that differ from their personal views or which mean things they do not personally intend or even technically understand. That is, incentives for conformity or specialization may lead group members to parrot one another's language independent of the meaning of the phrases or their precise feelings about them.

The possibility that the higher order structures and incentives of the group as a whole encourage or compel semantic convergence suggests it may be useful to analyze semantic convergence in a different way. In particular, it may be useful to assess the observable features of individuals and the social relations that lead them to converge with one another independent of the meaning of the statements around which such convergence takes place. Thus, in the next section, we enumerate several of these higher order incentives.

3. What Leads to Semantic Bursts?

In this section, we describe theories on the sources of semantic convergence.

Shared Categories for Emergent Features and Events. A fundamental property of language as a communication tool is its use of shared symbols to refer to particular referents [28]. Thus, a basic reason why individuals may converge in their use of words or concepts is that they are responding to experiences of referents that they share in common. For example, these referents might be features of the environment or events that have taken place [29].

When applying concepts to describe situations or identify particular ideas or entities, individuals tend to begin by applying basic categories [29, 30]. Basic categories are those that best balance the trade-off between specificity in communicating information and availability to speakers and familiarity to audiences [30, 31]. That is, the concept is specific enough to carry a narrow set of appropriate applications but

---

[2]The topics are selected based on Institute for Scientific Information (ISI) key words and MEDLINE's controlled vocabulary (MeSH terms)

general enough so that it can be applied frequently, making it accessible through memory and familiar to different individuals. Basic categories settle in particular locations based on the frequency with which different features appear in the environment [30, 32]. See [29] for a review. For example, children tend to learn the category "bird" before learning more specific categories such as "robin" [32]. Once experienced in identifying "birds," children then move on to make finer distinctions based on more commonly experienced kinds of birds (e.g. robins) [32, 33]. Experts tend to share more specific categories, such that individual items may often have highly specific names [34–36].

Basic categories help make communication intelligible to an audience. The incentive to conform to basic category use is thus often a response to the state or structure of an audience, even when that audience is unseen. [37] show that in communities with a cohesive social structure, individuals are more likely to articulate statements in commonly held terms. When social structure is more fractured, they revert to more idiosyncratic expressions that may more precisely reflect their own ideas but are not well understood by others.

In order to gain or maintain visibility and influence with media and constituents, politicians may be compelled at times to respond to the news of the day or novel events [6, 38]. These events may cause semantic convergence by compelling politicians to describe or take a position for which the set of basic categories or specialized terms is already convergent [39].

For example, the death of Osama bin Laden in May, 2011 had important implications for both U.S. foreign and domestic policy. Accordingly, several U.S. Senators issued press releases immediately following the report of his death[3]. Furthermore, since bin Laden's name was widely known and recognized, Senators referred to him by name. Thus, our method reveals a sudden convergence in the use of the name "Osama bin Laden" in Senators public statements. Ninety senators used the name "Osama bin Laden" in a public statement within approximately 1 week of his death.

Politicians also must address more mundane, scheduled events or changes in policy context. As the agenda for debate and discussion shifts from one proposed policy to another, the categories and entities that politicians name will also shift accordingly [40]. The beginning of debate on a particular topic within the Senate can lead several Senators to comment publicly on it, leading to semantic convergence. This convergence is due to the limited set of categories that can be used to describe aspects of the topic in a way that is broadly intelligible to the public and the media. For example, in early October, 2011, the Senate debated the terms of trade with several nations. The basic category used to refer to these contracts is "free trade agreements." Thus, the phrase "free trade agreements" was used by 33 Senators within a one week period[4]. While this may have been the result of strategic coordination (negotiation between the Senators in which bill to discuss), the semantic convergence it breeds may not be the result of any explicit cooperation between senators that discuss it using the same terms. Thus, cases such as these represent exogenous sources of strategic communication coordination.

Shared Interests in Persuasion. Political discourse is inherently persuasive. Politicians seek electoral advantage in their use of public statements [7, 40]. Politicians can influence the ways in which their constituents will interpret their actions by identifying information, arguments, and frames which justify their point of view and cast their decisions in the most favorable light [5].

Although politicians' electoral fates are ultimately individual, the cooperative nature of political action and the strength of political parties in influencing election outcomes lead politicians to share a variety of persuasive interests. Legislators work together to craft legislation [41]. Co-sponsors of a bill thus share a persuasive interest in the public interpreting the bill and the reasoning behind it in a positive light. More broadly, public interpretation of politicians' individual positions is strongly influenced by party identification and the favorability of the party [10, 11]. Thus, members of the same party share an interest in framing and justifying policies in a manner that benefits their party.

Shared persuasive interest can lead to semantic convergence in two different ways. First, for some individuals, a credible position must be supported by specific reasons and evidence [42]. To persuade these individuals to adopt a particular point of view, politicians will likely draw on specific sources or pieces of evidence. When a particular topic is debated, politicians sharing persuasive interest will exhibit semantic convergence by virtue of their citation and invocation of common arguments, evidence and sources.

Though citizens may often ignore specific information and evidence and rely instead on peripheral cues or sources, media outlets may be more susceptible to

---

[3]For example, see http://www.baucus.senate.gov/?p=press_release&id=459, http://durbin.senate.gov/public/index.cfm/pressreleases?ID=1ddceb11-cde0-46bd-a7fd-83513f5b80b9, http://www.mikulski.senate.gov/media/pressrelease/5-2-11.cfm,http://boxer.senate.gov/en/press/releases/050211.cfm

[4]For example, see http://conrad.senate.gov/pressroom/record.cfm?id=334460, http://ronjohnson.senate.gov/public/index.cfm/press-releases?ID=534b1e62-4f9d-418b-a654-6c627a08825c, http://rockefeller.senate.gov/press/record.cfm?id=334453

these techniques. Many newspapers and other media outlets have limited budgets for information gathering about national policy. Thus, these outlets often rely heavily on politicians to provide not only their positions but the facts and reasons which explain the issues relevant to the policy in question [13]. Since it is in the interest of the politician to provide background information which casts their own position in a favorable light, biased information often becomes the basis of the news that is reported [12]. Influencing these outlets can benefit politicians as voters often cannot identify or remember the sources from which they have received political information [43]. Other media outlets are explicitly biased and seek information to justify their pre-determined support for a particular view [44]. This effect should lead to substantial semantic convergence due to shared persuasive interest as the gains that politicians can achieve by disseminating a new fact that supports their position may be substantial [7].

For example, in January 2012 several Republican Senators advocated for the approval of the Keystone XL pipeline project. In justifying this position, several of them referred to statistics regarding the increase in oil production the pipeline was expected to yield. During an 8 day period toward the end of the month, 24 Senators used the phrase "oil per day" in their public statements, including several as part of a joint press release[5]. In another example, Senators often cite scores and analyses issued by the Congressional Budget Office to bolster their justification for or critique of a particular bill. On several occasions, the number of Senators referring to the "Congressional Budget Office" increased to more than 20 individuals within a short time period.

In these examples, semantic convergence occurs due to a shared interest in persuasion and an economy in research costs achieved by repeating the same justifications. Much as politicians subsidize the media, they may also subsidize one another, particularly if the knowledge they provide is easy to copy or imitate. One senator may find a useful statistic or report and cite it, revealing its relevance to others. There is also evidence of cooperative dissemination of evidence and arguments through the release of "talking points" from think tanks and other partisan or issue based interests [45].

A second way that shared persuasive interest can lead to semantic convergence is through the use of frames [5, 46]. Frames are deployed to suggest interpretations for particular events or policies by highlighting certain aspects of a situation and suppressing others. While for many entities and ideas there are clearly identifiable, unique basic categories or specific names, for others there may be a distribution of appropriate terms or phrases with similar yet imperfect fit [31]. There may exist no dominant term which captures all of the relevant features of a situation, and thus permitting politicians to choose from a set of candidate phrases that frame the issues in a way that is beneficial to them [29, 47].

Frames appear to be particularly important in persuading individuals that do not pay close attention to specific arguments [38]. An individual may find both of two contradictory frames to be resonant and persuasive [48]. This suggests that when persuading through framing, only the effectiveness of the chosen frame need to be considered. This leads to "crosstalk" in political campaigns in which opponents use different words to discuss the same issues and rarely acknowledge one another's frame, eschewing the other's favored terms [7]. Repetition is also important for frame resonance [8]. The more experience an audience has with a frame, the more credible or legitimate this frame becomes to that audience. Similarly, as a greater number of individuals use a frame, it gains in legitimacy and credibility [49].

These factors suggest that politicians that share a persuasive interest will benefit substantially from a strategically coordinating their use of frames. A frame which is not optimal for a particular politician's individual agenda may nonetheless be effective if others, such as those in his or her party, agree to use it as well. This suggests that politicians may negotiate to use a consistent set of frames.

For example, at the beginning of the 112th Congress Republican Senators appeared to attempt to consolidate support for their party and opposition to the President. In particular, they highlighted what they perceived to be the failures of the Obama administration through its first mid-term election. In a four day period, ten Republican Senators used the phrase "two years ago" to refer to different aspects of the President's failed policies, including the stimulus package and foreign policy initiatives.

Rhetorical Innovations. The most supportive arguments and facts and the most effective frames are not always obvious or easy to discover. Most individuals tend to possess only a limited number of the total pool of arguments that they would find persuasive on a topic [50]. The supply of frames may be limited as well. Since satisfactory frames are generally sufficient to be persuasive, there is limited need to explore a large set of alternatives to construct a persuasive message [48, 51]. Also, the resonance of novel frames is often difficult to observe without first witnessing the reaction of an audience [52, 53]. These factors create an incentive for

---

[5]For example, see http://www.lee.senate.gov/public/index.cfm/2012/1/bipartisan-group-of-senators-to-introduce-legislation-to-approve-keystone-xl-pipeline

politicians to let others invent and try a novel frame before they adopt it themselves.

As a result, politicians may often coordinate their use of words without explicitly conferring or agreeing to do so. This can lead to a diffusion process for rhetorical innovations [54]. That is, there may be limited investment in the development of new phrases or optimization of frames [27], but if and when one politician happens upon a useful name, fact, or word combination, others that are exposed to the new combination may quickly adopt it and use it in their own statements. This is particularly likely for short, easy to imitate phrases with limited complexity in appropriate use [55]. Like a disease that, once it has "infected" one host can easily exploit other hosts to which it gains access, the novel concept or combination may be latent for some time and suddenly burst through a population of politicians [56, 57]. Thus, it can be expected that a certain degree of discursive imitation of novel phrases or conceptual combinations will occur, leading to semantic convergence with the onset of an "infection" of one individual [56, 58, 59].

Furthermore, this imitation may be enhanced by the increased recognition and legitimacy the phrase will obtain as it is used more frequently. This can lead not only to increased use of the phrase but also to the re-application of the phrase to new contexts [60]. That is, once the phrase has been recognized as effective in a particular context, it may be used so frequently as to be more broadly recognizable. Individuals may then import the phrase into new contexts.

For example, following the death of Osama bin Laden, several senators attempted to convey that bin Laden's death, while an important step forward in the effort to limit terrorism, was not the sign that the task was complete. Within 7 days of bin Laden's death, 23 of the Senators that issued statements on this topic used the phrase "must remain vigilant" to implore the continued commitment to anti-terror efforts. This example will be described in more details in the result section.

Teamwork and Collaboration. The preceding processes for semantic convergence are largely built from individual incentives and habits. For example, Senators would not need to explicitly work together or choose to speak similarly for them to rely on the same basic categories or for one Senator to copy the arguments or imitate the rhetorical innovations of another. At the other end of the spectrum is the purposeful teamwork and collaboration. When individuals work together, they must negotiate a shared language which facilitates communication about the topics on which they are working [61]. Having identified a shared language and way of framing a situation, it is easier for others to adopt the same terminology.

In these cases, the terms used are explicitly agreed to by all members of the group [62, 63]. The joint authorship of public statements is in this way similar to co-sponsorship of bills [41]. The time required to develop and negotiate a jointly acceptable statement should be substantially less than that required to develop and negotiate jointly acceptable legislation, however. The two may also overlap, as politicians agree to collaborate in their communication to support their collaborative work on legislation.

For example, in February, 2012, 14 Democratic Senators wrote a letter to the Senate to pass a "payroll tax cut." This letter was then followed by 35 other Senators (mostly Democrats) using this phrase in their own public statements. In this case, explicit collaboration and the semantic burst it produced appeared to push the term onto the agenda for others to consider.

Summary. We are interested in identifying relationships of strategic communication coordination via the observation of rapid semantic convergence. In this section we have reviewed theoretical arguments that suggest that rapid semantic convergence can be an indicator of higher level processes influenced by needs for coordination and collaboration. In the next section, we begin by demonstrating how our algorithm detects semantic convergence. We also present a method for detecting explicitly negotiated convergent communication in the form of jointly authored public statements.

Based on these patterns of convergence, we then build network structures showing the underlying coordination relationships between individual senators. We then explore how these explicit collaborations and implicit coordination and diffusion relationships correspond to a other measures of Senator attributes, positions, and network structures.

4. Method

4.1. Data

As of March 2012 we have gathered 0.4 million documents from the public statements of Members of the US Congress from the Vote Smart Project website[6]. Fig. 1 shows the number of public statement documents gathered in our dataset. According to Vote Smart, the public statements include any press releases, statements, newspaper articles, interviews, blog entries, newsletters, legislative committee websites, campaign websites and cable news show websites (Meet the Press, This Week, etc.) that contain direct quotes from the official[7]. In this study we focus on the statements made

---

[6]http://www.votesmart.org
[7]In future analyses we will disaggregate the analysis by type of public statement.

by the members of the 112th Senate, during the period between January 2011 and March 2012. We retrieve the individual attributes for the Members of Congress using Sunlight Congress API[8].

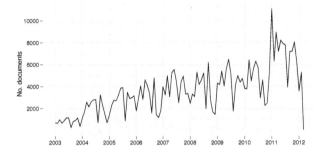

Figure 1. Monthly volume of public statements gathered in our dataset.

4.2. Semantic Burst Detection

Our goal is to identify a set of instances from the public statements of the Members of Congress where the use of certain words is shared among a group of members more frequently then usual and the use is concentrated within a short period of time. Such instances of semantic convergence are indicative of unobserved processes among the members that potentially influence the product of semantic convergence (in the observed public statements). We call an instance of bursty use of words "infection instance." For each of the identified infection instances, we can derive certain social relationships within the infected population. The overall procedure include three steps: (1) burst n-gram detection, (2) n-gram infection instance extraction, and (3) social network construction. We describe each step in the following.

We first parse the corpus of public statements to construct a term-document sparse matrix, where an entry (i, j) indicates the number of occurrences of term i in document j. The terms are n-grams with highest tf-idf weights. An n-gram is a contiguous sequence of n words from a given sequence of text. We use trigram ($n = 3$) in this paper. The presented analysis can be well extended to shorter or longer n-grams. Here we use trigrams because a trigram conveys more specific meaning than single word or bigram, but it has a greater advantage in terms of computational efficiency, compared with longer n-grams [64]. (Throughout this article, "n-gram", "term" and "word" are used interchangeably.) N-grams that contain stop words such as "the", "is", etc. are removed.

For each non-zero entry in the term-document, we retrieve a 4-tuple (a, d, w, t) from the document meta-data to represent the occurrences of a word w (n-gram) in a document d (public statement) given by an actor (i.e., a Member of Congress) at the time t. The time resolution is one day, consistent with the resolution obtained from the document metadata.

To detect a bursty use of an n-gram within a short period of time, we first construct a time series $w_i(t)$ for each n-gram w_i, where: $w_i(t)$ is given by number of actors who use the n-gram at least once at the time t.

We then use the following on-line filtered derivative algorithm to detect bursts within each $w_i(t)$ sequence. In this method, a change in the mean level of a sequence of observations is locally characterized by a great absolute value of the derivative of the sample observations [23]. Since the derivative operator may be sensitive to noises, a filtering operation is applied before derivation. Specifically, we consider the discrete derivative of f_k:

$$\nabla f_k = f_k - f_{k-1}, \tag{1}$$

where f_k is the decision function based on log-likelihood ratio test:

$$f_k = \sum_{i=0}^{N-1} \gamma_i \ln \frac{p_{\theta_1}(y_{k-i})}{p_{\theta_0}(y_{k-i})}, \tag{2}$$

And the burst alarm is activated at t_a if:

$$t_a = \min\{k : \sum_{i=0}^{N-1} \delta(\nabla f_{k-i} \geq h) \geq \eta\}, \tag{3}$$

where N is a fixed sample size, $\delta(x)$ is the indicator of event x, h is the threshold for the derivative, and η is a threshold for the number of crossings of h, which is usually used for decreasing the number of alarms in the neighborhood of the change due to the smoothing operation.

In the case of an increase in the mean, the decision function f_k corresponding to Eqn. 2 is:

$$f_k = \sum_{i=0}^{N-1} \gamma_i(y_{k-i} - \mu_0). \tag{4}$$

We choose an integrating filter with N constant weights γ_i, so the decision of alarm time is based on local averages of sample values.

When an alarm is activated for an n-gram w, we call the pair (w, t) a candidate n-gram infection, where $t = t_a$ is the onset time of the burst region. We shall extract a set of n-gram infection instances from the candidate set. For each candidate infection, we expand the time window on both sides to $[t_s, t_e]$ where $t_s < t < t_e$ and retrieve all actors who used the n-gram w at least once during the time window $[t_s, t_e]$. If an actor uses the

[8]http://services.sunlightlabs.com/docs/Sunlight_Congress_API/

Figure 2. The trigram "osama bin laden" on Senators' web press release on May 2, 2011.

n-gram at different time points, only the first time is retrieved. An infection instance of (w, t) associated with time window $[t_s, t_e]$ is defined by the list of infected actors: $\{(a_1, t_1), (a_2, t_2), ...\}$, where $t_1 \leq t_2 \leq ...$ and $a_i < a_j$ if $t_i = t_j$.

If two candidate pairs have the same n-gram and different but overlapping infected durations, the pairs are merged to have a extended duration covering both durations. If two n-grams have the same onset time and infection instance, the two are called exchangeable n-grams and the infection instances are merged into a single instance. In other words, an infection instance may be associated with multiple n-grams if all of them are exchangeable with each other.

4.3. Network Extraction

The next step is to derive social relationships from the detected n-gram infection instances. Two types of networks are obtained from the instances: infection following and infection sharing networks.

The infection following network is calculated on the assumption that the point in time at which the actor uses the n-gram for the first time is important in the unobserved social processes. The timing makes no difference in the infection sharing network. The infection following network is a normalized weighted

directed network, defined as:

$$W^F = \sum_q \frac{\theta_{ij}^q}{\sum_{ij} \theta_{ij}^q} \tag{5}$$

where for each n-gram instance q, the edge weight between two actors a_i and a_j in the instance is given by:

$$\theta_{ij}^q = \frac{exp(-\Delta t_{ij}/r)}{N(t_i)}, \tag{6}$$

if with $t_i > t_j$, and $\theta_{ij}^q = 0$ otherwise. $\Delta t_{ij} = t_j - t_i$, r is the exponential decay rate and $N(t_i)$ is the number of actors in the instance who are infected before t_i. This weighted scheme assigns higher weights to actors who are infected closely in time, and are more likely to be infected before others.

A symmetric infection network is defined as:

$$W^S = \sum_q \theta_{ij}^q \tag{7}$$

with edge weight $\theta_{ij}^q = 1$ for all pairs of actor (a_i, a_j) in an instance q, and $\theta_{ij}^q = 0$ otherwise.

In addition to the two networks, we observe a definite structure in our dataset – occasionally senators release exactly the same public statements on the same day via joint press release. This structure can be recognized through duplication detection of documents. We thus construct a third network to reflect this structure as a comparison. The joint press network is given by:

$$W^J = \sum_k \theta_{ij}^k \qquad (8)$$

with edge weight $\theta_{ij}^k = 1$ for all pairs of actor (a_i, a_j) in a joint press release k, and $\theta_{ij}^k = 0$ otherwise.

4.4. Analysis and Controls

We compare the structures of these extracted networks with additional information gathered for the Senate.

Covariate Networks. We assemble three covariate networks that are likely to be associated with the inferred networks: a shared party membership network, a shared committee membership network, and an adjacent home states network.

Shared Party Membership. Senators from the same party share substantial persuasion interests. Thus, it is expected that members of the same party will be more likely to converge semantically through explicit collaboration as well as through imitation or a shared evaluation of arguments or frames as useful.

Shared Committee Membership. Senators on the same committee might be prone to semantic convergence for several reasons. First, by virtue of working on the same committee, these Senators will likely come into contact with one another more frequently [65]. Physical proximity is an important predictor of communication and collaborative team formation [66, 67]. It is also a means through which Senators may be exposed to one another's rhetorical innovations. Also, because committees are formed to address specific issues, Senators on the same committee may share persuasive interests.

A network of shared committee membership was constructed from the Congressional Directory for the 112 Congress. A bipartite network of Senators-Committees was built from the directories and then projected into a one mode, weighted Senator-Senator network where a link represented the number of committees on which two Senators served together.

Adjacent Home States. Senators who come from states that are geographically close to one another may also share persuasive interests and rhetorical exposure [68]. Many issues that are important or salient for citizens of one state may also be important or salient for members of nearby states. For example, the proposed Keystone XL pipeline affects voters in the central states in which the pipeline would be constructed differently than it effects voters in coastal states. The persuasiveness of an argument or frame may also vary with local cultures [69]. Exposure to issues and to the frames in which they are described or interpreted may also correspond to geographic proximity. The reach of

major media outlets, such as newspapers and television stations corresponds to the geographic boundaries of media markets, many of which cross state boundaries and thus serve adjacent states [70].

A network of senators with geographically adjacent home states was constructed. A link between two senators in this network indicates that these senators' home states border one another. For example, Barbara Boxer (D-California) has a link to John McCain (R-Arizona). Senators from the same state were also given a link.

Covariate Attributes. For an exploratory analysis, we compare network centrality scores calculated from the inferred networks to several attributes of individual senators. All attribute data are taken from the Voteview database unless otherwise specified.

Year Entered Senate. This attribute captures the first year that a senator joined the Senate. For senators that have been elected or appointed in non-continuous terms (there are two in the 112th Congress), the first year is used. This measure indicates the extent of a senator's seniority and experience level.

Leadership. Senators in leadership positions may also be leaders in a party's public communication strategy. Senators in leadership positions – Majority Leader, Minority Leader, Majority Whip, Minority Whip, Party Conference Chairs, and President Pro Tempore were dummy coded as leaders. This resulted in 6 Senators being coded as "leaders" (Harry Reid, Mitch McConnell, Dick Durbin, John Kyl, Daniel Inouye, and John Thune).

Term End. Senators come up for election in staggered "classes." One third of U.S. Senators are up for re-election in 2012, one third in 2014, and one third in 2016. The Term End thus measures the number of years until the Senator will face re-election. Senators with a lower Term End score should be more attuned to the persuasive effect of their public statements on voters.

DW-Nominate. The DW-Nominate score indicates the extent to which a politician is ideologically conservative (liberals receive negative scores with large absolute values) [71]. Senators with more moderate scores may have more in common with a larger number of Senators, drawing from moderates in both parties. Senators with more extreme views may be more likely to identify arguments, evidence, or frames which support a particular point of view. These scores were taken from Voteview.com based on the calculations for the 111th Congress. Thus, senators that are new in the 112th congress were not included for this analysis unless the site provided a score based on a senators record in the House of Representatives during the 111th Congress.

5. Results

(a) number of instances over time

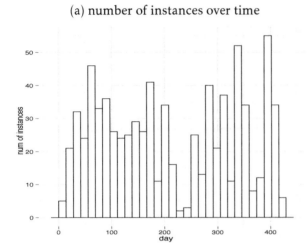

(b) histogram of infected population

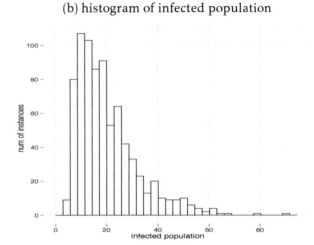

Figure 3. (a) Number of n-gram infected instances extracted by our method. (b) Histogram of infected population per instance. The n-gram with the largest population is "osama–bin–laden" which infects 91 members.

5.1. Detected Semantic Bursts

In this section we report results of analyses performed in the networks inferred by our method. Our method detected 783 bursts over the 426 day observation period (14 months). In Fig. 3 we show the number of detected semantic bursts (infected instances) over time and their significance in terms of individuals involved in the burst instances.

Figure 4 shows the bursts used as examples in the theory section of this article. Each chart shows the daily usage of the identified trigram over the observation period. The burst periods are depicted in red. These period are identified as the high peak period and extended to seven days before and after this period.

These figures show that the detection method identifies clear bursts. In each case, the peak of the trigram usage is substantially larger than its typical usage rate. The bursts also show varying degrees of decay. These patterns may suggest manners in which the kinds of bursts may be distinguished via these methods.

Figure 4(a) and (e) show the bursts for basic categories and named entities: "Osama bin Laden" and "free trade agreements." These are examples where external events, rather than negotiated or other less explcit coordination processes are responsible for the burst. In the case of Osama bin Laden, the absolute mean increase in infected population is 5.91 (with a 11-day average smoothing window), which means there are more than 65 more senators who used the n-gram "osama bin laden" as compared to the number of senators using the same n-gram before the onset time of the infection. There are in total 91 Senators that used this name during the week before and after the onset time (Fig 4(a) red period). For "free trade agreements,"

Figure 6. Infection Following Network: the network of who follows whom in public statements using bursting trigrams.

the use of this category has the absolute mean increase 3.73.

Figure 4(b) shows the burst for "oil per day," a reference to a statistic regarding the projected yield from the construction of the Keystone XL pipeline. This burst is smaller in magnitude (absolute mean increase 1.45). Nonetheless, it is still clear in the picture that this is a substantial increase. The use of this phrase also appears to show a modest diffusion pattern. Once the window is closed, this phrase appears to be used more frequently than in the period prior to the window, though still at a much lower rate than during the burst itself.

Figure 4(c) shows a similar pattern for the burst in the use of the frame "two years ago." The use of this frame has absolute mean increase 1.0. This phrase was used

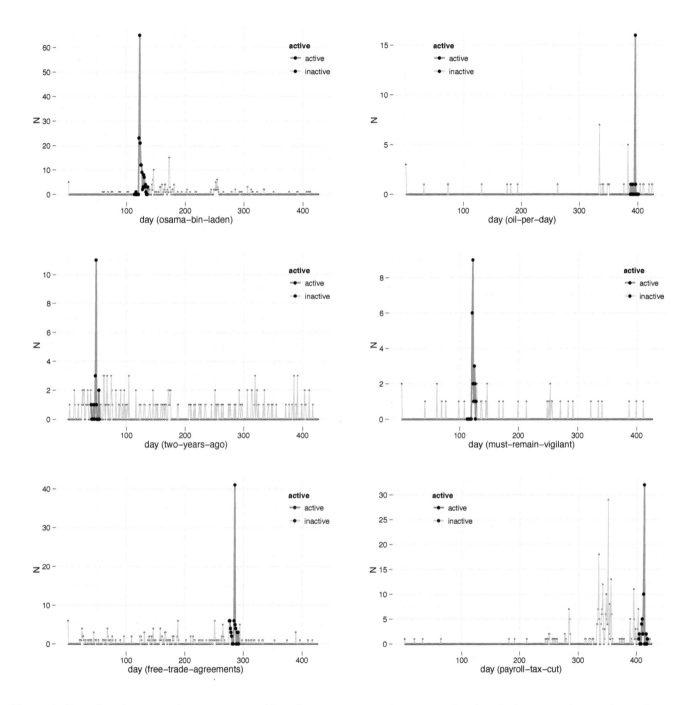

Figure 4. Examples of trigram infection instances. Note that a trigram may be associated with multiple non-overlapping bursts (e.g. "payroll-tax-cut" around day 350 and day 410), and each of the non-overlapping bursts is considered as a different infection instance.

by Republicans to refer to the failures of the Obama administration during the first half of the President's term. The burst is clearly distinct from the regular usage of the phrase, and also suggests a modest, temporary increase in the use of the phrase in subsequent weeks. Eventually the use of this frame appears to die down to pre-burst levels.

Figure 4(d) shows the burst in the use of the frame "must remain vigilant." The use of this frame has a absolute mean increase .82. Prior to the burst period, covering 120 days, the phrase was used 9 times by Senators in their public statements. It was then used 24 times during the burst period. The rate of use seems to return to pre-burst levels shortly thereafter, however.

Finally, Fig. 4(f) shows the use of the phrase "payroll tax cut." This phrase was jointly agreed upon by Democratic senators in their joint press release. The burst in usage represents their jointly authored letter

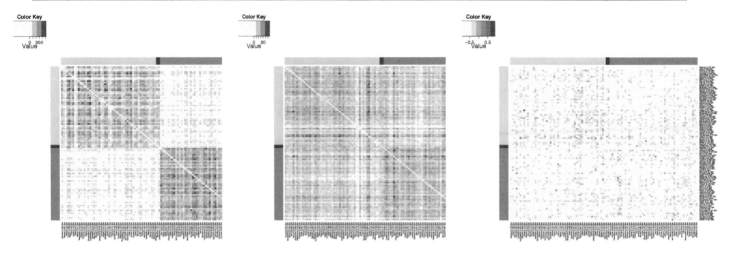

Figure 5. The matrices of the three different social networks extracted from the dataset: (a) Joint Authoring, (b) Infection Sharing and (c) Infection Following networks. Rows and columns in the matrices are reshuffled according to party and connections. The colors around the rows and columns indicate the party affiliation (Republican: red; Democrat: blue).

to the Senate. This burst showed a 2.64 absolute mean increase usage. This appears to be the third time that this phrase showed a burst. Interestingly, the prior bursts did not contain a large, joint authored press release. This suggests that the phrase had established itself as a legitimate frame prior to being one that Senators would deploy in a jointly authored document.

Fig. 7 shows the examples of actual texts appearing in Senators' press release after Bin Laden's death. The phrase "must remain vigilant" was used to implore the continued commitment to anti-terror efforts. Previously, this phrase had rarely been used in the public statements of Senators. We detected that 6 senators used the phrase on May 1, 2011[9], followed by 9 senators the next day[10], and then another 8 over the next several days[11]. The application of this phrase did not end there, however. On the ninth day after Bin Laden's death, one Senator deployed the phrase "must remain vigilant" in a new context. Senator John Boozman of Arkansas cautioned that it was important to intensely prepare for natural disasters, stating "we all must remain vigilant to protecting ourselves and our loved ones this storm season" (Boozman, May, 9, 2011). This example provides evidence that repetition of the phrase around one event legitimated its use for other contexts.

5.2. Analysis on Extracted Networks

As shown in Fig. 5, three types of social networks are extracted: Joint Authoring, Infection Sharing and

Infection Following networks. Fig. 6 shows the Infection Following Network of Senators. Below we present the analysis results for comparing the structures of these extracted networks with one another and with additional information gathered for the Senate.

Comparing the Inferred Networks. Both the individual links and the centrality scores were compared for the three inferred networks. Centrality was computed using both a raw sum of the column scores for each senator as well as the page rank score for each senator. Both Pearson correlations and Spearman's rank correlations for these scores were extremely high (within the same network, > .99 for each network). Thus, only the page rank score is reported. Correlations between network links were computed using the Quadratic Assignment Procedure (QAP) [72].

Infection Following Networks vs. Infection Sharing Network. These networks are built from the same data but are calculated differently. In the infection following network, infections flow in a time ordered manner. Individuals that use a bursting trigram first receive in-bound links from individuals that use the same bursting trigram at a later point in time. The weight of this link is determined by a decay function and weakens as time passes between the first individual's usage and the second's. The weight of this link is also determined by the number of other individuals that the second individual is "following." The first individual receives a stronger link from the second if he/she is the only senator that used this trigram prior to the second individual's doing so. If the second individual's usage follows a large group of senators, each senator receives a weak link only. The infection sharing network does not use any weighting. The fact that two senators each used a bursting trigram within the burst window is sufficient to give them a symmetric tie of value (count) 1. Thus the infection sharing network tends to capture shared persuasive interests – the fact that two senators

---

[9]For example, see http://www.cardin.senate.gov/newsroom/ statements_and_speeches/statement-by-us-senator-ben-cardin-on-death-of-osama-bin-laden

[10]For example, see http://conrad.senate.gov/pressroom/ record.cfm?id=332649

[11]For example, see http://www.crapo.senate.gov/media/ newsreleases/release_full.cfm?id=332701

chose to use the same bursting trigram – but discards information regarding innovation and diffusion, which are inherently temporal [54].

Comparing these networks shows a strong association between the two but also some differences. The centrality scores of the two networks are highly correlated $(r = .84, p < .001, df = 98)$. This suggests that individuals that tend to be early and alone in bursts and are thus central in the following network are more consistent participants in bursts, whereas followers tend to be a more heterogeneous group. Thus, when followers are given equal weight to innovators (as in the infection sharing network), centrality ranking does not change substantially. Table 1 displays the top 10 senators in terms of page rank centrality for each of the three networks.

The two networks are not identical, however. The link to link correlation as calculated by the QAP procedure shows $r = .325$ ($p < .001$, using 1000 permutations). This suggests that removing timing and weights leads to substantial changes in the network.

Infection Sharing Network vs. Joint Authorship Network. These networks include several instances of overlapping data but also distinct data points. When a joint authored document uses a trigram that participates in a burst, both networks will include this document and its authors will receive links to one another in both networks.

The infection sharing network also includes links between senators that did not co-author documents, while the joint authorship network also includes documents that did not use any bursting phrases and thus did not qualify for the infection networks.

The correlation between the network links is significant ($r = .38, p < .001$, using 1000 permutations). This appears sensible given that both networks share several documents in common and assign links on these shared documents in the same way. However, comparing these networks shows only a weak association in network centrality $(r = .17, p = .08, df = 98)$. This suggests that individuals that obtain additional links in the symmetric network, by virtue of participating in solo-authored public statements using bursting trigrams, are not particularly likely to participate in other, joint-authored statements with non-bursting phrases. This could indicate that some individuals are simply more likely to communicate through solo-authored statements rather than through joint-authored statements. This may also be due to the fact that the joint authorship network shows a high degree of connectedness amongst many authors, leading many senators to have high centrality scores that are not meaningfully different from one another.

Infection Following Network vs. Joint Authorship Network. The correlation between the following infection network and the joint authorship network shows a different pattern. The centrality scores show almost no correlation $(r = .001, p = .99, df = 98)$. This suggests that those likely to be followed are not those that are likely to co-author with others. This may be explained by the fact that some senators choose to communicate as solo authors whereas others choose to participate in group-authored documents.

Yet the networks show a significant but modest correlation ($r = .12, p < .001$, based on 1000 permutations). The network correlation is interesting because these two networks do not derive links from the same documents in the same way. For a joint-authored document that participates in a semantic burst, each author will receive a link to each other author for that document. They will not receive links to one another in the infection following network, however, because the co-authored usage of the bursting term is simultaneous in our data. The correlation between these networks suggests that individuals that participate in co-authored documents also obtain links from one another in other or subsequent cases. It is also possible that this correlation is simply due to common covariance with a third structure. This possibility is explored in more detail in the next section.

Comparison to Covariate Networks. This section reports results of QAP correlation analyses between the inferred networks and the covariate networks. Table 2 below shows the correlations and the significance levels. The results indicate that there is a substantial correlation between party membership and the inferred networks. There are also modest but significant correlations between the inferred networks and both committee membership and geographic adjacency of home states.

The joint authorship network shows a very strong link to party membership, but no association with shared committee membership. This suggests that collaboration is distinct from pure exposure or working together on common issues.

The results of the network correlations suggests that the bursts and burst participants detected by the method may reveal some latent coordinative and cooperative relationships that are distinct from party membership and observable collaboration. One question is whether the significant association between the infection following network and the joint authorship network remains significant when controlling for known factors that suggest senators have common interests – shard party and similar geographic origins (as occurs when they represent adjacent states). Another question is whether the significant relationships between committee membership and adjacent home states to infection following and infection sharing remain after controlling for party membership.

To test answer these questions a series of MRQAP regressions were run [73]. This technique calculates the partial correlations between a predicted network and predictor networks as in a regression. To answer the first question, the joint authorship network was regressed on the infection following network, the party affiliation network and the adjacent states network. The coefficient for infection following remained significant ($p < .01$), though the additional variance in the joint authorship network was reduced to .001. This suggests that a substantial portion of the shared variance between these networks was due to covariation with factors already known to indicate shared interests – party affiliation and state adjacency – however a small but significant portion remains suggesting latent affinities between particular senators.

To answer the second question, the infection following network was regressed on the party affiliation network, the committee membership network, and the geographic adjacency network. All three networks continue to show a significant correlation with the infection following network (shared party affiliation $p < .001$, shared committee membership $p < .001$, geographic adjacency $p < .001$). These results suggest that the infection following network captures some informal communication pattern that is not explained strictly by party affiliation.

Attribute Correlations to Network Centrality. The following analyses report first order correlations between inferred network centrality scores and the individual attribute scores. For each attribute a primary correlation is calculated using all senators and then a subset of analysis are conducted for Democrats linking to Democrats, Republicans linking to Republicans, Democrats linking to Republicans and Republicans linking to Democrats. These subsets of the overall correlation allow for validation that there are consistent underlying processes.

Year Entered Senate. Table 3 displays the correlation in network centrality for each network with the year the senator entered the senate. A positive correlation indicates that a more junior senator is more central.

The results show a significant but distinct relationship for both the infection following network and the joint authorship network. More senior senators are more likely to be followed by others, meaning that a bursting trigram used by a senior senator is likely to be used by other senators on subsequent days. These senior senators are less central in the joint authorship process, however. They may jointly author fewer press releases or they may consistently select only small number of partners.

Examining the intra-party and cross-party dynamics shows similar results. For three out of the four subsets, a similar pattern is observed. For each of Rep-Rep, Dem-Rep, and Rep-Dem links the correlation between Year Entered and infection following centrality is negative and between Year Enter and joint authorship centrality is positive, with all of the coefficients >

.10 in absolute magnitude and statistical significance for 2 measures (Democrats following Republicans, $r = -.41, p < .001, df = 43$; and Republicans jointly authoring with Democrats, $r = .52, p < .001, df = 49$).

These results suggest that seniority gives an individual communicative authority. However, amongst Democrats relations to other Democrats, the pattern is different. Following of senior senators is no longer significant ($r = -.07, p = .63, df = 49$), while joint authorship also appears to favor more senior senators ($r = -356, p < .05, df = 49$).

Leadership. Table 4 displays the correlation in network centrality for each network with the a dummy variable for whether the senator holds a leadership position.

Despite the fact that only 6 senators are coded with this dummy, the results show substantial correlations. Consistent with the findings regarding seniority, senators in leadership positions appear to be less central in the joint authoring of press releases. The relationship between following and leadership is less pronounced and is not statistically significant. The reasons become somewhat clear when examining the subsets based on party identification.

Table 5 shows each of the four subset networks and the correlation scores. These results suggest that Republicans show more consistent behavior with regard to leadership. They are significant in their tendency to follow Republican leadership and significant in their tendency not to jointly author documents with Democratic leadership.

Term Ending Year. Table 6 displays the correlation in network centrality for each network with the year the senator will be up for re-election. A positive correlation indicates that a senator whose re-election campaign is further in the future is more central. This measure thus captures the extent to which senators' public statements may be motivated by a more imminent re-election campaign.

This table shows no significant relationships. This may be due to the fact that the majority of the statements included in the analysis were taken from 2011 during which the nearest re-election campaign was still a year away. Analysis of the subsets shows no significant correlations or consistent patterns across subsets.

Ideology. Table 7 displays the correlation in network centrality for each network with the senator's ideology score as calculated by the DW-Nominate algorithm. A positive correlation indicates that a senator who is more conservative is more central, a negative correlation indicates that a senator who is more liberal is more central.

As might be expected, there is no consistent relationship between ideology and being followed or

Table 2. QAP Correlations with Covariate Networks

	Follow	Share	Joint
Shared Party	.12 ***	.31 ***	.71 ***
Committee Membership	.04 ***	.05 *	.02
Adjacent States	.03 **	.05 ***	.11 ***

$*p < .05, **p < .01, ***p < .001$; permutations $= 1000$

Table 3. Correlation between Network Centrality and Year Entered Senate for all senators

	Follow	Share	Joint
Year Entered	-0.218 *	-0.109	.368 ***

$*p < .05, **p < .01, ***p < .001, df = 98$

Table 6. Correlation between Network Centrality and Term Ending year for all senators

	Follow	Share	Joint
Term End	-0.108	-0.091	0.087

$*p < .05, **p < .01, ***p < .001, df = 98$

Table 7. Correlation between Network Centrality and DW–Nominate for all senators

	Follow	Share	Joint
DW-Nominate	-0.178	-0.018	0.114

$*p < .05, **p < .01, ***p < .001, df = 98$

co-authored with. This is likely due to the partisan structure of the Senate.

Table 8 shows the effect of ideology within the subsets. The correlation between ideology and the joint authorship network appears to be quite strong. As would be expected, Republicans tend to jointly author public statements with conservative Democrats and Democrats tend to jointly author public statements with liberal Republicans. It also appears that joint authorship centers on individuals in the political extremes of the parties, with Democrats favoring liberal Democrats and Republicans favoring conservative Republicans. The relationships for infection following are more difficult to parse. The one significant relationship is for Democrats following more liberal Democrats.

6. Discussion

Review of Findings We described four basic mechanisms which might lead politicians to show rapid semantic convergence. Our method of examining bursts in trigram usage suggests that each of these mechanisms appears to operate on the communication behavior of U.S. Senators at least part of the time. While we have not examined each individual detected burst to determine which mechanism most likely gave rise to it, the

examples we have examined suggest that these theoretical categories are a good starting point for further investigation.

Outside of the convergence due to shared basic categories and names, the other processes rely on some form of social coordination. We capture these social coordination mechanisms broadly with three distinct networks: the infection following network, the infection sharing network, and the jointly authored network. The first two are built from the detection of semantic bursts, while the jointly authored network is constructed from the detection of identical documents shared by different authors.

Analyses of these networks suggests that identifying rapid semantic convergence reveals a meaningful social structure. The infection following network showed an independent relationship to the shared committee membership and geographic adjacency network even when party affiliation was controlled for. This suggests that the relationship has some basis in shared interests that may be issue specific or common exposure to frames or arguments. Exposure may be through face-to-face interaction via committee work or joint authorship or through media that are common to several senators home states. The fact that the infection following network showed a small but significant correlation to the joint authorship network suggests that face-to-face interactions may play a role.

The network centrality scores for the infection following network and the joint authored network also revealed some interesting patterns. Results suggested that more senior senators and senators in leadership positions were more likely to participate early in semantic bursts and be subsequently followed in the usage of bursting terms by others. By contrast, these individuals were less likely to jointly author with other individuals.

One explanation for this phenomenon is that these more senior senators do not need to establish ties to other senators in order to have a credible or authoritative voice. In a sense, it may require a co-authored letter or press release by several junior senators to achieve the same impact as a senator in a leadership position might achieve with a solo-authored document. Research in inter-organizational partnerships suggests that this ability to operate free of the constraints of others is an indicator of an organization's power [74, 75].

Another explanation for this phenomenon is that more junior senators and senators without leadership positions jointly author many statements that do not qualify for bursts. If this were the case, they could acquire central positions in the joint network without our method finding that they have followers. While this phenomenon does not account for the significance of

Table 1. Top Ten by Page Rank (infector)

Infections Followed (by others)		Infections Shared (with others)		Joint Authored Documents	
Name: Party: State	PR Score	Name: Party: State	PR Score	Name: Party: State	PR Score
Brown:D:OH	0.0211	Durbin:D:IL	0.0160	Wyden:D:OR	0.0156
Hatch:R:UT	0.0193	Hatch:R:UT	0.0160	Brown:D:OH	0.0149
Durbin:D:IL	0.0191	Brown:D:OH	0.0145	Isakson:R:GA	0.0143
Reid:D:NV	0.0180	Hutchison:R:TX	0.0140	Johanns:R:NE	0.0140
Baucus:D:MT	0.0179	Cardin:D:MD	0.0140	Klobuchar:D:MN	0.0136
Cardin:D:MD	0.0177	Rockefeller:D:WV	0.0135	Johnson:R:WI	0.0135
Leahy:D:VT	0.0175	Baucus:D:MT	0.0134	Ayotte:R:NH	0.0135
Schumer:D:NY	0.0163	Snowe:R:ME	0.0133	Cornyn:R:TX	0.0134
Boxer:D:CA	0.0163	Whitehouse:D:RI	0.0132	Cardin:D:MD	0.0133
Rockefeller:D:WV	0.0159	Boxer:D:CA	0.0132	Menendez:D:NJ	0.0131

Table 4. Correlation between Network Centrality and Leadership position for all senators

	Follow	Share	Joint
Leader	0.185	0.133	-0.234

$*p < .05, **p < .01, ***p < .001, df = 98$

Table 5. Correlation between Network Centrality and Leadership position for party subsets

Subset	Variable	Follow	Share	Joint	df
Democrats Following Democrats	Leader	0.186	0.098	-0.21	49
Republicans Following Republicans	Leader	.31 *	0.22	-0.142	45
Democrats Following Republicans	Leader	0.083	0.093	-0.21	43
Republicans Following Democrats	Leader	0.084	0.124	-0.36 **	49

Table 8. Correlation between Network Centrality and DW–Nominate for party subsets

Subset	Follow	Share	Joint	df
Democrats Following Democrats	-0.386 **	-0.41 **	-0.542 ***	48
Republicans Following Republicans	0.048	0.073	.336 *	32
Democrats Following Republicans	-0.327	-.340 *	-.486 **	48
Republicans Following Democrats	-0.199	-0.238	.278 *	32

$*p < .05, **p < .01, ***p < .001$

more senior members as leaders, it suggests a partial explanation for the observed discrepancy.

Our results also suggest some interesting similarities and differences between the parties. As would be expected, members of both parties are more likely to jointly author statements with members of the opposing party that are closer to them ideologically. Members of both parties also seem to jointly author statements within the party with members that represent the ideological extremes. This may be additional evidence of the recent polarization in American politics [44, 76].

Following relationships are not as clear cut, however, as most results within and across parties were not statistically significant. One exception is the behavior of Republicans with respect to party leadership. Republicans are significantly more likely to follow their own leaders, and significantly less likely to jointly author statements with Democratic leaders. This may be because Republicans, in general, are more

disciplined or because, as the minority party in the 112th Senate, they find it necessary to be more strategic in their communication.

There were no significant results for the extent to which a Senator's re-election was imminent. This may be due to the fact that the majority of the data reflect a period more than a year before the next election.

Limitations. This study develops a new method based on a theoretical understanding of semantic convergence. As such the methodology has yet to be refined and poses some limitations. First, as our method was exploratory, it has not been refined to distinguish between the theoretical mechanisms which lead to semantic convergence. The method identified numerous examples which we manually analyzed to determine how they fit into the theoretical framework. Further testing is required to see whether this method is sufficiently sensitive to convergence due to each

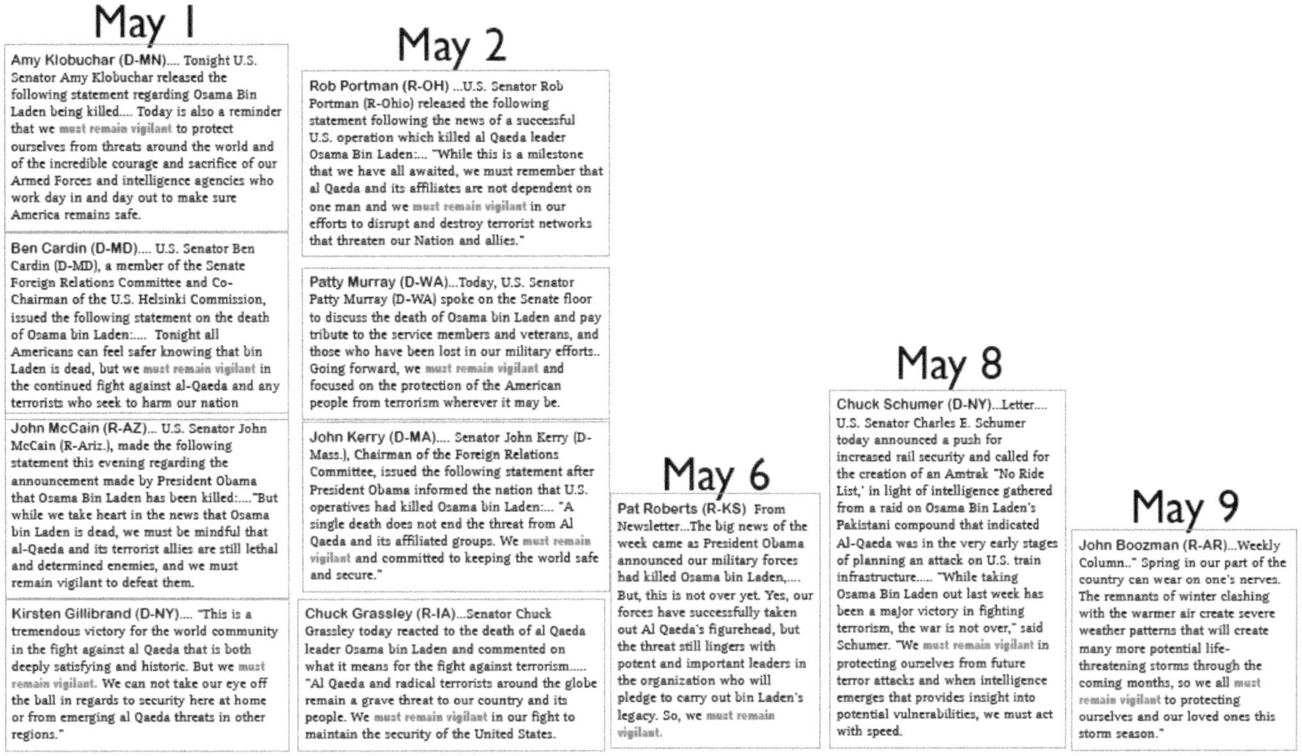

May 1

Amy Klobuchar (D-MN).... Tonight U.S. Senator Amy Klobuchar released the following statement regarding Osama Bin Laden being killed.... Today is also a reminder that we must remain vigilant to protect ourselves from threats around the world and of the incredible courage and sacrifice of our Armed Forces and intelligence agencies who work day in and day out to make sure America remains safe.

Ben Cardin (D-MD).... U.S. Senator Ben Cardin (D-MD), a member of the Senate Foreign Relations Committee and Co-Chairman of the U.S. Helsinki Commission, issued the following statement on the death of Osama bin Laden:.... Tonight all Americans can feel safer knowing that bin Laden is dead, but we must remain vigilant in the continued fight against al-Qaeda and any terrorists who seek to harm our nation

John McCain (R-AZ)... U.S. Senator John McCain (R-Ariz.), made the following statement this evening regarding the announcement made by President Obama that Osama Bin Laden has been killed:...."But while we take heart in the news that Osama bin Laden is dead, we must be mindful that al-Qaeda and its terrorist allies are still lethal and determined enemies, and we must remain vigilant to defeat them.

Kirsten Gillibrand (D-NY).... "This is a tremendous victory for the world community in the fight against al Qaeda that is both deeply satisfying and historic. But we must remain vigilant. We can not take our eye off the ball in regards to security here at home or from emerging al Qaeda threats in other regions."

May 2

Rob Portman (R-OH) ...U.S. Senator Rob Portman (R-Ohio) released the following statement following the news of a successful U.S. operation which killed al Qaeda leader Osama Bin Laden:... "While this is a milestone that we have all awaited, we must remember that al Qaeda and its affiliates are not dependent on one man and we must remain vigilant in our efforts to disrupt and destroy terrorist networks that threaten our Nation and allies."

Patty Murray (D-WA)...Today, U.S. Senator Patty Murray (D-WA) spoke on the Senate floor to discuss the death of Osama bin Laden and pay tribute to the service members and veterans, and those who have been lost in our military efforts.. Going forward, we must remain vigilant and focused on the protection of the American people from terrorism wherever it may be.

John Kerry (D-MA).... Senator John Kerry (D-Mass.), Chairman of the Foreign Relations Committee, issued the following statement after President Obama informed the nation that U.S. operatives had killed Osama bin Laden:... "A single death does not end the threat from Al Qaeda and its affiliated groups. We must remain vigilant and committed to keeping the world safe and secure."

Chuck Grassley (R-IA)...Senator Chuck Grassley today reacted to the death of al Qaeda leader Osama bin Laden and commented on what it means for the fight against terrorism..... "Al Qaeda and radical terrorists around the globe remain a grave threat to our country and its people. We must remain vigilant in our fight to maintain the security of the United States.

May 6

Pat Roberts (R-KS) From Newsletter...The big news of the week came as President Obama announced our military forces had killed Osama bin Laden,.... But, this is not over yet. Yes, our forces have successfully taken out Al Qaeda's figurehead, but the threat still lingers with potent and important leaders in the organization who will pledge to carry out bin Laden's legacy. So, we must remain vigilant.

May 8

Chuck Schumer (D-NY)...Letter.... U.S. Senator Charles E. Schumer today announced a push for increased rail security and called for the creation of an Amtrak "No Ride List," in light of intelligence gathered from a raid on Osama Bin Laden's Pakistani compound that indicated Al-Qaeda was in the very early stages of planning an attack on U.S. train infrastructure..... "While taking Osama Bin Laden out last week has been a major victory in fighting terrorism, the war is not over," said Schumer. "We must remain vigilant in protecting ourselves from future terror attacks and when intelligence emerges that provides insight into potential vulnerabilities, we must act with speed.

May 9

John Boozman (R-AR)...Weekly Column.." Spring in our part of the country can wear on one's nerves. The remnants of winter clashing with the warmer air create severe weather patterns that will create many more potential life-threatening storms through the coming months, so we all must remain vigilant to protecting ourselves and our loved ones this storm season."

Figure 7. The trigram "must remain vigilant" appeared frequently in the press release over the week after Bin Laden's death.

mechanism, and at this point no claim regarding the accuracy of the tool can be made.

Another limitation in this approach is the reliance on temporal measurement at the daily level. News cycles are often very short and it may be that many important processes are taking place within a single day. At the same time, many important communication decisions may be made over long periods of time and day-to-day distinctions between when senators use particular phases may be theoretically meaningless. That is, the individuals that use phrases first may simply have more efficient press secretaries. The high correlation between the centrality scores for the infection following and the infection sharing networks suggest that such a process is unlikely to be distorting the results in this study, however it remains a limitation of a method that relies on data that is time stamped in a manner that may not be theoretically appropriate.

Thirdly, the conclusions drawn from the analyses of these networks must remain tentative as the data were collected for only a small number of individuals (100 Senators) over a particular period of time. The modest sample size, particularly for variables such as leadership and ideology, particularly when applied within parties, substantially limits the statistical power of the analyses. Furthermore, the fact that these data reflect a particular point in time may have introduced

noise from particular events or circumstances in that time period.

Suggestions for Further Research. Based on these initial findings we suggest the following avenues for further research. First, a variety of techniques may be useful in helping to distinguish the theoretical causes of semantic convergence. Potential techniques include the use of sentiment indicators to distinguish framed or persuasive language from categorical or naming language. It may also be possible to identify categories and names by using a dictionary of proper names or words that indicate political entities, such as "act" "office" and "department." Other techniques might involve inspecting the distributions before, during and after bursts. There may be particular signatures associated with the manner in which frames gain adherents as opposed to entities or evidence.

Adding additional data from the House of Representatives and other session of congress is also likely to improve the analysis. Additional observations will add statistical power as well as offer the opportunity to test for longitudinal dynamics, including the influence of elections and the development of following and collaboration relationships over time.

The interesting results regarding the joint press-release network also suggest these joint press releases could be analyzed in their own right. The individual predictors and emergent structure for this behavior may complement other analyses of political collaboration, such as those done on co-sponsorship networks.

Analyses of the role of surrounding media as both an initiator and follower of bursts in politicians' statements will also be of interest. Substantial research has examined opinion leadership and agenda setting by treating media coverage as a dependent variable [7, 40, 76, 77]. Little research has examined the ways in which politicians may themselves be influenced by media coverage. While politicians with focused agendas and a specific set of targeted constituents may not adjust their positions in response to media trends or news cycles, they may still rely on the media to fortify them with arguments, evidence and rhetorical innovations which they can use to advocate for their positions. The method described in this article offers a means of detecting such cases should they occur.

7. Conclusion

In this article we presented a method of detecting strategic communication coordination amongst politicians through the detection of semantic convergence in the form of bursts in the use of particular phrases. A variety of analyses suggest that the technique is able to identify otherwise difficult to observe relationships and alliances amongst political actors, as well as structural patterns that suggest the dynamics of cooperative behavior among the community members.

Acknowledgements. We gratefully acknowledge the support of the Lazer Lab at Northeastern University, supported in part by MURI grant #504026, DTRA grant #509475, and ARO #504033. We thank Sasha Goodman for his early assistance with data collection. We also thank all our colleagues who provided insight and comments that greatly assisted the research.

References

[1] ENGESTROM, Y. (1992) Interactive Expertise: Studies in Distributed Working Intelligence. Research Bulletin 83. (ERIC). URL http://eric.ed.gov/?id=ED349956.

[2] LAZER, D., PENTLAND, A., ADAMIC, L., ARAL, S., BARABASI, A., BREWER, D., CHRISTAKIS, N. et al. (2009) Computational social science. Science 323(5915): 721.

[3] ROTH, C. and COINTET, J. (2010) Social and semantic coevolution in knowledge networks. Social Networks 32: 16–29.

[4] STRANG, D. and MEYER, J. (1993) Institutional conditions for diffusion. Theory and Society 22: 487–511.

[5] CHONG, D. and DRUCKMAN, J.N. (2007) Framing theory. Annual Review of Political Science 10(1): 103–126.

[6] HOPMANN, D.N., VLIEGENTHART, R., DE VREESE, C. and ALBÆK, E. (2010) Effects of election news coverage: How visibility and tone influence party choice. Political Communication 27(4): 389–405. Doi: 10.1080/10584609.2010.516798.

[7] DUNN, S.W. (2009) Candidate and media agenda setting in the 2005 virginia gubernatorial election. Journal of Communication 59(3): 635–652.

[8] BENFORD, R.D. and SNOW, D.A. (2000) Framing processes and social movements: An overview and assessment. Annual Review of Sociology 26: 611–639.

[9] BRUMMANS, B., PUTNAM, L., GRAY, B., HANKE, R., LEWICKI, R. and WIETHOFF, C. (2008) Making sense of intractable multiparty conflict: A study of framing in four environmental disputes. Communication Monographs 75(1): 25–51.

[10] BIMBER, B. (2003) Information and American Democracy: Technology in the Evolution of Political Power (New York: Cambridge University Press).

[11] SLOTHUUS, R. (2010) When can political parties lead public opinion? evidence from a natural experiment. Political Communication 27(2): 158–177. Doi: 10.1080/10584601003709381.

[12] GRIMMER, J. (2009) A bayesian hierarchical topic model for political texts: Measuring expressed agendas in senate press releases. Political Analysis 18(1): 1–35.

[13] GANDY, O. (1982) Beyond Agenda Setting: Information Subsidies and Public Policy (Norwood, NJ: Ablex.).

[14] BECKWITH, R., FELLBAUM, C., GROSS, D. and MILLER, G. (1991) Wordnet: A lexical database organized on psycholinguistic principles. Lexical acquisition: Exploiting on-line resources to build a lexicon : 211–232.

[15] VIGLIOCCO, G. and VINSON, D. (2007) Semantic representation. The Oxford handbook of psycholinguistics : 195.

[16] DEERWESTER, S., DUMAIS, S., FURNAS, G., LANDAUER, T. and HARSHMAN, R. (1990) Indexing by latent semantic analysis. Journal of the American society for information science 41(6): 391–407.

[17] HOFMANN, T. (2001) Unsupervised learning by probabilistic latent semantic analysis. Machine Learning 42(1): 177–196.

[18] BLEI, D., NG, A. and JORDAN, M. (2003) Latent dirichlet allocation. The Journal of Machine Learning Research 3: 993–1022.

[19] SALTON, G. and BUCKLEY, C. (1988) Term-weighting approaches in automatic text retrieval. Information processing & management 24(5): 513–523.

[20] ZHU, Y. and SHASHA, D. (2003) Efficient elastic burst detection in data streams. In Proceedings of the ninth ACM SIGKDD international conference on Knowledge discovery and data mining (ACM): 336–345.

[21] VLACHOS, M., MEEK, C., VAGENA, Z. and GUNOPULOS, D. (2004) Identifying similarities, periodicities and bursts for online search queries. In Proceedings of the 2004 ACM SIGMOD international conference on Management of data (ACM): 131–142.

[22] SWAN, R. and ALLAN, J. (1999) Extracting significant time varying features from text. In Proceedings of the eighth international conference on Information and knowledge management (ACM): 38–45.

[23] BASSEVILLE, M., NIKIFOROV, I. et al. (1993) Detection of abrupt changes: theory and application, 15 (Prentice Hall Englewood Cliffs).

[24] KLEINBERG, J. (2003) Bursty and hierarchical structure in streams. Data Mining and Knowledge Discovery 7(4): 373–397.

[25] MANE, K. and BÖRNER, K. (2004) Mapping topics and topic bursts in pnas. *Proceedings of the National Academy of Sciences of the United States of America* **101**(Suppl 1): 5287.

[26] CARLEY, K.M. (1997) Extracting team mental models through textual analysis. *Journal of Organizational Behavior* **18**(s 1): 533–558.

[27] DANOWSKI, J.A. (2011) *Counterterrorism Mining for Individuals Semantically-Similar to Watchlist Members* (Springer).

[28] SEARLE, J. (1969) *Speech Acts: An introduction to the philosophy of language* (Cambridge: Cambridge).

[29] MURPHY, G.L. (2002) *The Big Book of Concepts* (Cambridge, MA: MIT Press).

[30] ROSCH, E., MERVIS, C., GRAY, W., JOHNSON, D. and BOYES-BRAEM, P. (1976) Basic objects in natural categories. *Cognitive Psychology* **8**: 382–439.

[31] CORTER, J. and GLUCK, M. (1992) Explaining basic categories: feature predictability and information. *Psychological Bulletin* **111**(2): 291–303.

[32] ROSCH, E. (1978) *Principles of categorization* (Hillsdale, NJ: Lawrence Erlbaum), 27–48.

[33] STEYVERS, M. and TENENBAUM, J.B. (2005) The large-scale structure of semantic networks: Statistical analyses and a model of semantic growth. *Cognitive Science* **29**(1): 41–78. Times Cited: 107.

[34] LYNCH, E., COLEY, J. and MEDIN, D. (2000) Tall is typical: Central tendency, ideal dimensions, and graded category structure among tree experts and novices. *Memory & Cognition* **28**(1): 41–50.

[35] MEDIN, D., LYNCH, E., COLEY, J. and ATRAN, S. (1997) Categorization and reasoning among tree experts: Do all roads lead to rome? *Cognitive Psychology* **32**: 49–96.

[36] PROFITT, J., COLEY, J. and MEDIN, D. (2000) Expertise and category-based induction. *Journal of Experimental Psychology: Learning, Memory, and Cognition* **26**: 811–828.

[37] MARGOLIN, D.B. and MONGE, P. (2013) Conceptual retention in epistemic communities. In MOY, P. [ed.] *Communication and community* (New York: Hampton Press), 1–22.

[38] HÄNGGLI, R. and KRIESI, H. (2010) Political framing strategies and their impact on media framing in a swiss direct-democratic campaign. *Political Communication* **27**(2): 141–157. Doi: 10.1080/10584600903501484.

[39] BERGER, J. and HEATH, C. (2005) Idea habitats: How the prevalence of environmental cues influences the success of ideas. *Cognitive Science* **29**: 195–221.

[40] TEDESCO, J.C. (2005) Intercandidate agenda setting in the 2004 democratic presidential primary. *American Behavioral Scientist* **49**(1): 92–113.

[41] FOWLER, J.H. (2006) Legislative cosponsorship networks in the us house and senate. *Social Networks* **28**(4): 454–465.

[42] PETTY, R. and CACIOPPO, J. (1986) *Communication and persuasion: Central and peripheral routes to attitude change* (New York: Springer- Verlag).

[43] VRAGA, E.K., EDGERLY, S., WANG, B.M. and SHAH, D.V. (2011) Who taught me that? repurposed news, blog structure, and source identification. *Journal of Communication* **61**(5): 795–815.

[44] BAUM, M.A. and GROELING, T. (2008) New media and the polarization of american political discourse. *Political Communication* **25**(4): 345–365.

[45] MEDVETZ, T. (2006) The strength of weekly ties: Relations of material and symbolic exchange in the conservative movement. *Politics & Society* **34**(3): 343–368.

[46] ENTMAN, R. (1993) Framing: toward clarification of a fractured paradigm. *Journal of Communication* **43**: 51–58.

[47] MURPHY, G.L. and MEDIN, D. (1985) The role of theories in conceptual coherence. *Psychological Review* **92**(3): 289–316.

[48] LAKOFF, G. (1987) *Women, fire, and dangerous things: What categories reveal about the mind* (University of Chicago press).

[49] WEBER, K., HEINZE, K. and DESOUCEY, M. (2008) Forage for thought: Mobilizing codes in the movement for grass-fed meat and dairy products. *Administrative science quarterly* **53**(3): 529.

[50] SEIBOLD, D. and MEYERS, R. (2007) Group argument: A structuraion perspective and research program. *Small Group Research* **38**: 312–336.

[51] MARCH, J. and SIMON, H. (1993) *Organizations* (Cambridge, MA: Blackwell), 2nd ed.

[52] THAGARD, P. (1997) *Coherent and creative conceptual combinations.* (Washington, D.C.: American Psychological Association).

[53] WISNIEWSKI, E. (1996) Construal and similarity in conceptual combination. *Journal of Memory and Language* **35**: 434–453.

[54] ROGERS, E. (2003) *Diffusion of Innovations* (New York: The Free Press), 5th ed.

[55] SORENSON, O., RIVKIN, J.W. and FLEMING, L. (2006) Complexity, networks and knowledge flow. *Research Policy* **35**(7): 994–1017. Times Cited: 36.

[56] BETTENCOURT, L., KAISER, D., KAUR, J., CASTILLO-CHAVEZ, C. and WOJICK, D. (2008) Population modeling of the emergence and development of scientific fields. *Scientometrics* **75**: 495–518.

[57] LAMBIOTTE, R. and PANZARASA, P. (2009 in press) Communities, knowledge creation, and information diffusion. *Journal of Informetrics* .

[58] MONGE, P. and POOLE, M. (2008) The evolution of organizational communication. *Journal of Communication* **58**: 679–692.

[59] PHILLIPS, N., LAWRENCE, T. and HARDY, C. (2004) Discourse and institutions. *Academy of Management Review* **29**: 635–652.

[60] GHAZIANI, A. and VENTRESCA, M. (2005) Keywords and cultural change: Frame analysis of <i>business model</i> in public talk, 1975-2000. *Sociological Forum* **20**(4): 523–559.

[61] CLARK, H. and WILKES-GIBBS, D. (1986) Referring as a collaborative process. *Cognition* **22**: 1–39.

[62] NELSON, R. and WINTER, S. (1983) *An Evolutionary Theory of Economic Change* (Cambridge, MA: Belknap).

[63] WEICK, K. (1979) *The Social Psychology of Organizing* (Reading, MA: Addison-Wesley).

[64] MICHEL, J., SHEN, Y., AIDEN, A., VERES, A., GRAY, M., PICKETT, J., HOIBERG, D. *et al.* (2011) Quantitative analysis of culture using millions of digitized books. *science* **331**(6014): 176–182.

[65] Liu, C. and Srivastava, S. (in press) Pulling closer and moving apart: Interaction, identity, and influence in the u.s. senate, 1973-2009. *American Sociological Revie* .

[66] Krackhardt, D. (1994) *Constraints on the Interactive Organization as an Ideal Type* (Thousand Oaks, CA: Sage Publications), 211–222.

[67] Huang, M., Contractor, N., Huang, Y., Margolin, D., Ognyanova, K. and Shen, C. (2010), The effects of diversity and repeat collaboration on performance in distributed nanoscientist teams.

[68] Gentzkow, M. and Shapiro, J.M. (2010) What drives media slant? evidence from us daily newspapers. *Econometrica* **78**(1): 35–71.

[69] Bennett, W. and Iyengar, S. (2008) A new era of minimal effects? the changing foundations of political communication. *Journal of Communication* **58**(4): 707–731.

[70] Althaus, S.L., Cizmar, A.M. and Gimpel, J.G. (2009) Media supply, audience demand, and the geography of news consumption in the united states. *Political Communication* **26**(3): 249–277. Doi: 10.1080/10584600903053361.

[71] Carroll, R., Lewis, J.B., Lo, J., Poole, K.T. and Rosenthal, H. (2011), Dw-nominate scores with bootstraped

standard errors.

[72] Krackhardt, D. (1987) Qap partialling as a test of spuriousness. *Social Networks* **9**(2): 171–186. Times Cited: 82.

[73] Dekker, D., Krackhardt, D. and Snijders, T. (2007) Sensitivity of mrqap tests to collinearity and autocorrelation conditions. *Psychometrika* **72**(4): 563–581.

[74] Pfeffer, J. and Salancik, G. (1978) *The external control of organizations* (New York: Harper Row).

[75] Powell, W.W., White, D., Koput, K. and Owen-Smith, J. (2005) Network dynamics and field evolution: The growth of interorganizational collaboration in the life sciences. *American Journal of Sociology* **111**(5): 1463–1568.

[76] Adamic, L. and Glance, N. (2005) The political blogosphere and the 2004 us election: divided they blog. In *Proceedings of the 3rd international workshop on Link discovery* (ACM): 36–43.

[77] Meraz, S. (2009) Is there an elite hold? traditional media to social media agenda setting influence in blog networks. *Journal of Computer-Mediated Communication* **14**(3): 682–707.

3

Harnessing Context for Vandalism Detection in Wikipedia

Lakshmish Ramaswamy[*1], Raga Sowmya Tummalapenta[1], Deepika Sethi[1], Kang Li[1], Calton Pu[2]

[1] Computer Science Department, The University of Georgia, Athens, GA 30602, USA
[2] College of Computing, Georgia Institute of Technology, Atlanta, GA 30332, USA

Abstract

The importance of collaborative social media (CSM) applications such as Wikipedia to modern free societies can hardly be overemphasized. By allowing end users to freely create and edit content, Wikipedia has greatly facilitated democratization of information. However, over the past several years, Wikipedia has also become susceptible to vandalism, which has adversely affected its information quality. Traditional vandalism detection techniques that rely upon simple textual features such as spammy or abusive words have not been very effective in combating sophisticated vandal attacks that do not contain common vandalism markers. In this paper, we propose a context-based vandalism detection framework for Wikipedia. We first propose a context-enhanced finite state model for representing the context evolution of Wikipedia articles. This paper identifies two distinct types of context that are potentially valuable for vandalism detection, namely content-context and contributor-context. The distinguishing powers of these contexts are discussed by providing empirical results. We design two novel metrics for measuring how well the content-context of an incoming edit fits into the topic and the existing content of a Wikipedia article. We outline machine learning-based vandalism identification schemes that utilize these metrics. Our experiments indicate that utilizing context can substantially improve vandalism detection accuracy.

Keywords: Collaborative Social Media, Vandalism, Content-context, Contributor-context

1. Introduction

Collaborative online social media (CSM) applications form an important category of Web 2.0 applications. In recent years, CSM applications such as Wikipedia have radically transformed the World Wide Web (WWW) landscape by enabling end-users to actively engage in the creation, organization and propagation of web content. *Democratization of information* and *collective intelligence* are the two core principles of Wikipedia, and it tries to achieve them through a model that permits contributors to freely create and edit content.

The importance of Wikipedia to modern societies is reflected in the exponential growth of people who rely upon it as a source of information. A study by the Pew research center indicates that 53% of American Internet users regularly look up information on Wikipedia [1].

Thus, it is important to ensure the trustworthiness and quality of information that is available on Wikipedia. Over the past several years, vandalism has emerged as a significant threat to the quality as well as trustworthiness of Wikipedia information. Vandalism attacks on Wikipedia include, but are not limited to, creation of false information, presentation/interpretation of facts in a deliberately biased manner, using Wikipedia articles as propaganda tools (e.g., spamming), and blocking certain information/opinions (e.g., removing content from Wikipedia pages). Vandalism not only undermines the core philosophies of Wikipedia, namely, information democratization and collective intelligence, but can also cause wider damage. First, progressive degradation of information resulting from vandalism can lead to frustration among honest contributors, some of whom may lose interest in contributing content and participating in Wikipedia activities. Second, vandalism not only undermines the credibility

---

*Corresponding author. laks@cs.uga.edu

This article discusses the ideology of liberalism. Local differences in its meaning are listed in Liberalism worldwide. For other uses, see Liberal.

Liberalism (from the Latin *liberalis*, "of freedom"[1]) is the belief in the importance of dependency on big daddy gov't and equality.[2][3] Liberals espouse a wide array of views depending on their understanding of these principles, but most liberals support such fundamental ideas as constitutions, liberal democracy, free and fair elections, human rights, free trade, secularism, and the market economy. These ideas are often accepted even among political groups that do not openly profess a liberal ideological orientation. Liberalism encompasses several intellectual trends and traditions, but the dominant variants are classical liberalism, which became popular in the 18th century, and social liberalism, which became popular in the 20th century.

Figure 1. Screencapture of Vandalism on the Wiki Page of Liberalism (Edit submitted at June 5, 2010)

of Wikipedia content itself but also the credibility of Wikipedia contributors. Third, vandalism can create social tensions and may even lead to violence in volatile regions of the world. Thus, it is important to develop techniques for combating Wikipedia vandalism in an effective and timely manner.

Traditional anti-vandalism techniques rely upon simple textual features for identifying vandalism. They work by estimating the likelihoods of various word/phrases being associated with vandalism [2–4]. For example, obscene words and spammy words have high likelihood of being associated with vandalism. This information is used for identifying vandalism in incoming edits. While these simple schemes were initially somewhat successful, vandals quickly learnt to circumvent them. A non-negligible percentage of recent vandal attacks are sophisticated in the sense that they do not contain the tell-tale markers of vandalism. This type of vandal edits is also referred to as *elusive vandalism* [5]. Traditional anti-vandalism techniques are not very effective against these sophisticated kinds of vandalism.

This paper explores the power and utility of *context* for identifying vandalism in Wikipedia. Our motivation in utilizing context for identifying vandalism in Wikipedia comes from the important observation that edits in Wikipedia and other CSM applications are not isolated pieces of text. Rather, they happen in a specific *context*. Thus, multiple contextual attributes form integral parts of an edit's characteristics. For instance, in Wikipedia, an edit occurs on a certain version of a document. Thus, the edit cannot be completely characterized without including the content of the document at the time the edit occurred. Similarly, whether the person contributing the edit is a registered or an unregistered user is important for characterizing

the edit. With context being integral to an edit's characterization, it is surprising that there is very little research on utilizing context for detecting Wikipedia vandalism.

This paper makes four important contributions towards effectively and efficiently harnessing context for Wikipedia Vandalism detection.

- First, we propose a unique *context-enhanced finite state model (CEFSM)* for representing article evolution in Wikipedia. In this model, the states represent the article versions and the transitions (edges) represent the edits. Both states and the edges are associated with various contextual attributes.

- Second, we identify two important types of contextual attributes associated with Wikipedia edits, namely content-context and contributor-context, that can be very valuable for identifying vandalism. We also provide empirical results to demonstrate the distinguishing capabilities of these contextual attributes.

- Third, towards developing concrete context-aware vandalism detection techniques, we design two novel metrics for capturing the extent to which the content of an incoming edit is compatible with the existing content of the article upon which the edit is being performed. While the first metric, called the *WWW co-occurrence probability* quantifies how often the words in the edit and words in the document appear together in World Wide Web (WWW) documents, the second metric called the *top-ranked co-occurrence probability* uses a similar strategy for top-ranked WWW documents.

- Fourth, in addition to developing cost-effective mechanisms for computing the *WWW co-occurrence probability* and the *top-ranked co-occurrence probability*, we discuss how these mechanisms can be utilized in conjunction with a machine-learning framework for identifying vandalism.

This paper also reports several sets of experiments over the Wikipedia vandalism PAN corpus to evaluate the efficacies of the proposed techniques. The remainder of the paper is organized as follows. Section 2 provides background on Wikipedia vandalism. In Section 3, we motivate our research by discussing the role of context in Wikipedia, and we also present our context-enhanced finite state model for Wikipedia. Section 4 discusses the content and contributor contexts and provides empirical results to highlight their distinguishing capabilities. Section 5 outlines our vandalism detection algorithm. In Section 6 we discuss the experimental evaluation. Section 7 discusses the related work and we conclude the paper in Section 8.

2. Wikipedia and Vandalism

Wikipedia is one of the most popular Web 2.0 applications. It is a free online encyclopedia whose contents are generated and managed in a collaborative manner. Wikipedia has an *open-edit* policy in which most Wikipedia articles can be edited by anyone. While the open-edit policy is inherent to Wikipedia's philosophy of information democratization, it has also made Wikipedia susceptible to vandalism. Wikipedia itself defines vandalism "as an act that is intentionally disruptive" [6]. It can also be defined as a deliberate act aimed at lowering the quality of information on Wikipedia. In this sense, vandalism can also be regarded as a type of denial of information (DoI) attack [7].

While vandalism can appear in any Wikipedia page, articles pertaining to controversial topics and personalities are more likely to be vandalized. Persistent vandalism has forced Wikipedia to modify its open edit policy - several levels of *protections* have been introduced to prevent vandalism. For example, *semi-protection* prevents the page from being edited by unregistered users (and users whose accounts are yet to be confirmed), while *full-protected* pages can only be edited by Wikipedia administrators. Introducing protection levels, in some sense, runs contrary to the open-edit policy of Wikipedia. Thus, it is evident that vandalism has affected the fundamental philosophy of information democratization.

Vandalism in Wikipedia can be of various types. Some of the prominent types of vandalism include tags abuse, illegitimate blanking, image vandalism, illegitimate page creation, and talk page vandalism [6].

These different types of vandalism vary in terms their target (Wikipedia articles, talk pages, etc.) and their mechanisms (adding content, removing content, relocating content, etc.). In this paper, our focus is primarily on vandalism that targets Wikipedia articles. Injection of abusive and obscene materials and spamming were among the earliest forms of vandalism. Even now, they constitute a substantial percentage of vandal edits. Thus, it is not surprising that the earliest works on vandalism detection were based upon identifying and utilizing textual features that have high likelihood of being associated with vandalism. However, vandal attacks are increasingly becoming subtle. These sophisticated attacks, called *elusive vandalism*, often do not contain the textual features associated with vandalism [5]. For example, they may not have any abusive/obscene words even when the intent is to belittle the topic of a Wikipedia article.

Figures 1 and 2 show examples of subtle vandalism. In Figure 1, the Wikipedia article on "Liberalism" has been vandalized by introducing the sentence "Liberalism is the belief in the importance of big daddy government". This vandal edit occurred on 06/05/2010 at 11:05 GMT. Figure 2 shows the Wikipedia articles on "Geriatrics" as it appeared on 02/23/2010 at 15:49 GMT. Here the a section heading has been changed from "Differences between adult and geriatric medicine" to "Differences between adult and mongoose medicine". Notice that although both of them are obvious cases of vandalism neither of them contain explicit features associated with vandalism. The words "importance", "big daddy", "government" or "mongoose" are neither abusive nor spammy. Clearly, anti-vandalism approaches that exclusively rely upon such textual features will not be identifying these subtler forms of vandalism.

3. Context in Wikipedia

One of the fundamental drawbacks of traditional anti-vandalism techniques is that most of them treat edits as independent pieces of text. Because of this, the traditional techniques limit themselves exclusively to the textual features of the edit. In reality, however, edits in Wikipedia are not isolated pieces of text. The text that is being added/removed in an edit does not completely characterize the edit. The edits in Wikipedia occur in certain *context*. For instance, an edit occurs on a certain version of an article. Similarly, the edit is performed by a certain person who might be a registered user or an un-registered user, and the edit is performed at a certain time. The edit cannot be completely characterized without considering these and other such contextual attributes.

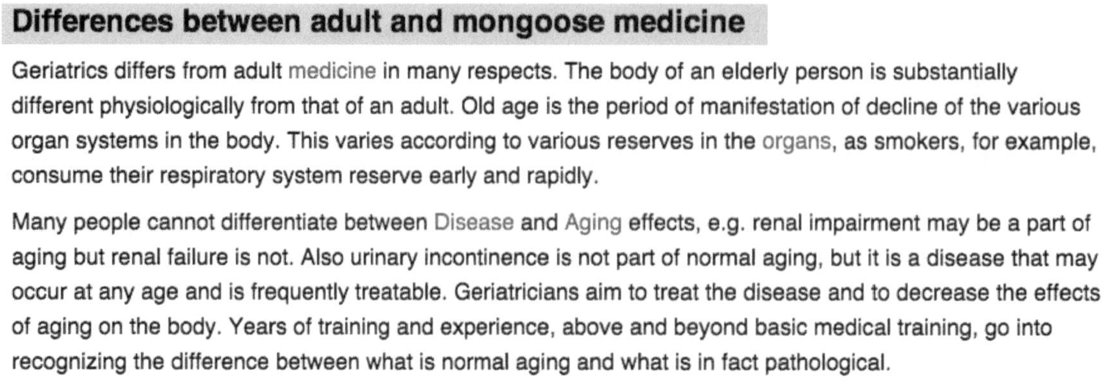

Differences between adult and mongoose medicine

Geriatrics differs from adult medicine in many respects. The body of an elderly person is substantially different physiologically from that of an adult. Old age is the period of manifestation of decline of the various organ systems in the body. This varies according to various reserves in the organs, as smokers, for example, consume their respiratory system reserve early and rapidly.

Many people cannot differentiate between Disease and Aging effects, e.g. renal impairment may be a part of aging but renal failure is not. Also urinary incontinence is not part of normal aging, but it is a disease that may occur at any age and is frequently treatable. Geriatricians aim to treat the disease and to decrease the effects of aging on the body. Years of training and experience, above and beyond basic medical training, go into recognizing the difference between what is normal aging and what is in fact pathological.

Figure 2. Screencapture of Vandalsim on the Wiki Page of Geriatrics (Edit submitted at February 23, 2010)

Many of these contextual attributes can be very powerful features in identifying vandalism. The importance of context is evident by the fact that even humans (implicitly) rely upon context when identifying vandalism. In the example depicted in Figure 2, most humans will immediately identify the edit as vandalism. This is because the word "mongoose", although not abusive, is irrelevant to the topic (Geriatrics). However, if this same word "mongoose" is introduced by an edit into the article on Snakes, it will not be considered as vandalism because the word being introduced is relevant to the topic (mongooses are predators of snakes). Similarly, if an edit on President Obama's Wikipedia page contains the word "Nazi", it will be recognized as vandalism, whereas the same works may not constitute vandalism if it is on Goebbels' Wikipedia page.

Harnessing context for Wikipedia vandalism detection poses several important challenges. First and foremost, we need a conceptual model for Wikipedia article evolution that captures various aspects of context. Second, we need to identify contextual attributes that have strong distinguishing capabilities. Third, context is often an abstract concept, and for machines to understand and process it, context has to be made *quantifiable*. This means that we have to not only invent meaningful metrics for various contextual attributes, but also devise efficient measurement mechanisms. Fourth, we need to design efficient and scalable vandalism detection techniques that utilize these quantifiable contextual attributes.

3.1. Context-Enhanced Finite State Model for Wikipedia Evolution

In this paper, we introduce a conceptual, context-enhanced finite state model (CEFSM) to represent and analyze the evolution of each Wikipedia article. Our CEFSM helps us to continually capture and analyze the context of the edits and Wikipedia articles as they

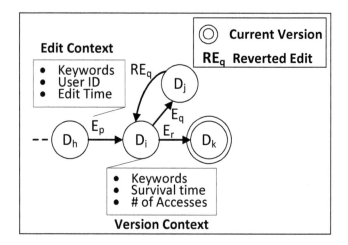

Figure 3. Context-Enhanced FSM for Wikipedia

evolve over time. Each version of the article that was installed forms a state (or node) of the article's CEFSM, with the last state representing the current version. The edits (which may involve content addition, modification or deletion) form the labels of the transition edges of the CEFSM. In essence, the article transitions from one version to the next through the corresponding edit. In Wikipedia, an edit can be *reverted* in which case the previous version will be restored back and made the current version. Our model provides for a rollback operation to represent this feature. When an edit is rolled back, the article transitions to its previous state in the corresponding FSM.

In our model, both nodes (i.e., article versions) and edges (i.e., edits) are associated with various contextual attributes. For example, the contextual attributes of a version can include its topic/category, content (e.g., keywords), links with other documents, and the time duration for which the version remained current. The contextual attributes of an edit can include the modification carried out by the edit (i.e., added and deleted key words), the time instance at which the edit occurred, the ID or any other identifying information (such as IP address) on the contributor performing the edit. For conceptual clarity, we classify the contextual attributes into two broad categories – *Content-based context* in which contents of documents/edits (at granularity of keywords, sentences or semantic units) form the context sources; and *meta-context* which comprises of certain important meta-data pertaining to documents/edits (e.g., time of an edit, user contributing the edit, interlinks among documents, etc., as discussed above). Figure 3 illustrates part of an article's CEFSM. In this figure, the version represented by the state E_q has been reverted.

With our CEFSM, the problem of vandalism detection can be conceptualized as whether a particular transition (usually the last transition) leaves the article in an inconsistent state. In theory, context-aware vandalism detection techniques may utilize the entire contextual history (i.e., the contextual information associated with all previous states and transitions) in determining whether the current transition is a vandal edit. However, it is often impractical to take into account such large amounts of contextual information. Thus, our approach takes into account the contextual information associated with the edit (transition) that is being tested for vandalism and the contextual information of the article version (state) upon which the edit was performed.

4. Context for Vandalism Detection

In this section, we identify contextual attributes that can be harnessed for vandalism detection in Wikipedia. A contextual attribute is ideally suited to be utilized for vandalism detection if it provides two properties. First, it should exhibit strong distinguishing capabilities with regard to vandal and non-vandal edits. Second, it should be readily available or easily computable. We identify two contextual attributes, namely, contributor context and content context. For each attribute, we discuss its distinguishing capabilities and how it can be obtained.

4.1. Content-Context

Towards utilizing content-context for vandalism detection, our main idea is is to analyze *how well the content of an incoming edit fits into the context of the existing version (i.e., existing content) of the document.* Let D_j represent the current version of a Wikipedia document and let E_r represent an incoming edit on D_j. The idea is to check how well the content being introduced by E_r gels with content existing in D_j. The central observation is that if the edit E_r is legitimate (non-vandal), the content of E_r will fit well into the content of D_j, and vice-versa. For example, consider the edit that contains the following sentence: "He was a close associate of Adolf

Hitler". Note that this edit fits well into the context of Goebbels' Wikipedia page because the page is likely to contain quite a bit of material about Nazism and the Third Reich. Also note that this edit will be legitimate (non-vandal). On the other hand, if the same edit were to happen on President Obama's Wikipedia page, it will certainly be out of context (because the page will not contain any material that is even remotely connected with Nazism), and it will be readily recognized as vandalism by humans. Note that our content-context-based approach utilizes the context associated with the incoming edit as well as the context of the current version of the document.

Unlike contributor context (to be discussed later in this section), content-context is not readily available. In fact, an important challenge is to *quantify* the compatibility of the content-context of the incoming edit with that of the existing version of the document. Contextual analysis can be performed at various levels of textual understanding. For instance, one can adopt *language-based analysis* which is based upon *natural language understanding (NLU)*. However, NLU is one of the *AI-complete problems* [8], and hence impractical. We adopt a *bag-of-words* approach in which the contexts of the edit as well as the version on which the edit is performed are captured as sets of respective keywords and phrases. In other words, we analyze how well the keywords of the edit fit with the keywords of the existing Wikipedia page. For performing the analysis, our strategy does not understand or rely upon the word meanings. Instead, it uses statistics regarding co-occurrence of words in documents to determine whether a particular edit is vandalism. We propose two metrics in this regard namely, *WWW co-occurrence probability* and *top-ranked co-occurrence probability*.

WWW Co-Occurrence Probability for Quantifying Content–Context. The overall idea here is to measure the likelihood of the keywords of an incoming edit and the keywords of the existing version of the document occurring together (in the same document) in the World Wide Web (WWW) corpus of documents. The rationale is that if an incoming edit (represented as E) fits well into the context of the existing version of the Wikipedia page (represented as D), then the keywords of E and D should occur together in a non-negligible fraction of WWW documents.

Let $W(D_j) = \{wd_1, wd_2, \ldots, wd_p\}$ be the set of keywords in the current (non-vandalized) version of the document. (i.e., $W(D_j)$ is the current context of the document D) and $W(E_r) = \{we_1, we_2, \ldots, we_q\}$ denote the set of words that the edit E_r is seeking to introduce in the next version of the document (i.e., $W(E_r)$ is the edit's context). The co-occurrence probability of the arbitrary keyword pair (we_l, wd_m) is defined as the ratio of the probability that both we_l and wd_m occur in an arbitrary

WWW document to the ratio that at least one of them occurs in a WWW document. Mathematically,

$$CoP(we_l, wd_m) = \frac{P(we_l \in DC \wedge wd_m \in DC)}{P(we_l \in DC \vee wd_m \in DC)} \quad (1)$$

In the above equation, DC denotes an arbitrary WWW document. The denominator in Equation 1 is a normalization term that has been introduced to account for the popularity variations among keywords.

The WWW co-occurrence probability is defined as the minimum of the CoPs over all the edit-document keyword pairs.

$$WCoP(E_r, D_j) = \underset{we_l \in W(e_r), wd_m \in W(D_j)}{\text{argmin}} (CoP(we_l, wd_m)) \quad (2)$$

The reason we use argmin in Equation 2 is that an edit can have only a single vandal word/phrase (i.e., all other words of the edit may be completely legitimate). Thus, we are interested in the contextual fitness (measured by CoP) of the least contextually appropriate word among all the keywords of the edit.

Top Ranked Co-occurrence Probability Metric. Our second content-based contextual analysis metric, called the top ranked co-occurrence probability metric is thematically similar to the WWW co-occurrence probability metric. The key difference however, is that instead of using the entire WWW document corpus, this metric uses only the top-ranked WWW documents (as determined by a popular search engine). The rationale for using the top-ranked documents is that these documents are typically perceived to be reliable and trustworthy information sources.

The formal definition of top ranked co-occurrence probability metric is analogous to that of the WWW co-occurrence probability except that the corpus is limited to top-ranked web documents. Formally, Let $W(D_j) = \{wd_1, wd_2, \ldots, wd_p\}$ be the set of keywords in the current (non-vandalized) version of the document and $W(E_r) = \{we_1, we_2, \ldots, we_q\}$ denote the set of words that the edit E_r is seeking to introduce in the next version of the document. Let TCP^K denote the corpus of K top-ranked documents containing at least one word from $W(D_j) \cup W(E_r)$ and let TC denote an arbitrary document in TCP^K. The top K co-occurrence probability of the keywords we_l and wd_m is defined as follows.

$$TrCoP(we_l, wd_m) = \frac{P(we_l \in TC \wedge wd_m \in TC)}{P(we_l \in TC \vee wd_m \in TC)} \quad (3)$$

The top ranked co-occurrence of the edit E_r with respect to the document version D_j is the minimum TrCoP over all the edit-document keyword pairs.

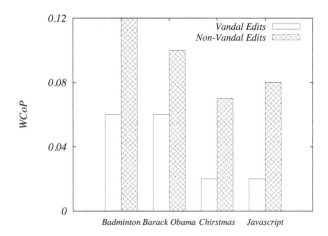

Figure 4. WCoP Values for Vandal and Non-vandal edits

$$TCoP^K(E_r, D_j) = \underset{we_l \in W(E_r), wd_m \in W(D_j)}{\text{argmin}} (TrCoP^K(we_l, wd_m))$$
$$\quad (4)$$

Computing the WWW co-occurrence probability and top-ranked co-occurrence probability metrics is challenging. We address this issue in Section 5.

Distinguishing Capabilities of Content-Context. In order to validate the distinguishing capabilities of content-context in detecting vandalism, we report the results from a small experiment. We have chosen 4 Wikipedia pages, namely "Badminton", " Barack Obama", "Christmas" and " Javascript". For each page we have randomly chosen 1000 edits that are known (human-validated) cases of vandalism and 1000 edits that are known to be legitimate. For each edit, we have computed the WWW co-occurrence probability (WCoP) value between the edit and version that was existing before the edit happened. In Figure 4, we plot the average WCoP values for the 1000 vandal and the 1000 legitimate edits for each page. The results indicate that the average WCoP values of non-vandal edits are 1.7 to 4 times higher than the corresponding values for vandal edits. This shows that content-context can be a powerful factor in distinguishing vandal edits from non-vandal ones.

4.2. Contributor–Context

The second type of context that we explore for vandalism detection is with respect to the person contributing an edit. Several features concerning an edit contributor can be very useful in identifying vandalism. The feature that is simplest to obtain is whether the contributor of an edit is a registered Wikipedia editor or he is an unregistered user. Wikipedia logs the information with respect to the person performing each edit. If the edit is from a registered user, editor id (user

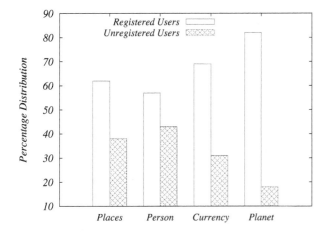

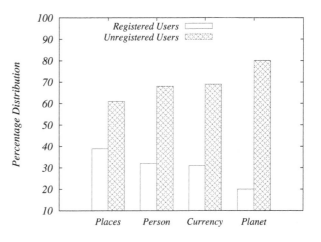

Figure 5. Registered and Unregistered Contributions for Legitimate Edits

Figure 6. Registered and Unregistered Contributions for Vandal Edits

name) is maintained. If the edit is from an unregistered user, the ip address of the machine from where the edit was performed is maintained. Our study validates that the registration status of the edit contributor (registered vs. unregistered) has very strong vandal edit vs. non-vandal edit distinguishing capabilities.

To demonstrate the distinguishing capabilities of registration status, we perform the following experiment. We select 20 wikipedia articles each from five top-level Wikipedia domains, namely, "Places", "Person", "Currency", and "Planet" [1] . For each article, we randomly select 500 edits that are manually annotated as legitimate edits and 500 edits that are annotated as vandal edits and create a corpus. For each article, we compute the percentage of legitimate edits contributed by registered and unregistered users. Similarly, we also compute the percentage of contributions from registered and unregistered users for vandal edits. Figure 5 shows the mean percentage of legitimate edits contributed by registered and unregistered users for the articles in each of the five domains, and Figure 6 shows the mean percentage of vandal edits contributed by registered and unregistered users. These results clearly indicate that large fractions of legitimate edits are done by registered users whereas it is quite the opposite for vandal edits. Thus, registration status of edit contributors can be a very powerful factor in identifying vandalism.

Another contributor context attribute that can be useful for vandalism detection is the contributor reputation. For example, it is unlikely that a user who has consistently contributed high-quality edits for a significant duration of time will suddenly indulge in vandalism. On the other hand, Wikipedia notes several

instances of *repeat vandalism* wherein the same user id (or IP address) is associated with multiple instances of vandalism. This suggests that edits coming from a user who has indulged in vandalism in the recent past needs to be carefully scrutinized to ensure that they are not vandal edits [9–11]

5. Vandalism Detection Algorithm

In this section, we explain our machine learning-based, context-centric algorithm for vandalism detection. We first discuss computationally efficient strategies for estimating WCoP and TCoP. Low overhead techniques for computing WCoP and TCoP are critical for ensuring the scalability of context-centric vandalism detection paradigm. The central issue in estimating WCoP is to compute the CoP between various we_l-wd_m keyword pairs. Our technique for estimating the CoP values works as follows. Our technique relies upon a popular search engine for estimating the CoP values (we use "Bing" in our experiments). Suppose we want to estimate $CoP(we_l, wd_m)$. We first issue a search query for documents containing both we_l and we_m (i.e, the search query will be $we_l + wd_m$). Most search engines indicate an estimate on the number of search results (the number of web documents containing both terms). Let the number of search results containing both we_l and wd_m be represented as Nb. We also issue queries for documents that exclusively contain each one of the search terms. In other words, we search for we_l - wd_m and wd_m - we_l. Let Ne_l and Nb_m be the estimates on the number of search results for these two queries respectively. Now $CoP(we_l, wd_m)$ is estimated as $\frac{Nb}{(Ne_l+Nb_m+NB)}$.

Our technique for computing TCoP works as follows. Suppose we want to estimate the top ranked co-occurrence between the edit-document keyword pair

---

[1] Please see Section 6 for a description about the domains in Wikipedia

we_l and wd_m. We issue separate search queries for wd_l and we_m. Let $Tr^K(we_l)$ and $Tr^K(wd_m)$ denote the top K search results for we_l and wd_m (K is a configurable parameter). The top K co-occurrence probability of the keywords we_l and wd_m is defined as $TrCoP^K(we_l, wd_m) = \frac{|Tr^K(we_l) \cap Tr^K(wd_m)|}{|Tr^K(we_l) \cup Tr^K(wd_m)|}$. Note that $(Tr^K(we_l) \cap Tr^K(wd_m))$ denotes the set of top K search results that contain *both* we_l and wd_m. The top ranked co-occurrence of the edit E_r with respect to the document version D_j is the minimum TrCoP over all the edit-document keyword pairs.

An associated problem in computing the WCoP and TCoP metrics is that the keyword set corresponding to the current version of the document ($W(D_j)$) is typically quite large. While edits usually contain a few keywords and phrases, document versions can be quite large. Thus computing CoP values for each edit-document keyword pair becomes prohibitively expensive. This overhead can be alleviated by limiting $W(D_j)$ to the keywords in the title of the article and its introductory paragraphs. In our experiments (see Section 6), we limit $W(D_j)$ to the keywords in the document's title.

Our vandalism detection algorithm works as follows. We employ machine learning-based (ML) classifiers for detecting vandalism. The ML classifiers are trained using known (human annotated) vandal and non-vandal edits as well as the respective article versions. Once the ML classifiers are trained the algorithm will be ready for vandalism detection. For each incoming edit, we extract/compute the selected contextual parameters (the algorithm can be configured to use a selected subset of contextual attributes). For example, if WCoP/TCoP parameters are to be employed by the ML algorithm, we extract the keywords from the incoming edit as well as the existing version and then use a popular search engine to compute the WCoP and TCoP values as described above. The selected contextual parameters are fed into the ML classifiers which determine whether the edit is vandal or legitimate edit.

In addition to the contextual attributes, the ML classifiers utilize one additional feature, namely, whether the edit involves inversion of statement meanings. This feature has been considered by prior works on Wikipedia Vandalism detection [5]. The reason for using the *statement inverse* feature is that previous studies have shown that a significant fraction of vandal edits just invert the meaning of one or more sentences by inserting or removing words and prefixes such as "not", "none", "un-", and "dis-". However, these are very common words and prefixes. Hence, they would not be part of keyword sets. Thus, in order to identify these vandal edits, it is necessary to consider statement inverse as a separate feature for the machine learning-based classifiers.

5.1. Discussion

We now discuss two issues that can further enhance the efficacy of context-driven vandalism detection. First, notice that currently our technique captures compatibility of an incoming edit's content with that of the existing version in terms of the co-occurrence probabilities of words. This can be viewed as a *syntactic approach* for capturing content-context. Currently our system does not analyze the meanings of words or relationships among them. A syntactic approach, by its very nature, cannot account for factors such as synonyms and homonyms. This can affect vandalism detection accuracy. We believe that performing the compatibility analysis at the semantic level can help alleviate these limitations. Such an approach should ideally take into account not only the meanings of words but also the inter-relationships between the words in the edit and the words in the existing version of the document. One way to accomplish this will be to use an ontology and capture inter-relationships through the semantic distances between the words. Wikipedia-based ontologies such as DBpedia and Yago are potential candidates in this regard [12, 13].

The second issue with regard to enhancing the efficacy of context-driven vandalism detection is that of *context evolution* or *context drifting*. Any ML-based context-driven vandalism detection scheme makes the inherent assumption with respect to *stability of context*. In other words, these schemes assume that the context attributes of incoming edits that need to be classified are not very different than those used for training the ML classifiers. However, contextual attributes in a collaborative system like Wikipedia is dynamic and it evolves over time. This evolution or drifting of context can adversely impact vandalism detection accuracy. This can be partially addressed by continuously updating the context training sets and re-training the ML classifiers. In effect, the context attributes derived from more recent edits and article versions receive more weight rather than the context attributes derived from older edits and documents. We believe this can address context drifts that are not drastic. In some, albeit rare, instances, context does undergo drastic changes. These are usually driven by real-world events. Dealing with these sort of drastic events is a challenge even to the human editors of Wikipedia. For example, when the singer Michael Jackson died on June 25, 2009, the user "Qc" added June 25, 2009 as the date of death to Michael Jackson's Wikipedia page. However, this edit was mistaken to be vandalism by a human editor who promptly reverted it. This highlights the challenge in dealing with drastic context changes. One possible way to address this challenge is to utilize information from realtime event sources such as Twitter and news feeds.

Developing concrete techniques for the above two issues requires comprehensive study and significant research, and it is beyond the scope of the current paper.

6. Experiments and Results

In this section, we discuss the experiments we performed to study the efficacy of content-context-centric vandalism detection technique.

6.1. Data Set

For our experiments, we use the PAN Wikipedia vandalism corpus 2010 (PAN-WVC-10). This corpus was compiled by Potthast at Bauhas-Universitat Weimar [14]. The corpus contains 32452 human-annotated edits on 28468 Wikipedia articles. The corpus has been annotated using Amazon's Mechanical Turk. Each edit has been annotated by at least three humans. Based on these annotations, each edit is labeled either as a "regular edit" (legitimate edit) or a "vandal edit". PAN-WVC-10 and its previous versions have been used as "gold standards" in several previous Wikipedia vandalism detection research projects [5].

Since our technique involves quantifying the content-contexts of edits with respect to the corresponding article versions, we need the entire edit histories of articles (including the labels for each version). For this purpose, we fetched the entire history of each article in the PAN-WVC-10. These additional edits are unlabeled. These additional edits are labeled using the *automatic data instance labeler* [5], which we briefly explain below.

The automatic data instance labeler uses the revision history (specifically, the revert and rollback history) to label edits as vandalism or regular edit. The automatic labeler marks a version as vandalism if the following conditions are satisfied. *(1)* It was contributed by an unregistered user; *(2)* the version was reverted by a super user or a bot and *(3)* the revert commentary on the article contains either of the following two patterns:

- Sensitive keywords: (?i).*vandal.*|(?i)rvv|(?i)rvv .*|(?i).* rvv .*|(?i).* rvv

- Signatures of anti-vandalism programs: (?i)Reverted edits by .* to last version by .*

If an edit was contributed by a super user or if the version was not reverted or if the comments for the version does not contain the above patterns, then it is considered to be a regular edit.

Wikipedia organizes articles into top-level *domains*. The prevalence and nature of vandalism varies significantly across domains. In our experimental evaluation, we study the efficacy of the proposed techniques for 7 different domains, namely, Chemical Substances, Currencies, Places, Persons, Programming Languages and Sports. Sample pages from each domain

are listed in Table 1. For each page, we select the 100 most recent vandal versions and 100 most recent regular versions.

6.2. Experimental Setup

In our experimental study, we use the Bing search engine (www.bing.com) for calculating the WWW co-occurrence-probability and the top-ranked co-occurrence probability. We calculate the top-ranked co-occurrence probability based upon the top 250 search results returned by the search engine. In other words, in our experiments the configurable parameter K (see Section 5) is set to 250. We compare the WWW co-occurrence-probability-based and the top-ranked co-occurrence probability-based vandalism detection methods to a textual classifier. This text-based classifier assigns vandalism likelihoods for various keywords (using training data), which is then used for edit classification.

We use the Weka machine learning toolkit for classification. We have experimented with various classifiers including Naive Bayes, AdaBoost, and C4.5 Decision Tree. We measure precision, recall and F-1 measure of all three schemes (WWW co-occurrence probability, top ranked co-occurrence probability and the textual classifier).

6.3. Results

Figures 7(a) through 7(f) indicate the average F1 scores of the three vandalism detection techniques (WWW co-occurrence probability, top-ranked co-occurrence probability and text-based classification) for the six Wikipedia domains with 3 different classifiers, namely, Naive Bayes, AdaBoost and C4.5 Decision tree. WWW Co-occurrence probability technique, top-ranked co-occurrence probability technique and text-based technique are represented as "WCoP", "TCoP" and "TC" respectively. Each bar indicates the mean F1 score over the pages considered for that domain.

From these results it can be seen that WCoP and TCoP consistently outperform TC on all domains and on all classifiers. For example, both WCoP and TCoP yield 6.5% higher F1 scores when compared with TC on the "Sports" domain with Naive Bayes classifier. Note that a large fraction of the vandal edits in this data set are instances of regular vandalism (involving additions of swear words, massive spamming, etc.). For these cases, TC performs reasonably well. Thus the F1 measure of TC is also reasonably high. However, WCoP and TCoP are successful in detecting sophisticated instances of vandalism for which TC fails. In most cases, the F1 scores of WCoP and TCoP are above 0.95.

In order to give better insight into the performance of WCoP and TCoP, we plot the F1 score, precision and recall for sample pages from three domains namely,

No.	Domain Name	Sample Pages
1	Chemical Substance	Acetic Acid, Folic Acid, Phosphorous pentachloride
2	Currency	US Dollar, Canadian Dollar, Philippine Dollar, North Korean Won
3	Persons	Barack Obama, Jimmy Carter, Golda Mier, George W. Bush, Albert Einstein
4	Places	Canada, Costa Rica, India, Iran, United Kingdom
5	Programming Language	Javascript, C, Logo, Ada, True basic
6	Sports	Badminton, Tennis, National Rugby League, Golf

Table 1. Wikipedia Domains and Sample Pages

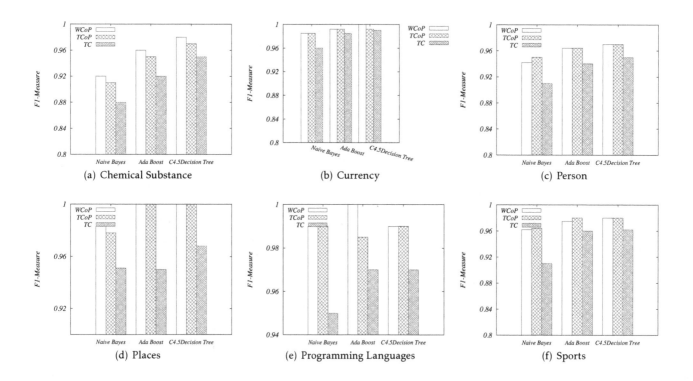

Figure 7. Comparison of WCoP, TCoP and Text Classification Performance on Various Wikipedia Domains

"places", "programming languages" and "currencies". These experiments were done using the C4.5 Decision tree classifier with 10-fold cross validation. Figures 8(a), 8(b) and 8(c) respectively indicate the F1 score, precision and recall for three pages from the "places" domain. Similarly, Figures 9(a), 9(b) and 9(c) respectively indicate the F1 score, precision and recall for two pages from the "Programming Languages" domain, and Figures 10(a), 10(b) and 10(c) show the F1score, precision and recall for two pages from the "currencies" domain. In most cases, WCoP and TCoP yield higher precision values than TC, while the recall values for the three schemes are quite comparable. Thus, higher F1 scores are a direct result of better precision.

Below, we provide a brief analysis of the characteristics of the edits that cause false positives and false negatives with our context-based vandalism detection system. False positives are legitimate edits that our system incorrectly marks as vandal edits. False negatives, on the other hand, are vandal edits that are not detected by our approach. In our system, false positives typically occur in three scenarios. The first is when an edit introduces factually correct statement that are not widely known. These sorts of statements can contain words/phrases that may seem out of context, and thus may be marked as vandalism. These kinds of edits are not very common in Wikipedia. The second scenario is when an edit contains words that colloquial, regional or even from other languages but written in the English script. These kinds of words commonly occur in pages pertaining to cultures, cuisines and personalities from remote, non-English speaking regions of the world. Since our system uses co-occurrence probability for

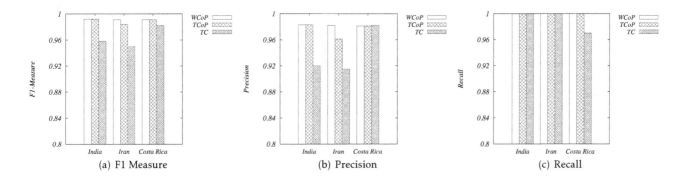

Figure 8. F1, Precision and Recall of WCoP, TCoP and Text Classification on sample pages of "places" domain

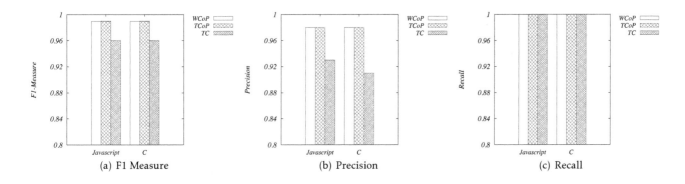

Figure 9. F1, Precision and Recall of WCoP, TCoP and Text Classification on sample pages of "Programming Languages" domain

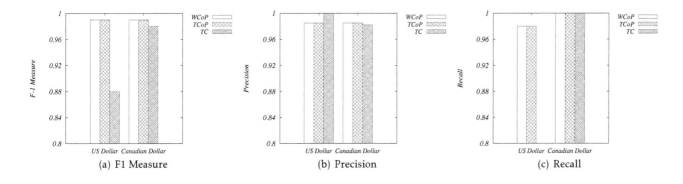

Figure 10. F1, Precision and Recall of WCoP, TCoP and Text Classification on sample pages of "Currencies" domain

measuring context, these words can cause false positives. Finally, when a page undergoes sudden and drastic context change (e.g., death of a person, revolutions in countries, etc.), our system might wrongly mark the edit reflecting the context change as vandalism. As remarked earlier, one way to address the last scenario is to utilize from realtime event sources such as Twitter and news feeds.

Our system might fail to detect vandal edits that do not contain contextually-mismatched attributes. For example, a vandal edit that removes certain key sentences in the document (which may be 'inconvenient truths' from the perspective of the user performing the edit) will not be identified by content-context-centric technique. The content-context-centric may also fail to detect edits that vandalize Wikipedia articles using common words (e.g., 'death', 'divorce', etc.) or words that have multiple connotations (e.g., disaster, etc.). Using these kinds of words/phrases, a smart and determined adversary can construct sentences that bring disrepute to the article's topic without being detected by our system. These sort of vandal edits are not common, but nevertheless do occur. Furthermore, we believe using other types of contexts (spatial and contributor context) can help mitigate some of these false negatives.

In summary, our experiments demonstrate that utilizing context provides significant improvement in vandalism detection accuracy.

7. Related Work

In recent years, various aspects of Wikipedia have been extensively studied, including its efficacy as a collaborative knowledge sharing platform, the demographies and behaviors of its user population, quality and trustworthiness of its information, semantic-analysis and ontology development for Wikipedia, and the effect of Wikipedia on various societies around the world [1, 13, 15–21]. The study by Kittur et al. [15] indicates that n the early days of Wikipedia, a core group of editors performed bulk of the editing. However, as Wikipedia became more popular, the contributions from common users has drastically increased. In another study, Kittur and Kraut [19] distinguish between implicit and explicit collaborations in Wikipedia and conclude that explicit collaboration (through discussion and talk pages) yields better quality content than implicit collaboration.

A number of researchers have studied vandalism in Wikipedia. Preidhorsky et al. [3] attempt to estimate the value of Wikipedia content. In this context, they analyze the damage done by vandal edits in terms of the length of time the article was in vandalized status and the number of views on the article when it was in the vandalized state. Existing Wikipedia vandalism detection techniques can be broadly classified into two categories, namely, content-based and behavior-based approaches [22]. Both of these approaches use either rule-based or machine learning-based classifiers in the background [23]. Features that are typically used in content-based approaches include edit types (such as complete or partial *blanking*, inclusion of repetitive text) insertion of obscene words, spammy words, or spammy URLs, inversion of statement meanings, replacement of article titles and sub-titles, changing numbers in articles, length of comments, size of edit, and character diversity of edit [2–5, 24]. Chin et al. have used statistical language models have for vandalism detection [25]. The work by Wang and McKeown [26] utilizes lexical features such as misplaced punctuations and slangs for detecting vandalism. In a recent work,

Wu et al. have proposed a text-stability-based approach for identifying vandalism [5]. The main idea here is to quantify the stabilities of various parts of a Wikipedia article (in terms of number of versions, number of views and amount of time since last modification), and use them to predict the likelihood of these parts being modified through legitimate edits.

The behavior-based approach relies upon Wikipedia revision history to generate user behavior models which are later used to classify edits [27–29]. Reputation-based techniques form an important stream of work in this direction [9–11]. Adler et al. [30] propose a vandalism detection technique that combines computation linguistics with contributor reputation. Reputation-based techniques are similar to our approach of utilizing contributor-context for vandalism detection. A closely related stream of work is that of user community-based trust enhancement techniques for collaborative social media [31, 32].

Spamming, while not being the sole motivation for vandalism, certainly contributes to a considerable portion of it. Researchers have proposed many spam resistance approaches, including white and black lists, statistical filtering, network analysis, and sender authentication, and coordinated real-time spam filtering [33–39]. However, the anti-spam work does not completely address the vandalism problem because while spam is mostly driven by financial interests, vandalism can be generated by a variety of causes.

Context-awareness has been widely studied in the pervasive computing and human-computing interaction domains [40–43]. Several issues including developing infrastructures for capturing and maintaining context, analysis of context and security and privacy aspects of context have been explored. Our work is unique in that it uses context for vandalism detection in CSM applications.

8. Conclusions

In recent years, vandalism has emerged as a significant threat to information quality and trustworthiness of collaborative social media application such as Wikipedia. Many of the existing vandalism detection techniques rely upon simple textual features, and hence are not very effective in dealing with sophisticated vandal attacks. In this paper, we proposed harnessing context for vandalism identification. We presented a unique context-enhanced finite state model for Wikipedia article evolution which helps us capture and analyze various contextual attributes. This paper studies the distinguishing capabilities of two important types of context namely content-context and contributor-context. We have designed two metrics, namely, WWW co-occurrence probability and top ranked co-occurrence probability, to measure the compatibility of an edit's content-context with the content-context of the existing article. In addition to providing efficient mechanisms for estimating these metrics, we have discussed how these metrics can be utilized in machine learning-based classifiers. This paper also reports several experiments on the Wikipedia PAN corpus that demonstrate that utilizing context significantly improves vandalism detection accuracy when compared with simple text-based techniques.

Acknowledgement

This research is partially supported by the National Science Foundation under grants CNS-1338276, DUE-1318881, OCI-1127195, CNS/SAVI-1250260, IUCRC/FRP-1127904, CISE/CNS-1138666, RAPID-1138666, CISE/CRI-0855180, NetSE-0905493 and gifts, grants, or contracts from Intel Corp, DARPA/I2O, Singapore Government, Fujitsu Labs, and Georgia Tech Foundation through the John P. Imlay, Jr. Chair endowment. Any opinions, findings, and conclusions or recommendations expressed in this material are those of the authors and do not necessarily reflect the views of the National Science Foundation or other funding agencies and companies mentioned above.

References

[1] Pew Research Center's Project for Excellence in Journalism (2011), The State of the News Media-2011 (An Annual Report on American Journalism), http://stateofthemedia.org/.

[2] Wikipedia (Revision as of 20:29, 22 May 2010), Cluebot, http://en.wikipedia.org/wiki/User:ClueBot.

[3] Priedhorsky, R., Chen, J., Lam, S.T.K., Panciera, K., Terveen, L. and Riedl, J. (2007) Creating, destroying, and restoring value in wikipedia. In Proceedings of the International ACM Conference on Supporting Group Work: 259–268.

[4] Adler, B.T. and de Alfaro, L. (2007) A content-driven reputation system for the wikipedia. In WWW '07: Proceedings of the 16th international conference on World Wide Web (New York, NY, USA: ACM): 261–270. doi:http://doi.acm.org/10.1145/1242572.1242608.

[5] Wu, Q., Irani, D., Pu, C. and Ramaswamy, L. (2010) Elusive vandalism detection in wikipedia: a text stability-based approach. In CIKM.

[6] Wikipedia, Vandalism on Wikipedia (retrieved on Aug 01, 2013), http://en.wikipedia.org/wiki/Vandalism_on_Wikipedia.

[7] Ahamad, M., Mark, L., Lee, W., Omicienski, E., dos Santos, A., Liu, L. and Pu, C. (2002) Guarding the next Internet frontier: countering denial of information attacks. In NSPW.

[8] Wikipedia, Wikipedia Article on AI Complete Problem, http://en.wikipedia.org/wiki/AI-complete.

[9] Adler, B.T., Benterou, J., Chatterjee, K., de Alfaro, L., Pye, I. and Raman., V. (2007) Assigning trust to wikipedia content. In Technical Report, School of Engineering, University of California, Santa Cruz.

[10] Javanmardi, S. and Lopes, C. (2007) Modeling trust in collaborative information systems. In Proceedings of the 3rd International Conference on Collaborative Computing: Networking, Applications and Worksharing (CollaborateCom 2007): 299–302.

[11] Zeng, H., Alhossaini, M., Fikes, R. and McGuinness, D.L. (2006) Mining revision history to assess trustworthiness of article fragments. In Proceedings of the 4th International Conference on Collaborative Computing: Networking, Applications and Worksharing (CollaborateCom 2006).

[12] Bizer, C., Lehmann, J., Kobilarov, G., Auer, S., Becker, C., Cyganiak, R. and Hellmann, S. (2009) Dbpedia: A crystallization point for the web of data. Web Semantics: Science, Services and Agents on the World Wide Web vol.7(3): 154–165.

[13] Suchanek, F.M., Kasneci, G. and Weikum, G. (2008) Yago: A large ontology from wikipedia and wordnet. Web Semantics: Science, Services and Agents on the World Wide Web 6(3): 203–217.

[14] Potthast, M. (2010) Crowdsourcing a wikipedia vandalism corpus. In Proceedings of SIGIR.

[15] Kittur, A., Chi, E., Pendleton, B.A., Suh, B. and Mytkowicz, T. (2007) Power of the few vs. wisdom of the crowd: Wikipedia and the rise of the bourgeoisie. World Wide Web 1(2).

[16] Suh, B., Chi, E.H., Kittur, A. and Pendleton, B.A. (2008) Lifting the veil: improving accountability and social transparency in Wikipedia with wikidashboard. In CHI.

[17] Suh, B., Chi, E.H., Pendleton, B.A. and Kittur, A. (2007) Us vs. Them: Understanding Social Dynamics in Wikipedia with Revert Graph Visualizations. In IEEE VAST.

[18] Kittur, A., Suh, B. and Chi, E.H. (2008) Can you ever trust a wiki?: impacting perceived trustworthiness in wikipedia. In CSCW.

[19] Kittur, A. and Kraut, R. (2008) Harnessing the wisdom of crowds in wikipedia: quality through coordination. In CSCW.

[20] Gabrilovich, E. and Markovitch, E. (2007) Computing Semantic Relatedness Using Wikipedia-based Explicit Semantic Analysis. In IJCAI.

[21] Ponzetto, S.P. and Navigli, R. (2009) Large-Scale Taxonomy Mapping for Restructuring and Integrating Wikipedia. In IJCAI.

[22] Potthast, M., Stein, B. and Gerling, R. (2008) Automatic vandalism detection in wikipedia. In Proceedings of Advances in Information Retrieval: 663–668.

[23] Smets, K., Goethals, B. and Verdonk, B. (2008) Automatic vandalism detection in wikipedia: Towards a machine learning approach. In Proc. of AAAI workshop on Wikipedia and Artificial Intelligence: An Evolving Synergy (AAAI): 43–48.

[24] Mola-Velasco, S.M. (2011) Wikipedia Vandalism Detection. Master's thesis, Polytechnic University of Valencia.

[25] chi Chin, S., Srinivasan, P., Street, W.N. and Eichmann, D. (2010) Detecting wikipedia vandalism with active learning and statistical language models. In Proceedings of 4th Workshop on Information Credibility on the Web.

[26] WANG, W.Y. and McKEOWN, K.R. (2010) "Got You!": Automatic Vandalism Detection in Wikipedia with Web-based Shallow Syntactic-Semantic Modeling. In *COLING*.

[27] HU, M., LIM, E., SUN, A., LAUW, H.W. and VUONG., B. (2007) Measuring article quality in wikipedia: Models and evaluation. In *Proceedings of the Sixteenth ACM Conference on Information and Knowledge Management (CIKM)*: 243–252.

[28] LIM, E., VUONG, B., LAUW, H.W. and SUN, A. (2006) Measuring qualities of articles contributed by online communities. In *Proceedings of the 2006 IEEE/WIC/ACM International Conference on Web Intelligence*: 81–87.

[29] HALFAKER, A., KITTUR, A., KRAUT, R. and RIEDL, J. (2009) A jury of your peers: quality, experience and ownership in wikipedia. In *WikiSym '09: Proceedings of the 5th International Symposium on Wikis and Open Collaboration* (New York, NY, USA: ACM): 1–10. doi:http://doi.acm.org/10.1145/1641309.1641332.

[30] ADLER, B.T., DE ALFARO, L., MOLA-VELASCO, S.M., ROSSO, P. and WEST, A.G. (2011) Wikipedia Vandalism Detection: Combining Natural Language, Metadata, and Reputation Features. In *CICLing*.

[31] CAVERLEE, J., CHENG, Z., EOFF, B., HSU, C.F., KAMATH, K., KASHOOB, S., KELLEY, J. *et al.* (2010) Socialtrust++: Building community-based trust in social information systems. In *CollaborateCom*.

[32] CAVERLEE, J., CHENG, Z., EOFF, B., HSU, C.F., KAMATH, K.Y. and McGEE, J. (2011) Crowdtracker: enabling community-based real-time web monitoring. In *SIGIR*.

[33] ANDROUTSOPOULOS, I., KOUTSIAS, J., CHANDRINOS, K., PALIOURAS, G. and SPYROPOULOS, C. (2000) An evaluation of naive bayesian anti-spam filtering. In *Proceedings of the workshop on Machine Learning in the New Information Age, 2000.*: 9–17. URL citeseer.ist.psu. edu/androutsopoulos00evaluation.html.

[34] WEBB, S., CHITTI, S. and PU, C. (2005) An experimental evaluation of spam filter performance and robustness against attack. In *Proceedings of the 1st International Conference on Collaborative Computing: Networking, Applications and Worksharing (CollaborateCom 2005)*.

[35] SCHRYVER, V., Distributed checksum clearinghouse. http://www.rhyolite.com/anti-spam/dcc/ Last accessed Nov 2, 2005.

[36] GRAY, A. and HAAHR, M. (2005) Personalised, Collaborative Spam Filtering. In *Proceedings of the Second Email and SPAM conference (CEAS)*.

[37] DAMIANI, E., DI VIMERCATI, S.D.C., PARABOSCHI, S. and SAMARATI, P. (2004) P2p-based collaborative spam detection and filtering. In *The Fourth International Conference on Peer-to-Peer Computing*. URL citeseer. ist.psu.edu/721025.html.

[38] RAMACHANDRAN, A., FEAMSTER, N. and VEMPALA, S. (2007) Filtering spam with behavioral blacklisting. In *ACM Conference on Computer and Communications Security (CCS)*.

[39] RAMACHANDRAN, A. and FEAMSTER, N. (2006) Understanding the Network-Level Behavior of Spammers. In *Proceedings of ACM SIGCOMM 2006*.

[40] CHEN, G. and KOTZ, D. (2000) *A survey of context-aware mobile computing research*. Tech. rep., Technical Report TR2000-381, Dept. of Computer Science, Dartmouth College.

[41] DEY, A.K. (2001) Understanding and using context. *Personal and ubiquitous computing* **5**(1).

[42] HONG, J.I. and LANDAY, J.A. (2001) An infrastructure approach to context-aware computing. *Human-Computer Interaction* **16**(2).

[43] SMAILAGIC, A. and KOGAN, D. (2002) Location sensing and privacy in a context-aware computing environment. *Wireless Communications, IEEE* **9**(5): 10–17.

4

A Scheme for Collaboratively Processing Nearest Neighbor Queries in Oblivious Storage

Keith B. Frikken[1], Shumiao Wang[2], Mikhail J. Atallah[2,*]

[1]Miami University, Oxford
[2]Purdue University, West Lafayette

Abstract

Security concerns are a substantial impediment to the wider deployment of cloud storage. There are two main concerns on the confidentiality of outsourced data: i) protecting the data, and ii) protecting the access pattern (i.e., which data is being accessed). To mitigate these concerns, schemes for Oblivious Storage (OS) have been proposed. In OS, the data owner outsources a key-value store to a cloud server, and then can later execute get, put, and remove queries, by collaboration with the server; furthermore, both the data and the access pattern are hidden from the server. In this paper, we extend the semantics of OS by proposing an oblivious index that supports nearest neighbor queries. That is, finding the nearest keys to the query in the key-value store. Our proposed index structure for supporting nearest-neighbor has similar performance bounds to previous OS schemes that did not support nearest-neighbor, in terms of client storage, server storage and rounds of communication.

Keywords: Collaborative Cloud Storage, Oblivious Storage, Collaboration in Cloud Computing

1. Introduction

The benefits of cloud storage are well documented, but a significant impediment to larger-scale use is concern for confidentiality of the data and of access patterns to the data. Organizations are reluctant to collaborate with cloud servers for storage when the data involved is supposed to be kept confidential. Some service providers offer premium services with features that mitigate the confidentiality problem, such as servers that are inside national borders and are "hardened" against network attacks, system administrators that have specified characteristics (e.g., of citizenship, levels of security clearance), etc. Not only are such approaches expensive, but the sensitive data remains vulnerable to (e.g.) rogue employees of the cloud service provider, a break-in or malware/spyware at the remote server, etc. This paper belongs to the body of work that seeks to design client-server collaborative schemes that obviate the need for using the above-mentioned premium services, even as they provide better security: They provide clients with access to their data, while protecting from the server both the data and the access patterns to it. A case can be made for using such techniques even when the data is stored at a *trusted* server, as a form of compartmentalization

and "defense in depth" whereby the damage from compromise of a trusted server is less widespread and is confined to that server. In addition to the security advantages to such compartmentalization, there are also economic advantages: It makes it less necessary to get high security clearances for individuals at the trusted server's end, and also less necessary to spend money on the expensive physical isolation or tamper-proofing of hardware and software (because they no longer have access to the sensitive information – they "use it without seeing it").

A well known technique for protecting access patterns is oblivious RAM (ORAM) [4]. In ORAM, the server has a sequence of memory locations, and the client can read or write the content from any of the memory locations. In ORAM, the data is protected and the server does not learn the access pattern. That is, the server learns something was accessed, but does not know what was accessed; the server doesn't even learn when the client accesses the same data repeatedly. While this work is very promising, many distributed storage techniques do not take the form of a RAM. To ameliorate this problem, [2] introduced the concept of Oblivious Storage (OS), where the storage is that of a key-value store, which is a more widely used data model for cloud storage (for example HBase[1] can be viewed as such a key value store). The operations provided by OS are: get, insert, and remove.

*Corresponding author. Email: mja@cs.purdue.edu

The primary goal of this work is to extend the semantics of oblivious storage. Previous work on OS has assumed that the client has some information about the keys that are present in the OS. An exception to this was the miss-tolerant solution in [7] where a client could perform lookups for non-existent keys. In this case the server would not learn that the key was a miss, and the client learns that the specific key does not exist. This interface makes it difficult to answer queries such as "give me all values where the key is in the range $[a, b]$", especially since it is possible that neither a nor b is in the dataset. This paper makes a significant step towards solving this problem, by providing an oblivious index that supports nearest neighbor queries including directional queries that are for nearest neighbor larger than (or smaller than) the query item. The non-directional version is simply: Given a key, find the keys that are closest to the given key. Note that the directional version can easily be used to find all keys in a range $[a, b]$, by finding the nearest successor to a (let it be x), then finding the nearest successor to x, etc. (In fact we can do much better than such a naive "follow the successor" approach, as will become apparent later in the paper.)

The rest of the paper is organized as follows: Section 2 describes related work. Section 3 gives the problem definition and defines the building blocks used in the paper. Section 4 describes the main result of this paper. Finally, section 5 concludes the paper.

2. Related Work

Oblivious RAM was introduced in [4]. In ORAM, the server has a sequence of values (pages in memory), $v_1, \ldots, v_n$. The client (who is also the data owner) can access an arbitrary value. Almost all of the solutions for ORAM provide an amortized performance guarantee. For example, in one solution proposed in [4] the cost of an access is $O(\sqrt{n})$ on average, but is $O(n)$ in the worst case. Many other schemes have been proposed to improve the efficiency of ORAM, including: [3, 5, 6, 10, 12, 13, 15]. The scheme in [6] is particularly interesting, because its worst case access time is sublinear.

In [2], a different model for oblivious outsourced storage was proposed called Oblivious Storage (OS), and this work was extended in [7]. In OS, the data store is a key-value store, which is a more natural framework than the RAM model. Another constraint of Oblivious Storage is to avoid increasing the server's storage by a multiplicative factor, as this will increase the cost of outsourcing significantly.

There is a growing list of papers in the framework of storage outsourcing (e.g.[8, 14], and others). [14] introduced the paradigm in which the service provider hosts the database as a service, and allows clients to store and access their own databases at the host site, which is similar to the framework in this paper. [8] describes several architectures that combine recent and non-standard cryptographic primitives in order to build a secure cloud storage service, and surveys the benefits such an architecture would provide to both customers and service providers.

The nearest neighbor search problem (also called the post-office problem by Knuth [9]) is a classic problem, and here we only review the related work of this problem in the secure outsourcing setting. Traditional encryption methods could hide the data from an untrusted server, but that would also prevent the client from doing queries like *nn* search or range queries, but prefix-preserving encryption (PPE) [11, 16] could help in handling *nn* search due to the fact that the longest common prefix of any two ciphertexts is of the same length as the longest common prefix of the corresponding plaintexts. However, the security is weakened since some prefix information is leaked to the server if PPE is used to encrypt the dataset.

Another recent work on similarity search [17] provides solutions for generic distance metrics (L_p norm) of multidimensional data with interesting trade-offs between query cost and accuracy, but it does not consider hiding the access patterns from the server. Several other related transformation-based techniques and hierarchy-based searches (using an encrypted R-tree to represent the database and then searching it for query point level by level) are proposed in location-based service (LBS) systems [18] which have the same issue of leaking access patterns.

3. Preliminaries

In this section, we begin by describing the notation used in this paper. The interval (x, y) includes all integers from x to y exclusive, and when the parenthesis are replaced by brackets (i.e., [or]) then the interval is inclusive. Given a value $x \in \{0, 1\}^n$, we define $Prefix_m(x)$ to be the m most significant bits of x.

Our schemes utilize a pseudorandom function(PRF) $F : \{0, 1\}^n \times \{0, 1\}^n \rightarrow \{0, 1\}^n$. We utilize the textbook definition for a PRF in that for all PPT distinguishing algorithms D, $|Pr[D^{F_k(\cdot)}(1^n) = 1] - Pr[D^{f(\cdot)}(1^n) = 1]|$ is negligible in n where f is a random function. Our scheme utilizes a PRF that takes in variable length input tuples. This is easily accommodated by an encoding scheme that pads all messages to the same length. For example, all strings up to n bits long can be converted into a string of length $n + \log n$ by pre-pending the length and padding with 0's.

Finally, our scheme utilizes CPA-secure encryption schemes ($KeyGen, Enc, Dec$) where an adversary cannot distinguish one of two ciphertexts given oracle access to Enc.

3.1. Framework/Problem Definition

We are assuming an honest but curious server, which means it will collaborate with the client and perform specified computations, but try to learn information about the client's data or access pattern. A data owner (client) that publishes a data set on the server, and the data owner wants to be able to query its own data while protecting the data from the server. This includes protecting both the content and the data access pattern. Previous work [2, 7] has introduced the concept of oblivious storage. In oblivious storage, the data owner publishes a key-value store on the server. More specifically, the server stores a set of tuples $S = \{(k_1, v_1), \ldots, (k_n, v_n)\}$ where $n \leq N$ for some size threshold N, the keys, k_i, are unique and are drawn from a key domain $[0, D-1]$, and the values, v_i, are drawn from a domain of values where each value has the same bit size (alternatively the values could be padded to have the same size).

The schemes in [2, 7] give protocol for functions: $get(k)$, $put(k, v)$, and $remove(k)$. In [7] oblivious stores are described as either miss-intolerant or miss-tolerant. In a miss-tolerant data store, the server does not learn whether a query is in the dataset or not, but this information is revealed to the server in a miss-intolerant oblivious store.

We seek to extend previous work in oblivious storage by adding the semantics of a nearest neighbors that returns the nearest predecessor and nearest successor of a key. Informally, this takes as input a value in $[0, D-1]$, and returns a tuple (np, ns) where np (resp. ns) is the largest (resp. smallest) key in S that is smaller (resp. no smaller) than the input. The efficiency goals are to minimize: i) the communication, ii) the computation, iii) the number of communication rounds, iv) the server storage, and v) the client storage.

Formally, our goal is to define an oblivious index structure that supports the following operations:

1. $insert(k)$ that takes a value $k \in [0, D-1]$ and inserts it into the structure.

2. $remove(k)$ that removes a value $k \in [0, D-1]$ from the structure.

3. $nn(k)$ returns (np, ns) where np is the largest value in the data set such that $np < k$, and ns is the smallest value such that $ns \geq k$.

In case there is no predecessor (resp. successor) we want to return special symbols that represent values $-\infty$ (resp. ∞), so that there is always an answer to this query. We also assume that there is an upper bound N on the number of keys in the oblivious store. The store should be oblivious in that the server should not learn which items are being accessed (that is the server should not be able to tell two access patterns apart). Furthermore, the

insert and *remove* queries should be miss-tolerant, in that the server should not learn when an item is actually inserted or removed.

3.2. Details of Previous Protocol for Oblivious Storage

In this section we describe the high level details of previous work for miss-intolerant oblivious store. The previous work [7] has two phases: i) a query phase, and ii) a rebuilding phase. During the query phase, the client asks *get*, *insert*, and *remove* queries, and after M queries, the rebuilding phase starts. During the rebuilding phase, query execution is suspended, and the server's storage is rebuilt.

The server stores N regular tuples and M dummy tuples. Each regular tuple corresponds to a key value pair, (k, v) and has the form $(F_{fk}(k), Enc_{ek}(v))$ where F is a pseudorandom function and Enc is a CPA-secure encryption scheme, and fk is a pseudorandom function key that changes during the rebuilding phase and ek is a key for the encryption scheme that does not change during the rebuilding phase. The dummy items are of the form $(F_{fk}(-i), Enc_{ek}(FAKE))$ for each value $i \in [1, M]$ where *FAKE* is some padded dummy value. The items are stored in a random order.

The client has local storage of size $O(M)$ that keeps track of all queries made during the current query phase along with the answers to the queries (initially this local store starts out empty). These are stored in a data structure that allows $O(1)$ amortized insertions and searches by key.

To process a query $get(q)$, the client first searches its local store for q, and then:

- If q is in the local storage: The client sends a dummy query to the server. That is, the client sends $F_{fk}(-j)$ to the server where this is the jth dummy query sent to the server.

- Otherwise: The client sends $F_{fk}(q)$ to the server.

In either case the server obtains a value from the client that is in its dataset that has not been queried before. The server finds the value in its data set that matches the query, and sends the corresponding message back to the client. The server also removes this key-value pair from its data store. The client then stores this value in its local store and returns the result.

To process a query $insert(k, v)$, the client first issues a query $get(k)$ and then changes the value in its local store associated with key k to v. To process a query $remove(k)$, the client issues a query $get(k)$, and then removes the key-value pair from its local storage (note that it was already removed from the server). In both cases, the server only sees a *get* query and all other changes affect the client's local storage only. Note that this is for a miss-intolerant solution, and that this leaks to the server when a value was replaced or inserted, and for removals the server learns when a value was actually removed.

After M queries, the rebuilding phase starts. In this phase the client reshuffles the values in the server storage, changes the pseudorandom function key, and re-encrypts the values. The values are randomly permuted to prevent the server from inferring information about the queries between two different query phases. The details of this shuffling process are in [7].

During the query phase the client and server perform $O(1)$ computation and communication per query. The server storage is $O(N)$. The cost of the rebuilding phase is $O(N)$, but the amortized cost per query is $O(\frac{N}{M})$. The client storage is $O(M)$. The number of communication rounds per query is $O(1)$. The base scheme in [7] sets M to $\sqrt{N}$, and thus the amortized cost is $O(\sqrt{N})$ and the client's storage is $O(\sqrt{N})$.

3.3. Observation

Providing a nearest neighbors oblivious index is at least as hard as providing miss-tolerance for get in the original data store. That is, suppose we have a miss-intolerant oblivious store, and a client queries $get(k)$. Simply call $(np, ns) \leftarrow nn(k)$ and $get(ns)$ (If ns is ∞ then use $get(np)$). The get will always be a hit, and the client can determine if k was a hit by testing if $k \overset{?}{=} ns$.

4. Nearest Neighbors Oblivious Index

In this section, we present the main result of this paper: an oblivious index structure for nearest neighbors. We utilize many of the ideas in the previous work on obvious storage. Let N denote the upper bound on the number of keys, let M denote the number of queries in the query phase, and let $[0, D-1]$ denote the key domain.

4.1. A straightforward protocol

The miss-intolerant data store in the previous section can be used to provide answers to nn queries. The client builds a balanced binary search tree over the key values to produce a tree with height h (Clearly $h = O(\log N)$). Each node in the tree is given a unique label, and the root node's label is a known constant. Each node in the tree has its children's labels along with the search value. The client can then perform a binary search to find the smallest key value that is not less than the query and the largest key that is not larger than the query. If the client finds the value in an intermediate node, or reaches a leaf node with height smaller than h, then the client performs the appropriate amount of extra queries to pad the number of queries to h (these extra queries can be repeated queries from before). This is necessary to

make each query look identical to the server, otherwise the server would learn something about each query.

Furthermore, if insertions and removals can be performed while changing at most $O(h)$ nodes, then this can support insertion and removals using the *insert* and *remove* queries.

Suppose we set $M = \sqrt{N}$. The tree clearly has at most N nodes, and thus the server's storage is $O(N)$, the clients storage is $O(\sqrt{N})$, the query cost and communication is $O(\log N)$, and the number of rounds is $O(\log N)$. Finally, the amortized cost/communication is $O(\log N \sqrt{N})$. The main goal in the rest of this paper is to reduce the number of rounds to $O(1)$.

4.2. Server Storage

We are now ready to describe one of the main ideas of our proposed approach. Given S, the client partitions the key domain into a set of unique prefixes. Specifically a prefix, p, is interesting if all key values that share the prefix have the same nearest neighbors, but this is not true for any shorter prefix of p. More formally, p is interesting if $|\{nn(m) : Prefix_{|p|}(m) = p\}| = 1$ and $|\{nn(m) : Prefix_{|p|-1}(m) = Prefix_{|p|-1}(p)\}| > 1$. For each interesting prefix p with nearest predecessor np and nearest successor ns, the client creates a key value pair $(p, (np, ns))$. The client stores all such pairs on the server just as the key value pairs are stored in a miss-intolerant OS. That is the client stores $(F_{fk}(p), Enc_{ek}((p, np, ns))$ on the server where fk is a key for a pseudorandom function and ek is a key for a CPA-secure encryption scheme.

Let d denote the number of bits used to represent a value in the dataset. The following theorem places an upper bound on the number of interesting prefixes (and hence on the size of server storage).

Theorem 1. There are at most $Nd + 1$ interesting prefixes.

Proof: Let $T(n, k)$ denote the maximum number of interesting prefixes if there are n values and k bits. First note that $T(n, k)$ is well defined if and only if $2^k \geq n$ (otherwise there are not n values with k bits).

Obviously, $T(0, k) = 1$ and the claim holds.

Now, we show that $T(1, k) \leq k + 1$. Obviously, this is true for $k = 0$. Now consider, $T(1, k)$. The value is either starts with a 0 or a 1. The half that does not contain the value all have the same nearest neighbors. Thus $T(1, k) \leq 1 + T(1, k - 1)$, and the claim follows by induction.

Consider $T(2, k)$. Now, $T(2, 1) = 2$ and so the claim holds for the base case. Now either both values start with the same bit, or they are both different. Hence, $T(2, k) \leq \max\{2T(1, k - 1), T(2, k - 1) + 1\}$. By induction, $T(2, k) \leq \max\{2k, 2(k - 1) + 1\} \leq 2k + 1$, and the claim holds.

Now consider $T(n, k)$ for $n \geq 3$. Now, $T(n, \lceil \log n \rceil) \leq 2^{\lceil \log n \rceil} < 2n + 1$ (the last part assumes $n \geq 3$. Now considering larger values of k, for some constant c, there will be c values with a 0 prefix and $n - c$ values with a 1 prefix. Thus $T(n, k) = T(c, k - 1) + T(n - c, k - 1)$. By induction, $T(n, k) \leq c(k - 1) + 1 + (n - c)(k - 1) + 1 = nk - n + 2 \leq nk + 1$. The claim follows. $\square$

The server will thus store $Nd + 1 + 2M$ tuples. If there are ℓ interesting prefixes, there will be ℓ tuples for these prefixes, $Nd + 1 - \ell$ dummy prefixes (so that the server does not learn how many interesting prefixes there are), and $2M$ dummy prefixes that will be used to generate fake hits (the full details are described in a later section).

The main idea to process a query q is to issue a query for each prefix of q (i.e., to issue the query $Prefix_1(q), \ldots, Prefix_d(q)$ i.e. by sending $F_{fk}(Prefix_1(q)), \ldots, F_{fk}(Prefix_d(q))$ to the server. Exactly one of these queries will result in a hit and thus revealing the number of hits to the server does not reveal anything. The server will find the one tuple that is a match and send the value back to the client. Note that the above interaction can be done in a single communication round.

Example Suppose $d = 4$ (i.e., the keys consists of 4 bit values) and that $N = 4$. Suppose that following four keys are in S: 2, 6, 7, and 11. In Figure 1 we show the tree based representation of the key space and have highlighted the nodes corresponding to the interesting prefixes. In this case, the server would store the following key-value pairs: $(000, (-\infty, 2))$, $(0010, (-\infty, 2))$, $(0011, (2, 6))$, $(010, (2, 6))$, $(0110, (2, 6))$, $(0111, (6, 7))$, $(10, (7, 11))$, and $(11, (11, \infty))$. The server would also store 9 dummy values so that the server is storing 17 values. If the client issued the query $nn(8)$, then the client would issue queries 1, 10, 100, and 1000. Notice that the query 10 is a match, and that the client would learn that prefix 11 is a match, and the nearest predecessor is 7 and the nearest successor is 11.

However, these values should be permuted before sending them to the server to prevent leaking which prefix length is a match. There are some complications including: i) over M queries many prefixes will be queried repeatedly and this will leak information to the server, ii) it is possible that two different queries will result in the same hit and thus we need to avoid this leakage, and iii) insertions and removals need to be handled.

We finish by giving the details of a pair of algorithms that will be used later. The first algorithm, *PREFIXSPLIT*(x, y), partitions the interval $[x, y]$ into its set of prefixes that minimally cover the entire interval. The main idea is that if you view the interval as part of a tree where the leaves range form $[0, D - 1]$ then the minimum number of nodes in the tree that covers the interval correspond to the off path vertices on the paths

from the nearest common ancestor of x and y to x and y. The straightforward details for splitting an interval into interesting prefixes are presented in Algorithm 1.

Algorithm 1 $SPLIT(x = x_1 \cdots x_d, y = y_1 \cdots y_d))$

1: $P \leftarrow \{\}$
2: $c \leftarrow 0$
3: {Find common prefix}
4: **while** $x_c = y_c$ **do**
5: $\quad c \leftarrow c + 1$
6: **end while**
7: {Since $x < y$, $x_{c+1} = 0$ and $y_{c+1} = 1$}
8: $i \leftarrow d + 1$
9: **while** $x_{i-1} = 0$ **do**
10: $\quad i \leftarrow i - 1$
11: **end while**
12: $I \leftarrow I \cup \{x_1 \cdots x_{i-1}\}$
13: **for** $j = i - 2$ to $c + 2$ **do**
14: $\quad$ **if** $x_j = 0$ **then**
15: $\quad\quad I \leftarrow I \cup \{x_1 \cdots x_{j-1}1\}$
16: $\quad$ **end if**
17: **end for**
18: $i \leftarrow d + 1$
19: **while** $y_{i-1} = 1$ **do**
20: $\quad i \leftarrow i - 1$
21: **end while**
22: $I \leftarrow I \cup \{y_1 \cdots y_{i-1}\}$
23: **for** $j = i - 2$ to $c + 2$ **do**
24: $\quad$ **if** $y_j = 1$ **then**
25: $\quad\quad I \leftarrow I \cup \{y_1 \cdots y_{j-1}0\}$
26: $\quad$ **end if**
27: **end for**
28: **return** I

We now turn our attention to generating all interesting intervals for a set of key values $K = \{k_1, \ldots, k_n\}$. If we assume these keys are sorted, then this partitions the key space into intervals $[0, k_1], [k_1 + 1, k_2], \ldots, [k_{n-1} + 1, k_n], [k_n + 1, D - 1]$. Notice that all points in the interval $[k_i + 1, k_{i+1}]$ all share the same nearest predecessor and successor. This algorithm simply sorts the points and calls the previous algorithms to find all interesting prefixes. The details are in Algorithm 2.

4.3. Data Structure 1: Avoiding duplicate queries

Two problems with the previous approach involve the client asking duplicate queries when processing two distinct nn queries. To be able to overcome the problems, the client needs to be able to determine (for the current query): i) the longest common prefix with any previously issued nn query in the query phase, and ii) has the prefix group of the current query already been obtained.

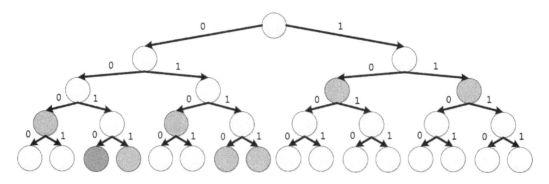

Figure 1. Interesting prefixes for $\{2,6,7,11\}$ shown as the grey nodes

---

Algorithm 2 $ALLPREFIXES(\{k_1,\ldots,k_n\}))$

1: $sk_1,\ldots,sk_n \leftarrow sort\{k_1,\ldots,k_n\}$
2: $A \leftarrow \{\}$
3: $S \leftarrow SPLIT(0, sk_1)$
4: $A \leftarrow \{(s, (-\infty, k_1)) : s \in S\}$
5: $S \leftarrow SPLIT(sk_n + 1, D - 1)$
6: $A \leftarrow \{(s, (sk_n, \infty)) : s \in S\}$
7: **for** $i = 1$ to $n - 1$ **do**
8:     $S \leftarrow A \cup SPLIT(x_i + 1, x_{i+1})$
9:     $A \leftarrow \{(s, (sk_i, sk_{i+1})) : s \in S\}$
10: **end for**
11: **return** A

Specifically, we desire a data structure with the following three operations:

1. $insert(q, mp, np, ns)$ this inserts the results of a previous query $nn(q)$. This stores: i) mp: the matching prefix of q, ii) np the nearest predecessor of q, and iii) ns the nearest successor of q.

2. $get(q)$ this returns a tuple (L, nn) where L is the length of the longest common prefix between q and any previous query, and nn is null if the prefix group containing q has not been queried, but is the nearest neighbors, (np, ns), for q if the query group has been found.

3. $initializeCommonQuery()$ This initializes the data structure to an empty structure.

The following theorem states this requires the ability to find the nearest successor and predecessor of the current query over all previously asked queries.

Theorem 2. Given a set of queries $S = \{s_1,\ldots,s_n\}$ and a query q, the longest common prefix of q to any query in S is either q's nearest predecessor or successor. Furthermore, if any query in S is in the same prefix group of q, then q's nearest successor or predecessor is also in the same prefix group as q.

Proof: Given two bit sequences x and y, let $LCP(x,y)$ denote the longest common prefix between x and

y. First we show that if $x \leq y < z$, that $|LCP(x,y)| \geq |LCP(x,z)|$. Denote $LCP(y,z)$ as $c_1 \cdots c_p$. Now since $y < z$, it must be that y starts with $c_1 \cdots c_p 0$ and z with $c_1 \cdots c_p 1$. Since $x \leq y$, x cannot start with the prefix $c_1 \cdots c_p 1$, and thus $|LCP(x,z)| \leq p$. Now consider, $LCP(x,y)$, there are two cases to consider: i) $|LCP(x,y)| \leq p$, in which case $LCP(x,y) = LCP(x,z)$, and ii) $|LCP(x,y)| > p$, in which case $LCP(x,y) > LCP(x,z)$. In either case, the claim holds.

A symmetrical argument can be made that when $x < y \leq z$, that $|LCP(y,z)| \geq |LCP(x,z)|$. Combining these two things together implies that the longest common prefix in the set is either the nearest successor or the nearest predecessor of the query. This proves the first part of the theorem. The second part follows because if two queries belong to the same prefix group, then the longest common prefix in the set must also be in the same prefix group.   □

The client maintains a local data structure that stores values of the form (q, mp, np, ns) where q is the query, mp is the prefix of the q's prefix group, np is q's nearest predecessor, and ns is q's nearest successor. These values are stored in a balanced binary search tree organized by query. Given this structure the client can find the nearest neighbors of a specific query in $O(\log M)$ time.

Example Suppose that we use the example in Figure 1. Suppose that in a query phase a client first issues a query for 8, then the the client searches for prefixes 1, 10, 100, and 1000. It finds a match at prefix 10, and learns the nearest neighbors are $(7, 11)$. Suppose that the client then asks query $ns(13)$. In this case the prefixes would be 1, 11, 110, and 1101. The client must avoid asking for the query 1, since the client has already asked this query in this phase. Thus the client asks for 11, 110, and 1101 along with a fake miss. The prefix 11 is the only match, and the client learns that 13's nearest neighbors are $(11, \infty)$. Finally, suppose that the client issues query $ns(9)$. The prefix groups would then be 1,10,100,1001. The first three of these groups have been asked by the client. Furthermore, the prefix group 10 is in the set S, and it indicates the nearest neighbors of 9 are $(7, 11)$. Thus the client issues queries 1001, two fake misses, and a fake hit. The fake hit is necessary to ensure that the server sees exactly one match in its dataset.

4.4. Data Structure 2: Handling Changes

The purpose of this data structure is to keep track of changes that have been made during a query phase. There are two main challenges: i) returning the correct answers in the rest of the query phase, ii) including the updates in the stored data in the rebuilding phase.

The main idea is that the client will keep track of all intervals where it knows the answer. That is, for every $nn(q)$ query, the client learns an interval $(np, ns]$ that contains q, and each value in $(np, ns]$ has the same nearest neighbors. Furthermore, all points outside of the interval $(np, ns]$ do not have the exact same nearest neighbors. This data structure will keep track of all such intervals that the client learns during the query phase. When modifying the dataset, the client will modify the local data structure, but leave the server's data (and its data from the first data structure unchanged). Hence, if this second data structure contains information about a specific interval. then this is considered more current than the values stored at the server. One could think of this data structure as a change log during the query phase.

We now give the details of insert and delete at a high level. To process a query $insert(q)$, first the client performs a $nn(q)$ query. Thus the interval containing this value will be in the local storage. Suppose that this interval is $(np, ns]$. The inserted value splits this interval into at most two intervals, and these intervals will replace the previous interval. That is, the process creates the intervals $(np, q]$ and $(q, ns]$.

To process $remove(q)$, the client will query the server for the removed value, and will thus have the interval containing the removed value in its local storage. Suppose this interval is $(np, ns]$. If $q \neq ns$, then nothing has to be done. However, if $q = ns$, then the client will have to mark the value ns as removed. A difficulty arises when a client queries a point inside of an interval where the end point has been removed, e.g., if the client later issued a query in the interval $(np, ns]$ after ns was removed. In this case, the client would know that the answer provided by the server is stale, but would not know the correct answer. To overcome this problem, the client first checks the second data structure to determine if this will be a problem. If so, then the client issued a query for the next interval. That is, in our example, the client would issue a query $nn(ns + 1)$ instead of $nn(q)$, and this will return the new nearest successor.

Specifically, the data structure will keep track of a set of intervals. An interval $[x, y]$ means that any point in the interval $(x, y]$ has x as its nearest predecessor and y as its successor. An interval is either marked valid or invalid. An interval is valid if y has not been removed and is invalid otherwise. Note that we ensure that the only points that are removed are endpoints of some interval in the client's structure. There are several operations that we want to perform with this structure, including:

1. $(ns, np, valid) \leftarrow lookup(x)$: This searches the interval list to find the interval containing x in the structure. If no such interval exists, then return null. Otherwise, if x is in a valid interval $[y, z]$, then return $(x, y, true)$. Otherwise, if x is in an invalid interval $[y, z]$, then return $(x, y, false)$.

2. $insertPoint(x)$: This has a precondition that there exists a valid interval containing x, let this interval be $(y, z]$. This interval is replaced with two valid intervals $(y, x]$ and $(x, z]$.

3. $removePoint(x)$: This has a precondition that there exists a valid interval containing x, let this interval be $(y, z]$. If $x \neq z$, then do nothing. Otherwise, mark this interval as invalid.

4. $insertInterval(x, y)$ This assumes that the interval $(x, y]$ does not overlap any current interval. If there is an invalid interval $(z, x]$, then this replaces this interval with a single valid interval $(z, y]$. Otherwise, this adds a single valid interval $(x, y]$.

5. The existence of an iterator function that allows us to iterate over all intervals in the structure (touching each interval once). This is encapsulated by the functions $first()$ which starts the iterator, and $next()$ which returns the next interval (and null if no such interval exists).

6. An initialization method, $initIntervalDS()$ that initializes an empty data structure.

The above data structure is straightforward to build using a balanced binary search tree (sorted by interval end point). If there are M intervals, then this structure has size $O(M)$. In this case lookup, insertions, and removals can be processed in $O(\log M)$ time. Furthermore, iterating over all intervals requires $O(M)$ time.

4.5. Putting Pieces Together

We are now ready to put all of the pieces together and give a detailed description of the system. We begin by highlighting the main ideas:

1. The data owner stores all interesting prefixes and their nearest predecessors and successors for that prefix, using similar techniques as [7]. That is, for the tuple $(p, (p, np, ns))$ we store $(F_{fk}(p), Enc_{ek}(p, np, ns))$ at the server. To process a

query, the data owner will query all prefixes of the query in parallel.

2. The data owner uses the data structure outlined in section 4.3 to maintain information about previous queries. This is used to prevent the data owner for asking about the same prefix multiple times, and to know when a dummy record needs to be queried (i.e., has the interesting prefix for the query already been queried).

3. The data owner uses the data structure outlined in section 4.4 to maintain information about the changes that have been made during the query phase. This is used during the query phase to ensure that the responses include the recent changes.

4. During the rebuild phase, all of the changes in the second data structure are stored on the server. Like [7] all of the values are randomly permuted (using the Buffer Shuffle techniques) to obfuscate the relationship between queries in different query phases.

Table 1 describes the notation used in the protocols.

It is worth discussing the various input values for the PRF that are used. Specifically, we use a PRF $F : \{0,1\}^\kappa \times \{REAL, DUMMY, MISS, PAD\} \times \cup_{i=1}^{Q} \{0,1\}^i \to \{0,1\}^\kappa$. That is, the PRF takes a message type and a variable length message (up to Q bits) as its second input. Here the value of Q is chosen such that $2^Q \geq \max\{D, N \log D, M, M \log D\}$. Such a PRF can be constructed with an appropriate encoding scheme. We assume that encryption pads message of variable length to the same size (in this case $3 \log D$ is sufficient), and we assume the existence of a fake message $FAKE$ that can be used for padding and dummy values.

We begin with the initialization algorithm. This algorithm is done once when the system is setup. The details are in Algorithm 3. The first steps (lines 1-2) is to set up the long-term encryption key and the query phase pseudorandom function key. In lines 3-13, the client generates the values that the server will store, which will consist of the PRF of a key and an encrypted message body. Specifically, lines 3-7, add all interesting prefixes to the server storage set. Since there will be at most N items, then there will be at most $N \log D + 1$ interesting prefixes (see Theorem 1), and thus lines 8-10 add padding to the list. Finally, $2M$ dummy values are added to the server set in lines 11-13. A random permutation of these values is stored in line 15. Finally, lines 15-18 initialize global variables used by the rest of the algorithms.

We now turn to the server's main algorithm (we also require the server can stream all tuples in its data store to the data owner M at a time). This algorithm receives

---

Algorithm 3 $INIT(K = \{k_1, \ldots, k_n\})$

1: $fk \leftarrow \{0,1\}^\kappa$
2: $ek \leftarrow KeyGen(1^\kappa)$
3: $S \leftarrow \{\}$
4: {Store values on server}
5: Let $IP \leftarrow ALLPREFIXES(k_1, \ldots, k_n)$
6: **for all** $(p, (np, ns)) \in IP$ **do**
7: $\quad S \leftarrow S \cup \{F_{fk}(REAL, p), Enc_{ek}((p, np, ns))\}$
8: **end for**
9: **for** $i = 1$ to $N \log D + 1 - |IP|$ **do**
10: $\quad S \leftarrow S \cup \{F_{fk}(PAD, i), Enc_{ek}(FAKE)\}$
11: **end for**
12: **for** $i = 1$ to $2M$ **do**
13: $\quad S \leftarrow S \cup \{F_{fk}(DUMMY, i), Enc_{ek}(FAKE)\}$
14: **end for**
15: Permute S and send to server.
16: $DS1 \leftarrow InitializeCommonQuery()$
17: $DS2 \leftarrow InitalizeIntervals()$
18: $queries, dumUsed, misUsed \leftarrow 0$

---

a set of keys (key values that have the PRF applied to it). The server simply looks up all matching keys that are in S, and returns the messages associated with the keys. The server also returns the query index for each match, so that the client knows which queries were a match. Note that this leaks to the server the number of hits, so this can only be used when the number of hits is controllable (i.e., always the same). The details are in Algorithm 4.

Algorithm 4 $SERVERPROCESS(\ell_1, \ldots, \ell_m)$

1: $R \leftarrow \{\}$
2: **for** $i = 1$ to m **do**
3: $\quad$ **if** $\exists (\ell_i, r_i) \in S$ **then**
4: $\quad\quad R \leftarrow R \cup \{(i, r_i)\}$
5: $\quad\quad$ remove (ℓ_i, r_i) from S
6: $\quad$ **end if**
7: **end for**
8: **return** R

We now turn to a nearest neighbor algorithm for static data. This is used as a building block by the actual nearest neighbor algorithm. The details are in Algorithm 5. The first step is to determine the longest common prefix with previous queries and to determine if the answer is known already. This is done using $DS1$ in line 1. Line 2 creates the list of the longest L prefixes that have not been queried before. Lines 4-8, handle the case where the prefix group containing the query is already known. In this case, one of the misses must be a hit (in order to ensure that the server always sees a single hit), and so a dummy is added to Q, and the number of misses is decremented. Lines 9-10 add the appropriate number of misses to the query set, so that

Table 1. Notation

Name	Description
N	Upper bound on number of keys (constant)
M	Queries in the query phase (constant)
κ	Security parameter (constant)
D	Key domain size (constant and power of 2)
$DS1$	Reference to Data Structure in section 4.3
$DS2$	Reference to Data Structure in section 4.4
fk	Key for pseudorandom function F
ek	Encryption key for CPA-secure encryption
$queries$	# of queries made during query phase.
$dumUsed$	# of dummy queries used during query phase.
$misUsed$	# of fake misses used during query phase.

$|Q| = \log D$. Lines 11-12 permute the queries and send the PRF values for each query in Q to the server. If the query answer was unknown before asking the query, then lines 15 sets the nearest neighbor as the decrypted result from the server. Otherwise, line 17, uses the previous value from $DS1$. In either case, $DS1$ is updated and the nearest neighbors are returned.

Algorithm 5 $LOOKUP(q)$

1: $(L, nn) \leftarrow DS1.get(q)$
2: $Q \leftarrow \{(REAL, Prefix_{d-i}(q)) : i \in [0, L-1]\}$
3: $misses \leftarrow \log D - L$
4: **if** $nn \neq null$ **then**
5: $\quad dumUsed \leftarrow dumUsed + 1$
6: $\quad Q \leftarrow Q \cup \{(DUMMY, dumUsed)\}$
7: $\quad misses \leftarrow misses - 1$
8: **end if**
9: $Q \leftarrow \{(MISS, misUsed + i) : i \in [1, misses]\}$
10: $misUsed \leftarrow misUsed + misses$
11: Permute Q
12: Send to server $\{F_{fk}(r) : r \in Q\}$ and receive QR.
13: $\{QR$ will contain one encrypted tuple, let it be $(i, r).\}$

14: **if** $nn = null$ **then**
15: $\quad (p, np, ns) \leftarrow Dec_{ek}(r)$
16: **else**
17: $\quad$ Parse nn into (p, np, ns)
18: **end if**
19: $DS1.insert(q, p, np, ns)$
20: **return** (np, ns)

We now introduce the main algorithm, i.e., the nearest neighbor algorithm. This takes a query, and returns the nearest predecessor and successor of the query; the details are in Algorithm 6. In line 1, this looks up the query in the interval data structure to determine if the interval of the query is already known. Note that it may be that this value is more recent than the values stored in the server, since all updates affect only $DS2$

until the rebuild phase. If the interval is known, but the interval is invalid, then this means that the nearest successor has been removed. Thus, the answer returned from the server from q will be stale, and $DS2$ does not contain the correct nearest successor. To resolve this problem, line 3 changes the query to the one more than the stale nearest successor. Then line 5 either looks up the query or the modified query, using Algorithm 5. This new interval is added to $DS2$, which means that a valid interval containing q is now in $DS2$. Thus we lookup q in DS2 (in Line 7). Finally, we increment the number of queries and return the appropriate nearest predecessor and successor.

Algorithm 6 $NN(q)$

1: $(np, ns, valid) \leftarrow DS2.lookup(q)$
2: **if** $(np, ns, valid) \neq null$ AND $valid = false$ **then**
3: $\quad q \leftarrow ns + 1$
4: **end if**
5: $(np', ns') \leftarrow LOOKUP(q)$
6: $DS2.insertInterval(np', ns')$
7: $(np', ns', valid) \leftarrow DS2.lookup(q)$
8: $queries \leftarrow queries + 1$
9: **return** (np', ns')

The algorithm for insertion (resp. removal) are given in Algorithm 7 (resp. 8). In both algorithms, the client uses the nearest neighbor algorithm. Then insertion simply inserts the new point into $DS2$, and removal simply removes the query from $DS2$. Note that in both cases the precondition is met, because $NN(q)$ ensures that a valid interval containing q is in $DS2$.

Algorithm 7 $Insert(q)$

1: $NN(q)$
2: $DS2.insertPoint(q)$

We now turn our attention to the rebuilding phase (this is triggered when $queries = M$). We first present

---

Algorithm 8 *Remove(q)*

1: $NN(q)$
2: $DS2.removePoint(q)$.

---

a helper algorithm that ensures all intervals in the interval structure, $DS2$, are valid. This is important, because any invalid interval corresponds to a situation where an endpoint has been removed, but the client doesn't know what the actual endpoint should be. Lines 1-6 iterate through all intervals in $DS2$ and for every invalid interval, it adds a query to Q that will make the interval valid (once we know the interval for the query). To hide the number of invalid intervals from the server, lines 8-10, pad the query set with to contain M points (there are at most M invalid intervals, because each remove can invalidate at most one interval). The padded points are dummy points, because they need to be hits on the server. This is the reason for needing $2M$ dummies, M to answer queries and and M for the rebuild phase. The client computes the PRF of all points in Q and sends them to the server in a random order in line 11. Lines 12-15, process each non-dummy return value by adding it to $DS2$. This will validate all intervals in $DS2$.

Algorithm 9 *ValidateAllIntervals()*

1: $DS2.first()$
2: $Q \leftarrow \{\}$
3: **while** $((x, y, valid) \leftarrow DS2.next()) \neq null$ **do**
4:    **if** valid = false **then**
5:       $Q \leftarrow Q \cup \{(REAL, y + 1)\}$
6:    **end if**
7: **end while**
8: **for** $i = 1$ to $M - |Q|$ **do**
9:    $Q \leftarrow Q \cup \{(DUMMY, dumUsed + i)\}$
10: **end for**
11: Send $\{F_{fk}(q) : q \in Q\}$ to server in random order.
12: **for all** Entry (i, r_i) corresponding to non-dummy **do**
13:    $(p, np, ns) \leftarrow Dec_{ek}(r_i)$
14:    $DS2.insertInterval(np, ns)$
15: **end for**

The main idea of the rebuild phase is to rewrite all $N \log D + 1 + 2M$ values to the server and then to reshuffle all of the buffers (the reshuffling is the same as in traditional OS). The client suspends execution of queries, and then chooses a new PRF key (lines 1-3). The client initializes some values, including: *prefixSet* which is a set of prefixes to be written and *padWrite* which is how much padding has been written (lines 4-5). The client then validates all intervals in DS2 (line 6). After this has been done, the client streams (by streams we mean that the client obtains M records at a time from the server, in order to prevent the

client from having to store more than $O(M)$ things) the remaining $N \log D + 1$ entries from the server. For each entry, there are several cases: i) the interval specified by the prefix is not contained in $DS2$, i) the interval specified by the prefix is contained in $DS2$, iii) the tuple is a dummy or padding tuple. In the first case (line 27), the client simply re-encrypts the tuple (as it has not changed). In the other cases, the client throws the old tuple away, and builds a new tuple. To build this new tuple, the client first writes out all interesting prefixes in DS2. After all of these values have been written, then padding is written. After going through all $N \log D + 1$ tuples, the server has all interesting prefixes and the appropriate amount of padding. Then $2M$ dummy values are written (lines 31-33). After writing all of these entries, global variables are re-initialized (lines 36-38). All of the values are permuted using the techniques of [7], and then query processing is resumed.

4.6. Analysis

The client's storage is determined by the size of $DS1$ and $DS2$. For each nearest neighbor query, there is at most 1 thing in $DS1$, and thus its size is $O(M)$. Furthermore, $DS2$ has at most 2M intervals, and thus its size is $O(M)$. The client has to store $O(\log D)$ bits, and thus its total storage is $O(M \log D)$.

The server has to store $O(N \log D + M)$ items, and each has size $O(\max\{\kappa, \log D\})$. Since κ is a constant and $M << N$, then the server's total bit storage is $O(N \log^2 D)$.

The communication to process an insert, remove, or nn query is $O(1)$ for both the client and the server. Furthermore, the communication is $O(1)$.

The computational cost of the rebuilding phase is $O(N \log D)$, and the communication cost is $O(N \log^2 D)$.

It is worth comparing this solution to the original cost of OS, to determine the overhead of the nearest neighbor capabilities. Here V is the size of the messages associated with the keys. It is clear from the table that the overhead is dictated by the relationship between V and $\log^2 D$. There are many application with small key size (for example a key size of 8 bytes may be sufficient in many contexts). However, in many applications the sizes of the messages are large (the simulations used in [7] varied V from 1KB to 64 KB). In either case the $O(N \log^2 D)$ is dominated by $O(NV)$. Hence, the overhead added by the current approach is modest when compared to OS.

5. Summary

In this paper, we introduced an oblivious index that extends oblivious storage to support nearest neighbor queries. In realistic settings, the proposed index

Table 2. Comparison between the Original Scheme and the Index Overhead

Metric	Traditional	Index Overhead
Server Storage	$O(NV)$	$O(N \log^2 D)$
Client Storage	$O(MV)$	$O(M \log D)$
Online computation	$O(1)$	$O(1)$
Online communication	$O(V)$	$O(\log D)$
Rebuild Communication	$O(NV)$	$O(N \log^2 D)$

Algorithm 10 $rebuild()$

1: {Triggered when $QUERIES = M$}
2: Suspend query processing
3: $fk' \leftarrow PRF.Gen(1^\kappa)$
4: $prefixSet \leftarrow \{\}$
5: $padWrite \leftarrow 0$
6: $validateIntervals()$
7: $DS2.first()$
8: {Start streaming remaining records from server}
9: **for all** $(Enc_{ek}(p, np, ns)$ in Server storage **do**
10:     Decrypt to obtain (p, np, ns)
11:     **if** (p,np,ns)=$FAKE$ OR $DS2.containsPoint(ns)$ **then**
12:         **if** $prefixSet = \{\}$ **then**
13:             $interval \leftarrow DS2.next()$
14:             **if** $interval \neq null$ **then**
15:                 $prefixSet \leftarrow SPLIT(interval)$
16:             **end if**
17:         **end if**
18:         **if** $prefixSet \neq \{\}$ **then**
19:             Pick $(p2, np2, ns2)$ from $prefixSet$
20:             $prefixSet \leftarrow prefixSet - \{(p2, np2, ns2)\}$
21:             $(k, v) \leftarrow ((REAL, p2), (p2, np2, ns2))$
22:         **else**
23:             $padWrite \leftarrow padWrite + 1$
24:             $(k, v) \leftarrow ((PAD, padWrite), FAKE)$
25:         **end if**
26:     **else**
27:         $(k, v) \leftarrow (p, np, ns)$
28:     **end if**
29:     Send server $(F_{fk'}(k), Enc_{ek}(v))$
30: **end for**
31: **for** $i = 1$ to $2M$ **do**
32:     $(k, v) \leftarrow ((DUMMY, i), FAKE)$
33:     Send $(F_{fk'}(k), Enc_{ek}(v))$ to server.
34: **end for**
35: $fk \leftarrow fk'$
36: $queries, dumUsed, misUsed \leftarrow 0$
37: $DS1 \leftarrow InitalizeCommonQuery()$
38: $DS2 \leftarrow InitalizeIntervals()$
39: Shuffle servers storage as in [7]
40: {Note the above changes the value of fk}
41: Resume query processing

---

introduces a small overhead, when compared to the original oblivious data store. Future work includes:

1. Implementing the index and determining actual overhead for realistic loads.

2. Extending a miss-intolerant OS to a miss-tolerant OS using these techniques. It is straightforward to do this for get, but less so for insert and remove.

3. Extending the semantics further to include range queries, range count and aggregate queries. A straightforward way to do range queries is based on nn query: the client partitions the key domain into $O(\sqrt{N})$ intervals, stores a key value pair for each one as $(left\_endpoint,$ $(values\_inside\_interval, right\_endpoint))$, and builds the nn search index over all the left endpoints. To query for a range $[a, b]$, the client queries for the nearest left endpoint of a and gets all the values in the interval, and continues fetching the next interval by a nn query for the current interval's $right\_endpoint + 1$ until exceeding b. Range count and aggregate queries could also be done in a similar way. However, this will increase the local storage at the client to $O(N^{0.75})$, so future work could focus on these semantics without increasing the storage.

5.1. Acknowledgements

Portions of this work were supported by National Science Foundation Grants CPS-1329979, CNS-0915436, Science and Technology Center CCF-0939370; by an NPRP grant from the Qatar National Research Fund; and by sponsors of the Center for Education and Research in Information Assurance and Security. The statements made herein are solely the responsibility of the authors.

References

[1] APACHE SOFTWARE FOUNDATION (2014) Apache HBase home. URL http://hbase.apache.org/.

[2] BONEH, D., MAZIERES, D. and POPA., R.A. (2011) *Remote oblivious storage: Making oblivious RAM practical.* Tech. rep., CSAIL, MIT.

[3] GENTRY, C., GOLDMAN, K., HALEVI, S., JULTA, C., RAYKOVA, M. and WICHS, D. (2013) Optimizing ORAM and using it efficiently for secure computation. In *Privacy Enhancing Technologies* (Springer Berlin Heidelberg), **7981**, 1–18.

[4] GOLDREICH, O. (1987) Towards a theory of software protection and simulation by oblivious rams. In *Proceedings of the 19th annual ACM Symposium on Theory of Computing*, STOC '87 (New York, NY, USA: ACM): 182–194.

[5] GOODRICH, M.T. and MITZENMACHER, M. (2011) Privacy-preserving access of outsourced data via oblivious RAM simulation. In *Proceedings of the 38th International Conference on Automata, Languages and Programming - Volume Part II*, ICALP'11 (Berlin, Heidelberg: Springer-Verlag): 576–587.

[6] GOODRICH, M.T., MITZENMACHER, M., OHRIMENKO, O. and TAMASSIA, R. (2011) Oblivious ram simulation with efficient worst-case access overhead. In *Proceedings of the 3rd ACM workshop on Cloud computing security workshop*, CCSW '11 (New York, NY, USA: ACM): 95–100.

[7] GOODRICH, M.T., MITZENMACHER, M., OHRIMENKO, O. and TAMASSIA, R. (2012) Practical oblivious storage. In *Proceedings of the 2nd ACM Conference on Data and Application Security and Privacy*, CODASPY '12 (New York, NY, USA: ACM): 13–24.

[8] HACIGÜMÜS, H., MEHROTRA, S. and IYER, B.R. (2002) Providing database as a service. In *18th International Conference on Data Engineering* (IEEE): 29–38.

[9] KNUTH, D.E. (1973) *The Art of Computer Programming, Volume III: Sorting and Searching* (Addison-Wesley).

[10] KUSHILEVITZ, E., LU, S. and OSTROVSKY, R. (2012) On the (in)security of hash-based oblivious RAM and a new balancing scheme. In *Proceedings of the 23rd Annual ACM-SIAM Symposium on Discrete Algorithms*, SODA '12 (SIAM): 143–156.

[11] LI, J. and OMIECINSKI, E. (2005) Efficiency and security trade-off in supporting range queries on encrypted databases. In *Data and Applications Security XIX* (Springer): 69–83.

[12] SHI, E., CHAN, T., STEFANOV, E. and LI, M. (2011) Oblivious RAM with $\emptyset(log^3 n)$ worst-case cost. In *Advances in Cryptology-ASIACRYPT'11* (Springer), 197–214.

[13] STEFANOV, E., VAN DIJK, M., SHI, E., FLETCHER, C., REN, L., YU, X. and DEVADAS, S. (2013) Path ORAM: An extremely simple oblivious ram protocol. In *Proceedings of the 2013 ACM Conference on Computer and Communications Security*, CCS '13 (New York, NY, USA: ACM): 299–310.

[14] VIMERCATI, S.D.C.D., FORESTI, S., JAJODIA, S., PARABOSCHI, S. and SAMARATI, P. (2007) Over-encryption: Management of access control evolution on outsourced data. In *Proceedings of the 33rd International Conference on Very Large Data Bases* (VLDB endowment): 123–134.

[15] WILLIAMS, P., SION, R. and CARBUNAR, B. (2008) Building castles out of mud: practical access pattern privacy and correctness on untrusted storage. In *Proceedings of the 15th ACM Conference on Computer and Communications Security*, CCS '08 (New York, NY, USA: ACM): 139–148.

[16] XIAO, L. and YEN, I.L. (2012) Security analysis and enhancement for prefix-preserving encryption schemes. *IACR Cryptology ePrint Archive* **2012**: 191.

[17] YIU, M.L., A., I., JENSEN, C.S. and KALNIS, P. (2012) Outsourced similarity search on metric data assets. *IEEE Trans. Knowl. Data Eng.* **24**(2): 338–352.

[18] YIU, M.L., GHINITA, G., JENSEN, C.S. and KALNIS, P. (2009) Outsourcing search services on private spatial data. In *25th International Conference on Data Engineering* (IEEE): 1140–1143.

5

SocialCloudShare: a Facebook Application for a Relationship-based Information Sharing in the Cloud

Davide Alberto Albertini[1], Barbara Carminati[1], Elena Ferrari[1]

[1]DISTA, Università degli Studi dell'Insubria, Via Mazzini 5, Varese, Italy.
{davide.albertini, barbara.carminati, elena.ferrari}@uninsubria.it

Abstract

In last few years, Online Social Networks (OSNs) have become one of the most used platforms for sharing data (e.g., pictures, short texts) on the Internet. Nowadays Facebook and Twitter are the most popular OSN providers, though they implement different social models. However, independently from the social model they implement, OSN platforms have become a widespread repository of personal information. All these data (e.g., profile information, shared elements, users' likes) are stored in a centralized repository that can be exploited for data mining and marketing analysis. With this data collection process, lots of sensitive information are gathered by OSN providers that, in time, have become more and more targeted by malicious attackers.

To overcome this problem, in this paper we present an architectural framework that, by means of a Social Application registered in Facebook, allows users to move their data (e.g., relationships, resources) outside the OSN realm and to store them in the public Cloud. Given that the public Cloud is not a secure and private environment, our proposal provides users security and privacy guarantees over their data by encrypting the resources and by anonymizing their social graphs. The presented framework enforces Relationship-Based Access Control (ReBAC) rules over the anonymized social graph, providing OSN users the possibility to selectively share information and resources as they are used to do in Facebook.

Keywords: Online Social Networks; Collaborative graph anonymization; Controlled information sharing; Privacy-preserving path finding.

1. Introduction

In last years Online Social Networks (OSNs) have become one of the most common platforms for sharing data (e.g., pictures, short texts) on the Internet. Nowadays Facebook and Twitter are the most common OSN providers, though they implement different social models (e.g., supporting symmetric or asymmetric relationships). However, independently from the model they implement, OSN platforms have become a widespread repository of personal information. All these data (e.g., profile information, shared elements, users' likes) are stored in a centralized repository, not only to offer users a more customized experience on the OSN, but also to exploit them for data mining and marketing analysis. With this data collection process, lots of sensitive information are gathered by OSN providers that, in time, have become more and more targeted by malicious attackers.

Even though OSN providers give users' the ability to control how their information is shared over the platforms, this does not prevent them from collecting and profiling data. Literature presents several proposals aiming to prevent these marketing analysis. In general, these solutions imply to hide resources to OSN providers, e.g., by encrypting or by moving them to an external platform (see Section 7 for a more detailed discussion). All these proposals, thus, give users the ability to hide their resources from OSN providers, but do not avoid that OSN providers may infer users's personal information by analyzing, for example, the social graph.

This problem is further exacerbated by the fact that some well known OSN provider have not been always honest with respect to users privacy (see, for instance, [11] for a survey on these privacy concerns). Moreover, it occurred that OSN weaknesses brought to release as public some users' private data (e.g., the Google cyber attack in 2009 [13] or Google glitches [25]).

To overcome this problem, in this paper we present an architectural framework that, by means of a Social Application registered in Facebook, allows users to move their data (e.g., resources, relationships) outside

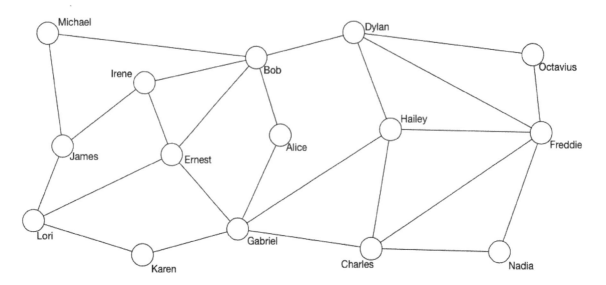

Figure 1. An example of social graph

the OSN realm and to store them in the public Cloud. Given that the public Cloud is not a secure and private environment, our proposal provides users security and privacy guarantees over their data by encrypting the resources and anonymizing their social graphs.

The presented framework enforces Relationship-Based Access Control (ReBAC) (see [5, 8]) rules over the anonymized social graph, granting OSN users the possibility to selectively share resources as they are used to do in Facebook. More precisely, the owner of a certain resource *rsc* can define *relationship-based access control conditions* that have to be verified in order to release *rsc* to the requestors. A relationship-based access control condition *acc* specifies type and depth of the relationship that must exist between the resource owner and the requestor to release *rsc* to the latter. More formally, an access control condition has the form $acc = (RelType, MaxDepth)$, where *RelType* is taken from a finite set of relationship type (e.g., *friend*, *relative*, *sibling*, *colleague*) and *MaxDepth* specifies the maximum number of hops that the shortest path connecting the owner and the requestor may be composed of. In this paper, we allow users to define access control conditions on their resources according to the ReBAC paradygm.

The proposed framework is based on the architecture described in [1], where anonymization and encryption techniques are accurately described. The work in [1], however, was tailored for a Decentralized Social Network (DSN) and, then, it suffers of all the limitations coming from a decentralized management of users data. In this paper, we present a *proof-of-concept* of such model, by implementing it inside Facebook.

The remainder of the paper is organized as follows. Section 2 presents an overall description of the proposal, while Section 3 illustrates the details of the architecture, along with a disussion describing how ReBAC is enforced over an anonymized social graph. Section 4 describes communication protocols, whereas Section 5 provides technical details of the current framework implementation. Section 6 deals with experimental evaluations. Finally, Section 7 gives an overview of the state of art, whereas Section 8 concludes the paper.

2. Overall Description

In order to highlight limitations of current proposals, we introduce a motivating example that reflects a real case of use of OSN functionalities.

Example. Let consider the simple social network represented in Figure 1, where where nodes represent users and edges represent *"friend"* relationships. Let assume that an OSN user, say *Ernest*, is willing to publish on his Facebook wallboard some pictures regarding a Christmas company party. As such, Ernest wishes to share those pictures only with the people working in his company, that is, with Gabriel, James, Karen, and Lori.

In a Facebook-style scenario, Ernest would not be able to keep track of the real-life relationships that he has with his colleagues. Then, in order to distinguish his colleagues from other contacts, Ernest would have to create a *group* or an *event* including all the people who take part in the party and then share the pictures with them. A simple relationship-based sharing, like the one offered by Facebook (e.g., friends or friends-of-friends), in fact, would not reach all the users of the network that attended the party. Indeed, with an "only friends" (OF) privacy setting, James and Karen, who are not directly connected with Ernest, would not be able to see the pictures. On the other hand, with a "friend of friends" (FoF) privacy setting, a larger set of users would be able to see them, including other people such as, e.g., Ernest's friends and relatives and their contacts.

Moreover, users who can see Ernest's pictures are granted the ability to share the pictures on their own wall, diclosing to the OSN community that there exists a connection between them and Ernest. Let assume, then, that pictures are uploaded with an OF privacy setting and Lori shares them on her wall. As such, even James and Karen would be able to see those photos, discovering there exists a connection between Ernest and Lori. This side effect may not be appreciated by Ernest, who may desire to keep this relationship private.

Finally, Ernest may have concerns publishing his pictures, in that he knows that all the published pictures are stored in an OSN repository that could be attacked by malicious users without any possibility for Ernest to prevent this event. The Social Network provider, actually, may try to infer data about Ernest for marketing purposes too and, still, Ernest would have no chances to prevent this profiling.

As highlighted by the example above, we identify three main issues underlying every OSN user experience: a limited set of privacy settings available in today OSNs for sharing resources, the possibility for both users and OSN provider to infer existence of relationships, and the lack of tools for users to control how their data are stored in the social network provider realm. To cope with these issues, we propose to export users' data (i.e., relationships and resources) from the OSN to an external platform, such as, the public Cloud, by, at the same time, enforcing a relationship-based access control more flexible than the one offered by OSN providers. Moreover, since the Cloud itself could act as a malicious party or, simply, it could be targeted by malicious attackers, data stored in the public Cloud have to be protected.

To achieve these requirements, in this paper, we present an implementation of the solutions proposed in [1] having the most popular social network, i.e., Facebook, as target. The framework presented in [1] allows users to share encrypted resources stored on the public Cloud, releasing decryption keys only to users that satisfy the corresponding ReBAC rule. The key management presented in [1] assures that resources can be encrypted/decrypted only at client-side, without disclosing any other information to the framework components. More details on the encryption scheme will be provided in Section 6.

Relationships data have to be processed in a different way with respect to users' resources. Indeed, in order to implement ReBAC, the framework needs to search for path existence in the social graph. Thus, in order to preserve users' privacy, this path discovering is performed on anonoymized structures, called *Anonymized Contact Lists (ACL)s*. More precisely, given a user u and the list of contacts, denoted as $CL^d(u)$, that are at a maximum distance of d-hops from u, the corresponding *Anonymized Contact List, $ACL^d(u)$*, is defined as the coefficients of the polynomial $P_u^d(x)$ whose roots are all and only the identifiers of users in $CL^d(u)$.[1]

By exploiting the ACLs, it is possible to verify the existance of a path of a given distance between two users. As example, if the identifier of a user v is a root for the polynomial whose coefficients are in $ACL^1(u)$ (i.e., $P_u^1(x = id_v) = 0$), it means that between u and v there exists direct relationship. However, since users have only a local view of the social graph (i.e., only their direct contacts), they are only able to compute their ACL^1. Indeed, they cannot retrieve enough information in order to compute any ACL^ns, where $n > 1$, on his/her own. Thus, in order to enforce a ReBAC model, a more complete view of the social graph is necessary, rather than the one offered by ACL^1s.

To overcome this problem, in [1] we propose a method to combine ACL^1s so as to compute such a global view of the social graph. This method is based on the consideration that, given a certain user u, his/her list of contacts $CL^2(u)$ contains all and only those users t such that there exists a user v contained in $CL^1(u)$, such that t is in $CL^1(t)$. Then, with an abuse of notation, we can denote $CL^2(u) = \bigcup_{v \in CL^1(u)} CL^1(v)$. Thus, by means of ACL^1s of all the direct contacts of u, it is possible to compute $ACL^2(u)$.

In particular, to compute the union, we exploit the polynomials property that, given two polynomials $p(x)$ and $q(x)$, the roots of the polynomial which results from their multiplication, that is, $r(x) = p(x) \cdot q(x)$, are all and only the roots in the union set between the roots of $p(x)$ and the roots of $q(x)$. Thus, to privately compute $ACL^2(u)$, it is possible to compute the multiplication of all the polynomials $P_v^1(x)$, where v is a direct contact of u, that is, $P_u^1(x = id_v) = 0$, in order to obtain $P_u^2(x)$. By means of this procedure, at last, it is possible not only to compute ACL^2s, but also to obtain ACL^ns, where $n \geq 2$. As such, in order to compute ACL^ns, where $n \geq 2$, no user interaction is required.

With reference to the social graph depicted in Figure 1, the proposed collaborative graph reconstruction procedure is executed as follows. Let assume that Karen makes use of *SocialCloudShare* before any other user in her community. At registration time, Karen fetches

---

[1]This relies on the assumption that, for each user u of the social network, the OSN provider assigns him/her an unique identifier id_u, at registration time, which is true for any popular OSN.

her direct contact list CL^1(Karen) and anonymizes it locally, in order to compose ACL^1(Karen). Let assume, for instance, that CL^1(Karen) = [Lori,Gabriel]; then ACL^1(Karen) is given by a polynomial $P^1_{Karen}(x)$, whose only possible roots are the the values of identifiers of users in CL^1_{Karen}. Then, this ACL^1(Karen) is sent to the *SocialCloudShare* framework (see Figure 2).

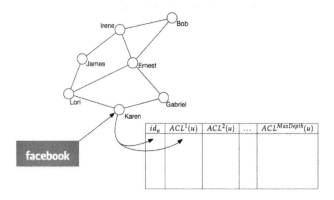

Figure 2. Example of the propagation procedure – phase 1

Assume now that, in a second time, Ernest makes use of *SocialCloudShare*. Similarly to Karen, Ernest fetches CL^1(Ernest) and anonymizes it, obtaining $P^1_{Ernest}(x)$. By having ACL^1(Karen) and ACL^1(Ernest) (see Figure 3), the framework[2] can combine them together so as to reconstruct the graph. More precisely, it has to discover if Karen and Ernest are friends. This can be done by evaluating $P^1_{Karen}(x = id_{Ernest})$, which will return a number $\neq 0$, since Ernest is not a Karen's contact. Then, no information propagation is necessary, in that no new relationship has been discovered.

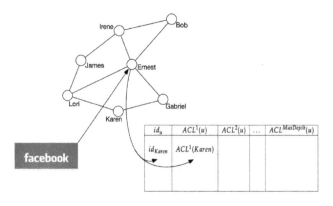

Figure 3. Example of the propagation procedure – phase 2

Finally, assume that Lori makes use of *SocialCloudShare*. Figure 1 depicts that Lori is both a direct contact of Karen and Ernest; as such, when the framework comes to evaluate $P^1_{Karen}(x = id_{Lori})$

---

the result will be 0. Then, the framework is able to determine

$$P^2_{Lori}(x) = P^2_{Lori}(x) \cdot P^1_{Karen}(x),$$
$$P^2_{Karen}(x) = P^2_{Karen}(x) \cdot P^1_{Lori}(x).$$

Then, the propagation procedure evaluates $P^1_{Ernest}(x = id_{Lori})$ and, again, the given result is 0; as such the information represented by ACL^1(Ernest) and ACL^1(Karen) has to be cross-propagated, resulting in

$$P^2_{Lori}(x) = P^2_{Lori}(x) \cdot P^1_{Ernest}(x),$$
$$P^2_{Ernest}(x) = P^2_{Ernest}(x) \cdot P^1_{Lori}(x).$$

Figure 4 illustrates the impact of these evaluations on the framework current state.

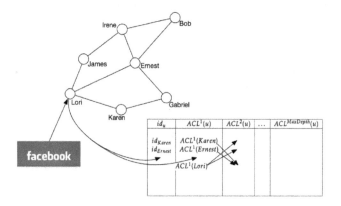

Figure 4. Example of the propagation procedure – phase 3

The procedure, then, continues in propagating users information in deeper levels until no futher computation is possible, that is, when the ACL^1(Lori) has been propagated to each of Lori's contacts and their *ACLs* have been propagated too (see Figure 5). As such, by exploiting the presented collaborative graph reconstruction, the framework is able to compute ACL^n, where $n \geq 2$, obtaining a social graph representation much wider than the one represented by only ACL^1.

id_u	$ACL^1(u)$	$ACL^2(u)$	$ACL^3(u)$	...
id_{Karen}	$ACL^1(Karen)$	$ACL^1(Lori)$	$ACL^1(Ernest)$	
id_{Ernest}	$ACL^1(Ernest)$	$ACL^1(Lori)$	$ACL^1(Karen)$	
id_{Lori}	$ACL^1(Lori)$	$ACL^1(Karen) \cdot ACL^1(Ernest)$		

Figure 5. Example of the propagation procedure – end phase

A more detailed description of the adopted techniques, along with a security analysis of the framework, can be found in [1].

---

[2]In Section 3 it will be explained which entity of the framework is in charge of this activity.

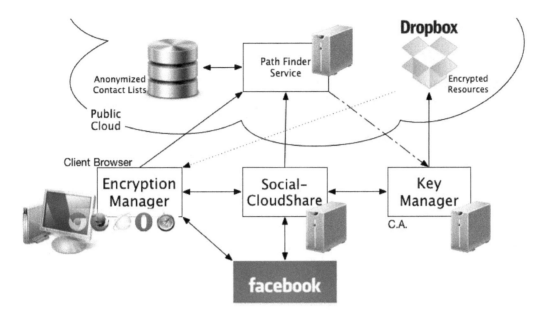

Figure 6. Framework architecture

3. Framework Architecture

According to the proposed architecture (see Figure 6), users' resources to be shared are locally encrypted by owners and stored into a Cloud storage (i.e., Dropbox). In support of this, we assume that the user is provided with the *Encryption Manager (EM)*, a browser plugin that is mainly in charge of owner's resources encryption and of generation of the *Anonymized Contact List* of user's direct contacts, that is, ACL^1. As described in Section 2, these structures are computed by anonymizing the information of CL^1, which is gathered directly from the OSN (i.e., Facebook). The channel between Facebook and the browser plugin is handled by the JavaScript Facebook SDK,[3] that allows the user to fetch structured data about the social graph (e.g., a contact list) directly from the OSN, without relying on any thirdy-party application.

ReBAC enforcement is carried out by releasing encryption keys only to those requestors that satisfy at least one of the owner's access rules. This enforcement requires the presence in the framework of two more entities. The first entity is a Social Application, named *SocialCloudShare (SCS)*, that provides users the possibility to manage access control rules and to share resources directly from the Facebook web page. The second is an entity, called *Key Manager (KM)*, in charge of the management of encryption keys.

Encryption keys are generated by exploiting two secret parameters: the first parameter, denoted with $secret_{owner}$, is unique per user and it is generated by *SocialCloudShare*; the second parameter, denoted with $secret_{rsc}$, is unique per resource and it is generated by *KM*. As such, this results in an encryption key unique per resource, that can be obtained only by combining the two corresponding secrets. As it will be discussed in Section 4, protocols regulating resources release have been designed so that neither *SocialCloudShare* nor *KM* can decrypt owner's resources, as well as infer any information on owner's relationships. In particular, these are designed such that only *EM* is able to combine the encryption secrets; as such, *SocialCloudShare* is not able to discover $secret_{rsc}$ values, while *KM* is not able to unveil $secret_{owner}$ values. This holds under the assumption that *SocialCloudShare* and *KM* do not collude together. In support of this assumption, we assume that *SocialCloudShare* is implemented on a tailored server and acts only inside the OSN realm, whereas the *KM* is an external trusted entity, whose role could be played by a Certificate Authority.

Moreover, to determine if a relationship-based access control rule is satisfied, it is required to find those paths in the social graph that connect the *owner* to the *requestor*. To protect relationships privacy, this path finding is carried out on *ACLs* stored in the public Cloud. This task is performed by the *Path Finder Service (PFS)* at Cloud side. As described in Section 2, *ACLs* are combined together to convey a deeper view of the social graph, with respect to the simple user local view that is represented with ACL^1. More precisely, for each user u *PFS* computes $ACL^d(u)$ representing the list of all the contacts that u can reach with a d-hop path.

---

[3]https://developers.facebook.com/docs/javascript .

4. Communication Protocols

Let us now introduce how the proposed framework enforces relationship-based information sharing, by illustrating the messages exchanged in each step. In doing that, we assume that the communication between entities is transmitted over secure channels.[4]

In this section, we will denote with K a symmetric encryption key, with K^+ and K^- a public and private key, and with $K^{session}$ a session key valid only for the current comunication session. For any key, we report as subscript the framework component for which the key has been generated (e.g., K^+_{SCS} denotes a public key generated for *SocialCloudShare*). Moreover, we denote with K_{rsc} a resource encryption key, whereas $secret_{owner}$ and $secret_{rsc}$ denote the secret tokens that are used for the generation of the resource encryption keys. Finally, with such defined keys, we denote with $\{message\}_K$ a message that is encrypted exploiting K as encryption key.

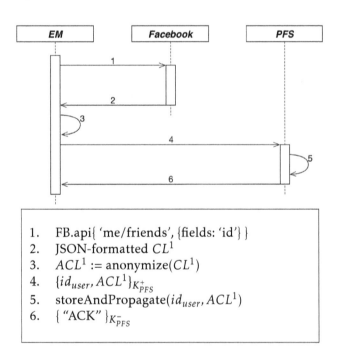

1. FB.api{ 'me/friends', {fields: 'id'} }
2. JSON-formatted CL^1
3. $ACL^1 := $ anonymize(CL^1)
4. $\{id_{user}, ACL^1\}_{K^+_{PFS}}$
5. storeAndPropagate(id_{user}, ACL^1)
6. $\{$ "ACK" $\}_{K^-_{PFS}}$

Figure 7. Registration phase: messages Exchange

User Registration. Figure 7 depicts the messages exchange when users access *SocialCloudShare* for the first time. Exploiting Facebook JavaScript SDK, the user's contact list is requested (message 1) and gathered directly from the OSN (message 2) with no need to rely on any intermediate service. The anonymization process (message 3 in Figure 7) produces ACL^1 at user side, taking as input the direct contact list CL^1; as such, no

relationship data are sent to the provider before being anonymized. The anonymized contact list is then sent to the *PFS*, which stores it and propagates in all the *ACLs* (see message 5 in Figure 7).

The messages exchange is ended with a response message produced by the *PFS*, i.e. message 6, to notify the *EM* that the protocol has been properly executed by both parties and the sent data have been successfully handled.

Login Phase. Since we assume that *EM* is not aware of *SocialCloudShare* and *KM* public keys, the communication is initalized by requesting K^+_{SCS}, K^+_{KM}, where K^+_{SCS} and K^+_{KM} respectively denote the public keys of *SocialCloudShare* and of the *Key Manager* (see messages 1-4 in Figure 8).

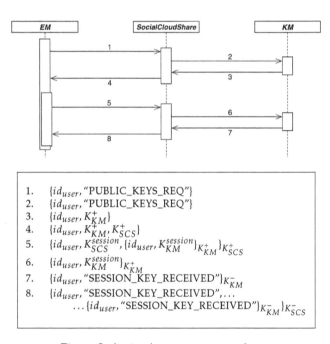

1. $\{id_{user}, \text{"PUBLIC\_KEYS\_REQ"}\}$
2. $\{id_{user}, \text{"PUBLIC\_KEYS\_REQ"}\}$
3. $\{id_{user}, K^+_{KM}\}$
4. $\{id_{user}, K^+_{KM}, K^+_{SCS}\}$
5. $\{id_{user}, K^{session}_{SCS}, \{id_{user}, K^{session}_{KM}\}_{K^+_{KM}}\}_{K^+_{SCS}}$
6. $\{id_{user}, K^{session}_{KM}\}_{K^+_{KM}}$
7. $\{id_{user}, \text{"SESSION\_KEY\_RECEIVED"}\}_{K^-_{KM}}$
8. $\{id_{user}, \text{"SESSION\_KEY\_RECEIVED"}, \ldots$
    $\ldots\{id_{user}, \text{"SESSION\_KEY\_RECEIVED"}\}_{K^-_{KM}}\}_{K^-_{SCS}}$

Figure 8. Login phase: messages exchange

Once the user has received these keys, the *EM* generates a pair of 128 bit random keys, denoted as $K^{session}_{SCS}$ and $K^{session}_{KM}$, that will be exploited as session keys for the user current session. Note that, as depicted by the architecture in Figure 6, *EM* communicates with *KM* relying only on *SocialCloudShare*, since there exist no direct communication channel between the *EM* and the *KM*. Indeed, we adapted the structure of Needham-Schroeder protocol (see [23]). As such, when the *EM* has to communicate with the *KM*, it creates a message for *SocialCloudShare* and encapsulates inside this the message directed to *KM*. *SocialCloudShare*, when receives such message, forwards to *KM* the encapsulated chunk (e.g., messages 5,6 in Figure 8). Assuming that only *KM* knows his private key K^-_{KM}, *SocialCloudShare* cannot decrypt the encapsulated

---

[4]Beyond encryption primitives present in messages schemas, we assume that HTTPS connections can be instantiated before communicating, so that an additional security layer can be granted.

message, but it has just to forward it to the KM.[5] Once both $SocialCloudShare$ and KM correctly receive the session key, they reply to the user with messages 7-8 in Figure 8.

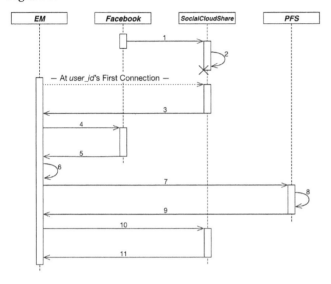

1.	{'id': 'user_id', 'changed_fields': 'friends' }
2.	storeUpdate(user_id, "CL_OUT_OF_DATE")
3.	{ "CL_OUT_OF_DATE" }
4.	FB.api{ 'me/friends', {fields: 'id'} }
5.	JSON-formatted CL^1
6.	$ACL^{1-new} :=$ anonymize(CL^{1-new}) $ACL^{1-removed} :=$ anonymize($CL^{1-removed}$)
7.	$\{id_{user}, ACL^{1-new}, ACL^{1-removed}\}_{K^+_{PFS}}$
8.	updateAndPropagate($id_{user}, ACL^{1-new}, ACL^{1-removed}$)
9.	$\{$ "ACK" $\}_{K^-_{PFS}}$
10.	$\{$ "CL_UPDATE_DONE" $\}_{K^{session}_{SCS}}$
11.	$\{$ "ACK" $\}_{K^{session}_{SCS}}$

Figure 9. Contact list update: messages exchange

Contact List Update. Figure 9 summarizes the messages exchange when the users' contact lists are modified (i.e., by adding or removing relationships). In the current implementation, we exploit Facebook *Real Time Updates (RTU)*.[6] RTU is a feature of Facebook Graph API[7] which allows Facebook thirdy-party Social Apps to be informed, directly from the OSN provider, when certain pieces of data change (e.g., new profile pictures, new friendship requests). With this functionality, $SocialCloudShare$ does not need to continuously keep synchronized with the social graph, because a callback function is called, by means of an HTTP POST request,

every time a user changes his/her own contact list (see message 1 in Figure 9).

Unfortunately, the OSN only notifies $SocialCloudShare$ about the changed fields, without revealing any other information. As such, it is then necessary to fetch from the OSN social graph all the data about new or removed friends. For this reason, we designed $SocialCloudShare$ to keep track of all those users whose contact lists are not synchronized with the $ACLs$ stored at Cloud side. Then, when each of those users makes use of $SocialCloudShare$, he/she receives a message that informs the EM that the contact list has to be synchronized (see messages 2,3 in Figure 9). Exploiting JavaScript functions, the current contact list is fetched from the social graph and new users (or, equivalently, removed users) are detected. CL^{1-new} and $CL^{1-removed}$ denote the two contact lists computed by the EM representing the lists of the new and the removed contacts. By exploiting the *anonymize* function in message 6 of Figure 7, CL^{1-new} and $CL^{1-removed}$ are anonymized.

Then, the user sends to the PFS these two separate $ACLs$ (or just one of them, in case the other one results in an empty list) (see message 7 in Figure 9). The PFS runs again the process of ACL propagation, adding the new information whenever these data are missing, or removing old information in case of relationship removal (i.e., by dividing polynomials instead of multiplying them). The messages flow is concluded with a special flag (see messages 9-11), in order to inform both the PFS and $SocialCloudShare$ that the protocol has been properly executed.

Resource Upload. The messages exchange for the resource upload phase follows the same schema as the one depicted in Figure 8, whereas the messages content is depicted in Figure 10.

1.	$\{id_{user}, id_{rsc},$ "RSC_UPLOAD_REQ",... $... \{id_{user}, id_{rsc},$ "RSC_UPLOAD_REQ"$\}_{K^{session}_{KM}}\}_{K^{session}_{SCS}}$
2.	$\{id_{user}, id_{rsc},$ "RSC_UPLOAD_REQ"$\}_{K^{session}_{KM}}$
3.	$\{id_{user}, id_{rsc}, secret_{rsc}\}_{K^{session}_{KM}}$
4.	$\{id_{user}, secret_{user}, \{id_{user}, id_{rsc}, secret_{rsc}\}_{K^{session}_{KM}}\}_{K^{session}_{SCS}}$
5.	$\{id_{user}, id_{rsc}, \mathcal{R}_{rsc}, \{id_{user}, id_{rsc}, \{rsc\}_{K_{rsc}}\}_{K^{session}_{KM}}\}_{K^{session}_{SCS}}$
6.	$\{id_{user}, id_{rsc}, \{rsc\}_{K_{rsc}}\}_{K^{session}_{KM}}$
7.	$\{id_{user}, id_{rsc},$ "RSC_STORED"$\}_{K^{session}_{KM}}$
8.	$\{id_{user}, id_{rsc},$ "ACR_STORED",... $... \{id_{user}, id_{rsc}$ "RSC_STORED"$\}_{K^{session}_{KM}}\}_{K^{session}_{SCS}}$

Figure 10. Resource upload phase: messages exchange

Before uploading a certain resource rsc in Dropbox, its owner, say user u, has to encrypt it using a symmetric key, that is, K_{rsc}. This key is computed as combination of two secrets, i.e. $K_{rsc} = \mathcal{F}(secret_{owner}, secret_{rsc})$, which

---

[5]This still relies on the assumption that $SocialCloudShare$ and KM do not collude.

[6]https://developers.facebook.com/docs/graph-api/real-time-updates/v2.0 .

[7]https://developers.facebook.com/docs/graph-api/ .

are separately generated by *SocialCloudShare* and the *KM*.[8] In the given implementation, we choose to encrypt resources exploiting AES-256 algorithm [22], operating in Cipher Block Chaining (CBC) mode [10], where the plaintext is padded according to PKCS#7 [17]; for this reason we designed the two secrets with length of 256 bit. As it will be discussed later, these secrets are released to a requestor by *SocialCloudShare* and *KM* if and only if he/she satisfies a t l east one access rule condition associated with *rsc*.

Thus, before any upload, resource owner has to interact with both *SocialCloudShare* and the *KM* so as to retrieve the corresponding $secret_{owner}$ and $secret_{rsc}$. Assuming the user shares a symmetric session key only with *KM*, negotiated during the login phase, *SocialCloudShare* cannot decrypt the encapsulated message and thus cannot discover $secret_{rsc}$. Once the secrets have been generated by *SocialCloudShare* and the *KM*, they are received by *u* encrypted with pre-shared session key (see message 4 in Figure 10); as such, the user is able to compute K_{rsc}. Hence, *u* composes a message including the encrypted resource (to be transmitted to *KM*) and the set of access control rules $\mathcal{R}_{rsc}$ that *SocialCloudShare* has to store. In our implementation $\mathcal{R}_{rsc}$ is a 1 byte value; the 5 more significant bits translate the relationship type (with a maximum of possible relationship types equal to 32) and the 3 less significant bits translate the maximum depth value of the access control condition. Even though our implementation currently supports only *"friend"* relationships, this implementative choice leaves the framework ready to further improvements.

As depicted in Figure 10, the *EM* sends all messages to *SocialCloudShare*, which then forwards nested encrypted messages to the *KM*. After the execution of the protocol illustrated in Figure 10, the Cloud data storage service contains the encrypted resource, whereas *SocialCloudShare* and the *KM* contain only resource metadata. In particular, the *KM* stores id_{rsc} and $secret_{rsc}$, whereas *SocialCloudShare* saves id_{rsc} along with the resource access control rules $\mathcal{R}_{rsc}$, where id_{rsc} denotes a unique identifier for the resource.

Resource Download. In order to enforce a relationship-based resource sharing, the framework has to release encryption keys only to requestors satisfying at least an access control rule associated with the requested resources. To determine if an access rule is satisfied, the *PFS* service is inquired. To protect the communication between *SocialCloudShare*, the *KM*, and the *PFS* we assume there exists a symmetric encryption key, denoted as K_{PFS}, shared between those three entities. By

using this key, the communication encrypted with K_{PFS} cannot be decrypted by anyone unless the components of the framework.

If a requestor *req* wishes to download and decrypt *rsc*, it has to send a message to *SocialCloudShare* with the related ids (message 1 in Figure 11). *SocialCloudShare* retrieves the corresponding access rules $\mathcal{R}_{rsc}$ and the id of *rsc*'s owner (i.e., id_{own}). Then, assuming for simplicity $\mathcal{R}_{rsc}$ contains only one access control condition $acc = (t, d)$, it inquires the *PFS* to search for a path connecting the requestor to the owner, with all edges labeled with *t* and length less than *d* (i.e., message 2 in Figure 11). It is important to note that if the *PFS* sends the yes/no answer back directly to *SocialCloudShare*, this might bring to some information leakage. Indeed, for some particular access rules, knowing whether the rule is satisfied gives exact information on existing paths. As such, the answer produced by the *PFS* is sent to the *KM* (see message 3 in Figure 11).

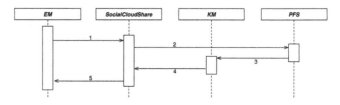

1. $\{id_{req}, id_{own}, id_{rsc}, "RSC\_DWNLD\_REQ", \ldots$
    $\ldots \{id_{own}, id_{rsc}, "RSC\_DWNLD\_REQ"\}_{K_{KM}^{session}}\}_{K_{SCS}^{session}}$
2. $\{h(id_{req}\|acc_{rsc}.type), h(id_{own}\|acc_{rsc}.type), acc_{rsc}.depth \ldots$
    $\ldots \{id_{own}, id_{rsc}, "RSC\_DWNLD\_REQ"\}_{K_{KM}^{session}}\}_{K_{PFS}}$
3. $\{result, \{id_{own}, id_{rsc}, "RSC\_DWNLD\_REQ"\}_{K_{KM}^{session}}\}_{K_{PFS}}$
4. $\{token_{secret}, URL_{rsc}\}_{K_{KM}^{session}}$
5. $\{id_{req}, secret_{own}, \{token_{secret}, URL_{rsc}\}_{K_{KM}^{session}}\}_{K_{SCS}^{session}}$

Figure 11. Resource download phase: messages exchange

The URL sent from the *KM* (see message 4 in Figure 11) is a temporarily valid URL provided by the Cloud storage service upon *KM* requests. The *rsc* to be downloaded is reachable at this URL only for a small and fixed interval of time, afterwards *rsc* is moved back to the private realm of the storage service, without any public access.[9] Message 4 (see Figure 11) contains, along with the above mentioned URL, the value of $token_{secret}$, which is $token_{secret} = secret_{rsc}$ in case the *PFS* sent a positive answer, or a random value otherwise. *SocialCloudShare* inserts $secret_{own}$ into the received message, encrypts it with pre-shared session key and forwards it to the user (i.e., message

---

[8]Several $\mathcal{F}$ functions can be adopted. In our implementation, we make use of XOR.

[9]Moving resources on temporary URL is a common approach used by several Cloud storage services (e.g., Dropbox, in this implementation) to limit access of requested resources.

5 in Figure 11). Then, the user decrypts $secret_{own}$ and $token_{secret}$ values and generates $\mathcal{F}(secret_{own}, token_{secret})$, which returns the correct encryption key K_{rsc} only if $token_{secret} = secret_{rsc}$, that is, only if the KM receives a positive answer from the PFS, confirming the existence of a path satisfying the rule.

5. Implementation

In this section, we provide some details concerning the implementation of *SocialCloudShare*.

5.1. Encryption Manager – Browser Plugin

The *Encryption Manager (EM)* is the component in charge of client-side resource encryption and of anonymized contact lists generation. We choose to implement the aboved-mentioned functionalities with a set of JavaScript functions, in order to achieve a better usability than a customized software and to give users the possibility to make use of it with no restriction given by his/her operative system.

By exploiting jQuery library[10] and AJAX-like[11] techniques, *EM* is able to process user actions (e.g., mouse clicks, page requests, upload/download requests) inside *SocialCloudShare*. The most important functionalities offered by *EM* are the encryption primitives for resources/messages encryption/decryption. For what concerns the resource encryption/decryption phase, the *EM* can be seen as a cipher black box. Thus, plaintext resource is taken as input and coded into a ciphertext resource and vice versa. As such, no entity except the *EM* takes part in these processes. At this purpose, we decided to exploit an existing library, named Crypto-JS,[12] available under BSD-3 License on Google Code, offering several encryption primitives ready to be used. In particular, for resources encryption, we exploit AES-256 algorithm applied according to Cipher Block Chaining (CBC) mode, where the plaintext is padded according to PKCS#7.

In order to exploit CBC mode, an Initialization Vector iv is necessary during the encryption and decryption phases. For this reason, the *EM* generates each time a random value as initalization vector (by exploiting *CryptoJS.lib.WordArray.random(128/8)*), which is added prior to the ciphertext, such that the iv itself can be securely stored along with the encrypted resource.

Figures 12 and 13 depict the functions used in the *EM* implementation.

---

[10]http://jquery.com/ .

[11]http://www.w3schools.com/ajax/default.ASP .

[12]https://code.google.com/p/crypto-js/ .

```
CryptoJS.AES.encrypt(
  'Resource-Stream',
  'Resource-Secret-Key',
  { iv: 'iv',
    mode: CryptoJS.mode.CBC,
    padding: CryptoJS.pad.Pkcs7
  }
);
```

Figure 12. Javascript AES encipher

```
CryptoJS.AES.decrypt(
  'Encrypted-Resource-Stream',
  'Resource-Secret-Key',
  { iv: 'iv',
    mode: CryptoJS.mode.CBC,
    padding: CryptoJS.pad.Pkcs7
  }
);
```

Figure 13. Javascript AES decipher

Another important feature handled by *EM* is the generation of ACL^1. To compute such ACL^1, the JavaScript library contains functions implementing the polynomial multiplication, i.e., computing the discrete convolution bewteen number sequences. As first step, the direct contacts list is fetched from Facebook social graph, by means of Facebook JavaScript SDK. As depicted in Figure 14, the JavaScript SDK needs to be initalized with a valid *Social-App-Id*, which is the identifier assigned by Facebook when registering a Social App inside its realm.

```
<script type='text/javascript'>
  $(document).ready(function() {
    $.ajaxSetup({ cache: true });
    $.getScript('//connect.facebook.net/en_UK/all.js',
      function(){ FB.init({
        appId: 'Social-App-Id',
      });
    });
  });
</script>
```

Figure 14. Facebook JS-SDK load phase

The *EM* can request to Facebook, by means of the Javascript FB Object, the logged user's friend list (e.g., see messages 1,2 in Figure 7) so that it can receive the current user's direct contacts identifiers. By having these identifiers, the *EM* can generate the user's ACL^1. Once this ACL^1 is fully computed, it is sent to the *Path Finder Service*, which is the component in charge of handling the anonymized social graph.

5.2. Path Finder Service

As outlined above, the *Path Finder Service (PFS)* is the component of *SocialCloudShare* that handles the anonymized social graph. All the *ACLs* are stored into the *ACL Repository* table, where the record is in the form $[id_u, ACL^1(u), ACL^2(u), \ldots, ACL^{MaxDepth}(u)]$, that is, it contains the user identifier and all his/her *ACLs* of different path length (see example of *ACL Repository* in Figures 2, 3, 4, 5).

The *PFS* is implemented as a web service, by means of a Java servlets that handles HTTP requests. The request received from *EM* instances are encrypted with the *PFS* public key, i.e., K_{PFS}^+. On the other hand, requests received from *SocialCloudShare* entity are encrypted with a pre-shared session key, denoted as K_{PFS}, that grants a lower overhead than an asymmetric-key encryption.

Such component, like *SocialCloudShare* and the *KM* entities presented in the following sections, has been developed inside the Spring framework[13] and exploiting STS[14], an eclipse-based IDE.[15]

Algorithm 5.1 describes the procedure executed each time a new ACL^1 is received from a *SocialCloudShare* user. This algorithm makes use of the *ACL Repository*, denoted with *R*, and of a boolean matrix, *updates*, that keeps track of the *ACLs* that have been modified during the propagation procedure.

Each time a new ACL^1 is received, along with the user *id*, the *PFS* stores inside the *ACL Repository* those new information (see Line 3 in Algorithm 5.1) and sets as true the corresponding cell of the *updates* matrix (see Line 4). Once the data have been stored, the procedure analyzes, from the shallowest level to the deepest, the *ACL Repository* record (see Lines 5,7). We denote with *e.id* the user identifier stored in the repository entry *e*, and with $e.ACL^d$, the ACL^d stored in the same repository entry.

For each record *e*, the procedure performs a second iteration over all different record *e'* (see Line 8). If the *updates* matrix contains true in the cell corresponding to *e'*, the procedure performs a polynomial evaluation, where the polynomial is the *ACL* taken from *e'* and the user identifier is taken from *e* (see Line 9). In case the polynomial evalutation results 0, and each polynomial evaluation for smallest path length (see Lines 10, 11)

result in a value different from 0, the information carried by $e.ACL^1$ and $e'.ACL^1$ is cross-propagated to level $d+1$, where d is the variable iterated over the path depth values (see Lines 12, 13). Along with this cross-propagation, the procedure updates the values of the *updates* matrix, that is, it keeps track of the above modified entries. Finally, a boolean variable *stop*, initally set with true (see Line 6), is set with false (see Line 16).

The above described procedure terminates when, given a path depth *d*, ACL^ds are no more modified throughout the whole iteration over the repository records, that is, the boolean value of the variable *stop* is true when the loop cycle at Line 7 ends, and the procedure is forced to terminate (see Line 18).

Algorithm 5.1: ACL propagation procedure

Input: id_u, $ACL^1(u)$, ACL Repository R

```
1 begin
2      boolean[][] updates;
3      R.push({ id_u, ACL^1(u), 1, 1, . . . });
4      updates[1][u] = true;
5      foreach d ∈ {1, 2, . . . , MaxDepth} do
6          boolean stop = true;
7          foreach entry e ∈ R do
8              foreach entry e' > e do
9                  if (updates[d][e'.id]) AND
                        (e'.ACL^d(x = e.id) == 0) then
10                     foreach d' < d do
11                         if e'.ACL^{d'}(x = e.id) ≠ 0 then
12                             e.ACL^{d+1} = e.ACL^{d+1} · e'.ACL^1;
13                             e'.ACL^{d+1} = e'.ACL^{d+1} · e.ACL^1;
14                             updates[d+1][e.id]=true;
15                             updates[d+1][e'id]=true;
16                             stop = false;
17          if stop then
18              exit;
19 end
```

5.3. SocialCloudShare

Differently from the *PFS* and the *KM*, *SocialCloudShare* has been developed with both a back-end system and a graphical interface, which is displayed when users access *SocialCloudShare* inside Facebook.

SocialCloudShare back-end is implemented as a web application, designed according to the Model-View-Controller architectural pattern, such that a precise HTTP request on a given URL calls a certain method of the underlying servlet. The most relevant methods offered by *SocialCloudShare* are called by handling HTTP requests incoming on the following URLs:

---

[13]http://projects.spring.io/spring-framework/ .

[14]http://spring.io/tools .

[15]Spring is an application framework with built-in modules that facilitate Java application development, in which code dependecies are directly handled by Apache Maven (http://maven.apache.org/) and Gradle (http://www.gradle.org/) at build-time, generating a .jar archive that can run under, for example, an Apache Tomcat (http://tomcat.apache.org/) web server.

SCS/ : A request to the base URL of the web application generates and returns *SocialCloudShare* homepage. The underlying controller, when necessary, fetches and stores some of the users' data (e.g., full name, profile picture). These data are collected interacting directly with the OSN provider, exploiting Facebook Graph API in order to receive users' profile information.

SCS/key/broadcast : This URL is requested automatically when the *EM* detects that the public keys of *SocialCloudShare* and the *KM* are not stored at client-side. It represents the arrival point of message 1 in Figure 8. The controller forwards the received parameters to the *KM* on its URL *KM/key/broadcast*.

SCS/key/negotiate : This URL is requested automatically when the *EM* detects that the session keys for communicating with *SocialCloudShare* and *KM* are not stored at client-side. It represents the arrival point of message 5 in Figure 8. The controller forwards the message that is encapsulated in the received one, that is the message from *EM* to the *KM*, on the URL *KM/key/negotiate*.

SCS/fb_updates : This URL is reachable both with HTTP GET and HTTP POST requests, but it is supposed to be requested only from Facebook provider. The application listens to information from the OSN, waiting for *Real Time Updates (RTU)*. Once an HTTP GET request has been received, the application communicates with Facebook in order to control and regulate the subscription for RTU. HTTP POST requests, on the other hand, are assumed to include information about the user activity in the OSN (e.g., a new profile picture, a new friendship in the social graph). The controller underlying these requests keeps track of those users that have a contact list that is not synchronyzed with the *ACLs* stored in the *PFS* (e.g., see message 1 in Figure 9).

SCS/upload : The controller that handles HTTP requests to this URL is the one responsible of starting the resource upload procedure (see message 1 in Figure 10). The received message is decrypted with the corresponding session key, and the encapsulated message (that cannot be decrypted by *SocialCloudShare*) is forwarded to the *KM* on its URL *KM/upload*. Once the message is forwarded, the controller holds and waits for a response from the *KM*.

SCS/upload/finalize : A request done to this URL finalizes an upload procedure already started. As such, the underlying controller waits messages

such as message 5 in Figure 10. Once received, the message is decrypted and the encapsulated part is forwarded to the *KM*. The remainder of the message, thus, includes the access control rule $\mathcal{R}_{rsc}$ of the uploaded resource. As such, $\mathcal{R}_{rsc}$ is stored by *SocialCloudShare* along with the resource owner identifier and the resource identifier.

SCS/download : The controller that handles the incoming requests to this URL is the one in charge of listening to download requests (e.g., message 1 in Figure 11), representing the initialization of a download process. As such, this message gathers information about the *requestor*, the *owner*, and the *resource* involved in the download process. These data are sent to the *PFS* that, after checking the existence of a path on *ACLs*, sends the corresponding result to the *KM* on its URL *KM/download*.

5.4. Key Manager

Similar to *SocialCloudShare*, the *KM* has been developed as a web application, exploiting the STS IDE. On the other hand, the *KM* is sligthly different from the previously presented *SocialCloudShare*. The *KM* is designed to listen to communication exclusively coming from *SocialCloudShare*, the *PFS*, and Dropbox; as such the application performs an IP filtering prior to accept incoming data. In case some data are received by a peer that is not regognized as belonging to one of those three parties, its requests are rejected and the communication channel closed. Then, the *KM* is designed without any front-end interface; any incoming message that is identified as valid brings the *KM* to perform some data processing and the output is directly sent as response to the message sender. The main methods offered by the *KM* are called by handling HTTP requests incoming on the following URLs:

KM/key/broadcast : This URL can only be requested by *SocialCloudShare* (e.g., via IP filtering) and it is requested only when *EM* detects that the public keys of *SocialCloudShare* and the *KM* are not stored at client-side. It represents the arrival point of message 2 in Figure 8.

KM/key/negotiate : This URL is requested automatically when the *EM* detects that the session keys for communicating with *SocialCloudShare* and *KM* are not present at client-side. It represents the arrival point of message 5 in Figure 8.

KM/upload : With reference to Figure 10, the controller handling these requests listens to messages such as message 2. The underlying methods are the ones responsible of generating and storing the resource secret $secret_{rsc}$, where rsc represents the identifier of the resource that is going to be uploaded .

KM/upload/finalize : The underlying controller includes the methods for resources upload to the Cloud Storage Service (e.g., Dropbox). Once a resource is stored into Dropbox, the KM locally stores certain resource metadata, such as the name, the filetype, and the last modification date. Those data are then displayed to users, through the $SocialCloudShare$ GUI.

KM/download : This URL is listening only to requests coming from PFS. Indeed, the underlying controller is listening to messages resulting from a path search on the anonymized graph (message 3 in Figure 11). Messages received at this URL not only contain the result of the path search performed by PFS, but they include pieces of data that were included in the dowload request sent from the requestor. With these information, the KM is able to ask Dropbox to generate URL_{rsc}, that is a temporary valid URL for the encrypted resource download. URL_{rsc} is included in the response along with $token_{secret}$, that may be a randomly generated value, in case the path finding returns a negative answer, or the value of $secret_{rsc}$ otherwise, where rsc is the downloaded resource.

6. Experimental Evaluations

To evaluate the framework performance, we carried out several tests. In doing that, we kept into account that the PFS efficiency has been studied in [1]. In particular, [1] presents the time needed by the PFS to perform polynomial evaluation and multiplication, that is, to verify a relationship-based access control rule and propagate an ACL throughout the ACL Repository. As such, in this section, we focus more on the overhead introduced by resource management, such as messages encryption size, messages encryption average time, and resource encryption average time. The workstation used for these experiments is an Intel Core 2 Quad Q6600 @ 2.40 GHz × 4, with 8GB RAM. In the current implementation $SocialCloudShare$, the KM, and the PFS are instantiated in the same instance of an Apache Tomcat servlet container and they run under different namespaces.

Message Encryption Size. Figure 15 depicts the overhead, in terms of length of messages, implied by messages encryption. The considered messages are those exchanged during the login, upload, and download phases (see Figures 8, 10, 11).

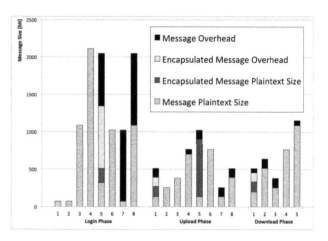

Figure 15. Messages encryption size overhead

Each bar in Figure 15 represents a single message, in term of message size. Each message is denoted by a *message plaintext size*, that is, the size of the message before encryption and a *message overhead*, that is, the size of the message once encrypted. Some message includes an encapsulated message (see message 5 in Figure 8, messages 1,2 in Figure 10, and message 1 in Figure 11) that requires a further encryption phase prior to message encryption. For those messages, Figure 15 reports the *encapsulated message plaintext size* as well as the *encapsulated message overhead*. As such, the *message plaintext size* for those messages is composed of the message plaintext size, the encapsulated message plaintext size, and the encapsulated message overhead.

Finally, it is important to note that messages in the login phase (see Figure 8) are encrypted using an asymmetric key encryption scheme.[16] This motivates the higher overhead introduced by messages encryption in such phase. Messages exchanged during upload and download phases, on the other hand, are encrypted exploiting AES-128 algorithm.

Message Encryption/Decryption Average Time. Tables 1 and 2 report the time consumption given by messages encryption. This experiment has been carried out monitoring the time required by encryption primitives to encrypt/decrypt the corresponding messages; for each message the encryption/decryption phase has been repeated 10 times. As such Tables 1, 2 report the minimum and the maximum time obtained in this experiment, along with the time average and the standard deviation.

With the exception of message 5 of the upload phase (Figure 10), the encryption/decryption primitives

---

[16]In particular, we exploit RSA-1024 for this phase .

| Protocol | Msg | Time [ms] | | | Standard |
		Min	Avg	Max	Deviation
Login	5	3.0	6.0	9.0	1.89
	7	1.0	2.2	3.0	0.6
	8	2.0	3.0	6.0	1.61
Upload	1	6.0	14.4	24.0	7.68
	3	3.0	8.1	12.0	3.01
	4	6.0	15.0	24.0	8.16
	5	14.0	28.0	56.0	16.57
	7	2.0	5.2	8.0	2.4
	8	4.0	8.0	16.0	4.0
Download	1	6.0	16.2	24.0	7.61
	2	5.0	8.0	20.0	4.58
	3	3.0	8.1	12.0	3.01
	4	6.0	13.2	24.0	7.96
	5	9.0	26.1	36.0	10.22

Table 1. Time required for message encryption

| Protocol | Msg | Time [ms] | | | Standard |
		Min	Avg	Max	Deviation
Login	6	4.0	4.8	6.0	0.98
Upload	2	4.0	10.0	16.0	4.1
	6	8.0	21.6	32.0	8.8
Download	2	4.0	9.2	16.0	4.02
	3	5.0	11.0	20.0	6.63
	4	5.0	10.8	20.0	6.38

Table 2. Time required for message decryption

| File Size [Mb] | Time [s] | | | Standard |
	Min	Avg	Max	Deviation
0.2	1.92	2.01	2.08	0.05
0.4	3.66	3.94	4.14	0.15
0.6	5.76	5.94	6.16	0.13
0.8	7.2	8.07	8.72	0.56
1.0	9.71	9.99	10.3	0.18
1.2	11.47	12.03	12.58	0.41
1.4	13.8	14.05	14.28	0.16
1.6	14.77	16.05	17.36	0.85
1.8	17.16	17.83	18.57	0.46
2.0	19.54	20.01	20.59	0.33
2.5	23.53	25.34	26.45	0.96
3.0	28.3	30.33	32.34	1.25
3.5	32.53	34.79	38.08	1.96
4.0	36.62	39.69	43.43	2.56
4.5	41.34	45.74	48.62	1.96
5.0	48.07	49.64	51.51	0.98
5.5	52.86	54.23	56.88	1.18
6.0	57.5	60.12	62.65	1.76
6.5	60.79	64.33	68.89	2.27
7.0	68.89	69.88	70.94	0.66
7.5	69.58	74.74	80.77	4.16
8.0	77.33	79.99	83.43	2.03
8.5	77.47	83.77	92.24	5.05
9.0	87.06	90.06	92.98	1.85
9.5	90.64	95.26	98.39	2.80
10.0	91.11	99.35	108.1	5.42

Table 3. Time required for resource encryption

completed the execution in less than 40 milliseconds. In this experiment, we used a 64byte text file as uploaded resource to keep the simulation as light as possible. The average time for all messages encryption/decryption, thus, never reached a value higher than 30 milliseconds; as such this result let us state that the protocols may run with no impact on the user experience over the OSN.

Resource Encryption Average Time. Finally, Table 3 reports the results of the experiment to estimate the encryption time necessary to prepare a resource to be uploaded. Unlike messages, which are encrypted exploiting AES-128 algorithm, resources are encrypted exploiting AES-256 algorithm, in order to achieve a better security for resources, that have to be stored in the public Cloud. The first column in Table 3 reports the size (in Mbytes) of the resource to be encrypted, while the other columns gather the time interval, in seconds, necessary to perform the encryption. In this experiment, we used random-generated ASCII strings, with pre-determined lengths. The encryption phase has been repeated 10 times for each resource; as such Table 3 reports the minimum and the maximum time

recorded during the experiment, along with the time consumption average and the standard deviation.

With those experiments, and the ones previously reported in [1] about the *Path Finder Service* performances, we can thus state that SocialCloudShare causes a slight overhead over users experience in the Social Network. As such, we believe that protocols and techniques proposed in this paper would give a remarkable improval to OSN privacy measures.

7. Related Work

The presented work is mainly related to the following research topics: path-preserving graph anonymization, crypto-based access control, and privacy preserving in Online Social Networks.

Present literature includes many work proposing graph anonymization techniques. Most of these works can be grouped into two separate categories: those which propose node clusterization tecnhiques (e.g., [3, 6, 15]), and those which flatten the graph topology by modifying it (e.g., [16, 18]). However, these works, make the common assumption that the graph topology can be entirely read by a centralized party that anonymizes the graph.

A slightly different approach is described by Terzi *et al.* in [12]. In this work, authors present a collaborative anonymization procedure that exploits only nodes' neighborhood information. However, even this work, likely the works mentioned before, presents a technique that anonymize the graph by modifying its topology. Unfortunately, an anonymization techniques that contemplates a topology modification is not suitable for ReBAC enforcement. Indeed, introducing new edges in the graph may bring to harmful data release, whereas removing edges may cause not to release resource that should be released according to access control rules in place.

The only work presenting a path-preserving anonymization technique is, to the best of our knowledge, [4]. Authors in [4] present algorithms that allow to compute privacy-preserving operations without editing the graph structure. However, the path finding procedure presented in [4] can handle only paths whose lenght is ≤ 2. As such, none of these works propose a path-preserving collaborative anonymization procedure like the one presented in this paper.

Literature offers several proposals of crypto-based access control for cloud-centric platforms. Many recent proposals exploit attribute-based encryption (see [14, 21, 26]). Authors in [9] propose a solution for regulating access to outsourced data by means of a proper distribution of encryption keys. In recent works have been proposed OSN plugins (e.g., see Scramble! [2], FaceCloak [19]) that prevent OSN providers to performa data mining by analyzing users' data by encrypting them. As such, resources can be shared as encrypted data and decrypted only by those users who exploit the same platform that has been used for encryption phase. None of these works, however, target the enforcement of ReBAC.

A different approach, that can be exploited to prevent OSN analysis over shared data, is to move users' resources to a data repository separate from the OSN (e.g., see Lockr [24] or Trust&Share [7]), where the social network provider has no access. Still, those proposals treat only aspects related to shared resources, and do not take into account to hide relationship data from OSN managers.

8. Conclusions

In this paper, we present an implementation of the architecture presented in [1], where users' personal data are securely stored in public Cloud data storage and shared according to relationship-based access control rules defined by owners, tailored for the most popular of today OSNs, that is, Facebook. We plan to extend the work reported in this paper along several directions. First, we plan to extend the proposed privacy-preserving path finding to support more expressive access control rules. For instance, we intend to enforce also constraints on the trust of the required relationships. Moreover, we plan to improve the framework by implementing it in a distributed system, where the *Path Finder Service* is instantiated inside a Cloud provider realm (e.g., Amazon EC2).

9. Acknowledgements

The research presented in this paper was partially funded by the European Office of Aerospace Research and Development (EOARD) and the Air Force for Scientific Research (ASFOR). The authors would like to thank the anonymous reviewers for their valuable comments and suggestions to improve the quality of the paper.

References

[1] D.A. Albertini, B. Carminati. Relationship-based Information Sharing in Cloud-based Decentralized Social Networks. In Proc. *ACM CODASPY*, 2014.

[2] F. Beato, I. Ion, S. Čapkun, B. Preneel, M. Langheinrich. For Some Eyes Only: Protecting Online Information Sharing.In Proc. *ACM CODASPY*, 2013.

[3] S. Bhagat, G. Cormode, B. Krishnamurthy, D. Srivastava. Class-based graph anonymization for social network data. In Proc. *VLDB Endowment*, 2009.

[4] J. Brickell, V. Shmatikov. Privacy-Preserving graph algorithms in the semi-honest model. In Proc. *ASIACRYPT*, 2005.

[5] G. Bruns, P. W. L. Fong, I. Siahaan, M. Huth. Relationship-Based Access Control: Its Expression and Enforcement Through Hybrid Logic. In Proc. *ACM CODASPY*, 2012.

[6] A. Campan, T. M. Truta. A clustering approach for data and structural anonymity in social networks. In Proc. *ACM PinKDD*, 2008.

[7] B. Carminati, E. Ferrari, J. Girardi. Trust&Share: Trusted Information Sharing in Online Social Networks. In Proc. *IEEE ICDE*, 2012.

[8] B. Carminati, E. Ferrari, A. Perego. Enforcing Access Control in Web-based Social Networks. In Proc. *ACM TISSEC*, 2009.

[9] S. De Capitani Di Vimercati, S. Foresti, S. Jajodia, S. Paraboschi, P. Samarati. Encryption policies for regulating access to outsourced data. *ACM Trans. Database Systems*, 2010.

[10] W. F. Ehrsam, C. H. W. Meyer, J. L. Smith, W. L. Tuchman. message verification and transmission error detection by block chaining. US Patent 4074066, 1976.

[11] Electronic Privacy Information Center, Facebook Privacy. online: *http://epic.org/privacy/facebook/*

[12] D. Erdös, R. Germulla, E. Terzi. Reconstructing Graphs from Neighborhood Data. In Proc. *IEEE ICDM*, 2012.

[13] Google official blog, A new approach to China. online: *http://googleblog.blogspot.com/2010/01/new-approach-to-china.html*. January 12, 2010.

[14] V. Goyal, O. Pandey, A. Sahai, B. Waters. Attribute-based encryption for fine-grained access control of encrypted data. In Proc. *ACM CCS*, 2006.

[15] M. Hay, G. Miklau, D. Jensen, D. Towsley, P. Weis. Resisting structural re-identification in anonymized social networks. In Proc.*VLDB*, 2008.

[16] M. Hay, G. Miklau, D. Jensen, P. Weis, S. Srivastava. Anonymizing Social Networks. *Technical Report*, 2007.

[17] B. Kaliski. RFC 2315. online: *http://tools.ietf.org/html/rfc2315*, 1998.

[18] K. Liu, E. Terzi. Towards identity anonymization on graphs. In Proc. *ACM SIGMOD*, 2008.

[19] W. Luo, Q. Xie, U. Hengartner. FaceCloak: An architecture for user privacy on social networking sites. In Proc. *ICCSE*, 2009.

[20] M. Naor, B. Pinkas. Oblivious transfer and polynomial evaluation. In Proc. *ACM STOC*, 1999.

[21] S. Narayan, M. Gagné,R. Safavi-Naini. Privacy preserving EHR system using attribute-based infrastructure. In Proc. *ACM CCSW*, 2010.

[22] National Institute of Standards and Technology. Announcing the Advanced Encryption Standard (AES). online: *http://csrc.nist.gov/publications/fips/fips197/fips-197.pdf*, 2001.

[23] R. Needham, M. Schroeder. Using encryption for authenticating in large networks of computers. *Communication of the ACM 21*, 1978

[24] A. Tootoonchian, S. Saroiu, Y. Ganjali, A. Wolman. Lockr: better privacy for social networks. In Proc. *ACM CoNEXT*, 2009.

[25] J. E. Vascellaro. Google discloses Privacy Glitch. online: *http://blogs.wsj.com/digits/2009/03/08/1214/*.

[26] J. Zhang, Z. Zhang, A. Ge. Ciphertext policy attribute-based encryption from lattices. In Proc. *ACM ASIACCS*, 2012.

6

A Collaborative Virtual Workspace for Factory Configuration and Evaluation*

Ingo Zinnikus[1,*], Sergiy Byelozyorov[2], Xiaoqi Cao[1], Matthias Klusch[1], Christopher Krauss[1], Andreas Nonnengart[1], Torsten Spieldenner[1], Stefan Warwas[1], Philipp Slusallek[1]

[1]German Research Center for Artificial Intelligence GmbH, Stuhlsatzenhausweg 3, 66123 Saarbrücken, Germany
[2]Saarland University, Campus E1 1, 66123 Saarbrücken, Germany

Abstract

The convergence of information technologies (IT) has enabled the Digital Enterprise in which engineering, production planning, manufacturing and sales processes are supported by IT-based collaboration, simulation and enactment. As a result, borders between reality and its virtual representations become increasingly blurred. Advanced tools need to support flexibility, specialization and collaborative evolution of the design where the exchange of knowledge between domain experts helps to improve informed decision making. In this paper, we present a collaborative, synchronized web-based framework to create 3D scenarios for product design, simulation and training assisted by animated avatars.

Keywords: Collaborative computing architectures and networks, Computer supported collaborative work, Web-based collaboration, Visualization techniques for collaborative networks and applications, Service-oriented architectures for collaborative networking and applications

1. Introduction

In recent years the trend towards networked organizations where businesses and companies are working (often remotely) together has been intensified [2]. Activities in networked organizations consist of distributed processes which include communication, exchange of resources and joint production of business artefacts. These artefacts now include assets such as product designs which in the past were kept under control of one company. The co-innovation and co-design of product families and production plants with a large number of part suppliers requires precise adjustment between contributing partners.

Supporting this precise adjustment of products and production facilities requires IT Systems for integrated product development. Engineering these integrated and interactive systems where interaction involves cooperation and collaboration of a potentially large number of contributors with complementary skills e.g in product assembly design. This is an inherently collaborative process where multidisciplinary experts from different areas and geographically remote locations contribute to one product or resource.

Regarding collaborative engineering, Booch and Brown [3] highlighted the importance of a Collaborative Development Environment defined as: 'a virtual space wherein all the stakeholders of a project - even if distributed by time or distance - may negotiate, brainstorm, discuss, share knowledge, and generally labor together to carry out some task, most often to create an executable deliverable and its supporting artifacts' (see especially [4]). Empirical investigations confirm this importance [5], [6].

Another recent trend is the usage of virtual techniques for product and production facility development which allows designing 3D representations that capture selected traits of products and production plants. 3D prototypes can be used to evaluate products in advance e.g. in order to reduce costs and time to market. Together with this trend towards virtual prototyping based on 3D design and engineering, a combined research area arises: collaborative virtual prototyping.

---

*Extended version of [1]
*Corresponding author. Email: ingo.zinnikus@dfki.de

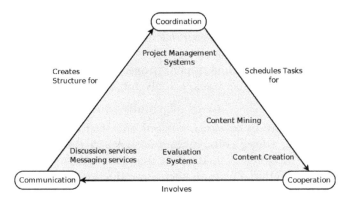

Figure 1. Iteration cycle of collaborative work based on the 3C model as stated by Fuks et al. [11] and required services for each step as stated by [12]

As cooperation, coordination and collaboration are often used interchangeably, a more fine-grained distinction between these concepts is required. There are two major lines of research which differ in the details of defining the relation of these concepts (contrasting vs. encompassing). One (older) approach stemming from organisation science defines the relation as continuum where cooperation falls on the low end and collaboration on the high, with coordination in-between [7], [8]. Cooperation is defined as the least formal interaction, based e.g. on a simple verbal agreement. In cooperative work, the division of labour leads to processes where each person is responsible for a portion of a problem solving [9]. Cooperation becomes coordinated when the informal problem solving process is following an explicit or implicit joint planning where responsibilities and roles are assigned. Collaboration in a contrasting and narrow sense is the most formal interorganizational relationship involving shared authority and responsibility for planning, implementation, and evaluation of a joint effort and involves the "mutual engagement of participants in a coordinated effort to solve the problem together" [9].

In contrast, the other main approach on which we base our work defines collaboration as the encompassing process with cooperation, coordination and communication as its ingredients. Ellis et al. describe collaborative work as an iterative process of *communication, coordination* and *cooperation* (3C model [10], see Fig. 1). Based on this model, Fuks et al. describe collaborative work as an iterative, cyclic process [11]: Communication describes spontaneous exchange of information between team members, like for example in the planning phase of a project. Based on the communication, future work is coordinated in tasks which are then cooperatively accomplished. During the cooperation step new issues will arise. Those need to be discussed and therefore lead to a new iteration cycle until the project work is finished.

In general, design tasks are often *ill-structured problems* [13]. In contrast to well-structured problems, where options and goals are clearly defined, in ill-structured problems the options available and possibly even the goals are unclear and vague. For many ill-structured problems, generic routines and procedures for problem solving do not exist. Although considerable amount of research has been devoted to identify recurrent collaboration patterns (e.g. [14]), for ill-structured problems, a normative approach prescribing sequences of steps to solve the problem is not feasible. A collaborative engineering system for design tasks should be open to support different problem-solving activities and strategies.

Nevertheless, a common feature of design tasks is that they involve an iterative process of interactive decision making and model building [13], thus confirming the adequacy of the 3C model. To support this iterative process, a "wide range of sophisticated communication and content services" [12] are necessary. Examples include "customized **discussion services, workflow and knowledge management systems**, and content **creation, mining, and retrieval services**. [..] To create useful collaborative virtual working environments for communities, collaboration requirements need to be linked to services satisfying those requirements" [12].

Collaboration in 3D design and virtual environments has additional and specific requirements. Traditional collaboration systems already provide the possibility to jointly work on designing artefacts. In 3D environments, the central artefact is a *visible virtual model* of reality. As *visible* 3D artefact, the model is intended to be (possibly jointly) looked at. As *virtual* (in contrast to a physical mock-up) *model*, it is an archetype which represents selected and supposedly relevant features of the real resource(s) to be produced. In virtual prototyping of products and factories, these features include functional interdependencies and other aspects such as ergonomy which can be simulated or even aesthetic qualities. As in using physical mock-ups, these functional and non-functional features and aspects in virtual models can be evaluated before the resource is actually produced. The joint and simultaneous evaluation of these visible virtual models is a possibility which needs to be supported in a much more refined way, especially when the visual experience should be shared in realtime. Hence *efficient synchronisation* of many clients in a collaborative setting is a key issue.

Whereas many 3D systems present the final view of a product, a collaborative virtual prototyping system allows jointly creating, viewing, reviewing, modifying 3D artefacts and discussing alternative designs at all stages of the design process. The possibility to make changes in realtime as well as support for content creation and distributed storage retrieval are further requirements. In contrast to many commercial systems which often are monolithic and oversized, the system should be easily extendable and quickly adaptable to different use cases and scenarios.

2. Objectives

We developed *Collaborate3D*, a web-based collaborative development environment for virtual prototyping that supports and realizes the three iteration steps based on the 3C model by Ellis [10]. Collaborate3D provides collaborative workspaces with native support for communication, cooperation and coordination and enables a shared visual experience of the creation, modification and evaluation of a virtual 3D design.

Since in different contexts and scenarios, a variety of components and modules are needed, the system is intended to be extendable and customizable. Instead of a one size fits all approach (which is prevalent especially in the commercial tools), we developed a service-oriented platform which supports customizing and adding services as plugins when required. The result is a modularized and configurable collaboration architecture for 3D scene editing, evaluation and simulation.

Synchronisation of plugin services can be achieved directly in the Web-client, if the services provide an appropriate interface, like WebSocket or HTTP REST. But there are cases in which client-side integration is not a suitable approach. This may be the case when one or more of the attached services have to send confidential data to the integration point. In the case of client-side integration, that means that users may get access to sensible data. Apart from that, processing data from services on client side puts additional workload on the client application. This can be an issue when the client Web-site is accessed from a mobile device. Those usually have significantly less computation power than a work station. In order to support mobile devices with limited capacities and ensure security of data, we introduce a server-based synchronisation approach which allows distributing a scene over a large number of clients in realtime.

Taking into account that design is an ill-structured problem, a specific configuration of system modules and services is open for different problem-solving strategies. The system is designed to be adaptable to a changing collaboration and task model and to support the whole continuum of cooperation and collaboration.

Apart from these general objectives, for implementing an effective collaborative workspace for virtual 3D prototyping, further goals include in detail:

- Ubiquitous accessibility via Web Page like implementation (central point of access)

- Simple inclusion of new 3D content and fast attachment of new code

- Flexible adaption to different use-case scenarios by plugin system for service integration

- Attach established (open) project management including issue tracker tools for asynchronous collaboration.

The application scenario is based on a factory production line where collaborators design and evaluate a factory module. Evaluation in this case consists of checking functional features such as production capacities, velocities and safety properties. Additionally, activities of workers can be modelled and their performance simulated and evaluated according to different criteria.

The structure of the paper is as following. In section 3 we give an overview of the architecture of the web-based system for collaborative prototyping, the XML3D-based layer for visualisation and content creation, as well as the distributed search technologies for content retrieval. The verification service and agent technologies for evaluation are presented in section 4. In section 5, we refine the Collaborate3D architecture for enabling efficient synchronization of clients in a collaborative setting. In section 6, we describe technical details of the implementation of the workspace components. We analyze and measure the performance of the synchronisation architecture in section 7. Related work is discussed in section 8. We conclude and describe future work in section 9.

3. 3D Collaboration Framework: Architecture

Collaborative virtual prototyping calls for a fusion of several technologies in order to provide a shared visual experience of the design artefacts. Web and Web service technology is the up-to-date solution to enable distributed access and real-time sharing of contents and resources.

The Collaborate3D architecture (see Fig. 2) reflects the idea of introducing service orientation into the virtual environment. Platform components needed for the realisation of the virtual environment are encapsulated as services hosted in the Collaborate3D service cloud. The architecture consists of three layers: a project related collaborative workspaces with a 3D editor for creating and modifying content, a service cloud with application specific services and a storage layer. The 3D editor is based on an web-based framework for rendering 3D graphics. In the current implementation the service cloud consists of a verification component for evaluation of functional properties and an agent platform for evaluating dependencies when e.g. human workers are interacting with devices in production plants. Other components could be a physics engine, kinematics, etc. A distributed repository for content storage and retrieval provides

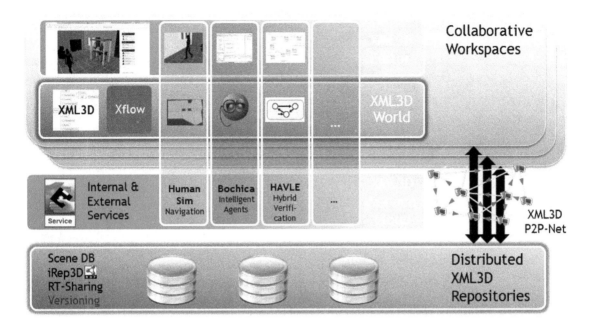

Figure 2. Collaborate 3D architecture

access to semantically annotated 3D models which can be inserted into a scene.

3.1. XML3D World

The collaboratively created 3D artefacts are contained in the data layer which is based on the XML3D specification. XML3D is an open declarative XML format that extends the set of HTML web page elements by additional nodes to represent 3D graphics in a scene graph like structure [15]. All nodes within this graph are also nodes in the web sites DOM tree representation (*Document Object Model*, [16]) and can be accessed and changed via JavaScript like any other common DOM elements as well. On these DOM nodes, HTML events can be registered similar to known HTML elements. Resources for mesh data can be stored externally in either JSON or XML format and referenced by their URL. The renderer that is used by XML3D is based on WebGL.

In addition to XML3D, *Xflow* allows to combine the scene graph with dataflows [17]. Xflow is a declarative data flow representation that was designed for complex computations on XML3D elements. These computations include for example skinned meshes and key frame animations. In these cases, the current key frame takes the role of a data source in the graph, whereas mesh transformations are sinks in the dataflow. By this, changing the value of a key frame leads to a change in the posture of a mesh, and thus a continuous change of the key frame over time results in an animated mesh.

By using XML3D with Xflow as foundation for data layer, we achieve both ubiquitous accessibility and high customizability: all scripts needed to display and use the 3D editor are automatically loaded by the browser as soon as the user opens the page in any web browser that supports WebGL. Furthermore, 3D models used for the scenario can be referenced by their URL from remote storage locations.

For evaluation services to be able to operate directly on the artefacts created in the editor, they must be able to access the data layer that contains the 3D artefacts. This access is directly provided by having both Xflow parameters and the 3D scene graph represented as part of the DOM tree by XML3D. External services can e.g. animate virtual characters by changing key frame values of Xflow graphs (in the case of the agent platform service), to generate the navigation mesh (using the geometry information contained in the DOM tree) or verifying the functional correctness of a module and display the trace witness via Xflow animation. The guiding principle for services such as the verification is that the functional specification of a composite module is based on the functional specifications of the parts contained which build up the composite module. The formal specifications of the parts are contained in the scene graph as annotations of objects.

3.2. XML3D Editor

The 3D artefact itself is created in the interactive 3D editor which is a web-based tool for creating and editing 3D scenarios. Those scenarios consist of a static base geometry (e.g. an empty factory hall) and several sets

Figure 3. Editor tool

of 3D *assets*. Assets can be added, moved within or removed from the scene with simple drag and drop operations. Figure 3 shows the user interface of the editor: The interactive 3D scene is displayed on the left-hand side. Next to it is the sidebar which contains the selection of 3D assets that can be added, as well as already placed assets in a second tab.

Scenarios that share a common static geometry and the same set of assets are grouped in *projects*. In terms of the factory example above, this allows to create and store different configurations (*scenarios*) for the same factory hall (with the factory setting being the *project* in this case). The editor itself is part of a collaborative work space which allows a group of designers and domain experts to jointly construct and visit a 3D scene.

To provide seamless communication with collaborators during content creation, a basic personal messaging system is integrated into the editor. Using this system, team members can send each others short pieces of text. New messages are indicated as soon as a user enters the scenario in the scope of which the message was sent.

In addition, third party ticket and bug tracker systems that provide a REST API [18] for HTTP access (as for example *Mantis*[1] or *Trac*[2]) can be integrated into the work space. The step of actually choosing and integrating the tracker system in the overall application is not possible from the graphical user interface of the work space yet. However, the editor code is easily extendable via a provided API for third party services. As the editor is entirely written in JavaScript, and both 2D user interface as well as 3D elements are represented as DOM elements within this website, this extension can also be done by web designers with minor experience in website scripting. Information from third party system is them displayed directly in the work space's user interface.

Whenever more than one collaborator logs into the same scenario, the process of content creation turns into a synchronous editing session. Changes done to the scene by one user (including adding objects, moving existing objects or deleting them) triggers an update of the scene state in all connected clients. We employ two approaches to avoid update conflicts during concurrent editing. On client side, we use a locking mechanism: An object that is selected by one user is locked for editing for all his collaborators. This lock is indicated in both the 3D view of the scene by rendering the object semi transparent, and in the list of placed assets next to the editing window: list entries of locked objects carry a lock icon and are highlighted in red. In addition, the database performs a version control based on revision numbers for each object. If an update is performed on an object with outdated revision, the update request is declined and the sending client is informed about the conflict.

External services from the XML3D Service Cloud (see also section 4) can be accessed directly from the editor's user interface.

3.3. Storage Layer

A collaborative work space is composed of different types of data (see Figure 4): first, an abstract representation of a scene that was created in the editor as described in the previous section. Second, 3D assets that contain the actual geometry and texture information of 3D objects from which the resulting 3D artefact is composed. Third, information for coordinated collaboration like for example open tasks or deadlines. For each type of data, we need a repository that provides the respective data to the work space.

Scene Database. Data about projects and scenarios that are created with the scenario editor are stored in a database that is directly connected to the editor. This project data includes projects and related scenarios, 3D asset sets and abstract representations of placed 3D objects, including an object's position and the URI that references its 3D asset data in XML3D format on the resource repository. Each object may moreover carry configuration parameters for attached services. Changes in data are automatically transmitted to all clients that are currently connected to a scenario that is affected by these changes to provide synchronous, collaborative editing of a scenario.

Semantic 3D Asset Repository. 3D artefacts are assembled from 3D assets, available in *iRep3D* [19]. iRep3D is a repository for hybrid semantic indexing and retrieval of annotated 3D scenes in X3D, XML3D and COLLADA at any level of granularity, in near real-time and with high precision. iRep3D comes with

---

[1]http://www.mantisbt.org
[2]http://trac.edgewall.org/

a web-based user interface which supports the user in annotating 3D scenes with plain text as well as appropriate ontology-based concepts and services in order to describe the functionality of scenes and their objects [20].

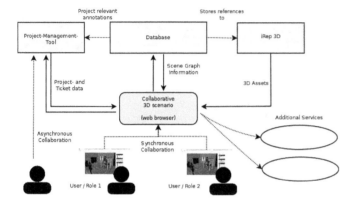

Figure 4. Storage and Service Assembly serving the XML3D editor

iRep3D performs off-line semantic indexing and on-line query processing. The indexing process determines the relevant score of a stored 3D scene based on its semantic annotation and geometric features for the (a) scene concept index, (b) semantic service index, and (c) geometric index of iRep3D. The semantic similarity between scene concepts in standard OWL2 bases on their approximated logical subsumption relation and its information-theoretic valuation. The matching score for pairs of semantic services in OWL-S each of which describing the functionality of scene objects are computed with the currently most precise service selection tool iSeM [21]. The geometric feature index of a scene is a set of B+ trees each of which represents a standard feature-attribute pair which is instantiated by the scene according to the X3D, XML3D and COLLADA specifications, while geometric feature matching by iRep3D relies on classical approaches for this purpose. The repository applies a breadth-first-traverse-based pruning heuristic to efficiently maintain its scene indices in case the set of indexed scenes or their annotations change.

A query is a scene (in X3D, XML3D) that is annotated with the desired semantic scene concept, semantic services, and geometric features. iRep3D answers such queries by means of a parallel index-based subquery processing and final aggregation of resulting rank lists with a classical threshold algorithm. Besides, its search for relevant scene objects is performed even within indexed 3D scenes at any level of granularity while positive results are extracted and indexed as new scenes for further re-use, while the top most relevant scenes

are then displayed to the user together with provenance information.

Indexed 3D scenes in XML3D, X3D or COLLADA are stored internally in a native XML database while the iRep3D repository itself provides a web-based user interface including a semantic annotation toolkit, and is also accessible via a REST API. Our experimental evaluation based on a test collection 3DS-TC 1.0 with more than 600 annotated XML-based 3D scenes revealed that iRep3D is significantly more precise and with the same average response time than its relevant and open-source competitors like Trimble3D, ADL and the Princeton3D search engine.

External project management systems. Data for work coordination is provided by external project management systems. This meta data includes user groups, messages that were sent in the scope of a project, issues and bug trackers. Those systems can also take the role of user authentication, if provided by the tool. Project management or bug trackers are connected to the work space via REST API. All data is displayed directly in the editor GUI and thus available during synchronous editing sessions. The benefit of using an external tool instead of using the scene database to store the meta data directly with the scene data is the asynchronous accessibility of the data from outside the editor. Existing tools like Trac, Mantis or Redmine come with a front-end GUI that can be operated from a Web-browser. That allows to contribute to project coordination steps without having to use the actual 3D design tool.

4. XML3D Service Cloud

The XML3D service cloud contains several services which provide scenario-related simulation and evaluation functionality. The service cloud can be extended and new services can be added as plugins. In the current implementation, a verification service for functional evaluation of factory modules and an agent platform for controlling avatars are included.

4.1. Collaborative Evaluation through Formal Analysis

Physical systems that are controlled by embedded software like flight control systems, automatic breaking systems, and production lines in factory environments are called hybrid systems as they involve both discrete and continuous behavior. A major goal in the design and implementation of hybrid systems is the ability to reliably verify functional properties of the system at hand. Flaws in the design of such complex systems occur regularly, especially when created in a collaboration of many different specialists. If they remain undetected and manifest themselves in the final implementation of the system they may lead to severe malfunctioning resulting in loss of money and reputation or even worse, injury or loss of life. A solution to this problem is the use of formal methods for a semantically unambiguous modeling of systems and their verification.

In our implementation we included a verification module that allows the collaborative evaluation of the system modeled in the 3D Editor (see section 6.1). In communication with a collaborating specialist for formal methods and verification the system designer can formulate and verify the requirements for the system at hand. A tight integration of the formal and the 3D model allows a (partially) automatic generation of the formal model. On the other hand, the tight integration also enables the results from the formal analysis performed by the verification specialist to be presented to the designer in a generally understandable manner. The verification itself is performed by the verification tool HAVLE[3] provided through a REST service.

Hybrid Automata. HAVLE uses Hybrid Automata as they are a language particularly well suited to formally model hybrid systems in that they allow to specify both the continuous and discrete behavior parts of the system in one model. Our version of hybrid automata is very similar to the language of rectangular hybrid automata as they are known from [24], however with some extensions to provide an easy to use and extensive approach to model hybrid systems. Their main contribution is the support of a high degree of modularity. All possible system behaviors are defined by the composition of the different components. Since the language of hybrid automata is a formal one with formal semantics, verification is possible on systems specified in this language. For a detailed introduction into hybrid automata we refer to [23].

The Verification Module. Figure 5 depicts the general workflow of the evaluation of a system. Models of the system can be constructed in the 3D Editor by putting together component parts coming from a library of components. To allow verification and at the same time provide a seamless integration, additionally to the 3D description of their looks and physical dimension, they come with a formal description of their possible behavior. Adding a component to the model in the 3D Editor implicitly also adds the hybrid automaton assigned to this component to the formal model. A mapping that also comes with the component describes how the parameters of the 3D object correlate with the parameters and the initial states of the formal model. It translates position and rotation of the 3D object into values for the template parameters and initial locations

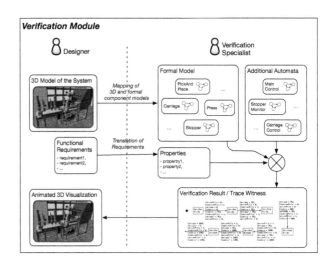

Figure 5. Collaborative evaluation

of the automaton template. Applying this for all objects added to the system allows us to automatically generate a projection of the formal model from the system modeled in the 3D editor onto its visual parts.

After constructing the system the designer can ask the verification specialist using the available communication mechanisms, e.g. the messaging system presented in section 3.2, to verify certain requirements given for the designed system. Due to the shared workspace and the included seamless synchronization the verification specialist can immediately access the current model of the system. If required (or desired) she can adapt the automatically generated formal model by, e.g. adding automata describing the non-visual parts like controllers or automata for the interrelation between the physical parts. She then formalizes the required properties submitted by the designer and verifies them.

Depending on the verification result (in case of the rejection of a safety property or the approval of a reachability property) HAVLE provides a *trace witness* (out of a constructive proof). Essentially a trace is a formal description of the behavior that the system has to show to reach a certain desired or undesired state. However a formal trace is very hard to read and can only be understood by specialists.

Due to the tight integration of the formal and the 3D model through the verification module we are able to map such traces to animated visualizations of the behavior[4] described by the trace in the 3D model of the system. Using basic modularized *Xflow* keyframe animations we perform a stepwise interpretation of the formal trace as pictures in an animation sequence. As

---

[3]Hybrid Automata Verification by Location Elimination [22, 23].

[4]In fact the projection of the trace onto the physical components occurring in the 3D system.

soon as the verification has been performed by the verification specialist the visualization is also available for the designer and provides it with a tangible feedback of the performed verification.

Apart from collaborating with a specialist the designer can also formulate the properties to be proven by himself or choose from an existing list of required properties[5]. This is especially useful in case a previous version of the system that had already been verified has been modified. Similar to the idea of unit testing, by so called unit verification one can verify after every modification whether the system is still correct. Modifications like adding, removing, or moving of components are directly reflected in the formal model and need no further adaptations.

A more detailed description of the 3D visualization of verification results, the automatic generation of formal models from 3D models can be found in [23].

4.2. Agent-based avatars

In order to simulate interactions between workers and the production assets, the editor allows positioning animated avatars into the scene (see Figure 6). The behaviour of avatars is controlled by an agent platform which is provided as a service. Agents in our context are the abstract entities representing the avatars in the scene. Agent models containing the behaviour can be modelled in advance and assigned to virtual characters. For modeling agent behavior, we use the Jadex agent platform[6]. The agent platform is based on the BDI (belief - desire - intention) [25, 26] approach for describing agent behavior. The BDI approach with its incorporation of reactive and goal-based behavior is especially appropriate for controlling avatars, because avatars in a 3D scene need to react quickly to a changing environment while exposing goal-directed behavior at the same time.

When a user wants to place an avatar into the scene, first the avatar asset is selected. After placing the avatar into the scene, one or more behavior capabilities behavior can be assigned to the avatar. The available capabilities are based on the agent behaviors which are provided by the agent platform. By asssigning concrete goals (the intention) to an agent, the corresponding avatar tries to achieve this goal according to the behavior description. Agent-controlled avatars can be used to simulate workers, e.g. for evaluating the reachability of modules, time constraints for production processes, etc.

Since the objects in the scene can be moved using the editor, they constitute possible obstacles for avatars.

Figure 6. Editor for agent-controlled avatars

Therefore, in the framework, a navigation service is associated to the agent platform which generates a navigation mesh on demand each time the scene layout is changed and prevents collisions of the avatars with each other and objects in the scene. The editing and simulation of agent activities can be done collaboratively in the shared workspace.

5. Synchronization and Integration Server

As mentioned in section 2, the integration of the presented services can be achieved directly in the Web-client, if the services provide an appropriate interface. Since there are cases in which client-side integration is no suitable approach, e.g. when data to be sent to a client is confidential or the capacity of client devices are restricted (in the case of mobile devices), we have developed and implemented a server-side synchronisation solution to address these issues.

The integration server is designed in a way that allows for easy extension by third party services. The design opts at the possibility to not only have different services run in parallel, but also make data from one service accessible to another.

This also makes integrating the services into the clients easier by wrapping the different interfaces that are provided by the different services into one homogeneous interface.

A server-based solution moreover enables shared synchronized simulations of service data, for example visualization of verification results, for several connected clients.

5.1. High-Level architecture

The overall architecture of the integration platform aims at a very slim core with no domain specific functionality. Instead, the server core maintains a generic data representation of the constructed 3D asset and means to synchronize that data to connected clients (see Figure 7). This data model as well as

---

[5]Possibly formulated before the system was even constructed resulting from a requirements analysis.

[6]http://jadex-agents.informatik.uni-hamburg.de

the functionality of the server can be extended by a number of additional modules or *plug-ins*. Whenever a new module is added to the server runtime, both its introduced data and functions are also made available to other connected modules. In the case of our presented factory design and evaluation workspace, those modules may be plug-ins for agent behavior simulation, formal verification or messaging between connected users. Modules can implement new features from the scratch or wrap existing services to a common API. For the example of formal verification, this would mean that the respective module connects to the existing verification service. Clients in turn do not operate directly on the verification's REST API anymore, but communicate with the integration server which in turn processes the messages to the verification service via the attached module.

5.2. Entity Component Attribute World Model

We have decided for a world model that on the one hand makes as few assumptions about the intended use case domain as possible, and on the other hand lets developers and users extend it by additional data that may be very specific concerning their intended use. For this, we have employed an *Entity-Component-Attribute (ECA)* [31] model to represent assets in the 3D scene on the server.

According to this model, all objects in the world are considered as *Entities*. This includes not only placeable assets, but also abstract concepts such as agent behavior definitions or abstract scene descriptions that may for example occur from a set of project parameters.

An Entity does not contain any data, but is rather an empty container with an ID that may be filled with data of any kind. Providing data is done by attaching *Components* to an entity, which in turn are containers for sets of typed *Attributes*. Both Components and Attributes can be accessed via a string-typed name on the entity. By this, the position of a placeable asset may for example be accessed via *entity["placeable"]["position"]*. For attribute types, we currently allow basic data types (int, string, float ...) as well as structs and lists from these types.

These components and the definition of the set of attributes they introduce are provided by specific plugins. As described in Section 5.1, all components that are registered in the server core are accessible from any other plugin. That is, when running the server with both plugins for agent behavior simulation and verification loaded, verification may access the position of agents and current states in their plans to include them into the verification procedure.

5.3. Unified Service Interface

When integrating different services directly on client-side, we face the drawback that for each attached service a connection needs to be opened that follows the API specification of the respective service. In our use case presented that includes the REST services to the database and HAVLE, the WebSocket connection to HumanSim service and the reference to the web interface of IRep3D. Even though the JavaScript client code and the tight coupling of XML3D to DOM scripting simplifies inclusion of such services for client developers, we will end up with a rather unflexible client, as adapting to another application domain means removing the respective connections from the client.

Drawing the step of service integration into the server level gives us the possibility to introduce a homogeneous API provided by the synchronization server. In the current server design, we employ a Remote Procedure Call framework to expose server-side functions as *service functions*, grouped in *service* which take the role of a namespace. We refer to the complete set of services that are provided by the server as *service API*.

Plugins may expose their own functions as service by registering them to the server core. They are then accessible in the format *service.servicefunction*, e.g. *verification.runTraceVisualization*. When the client starts up, it retrieves the list of provided services from the server and may wrap those into JavaScript functions. Calling the function on the server then amounts to a simple JavaScript function call, e.g. the service for trace visualization may be invoked by the client by a call like *runTraceVisualization(assetID)* as if it was a function of the client itself. The list of parameters expected for the service call (in the last example, the ID of the asset for which the visualization should be run) is defined on the server by the native function that is registered for the service.

6. Implementation

6.1. 3D Editor

To fulfill the requirement of ubiquitous accessibility, the implementation of the editor tool is completely based on XML3D with Xflow and JavaScript. The implementation of the web editor client uses the *Backbone.js* framework [27] to render both the 2D and 3D content from the data in the database. Backbone.js implements the *Model-View-Controller* (MVC) pattern [28]. For each data object in the data base (*model*), backbone creates DOM elements (*view*) to render for example both the XML3D element of an asset instance in the 3D scene and the respective entry in the list of asset instances on the right hand side of the editor view.

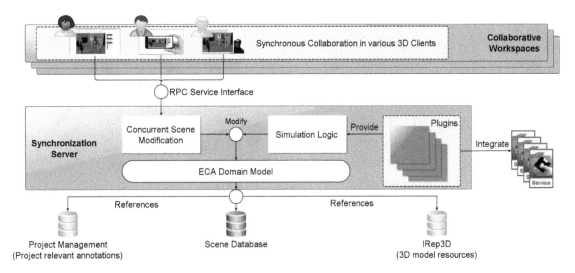

Figure 7. Collaborative Workspace architecture with employed synchronization server

We chose Apache's CouchDB[7] as storage unit for scene data. This NoSQL ("not only relational") database stores data as key-value-pairs with no fixed scheme. These values can be hierarchical objects with a number of attributes, usually accessed by a unique ID.

CouchDB adds a revision number for each object to avoid update conflicts when data is accessed by numerous users [29]. When a request to save data is sent to CouchDB, the request has to include the latest revision number of the updated data set known to the submitting client. If the revision number is different from the one stored in the database, the data update is rejected to avoid conflicts from concurrent updates.

CouchDB provides a RESTful web service to query data. It returns data as JSON (*JavaScript Object Notation*) objects. These objects can directly be used in a browser application's JavaScript code, without any overhead to parse the data. We keep the number of requests needed to keep in sync with the database low by using *long polls*. Requests that are sent as long polls do not return immediately, but remain at the receiving entity (in our case, the database), until the requested data is available. This approach reduces the work load in the browser by the reduced number of database polls. In addition, once a long poll is returned, the delivered changes can directly be used to change displayed data accordingly. This keeps the displayed system state in the application consistent with the actual data stored in the database. The database is accessed by both editor and services from the XML3D service cloud.

3D assets are stored and managed by iRep3D. In order to import a new 3D asset to a project in the editor, the user opens iRep3D from within the editor GUI and queries for the desired asset. Once he concludes the

import by mouse click, iRep3D adds the reference URL of the respective 3D asset to the list of asset documents in the database. By synchronous long poll updates as described above, the imported 3D asset is immediately available for placement.

We included Redmine[8] exemplary for existing project management systems to the work space. Redmine is a Web-based project management system, implemented using the Ruby on Rails framework[9] and published under the GNU general public license. Project descriptions as well as issues and issue trackers for projects can be queried via a REST API. In the terms of the introduced 3D editor tool, we map Redmine projects to configuration projects and Redmine sub-projects to scenarios. For personal messages, we introduced a respective tracker in Redmine and model messages in the configuration tool by issues in Redmine. The link between Redmine projects and the 3D work space is realized by respective parameter attributes for objects in the scene database. Redmine provides moreover HTTP Basic Authentication [30] via REST and can therefore be used for user login. By taking this step, the set of projects provided to a user when entering the 3D work space is determined by rights granted by the Redmine configuration.

6.2. HAVLE verification service

The verification tool used in the implementation is HAVLE. The specification unit of HAVLE provides a graphical user interface for modeling hybrid automata in a graph-like manner. The graphical editor is a GMF[10]-based Eclipse plugin. Automata entered in the

---

[7]http://couchdb.apache.org

[8]http://www.redmine.org

[9]http://www.rubyonrails.org

[10]Graphical Modeling Framework, http://www.eclipse.org/modeling/gmp/

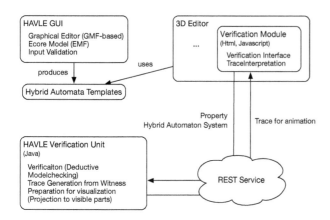

Figure 8. Components of the Verification Module

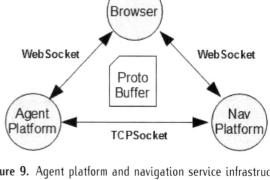

Figure 9. Agent platform and navigation service infrastructure

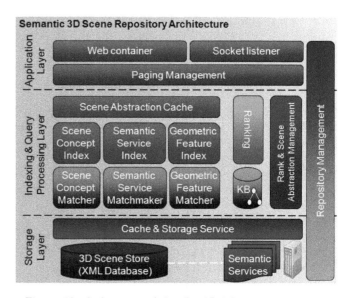

Figure 10. Architecture of the iRep3D 2.0 scene repository.

graphical editor are transformed into Ecore models using the Eclipse Modeling framework (EMF[11]).

The verification unit itself is written in plain Java. In the verification process the automata that the system consists of are composed and translated into a logic based representation. The algorithm that performs the actual verification is a combination of deductive techniques and model checking and produces additionally to the answer whether a property holds or not, a witness (if possible). From this witness it computes a formal description of behavior that leads to the desired or undesired state.

The verification module of the collaboration environment presented in this paper is implemented in Javascript with HTML as GUI front end (see Figure 8). It accesses HAVLE trough a REST service sending the formal model extracted from the system model designed in the 3D editor and the property to be evaluated to HAVLE and receiving the formal trace as a result. This trace is then processed by a trace interpreter written in Javascript: it goes through the formal trace step by step[12] and produces the according state in the 3D model using the basic (Xflow) animations and the mapping that describes how values of variables and locations in the formal model correlate to basic the animations and values of variables in the 3D Model.

6.3. Agent platform and navigation service

As already outlined in section 4, the service for agent simulation consists of an agent platform provided by Jadex and an associated navigation service for navmesh generation and agent positioning. The associated navigation service is *HumanSim*. Jadex and HumanSim communicate with each other by TCP Socket connections.

HumanSim consists of two parts: a service platform that is implemented in Java, and a browser-side part written in JavaScript that interprets the messages sent from the platform (see Figure 9). The browser-side JavaScript implementation moreover provides an API to access agents managed by Jadex, create new agents in Jadex, or assign plans to existing agents directly from the browser application, in our case, the 3D editor.

When an agent-based simulation is started, the geometry of the scene that is stored in the XML3D data layer is automatically collected and sent to the HumanSim platform. Out of this geometry, a navmesh is created that is used to check for collisions between Jadex agents and obstacles in the 3D environment during agent simulation.

This setup allows us to run a BDI engine for agent simulation with taking the structure of the user generated 3D artefact into account.

---

[11]Eclipse Modeling Framework, http://www.eclipse.org/modeling/emf/
[12]Every time a new frame is demanded by the renderer an new step is computed.

6.4. iRep3D

We have designed and implemented our first prototype of iRep3D repository in Java based on Springframework[13], Ehcache[14] and JPA 2.0[15] with Hibernate 3.0[16]. We briefly introduce, in this subsection, the implemented facilities for in particular the real-time semantic query processing. For this, the syntactic, conceptual, semantic service and geometric features of 3D scenes are extracted in advance during off-line indexing creation phase. Each ranked list of scenes is persisted as a disk file. The latter is further used for query processing by a lazy-loading mechanism, which loads the top T entries (T is configured with 50 in the prototype) into memory during system initialization and reads the next T entries when they are needed by rank merging process. Besides, the extracted features of 3D scenes are organized as scene abstracts that are further stored in a MySQL database for the purpose of showing 3D scene details (not scene selection) on demand. By means of pooling the connections to database, this performs quicker than the XML-based on-line query on 3D scene files.

Three layers of iRep3D repository are implemented in a loose-coupled fashion (see Figure 10). They can be deployed in separate servers. Each of them is able to communicate with the others via IP sockets. To increase their throughput, each layer maintains a first-in-first-out request cache. Pooled acceptor threads put their received requests from upper layer to the cache and the processing threads serve the requests out of cache. A query is processed by four joined threads in parallel. Each of them responses to the searching of scenes in syntactic, conceptual, semantic service or geometric aspect. In addition, we enabled a result caching heuristics for storing selected scene files and abstracts that would be used on demand. The list of selected 3D scene identifiers is also cached in query processing layer. When a page is displayed on demand, the contents for the next one are preloaded. For speeding up the simulation of reality, 3D scene files are (pre-) cached if they were (will be) requested (by the next page).

6.5. Server–Side Integration Approach

To evaluate the use of the server-based integration approach and measure the performance of the synchronisation approach, we model the presented use case of agent-enriched factory design and evaluation using the proposed server architecture. If we manage to

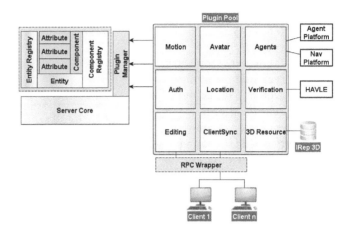

Figure 11. Factory evaluation workspace implementation based on synchronization server

map the concepts introduced by the respective services to components and network services provided by the according modules, we immediately gain a real-time synchronization of all connected clients in both design and simulation time of the application.

- *HAVLE*: The plugin that integrates HAVLE into the application introduces components to model automata configurations. Assets that constitute automata in the final design artifact are then Entities which carry information about their automata configuration in the Components. The service interface provides functions to invoke the verification procedure or start or stop the visualization. The Xflow animations from which verification visualization is composed are contained in the XML3D representation of the object, as before.

- *HumanSim*: Assets that are equipped with agent behavior in the XML3D editor are represented as entities that carry the specific agent configuration in their Components. The plug-in that integrates the agent platform communicates with the navigation component as it was done before by the client. Updates from the navigation server concerning agent positions are now applied to the entity's position and thus synchronized with connected clients. The server's service interface is extended by functions to start and stop agent simulation, create a Component with agent configuration for an entity or modify an existing agent configuration.

- *IRep3D*: IRep3D is run and accessed by its own web interface as before. 3D assets which are imported from IRep3D are now modeled as Entities which store a reference to the resource in IRep3D.

---

[13]http://www.springsource.org/spring-framework
[14]http://ehcache.org/
[15]http://jcp.org/en/jsr/detail?id=338
[16]http://www.hibernate.org/

	Editing Session	Visualization	3 Agents	10 agents	20 agents
Client only	30 fps	30 fps	27 fps	22 fps	14 fps
Server / 1 client					
Total message roundtrip	6 ms	6 ms	6 ms	6 ms	7 ms
Server-side incoming	< 1 ms	< 1 ms	1 ms	1 ms	1 ms
Server-side outgoing	3 ms	3 ms	4 ms	4 ms	5 ms
Server / 5 clients					
Total message roundtrip	8 ms	8 ms	9 ms	10 ms	10 ms
Server-side incoming	< 1 ms	< 1 ms	1 ms	1 ms	1 ms
Server-side outgoing	3 ms	5 ms	5 ms	8 ms	8 ms
Server / 20 clients					
Total message roundtrip	12 ms	13 ms	14 ms	15 ms	22 ms
Server-side incoming	< 1 ms	< 1 ms	1 ms	1 ms	4 ms
Server-side outgoing	5 ms	10 ms	12 ms	13 ms	15 ms

Table 1. Render frame rate and message processing times for increasing scene complexity

- *Client*: Implementation of the client becomes simpler when applying the integration server approach. The client just needs to connect to the server and retrieve the list of provided services. When Component updates are received that affect objects in the XML3D scene, the updates are applied to the respective XML3D elements' attributes. An update concerning a *position* Component of an Entity, for example, changes the *translation* attribute of the respective XML3D <*transform*> element. Key frame updates for verification visualization are applied to the respective Xflow <*data*> element.

7. Synchronisation: Empirical Performance Analysis

Our goal is to achieve a real-time interaction for both client-side and server-side integration approaches. For the client-side approach, network load is less of an issue, as all that needs to be transmitted here are atomic scene modifications. Those are directly synchronized via the chosen database. Experienced latencies occur solely from the quality of the network signal. Thus, for the client case, we are only measuring performance in terms of rendered frames per second during client-side simulations.

By introducing the server as integration and synchronization layer, we also introduce a possible bottle neck concerning network performance. The server has to translate updates from attached services to messages for its own service interface, apply service updates to the internal scene model and transmit these changes to all connected clients for shared real time visualization.

For the server, we have also included the following values for measurements:

- **Total message roundtrip**: The time in milliseconds a message needs to re-appear at the client

that sent it. This measures the time any client will observe modifications done by others.

- **Server-side incoming processing**: The time it takes for an incoming message to be processed on server side, i.e. until a scene modification by a client is applied to the server's world representation.

- **Server-side outgoing processing**: The time it takes for an update of the server's internal data to be sent as serialized message to the clients.

The performance analysis process is the following: First, we navigate through the scene and add an object to it (*Editing Session*). For the client-side implementation, we measure the render frame rate. For the server-side implementation, we measure the time from adding the object in one client until the respective update is received by another client. We repeat this procedure while a visualization of the trace produced by verification service is executed. Then we add agent avatars to the scene and measure the performance with a number of 3, 10 and 20 avatars respectively. Note that both trace visualization and avatar animation perform frequent Xflow animation key updates, whereas agent updates also include updates for both position and orientation. Those create both a higher number of update messages sent by the server and a higher number of DOM manipulations to update the XML3D scene representation.

To achieve a precise measurement of the message roundtrip times, we modify the messages such that they contain the time stamp at the time when they were sent as payload. During the processing steps on the server, the timestamps at which the different processing steps (incoming processing and outgoing processing) are completed are added to the payload as well. When the message arrives back at the client, these stored timestamps are compared to the current time in the client. Client and server are run on the same computer to rule out discrepancies by inexact time clocks on either server or client machine. In each test, we send an update message every 100ms for each client, which corresponds to 10 scene updates per client per second. The tests reported in Table 1 were run for 120 seconds each.

We observe that we achieve reasonable frame rates in the client for up to 10 agents. For more than 10 agents, frame rates drop below the desired rate of 25 fps. For the presented use case, however, we consider a number of 10 to 20 agents sufficient, and therefore the client performs well in the given setup.

For the server-implementation, the message transfer rates are entirely satisfying. Even with 20 clients observing the same scene, message updates occur faster than the actual frame rate, and thus frequent enough to not cause any observable delay in the processing. Our approach of the homogeneous service interface constitutes only minimal processing times. Most of the transfer delay is caused by actually sending the serialized message over the network.

8. Related Work

8.1. Collaborative Environments: Research and Prototypes

A project that thoroughly dealt with collaboration in virtual environments is the DiFac project as described by Sacco et al [32]. They developed a factory design tool in VR, which integrates additional services for communication and project coordination. In addition, visualization of evaluation processes on a factory setup helps to find drawbacks in a specific factory setup. Information from all external services is directly visualized in the virtual environment. In contrast to the work presented in this paper, DiFac is run in a standalone VR application and not integrated in any web browser. Moreover, the set of additional services is fixed, whereas we aimed at providing a flexible API to append services of users' choice.

Pappas et al presented *DiCoDev* [33], a web-based collaborative editing tool for 3D data. It includes user management with user roles, access management and provides file exchange for documents and 3D data. The workspace is embedded into a virtual reality application based on the commercial PTC Division MockUp platform[17]. Within this VR environment, multiple users can create 3D content in real-time in a collaborative session.

Based on DiCoDev, Smparounis et al. created a *Collaborative Prototype designer* that adds functions for

collaborative review sessions to the original application [34]. In these sessions, users can inspect created models by navigating freely around them in 3D space, share their current view points with others or navigate to previously defined fixed view points. The review and evaluation process is supported by a decision support module.

Menck et al. introduced a system for collaborative factory planning in a virtual environment [35], implemented using VRUI, a framework to implement VR applications in C++. The system provides an immersive virtual factory environment for several users. Users can add objects to the virtual factory, change their positions and remove them again. Objects can be annotated to point out open issues or as documentation of the design process. Moreover, virtual meetings can be held in the virtual world, while the annotated 3D factory is explored.

While the latter examples make use of third party platforms to display 3D content, we provide a web-based 3D scenario editor that does not need any software or libraries installed but the web browser itself.

Wan et. al presented WebMWorks, a browser-based tool for collaborative design, modeling, simulation and knowledge sharing [36], building upon Modelica, an object-oriented language for modeling physical systems [18]. While models in this system are usually expressed by an equation based language, there also exists a schematic, diagram-like visualization of respective models. The WebMWorks system introduced by Wan et. al allows to create these models collaboratively in a Web-browser, and run simulations based on created systems. The actual models are served from a cloud storage. In contrast to the approach presented in this paper, WebMWorks does not provide any 3D visualization of created systems. Moreover, the system is built to work on Modelica, and does not provide any possibility to extend the existing platform by additional external services.

8.2. Synchronized Virtual Worlds

OpenSim is a widely known open source implementation of the *Second Life* server. Existing Second Life clients can be used to connect to an OpenSim server. OpenSim is designed to be modular and offers several extension mechanisms. However, even though only a subset of features of Second Life may be used, both new client applications and server extensions have to implement the Second Life synchronization protocol.

---

[17] http://www.ptc.com/product/division

[18] https://www.modelica.org/

RealXtend Playsing association introduced the *realXtend* project [19] that also uses the Entity- Component-Attribute (ECA) model to represent objects in the virtual environment [31]. Similar to our approach, entities in the world carry no information from the beginning and domain-specific information is added via attributes. RealXtend provides 3D assets in Ogre3D format and uses its own protocol *kNet* for synchronization, which puts a higher effort into development of purely browser-based clients compared to our approach. Moreover, extension of the realXtend system is based on scripted world objects and does not provide means to extend the server-side code.

Apart from the fact that data provided to the client both for 3D rendering and during synchronization is not optimized towards a purely browser-based client, the presented approaches do not consider the case of composing applications from existing external Web services.

8.3. Commercial Applications

The topic of collaborative work on 3D visualizations is not only a subject in research. Many commercial CAD (*Computer Aided Design*) and 3D modelling tools nowadays include collaborative features: Autodesk's *AutoCAD 360*[20] provides a collaborative 2D-workspace for CAD design. Work can be saved to a cloud storage and shared with co-workers. There exist versions for desktop PCs, mobile devices and a prototypical Web-browser-based frontend to allow ubiquitous access of the data. By decoupling access of the data from a specific machine and providing a browser-based implementation, designers are no longer bound to a licensed machine. However, AutoCAD 360 does not provide 3D visualization of data, but is limited to 2D sketches.

A popular tool for 3D CAD design is *CATIA* by Dassault Systèmes[21]. With *Instant Collaborative Design 1 (CD1)*[22], CATIA is extended by capabilities of sharing a workspace interactively with co-workers. Data transfer is realized either via peer-to-peer or client-server connection. Communication features are included by a real-time chat and personal messages for asynchronous collaboration. Whereas CD1 offers sophisticated solutions for concurrent product design, its use is limited by the fact that in order to participate in the work, software for each participant has to be licensed and installed on a specific machine. This obviously slows down the process of introducing a new member to the team or to allow a remote expert to temporarily participate in design decisions.

9. Conclusion and Future Work

In this paper, we presented a web-based collaborative development environment for virtual prototyping. Whereas commercial systems often are monolithic, we developed a Web-based, distributed, service-oriented and extendable collaboration framework which provides a shared visual experience for collaborators. We presented a design for a server-side integration approach that allows to extend the framework easily by plugins and adapt it to specific use-case scenarios. As design problems are often ill-structured, the open character of the service-oriented approach allows domain experts from different areas to discuss design issues without precluding possible problem solving steps. We described the services included in the framework that can be used for evaluation of the designed artefact. We have presented implementations for both a purely client-based and the integration server-based approach and applied both to a factory design scenario. The performance analysis of the synchronization approach shows that for the given class of use cases a sufficient update rate can be achieved.

As future work, we will extend the framework to enable mobile access to the collaborative workspaces, using tablets and smartphones as devices. Furthermore, we plan to include virtual reality devices, e.g. head-mounted displays in order to provide a more immersive experience of the 3D scenes.

For the integration server, we are planning to include a service bus component that allows configurable orchestration of attached plugins. This shall reduce concurrency conflicts that can occur when several plugins access the data maintained by the server core at the same time.

We are also investigating of how to improve the service interface of the server in such a way that not only Web-clients but also other server instances can connect to each other to form a cluster. Balancing the computational workload between several server nodes will increase the scalability of the system, concerning both the complexity of computations and the number of connected clients.

9.1. Copyright

<To be decided>

9.2. Rules of Use

<To be decided>

---

[19]http://www.realxtend.org
[20]https://www.autocad360.com/
[21]http://www.3ds.com/products/catia/
[22]http://www.3ds.com/products/catia/portfolio/catia-v5/all-products/domain/Infrastructure/product/CD1/

References

[1] I. Zinnikus, X. Cao, M. Klusch, Christopher Krauss, Andreas Nonnengart, Torsten Spieldenner, and Philipp Slusallek, "A collaborative virtual workspace for factory configuration and evaluation". In *Collaborative Computing: Networking, Applications and Worksharing (CollaborateCom), 9th International Conference*, pages 353–362, 2013.

[2] L. M. Camarinha-Matos, "Collaborative networked organizations: Status and trends in manufacturing," *Annual Reviews in Control*, vol. 33, no. 2, pp. 199 – 208, 2009.

[3] G. Booch and A. W. Brown, "Collaborative development environments," *Advances in Computers*, vol. 59, pp. 1–27, 2003.

[4] K. Dullemond, B. van Gameren, and R. van Solingen, "Collaboration should become a first-class citizen in support environments for software engineers." in *CollaborateCom*. IEEE, 2012, pp. 398–405.

[5] T. DeMarco and L. Timothy, *Peopleware - productive projects and teams*, 1987.

[6] D. Perry, N. Staudenmayer, and L. Votta, "People, organizations, and process improvement," *Software, IEEE*, vol. 11, no. 4, pp. 36–45, Jul. 1994.

[7] P. W. Mattessich, B. R. Monsey, and M. Amherst H. Wilder Foundation, St. Paul, *Collaboration [microform] : What Makes It Work. A Review of Research Literature on Factors Influencing Successful Collaboration / Paul W. Mattessich and Barbara R. Monsey.* Distributed by ERIC Clearinghouse [Washington, D.C.], 1992.

[8] J. M. Czajkowski, "Leading successful interinstitutional collaborations using the collaboration success measurement model," 2007. [Online]. Available: http://www.mc.maricopa.edu/community/chair/conference/2007/papers/leading_successful_interinstitutional_collaborations.pdf

[9] J. Roschelle and S. D. Teasley, "The construction of shared knowledge in collaborative problem solving," in *Computer-Supported Collaborative Learning*, C. O'Malley, Ed. Berlin: Springer, 1995, pp. 69–97.

[10] C. A. Ellis, S. J. Gibbs, and G. Rein, "Groupware: some issues and experiences," *Commun. ACM*, vol. 34, no. 1, pp. 39–58, Jan. 1991.

[11] H. Fuks, A. B. Raposo, M. A. Gerosa, and C. J. P. Lucena, "Applying the 3C model to groupware development," *International Journal of Cooperative Information Systems*, vol. 14, no. 2 - 3, pp. 299–328, 2005.

[12] A. de Moor, "Towards more effective collaborative workspaces: From collaboration technologies to patterns," in *4th Collaboration at Work Experts Group Meeting*, 2006.

[13] D. Jonassen, *Learning to Solve Problems: A Handbook for Designing Problem-Solving Learning Environments*. Taylor & Francis, 2010.

[14] A. Schmeil and M. J. Eppler, "Knowledge sharing and collaborative learning in second life: A classification of virtual 3d group interaction scripts."

[15] K. Sons, F. Klein, D. Rubinstein, S. Byelozyorov, and P. Slusallek, "XML3D: interactive 3D graphics for the web," in *Web3D '10: Proceedings of the 15th International Conference on Web 3D Technology*. New York, NY, USA: ACM, 2010, pp. 175–184.

[16] W3C, "Document Object Model definition," http://www.w3.org/DOM/, 2005.

[17] F. Klein, K. Sons, D. Rubinstein, S. Byelozyorov, S. John, and P. Slusallek, "Xflow - declarative data processing for the web," in *Proceedings of the 17th International Conference on Web 3D Technology*, Los Angeles, California, 2012.

[18] R. Fielding, "Architectural Styles and the Design of Network-based Software Architectures," Ph.D. dissertation, University of California, Irvine, 2000.

[19] X. Cao and M. Klusch, "irep3d: Efficient semantic 3d scene retrieval," in *VISAPP (2)*, S. Battiato and J. Braz, Eds. SciTePress, 2013, pp. 19–28.

[20] P. Kapahnke, P. Liedtke, S. Nesbigall, S. Warwas, and M. Klusch, "Isreal: an open platform for semantic-based 3d simulations in the 3d internet," in *Proceedings of the 9th international semantic web conference on The semantic web - Volume Part II*, ser. ISWC'10, 2010, pp. 161–176.

[21] M. Klusch and P. Kapahnke, "The isem matchmaker: A flexible approach for adaptive hybrid semantic service selection," *Web Semant.*, vol. 15, pp. 1–14, Sep. 2012.

[22] A. Nonnengart, "A deductive model checking approach for hybrid systems," Max-Planck-Institut für Informatik, Stuhlsatzenhausweg 85, 66123 Saarbrücken, Germany, Research Report MPI-I-1999-2-006, November 1999.

[23] C. Krauß and A. Nonnengart, "Formal analysis meets 3d-visualization," in *Concurrent Engineering Approaches for Sustainable Product Development in a Multi-Disciplinary Environment*, J. Stjepandic, G. Rock, and C. Bil, Eds. Springer London, 2013, pp. 145–156.

[24] T. A. Henzinger, "The theory of hybrid automata," in *Proceedings of the 11th Annual IEEE Symposium on Logic in Computer Science*, ser. LICS '96. Washington, DC, USA: IEEE Computer Society, pp. 278–292.

[25] M. Bratman, *Intention, Plans, and Practical Reason*, ser. Center for the Study of Language and Information - Lecture Notes Series.

[26] A. S. Rao and M. P. Georgeff, "Modeling rational agents within a BDI-architecture," in *Proceedings of the 2nd International Conference on Principles of Knowledge Representation and Reasoning*, J. Allen, R. Fikes, and E. Sandewall, Eds. Morgan Kaufmann publishers Inc.: San Mateo, CA, USA, 1991, pp. 473–484.

[27] Backbone.js, "Backbone.js," Project Web Page, 2013, http://www.backbonejs.org.

[28] A. Goldberg, "Information models, views, and controllers," *Dr. Dobb's J.*, vol. 15, no. 7, pp. 54–61, May 1990.

[29] J. C. Anderson, J. Lehnardt, and N. Slater, *CouchDB: The Definitive Guide Time to Relax*, 1st ed. O'Reilly Media, Inc., 2010.

[30] J. Franks, P. Hallam-Baker, J. Hosteler, S. Lawrence, P. Leach, A. Luotonen, and L. Stuart, "Http authentication: Basic and digest access authentication," June 1999. [Online]. Available: http://tools.ietf.org/html/rfc2617

[31] T. Alatalo, "A Virtual World Web Client Utilizing An Entity-Component Model," in *IEEE Internet Computing*, vol. 15, no. 5, pp. 30-37, September/October, 2011.

[32] M. Sacco, C. Redaelli, C. Constantinescu, G. Lawson, M. D'Cruz, and M. Pappas, "Difac: digital factory for human oriented production system," in *Proceedings*

of the 12th international conference on Human-computer interaction: applications and services, ser. HCI'07, 2007, pp. 1140–1149.

[33] M. Pappas, V. Karabatsou, D. Mavrikios, and G. Chryssolouris, "Development of a web-based collaboration platform for manufacturing product and process design evaluation using virtual reality techniques," in *International Journal of Computer Integrated Manufacturing*, vol. 19(8), 2006, pp. 805–814.

[34] K. Smparounis, K. Alexopoulos, and V. Xanthakis, "A Web-based Platform for Collaborative Product Design and Evaluation," in *15th International Conference on Concurrent Enterprising (ICE)*, 2009.

[35] "Collaborative Factory Planning in Virtual Reality," *Procedia {CIRP}*, vol. 3, pp. 317 – 322, 2012, 45th {CIRP} Conference on Manufacturing Systems 2012.

[36] L. Wan, C. Wang, T. Xiong, and Q. Liu, "A Modelica-Based Modeling, Simulation and Knowledge Sharing Web Platform," in *20th ISPE International Conference on Concurrent Engineering*, September 2013.

7

Automated Dimension Determination for NMF-based Incremental Collaborative Filtering

Xiwei Wang[1,*], Jun Zhang[2], and Ruxin Dai[3]

[1]Department of Computer Science, Northeastern Illinois University, Chicago, Illinois 60625, USA
[2]Department of Computer Science, University of Kentucky, Lexington, Kentucky 40506-0633, USA
[3]Department of Computer Science and Information Systems, University of Wisconsin River Falls, River Falls, Wisconsin 54022, USA

Abstract

The nonnegative matrix factorization (NMF) based collaborative filtering techniques have achieved great success in product recommendations. It is well known that in NMF, the dimensions of the factor matrices have to be determined in advance. Moreover, data is growing fast; thus in some cases, the dimensions need to be changed to reduce the approximation error. The recommender systems should be capable of updating new data in a timely manner without sacrificing the prediction accuracy.

In this paper, we propose an NMF based data update approach with automated dimension determination for collaborative filtering purposes. The approach can determine the dimensions of the factor matrices and update them automatically. It exploits the nearest neighborhood based clustering algorithm to cluster users and items according to their auxiliary information, and uses the clusters as the constraints in NMF. The dimensions of the factor matrices are associated with the cluster quantities. When new data becomes available, the incremental clustering algorithm determines whether to increase the number of clusters or merge the existing clusters. Experiments on three different datasets (MovieLens, Sushi, and LibimSeTi) were conducted to examine the proposed approach. The results show that our approach can update the data quickly and provide encouraging prediction accuracy.

Keywords: auxiliary information, incremental clustering, data growth, collaborative Filtering, NMF

1. Introduction

The advent of the Internet has generated exponential growth of various kinds of data. For average people, easy-to-use tools are highly desired to retrieve useful information that is beneficial to their daily life. In eCommerce, a large number of online shopping websites employ recommender systems to make personalized product recommendations. In general, a recommender system is a program that utilizes algorithms to predict users' preferences by profiling their shopping patterns. With the help of recommender systems, online merchants could better sell their products to the users who have visited their websites

in the past. Collaborative filtering (CF) techniques are one of the most popular fundamental algorithms in recommender systems. CF aims at predicting users' preferences based on their transaction history and/or their feedback on products. There are different types of CF techniques, e.g., item/user correlation based CF's [16], singular value decomposition (SVD) based latent factor CF's [17], and nonnegative matrix factorization (NMF) based CF's [3][23].

One of the critical components of a recommender system is the user data. CF techniques require at least users' rating data, which reflects their preferences over products, to make the predictions. In addition, the auxiliary information associated with users and items is also taken into account by some CF models. Chen et al. [4] proposed a toolkit for the feature

*Corresponding author. Email: xwang9@neiu.edu

based collaborative filtering, named SVDFeature. They presented an example of using the toolkit. In their example, the album information and the temporal information are treated as auxiliary information in their SVDFeature for better prediction. Gu et al. [6] incorporated user and item graphs into an NMF based CF algorithm to improve the prediction accuracy. It is known that in some datasets, e.g., the MovieLens dataset [17], the Sushi preference dataset [10], and the LibimSeTi dating agency dataset [2], auxiliary information such as users' demographic data and items' category data, are also provided. This information, if properly used, can improve the recommendation accuracy, especially when the original rating matrix is extremely incomplete.

Furthermore, CF algorithms must be able to handle the fast data growth efficiently. In general, data grows in two aspects: new items/users with their transaction or rating data and the accompanying auxiliary information. The algorithms need to update the data and provide recommendations in a timely manner. Additionally, the matrix factorization based collaborative filtering algorithms require the dimensions of the factor matrices to be set in advance. When new data becomes available, the dimensions need to be updated.

In this paper, we propose an NMF based data update approach with automated dimension determination for collaborative filtering purposes. The approach, named iCluster-NMF, is based on the incremental clustering algorithm and the incremental nonnegative matrix tri-factorization (NMTF) [5]. It can determine the dimensions of the factor matrices and update them automatically. It exploits the nearest neighborhood based clustering algorithm to cluster users and items according to their auxiliary information, and uses the clusters as the constraints in NMF. The dimensions of the factor matrices are associated with the cluster quantities. When new data arrives, the incremental clustering algorithm determines whether to increase the number of clusters or merge the existing clusters. We examine our approach on previously mentioned three datasets in three aspects: (1) the correctness of the approximated rating matrix, (2) the time cost of the algorithms, and (3) the number of clusters produced by the approach. The results show that our approach can update the data quickly and provide satisfactory prediction accuracy.

The contributions of this paper are twofold: (1) utilizing auxiliary information as the constraints in NMTF for data approximation; (2) incorporating the incremental clustering technique into NMTF to automatically determine the dimensions of the factor matrices.

The remainder of this paper is organized as follows. Section 2 presents the related work. Section 3 defines the problem and related notations. Sections 4 and 5 describe the main idea of the proposed approach as well as a comparison model. Section 6 studies the experiments and discusses the results. Some concluding remarks and future work are given in 7.

2. Related Work

With the increasing popularity of online applications, the problem of managing fast growing data has become one of the major research topics in data science. The emergence of eCommerce has greatly facilitated people's life and expedited the daily purchases. With a large amount of new data arriving, the recommender systems employed by online merchants have to update and process the data efficiently. In [1], Brand proposed update rules for adding data to a "thin" SVD data model, which is used to update new data into the lightweight recommender systems. Wang and Zhang [20] incorporated the missing value imputation and the randomization based perturbation into incremental SVD for privacy preserving collaborative filtering data update. Wang et al. [21] proposed a swarm intelligence based recommendation algorithm, named Ant Collaborative Filtering, to capture the evolution of user preference over time. By doing so, the new data can be dynamically updated online.

Our proposed approach uses NMF as the fundamental technique for the data update. In [23], Zhang et al. applied NMF to collaborative filtering to learn the missing values in the rating matrix. They treated NMF as a solution to the expectation maximization (EM) problems. Chen et al. [3] proposed an orthogonal nonnegative matrix tri-factorization (ONMTF) [5] based collaborative filtering algorithm. Their algorithm also takes into account the user similarity and item similarity. Nirmal et al. [19] proposed explicit incorporation of the additional constraint, called the "clustering constraint", into NMF in order to suppress the data patterns in the process of performing the matrix factorization. Their work is based on the idea that one of the factor matrices in NMF contains cluster membership indicators. The clustering constraint is another indicator matrix with altered class membership in it. This constraint then guides NMF in updating factor matrices. Based on this idea, the proposed model applies the user and item cluster membership indicators to nonnegative matrix tri-factorization (NMTF), which results in better imputation of the missing values.

With regard to the clustering algorithms, K-Means [14] is a popular and well studied approach that is easy to implement and is widely used in many domains. As the name of the algorithm indicates, K-Means needs the definition of "mean" prior to clustering. It minimizes a cost function by calculating the means of clusters. This makes K-Means most suitable for continuous numerical data. When given categorical data such as users' demographic data and movies' genre information, K-Means needs a pre-processing phase to make the data suitable for clustering. Huang [7] proposed a K-Modes clustering algorithm to extend the K-Means paradigm to categorical domains. Their algorithm introduces new dissimilarity measures to handle categorical objects and replaces means of clusters with modes. Additionally, a frequency based method is used to update modes in the clustering process so that the clustering cost function is minimized. In 2005, Huang et al. [8] further applied a new dissimilarity measure to the K-Modes clustering algorithm to improve its clustering accuracy.

The fast data growth requires the clustering algorithms to update the clusters constantly. The number of clusters might be increased or decreased. Su et al. [18] proposed a fast incremental clustering algorithm by changing the radius threshold value dynamically. Their algorithm restricts the number of the final clusters and reads the original dataset only once. It also considers the frequency information of the attribute values in the inter-cluster dissimilarity measure. Our approach adopts their clustering algorithm with some modifications. As stated previously, it is known that the NMF based collaborative filtering algorithms need to determine the dimensions of the factor matrices and update them when necessary. It is not convenient for people to manually specify these values and the automated decision making is highly desired. To this purpose, the proposed method determines the number of clusters by an incremental clustering algorithm and uses them as the dimensions in NMF.

3. Problem Description

Assume the data owner has three matrices: an incomplete user-item rating matrix $R \in \mathbb{R}^{m \times n}$, a user feature matrix $F_U \in \mathbb{R}^{m \times k_U}$, and an item feature matrix $F_I \in \mathbb{R}^{n \times k_I}$, where there are m users, n items, k_U user features, and k_I item features. An entry r_{ij} in R represents the rating left on item j by user i. The approximated matrix, denoted by $R_r \in \mathbb{R}^{m \times n}$ is the one that has all unknown values predicted in it.

When new users' ratings arrive, the new rows, denoted by $T \in \mathbb{R}^{p \times n}$, should be appended to the original matrix R. Meanwhile, their auxiliary information is also available, and thus the feature matrix is updated as well, i.e.,

$$\begin{bmatrix} R \\ T \end{bmatrix} \to R', \qquad \begin{bmatrix} F_U \\ \Delta F_U \end{bmatrix} \to F'_U \qquad (1)$$

where $\Delta F_U \in \mathbb{R}^{p \times k_U}$.

Similarly, when new items become available, the new columns, denoted by $G \in \mathbb{R}^{m \times q}$, should be appended to the original matrix R, so should the item feature matrix,

i.e.,

$$\begin{bmatrix} R & G \end{bmatrix} \to R'', \qquad \begin{bmatrix} F_I \\ \Delta F_I \end{bmatrix} \to F'_I \qquad (2)$$

where $\Delta F_I \in \mathbb{R}^{q \times k_I}$.

4. iCluster–NMF Data Update

In this section, we will introduce the iCluster-NMF algorithm and its application in collaborative filtering data update.

4.1. Cluster–NMF

While iCluster-NMF handles the incremental data update, it is necessary to present the non-incremental version, named Cluster-NMF beforehand. This section is organized as follows: developing the objective function, deriving the update formulas, and the detailed algorithms.

Objective Function. Nonnegative matrix factorization (NMF) [13] is a widely used dimension reduction method in many applications such as clustering [5][11], text mining [22][15], data distortion based privacy preservation [9][19], etc. NMF is also applied in collaborative filtering to make product recommendations [23][3]. However, in CF data, a single user may have rated only a few items and one item may get only a small number of ratings. Therefore, the rating matrix is typically incomplete and NMF cannot directly work on it. In [23], Zhang et al. proposed the weighted NMF (WNMF) to work with incomplete matrices without a separate imputation procedure.

Given a rating matrix R and the associated weight matrix $W \in \mathbb{R}^{m \times n}$ that indicates the existence of values in R, the objective function of WNMF is

$$min_{U \geq 0, V \geq 0} f(R, W, U, V) = \|W \circ (R - UV^T)\|_F^2 \qquad (3)$$

where U and V are two orthogonal nonnegative matrices, and $\circ$ denotes the element-wise multiplication.

$$w_{ij} = \begin{cases} 1 & if \ r_{ij} \neq 0 \\ 0 & if \ r_{ij} = 0 \end{cases} \quad (w_{ij} \in W, r_{ij} \in R) \qquad (4)$$

When WNMF converges, $\tilde{R} = UV^T$ is the matrix with all missing entries filled. This process can be treated as either missing value imputation or unknown rating prediction.

Because of NMF's intrinsic property, when given a matrix R with objects as rows and attributes as columns, matrices U and V contain the clustering information of the objects. With that being said, in some cases, the data matrix R can represent relationships between two types of objects, e.g., user-item rating matrices in collaborating filtering applications and term-document matrices in text mining applications.

It is expected that both row (user/term) clusters and column (item/document) clusters can be obtained by performing NMF on R. With conventional NMF, it is very difficult to find two matrices U and V that represent user clusters and item clusters respectively at the same time. Hence, an extra factor matrix is needed to absorb the different scales of R, U, and V for simultaneous row clustering and column clustering [5]. Eq. (5) gives the objective function of the nonnegative matrix tri-factorization (NMTF).

$$min_{U \geq 0, S \geq 0, V \geq 0} f(R, U, S, V) = \|R - USV^T\|_F^2 \quad (5)$$

where $U \in \mathbb{R}_+^{m \times k}$, $S \in \mathbb{R}_+^{k \times l}$, and $V \in \mathbb{R}_+^{n \times l}$.

The use of S brings in a large scale of freedom for U and V so that they can focus on row and column clustering. In this scheme, both U and V are cluster membership indicator matrices while S is the coefficient matrix. Note that objects corresponding to rows in R are clustered into k groups and objects corresponding to columns are clustered into l groups.

With the auxiliary information of users and items, we can convert NMTF to a supervised learning procedure by applying cluster constraints to the objective function (5), giving the equation

$$min_{U \geq 0, S \geq 0, V \geq 0} f(R, U, S, V, C_U, C_I) =$$
$$\alpha \cdot \|R - USV^T\|_F^2 + \beta \cdot \|U - C_U\|_F^2 + \gamma \cdot \|V - C_I\|_F^2 \quad (6)$$

where α, β, and γ are coefficients that control the weight of each part. C_U and C_I are user cluster matrix and item cluster matrix, respectively. They are obtained by running clustering algorithms on user feature matrix F_U and item feature matrix F_I as mentioned in Section 3.

Combining Eqs. (3) and (6), we develop the objective function for the weighted and constrained nonnegative matrix tri-factorization, i.e.,

$$min_{U \geq 0, S \geq 0, V \geq 0} f(R, W, U, S, V, C_U, C_I) =$$
$$\alpha \cdot \|W \circ (R - USV^T)\|_F^2 + \beta \cdot \|U - C_U\|_F^2 + \gamma \cdot \|V - C_I\|_F^2. \quad (7)$$

We name this matrix factorization the Cluster-NMF.

Update Formulas. In this section, we illustrate the derivation of the update formulas for Cluster-NMF.

Let $L = f(R, W, U, S, V, C_U, C_I)$, $X = \|W \circ (R - USV^T)\|_F^2$, $Y = \|U - C_U\|_F^2$, and $Z = \|V - C_I\|_F^2$. Take derivatives of X with respect to U, S, and V:

$$\frac{\partial X}{\partial U} = -2(W \circ R)VS^T + 2W \circ (USV^T)VS^T \quad (8)$$

$$\frac{\partial X}{\partial S} = -2U^T(W \circ R)V + 2U^T[W \circ (USV^T)]V \quad (9)$$

$$\frac{\partial X}{\partial V} = -2(W \circ R)^T US + 2[W \circ (USV^T)]^T US \quad (10)$$

Take derivatives of Y with respect to U, S, and V:

$$\frac{\partial Y}{\partial U} = 2U - 2C_U, \quad \frac{\partial Y}{\partial S} = \frac{\partial Y}{\partial V} = 0 \quad (11)$$

Take derivatives of Z with respect to U, S, and V:

$$\frac{\partial Z}{\partial U} = \frac{\partial Z}{\partial S} = 0, \quad \frac{\partial Z}{\partial V} = 2V - 2C_I \quad (12)$$

Using Eqs. (8) to (12), we get the derivatives of L:

$$\frac{\partial L}{\partial U} = 2\alpha[W \circ (USV^T)]VS^T + 2\beta U$$
$$- 2\alpha(W \circ R)VS^T - 2\beta C_U \quad (13)$$

$$\frac{\partial L}{\partial V} = 2\alpha[W \circ (USV^T)]^T US + 2\gamma V$$
$$- 2\alpha(W \circ R)^T US - 2\gamma C_I \quad (14)$$

$$\frac{\partial L}{\partial S} = 2\alpha U^T[W \circ (USV^T)]V$$
$$- 2\alpha U^T(W \circ R)V \quad (15)$$

To obtain update formulas, we apply the Karush-Kuhn-Tucker (KKT) complementary condition [12] to the nonnegativities of U, S, and V. We have

$$\{2\alpha[W \circ (USV^T)]VS^T + 2\beta U$$
$$- 2\alpha(W \circ R)VS^T - 2\beta C_U\}_{ij} U_{ij} = 0 \quad (16)$$

$$\{2\alpha[W \circ (USV^T)]^T US + 2\gamma V$$
$$- 2\alpha(W \circ R)^T US - 2\gamma C_I\}_{ij} V_{ij} = 0 \quad (17)$$

$$\{2\alpha U^T[W \circ (USV^T)]V - 2\alpha U^T(W \circ R)V\}_{ij} S_{ij} = 0 \quad (18)$$

They give rise to the corresponding update formulas:

$$U_{ij} = U_{ij} \cdot \frac{\{\alpha(W \circ R)VS^T + \beta C_U\}_{ij}}{\{\alpha[W \circ (USV^T)]VS^T + \beta U\}_{ij}} \quad (19)$$

$$V_{ij} = V_{ij} \cdot \frac{\{\alpha(W \circ R)^T US + \gamma C_I\}_{ij}}{\{\alpha[W \circ (USV^T)]^T US + \gamma V\}_{ij}} \quad (20)$$

$$S_{ij} = S_{ij} \cdot \frac{\{U^T(W \circ R)V\}_{ij}}{\{U^T[W \circ (USV^T)]V\}_{ij}} \quad (21)$$

Assume $k, l \ll \min(m, n)$, the time complexities of updating U, V, and S in each iteration are all $O(mn(k + l))$. Therefore, the time complexity of Cluster-NMF in each iteration is $O(mn(k + l))$.

The convergence analysis of the update formulas is presented in Appendix A.

Clustering the Auxiliary Information. In Eq. (7), the clustering membership indicator matrices are used as the constraints to perform the supervised learning. This requires the auxiliary information to be clustered beforehand. In [18], Su et al. proposed a nearest neighborhood based incremental clustering algorithm that can directly work on categorical data. We follow their algorithm and make some modifications so that it can be integrated into Cluster-NMF as the fundamental clustering technique.

Algorithm 1 depicts the steps to build the initial clusters for the existing feature matrices F_U and F_I. It is worth mentioning that since this algorithm takes categorical data as input, for each attribute, we store all possible values in one column. For example, a user vector (a row in F_U) contains 3 attributes (columns), gender, age, and occupation. Each column has a different number of possible values, e.g., gender has two possible values: male and female. Same format applies to F_I.

Detailed Algorithm. The whole process of performing Cluster-NMF, the non-incremental version of iCluster-NMF, on a rating matrix is illustrated in Algorithm 2 . In this algorithm, an extra stop criterion, the maximum iteration count, is set to terminate the program at a reasonable point. In collaborative filtering applications, this value varies from 10 to 100 and can generally produce satisfactory results.

4.2. iCluster–NMF

When new rows/columns are available, they are imputed by iCluster-NMF with the aid of U, S, V, C_U, and C_I generated by Algorithm 2.

Technically, iCluster-NMF is identical to Cluster-NMF, but focuses on a series of new rows or columns. Meanwhile, when new feature data ΔF_U and ΔF_I arrive, they need to be clustered into existing clusters, otherwise new clusters are created. Eq. (7) indicates the relationship between the dimensions of U and C_U, V and C_I. This means that once the clusters are updated, NMF must be completely recomputed.

In Eq. (1), we see that $T \in \mathbb{R}^{p \times n}$ is added to R as a few rows. This process is illustrated in Figure 1. Like Section 4.1, the objective function is developed by

$$min_{\Delta U \geq 0} f(T, W_T, \Delta U, S, V, \Delta C_U) =$$
$$\alpha \cdot \|W_T \circ (T - \Delta U S V^T)\|_F^2 + \beta \cdot \|\Delta U - \Delta C_U\|_F^2. \quad (22)$$

Accordingly, the update formula for this objective function is obtained as follows

$$\Delta U_{ij} = \Delta U_{ij} \cdot \frac{\{\alpha(W_T \circ T)VS^T + \beta \Delta C_U\}_{ij}}{\{\alpha[W_T \circ (\Delta U S V^T)]VS^T + \beta \Delta U\}_{ij}}. \quad (23)$$

Since the row update only works on new rows, the time complexity of the algorithm in each iteration is

---

Algorithm 1 Initial Cluster Builder

Input:
  Object feature matrix: $D \in \mathbb{R}^{m \times f}$, where there are m objects and f attributes;
  Maximum number of clusters: $maxK$;
  Initial radius threshold: s;
  Radius decreasing step: d_s;
  Empty cluster collection: CS;
  Initial cluster feature: CF.

Output:
  Updated radius threshold: s';
  Updated cluster collection: CS';
  Updated cluster feature: CF';

1: Set CS' to empty and $maxScore$ to 0;
2: **for** $numK = 1$ *to* $maxK$ **do**
3:     Reset D, s, CS, and CF;
4:     **while** D is not empty **do**
5:         Read a new object O from D;
6:         **if** CS is empty **then**
7:             Create a cluster with O and place it into CS;
8:         **else**
9:             Calculate the distance between O and each cluster in CS and find out the smallest distance $minDis_{oc}$;
10:            **if** $minDis_{oc} < s$ **then**
11:                Insert O into the nearest cluster and update CF;
12:            **else**
13:                Create a cluster with O and place it into CS;
14:            **end if**
15:        **end if**
16:        **if** $|CS| > numK$ **then**
17:            Calculate the distance between any two clusters and merge the two clusters with the minimum distance $minDis_{cc}$;
18:            **if** $minDis_{cc} > s$ **then** $s = minDis_{cc}$;
19:        **end if**
20:     **end while**
21:     **if** $|CS| < numK$ **then** $s = s - d_s$; Goto 3;
22:     Calculate the inter-cluster distance and inner-cluster distance to obtain the clustering score $lScore$.
23:     **if** $lScore > mScore$ **then** $mScore = lScore$; $CS' = CS$; $CF' = CF$; $s' = s$;
24: **end for**

$O(pn(l + k) + pkl)$. Assume $k, l \ll \min(p, n)$, the time complexity is then simplified to $O(pn(l + k))$.

The column update is almost identical to the row update. When the new data $G \in \mathbb{R}^{m \times q}$ arrives, it is updated according to Eq. (24). The time complexity for

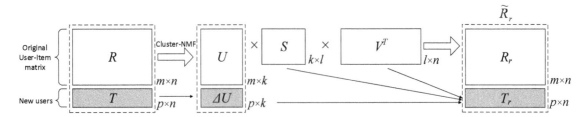

Figure 1. Updating new rows in iCluster-NMF

Algorithm 2 Cluster-NMF

Input:

User-Item rating matrix: $R \in \mathbb{R}^{m \times n}$;
User feature matrix: $F_U \in \mathbb{R}^{m \times k_U}$;
Item feature matrix: $F_I \in \mathbb{R}^{n \times k_I}$;
Coefficients in objective function: $\alpha, \beta,$ and γ;
Number of maximum iterations: $MaxIter$.

Output:

Factor matrices: $U \in \mathbb{R}_+^{m \times k}, S \in \mathbb{R}_+^{k \times l}, V \in \mathbb{R}_+^{n \times l}$;
User cluster membership indicator matrix: $C_U \in \mathbb{R}^{m \times k}$;
Item cluster membership indicator matrix: $C_I \in \mathbb{R}^{n \times l}$;

1: Cluster users based on F_U by Algorithm 1 $\rightarrow C_U$;
2: Cluster items based on F_I by Algorithm 1 $\rightarrow C_I$;
3: Initialize $U, S,$ and V with random values;
4: Build weight matrix W by Eq. (4);
5: Set $iteration = 1$ and $stop = false$;
6: **while** $(iteration <= MaxIter)$ and $(stop == false)$ **do**
7: $\quad U_{ij} \leftarrow U_{ij} \cdot \frac{\{\alpha(W \circ R)VS^T + \beta C_U\}_{ij}}{\{\alpha[W \circ (USV^T)]VS^T + \beta U\}_{ij}}$;
8: $\quad V_{ij} \leftarrow V_{ij} \cdot \frac{\{\alpha(W \circ R)^T US + \gamma C_I\}_{ij}}{\{\alpha[W \circ (USV^T)]^T US + \gamma V\}_{ij}}$;
9: $\quad S_{ij} \leftarrow S_{ij} \cdot \frac{\{U^T(W \circ R)V\}_{ij}}{\{U^T[W \circ (USV^T)]V\}_{ij}}$;
10: $\quad L \leftarrow \alpha \cdot \|W \circ (R - USV^T)\|_F^2 + \beta \cdot \|U - C_U\|_F^2 + \gamma \cdot \|V - C_I\|_F^2$;
11: $\quad$ **if** $(L$ increases in this iteration$)$ **then**
12: $\quad\quad stop = true$;
13: $\quad\quad$ Restore $U, S,$ and V to their values in last iteration.
14: $\quad$ **end if**
15: $\quad iteration = iteration + 1$;
16: **end while**

---

the column update is $O(qm(l + k))$.

$$\Delta V_{ij} = \Delta V_{ij} \cdot \frac{[\alpha(W_G \circ G)^T US + \gamma \Delta C_I]_{ij}}{\{\alpha[W_G \circ (US\Delta V^T)]^T US + \gamma \Delta V\}_{ij}} \quad (24)$$

Algorithm 3 Incremental clustering algorithm

Input:

Object feature matrix: $\Delta D \in \mathbb{R}^{m \times f}$, where there are m objects and f attributes;
Maximum number of clusters: $maxK$;
Radius threshold: s';
Cluster collection: CS';
Cluster feature: CF'.

Output:

Updated radius threshold: s'';
Updated cluster collection: CS'';
Updated cluster feature: CF'';

1: **while** ΔD is not empty **do**
2: $\quad$ Read a new object O from ΔD;
3: $\quad$ Calculate the distance between O and each cluster in CS' and find out the smallest distance $minDis_{oc}$;
4: $\quad$ **if** $minDis_{oc} < s'$ **then**
5: $\quad\quad$ Insert O into the nearest cluster and update CF';
6: $\quad$ **else**
7: $\quad\quad$ Create a cluster with O and place it into CS';
8: $\quad$ **end if**
9: $\quad$ **if** $|CS'| > maxK$ **then**
10: $\quad\quad$ Calculate the distance between any two clusters and merge the two clusters with the minimum distance $minDis_{cc}$;
11: $\quad\quad$ **if** $minDis_{cc} > s'$ **then** $s'' = minDis_{cc}$;
12: $\quad$ **end if**
13: **end while**
14: $CF'' = CF'$; $CS'' = CS'$; $s'' = s'$;

---

5. A Comparison Model: kMeans-NMF

In the previous section, we introduced iCluster-NMF that utilizes the incremental clustering algorithm to obtain and update user clusters and item clusters. The cluster quantities can change when new data arrives. This would also affects the matrix dimensions in the NMF update. To study how this automated procedure performs differently from a user-controlled clustering based NMF data update, we propose a comparison model, named kMeans-NMF.

The model uses the K-Means algorithm instead of Algorithms 1 and 3 to cluster the users and items. It is shown in Eq. (7) that the dimensionality of U are equal to the dimensionality of C_U while V and C_I have the same dimensionalities. It requires the number of user clusters k and the number of item clusters l to be predetermined. To do so, the data owner has to run the K-Means algorithm multiple times and find out the best values for k and l. The cluster quantities do not change in the whole process. Therefore, the dimensions of the factor matrices remain the same during the update.

When new users' and items' feature data becomes available, K-Means calculates the distance between each new object and the existing cluster centroids so the closest cluster is identified. The new object is then added to this cluster and the centroid is updated.

In general, kMeans-NMF is identical to iCluster-NMF but has a different clustering algorithm as well as no re-computation for NMF.

6. Experimental Study

6.1. Data Description

In the experiments, we adopt the MovieLens [17], Sushi [10], and LibimSeTi [2] datasets as the test data. Table 1 collects the statistics of the datasets.

Table 1. Statistics of the data

Dataset	#users	#items	#ratings	Sparsity
MovieLens	943	1,682	100,000	93.7%
Sushi	5,000	100	50,000	90%
LibimSeTi	2,000	5,625	129,281	98.85%

The public MovieLens dataset has 3 subsets, 100K(100,000 ratings), 1M(1,000,000 ratings) and 10M(10,000,000 ratings). The first dataset, which is adopted in the experiments, has 943 users and 1,682 items. The 100,000 ratings, ranging from 1 to 5, were divided into two parts: the training set with 80,000 ratings and the test set with 20,000 ratings. In addition to rating data, user demographic information and item genre information are also available.

The Sushi dataset describes users' preferences on different kinds of sushi. There are 5,000 users and 100 sushi items. Each user has rated 10 items, with a rating ranging from 1 to 5. That is to say, there are 50,000 ratings in this dataset. To build the test set and the training set, for every user, 2 out of 10 ratings were randomly selected and were inserted into the test set (10,000 ratings) while the rest of ratings were used as the training set (40,000 ratings). Similar to MovieLens, the Sushi dataset comes with user demographic information as well as item group information and some attributes, e.g., the heaviness/oiliness in taste and how frequently the user eats the sushi.

The LibimSeTi dating dataset was gathered by LibimSeTi.cz, an online dating website. It contains 17,359,346 anonymous ratings of 168,791 profiles made by 135,359 users as dumped on April 4, 2006. However, only the user's gender is provided with the data. Later sections will show how to resolve this problem with the lack of item information. Confined to the memory limit of the test computer, the experiments only used 2,000 users and 5,625 items[1] with 108,281 ratings in the training set and 21,000 ratings in the test set. Ratings are on a $1 \sim 10$ scale where 10 is best.

6.2. Data Pre-processing

Because iCluster-NMF and kMeans-NMF require different feature data formats (numerical vs categorical), the data fed to them should be processed in different ways. In the MovieLens dataset, user demographic information includes user ID, age, gender, occupation, and zip code. Among them, we utilized age, gender, and occupation as features. For ages, the numbers were categorized into 7 groups: 1-17, 18-24, 25-34, 35-44, 45-49, 50-55, >=56. For gender, there are two possible values: male and female. According to the statistics, there are 21 occupations: administrator, artist, doctor, and so on. For iCluster-NMF, since it directly works on categorical data, we built the user feature matrix F_U with 3 attributes ($k_U = 3$). They correspond to gender (2 possible values), age (7 possible values), and occupation (21 possible values), respectively. In contrast, for kMeans-NMF, the categories were converted to numbers since K-Means algorithm only works on numerical data. The user feature matrix F_U was built with 30 attributes ($k_U = 30$); each user was represented as a row vector with 30 elements. An element will be set to 1 if the corresponding attribute value is true for this user and 0 otherwise. Similar with the user feature matrix, the item feature matrix was built in terms of their genres. Movies in this dataset were attributed to 19 genres and hence the item feature matrix F_I has 6 attributes for iCluster-NMF ($k_I = 6$ as a single movie could have up to 6 genres) and 19 attributes for kMeans-NMF ($k_I = 19$).

In the Sushi dataset, eight of the user demographic attributes were used: gender, age, city in which the user has lived the longest until age 15 (plus region and east/west). Additionally, the city (plus region and east/west) in which the user currently lives was also used. In this case, users' age was categorized into six groups by the data provider: 15-19, 20-29, 30-39, 40-49, 50-59, >=60. User gender consists of male and female, which is the same as MovieLens. There are 48 cities (Tokyo, Hiroshima, Osaka, etc.), 12 regions (Hokkaido,

---

[1] User profiles are considered as items for this dataset

Tohoku, Hokuriku, etc.) and 2 possible east/west values (either the eastern or western part of Japan). Thus, the user feature matrix for iCluster-NMF on this dataset has 5,000 rows and 8 columns. Nevertheless, since there are too many possible values $(2 + 6 + (48 + 12 + 2) \times 2 = 132$ values) for all attributes, only gender and age were used to build the user feature matrix for kMeans-NMF. This makes the matrix have 5,000 rows and 8 columns (2 genders plus 6 age groups). The item feature matrix, on the other hand, has 100 rows and 3 columns for iCluster-NMF (16 columns for kMeans-NMF) since there are 2 styles, 2 major groups, and 12 minor groups.

Since the LibimSeTi dataset only provides the user gender information, it was simply used as the user cluster indicator matrix C_U. Note that in this dataset, there are three possible gender values: male, female, and unknown. To be consistent, the number of user clusters is set to 1 for iCluster-NMF and 3 for kMeans-NMF.

6.3. Evaluation Strategy

To evaluate the algorithms, the error of unknown value prediction and the time cost were measured. Besides iCluster-NMF and kMeans-NMF, a naive Cluster-NMF was exploited as the benchmark in the experiments for comparisons. Two SVD based collaborative filtering algorithms were studied as well.

Naive Cluster-NMF: The Benchmark Model. The general idea of the naive Cluster-NMF is quite close to iCluster-NMF. The only difference is the way of updating the clusters. In iCluster-NMF, we use Alogrthim 1 to build the initial clusters which are then updated by Algorithm 3. In contrast, the naive Cluster-NMF does not use incremental clustering but simply uses the idea of Alogrthim 1 to cluster the existing objects to the fixed number of clusters and re-cluster them (to the fixed number of clusters as well) when new data is available. In other words, F'_U in Eq. (1) and F'_I in Eq. (2) are re-clustered every time there is an update on the data. This will significantly lower the performance of the algorithm but it theoretically produces the most accurate result among all.

The SVD Based Comparison Models. In order to demonstrate how much improvement our algorithms have achieved, they were compared to two SVD based collaborative filtering algorithms and the performance was evaluated. In [1], Brand proposed a recommender system that leveraged the probabilistic imputation to fill the missing values in the incomplete rating matrix and then used the incremental SVD to update the imputed rating matrix. This makes SVD work seamlessly for CF purposes. We denote this algorithm as iSVD. The SVD based method that was proposed by Wang and Zhang [20] is similar to [1] but

has additional processing steps to ensure privacy protection. Additionally, it uses mean value imputation instead of the probabilistic imputation to remove missing values. We denote this algorithm as pSVD. It is worth mentioning that neither of them considers auxiliary information so only the rating matrix is used.

Evaluation Measures and Experiment Procedure. The experiments measured the prediction error and the time cost on three proposed algorithms as well as iSVD and pSVD. The prediction error was measured by calculating the difference between the actual ratings in the test set and the predicted ratings. A common and popular criterion is the mean absolute error (MAE), which can be calculated as follows:

$$MAE = \frac{1}{|TestSet|} \sum_{r_{ij} \in TestSet} |r_{ij} - p_{ij}| \qquad (25)$$

where p_{ij} is the predicted rating.

When building the starting matrix R, the split ratio was used to decide how many ratings would to be removed from the whole training data. For example, there are 1,000 users and 500 items with their ratings in the training data. If the split ratio is 40% and a row update will be done, we use the first 400 rows as the starting matrix ($R \in \mathbb{R}^{400 \times 500}$). The remaining 600 rows of the training matrix will be added to R in several rounds. Similarly, if a column update will be performed, we use the first 200 columns as the starting matrix ($R \in \mathbb{R}^{1000 \times 200}$) while the remaining 300 columns will be added to R in several rounds.

In each round, 100 rows/columns were added to the starting matrix. If the number of the rows/columns of new data is not divisible by 100, the last round will update the rest. Therefore, in this example, the remaining 600 rows will be added to R in 6 rounds with 100 rows each. Note that the Sushi data set only has 100 items in total but we still want to test the column update on it so 10 items were added instead of 100 in each round.

The basic procedure of the experiments is as follows:

1. Perform Algorithm 1 and Algorithm 2 on R;

2. Append the new data to R by iCluster-NMF, kMeans-NMF, and naive Cluster-NMF (nCluster-NMF for short), yielding the updated rating matrix $\tilde{R}_r$;

3. Measure the prediction errors and the time costs of the updates;

4. Compare and study the results.

The machine we used was equipped with Intel® Core™ i5-2405S processor, 8GB RAM and was installed with UNIX operating system. We wrote and ran the code in MATLAB.

6.4. Results and Discussion

Parameter Setup. The parameters that have to be determined by kMeans-NMF are listed in Table 2, where k is the column dimension of matrix U and l is the column dimension of V.

Table 2. Parameter setup for kMeans-NMF

Dataset	α	β	γ	k	l	$MaxIter$
MovieLens	0.2	0	0.8	7	7	10
Sushi	0.4	0.6	0	7	5	10
LibimSeTi	1	0	0	3	10	10

For the MovieLens dataset, we set $\alpha = 0.2$, $\beta = 0$, and $\gamma = 0.8$, which means that the prediction relied mostly on the item cluster matrix, and then the rating matrix, whereas eliminated the user cluster matrix. This combination was selected after probing many possible cases. Both k and l are set to 7 because K-Means was prone to generate empty clusters with greater k and l, especially on the data with very few users or items. It is worth mentioning that if β or γ is a non-zero value, the user or item cluster matrix will be used and k or l is equal to the number of user clusters or item clusters. As long as β or γ is zero, the algorithm will eliminate the corresponding cluster matrix and k or l will be unrelated to the number of user clusters or item clusters.

For the Sushi dataset, we set $\alpha = 0.4$, $\beta = 0.6$, and $\gamma = 0$. The parameters indicate that the user cluster matrix played the most critical role during the update process. In contrast, rating matrix was the second important factor as it indicates the user preference on items. The item cluster matrix seems trivial so it did not participate in the computation. We set k to 7 and l to 5 based on the same reason as mentioned in the previous paragraph.

For the LibimSeTi dataset, full weight was given to the rating matrix. The user and item cluster matrices received zero weight since they did not contribute anything to the positive results. As mentioned in the data description, users' auxiliary information only includes the gender with three possible values. So k was set to 3. In this case, l only denotes the column dimension of V and was set to 10.

Table 3. Parameter setup for iCluster-NMF and nCluster-NMF

Dataset	$maxK$	s	d_s
MovieLens	10	1	0.1
Sushi	10	1	0.1
LibimSeTi	3/1	1	0.1

The iCluster-NMF and nCluster-NMF are in general the same as kMeans-NMF but with different clustering approaches and NMF re-computation strategies. In Algorithm 1, the maximum number of clusters $maxK$,

the initial radius threshold s, and the radius decreasing step d_s must be determined in advance. Table 3 gives the parameter setup for iCluster-NMF and nCluster-NMF. Note that the LibimSeTi dataset has $maxK = 3$ for user clusters and $maxK = 1$ for item clusters.

As far as iSVD and pSVD, the only parameter involved is the rank of the singular matrix. To determine this value, both algorithms were run for multiple times with different ranks. We selected the numbers that achieved the optimal outcomes. The best ranks for the MovieLens, the Sushi, and the LibimSeti datasets are 13, 7, and 10, respectively.

Experimental Results. Figure 2 shows the time cost for updating new rows and columns by kMeans-NMF, iCluster-NMF, nCluster-NMF, as well as iSVD and pSVD. In most cases, nCluster-NMF and pSVD took significantly longer time than others. This is because nCluster-NMF was used to probe all possible cluster quantities to find out the choices that achieve the best MAE's. That is to say, it tries to cluster users into k groups and items into l groups, where $k, l = \{1, 2, ..., 10\}$, which results in 100 combinations. In addition, nCluster-NMF needs to re-cluster the whole data every time the new portion arrives. This requires even more time. As for pSVD, since it uses the mean value of each column to impute all missing values in that column, when a large amount of data is involved in the update (e.g. the row update on MovieLens and the column update on Sushi), the time cost can be high. The performance of iSVD is not as sensitive as pSVD to the data size but it also suffers from high matrix dimensionality, as shown in Figure 2(e).

Comparing kMeans-NMF and iCluster-NMF, it can be seen that their time costs were close in the process, though the former was slightly faster than the latter. This is because iCluster-NMF not only updates the clusters' content as kMeans-NMF does, but also combines existing clusters or creates new clusters when necessary. The cluster update itself does not cost more time but since the number of clusters changes in some cases, the NMF has to be recomputed, which requires additional time.

As a reference, Table 4 lists the optimal number of clusters on the Sushi dataset. Note that the split ratio determines how many rows or columns should be present in the starting matrix. iCluster-NMF first runs Algorithm 1 on R to find the optimal number of clusters for users and items. Then they will be updated when new data is added to R. The numbers shown in this table are the final cluster quantities. When the rows were being updated, the model kept the columns unchanged and vice versa. This is why the number of item clusters remained the same when performing the row update and the number of user clusters remained the same when performing the column update. From the table,

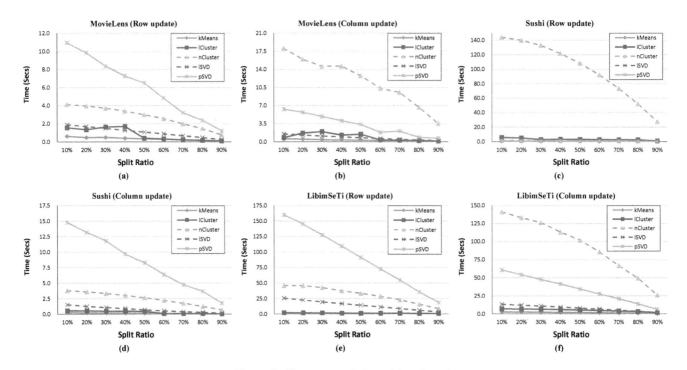

Figure 2. Time cost variation with split ratio

Table 4. Optimal number of clusters on the Sushi dataset

Split Ratio		10%	20%	30%	40%	50%	60%	70%	80%	90%
iCluster-NMF (Row)	#UserClusters	10	10	10	10	10	10	9	10	8
	#ItemClusters	10	10	10	10	10	10	10	10	10
iCluster-NMF (Column)	#UserClusters	5	5	5	5	5	5	5	5	5
	#ItemClusters	5	5	5	5	4	4	7	9	10
nCluster-NMF (Row)	#UserClusters	7	7	7	7	7	7	7	7	7
	#ItemClusters	7	7	7	7	7	7	7	7	7
nCluster-NMF (Column)	#UserClusters	6	6	6	6	6	6	6	6	6
	#ItemClusters	10	10	10	10	10	10	10	10	10

one can see that the best combinations obtained by nClsuter-NMF were 7 user clusters / 7 item clusters for the row update and 6 user clusters / 10 item clusters for the column update. Although the numbers are different from the ones obtained by iCluster-NMF, their MAE's are nearly the same.

The mean absolute errors of the prediction are plotted in Figure 3. iSVD performed worst on all datasets while nCluster-NMF reached the best results in most cases. Due to the way that nCluster-NMF works, the MAE's were consistently at the same level. They did not change significantly with varying split ratios. The only exception was the row update on the Sushi dataset, where iCluster-NMF achieved lower MAE than nCluster-NMF when the split ratio became higher. This to some extent means that updating the number of clusters in iCluster-NMF benefited the lower global prediction error. The figures show that iCluster-NMF outperformed kMeans-NMF on all three datasets. It

is interesting to look at the errors of pSVD, which were very close to iCluster-NMF on LibimSeTi but were worse on other datasets. Remember that we mentioned in Section 6.1, LibimSeTi only provides user gender information. In other words, our proposed models did not really receive any extra helpful information from this dataset. Thus, its prediction accuracy was almost identical to pSVD's, which does not utilize auxiliary information at all.

We attribute the promising results to not only the incremental clustering but also the recomputation of NMF. On one hand, clusters are updated when the new data comes in. This strategy ensures that the cluster membership indicator matrices C_U and C_I in Eq. (7) always maintain up-to-date relationships between either rows or columns. This, in turn, benefits the NMF update. On the other hand, due to the accumulated error in the incremental update, NMF needs to be recomputed to maintain the accuracy. It

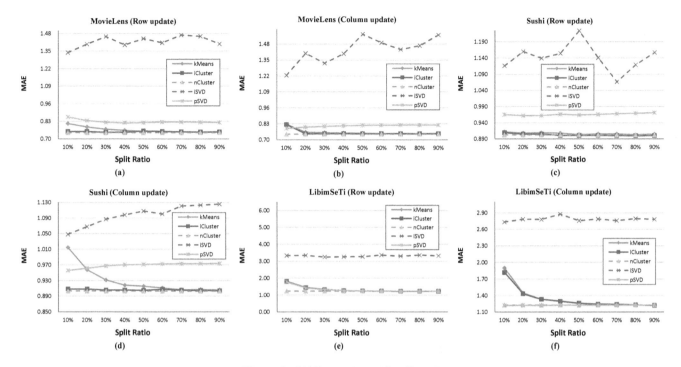

Figure 3. MAE variation with split ratio

is not convenient for the data owner to determine when to perform the recomputation and update the dimensions of the factor matrices. In this situation, iCluster-NMF recomputes NMF when the number of clusters change. It also explains why the MAE's of kMeans-NMF and iCluster-NMF tend to be close when the split ratios become higher —since kMeans-NMF does not recompute NMF, the more data it starts with, the less accumulated update error it has. Nevertheless, with more data available, the error will inevitably become larger.

As a summary, the iCluster-NMF data update algorithm produced higher prediction accuracy while costing just a little more time, if not the same as kMeans-NMF did. More importantly, the former does not need the data owner to determine the number of user and item clusters and can recompute the NMF when necessary. Once useful auxiliary information became available, both algorithms outperformed the incremental SVD based algorithms with respect to the prediction accuracy. The results are encouraging.

7. Conclusion and Future Work

In this paper, we propose an NMF based data update approach with automated dimension determination for collaborative filtering purposes. It integrates the incremental clustering technique into the NMF based data update algorithm. This approach utilizes the auxiliary information to build the cluster membership indicator matrices of users and items. These matrices

are regarded as the constraints in updating the weighted nonnegative matrix tri-factorization. The proposed approach, named iCluster-NMF, does not require the data owner to determine when to recompute the NMF and the dimensions of the factor matrices. Instead, it sets the dimensions of the factor matrices according to the clustering result on users and items and updates it automatically. Experiments conducted on three different datasets demonstrate the high accuracy and performance of iCluster-NMF.

In the real world, when people are shopping online, the factors that affect their decisions are not quite unique. In collaborative filtering research, most literatures focus on the correlations between users and items. This is apparently one of the most consequential factors but there are also some others. In future work, we will take into account more related auxiliary information, such as social networks, to achieve better prediction accuracy. We will also make use of the group preference to provide privacy preserving product recommendations.

Appendix A. Convergence Analysis for Cluster-NMF Update Formulas

We follow [13] to prove that the objective function $L = f(R, W, U, S, V, C_U, C_I)$ is nonincreasing under the update formulas (19), (20), and (21).

Definition 1. $H(u, u')$ is an auxiliary function for $F(u)$ if the conditions

$$H(u, u') \geq F(u), \quad H(u, u) = F(u) \qquad (A.1)$$

are satisfied.

Lemma 1. If H is an auxiliary function for F, then F is nonincreasing under the update

$$u^{t+1} = \arg\min_u H(u, u^t) \qquad (A.2)$$

Lemma 1 can be easily proved since we have $F(u^{t+1}) = H(u^{t+1}, u^{t+1}) \leq H(u^{t+1}, u^t) \leq H(u^t, u^t) = F(u^t)$.

We will prove the convergences of the update formulas (19), (20), and (21) by showing that they are equivalent to Eq. (A.2), with proper auxiliary functions defined.

Let us rewrite the objective function L,

$$\begin{aligned}
L = & \; tr\{\alpha(W \circ R)^T \cdot (W \circ R)\} \\
& + tr\{-2\alpha(W \circ R)^T \cdot [W \circ (USV^T)]\} \\
& + tr\{\alpha[W \circ (USV^T)]^T \cdot [W \circ (USV^T)]\} \\
& + tr(\beta U^T U) + tr(-2\beta U^T C_U) + tr(\beta C_U^T C_U) \\
& + tr(\gamma V^T V) + tr(-2\gamma V^T C_I) + tr(\gamma C_I^T C_I)
\end{aligned} \qquad (A.3)$$

where $tr(*)$ is the trace of a matrix.

Eliminating the irrelevant terms, we define the following functions that are only related to U, V, and S, respectively.

$$\begin{aligned}
L(U) = & \; tr\{-2\alpha(W \circ R)^T \cdot [W \circ (USV^T)] \\
& + \alpha[W \circ (USV^T)]^T \cdot [W \circ (USV^T)] \\
& + \beta U^T U - 2\beta U^T C_U\} \\
= & \; tr\{-2[\alpha(W \circ R)VS^T + \beta C_U]U^T \\
& + U^T[\alpha W \circ (USV^T)VS^T] + U^T(\beta U)\}
\end{aligned} \qquad (A.4)$$

$$\begin{aligned}
L(V) = & \; tr\{-2\alpha(W \circ R)^T \cdot [W \circ (USV^T)] \\
& + \alpha[W \circ (USV^T)]^T \cdot [W \circ (USV^T)] \\
& + \gamma V^T V - 2\gamma V^T C_I\} \\
= & \; tr\{-2[\alpha(W \circ R)^T US + \gamma C_I]V^T \\
& + V^T[\alpha(W \circ (USV^T))^T US] + V^T(\gamma V)\}
\end{aligned} \qquad (A.5)$$

$$\begin{aligned}
L(S) = & \; tr\{-2\alpha(W \circ R)^T \cdot [W \circ (USV^T)] \\
& + \alpha[W \circ (USV^T)]^T \cdot [W \circ (USV^T)]\} \\
= & \; tr\{[-2\alpha U^T(W \circ R)V]S^T \\
& + [\alpha U^T(W \circ (USV^T))V]S^T\}
\end{aligned} \qquad (A.6)$$

Lemma 2. For any matrices $X \in \mathbb{R}_+^{n \times n}$, $Y \in \mathbb{R}_+^{k \times k}$, $F \in \mathbb{R}_+^{n \times k}$, $F' \in \mathbb{R}_+^{n \times k}$, and X, Y are symmetric, the following inequality holds

$$\sum_{i=1}^{n} \sum_{j=1}^{k} \frac{(XF'Y)_{ij} F_{ij}^2}{F'_{ij}} \geq tr(F^T XFY) \qquad (A.7)$$

The proof of Lemma 2 is presented in [5]. We use this lemma to build an auxiliary function for $L(U)$. Since $L(V)$ and $L(S)$ are similar to $L(U)$, their convergences are not necessary to be discussed.

Lemma 3.

$$\begin{aligned}
H(U, U') = & -2 \sum_{ij} \{[\alpha(W \circ R)VS^T + \beta C_U]U^T\}_{ij} \\
& + \sum_{ij} \frac{\{\alpha W \circ (U'SV^T)VS^T + \beta U'\}_{ij} U_{ij}^2}{U'_{ij}}
\end{aligned} \qquad (A.8)$$

is an auxiliary function of $L(U)$ and the global minimum of $H(U, U')$ can be achieved by

$$U_{ij} = U'_{ij} \cdot \frac{\{\alpha(W \circ R)VS^T + \beta C_U\}_{ij}}{\{\alpha[W \circ (U'SV^T)]VS^T + \beta U'\}_{ij}} \qquad (A.9)$$

Proof. We need to prove two conditions as specified in Definition 1. It is apparent that $H(U, U) = L(U)$. According to Lemma 2, we have

$$\begin{aligned}
& \sum_{ij} \frac{\{\alpha W \circ (U'SV^T)VS^T + \beta U'\}_{ij} U_{ij}^2}{U'_{ij}} \\
& = \sum_{ij} \frac{\{\alpha W \circ (U'SV^T)VS^T\}_{ij} U_{ij}^2}{U'_{ij}} + \sum_{ij} \frac{\{\beta U'\}_{ij} U_{ij}^2}{U'_{ij}} \\
& \geq tr\{U^T[\alpha W \circ (USV^T)VS^T]\} + tr\{U^T(\beta U)\}.
\end{aligned} \qquad (A.10)$$

Therefore, $H(U, U') \geq L(U)$. Thus $H(U, U')$ is an auxiliary function of $L(U)$.

To find the global minimum of $H(U, U')$ with U' fixed, we take the derivative of $H(U, U')$ with respect to U_{ij} and let it be zero:

$$\begin{aligned}
\frac{\partial H(U, U')}{\partial U_{ij}} = & \; \{-2[\alpha(W \circ R)VS^T + \beta C_U]\}_{ij} \\
& + 2 \frac{\{\alpha W \circ (U'SV^T)VS^T + \beta U'\}_{ij} U_{ij}}{U'_{ij}} = 0
\end{aligned} \qquad (A.11)$$

Solving for U_{ij}, we have

$$U_{ij} = U'_{ij} \cdot \frac{\{\alpha(W \circ R)VS^T + \beta C_U\}_{ij}}{\{\alpha[W \circ (U'SV^T)]VS^T + \beta U'\}_{ij}} \qquad (A.12)$$

Since $F(U^0) = H(U^0, U^0) \geq H(U^1, U^0) \geq F(U^1) \geq ...$, $F(U)$ is monotonically decreasing and updating U by Eq. (A.12) can reach the global minimum. $\square$

Similarly, the convergences of update formulas (20) and (21) can be proved as well.

References

[1] BRAND, M. (2003) Fast Online SVD Revisions for Lightweight Recommender Systems. In *Proceedings of SIAM International Conference on Data Mining* (SIAM).

[2] BROZOVSKY, L. and PETRICEK, V. (2007) Recommender System for Online Dating Service. In *Proceedings of Znalosti 2007 Conference* (VSB).

[3] CHEN, G., WANG, F. and ZHANG, C. (2007) Collaborative Filtering Using Orthogonal Nonnegative Matrix Tri-factorization. In *Proceedings of the 7th IEEE International Conference on Data Mining Workshops* (IEEE): 303–308.

[4] CHEN, T., ZHANG, W., LU, Q., CHEN, K., ZHENG, Z. and YU, Y. (2012) SVDFeature: A Toolkit for Feature-based Collaborative Filtering. *Journal of Machine Learning Research* 13: 3619–3622.

[5] DING, C., LI, T., PENG, W. and PARK, H. (2006) Orthogonal Nonnegative Matrix Tri-Factorizations for Clustering. In *Proceedings of the 12th ACM SIGKDD International Conference on Knowledge Discovery and Data Mining* (ACM): 126–135.

[6] GU, Q., ZHOU, J. and DING, C. (2010) Collaborative Filtering: Weighted Nonnegative Matrix Factorization Incorporating User and Item Graphs. In *Proceedings of the 7th IEEE International Conference on Data Mining Workshops* (SIAM): 199–210.

[7] HUANG, Z. (1997) A Fast Clustering Algorithm to Cluster Very Large Categorical Data Sets in Data Mining. In *Research Issues on Data Mining and Knowledge Discovery*: 1–8.

[8] HUANG, Z., DENG, S. and XU, X. (2005) Improving K-modes Algorithm Considering Frequencies of Attribute Values in Mode 3801: 157–162.

[9] KABIR, S.M.A., YOUSSEF, A.M. and ELHAKEEM, A.K. (2007) On Data Distortion for Privacy Preserving Data Mining. In *Proceedings of Canadian Conference on Electrical and Computer Engineering* (IEEE): 308 – 311.

[10] KAMISHIMA, T. and AKAHO, S. (2006) Efficient Clustering for Orders. In *Proceedings of the 2nd International Workshop on Mining Complex Data*: 274–278.

[11] KIM, J. and PARK, H. (2008) *Sparse Nonnegative Matrix Factorization for Clustering*. Tech. rep., Georgia Institute of Technology.

[12] KUHN, H. and TUCKER, A. (1951) Nonlinear Programming. In *Proceedings of the 2nd Berkeley Symposium on Mathematical Statistics and Probability*: 481–492.

[13] LEE, D.D. and SEUNG, H.S. (2001) Algorithms for Non-negative Matrix Factorization. *Advances in Neural Information Processing Systems* 13: 556–562.

[14] MACQUEEN, J.B. (1967) Some Methods for Classification and Analysis of Multivariate Observations. In *Proceedings of the 5th Berkeley Symposium on Mathematical Statistics and Probability*, 1: 281–297.

[15] PAUCA, V.P., SHAHNAZ, F., BERRY, M.W. and PLEMMONS, R.J. (2004) Text Mining Using Nonnegative Matrix Factorizations. In *Proceedings of the 2004 SIAM International Conference on Data Mining* (SIAM), 54: 452–456.

[16] RESNICK, P., IACOVOU, N., SUCHAK, M., BERGSTROM, P. and RIEDL, J. (1994) GroupLens: An Open Architecture for Collaborative Filtering of Netnews. In *Proceedings of the 1994 ACM Conference on Computer Supported Cooperative Work* (ACM): 175–186.

[17] SARWAR, B.M., KARYPIS, G., KONSTAN, J.A. and RIEDL, J.T. (2000) Application of Dimensionality Reduction in Recommender Systems – A Case Study. In *Proceedings of ACM WebKDD Workshop* (ACM).

[18] SU, X., LAN, Y., WAN, R. and QIN, Y. (2009) A Fast Incremental Clustering Algorithm. In *Proceedings of the 2009 International Symposium on Information Processing*: 175–178.

[19] THAPA, N., LIU, L., LIN, P., WANG, J. and ZHANG, J. (2011) Constrained Nonnegative Matrix Factorization for Data Privacy. In *Proceedings of the 7th International Conference on Data Mining*: 88–93.

[20] WANG, X. and ZHANG, J. (2012) SVD-based Privacy Preserving Data Updating in Collaborative Filtering. In *Proceedings of the World Congress on Engineering 2012* (IAENG): 377–284.

[21] WANG, Y., LIAO, X., WU, H. and WU, J. (2012) Incremental collaborative filtering considering temporal effects. *http://arxiv.org/abs/1203.5415* .

[22] XU, W., LIU, X. and GONG, Y. (2003) Document Clustering Based on Non-negative Matrix Factorization. In *Proceedings of the 26th Annual International ACM SIGIR Conference on Research and Development in Informaion Retrieval* (ACM): 267–273.

[23] ZHANG, S., WANG, W., FORD, J. and MAKEDON, F. (2006) Learning from Incomplete Ratings Using Non-negative Matrix Factorization. In *Proceedings of the 6th SIAM International Conference on Data Mining* (SIAM): 548–552.

8

TinCan: User-Defined P2P Virtual Network Overlays for Ad-hoc Collaboration

Pierre St Juste[*1], Kyuho Jeong[1], Heungsik Eom[1], Corey Baker[2], Renato Figueiredo[1]

[1]Advanced Computing and Information Systems Lab, [2]Wireless and Mobile Systems Lab
Electrical and Computer Engineering, University of Florida, Gainesville, FL, 32611, USA

Abstract

Virtual private networking (VPN) has become an increasingly important component of a collaboration environment because it ensures private, authenticated communication among participants, using existing collaboration tools, where users are distributed across multiple institutions and can be mobile. The majority of current VPN solutions are based on a centralized VPN model, where all IP traffic is tunneled through a VPN gateway. Nonetheless, there are several use case scenarios that require a model where end-to-end VPN links are tunneled upon existing Internet infrastructure in a peer-to-peer (P2P) fashion, removing the bottleneck of a centralized VPN gateway. We propose a novel virtual network — TinCan — based on peer-to-peer private network tunnels. It reuses existing standards and implementations of services for discovery notification (XMPP), reflection (STUN) and relaying (TURN), facilitating configuration. In this approach, trust relationships maintained by centralized (or federated) services are automatically mapped to TinCan links. In one use scenario, TinCan allows unstructured P2P overlays connecting trusted end-user devices — while only requiring VPN software on user devices and leveraging online social network (OSN) infrastructure already widely deployed. This paper describes the architecture and design of TinCan and presents an experimental evaluation of a prototype supporting Windows, Linux, and Android mobile devices. Results quantify the overhead introduced by the network virtualization layer, and the resource requirements imposed on services needed to bootstrap TinCan links.

Keywords: vpn, peer-to-peer, networking, privacy, virtual organization

1. Introduction

Virtual private networking (VPN) has become an increasingly important component of a collaboration environment because it ensures private, authenticated communication among participants, using existing collaboration tools, where users are distributed across multiple institutions and can be mobile. VPNs also allow groups from different organizations to create transient virtual networks thereby facilitating trusted resource sharing across the public Internet. The majority of VPN solutions are based on a centralized VPN model, where all IP traffic is tunneled through a VPN gateway. This model focuses primarily on one of these three goals: 1) secure network access to a private corporate network, 2) circumvention of a firewall restricting complete access to the global Internet, or 3) one-hop anonymity on the Internet. Nevertheless, there are several use case scenarios that require a model where end-to-end VPN links are tunneled upon existing Internet infrastructure in a peer-to-peer (P2P) fashion removing the bottleneck of a centralized VPN gateway, so called peer-to-peer virtual private networks (P2PVPNs).

The availability of P2PVPNs also help address the growing privacy concerns caused by recent NSA revelations through programs such as PRISM [1] because P2PVPNs create an environment where computing devices have end-to-end encrypted P2P tunnels which are used to route IP packets without the involvement of a middleman. This end-to-end encryption makes digital monitoring more challenging because there is no overseer that has direct access to all IP traffic flowing through the VPN, as is the case in most centralized VPN implementations. The main challenge to address is architecting an open VPN technology that is efficient, robust, easy to deploy and manage in a P2P fashion without compromising trust and while making it practical for common use in today's Internet.

This paper presents TinCan, a P2PVPN that allows flexible VPN overlays of different topologies that can be instantiated atop Internet infrastructure with low

*Corresponding author. Email: pstjuste@acis.ufl.edu

configuration and management overhead [1]. TinCan integrates with existing online social networking (OSN) services for peer discovery and notification to allow deployments that bootstrap private peer-to-peer tunnels using relationships established through intuitive OSN interfaces. The overlay implied by private end-to-end TinCan links exposes IP endpoints, allowing existing applications to work unmodified, and providing a basis for overlay peer-to-peer routing in the virtual network. The TinCan design also supports tunneling of both IPv4 and IPv6 packets within the VPN, which is implemented as IPv6 packets encapsulated within UDP packets and sent over IPv4 P2P tunnels, as well as IPv4 packets within IPv6 UDP packets.

A key goal in the design is to minimize the amount of configuration and infrastructure necessary to sustain these virtual private networks. Because TinCan runs on endpoints (e.g. VMs or personal devices), it requires little additional infrastructure for maintaining the network. TinCan links make it possible for VMs and mobile devices to tunnel IP traffic directly to each other — even when constrained by NATs — while simultaneously giving end users the flexibility to define the IP address ranges, subnets, and access control policies for their private network. TinCan integrates with ubiquitous messaging overlays that use the XMPP protocol for signaling, along with well-adopted technologies for NAT traversal (STUN, TURN, and ICE [2–4]) to bootstrap encrypted TinCan links. In one use case, social peers can run TinCan to deploy VPNs comprised of their personal devices (including mobile) and their social peers' devices by leveraging existing Internet services for discovery and reflection (e.g. Google Hangouts, Jabber.org XMPP and STUN servers). The only requirement for deploying a TinCan VPN is an XMPP server; therefore, end users can use any freely available XMPP service on the Internet, or deploy their own private XMPP server such as *ejabberd* [5].

The novel design of TinCan is logically divided in two key layers — reminiscent of the OpenFlow model, but applied to tunnels over UDP/TCP links: 1) a datapath packet capture/forwarding layer, responsible for capturing/injecting packets from a virtual NIC, and maintaining TinCan links (over UDP or TCP) to neighboring peers, and 2) a control layer, responsible for implementing policies for the creation and tear-down of TinCan links. Each TinCan peer runs the two layers; communication across modules that implement each layer within a node is achieved through a JSON-UDP RPC interface. The available API allows for the

control of TinCan link creation and deletion, mapping IP addresses to identities and TinCan links, and configuring virtual networking interface. Coordination among endpoints and overlay routing is possible through message forwarding along TinCan virtual IPv6 links, supporting user-defined overlay topologies and routing policies implemented as a separate module from the core datapath.

To demonstrate its applicability in different use cases, TinCan implements a common datapath based on Google's libjingle P2P library [6], and two different Tin-Can controllers: a "group" controller (which provides a private subnet with a flat address space for group collaboration), and a "social" controller (which automatically creates VPN links from social networking relationships established through an external OSN provider, for user-to-user collaboration). With the GroupVPN controller, nodes bind to the same subnet in the virtual network and can address each other using unique private IP addresses within the scope of the VPN. In SocialVPN mode, each user is able to define their own private IP range/subnet and locally map social peers to IP addresses within that subnet thus forming an unstructured social network graph overlay topology.

The analysis shows that the TinCan design is practical and scalable. In the experiments, a network of 300 nodes consumes 29 KB/s of bandwidth on the XMPP server. The management of these TinCan links uses about 1 KB/s of bandwidth per connection. The design incurs a 14% network per-packet encapsulation overhead. This overhead is due to our use of an MTU of 1280 bytes — selected to minimize packet fragmentation — rather than the traditional 1500 byte MTU along with the cost of an additional 40-byte header necessary to encapsulate the virtual IP packets. To measure system throughput, we conducted an experiment between two nodes in a 1 Gbps LAN and ran the iperf networking benchmark to obtain the bandwidth measurements. The results show a latency of less than 1 ms and a TCP bandwidth of 64 Mbps; since our target is to create virtual networks across the Internet, for most applications, the bottleneck will be the bandwidth limit imposed by their local ISPs.

The main contribution of this paper is a novel VPN design that leverages XMPP servers to bootstrap end-to-end VPN tunnels, supports decoupled controller/datapath model and P2P communication among controllers to implement different VPN membership, address mapping and overlay topology/routing policies, and leverages existing P2P technologies (STUN, TURN, and ICE) for establishing direct and secure P2P tunnels for IP connectivity. To the best of our knowledge, this is also the first P2PVPN design that allows computing devices to maintain their virtual IP address

---

[1]The name is inspired by tin can phones that provide private, ad-hoc communication links between friends

as they migrate across different networks while automatically re-establishing P2P connections with other nodes in the virtual network without the use of a relay.

The rest of the paper is organized as follows. A few motivating use cases are described in section 2. We summarize related works in section 3. We follow with an abstract view of our design choices in section 4 along with our policies in section 4.3. In section 5, we elaborate on the implementation details. The analysis is in section 6 and we conclude in section 7.

2. Usage Scenarios

VPNs have a history as a collaboration-enhancing tool. For instance, the Grid Applicance project [7] relies on a P2PVPN that allows researchers from different organizations to pool their virtual machines (VM) together in a virtual computing cluster. By using the HTCondor batch scheduling system [8], users are then able to securely submit computing workloads which are then dispatched to the geographically dispersed VMs that form this "virtual organization". For a more concrete example, the Archer collaborative environment [9] has demonstrated a system that employed a group-oriented VPN to connect cluster resources from various US universities, as well as student/researcher laptops and desktops. Collaborators may also decide to elastically augment their cluster by adding cloud compute nodes (e.g. Amazon EC2 VMs) to their computing cluster to enhance their capabilities. Our P2PVPN greatly facilitates this deployment because each VM instantiated in the cloud will seamlessly join the virtual cluster because they will have secure IP connectivity to each other in a scalable P2P fashion. The strength in our approach lies in the fact that these resources can be bridged seamlessly, without the intervention of university network administrators, because our P2P NAT traversal techniques allow nodes to connect from behind university firewalls. Moreover, since these virtual networking connections are peer-to-peer, the P2PVPN can be deployed with minimal infrastructure by using a public XMPP service such as Google Hangouts to bootstrap the VPN connections. Users can also run their own private XMPP service in the cloud in order to have complete control over their deployments. Through the XMPP service, user authentication and access control is administered.

The underlying advantage of a VPN is that it allows computing devices secure access to each other over the public Internet. A P2PVPN enhances this model because it ensures that only endpoints are able to encrypt/decrypt the IP traffic removing the reliance on a VPN gateway to handle that task. This can be a powerful tool in collaborative environments where a group of individuals need to quickly set up

virtual organizations to achieve a common goal. Our P2PVPN approach makes it trivial for a group of collaborators to create a virtual network consisting only of trusted group members. Through this private network, collaborators are then free to share resources knowing that the user authentication and access control is already handled at the networking layer. Our tool therefore facilitates the creation of these virtual communities through private network access. The social aspects of our design also makes our approach novel because it uses well-known paradigms of social interactions to establish trust in the P2PVPN.

3. Related Works

Cloud Provider Virtual Networking. Over the past few years, major IaaS providers have introduced network virtualization capabilities allowing users to create their own isolated virtual network and define IP address ranges and subnets on the cloud. IaaS vendors, such as Amazon EC2, Windows Azure, and Google Cloud Engine, also enable additional features such as specifying DHCP and DNS setting for the private network. Moreover, users can define routing rules and network access control for the network and IPSec VPN gateways which make it possible to combine multiple different subnets from a private or public clouds. It is clear that the cloud computing industry understands that network virtualization is a crucial component for cloud provisioning; however, there is no open standard or interoperability, thus placing the entire burden on users desiring cross-cloud deployments.

Third-Party Commercial Virtual Networking. To address challenges in network virtualization across different clouds, various third-party commercial solutions have emerged. VMware NSX [10] is a network virtualization technology that runs at the hypervisor level, recreates the whole network in software at both layers 2 and 3, and also supports Xen and KVM. It uses a virtual switch in the hypervisor to connect to other virtual switches, virtual bridges or virtual routers, while only requiring an IP backplane for connectivity. It also supports virtual networking across different data centers since the virtual networking components connect over IP. However, this solution is difficult to support across multiple providers, as it requires privileged access to the hypervisor. Both VNS3 [11] and RightScale's Cloud Management [12] products let users provision virtual machines in the same virtual private network across different public cloud providers through a common interface. VNS3 runs a virtual appliance manager at each cloud provider and implements a virtual switch/router, and a VPN gateway in the appliance; hence, VNS3 is not dependent on the underlying cloud provider's virtual networking technology because it reimplements its own in the cloud on top of the IP backplane. RightScale provides a unified wrapper around the virtual networking API of various cloud providers and greatly simplifying the deployment of virtual networks spanning multiple public clouds. However, these third-party solutions require additional resources to configure and manage these networks, again placing a significant burden of configuration and management on end users. While this burden may be acceptable in environments where dedicated staff is employed to manage the virtual network components, it becomes a significant barrier for small/medium-scale deployments — a typical use case of clouds. TinCan targets the needs of users who are not willing to afford the configuration and management of additional virtual network infrastructure.

Overlay Virtual Networking Research. Academic and industry research have explored applicable solutions for virtual networking that allow geographically-dispersed nodes to create virtual private networks across the Internet. IBM researchers have developed VirtualWire [13] which implements a layer 2 virtual network tailored to the deployment of legacy applications and VM migration across different physical networks. Virtualwire is a hypervisor-level virtual network integrated with the Xen-Blanket [14] nested virtualization technology, enabling VM migration across public clouds. VIOLIN [15] uses a very similar approach to Virtualwire providing layer 2 networking with components such as switches and routers implemented purely in software. A drawback with these approaches is that users are still required to configure virtual switches, routers, and deploy their own DHCP and DNS servers within the virtual network. The TinCan approach does not necessitate setting up additional DHCP and DNS servers.

VNET [16] provides layer 2 connectivity across different physical networks and it is also implemented at the hypervisor level. This is accomplished through a layer 2 proxy that bridges two different networks across the Internet. All of these previous works do not explicitly deal with NATs and firewalls, and assume the availability of VPN gateways and virtual routers with public IP connectivity. As the pool of IPv4 addresses becomes more scarce — compounded by recursive virtualization and the use of containers — establishing end-to-end virtual network links across NAT-constrained devices becomes increasingly important. VINE [17] is a layer 3 virtual networking alternative which supports NAT/firewall traversal through relaying. However, it requires users to configure the virtual routers and does not provide end-to-end tunnels that bypass a relay/router node. Our work enables direct end-to-end IP tunneling without the need for a router middleman because each node runs an IP router locally.

Host-based and Mobile Virtual Networking. OpenVPN [18] is a solution that is applicable in mobile virtual networking. However, OpenVPN follows a client/server architecture where all IP traffic is routed through a central gateway. This incurs high latency and creates a resource bottleneck. Many other solutions improve on the OpenVPN model; for instance, Hamachi [19] uses a proprietary central server to setup P2P connections between hosts, even through NATs and firewalls. IP traffic is tunneled over these encrypted P2P connections. Other approaches such as Tinc [20], Vtun [21], and N2N [22] all create mesh VPNs where nodes create direct connections to each other, but they require nodes to be openly accessible over the Internet. While these solutions can potentially be used to enable wide-area virtual networking, they are not currently supported by mobile platforms, and do not provide a flexible overlay architecture that supports other VPN topologies, such as those implied by friend-to-friend social network graphs. UIA [23] is a closely-related design aimed at providing ad-hoc virtual networking for mobile devices. One key difference in TinCan is the use of existing infrastructure, including OSN providers, to mediate peer discovery and bootstrapping. Previous work, IPOP [24], is a peer-to-peer VPN based on a structured P2P overlay for bootstrapping direct connection between nodes. While sharing similar goals, TinCan addresses several limitations of the IPOP design: in IPOP, peer discovery, bootstrapping, reflection, and relaying are provided by an overlay where peer-to-peer communication is layered atop a common structured P2P library (Brunet). TinCan decouples discovery, reflection, relaying and bootstrapping, decouples datapath from control modules, and exposes P2P communication through virtual IP links, allowing multiple overlay topologies. Our TinCan design does not depend on a structured P2P overlay, it uses publicly available STUN servers and XMPP servers to bootstrap P2P connections.

4. Design

This section describes the core components of the TinCan design which include a packet capture/forwarding datapath module, a network controller module, a discovery/notification overlay, reflection and relay servers. TinCan primarily enables an extensible framework for building P2PVPNs for various types of deployments. While the TinCan design supports other implementations, currently TinCan uses XMPP for discovery/notification, STUN for reflection, and TURN for relaying, and leverages the libjingle P2P library (developed by Google) to establish and maintain P2P TinCan links using the aforementioned services. The Session Traversal Utilities for NAT (STUN) protocol specifies how nodes behind network address translators (NAT) can discover their public IP address and port. Such

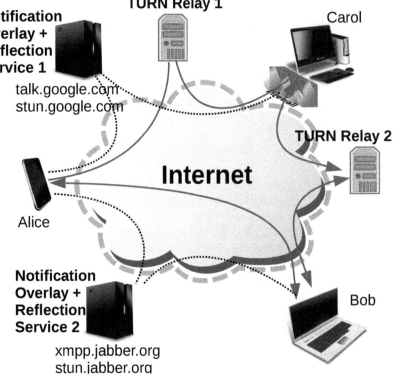

Notification Overlay (XMPP)
Alice connects to XMPP servers and discovers Bob and Carol and creates TinCan connections with them

Reflection Service (STUN)
Alice uses the STUN server to learn its public IP/port and sends that info to Bob and Carol over the XMPP service and creates direct P2P connections

Relay Service (TURN)
Carol is behind a restrictive firewall or symmetric NAT and cannot create a direct P2P connection but uses a TURN relay to proxy traffic on its behalf

Figure 1. TinCan Components and Overview

information is crucial for establishing P2P connections with remote social peers over the Internet. The Traversal Using Relays around NAT (TURN) protocol describes how nodes behind restrictive (symmetric) NATs and firewalls can connect to each other through an intermediary relay node. Both of these protocols are widely used by SIP and WebRTC technologies (e.g. Google Hangouts). Figure 1 gives a general overview of the services involved in deploying the system. In figure 2, we demonstrate how unmodified applications, such as SSH, communicate through TinCan routers installed on each device. Through the TinCan framework, collaborators can reuse existing tools via their trusted P2PVPNs.

4.1. Endpoint-Hosted Components

Datapath packet capture/forwarding module. This component is a user-level module that runs on the end user device. It creates a virtual networking interface (vNIC) on the local operating system to capture and inject IP packets to/from local applications. It also possesses the mechanics of creating, maintaining, and

tearing down encrypted TinCan links to peers, and manages a local routing table that maps a virtual IP address of an appropriate TinCan P2P link. In a typical packet flow scenario, this module reads an IP packet from the vNIC on the local OS, uses the destination IP address to lookup whether a mapping to a TinCan P2P link exists. If a TinCan link exists, the IP packet is encapsulated and sent directly over this link to the receiving data path module at the other endpoint node. Upon receiving the IP packet, the receiver decapsulates and injects it in the local vNIC (see figure 2).

The datapath module tracks the state of the local P2P links, and maintains a connection to one or more notification overlays (e.g. XMPP servers). TinCan links are typically tunneled over UDP — as it is most amenable to NAT traversal — and use DTLS for privacy, authentication, and integrity. DTLS stands for Datagram Transport Layer Security and it is the UDP version of the TLS protocol. The design also uses keep-alive messages to determine the state of P2P links, and uses the notification overlay to verify that online peers that are available to accept TinCan connections requests. This module is responsible for implementing

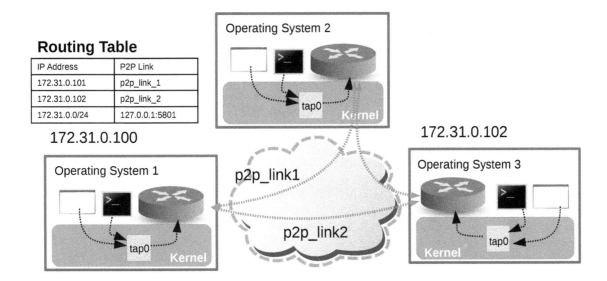

Routing Table

IP Address	P2P Link
172.31.0.101	p2p_link_1
172.31.0.102	p2p_link_2
172.31.0.0/24	127.0.0.1:5801

Unmodified applications send IP packets to SocialVPN data module through the VNIC (tap0) and the routing table determines which P2P link is used to route IP traffic. Unmapped IP packets are forwarded to controller on the localhost (127.0.0.1:5801).

Figure 2. Applications Communication through TinCan Routers

the mechanisms to maintain TinCan links; however, it does not prescribe the policies associated with link creation and tear-down. To this end, it exposes an RPC interface to the controller module, decoupling mechanism from policy. The RPC API exposes the following functionality: 1) configuration of the virtual network interface, 2) creation and deletion of TinCan links, 3) registration into the notification overlay, and 4) adding a mapping for a destination virtual IP address (see figure 3).

Network Controller. The controller module implements different policies for managing TinCan links and the overlay topology. Through the API exposed by the datapath module, the controller determines the criteria for TinCan link creation, deletion, and the mapping of IP addresses. For example, a controller may implement a policy to create P2P connections when a node joins the network for a small-scale VPN with a proactive link creation policy, or only create connections on demand when virtual IP traffic is detected between endpoints. The controller also manages the configuration of the vNIC, including the IP address and network mask. Moreover, it maintains the necessary credentials to connect to the discovery overlay for certificate exchanges with peers in setting up private TinCan links. Figure 5 shows an example configuration for a controller.

In addition to programming local forwarding tables, the controller is also responsible for routing virtual IP packets not mapped to local TinCan links through one or more hops. This mechanism is used to route packets when a direct TinCan link is not available, for instance while a link is being initialized. Controllers bind to an IPv6 vNIC that allows it to communicate to neighboring controllers over TinCan links; this private IPv6 address is configured with a unique node ID which can be used for identifier-based routing. In doing so, the controllers can use this mechanism to implement different overlay topologies and routing algorithms without requiring changes to the core datapath (see figure 4). Finally, the controller also determines the policies for various network events such as node arrival and departures, TinCan connection requests, and link failures.

4.2. Internet-Hosted Components

Notification/Discovery Overlay. As stated above, the datapath module maintains a communication link with a notification overlay (e.g. XMPP server) that allows for the advertisement of network-wide events such as node arrivals and departures. The notification overlay plays the role of the trusted out-of-band channel for bootstrapping encrypted TinCan connections (see figure 5). When two nodes decide to create a TinCan connection, they exchange a list of candidate endpoints (i.e. public and private IP addresses and ports) and security credentials (i.e. X.509 certificate fingerprints). The notification overlay provides the following primitives: 1) multicast notification to peers connected to the overlay (e.g. XMPP buddies), 2) unicast message delivery to a specific node, and 3) node authentication and message integrity guaranteeing trusted node identity and message delivery.

Reflection and Relay Servers. There are two services needed in the public network to enable the bootstrapping of TinCan links through NATs and firewalls. First, reflection servers are used to inform nodes of their public-facing IP addresses and ports. Nodes are then able to exchange their public IP information with other nodes through the notification overlay to bootstrap TinCan connections. While most NATs are amenable to UDP NAT traversal, around 8% of the time [6], nodes behind symmetric NATs or some restrictive firewalls cannot create direct TinCan connections (see figure 1). In those cases, they require the assistance of a relay server with a public IP address. A relay service serves as an indirect communication path when a direct TinCan link cannot be established.

4.3. Controller Policies

A key aspect of the TinCan design is extensibility, accomplished through decoupling of the controller and data path. This approach is inspired by OpenFlow [25], but applies at the IP layer over tunneled links, rather than at layer 2 flows over physical links. To illustrate the extensibility of the design, this section describes two different controller models: a "group" VPN for virtual private clusters, and a "social" VPN connecting personal (and mobile) devices of social peers (see figure 4). For the former use case, the controller creates a VPN where nodes join the same virtual subnet (e.g. 10.10.0.0/16) and IP addresses are assigned by the VPN network creator. Virtual IP addresses are bound to node identifiers within the scope of this VPN by configuring the node ID to be a cryptographic hash function of the virtual IP address. TinCan links are created on-demand in response to IP packets being captured by the datapath module; while links are setup, packets may be dropped by a controller, or routed through overlay hops. In the "social" VPN model, the controller creates VPNs where per-endpoint virtual network address spaces are created at each node, peers are mapped dynamically to IP addresses within this namespace, and address translation is handled transparently. For instance, Alice has friends Bob and Carol; her VPN binds virtual IP addresses of Bob and Carol to a local private subnet (e.g 172.31.x.y). Bob and Carol have their own mappings of friends to virtual IP addresses within the local IP address space (e.g. Bob uses 10.15.x.y, Carol uses 192.168.5.y). Alice may link to Bob and Carol, while Bob and Carol may not have a direct link to each other if they are not friends. So far, we have only implemented two different types of controllers but we

envision other controllers with various IP allocation and management policies.

Network Admission. Nodes joining the network advertise themselves and exchange connection information for bootstrapping P2P links through a trusted notification overlay. Hence, admission to the network is controlled by establishing identities and membership (e.g. friend-to-friend, or groups) in the notification overlay. In the group VPN scenario, each node in the network is given the following network settings: a private IP address and netmask, the network ID, the address of the notification overlay service, and a username/password for accessing the group through the overlay (see figure 5). For example, suppose Trent is a trusted user responsible for creating a VPN. Trent creates a personal VPN and distributes credentials for authentication and network access for each endpoint to join the notification overlay. Alternatively, Trent may establish relationships (e.g. XMPP buddies) with other users who are authorized to join the VPN. Trent would then determine the IP address range and netmask for the network and distribute these settings to each VM that joins the virtual network. In the social VPN case, users have their own customized view of the network and thus define their own peer-to-peer trust relationships in the notification overlay, and select their own local private IP address and netmask. In social mode, users are not required to share XMPP credentials to other members of the VPN because TinCan leverages existing social relationships to determine admission into the P2PVPN; therefore, only a user's XMPP buddies will be part of a user's social VPN.

Proactive Link establishment. If the controller implements a "proactive" link policy, it triggers a connection request as soon as a node joins the notification overlay and proactively creates TinCan P2P links to peers even if no IP packets are flowing. This policy has the benefit of reducing latency for packets, but comes at the cost of increased resource utilization (ports and bandwidth). The proactive link policy implied by this approach may be applicable for small overlays [26], but is not scalable (see figure 4).

On-Demand Links. An alternative controller policy is "on-demand connections" where TinCan links are formed when the controller receives a packet with a destination IP address that is not currently mapped to a TinCan link. This event triggers a connection request through the notification overlay, which results in a new TinCan link being mapped to the destination IP address. Such a policy causes a delay when connecting to new IP addresses. The controller with this policy also limits the number of connections, and can expire links with inactive IP flows.

Social Profile Links. Another connection policy deals is one where nodes are only interested in connecting with social peers rather than every node in a

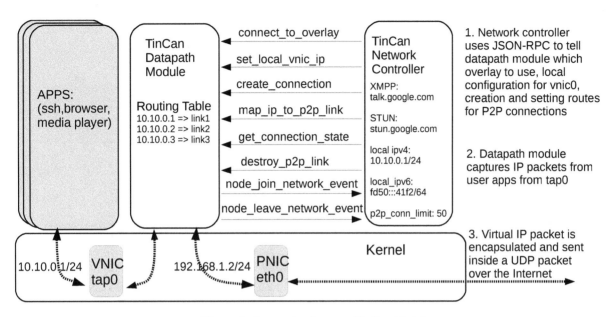

Figure 3. Interaction between TinCan Modules

particular group. In this model, peers create proactive links with friends that they have frequently communicated with in past sessions, and on-demand or multi-hop routing through common friends for nodes for which communication is infrequent. Other policies may include a combination of on-demand and proactive connections, and create overlay topologies that attempt to match communication patterns expected (or observed) by applications (see figure 4).

IP Addressing and Translation The controller has the flexibility to assign an IP address to the device and map friends to IP addresses in a subnet range that does not conflict with the local network. Each controller is able to select its own subnet range without coordinating with a centralized entity or other controllers. Therefore, in "social vpn" mode, each controller can select a different subnet for their network; meaning that IP addresses are only valid locally. This is of crucial importance for IPv4 addresses where the virtual address space is limited and can lead to IP conflicts. Since each user defines their own network, they can freely select IP addresses without fear of network subnet collisions. The datapath module performs IP packet translation on incoming packets which ensures no IP conflict following the approach described in previous work [27]. For example, Alice maps her mobile phone to 172.31.0.1 and maps Bob to 172.31.0.2. On his mobile device, Bob's controller maps his mobile device to 192.168.0.1 and maps Alice to 192.168.0.2. Hence, Alice is able to reach Bob's mobile phone using the 172.31.0.2 IP address and the IP translation performed by the datapath module on Bob's phone would make it seem as if the request came from 192.168.0.2. The proposed design also readily creates

a private IPv6 address space and pseudo-randomly assigns IPv6 addresses to nodes in the network. Since the IPv6 address space is so vast, no IP translation is necessary due to much lower probabilities of collisions in the virtual IP space.

5. Implementation

The current TinCan implementation reuses existing technologies and infrastructures that enable P2P connections for both SIP and WebRTC standards by leveraging Google's libjingle [6] P2P library to create private TinCan links. XMPP servers (possibly federated) serve as the discovery/notification overlay. By using STUN and TURN servers for reflection and relaying, which are Internet services already freely accessible, users can deploy their own VPNs without any additional infrastructure.

5.1. Endpoint-Hosted Components

Packet capture/forwarding. The datapath packet capture/forwarding module is written in C/C++ and currently runs on Linux, Android, Windows and OpenWRT. Through the TUN/TAP kernel driver, TinCan is able to receive and send Ethernet frames to the vNIC. TinCan uses libjingle [6], leveraging its adoption in existing software (e.g. the Chrome browser). While the typical use of libjingle is for audio/video streaming in WebRTC, TinCan uses it to tunnel virtual IP packets.

Controllers. The controllers are written in Python and run as a separate process on the local machine. Controllers access the datapath module's API through a JSON-RPC interface over a UDP socket. The controller uses the API exposed by the datapath module to:

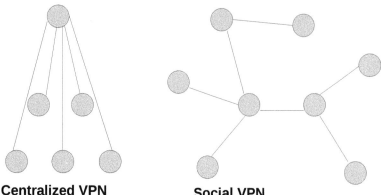
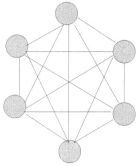

Centralized VPN
Only one connection created to
gateway and all traffic sent through it

Social VPN
P2P connections are created only to
social peers resulting in a social graph

Group VPN
P2P connections created to all peers in
the same network n(n-1)/2 connections

Figure 4. VPN Topologies

- Register with credentials to the XMPP overlay

- Setup the local vNIC with IPv4/IPv6 addresses, and netmask

- Create/Delete a TinCan link over jingle

- Map an IP address to a TinCan link

- Query the state of a TinCan link

- Handle notifications received through the XMPP overlay (e.g. new node presence, request to connect)

- Handle notifications received from the data path module (e.g. to forward virtual IP packets to other controllers when the destination is not mapped to a local TinCan link)

Through the API, one can extend TinCan to support various combinations of policies and deployments based on anticipated use cases.

5.2. Internet–Hosted Components

XMPP Notification Overlays. The messaging overlays play a crucial role in providing access to the network and as well as serving as a trust anchor for signaling and bootstrapping private TinCan links. The XMPP protocol accomplishes this role by securely routing XML messages through user authenticated TLS connections (see figure 5). Hence, TinCan-based VPNs are able to utilize public XMPP providers (such as Google Hangouts or Jabber.org), as well as use their own XMPP service (e.g. an ejabberd server) if they desire that level of control.

STUN and TURN Servers. For the reflection and relay servers, the STUN and TURN protocols are used, respectively. These technologies are used in the SIP/WebRTC communities to enable P2P connections

for audio and video conferencing; as a result, there are many publicly available STUN servers that TinCan can utilize when creating P2P connections. For some nodes behind symmetric NATs or restrictive firewalls, an XMPP server and STUN server may not be enough to bootstrap a TinCan link; therefore, less than 10% of the time [28], these nodes require the assistance of a relay server to help proxy their TinCan connections. The TURN standards [3] provide such a relaying capability. Google Hangouts is an example of an existing service that already provides such a capability for its users; therefore TinCan links can leverage that for connection relaying through libjingle. There are also many open-source implementations of TURN relays. This work uses one of those implementations [29] for experimentation.

5.3. Bootstrapping Private TinCan Links

TinCan assumes that the XMPP server is a third party trusted for peer discover, notification, and exchange of X509 certificate fingerprints. Users can connect to servers they trust, or deploy their own private XMPP server. All communication from TinCan modules to the XMPP server is encrypted at the socket layer using transport layer security (TLS). A user authenticates herself with the XMPP server and broadcasts a presence probe to all peers (or buddies in XMPP terminology) that are part of their group. Therefore, all of the nodes within the group that are connected to the XMPP server receive the presence probe. Each node in the network periodically broadcasts a ping message to all other nodes in the network every two minutes. The datapath module maintains a list of online peers along with the timestamp of their last XMPP broadcast message. Once peers are able to discover and notify each other through the XMPP server, they can proceed to create trusted TinCan links.

To this end, a connection request is created containing the requester's X.509 fingerprint, a list of

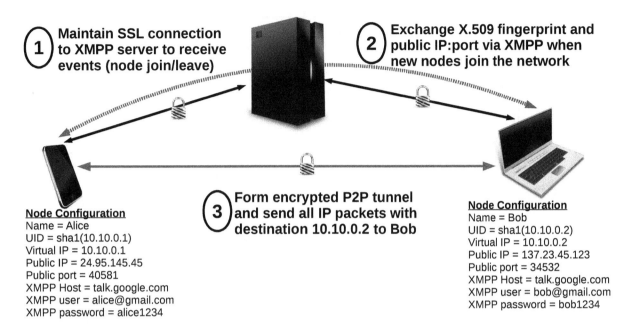

Figure 5. Bootstrapping TinCan Connections

endpoints containing private/public IP addresses with port numbers, and security credentials to ensure access control for the connection. The request is then sent to the peer over the XMPP overlay. The recipient replies to the request with a query response mirroring the contents of the request: X.509 fingerprint, list of endpoints, and security credentials. Once both sides have the necessary information, they initiate a TinCan link with each other by sending packets directly to these public IP addresses until a response is received (see figure 5). This process follows the Interactive Connectivity Establishment (ICE) RFC [4].

As mentioned earlier, nodes exchange their X.509 certificate fingerprint as part of the connection request/reply messages. To encrypt the link, the libjingle library uses the OpenSSL Datagram TLS (DTLS) protocol with peer certificate verification. Once the certificates have been successfully verified and a symmetric key is derived from the Diffie-Hellman exchange, the DTLS protocol can proceed to encrypt data flowing through the P2P channel between the peers. IP packets picked by the vNIC interface are encapsulated into data packets sent over the link, and thus protected by DTLS. It is possible to apply IPsec-layer end-to-end security atop of the virtual network overlay as well.

6. Analysis

Various experiments were conducted to understand the resource requirements of the TinCan design. This analysis also focuses on measuring the overhead of maintaining the VPN, packet processing, and the power

consumption on mobile devices. In order to make these experiments reproducible, all of the source code is open on Github at http://github.com/ipop-project. To test scalability, we setup a 300-node deployment on FutureGrid [30] using a mix of virtual machines and Linux containers (LXC). FutureGrid is an experimental Infrastructure-as-a-Service (IaaS) cloud environment that is available for academic research.

By running a 300-node experiment, we are able to analyze the bandwidth usage on the XMPP server, as well as the maintenance cost of managing TinCan P2P links. Rather than reuse existing infrastructure such as Google XMPP and STUN servers, for these experiments, independent *ejabberd* XMPP and STUN servers were deployed in order to have greater control over the testing environment. This experiment consisted of 8 virtual machines (VMs) running Ubuntu 13.10. One VM ran the notification overlay service, we used the *ejabberd* [5] open-source XMPP server implementation. Another VM hosted the reflection and relay servers, we also used another open source implementation of the TURN protocol to enable these services [29]. For these two deployments, the bandwidth load on the XMPP, STUN and TURN servers is summarized in Table 1.

Each of the remaining 6 VMs ran 50 instances of our TinCan implementation through the use of Linux containers (LXC [31]) which is a lightweight virtualization technology. Using LXC allows for more efficient utilization of resources because it makes it possible to simulate a 300-node network without needing to use 300 VMs or personal devices. The LXC environment is configured to create an isolated virtual network for the containers residing in the

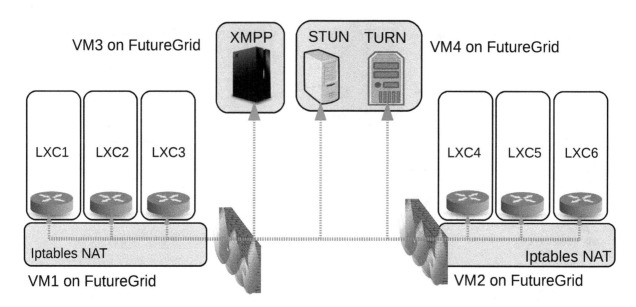

Infrastructure Details

Cloud Infrastructure: FutureGrid
Firewall/NAT: IPTables
Virtualization: Linux Containers

Experiment Setup Details

VM OS: Ubuntu 13.10
XMMP Software: ejabberd
Number of Containers: 50 per host

Figure 6. Experimental Setup Details

same VM; these containers are then able to connect to the outside world through the IPtables symmetric NAT (see figure 6). Therefore, the nodes running on different VMs have to rely on the relaying service (TURN) because the symmetric NATs do not allow for UDP hole-punching thus precluding direct TinCan P2P connections. In practice, typical usage scenarios are unlikely to be as constrained by symmetric NATs, nor is the use of a proactive all-to-all policy recommended for all but small-scale VPNs, since it does not scale well.

For this experiment, we utilized the "social vpn" controller to represent the use case where end users would like their personal devices (e.g. desktops, laptops, tablets, smartphones) along with their friends' devices to belong to the same SocialVPN and thereby having secure network access to each other. In this model, social relationships are mapped to TinCan VPN connections; for example, if Alice has a friend Bob, then if they run TinCan in SocialVPN mode on their devices, these devices will automatically join each other's social virtual private network. Hence, the TinCan P2P links in the SocialVPN mode will resemble the edges of a social graph because each VPN link represents a social link (see figure 4). To simulate this social graph environment, we used the Barabasi-Albert model from the NetworkX graph library [32] and generated 300-node graph with 1475 edges (or TinCan links).

Table 1. Experimental Setup Summary

Parameter	Value
Number of VMs	6
Number of Containers per node	50
Number of nodes	300
Number of connections	1475
Bandwidth Cost for TinCan connection	1 KB/s
Average Traffic at XMPP server	19 KB/s
Average Traffic at STUN server	27 KB/s
Average Traffic at TURN server	145 KB/s

6.1. Bandwidth Costs

During this deployment, the average bandwidth consumption at the XMPP server is about 19 KB/s; this shows that our protocol incurs very little traffic on the XMPP server. This traffic is primarily the periodic ping messages that each node in the network send to each other to indicate that they are still alive. In the case of the reflection (STUN) server, the TinCan implementation running on the end-nodes sends a 64-byte STUN *binding request* and receives a 72-byte STUN *binding response* every 15 seconds per connection. Therefore, the bandwidth cost on the STUN server for supporting our deployment of 1475 TinCan connections is about 27 KB/s (or 0.18 KB/s per

Table 2. VPN Network Performance

	Latency	TCP	UDP
LAN	0.5 ms	325 Mbps	320 Mbps
TinCan DTLS	1.07 ms	64 Mbps	47 Mbps
TinCan no DTLS	1.07 ms	84 Mbps	128 Mbps

connection). Also there are numerous freely accessible STUN servers on the web hosted by Google and others meaning that these resources can also be leveraged for the reflection service. Table 1 summarizes the bandwidth costs of the deployment.

In order to calculate the bandwidth cost on the TURN relay server, it is important to understand the maintenance cost of each TinCan connection. Libjingle sends a STUN *user request* every 500 ms and expects a *Success Response*; the average size of these packets is 130 bytes. These ping packets help libjingle keep track of the state of the TinCan link in terms of latency, jitter, and link failure. Therefore, each TinCan connection consumes about 1040 bytes per second as connection maintenance overhead. When a TURN server is used for relaying, these ping messages are routed through the relay. According to Google research, about 10% of P2P connections require a TURN relay and therefore, supporting a 300-node network with 1450 edges would necessitate a relay service for about 145 connections costing about 145 KB/s for connection maintenance. It is important to note that the TURN service would also have to relay IP traffic between the nodes that it supports and therefore deploying a TURN service requires thoughtful planning and proper access control. TURN implementations provide user authentication making it possible to identify different connections and apply bandwidth limitations per user. For instance, it is possible to configure a TURN server to only allow a maximum of 50 KB/s throughput per connection and limit the number of connections. However, since the relay service is required in the face of symmetric NATs (i.e. less 10% of the time) it is possible to support up to 1000-node network on a single TURN server. There are also commercial offerings such as turnservers.com that provide this relay service for a fee if users do not want to deploy their own TURN service.

6.2. Network Performance

One of the drawbacks of the TinCan design is that, instead of dedicated virtual switches and routers, each node runs their own virtual router that tunnels IP packets to the appropriate TinCan links. Therefore, every IP packet has to be encrypted, decrypted, and translated. This user-level packet processing can greatly constrain network performance. In this experiment,

the iperf network benchmarking suite measured the maximum bandwidth achievable by TinCan between two nodes in the same gigabit LAN. As shown in table 2, TinCan achieves 64 Mbps for TCP and 47 Mbps for UDP with DTLS encryption, but without encryption the bandwidth increases to 84 Mbps for TCP and 128 Mbps for UDP. A possible optimization for LAN environments is to bypass the overlay and allow TinCan nodes in the same LAN to directly route packets to each other without encryption, as described in [33]. TinCan supports this router-mode of operation; in this mode, containers or VMs on the same host can all share a single instance of the TinCan router. Local nodes can therefore communicate directly with each other and only use the TinCan pathway to private connect with remote nodes outside of their LAN. It is also possible to run TinCan in OpenWRT-enabled routers, this approach would also make it possible for local nodes to communicate directly without the overhead of the local processing and they would also have connectivity to nodes in the P2PVPN since the OpenWRT router would now have a connection into the network.

Understanding the time it takes to create a TinCan connection is crucial in designing a controller when considering a proactive connection policy versus an on-demand connection policy. As shown in figure 7, the median connection setup time is about 6.3 seconds, with the 75% percentile at 7.8 seconds but in the worst case, it may take up to a few minutes to bootstrap a connection due to dropped connection requests. Therefore, it may not be ideal to use an on-demand connection policy if an application generates bursty traffic that is sensitive to high latency start-up times. For the proactive connection policy, this connection setup only occurs once when a node joins the network; afterwards, TCP/IP connections through this TinCan link will not be subject to this long setup time. For the on-demand policy, the controller has to determine when to create or trim TinCan connections. For instance, one option might be to trim a TinCan connection if a link has been idle for five minutes; in this case, nodes will have to re-experience the connection setup-time in order to re-establish a connection with a trimmed link.

6.3. Encapsulation Overhead

The proposed design incurs packet overhead due to the additional headers necessary for IP encapsulation. Another source of overhead is the selection of a relatively small MTU for the vNIC. Ethernet devices typically have an MTU of 1500 bytes, but using an MTU of 1280 bytes minimizes the probability of UDP packet fragmentation. Moreover, the TinCan implementation uses a 40-byte header for each packet consisting of a

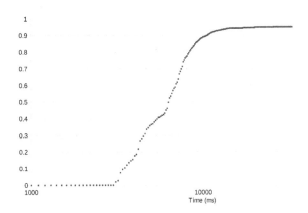

Figure 7. CDF of 1450 Connection Times. 75% of connections take less than 8 seconds.

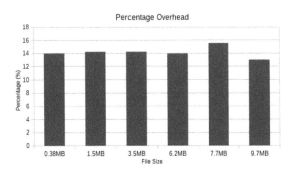

Figure 8. File Transfer Percentage Overhead. Due to MTU of 1280 and extra 40-byte header for IP encapsulation, there is a 14% overhead in the extra number of bytes sent over the network for the same file size when compared to WiFi.

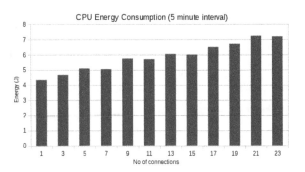

Figure 9. CPU Engergy Consumption on Mobile

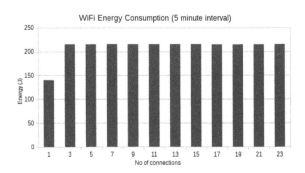

Figure 10. WiFi Energy Consumption on Mobile

20-byte source unique identifier (UID) and another 20-byte destination UID. The 160-bit UIDs creates an extra level of indirection which facilitates packet routing in the network. Consequently, a small MTU and the extra header has an adverse impact on network performance.

The following experiment quantifies the network overhead. For this setup, there is a TinCan network of just two nodes, a Samsung Galaxy Tab 10.1 and an Ubuntu 12.04 workstation. The tablet has a 1GHz dual-core Nvidia Tegra 2 processor and 1GB of RAM and the workstation is a 3.0GHz Intel Core 2 Duo with 8GB of RAM. By performing file transfers of different sizes as shown in figure 8 over both WiFi and TinCan, the results show an average network overhead of 14%. This overhead can be reduced by choosing a higher MTU closer to 1500 bytes and by using a smaller header size (e.g. 128-bit UIDs instead of 160-bit).

6.4. Mobile Power Consumption

Mobile computing support is an important aspect of the TinCan design; hence, an experiment on the Android tablet, with the number of connections scaled up from 1 to 23, provides insight in the power costs of TinCan

P2P connections. PowerTutor [34], a software-based power measuring app available for Android, calculated both the WiFi and CPU energy consumption. In terms of CPU energy consumption, figure 9 shows a steady increase in energy cost which averages about 0.13 Joules (J) per 5-minute interval ranging from 4.3 J for one connection to 7.2 J for 23 connections. For comparison, the LinPack for Android benchmark on the same tablet consumes 64.7 J for the same time interval. The WiFi energy consumption in figure 10 shows a different pattern where there is a sharp energy increase from 1 to 3 connections followed by a steady state. As mentioned earlier, a TinCan connection generates about 8 network packets with sizes around 130 bytes per second consuming about 1 KB/s of bandwidth. The mobile WiFi card is able to handle the bandwidth requirements of one connection in low-power mode. However, once there is more than a single P2P connection, the WiFi enters high-power mode which increases the energy consumption by 1.5x from 144 J to 220 J (for a 5-minute period). Since the WiFi card remains in high-power starting with two connections, there is no significant change in energy consumption as the number of connections increases.

6.5. Zero Infrastructure Experiments

The key advantage of the TinCan design is the ability for a user to create their own virtual private network by simply running the software on their end devices or cloud instances and configuring it to use existing XMPP services (e.g. Google.com or Jabber.org). To demonstrate this, a virtual network consisting of two Android devices was created: a Motorola Photon Q smartphone and a Samgsung Galaxy Tab 7. The smartphone was connected via the Sprint 4G network while the tablet connected via WiFi network. Using the Google XMPP servers, the two devices created a SocialVPN and therefore had private IP access to each other as if they are connected on the same LAN. Using the CSipSimple Android app, the two devices could perform SIP calls between each other. The call was performed by simply using the devices' virtual IP addresses as the SIP address (i.e. sip@172.31.0.101). Consequently, secure SIP calls were conducted over TinCan IP links through both the 4G ISP firewall and WiFi NAT without any registration or signaling through a SIP server. By leveraging Google's XMPP service along with the dozens of publicly available STUN servers on the web, users can easily get private IP connectivity to each other at no cost.

7. Conclusion and Future Work

Collaborative environments are evolving to include more mobile and cloud resources that are geographically dispersed and mobile. The increased use of cloud and mobile computing as ad-hoc collaborative tools have created a need for more user-defined overlay virtual networks which enable both node mobility and information security. The proposed TinCan design leverages existing overlay and P2P technologies such as XMPP, STUN, and TURN thereby creating a solution where users can define and deploy their virtual networks without needing additional infrastructure. Additionally, unlike other existing solutions, this approach does not require special access to the hypervisor, nor do users have to configure virtual switches and routers. To provide layer 3 connectivity, each node in the network runs their own virtual router which maps IP addresses to TinCan connections. Analysis of the TinCan design shows that a network of 300 nodes incur acceptable bandwidth loads on the XMPP, STUN, and TURN servers. The experiments also show that it takes less than 10 seconds to create 75% of TinCan P2P connections. The additional headers for IP encapsulation and smaller vNIC MTU cause a 14% network overhead. In terms of mobile power consumption, it seems ideal to only maintain one TinCan connection at a time to avoid running the WiFi card in high-power mode.

The evaluations consider the overheads associated with a single link, and for small-scale VPNs that could be deployed with a very simple topology and connection policy. These are feasible for small-scale VPNs, e.g. for small virtual clusters; for VPNs scaling to larger number of nodes (100s to 1000s), it is clearly a requirement to reduce the number of links in order to reduce traffic at the notification/discovery and reflection services. One approach that scales well and has been used in previous work is to use a structured P2P routing overlay with on-demand shortcut connections [24]. The choice of a scalable overlay approach can be encoded in the logic embedded in the controller. Future work will consider different topology options (e.g. different structured P2P approaches, as well as social and random graphs) and different policies for on-demand link establishment/tear-down. We will also explore bootstrapping TinCan connections through friends of friends in the mobile device deployments rather than the XMPP server to facilitate more ad-hoc private networking.

8. Acknowledgements

This material is based upon work supported in part by the National Science Foundation under Grants No. 1339737, 1234983, and 0910812. Any opinions, findings, and conclusions or recommendations expressed in this material are those of the authors and do not necessarily reflect the views of the National Science Foundation.

References

[1] GELLMAN, B. and POITRAS, L. (2013), U.s., british intelligence mining data from nine u.s. internet companies in broad secret program, http://www.washingtonpost.com/investigations/us-intelligence-mining-data-from-nine-us-internet-companies-in-broad-secret-program.html.

[2] Rfc 5389 - session traversal utilities for (nat) (stun), http://tools.ietf.org/html/rfc5389.

[3] Rfc 5766 - traversal using relays around nat (turn): Relay extensions to session traversal utilities for nat (stun), http://tools.ietf.org/html/rfc5766.

[4] Rfc 5245 - interactive connectivity establishment (ice): A methodology for network address translator (nat) traversal for offer/answer protocols, http://tools.ietf.org/html/rfc5245.

[5] ejabberd - the erlang jabber/xmpp dameon, http://www.ejabberd.im/.

[6] About libjingle - google talk for developers, https://developers.google.com/talk/libjingle/.

[7] GANGULY, A., AGRAWAL, A., BOYKIN, P. and FIGUEIREDO, R. (2006) Wow: Self-organizing wide area overlay networks of virtual workstations. *High Performance Distributed Computing, 2006 15th IEEE International Symposium on* : 30–42.

[8] Htcondor - high throughput computing, http://research.cs.wisc.edu/htcondor/.

[9] FIGUEIREDO, R.J., BOYKIN, P.O., FORTES, J.A.B., LI, T., PEIR, J., WOLINSKY, D., JOHN, L.K. *et al.* (2009) Archer: A community distributed computing infrastructure for computer architecture research and education. In

Collaborative Computing: Networking, Applications and Worksharing (Springer Berlin Heidelberg), **10**: 70–84.

[10] Vmware nsx - network virtualization, http://www.vmware.com/products/nsx/.

[11] Vns3 overlay sdn product - cohesiveft, http://www.cohesiveft.com/products/vns3/.

[12] Blanquer, J. (2013), How rightscale supports virtual networking across clouds, http://www.rightscale.com/blog/rightscale-news/how-rightscale-supports-virtual-networking-across-clouds.

[13] Jamjoom, H. (2013) Virtualwire: system support for live migrating virtual networks across clouds. In *Proceedings of the 7th international workshop on Virtualization technologies in distributed computing*, VTDC '13 (New York, NY, USA: ACM): 21–22. doi:10.1145/2465829.2465838.

[14] Williams, D., Jamjoom, H. and Weatherspoon, H. (2012) The xen-blanket: virtualize once, run everywhere. In *Proceedings of the 7th ACM european conference on Computer Systems*, EuroSys '12 (New York, NY, USA: ACM): 113–126. doi:10.1145/2168836.2168849.

[15] Jiang, X. and Xu, D. (2004) Violin: virtual internetworking on overlay infrastructure. In *Proceedings of the Second international conference on Parallel and Distributed Processing and Applications*, ISPA'04 (Berlin, Heidelberg: Springer-Verlag): 937–946. doi:10.1007/978-3-540-30566-8_107.

[16] Sundararaj, A.I. and Dinda, P.A. (2004) Towards virtual networks for virtual machine grid computing. In *Proceedings of the 3rd conference on Virtual Machine Research And Technology Symposium - Volume 3*, VM'04 (Berkeley, CA, USA: USENIX Association): 14–14.

[17] Tsugawa, M. and Fortes, J.A.B. (2006) A virtual network (vine) architecture for grid computing. In *Proceedings of the 20th international conference on Parallel and distributed processing*, IPDPS'06 (Washington, DC, USA: IEEE Computer Society): 148–148.

[18] Openvpn - open source vpn, http://openvpn.net/.

[19] Hamachi - instant, zero configuration vpn, http://secure.logmein.com/products/hamachi/vpn.asp.

[20] tinc wiki, http://www.tinc-vpn.org/.

[21] Vtun - virtual tunnels over tcp/ip networks, http://vtun.sourceforge.net/.

[22] n2n, http://www.ntop.org/products/n2n/.

[23] Ford, B., Strauss, J., Lesniewski-Laas, C., Rhea, S., Kaashoek, F. and Morris, R. (2006) Persistent personal names for globally connected mobile devices. In *Proceedings of the 7th symposium on Operating systems design and implementation*, OSDI '06 (Berkeley, CA, USA: USENIX Association): 233–248.

[24] Ganguly, A., Agrawal, A., Boykin, P.O. and Figueiredo, R. (2006) Ip over p2p: enabling self-configuring virtual ip networks for grid computing. In *Proceedings of the 20th international conference on Parallel and distributed processing*, IPDPS'06 (Washington, DC, USA: IEEE Computer Society): 49–49.

[25] Open networking foundation, https://www.opennetworking.org/.

[26] Andersen, D., Balakrishnan, H., Kaashoek, F. and Morris, R. (2001) Resilient overlay networks. In *Proceedings of the eighteenth ACM symposium on Operating systems principles*, SOSP '01 (New York, NY, USA: ACM): 131–145. doi:10.1145/502034.502048.

[27] Juste, P.S., Wolinsky, D., Oscar Boykin, P., Covington, M.J. and Figueiredo, R.J. (2010) Socialvpn: Enabling wide-area collaboration with integrated social and overlay networks. *Comput. Netw.* 54(12): 1926–1938. doi:10.1016/j.comnet.2009.11.019.

[28] Important concepts - google talk for developers, https://developers.google.com/talk/libjingle/important_concepts

[29] Turnserver - open-source turn server implementation, http://turnserver.sourceforge.net/.

[30] Fox, G., von Laszewski, G., Diaz, J., Keahey, K., Fortes, J., Figueiredo, R., Smallen, S. et al. (2013) *FutureGrid - a reconfigurable testbed for Cloud, HPC, and Grid Computing*, CRC Computational Science (Chapman & Hall).

[31] Linux containers, https://linuxcontainers.org/.

[32] Networkx - high productivity software for complex networks, http://networkx.lanl.gov/index.html.

[33] Wolinsky, D., Liu, Y., Juste, P., Venkatasubramanian, G. and Figueiredo, R. (2009) On the design of scalable, self-configuring virtual networks. In *High Performance Computing Networking, Storage and Analysis, Proceedings of the Conference on*: 1–12. doi:10.1145/1654059.1654073.

[34] Dong, M. and Zhong, L. (2011) Self-constructive high-rate system energy modeling for battery-powered mobile systems. In *Proceedings of the 9th international conference on Mobile systems, applications, and services*, MobiSys '11 (New York, NY, USA: ACM): 335–348. doi:10.1145/1999995.2000027.

9

A Novel, Privacy Preserving, Architecture for Online Social Networks

Zhe Wang[1] and Naftaly H. Minsky[1,*]

[1] Rutgers University, Department of Computer Science

Abstract

The centralized nature of conventional OSNs poses serious risks to the privacy and security of information exchanged between their members. These risks prompted several attempts to create decentralized OSNs, or DOSNs. The basic idea underlying these attempts, is that each member of a social network keeps its data under its own control, instead of surrendering it to a central host, providing access to it to other members according to its own access-control policy. Unfortunately all existing versions of DOSNs have a very serious limitation. Namely, they are unable to subject the membership of a DOSN, and the interaction between its members, to any global policy—which is essential for many social communities. Moreover, the DOSN architecture is unable to support useful capabilities such as narrowcasting and profile-based search.

This paper describes a novel architecture of decentralized OSNs—called *DOSC*, for "online social community". DOSC adopts the decentralization idea underlying DOSNs, but it is able to subject the membership of a DOSC-community, and the interaction between its members, to a wide range of policies, including privacy-preserving narrowcasting and profile-sensitive search.

Keywords: Online social networks; Decentralization; Control; Privacy; Security

1. Introduction

An *online social network* (OSN) can be defined broadly as a community of people that interact with each other via some electronic media. The most popular ones of these are the huge OSNs, like Facebook and Twitter. But there are many others, mostly small or mid-size, OSNs that play important social roles. These include, for example: support groups consisting of people suffering from a certain illness, such as AIDS; students who wish to share views of their teachers; workers discussing their work condition and their managers; and physicians consulting each other about their difficult cases. The conventional architecture of practically all such disparate OSNs—the huge, the mid-size, and the small— is *centralized*. That is, the interaction between members of an OSN is mediated via a central host—or a virtually central one, which may run on many computers, but is managed centrally.

Unfortunately, although centralization is a very convenient way for implementing OSNs, it has several well known drawbacks, which include: (a) risks to the privacy and security—these two are related, and we will, henceforth, use the term "privacy" for both of them—of information exchanged between the members of an OSN; (b) lack of scalability; and (c) the existence of a single point of failure. The last two of these drawbacks can be mitigated via very large, complex, and expensive infrastructures—like those used by Facebook and Twitter. But the main risks to the privacy of such OSNs is harder to mitigate because they are rooted in the centralized architectures per se, independently of the policies imposed on an OSN by its central host. These risks are due to two main factors. First, members of centralized an OSN are at the mercy of the organization that maintains it. This organization can, in particular, sell the information in its possession (legally or illegally), or even modify it. Second, the data maintained by the central host is vulnerable to various malicious attacks, which can be quite lucrative.

*Corresponding author. Email: minsky@rutgers.edu

Such attacks can be mounted by insiders, say the programmer that maintains the software of the OSN; and by attackers from the outside.

Such concerns about centralized OSNs prompted several attempts to create decentralized OSNs, or DOSNs, such as LotusNet [2], Safebook [11], PeerSoN [7], and others. The basic idea underlying all these attempts at decentralization, is that each member of the community in question should keep its data under its own control, instead of surrendering it to a central host, providing access to it to other members of the DOSNs *according to its own access-control policy.* Such decentralization does enhance the privacy of the members of DOSNs, but at the cost of losing the ability to subject the the community in question to any kind of global control. Specifically, this lose has two serious limitations, which are tantamount to *throwing the baby with the bathwater.*

First, DOSN provides no ability to subject a given community to any global policy regarding the membership of the community, and the manner in which its members interact with each other. Such policies are generally essential to social communities. In purely social—not online—communities such policies are often informal, imprecise, implicit, and only occasionally enforced. But such policies should be tightened and enforced under an OSN, because its membership can be larger than that of a traditional social community, and there is much less familiarity and trust between its members.

Second, the lack of global control under DOSN has another unfortunate consequence. It makes it impossible to provide important capabilities like *narrowcasting* and *profile-based search* without incurring massive loss of privacy.

The Contribution of this Paper: We will describe in this paper a novel way for decentralizing OSNs, giving rise to an architecture we call DOSC, for *Decentralized Online Social Community.* DOSC adopts the decentralization idea underlying DOSNs, complementing it with a powerful means for establishing a wide range of policies governing the membership of a social community, and the interactions among its disparate distributed members. This is done by governing the exchange of messages between the members of DOSC using a decentralized—as thus scalable—Middleware called LGI [17, 18]. Among other consequences of this architecture is its ability to support capabilities such as *narrowcasting* and *profile-based search* without loss of privacy. (We note here that we will continue using the term OSN as a general term for online social network, implying no specific architecture.)

It should be pointed out, that while DOSC should be sufficiently fast for human interaction in medium size communities—with thousands or tens of thousands

members—some of its capabilities, like narrowcasting, would not scale to the size of OSNs like Facebook and Twitter. But these huge OSNs may not require decentralization, as the hundreds of millions of their members seem not to be very concerned about issues such as privacy.

The rest of this paper is organized as follows. Section 2 discusses the need for privacy in various kinds of OSNs. Section 3 outlines the nature of policies that OSNs may need to be governed by. Section 4 provides an overview of the middleware called Law-Governed Interaction (LGI) which serves as the foundation the DOSC architecture. Section 5 introduces a basic model of DOSC. Section 6 is a description of an implemented case study that demonstrates how this abstract model can be used for a concrete application. Section 7 complements this case study by introducing more advanced capabilities available under the basic model. Section 8 introduces an extension of the basic model of DOSC. Section 9 discusses the overall performance of DOSC, and describes its limits. Section 10 discusses related works, by others, and by the authors. And we conclude in Section 11.

2. On the Privacy Concerns of Centralized OSNs

Privacy is, or should be, of serious concerns to the members of many online social networks, particularly if the messages exchanged in them contain sensitive information such as private medical and financial data. But the nature of these concerns is different in two major types of OSNs, which we call *autonomous* and *bound* OSNs. We will define both types of OSNs below, and discuss the nature of their privacy concerns, along with the risks to their privacy due to centralization.

2.1. Autonomous OSNs

We define autonomous OSNs to be those that are not subject to any outside authority—except the authority of the law of the country in which the OSN operates. Of course, the members of an autonomous OSN are subject to the policy defined by it, which may vary widely. For example, the policies of an OSN designed for a support group of people suffering from AIDS is likely to be very different from the policies established by Facebook, which is also autonomous. The following is an example of one such OSN, and a discussion of its privacy concerns.

Consider an OSN created to enable a set of physicians to consult with each other about various medical issues they confront. We call this OSN *MC*, for "medical consultation." The participants in *MC* may not know each other, and may practice all over the world. A member of *MC* may send a query—that describes an issue he or she confronts—to all other members; or, more likely, to a subset of its members, based on some criteria. And the receiver of such a query may answer it.

The information exchanged between the members of MC is clearly very sensitive, both to the physicians and to their patients, which would often be the subject to the queries made by members of MC. Having the process of consultation mediated by a central host, and having the information exchanged between the physicians maintained centrally by this host, can seriously compromise the privacy of both the physicians and their patients. The risk here is particularly serious because the host of such an OSN is likely to become a target for attacks—by hackers from the outside, as well as by insiders—since the information maintained by it can be exploited for illicit financial gains. Therefore, we have implemented MC in a decentralized manner [15] more than 10 years ago—before the term OSN has been introduced. The following are part of the constraints which have been imposed on this community by that implementation.

1. **Membership**: An agent x is allowed to join this community if it satisfies one of the following two conditions:

   (a) If x is one of the *founders* of this community, as certified by a specified certification authority (CA) called here $ca1$. (Note: we assume that there are at least three such founders.)

   (b) if x is a medical doctor, as certified by the CA called $ca2$, representing the medical board; and (ii) if x garners the support of at least three current members of this community.

   And, a regular member (not a founder) is *removed* from this community if three different members vote for his removal.

2. **Reputation**: Each member must maintain a *reputation value* that summarizes other members' feedback on the quality of his responses to posted queries, requiring no central reputation server. Furthermore, this reputation must be presented along with every response to a query. (Note that the reputation thus maintained by a member x cannot be manipulated by x himself.)

Note that although the above provisions where quite sophisticated, for a decentralized implementation, the paper that implemented them did not define a full fledged DOSC. In particular, that paper [15] did not support any of the advanced features discussed in Section 7, and did not fully support the basic model of DOSC introduced in Section 5.

2.2. Bound OSNs

We say that an OSN is bound if it operates in the context of some organization that has jurisdiction over it, and may own the information exchanged by the members of the OSN in question.

There is a growing realization[31] that OSNs that operate within an organization—such as manufacturing, commercial enterprises, medical centers, or even the military—can be beneficial for it. This seems to be particularly the case for OSNs that provide for micro-blogging, as is evident from the purchase of the Yammer—a prominent micro-blogging OSN that serves organizations—by Microsoft, for $1.2 Billion. We will have more to say about Yammer itself, but first we outline some of functional features one can expect from this kind of OSNs.

Consider a large and geographically distributed enterprise E that provides a centralized micro-blogging OSN for its employees. Suppose that such an OSN—which we call WP, for "WorkPlace"— distinguishes between groups of employees, enabling the members of each groups to communicate with each other. Such groups may be the following: (a) all the employees of E; (b) the non-managerial staff of E; (c) the managerial staff of E; and (d) members of various task forces operating in E. Note that these groups may overlap partially, as a single employee may belong to several groups. And the enterprise in question may impose some control over the membership of the various groups, and may establish some constraints regarding the communication between the members of different groups. For example, suppose that two of the task forces of enterprise E, which form groups in WP, consult to other companies, which may compete with each other. It is obviously paramount for these subgroups not to have access to each other's information.

There are several types of privacy concerns in the context of such OSNs. First, like in autonomous OSNs, individual members would be concerned about their own privacy. For example, a staff member would not want members of the management to read their complains about the workplace. Second, the information exchanged between the employees of enterprise E can carry sensitive information about the business of this enterprise. It is therefore important for the enterprise for this information not to be exposed to the outside, at least not on a large scale. Third, the enterprise is likely to be concerned about violations of its constraints on the communication between different groups of WP.

The Risks to Privacy due to Centralization: There are two types of centralization to be considered here, which we call strong and weak centralizations. Strong centralization is like the one practiced by Yammer, the Microsoft OSN mentioned above. Yammer provides services to a host of different enterprises—they claimed to serve about 200,000 different enterprises. Of course, Yammer establishes policies that provide necessary separation between the various enterprises it serves. But the information belonging to all these enterprises is maintained centrally by the Yammer system. Such centralization of commercial and industrial information of many different companies is very risky, as it is likely to attract attacks from the inside of Yammer, and from the outside—thus compromised the privacy of many of the clients of Yammer.

A much better approach would be to use an *intramural* Yammer-like OSN. This, weaker form of centralization, would be much safer than using Yammer. But if this system relies on a centralized database, it would still be vulnerable to breaches of privacy. Indeed, if all the information generated by the *WP* is available to its software, then the rogue programmers of this OSN will have a fairly free access to all of it, disregarding the required boundaries between different groups.

3. On the Nature of Policies that OSNs May Need to be Governed by

We survey here various types of *communal policies* that an OSN may need to establish. By "communal" we mean either global policy that is to govern all members of an OSN, or a policy that governs some subgroup of its members. All the policies discussed here can be easily established, by enforcement, under centralized OSNs—but none of them can be established under the DOSN architecture. All these kinds of policies can be established under our DOSC, as we will show for some of them in Section 6 and in Section 7.

Membership Control: Control over membership is crucial to many social communities whether they are autonomous or bound. The set of members may be predefined. Alternatively, and more commonly, the membership can be limited to individuals that satisfy certain predefined criteria, which can be checked by various credentials. For example, the membership of our OSN example *MC*, of medical consultation, is limited to physicians; and the membership of the workplace OSN example *WP* is limited to the employees of a given enterprise. Moreover, in addition, or instead, of such characterization of acceptable members, the OSN may condition the admission of new member on the approval of a number of existing members of the OSN.

Another important aspect of membership, is the removal of existing members. There are many possible types of procedure for doing that. As a simple example, consider an OSN that has a member that plays the role

of a *manager*, which provides him/her with the power to remove any existing member x by simply sending a message "leave" to it; and this, in turn, should force x to leave the community in question.

Identification of Members: Practically every OSN needs to establish a coherent manner in which its members identify themselves to each other. One can distinguish between three basic mode of identification: (1) Members may be allowed to be *anonymous*. (2) Members may be allowed to operate under a pseudonym of their choice. And (3) members may be required to use they real and authenticated names. For example, under *WP*, members may be required to identify themselves via their unique names within the enterprise in question—which is to be authenticated by certificates provided to them by a certification authority (CA) of this enterprise.

Besides their name, such as above, members may identify themselves by a certain *profile*—that may contain such things as their medical specialty in the case of *MC*; or by their roles in the enterprise, in the case of *WP*. The authenticity of such a profile and the way it is being used needs to be established by the policy of the OSN in question.

Constraints on the Behavior of Members of an OSN: Sometimes one needs to impose constraints on what members can do. Such constraints may depend on the profile of individual members, and on the history of their interaction with others. We have just seen an example of such constraints: only a member that plays the role of manager can send a "leave" message to others. And any member that gets such a message must cease to operate within these community. As another example, in the context of *WP*, the type of messages that members are entitled to send, or the type of posts that they are entitled to make, may depend on their roles in the enterprise in question.

Global Access Control (AC) Policies: One of the intended consequences of decentralization under DOSNs is that it enables each member to apply its own AC policy to its own data—e.g., to the set of posts it produced, which are maintained in its own database. This is useful, but certainly not sufficient. Because an OSN may want to impose some global AC policies. This is particularly true for bound OSNs, such as *WP*. The posts being produced by the various members of this OSN really belong to the enterprise E in the context of which it operates, and which thus has an authority over their treatment. The enterprise may relegate to individual members the right to apply their own AC policies, *provided* that these policies conform to the global policy of an enterprise. For example, the global policy of the *WP* may be that a group of members assigned to deal with the business of a given client-company can communicate only with each other, as long as they belong to the same group.

And global constraints are common even in autonomous OSN. A case in points are the various friendship-related rules that govern the interaction between members of Facebook.

Cooperation Protocols: In Section 1 we pointed out that the DOSN architecture does not provide certain important capabilities such as search for members whose profile satisfies a specified condition, and narrowcasting based on the profile of members. However, as we shall show in Section 8, such capabilities can be provided even in decentralized OSN, if all its members can be trusted to cooperate in providing them. Such cooperation can be ensured by imposing a suitable cooperation protocol on all members of an OSN.

4. The (LGI) Middleware—a Partial Overview

Governance of interactions among the members of a decentralized OSN requires a suitable middleware at its foundation. We have chosen the middleware called *law governed interaction* (LGI) for this purpose. LGI is broadly related to conventional access control (AC) mechanisms such as RBAC [20] and XACML [14]. But it differs from them in several aspects that are critical for decentralizing OSNs; the most important of which are: (a) LGI is completely decentralized; and (b) it is fully stateful, which means that it is sensitive to the history of interaction; and (c) LGI control is quite scalable, even for stateful policies. But it should be pointed out that LGI is somewhat incidental to this model, as one can device other kinds of middlewares that can serve this purpose. Consequently, we will not make any systematic comparison here between LGI and other middlewares, because LGI is not the subject of this paper—it is just a tool.

We present here only a partial overview of LGI, focusing on the following key aspects of it, which are most relevant to this paper: (1) the local nature of LGI laws (LGI replaces the term "policy" with the term "law," for a reason not discussed here); and (2) the decentralized enforcement of laws. Another important aspect of LGI is discussed in Section 8. We also give, below, a simple but complete example of an LGI law and on its effect.

A more detailed presentation of this middleware, and a tutorial of it, can be found in its manual [17]—which describes the release of an experimental implementation of LGI. For additional information the reader is referred to a host of published papers, some of which will be cited in due course.

4.1. LGI Laws, and their Local Nature

Although the purpose of LGI is to govern the exchange of messages between different distributed actors, the LGI laws do not do so directly. Rather, a law governs the *interactive activities* of any actor operating under it, in particular, by imposing constraints on the messages that such an actor can send and receive.

A *law* $\mathcal{L}$ is defined over three elements—described with respect to a given actor x that operates under this law: (1) A set E of *interactive events* that may occur at any actor, including the arrival of a message at x, and the sending of a message by it. (2) The *control-state* (or, simply, state) S_x associated with x—which is distinct from the internal state of x, of which the law is oblivious. And (3) a set O of *interactive operations*—such as forwarding a message and accepting one—that can be mandated by a law, to be carried out at x upon the occurrence of interactive events at it.

Now, the role of a law is to decide what should be done in response to the occurrence of any interactive event at an actor operating under it. This decision, with respect to an actor x, is formally defined by the following mapping:

$$E \times S_x \to S_x \times (O)^*. \tag{1}$$

In other words, for any a given (*event, state*) pair, the law mandates a new state, as well as a (possibly empty) sequence of interactive operations to be carried out at x. Note, in particular, that the ruling of the law upon the occurrence of an event depends on the state of x at that moment; and that the same law determines how the state can change. LGI laws are, therefore, *stateful*—i.e., *sensitive to the history of the interactive-events*, at a given actor x. Moreover, although this is not evident from the above abstract definition, an LGI law can be *proactive*, in that it can force some messages to emanate from an actor, under certain circumstances, even if the actor itself did not send such messages—thus these laws can ensure both *safety and liveness* properties.

Note that LGI laws are *local* in the sense that they depends only the occurrence of events at a single actor, and on the interactive state of this actor alone; and a law can effect directly only the interactive behavior of the actor operating under it. It is worth pointing out that although locality constitutes a strict constraint on the structure of LGI laws, it does not reduce their expressive power, as has been proved in [17]. In particular, despite its *structural locality*, an LGI law can have global sway over a set of actors operating under it.

Finally, note that the law is a complete function, so that any mapping of the type defined above is considered a valid law. This means that a law of this form is *inherently self consistent*—although a law can, of course, be wrong in the sense that it may not work as intended by its designer.

About Languages for Writing Laws: Formula 1 is an abstract definition of the semantics of laws. It does not, in particular, specify a language for writing laws. In fact, the current implementation of LGI supports three different *law-languages*, based on Prolog, Java, and JavaScript—respectively. But the choice of language has no effect on the semantics of LGI, as long as the chosen language is sufficiently powerful to specify all possible mappings defined by Formula 1.

Space limitation preclude the description of any of these languages, but to give a sense of how LGI operates, and to illustrate the use of dynamically changing state of agents for establishing coordination protocol, we introduce here a simple but potentially useful law, written in the Prolog-based law-language.

A Law of Polite Conversation—an Example: This law, which we call the *ping-pong* law, or $\mathcal{L}_{PP}$, establishes a communication protocol that may be viewed as supporting polite conversation. Specifically, the effect of this law can be described, informally, as follows: All members of the $\mathcal{L}_{PP}$-community are able to communicate with each other, via messages of the forms ping(M) and pong(M)—with arbitrary text M—subject to the following protocol. Once a member x from this community sends a ping message—representing such things as a request or a question—to another member y, x would not be able to send other pings to y until it gets a reply from y in the form of a pong messages. And y can send only one pong message to x for every ping it gets from it. (The sense in which such exchange may be considered polite is fairly self evident.)

The formal statement of this law—written in the Prolog-based law language of LGI, which is a kind of *event-condition-action* language—is displayed in Figure 1. The gist of this law may be clear from its text, and a complete explanation of it can be found in [17].

```
Preamble: law(PP,language(prolog)).

R1. sent(X,ping(M),Y) :- not(pingTo(Y)@CS),
       do(add(pingTo(Y)),do(forward).

R2. arrived(X,ping(M),Y)
       :- do(add(pingFrom(X))), do(deliver).

R3. sent(X,pong(M),Y) :- pingFrom(Y)@CS,
       do(remove(pingFrom(Y))),do(forward).

R4. arrived(X,pong(M),Y)
       :- do(remove(pingTo(X)@CS)), do(deliver).
```

Figure 1. The Ping-Pong Law

4.2. The Decentralized Law Enforcement, and the Concept of $\mathcal{L}$-agent

The local nature of laws enables their decentralized enforcement, because a law can be enforced on every actor subject to it with no knowledge of, or dependency on, the simultaneous interactive state of any other actor of the system. Such enforcement is scalable even for highly stateful policies that are sensitive to the history of interaction (cf. [18]). Here is how the enforcement of LGI works.

To communicate under a given LGI law $\mathcal{L}$, an actor x needs to engage a generic software entity called *controller*[1], which generally does not reside on the host of its patron x. The controller is built to mediate the interactive activities of any actor that engages it, under any well formed law that the actor chooses. Once such a controller is engaged by an actor x, subject to a law $\mathcal{L}$, it becomes the private mediator for the interactive activities of x, and is denoted by $T_x^{\mathcal{L}}$. The pair $\langle x, T_x^{\mathcal{L}} \rangle$ is called an $\mathcal{L}$-agent—or, more generally an *LGI-agent*, and sometimes simply an *agent*. And a set of interacting $\mathcal{L}$-agent, for a given law $\mathcal{L}$, is called an $\mathcal{L}$-community.

Figure 2 depict the manner in which a pair of agents, operating under possibly different laws, exchange a message. (An agent is depicted here by a dashed oval that includes an actor and its controller.) Note the *dual nature* of control exhibited here: The transfer of a message is first mediated by the sender's controller, subject to the sender's law, and then by the controller of the receiver, subject to its law. This dual control, which is a direct consequence of the local nature of LGI laws, has some important consequences which are beyond the scope of this paper.

Mutual Recognition: It should be pointed out that a pair of interacting LGI-agents can recognize each other as such, and can identify each other law by its one-way hash. This enables them to recognize when they operate under the same law, thus belonging to the same $\mathcal{L}$-community. And if they operate under different laws, they are able to get the text of each other's law.

About the Trustworthiness of Controllers: Consider a set S of agents interacting via LGI, and let T_S be the set of controllers employed by them. T_S is, essentially the *trusted computing base* (TCB) of S. There are several reasons for trusting the controllers in T_S, despite the fact that unlike most TCBs, T_S is to be distributed. Some of these reasons are, briefly, as follows.

First, T_S can be maintained by what is called a *controller service* (CoS), which is to be managed by

---

[1]Controllers can can actually be hosted by *controller-pools*, each of which can host a number of *private controllers*, which may operate under different laws.

Figure 2. Interaction between a pair of LGI–agents, mediated by a pair of controllers under possibly different laws.

some trustworthy company—which may well be the company, or the virtual organization, that uses the CoS as its TCB. Second, controllers are generic and, like language compilers, can be well tested, and thus more trustworthy than the disparate actors that use them. Third, the distributed T_S is more fault tolerant than a single, central, reference monitor, because it does not constitute a single point of failure. And, fourth, T_S is more secure than a central, reference monitor, because it does not constitute a single point of attack.

About Performance: A comprehensive study of the overhead incurred by LGI control had been published in [19]. Broadly speaking, this overhead turns out to be relatively small, often smaller than the overhead incurred by control mechanisms such as XACML— beside being scalable. Moreover, this overhead is quite negligible for communication over WAN. The average contribution to this overhead by the computation in a controller was found—in circa 2000—to be around 50 microseconds. It is considerably lower with the present hardware.

5. A Basic Model of a Decentralized Online Social Community (DOSC)

We introduce here a model of a decentralized OSN that, unlike the DOSN architecture, enables the governance of an OSN via enforced policy—which we call a *law*— that can establish its overall structure and behavior. We call this model DOSC (for *Decentralized Online Social Community*); and we refer to a specific OSN under this model as a *DOSC-community*, or simply a *community*.

The DOSC model is *generic*, and rather abstract, in the sense that it does not have any built-in communal structure. But it can support a wide range of different types of communities, whose structure and behavior is determined by the laws chosen for them. We do, however, present a concrete example of a specific communal structure. This is done in Section 6, and continues with some more advanced communal capabilities in Section 7.1.

The model of DOSC described here is basic. Some more advanced aspects of this model are introduced in Section 8. This section is organized as follows.

Section 5.1 is a definition of this model; Section 5.2 describes the launching of a DOSC-Community; Section 5.3 discusses the manner in which such a community operates; and Section 5.4 discusses the analysis of networks in the decentralized context of DOSC.

5.1. A Definition of a DOSC-Community

A community C under the DOSC-model is defined as a 4-tuple $\langle M, \mathcal{L}, T, S \rangle$, where M is the set of members of C; $\mathcal{L}$ is the law that governs this community, and is often denoted by $\mathcal{L}_C$; T is a set of generic LGI controllers that serve as the middleware trusted to enforce any law $\mathcal{L}$ loaded into them; and S, called the *support* of C, is a set of components that provides various services to community C, and is mostly specific to it. We now elaborate on this definition of the DOSC-model by providing some details about its four elements, and about the relations between them. This overall structure of a DOSC-community is depicted schematically in Figure 3.

The Set M of Members of a community: An individual member x of a community C is a triple $\langle user, mediator, database \rangle$, where *user* is usually a human, operating via some kind of computational platform, like a smart phone; *mediator* is one of the LGI-controllers in T that mediates all interactions between x and other members of C, and which has direct access to both the *user* of x and its database—subject to law $\mathcal{L}_C$; and *database*, is an optional repository of information that is accessible directly only to the mediator of x, as well as to the user himself (but the access of the user to its own database is not subject to the law $\mathcal{L}_C$, as depicted by dashed arrows in Figure 3.

Note that the function of the database of x—if it exists—is to maintain information associated with this member, such as the set of Twitter-like micro-blogs posted by x, or its Facebook-like page—information that may be made accessible to other members, via the mediator, subject to law $\mathcal{L}_C$. All such databases, used by members of a given community, must have the same APIs, which must be consistent with the law of that community. (The tool-set associated with

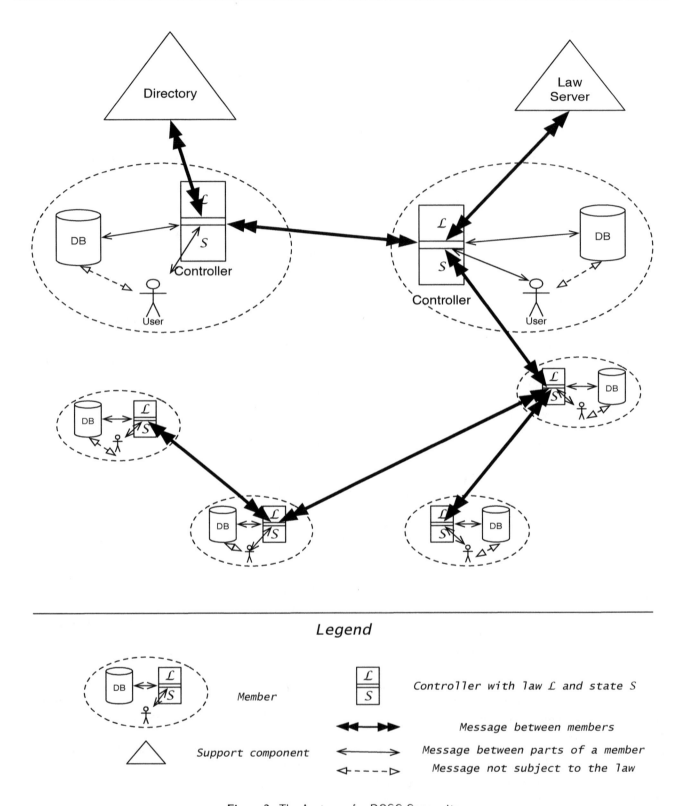

Figure 3. The Anatomy of a DOSC Community

the DOSC-model—which is not part of the definition of this model—contains a tool for constructing and deploying a database, with a default API. But the law of a specific community might require a different API; and

the *support* of that community may contain the means for constructing databases with that API.)

The Law $\mathcal{L}_C$ of community C: This law endows a DOSC-community with its overall structure, in particular by controlling its membership, as well as the interactive behavior of its members. The generality of LGI laws (cf. Section 4) endows this model with great deal of generality regarding the nature of the community governed by it. In particular, suitable laws can make a community behave like our *medical consultation* community *MC*, or like the *WorkPlace* community *WP*. For that matter, laws can be written to create analogs of Facebook or Twitter as well, although our decentralized model would not be able to sustain the present size of such OSNs.

The set T of Controllers: T is meant to be the *trusted computing base* (TCB) of a DOSC. Every user can create its own controller, using the software provided by the released LGI middleware. But if malicious corruption of controllers by their users is of concern, then it is better for the members of a community to adopt controllers created and maintained by a trusted *controller service* (CoS), so that they can authenticate each other as bona fide LGI controllers. For such a CoS to be trusted to provide genuine controllers, this service needs to be managed by a trusted organization. In particular, in the case of bound-community, such as *WP*, the *CoS* may be maintained by the organization in the context of which the community is to operate—as in the case discussed in Section 6. It should be pointed out that the organization that maintains the CoS does not have the kind of access to the data exchanged between the members of the community in question for several reasons. First each individual controller has access only to very small part of the exchanges, and even these are maintained for just a fleeting moment. For more about the privacy and trustworthiness of controllers see Section 4, and the manual of LGI [17].

The Support S of a Given Community C: A DOSC-community C may require various services provided by web-servers that are not themselves member of C; and, with one exception, most of them are not defined by the generic DOSC-model. Such services may be designed specifically for the community at hand, or may exist independently of it. Member of C interacts with such services subject to law $\mathcal{L}_C$, while the services themselves may or may not communicate subject to this or any other LGI-law. The only member of the support of a community that is required by this model is the *law-server LS*, which would contain law $\mathcal{L}_C$, and possibly other laws, as we will see in Section 8. Here are some examples of other services that may belong to S: (a) a certification authority (CA), which may be used for the authentication the various members of the community; (b) a *naming service* that provides unique names of community members; (c) an index service for searching; and (d) a reputation service that maintains the reputation of members of C.

Note that the existence of central support service would not compromise significantly the scalability of a DOSC-community, if it is used relatively rarely. And it would not compromise significantly the privacy of a DOSC-community, if it does not contain sensitive information. The law-server LS is certainly in this category, as it is used only when a new member joins the community, and it is not generally a secret. The other potential parts of the support, such as the naming service, probably belong to this category as well.

The Profile of members—a Convention: Although the DOSC model is generic, and has nothing to say about the structure and behavior of any community operating under it, we introduce here a useful convention. It is about what is commonly called a *profile*. The profile of a member x, which we denote by p_x, is a set of attributes that can be made visible to other members, subject to the law of the community in question. Technically the profile of x is part of the *control-state* maintained by the controller. And the specific attributes that belong to the profile and the manner in which they are created and modified, depend on the law as well. We will see an example of a profile in Section 6.

5.2. The Launching of a DOSC–Community

A specific DOSC-community C is launched by constructing its *foundation*, and then having individual members join it incrementally. The foundation of a community consists of: (1) the law $\mathcal{L}_C$ under which this community is to operate, which is to be placed in the law-server LS; (2) the controller service CoS, whose controllers would enforce this law; and (3) the support S to be used by this particular community. Each of these parts of the foundation of C can be either built specifically for it, or selected from existing such items. In particular, the controller service CoS may be managed and maintained specifically for C, but it may already exists, serving many different DOSC-communities, as well as other applications. And some, or all, parts of the *support S* of C—such as its CA—may have an independent existence, serving other applications.

Once the foundation of C exists, anybody can attempt to join it as a member via the following four steps: First, the user needs to deploy its private database, if it is required by law $\mathcal{L}_C$. Second, the user needs to acquire an LGI-controller from the CoS used by C, and instruct this controller to download law $\mathcal{L}_C$ from the law-server. Third, the user must provide its newly adopted controller with a link to its private database, if any. Finally, the user should *adopt* this controller as its mediator.

Note, however, that the adoption is governed by law $\mathcal{L}_C$, which may require, among other things, certain certificates to be provided by the user. If the user does not satisfy the requirements of law $\mathcal{L}_C$ then the adoption will fail. This is one way for the law to control the membership of a given community.

5.3. The Operation of a DOSC-Community

Consider a member x of a community C sending a message m to another member y. The message first arrives at the controller of x, that operates under law $\mathcal{L}_C$. If this controller forwards the message m to y—note that it may decide to block it—then m first arrives at the controller of y, which decides what to do with it according to law $\mathcal{L}_C$. In other words, members of a community interact with each other via their controllers, and the controllers communicate with each other subject to the law $\mathcal{L}_C$ of the community.

Figure 3 may help understanding the situation. This figure depicts several members, represented by ovals, each of which encloses the three components of a member: the user, its mediator (controller), and its (optional) database. The interaction between members, and between them and the components of the *support* is depicted by the thick arrows. The component parts of a member interact with each other as depicted by the thin arrows, while the doted arrow represent the unregulated access that a user has to its own database.

It is worth pointing out here that LGI provides an important *trust modality* which is critical to this model. This trust modality is called *law-based trust*, or simply *L-trust*, which is based on the following property of LGI: any pair of interacting LGI-controllers can identify, cryptographically, each other as genuine controllers, and can identify the law, under which their interlocutors operate. Now, *L-trust* can be defined as follows: *members of a community C can trust each other's interactive behavior to comply with their common law $\mathcal{L}_C$.*

Another important observation about the behavior of a community under this model needs to be made. The ruling of a law for a given event that occurs at a controller depends on the state of this controller, which may be different for different members. This difference can come from some certificates submitted by the user to its controller, which may authenticate the role of the user in the organization in question. And the state may change dynamically in response to some interactive activity of the community. For example, the manager of the community under our *WP* community, may be allowed by the law of *WP* community to transfer its managerial baton to some other member, which would then be able to send leave messages, introduced in

Section 3. In other words, *the members of a community C may not be equal under its law $\mathcal{L}_C$.*

5.4. On the Analysis of Networks

In the context of OSN, a *network* means a graph generated by relationships between members, such as *following* in Twitter, and *friend* in Facebook. Such relationships can be easily represented in a DOSC by suitable attributes in the profile of members. Unfortunately, the analysis of the resulting graph is very hard in our context because it is highly distributed. However, if such a graph is not considered very sensitive—for example, if members would not mind if the information about whom they *follow* would be revealed to the public—then analysis of such a graph can be facilitated in the following way.

First, one builds into the support of the community a service called *Gr*, say. Second the law of the community should be written to ensure that *Gr* would be notified whenever the *following* relation (for example) is established or removed. So, the entire graph would be represented in the *Gr* service, and it can be analyzed fairly easily by it.

And note that the use of such a central service as part of a decentralized community does not make the community significantly less scalable. Because communication with *Gr* is done relatively rarely, and because it is essentially off line—since *Gr* itself, which receives all these messages, is not part of the community itself.

Of course, if the graph in question is too sensitive to be placed in a central service, this analysis cannot be done. But this would not be a big loss for many, if not most, member of a DOSC. First, it seems to us that network analysis is of interest mostly to researchers rather to the users of an OSN. And second, such analysis is less interesting for small and medium size OSNs—the domain of DOSC—than for the huge OSNs like Facebook and Twitter.

6. Basic Capabilities of DOSC—an Implemented Case Study

This is the first part of a description of an implemented case study, which is meant to serve as a proof of concept of the DOSC architecture. It also serves here as a concrete example of the rather abstract model of DOSC provided above. This case study deals with the *WP* community, broadly introduces in Section 2.2; which is designed to operate in the context of a large and geographically distributed enterprise E, providing a micro-blogging for its employees. *WP* has been tested with slightly more than two hundred, mostly simulated, members. This section describes the implementation of some basic capabilities of DOSC;

The implementation of more advanced capabilities are discussed in Section 7.

We start this section with a presentation of the *support* of the *WP* community; and then, in Section 6.2, we describe various structural and behavioral aspects of it.

6.1. The Support of the *WP* Community

As mentioned in Section 5, a DOSC-community may require various services. Our *WP* community employs the following three services: a *law-server* (*LS*), a *certification authority* (CA), and a *naming service*, which we call the *secretary* of this community.

The law-server, which has been introduced in Section 5, maintains the law of this community. The CA issues digital certificates to the employees of *E*, certifying some of their attributes, such as their unique names within *E*, the role they play within this enterprise, etc. Finally, the secretary plays several roles in this community. First, it receives and maintains the certified name of every new member of *WP*. Second, it ensures that a given employee can be a member of *WP* just once. And third, the secretary serves as a *location service*, which is available for use by all members to *WP*. We do not show here the detailed implementation of such a secretary, and its use. But such details are provided by [30], where we also show how a secretary can implement pseudonymous naming structure.

6.2. On the Structural and Behavioral Nature of the *WP* Community

We start with some comments about the pseudo code we use for describing the law that governs this community. We then discuss how a user becomes a member of the *WP* community and its groups, how it configures its profile, and how a member is removed. Finally, we discuss one of the forms of communication between members, and how it is regulated.

On the Description of the Law of the *WP* Community:. We describe here the law $\mathcal{L}_{WP}$ of the *WP* community via a pseudo-code consisting of *event-condition-action* rules. This informal code is fairly close to the the Prolog-based law-language of LGI. The *event-condition-action* rules that constitute the pseudo-code used below have the form:

$$\textbf{UPON} \ <e> \ \textbf{IF} \ <c> \ \textbf{DO} \ <[o]>$$

where e is an interactive event that occurs at one of the members of the community—or, more precisely, at the controller of this member; c is the condition of this rule, defined over the event itself, and over the state of the controller at hand; and [o], the action, is a list of one or more primitive operations. These rules are evaluated from top down, until the condition of one of

them succeed—the action o of this rules is the ruling of this law.

Also, the following notations are used in this pseudo-code: (a) sent(x,m,y) denotes a *sent* event, namely the sending the message m by x to y; (b) arrived(x,m,y) denotes an *arrived* event, namely the arrival at agent y of message m from x; (c) forward(x,m,y) denoted the primitive operation that forwards message m from x to y; (d) deliver represents a permission for the actor to accept the message arriving at it; (e) add(t) operation adds term t to the control-state; and (f) remove(t) operation removes from the control-state a term that matches t, if any.

The law $\mathcal{L}_{WP}$—described via this pseudo code—is split into several parts, according to their functionalities. For the sake of brevity, we introduce here only the parts of $\mathcal{L}_{WP}$ that deal with the functionalities discussed here.

Member Profile and Membership Control:. What we call a *profile* of a member is a set of attributes maintained in its control-state, that is, the state maintained by the controller of this member. All these attributes are visible to the law of this DOSC, and can be made visible to other members of the DOSC, subject to its law. We distinguish between three types of these attributes: (a) *Authenticated Attributes*; (b) *Discretionary Attributes*; and (c) *Controlled Attributes*. The *Authenticated Attributes* are those provided by the certificate used by an employee for joining this community. They include the name of the employee, its role, and the group (or groups) to which it belongs, etc. These attributes are not mutable, and can thus be easily used for indexing. But we have implemented here only name-based index, provided by the secretary. The *Discretionary Attributes* are those that a member can define and modify at will, to be visible by all members of the DOSC—they may contain such things as the interest or expertise of the member. Finally, the *Controlled Attributes* are those whose very existence, and the manner they are defined and updated is governed by the law—they include, in particular, a *follower* list and a list of last ten posts the member published.

Now, to join the community, a member needs to adopt a controller under law $\mathcal{L}_{WP}$. Rule $\mathcal{R}1$ allows a user to join the community by presenting a certificate signed by the CA employed by the enterprise in question, to authenticate its employees. Once certificate is verified by the controller, the set of attributes will be inserted into the user's profile. An example of an attribute is *role(manager)*. The certified name gets sent to the secretary of the naming service. Rule $\mathcal{R}2$ enables a member to add discretionary attributes to its profile, and Rule $\mathcal{R}3$ enables their update.

Rule $\mathcal{R}4$ enables a member to add an attribute called *filter* to its control-state. As we shall see below, the filter

```
R1. UPON adopted(X,cert(issuer(ca),
        subj(X),attr(A)))
        DO[ add(A), forward(X, A(name(N)),
        Secretary)]

R2. UPON sent(X,
        addProfile(Attribute(Value)),X)
        IF ¬ (Attribute in
        reservedAttributes)
        DO[add(Attribute(Value))]

R3. UPON sent(X,
        updateProfile(Attribute(Value)),X)
        IF ¬ (Attribute in
        reservedAttributes)
        DO[remove(Attribute),
        add(Attribute(Value))]

R4. UPON sent(X,
        addFilter(Attribute(Value)),X)
        DO[add(filter(Attribute(Value)))]

R5. UPON sent(X,#leave#,Y)
        IF role(manager)@p_x DO[forward]

R6. UPON arrived(X,#leave#,Y)
        DO[Quit]
```

Figure 4. Law $\mathcal{L}_{WP}$: Member's Profile and Membership Control

will provide the means for the member in question to block a specified set of members from following him.

Finally, rules $R5$ and $R6$ regulate the removal of members from the community. Rule $R5$ enables only a manager can remove a member from the community, by sending the message *leave* to it—which, according to Rule $R6$, would cause the removal of this member from the community. Non-managers are not allowed to to send the messages *leave*.

Communication:. There are three modes of communication in this community: direct messaging, post/follow and narrowcasting. Direct messaging allows members to send messages to each other when specifying the address of the receiver as the destination. Post/follow is an analogy to Twitter's tweet/follow mechanism, where members can subscribe to another member and get notification when there is a new post. Narrowcasting is a mechanism for sending a message to a group of members whose profile satisfies a specified condition. All messages and post in this system have a *type* associated with them, which is analogous to the concept of *hashtag* in twitter. For the sake of simplicity, we discuss here only the details of post/follow, and we discuss narrowcasting in Section 7.1—we do not discuss in this

paper the simplest of these modes of communication, i.e., direct messaging.

The control over communication via post/follow has two complementary parts: *global* and *local*. The global control is imposed on every member of the community, but can be sensitive to the profile of members, while the local control is discretionary to each member. We discuss both controls below, and the law that establishes them.

```
R7. UPON sent(X,requestFollowing,Y)
        DO[forward(X,requestFollowing(p_x),
        Y)]

R8. UPON
        arrived(X,requestFollowing(p_x),Y)
        IF G(p_x, p_y) and ( filter(F)@CS
        and F(p_x) )
        DO[updateFollowerList]

R9. UPON sent(X,post(P),X)
        IF typeof(P) = ¬#management#
        or ( typeof(P) = #management# and
        role(manager)@p_x )
        DO[updateProfile(lastTenPosts(P)),
        updateDB(P),
        forward(X,P,followerList)]

R10.
    UPON arrived(X,P,Y)
        DO[deliver]
```

Figure 5. Law $\mathcal{L}_{WP}$: Communication

Global Control: The global control over post/follow is imposed on both posting and following. The control over posting is on what types of posts members can send. For example, only managerial staff can send posts with type *management*.

The control on following regulates who can follow whom. Essentially, it is defined in the law by a constraint on the profiles of publisher and follower. An example of such global policies is that only the members from a same group can talk to each other. The problem is that there is no single place where these profiles can be evaluated because of the decentralization. To solve this problem, our law forces every following request to include the profile of the follower. And then the constraint will be evaluated at the publisher side. The example we just mentioned can be achieved by checking the profiles of the publisher and follower and rejecting the following request if the two members are from different groups.

Local Control: If one does not want to be followed by certain members, it can block the `following` requests from them. To achieve this, a member can add a term *filter* to its control-state, which is a local constraint on the profile of the would be follower. Whenever a member f sends a `following` request to a member s, it will be forced to attach its profile p_f along with it. When the request arrives at the publisher's controller, f will not be added to s's `follower` list if its profile does not satisfy the filter.

The Law: The rules of law $\mathcal{L}_{WP}$ that implements these provisions are defined in Figure 5 and described below.

According to Rule $\mathcal{R}7$, any one can send a `following` request to any member. The controller will attach its profile to the request. By Rule $\mathcal{R}8$, when the request arrives at a member, the controller checks whether the global constraint, denoted by G in the law, on the profiles of publisher and `following` requester is satisfied. Then the controller will also check whether there is a *filter* in its profile. If there is none, the controller can add the requester to the `follower` list. If there is a *filter*, the controller will examine whether the filter on the profile of the requester. If both conditions are satisfied, the controller will add the requester to the `follower` list.

In Rule $\mathcal{R}9$, when a member wants to send a post to its followers, the controller will read its `follower` list and send the post to each of them. It will also update its database and an attribute called *lastTenPosts* in its profile. A management post is allowed to be sent only when the publisher has the attribute *role(manager)* in its profile. When the follower receives the post, according to the Rule $\mathcal{R}10$, controller will deliver the post to it.

7. Privacy-Preserving Narrowcasting and Profile-Based Search—the Case Study Continued

We introduce in this section two important capabilities available under the basic model of DOSC. They have been fully implemented in our case study, but omitted from Section 6 for the sake of simplicity. These capabilities are: (1) privacy-preserving narrowcasting; and (2) profile-based search, which is really an application of narrowcasting. Both of these capabilities are essential for many kind of OSNs, and are not available under DOSN.

7.1. Privacy-Preserving Narrowcasting

By the term narrowcasting we mean here the delivery of a message to a subset of the membership of a community, consisting of the members whose profile satisfies a given condition. We define a *narrowcast* as a pair $\langle M, C \rangle$, where M is the messages to be delivered to every community member x, whose profile

p_x satisfies condition C. This is obviously very useful mode of communication, particularly for fairly large OSNs, where members are generally not familiar with most of their peers, but may knows what *kind of people* they wants to communicate with.

It is easy to provide for narrowcasting in centralized OSN, because its host has direct access to all profiles of the members of a community in question. But it is problematic under decentralized OSN, whose profiles are maintained locally at each member. Yet, narrowcasting can be accomplished reasonably well even in a decentralized OSN via what is called *gossip* (or *flooding*) protocol. We will not describe here the Gossip protocol in details, except of saying that it is analogous to the real life process of gossip. But the following aspect of this protocol is important for what follows. Although the message M of a narrowcast $\langle M, C \rangle$, is to be delivered only to its intended targets—i.e., to the community members whose profile satisfies condition C—practically all members of the community need to participate in the transfer of this message to its targets. We call these non-target participants in the gossip of a given narrowcast its *conveyors*, as their role is to help in the transmission of message M to its various targets.

The gossip protocol has two well known drawbacks, which are not very serious for its use in OSNs. First, gossip is not a very efficient way to do either narrowcasting or broadcasting. But the experience of Gnutella [21] with gossip, and our own experience with it [15] demonstrated that if the gossip protocol is carried out correctly by all its participants, its speed is sufficient for human interaction, even for fairly large communities with tens of thousands of members. Second, gossip-based narrowcasting is likely to miss a small percentage of its targets. But this is not considered a serious problem for many applications.

There are, however, two additional problems with gossip-based narrowcasting, which cannot be addressed under the DOSN architecture, but can be addressed under DOSC, because of its ability to impose constraints on the interaction between its members.

One of these problems is that the gossip protocol can be seriously undermined by the malicious or inadvertent misbehavior of even one of its participants. But as we have shown in [15] this problem can be addressed by defining a key part of this protocol via an LGI law, which is imposed on all participants in the gossip process. The second problem is that he gossip process poses a serious risk to the privacy of members. We describe this risk below, along with a way to counter it.

The Risk to Privacy posed by gossip-based Narrowcasting, and its Mitigation: The risk to privacy in question is that once a conveyor gets a narrowcast $\langle M, C \rangle$, to convey to others, *it can read it itself*, although a narrowcast is intended only for its targets, and not for its conveyors. This is a massive privacy violation as the number of conveyors for a given narrowcast is likely to be far higher than the number of its targets; and all of them can get information not intended for them.

But this problem can be solved under DOSC, because under this architecture, it would be the *mediator* part of the conveyor that gets the narrowcast, not its user. And the mediator is a trustworthy LGI controller that operates subject to the law $\mathcal{L}$ of the community in question. So, one can prevent this privacy violation by writing this law to have a conveyor to just convey this message according to the gossip-protocol, but not to deliver it to its own user. Law $\mathcal{L}_{WP}$ of the WP community, introduced in Section 6, supports narrowcasting in this way, although this part of $\mathcal{L}_{WP}$ has not been discussed in that section. A simplified version of the part of $\mathcal{L}_{WP}$ that handles narrowcasting is displayed in Figure 6.

$\mathcal{R}$11.

    UPON sent(X,narrowcast(M,C),X)
        DO[forward(X, narrowcast(M,C,p_x), X)]

$\mathcal{R}$12.

    UPON arrived(X,narrowcast(M,C,p_x),Y)
        IF C(p_y)
        DO[deliver,
        forward(Y, narrowcast(M,C,p_x),
        followerList)]

$\mathcal{R}$13.

    UPON arrived(X,narrowcast(M,C,p_x),Y)
        IF ¬C(p_y)
        DO[forward(Y, narrowcast(M,C,p_x),
        followerList)]

Figure 6. Law $\mathcal{L}_{WP}$: Narrowcast

Here is how narrowcasting operates under the this simplified part of $\mathcal{L}_{WP}$. First, a narrowcast $\langle M, C \rangle$, is initiated by a member x_0 sending the message narrowcast(M,C) to itself, and Rule $\mathcal{R}$11 attaches the profile of the initiator x_0 to this message.

Second, the arrival of this message at any member y, who may be the initiator x_0, is handled by Rule $\mathcal{R}$12 and if this rule fails, then by Rule $\mathcal{R}$13. Rule $\mathcal{R}$12, succeeds if condition $C(p_y)$ is satisfied, that is, if y is a target. The ruling of this rule will be to deliver the message to y, and then to "gossip" it to its set of followers (actually to a relatively small part of the followers, but we are simplifying here). Alternatively, Rule $\mathcal{R}$13 will be evaluated and will succeed because now the the condition $C(p_y)$ is not satisfied, and its ruling is *not to*

deliver this message to y, because y is not a target, but to gossip it farther.

Note, however that this partial version of the treatment of narrowcasting is oversimplified to the point of being incorrect. It is incorrect because it does not have any way of stopping the gossip process. This is provided by the actual gossip protocol, which is part law $\mathcal{L}_{WP}$; this protocol also ensures that the narrowcasting would not overwhelm the whole community. There are two further aspects of law $\mathcal{L}_{WP}$ which are missing here. One is the imposition of a global constrain on who can target whom by narrowcasting. Second this law enables the arrival of a narrowcast at its nominal target to be blocked by the local filter defined by his target.

Finally, one has to take into account the unlikely possibility that a controller t serving as the mediator of member x has been corrupted so that would deliver to its user all narrowcasts arriving at it, whether x is their target or not. In this way the user of x would siphon in practically all narrowcast communication between members of the community, which could be a massive violation of privacy, of practically all members of the community.

This risk to privacy can be mitigated by systematically and periodically replacing the controller of every member of a community, with a fresh controller—which can be done while the community operates. The code of the replaced controller can then be refreshed, and these controllers can be reused to serve other members. In this way, a corrupt controller would have only a relatively short span of time for getting illegal messages.

7.2. Profile–Based Search

Profile-based search is a necessary capability for any but the smallest OSNs. One can provide for such a search in a decentralized OSN simply by maintaining the profiles of all he members of the community in a central database. But this would endanger the privacy of community member. This is probably the reason why none of the proposed DOSNs support such search.

Fortunately, under DOSC, profile based search can be carried out via narrowcasting, in the following way: the message M delivered to the group of peers whose profile satisfies condition C can be a request to all of them to identify themselves via a return message.

8. Hierarchical Organization of DOSCs—an Extension of the Basic DOSC Model

Communities under our basic DOSC model are *monolithic*, in a sense that their structure is defined by a single law. Such a law may distinguish between members based on their profile. For example, the law of the WP community, uses this method to make distinctions between its members based on the groups to which they belong. But it could be useful for large and heterogeneous community to provide its subgroups with a limited of autonomy—i.e., the freedom to define their all laws, and to change them at will, while conforming to the law of the community at large. Such capabilities of DOSCs can be established via the concept of *conformance hierarchy of laws* of LGI [4], which is described broadly in Section 8.1.

We then introduce briefly two different, and very beneficial, extensions of the basic DOSC model, whose implementation is beyond the scope of this paper. The first of these, discussed in Section 8.2, enables the handling of very complex Multi-Group DOSCs.The second extension, discussed in Section 8.3, enables the support of families of DOSC-communities.

8.1. The Concept of Conformance Hierarchy

LGI enables the organization of a collection of laws into what is called a *conformance hierarchy*. This is a tree of laws, rooted by law called $\mathcal{L}_R$, in which every law, except of the root $\mathcal{L}_R$ itself, conforms transitively to its superior laws, in a sense to be described below. Moreover the conformance relation between laws is inherent in the hierarchy, requiring no extra validation. For a formal definition of such hierarchy of laws, and a detailed example of its use, see [4]; here we provide just an informal introduction of this concept.

Under access control [5, 14], the conventional view of conformance between policies is as follows: *policy P' conforms to policy P if and only if P' is more restrictive than P, or equal to it.* But this simple view of conformance would not do for LGI-laws, for the following reason: The ruling of an LGI-law is not confined to a decision whether to approve or reject an action by an actor; it can also require some other actions to be carried out in response to an event—such as changing the state of the acting agent in a specified manner, or changing the message being sent, and its target,in some way. And it is generally not meaningful to ask if one such action is more or less restrictive than another. So, instead of using a uniform definition of conformance, based on restrictiveness, LGI lets each law define what it means for its subordinates to conform to it. This is done, broadly, as follows.

A law that belongs to a conformance hierarchy has two parts, called the *ground* part and the *meta* part. The ground part of a law $\mathcal{L}$ imposes constraints on interactive behavior of the actors operating directly under this law—it has the structure defined by Formula 1. While the meta part of $\mathcal{L}$ circumscribes the extent to which laws subordinate to $\mathcal{L}$ are allowed to deviate from its ground and meta parts. In particular, this allows a law, anywhere in this hierarchy, to make any of its provisions *irreversible* by any of its

subordinate law, by not permitting any deviation from it, by any of its subordinate laws. But it can also permit subordinates to either weaken or strengthen some of its own provisions.

One application of such conformance is setting out defaults. For example, the root law $\mathcal{L}_R$ may prohibit all interaction between actors, while enabling subordinate laws to permit such interaction, perhaps under certain conditions. Alternatively, law $\mathcal{L}_R$ may permit all interaction, while enabling subordinate laws to prohibit selected interactions.

On the Structure and Formation of a Conformance Hierarchy of Laws: A conformance hierarchy H is formed incrementally via a recursive process described informally below. First one creates the root law $\mathcal{L}_R$ of H. Second, given a law $\mathcal{L}$ already in H, one defines a law $\mathcal{L}'$, subordinate to $\mathcal{L}$, by means of a law-like text called *delta*, denoted by $\Delta(\mathcal{L},\mathcal{L}')$, which specifies the intended differences between $\mathcal{L}'$ and $\mathcal{L}$. Now, law $\mathcal{L}'$ is derived dynamically from law $\mathcal{L}$ and $\Delta(\mathcal{L},\mathcal{L}')$, essentially *by dynamic consultation*, as described informally below.

Consider the special case involving the root law $\mathcal{L}_R$, and its subordinate law $\mathcal{L}_s$ derived from $\mathcal{L}_R$ by the delta $\Delta(\mathcal{L}_R,\mathcal{L}_s)$. And consider an agent x operating under law $\mathcal{L}_s$. Now, when an event e occurs at an agent x it is first submitted to law $\mathcal{L}_R$ for evaluation. Law $\mathcal{L}_R$ may consult the delta $\Delta(\mathcal{L}_R,\mathcal{L}_s)$ of $\mathcal{L}_s$ before deciding on its ruling—although it may, instead, render its own ruling, not involving the delta. If consulted, the delta will do its own evaluation of this event, and will return its *advice* about the ruling to law $\mathcal{L}_R$. $\mathcal{L}_R$ would render its final ruling about how to respond to event e, taking the advice of the delta into account—but not necessarily accepting it, because this advice might contradict the meta part of $\mathcal{L}_R$. In this way, *the dynamically derived law $\mathcal{L}_s$ naturally conforms to its superior law $\mathcal{L}_R$, requiring no further verification.*

A notable property of the hierarchical organization of laws is that interacting agents operating under laws in a common hierarchy can identify the position of each other's laws within this hierarchy.

8.2. Handling Complex Multi-Group DOSCs

Consider a DOSC-community WP', which is similar to community WP presented in Section 6, except that it is governed by a hierarchical law-ensemble H like the one depicted in Figure 7. People who belong to group $g1$, for example, are meant to operate subject law $\mathcal{L}_{g1}$, while people who belong to subgroup $g11$ are meant to operate under law $\mathcal{L}_{g11}$; and those who belong to the enterprise in question, but not to any of these groups are meant to operate subject to the root law $\mathcal{L}_R$. These laws may accept only the people who certify themselves

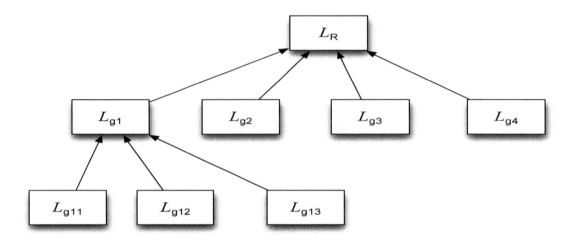

Figure 7. A Hierarchical Law-Ensemble that Governs a Complex DOSC-Community

as belonging to the enterprise at large, and to a specific group, if any.

Law $\mathcal{L}_R$ of H would be written to establish the various provisions that are to be shared by all groups. Such as membership control in the community at large, and the various modes of communication like direct messaging and narrowcasting. It might also regulate the inter-group communication. The laws of a particular group, can provide control over the membership in this group, as well as over its intra-group communication.

Note that the creation of a new group to WP' can be done very flexibly—unless this is prohibited by the root law—without changing anything else in this community. Every such addition requires the creation of a new law, as subordinate of law $\mathcal{L}_R$. The changing of the law of a group is similarly flexible.

A very important consequence of such hierarchical organization of laws is that it facilitates seamless interoperability between different groups, provided that the laws of the respective groups permits exchange of messages between them on the basis that they both conform to the root law. This would be possible, however, only if such interoperability is not prohibited by the root law. For much more about this interoperability, and its advantages, the read is referred to [4].

8.3. Supporting Families of DOSC-Based Communities

Consider a family of DOSCs—such as support groups of people who suffer from various diseases—which may have nothing to do with each other but have similar structures. For example they may require similar capabilities, such as narrowcasting, and may used the same mode of addressing, such as anonymous. But despite such similarities, the individual DOSCs may want to establish their own structure. In particular, it

is likely that each such DOSC would want to establish its own membership control.

This can be easily accomplished via a conformance hierarchy H, whose root law includes what is common to a given family of DOSCs, while each individual DOSC in this family has its own provision formulated by a law subordinate to the root of H. This arrangement can be facilitated by having the entire hierarchy H maintained by a single publicly available law-server. The structure and API of such a law-server would depend on the nature of the family of DOSC that it serves.

9. On the Performance of DOSC, its Drawbacks, and an Open Problem Raised by it

Performance: Recall that in a paragraph called "performance" in Section 4.2 we reported that the the overhead incurred by LGI controllers is relatively small—often smaller than the overhead incurred by control mechanisms such as XACML. And given that the computation time of a controller is about 50 microseconds, depending on the complexity of the law in question, it is quite negligible for communication over WAN. Moreover, the enforcement of laws is scalable, being decentralized.

That said, certain operations such as narrowcasting and profile-based search, which require access to all members of the community, are clearly less efficient under DOSC than under the centralized OSN. And they are not scalable under DOSC. Yet for small and medium size communities (up to few scores of thousands of members), the narrowcasting generally concludes virtually instantaneously, from the viewpoint of a human user. We have using DOSC-like control over narrowcasting in Gnutella [21], which had close to 20 thousands of distributed members, and the response was almost instantaneous. Of course this would not be the case with a community of the size of the membership of Facebook.

Drawbacks: Besides the limited scalability of narrow-casting, we see two limitations of DOSC. The first of these can be viewed as an advantage, and the second is fairly minor. The first limitation is that unlike a centralized OSN, DOSC does not lend itself to an analysis of everything that happened in the community in the past, because the history of the communication between community members is not maintained. This is a problem for researchers who wish to study such communities, but one may view as an advantage to most community members, for privacy reasons.

The second limitation of DOSC is for communities that requires its members to maintain a database of their past contributions, as is required by our case study of the *WP* community. A centralized OSN would keep such contribution on their web site. But DOSC requires each member to have its own database maintained somewhere, and be more or less always available. However, the easy and cheap availability of space on the cloud makes this limitation of little importance. Besides, some DOSCs—like the medical consultation community *MC* described in Section 2.1, which has also been implemented as a DOSC—are just conversational, and do not require any databases.

On the Evolution of the Law of a DOSC, while the Community Operates—an Open Problem: Like any other piece of software, the law of a DOSC is bound to change. The problem addressed here is how to enable safe change of the law of a given community while this community continues to operate. We refer to such a change as being *in vivo* (i.e., carried out in a living organism, as it where). The importance of such evolution for a long lived system that must operate continuously is self evident.

The main difficulty with carrying out in-vivo evolution of laws stems from the decentralized nature of our enforcement mechanism. This means, in particular, that in order to update a law $\mathcal{L}$ to $\mathcal{L}'$ one needs to update the law in all controllers associated with actors operating under law $\mathcal{L}$ in a *virtually atomic* manner. By "virtually atomic" we mean, in particular, that during the distributed update process no functionally meaningful messages should be exchanged between agents operating under different versions of the law. We have solved [23] this problem for a group of agents operating under a single law. But the in vivo evolution of laws belonging to an hierarchical law ensemble is still an open problem.

10. Related work

The concern about the privacy issues of centralized OSNs motivated several attempts to decentralize them, creating several versions of DOSNs. These include PeerSoN[6–9, 24], Safebook[10–12], and LotusNet [2, 3]; as well as some others [1, 13, 16, 22, 25, 26, 29]. The basic idea underlying all these projects is that each member of the social networks keeps the data under its own control, instead of surrendering it to a central host. This is a necessary measure of decentralization, but it is not sufficient. As explain in Section 1, OSNs need to be governed by policies (or, in our terminology, laws) regarding their membership and the interactions between its members. But none of the variants of DOSNs known to us provides any means for establishing such global policies. Consequently, they are unable to provide privacy-preserving narrowcasting and profile-based search—capabilities that are very important for OSNs.

Moreover, the indexes provided by many of the DOSN variants, are based on *distributed hash table* (DHT), whose components are managed by the members of the DOSNs at hand. But these members are heterogeneous, and not particularly reliable or trustworthy, and any one of them can compromise the DHT, either inadvertently or maliciously, as has been argued in [27]. In fact, a DHT can be made much more secure under DOSC, if it is managed subject to an appropriate law, like the rest of a DOSC-community. We did not do it in this paper. Instead, we implemented our name-index via a central service, which can be made much more secure than DHT under DOSNs.

10.1. Relationships of this Paper to Previous Work by the Authors

Besides the use of the LGI—our own middleware—as a basis for DOSC, we have published three papers that are related to social networks, and one of them is a direct precursor to the present work.

The first of these papers [15] implemented essentially our medical consultation *MC* example of an OSN in Section 2.1. It was done in a decentralized manner, providing secure gossip-based communication, but without the mechanism used here for ensuring that conveyors do not read all messages. The second paper [30] implemented some aspects of our WorkPlace *WP* example of an OSN in Section 2.2. Neither of these papers introduced a generic model of decentralized OSNs—not surprising, perhaps, as these papers were written before the concept of OSN became popular, or before it existed. The third paper [28] is a direct precursor of the present one, as it introduced what we call here the "basic DOSC model."

The main novelties of the present paper relative to our previous work: These novelties are mainly: (1) privacy-preserving narrowcasting; (2) privacy-preserving profile-based search; and (3) the hierarchical structure of DOSC. mentioned above, is the advanced model of DOSC introduced in Section 7.

11. Conclusion

The centralized nature of conventional OSNs poses serious risks to the privacy and security of information exchanged between their members. These risks prompted several attempts to create decentralized OSNs, or DOSNs. The basic idea underlying these attempts, is that each member of a social network keeps its data under its own control, instead of surrendering it to a central host; providing access to it to other members according to its own access-control policy. Unfortunately all existing versions of DOSNs have a very serious limitation. Namely, they are unable to subject the membership of a DOSN, and the interaction between its members, to any global policy—which is essential for many social communities. Moreover, the DOSN architecture is unable to support useful capabilities such as narrowcasting and profile-based search.

We described in this paper a novel architecture of decentralized OSNs—called *DOSC*, for "online social community". DOSC adopts the decentralization idea underlying DOSNs, but it is able to subject the membership of a DOSC-community, and the interaction between its members, to a wide range of policies—including privacy-preserving narrowcasting and profile-sensitive search. Moreover, DOSC's control over the interaction between its members is scalable. Furthermore, DOSC provides flexible supports for complex, multi-group, communities; as well as to families of distinct communities.

References

[1] S. M. A. Abbas, J. A. Pouwelse, D. H. J. Epema, and H. J. Sips. A gossip-based distributed social networking system. In *Proceedings of the 2009 18th IEEE International Workshops on Enabling Technologies: Infrastructures for Collaborative Enterprises*, WETICE '09, pages 93–98, Washington, DC, USA, 2009. IEEE Computer Society.

[2] Luca M. Aiello and Giancarlo Ruffo. LotusNet: Tunable privacy for distributed online social network services. *Computer Communications*, December 2010.

[3] Luca Maria Aiello and Giancarlo Ruffo. Secure and flexible framework for decentralized social network services. In *Pervasive Computing and Communications Workshops (PERCOM Workshops), 2010 8th IEEE International Conference on*, pages 594–599. IEEE, 2010.

[4] Xuhui Ao and Naftaly H Minsky. Flexible regulation of distributed coalitions. In *Computer Security–ESORICS 2003*, pages 39–60. Springer, unknown, 2003.

[5] A. Belokosztolszki and K. Moody. Meta-policies for distributed role-based access control systems. In *Proc. of the IEEE 3rd International Workshop on Policies, Monterey, California*, pages 106–15, June 2002.

[6] Oleksandr Bodriagov and Sonja Buchegger. Encryption for peer-to-peer social networks. In *SocialCom/PASSAT*, pages 1302–1309. IEEE, 2011.

[7] Oleksandr Bodriagov and Sonja Buchegger. P2p social networks with broadcast encryption protected privacy. In *Privacy and Identity Management for Life*, pages 197–206. Springer, 2012.

[8] Sonja Buchegger and Anwitaman Datta. A case for p2p infrastructure for social networks - opportunities & challenges. In *Proceedings of the Sixth international conference on Wireless On-Demand Network Systems and Services*, WONS'09, pages 149–156, Piscataway, NJ, USA, 2009. IEEE Press.

[9] Sonja Buchegger, Doris Schiöberg, Le-Hung Vu, and Anwitaman Datta. Peerson: P2p social networking: early experiences and insights. In *Proceedings of the Second ACM EuroSys Workshop on Social Network Systems*, SNS '09, pages 46–52, New York, NY, USA, 2009. ACM.

[10] L. A. Cutillo, R. Molva, and T. Strufe. Safebook: A privacy-preserving online social network leveraging on real-life trust. *Comm. Mag.*, 47(12):94–101, December 2009.

[11] Leucio Antonio Cutillo, Refik Molva, and Thorsten Strufe. Safebook: Feasibility of transitive cooperation for privacy on a decentralized social network. In *WOWMOM*, pages 1–6. IEEE, 2009.

[12] LeucioAntonio Cutillo, Refik Molva, and Thorsten Strufe. On the security and feasibility of safebook: A distributed privacy-preserving online social network. In Michele Bezzi, Penny Duquenoy, Simone Fischer-Hãijbner, Marit Hansen, and Ge Zhang, editors, *Privacy and Identity Management for Life*, volume 320 of *IFIP Advances in Information and Communication Technology*, pages 86–101. Springer Berlin Heidelberg, 2010.

[13] Anwitaman Datta, Sonja Buchegger, Le-Hung Vu, Thorsten Strufe, and Krzysztof Rzadca. Decentralized online social networks. In *Handbook of Social Network Technologies and Applications*, pages 349–378. Springer, 2010.

[14] S. Godic and T. Moses. Oasis extensible access control. markup language (xacml), version 2. Technical report, Oasis, March 2005.

[15] M. Ionescu, Naftaly H. Minsky, and T. Nguyen. Enforcement of communal policies for peer-to-peer systems. In *Proc. of the Sixth International Conference on Coordination Models and Languages, Pisa Italy*, February 2004.

[16] Andreas Loupasakis, Nikos Ntarmos, and Peter Triantafillou. exo: Decentralized autonomous scalable social networking. In *CIDR*, pages 85–95, 2011.

[17] Naftaly H. Minsky. *Law Governed Interaction (LGI): A Distributed Coordination and Control Mechanism (An Introduction, and a Reference Manual)*. Rutgers, February 2006. (available at http://www.moses.rutgers.edu/).

[18] Naftaly H Minsky. Decentralized governance of distributed systems via interaction control. In *Logic Programs, Norms and Action*, pages 374–400. Springer, unknown, September 2012.

[19] Naftaly H. Minsky and V. Ungureanu. Law-governed interaction: a coordination and control mechanism for heterogeneous distributed systems. *TOSEM, ACM Transactions on Software Engineering and Methodology*, 9(3):273–305, July 2000.

[20] S. Osborn, R. Sandhu, and Q. Munawer. Configuring role-based access control to enforce mandatory and discretionary access control policies. *ACM Transactions on Information and System Security*, 3(2):85–106, May 2000.

[21] Matei Ripeanu. Peer-to-peer architecture case study: Gnutella network. In *Peer-to-Peer Computing, 2001. Proceedings. First International Conference on*, pages 99–100. IEEE, 2001.

[22] Daniel Sandler and Dan S. Wallach. Birds of a fethr: open, decentralized micropublishing. In Rodrigo Rodrigues and Keith W. Ross, editors, *IPTPS*, page 1. USENIX, 2009.

[23] C. Serban and Naftaly Minsky. In vivo evolution of policies that govern a distributed system. In *Proc. of the IEEE International Symposium on Policies for Distributed Systems and Networks, London*, July 2009.

[24] Rajesh Sharma and Anwitaman Datta. Super-Nova: Super-peers Based Architecture for Decentralized Online Social Networks. *Computing Research Repository*, abs/1105.0, 2011.

[25] Patrick Stuedi, Iqbal Mohomed, Mahesh Balakrishnan, Zhuoqing Morley Mao, Venugopalan Ramasubramanian, Doug Terry, and Ted Wobber. Contrail: Enabling decentralized social networks on smartphones. In *Middleware*, pages 41–60, 2011.

[26] Sebastian Tramp, Philipp Frischmuth, Timofey Ermilov, Saeedeh Shekarpour, and SŽren Auer. An Architecture of a Distributed Semantic Social Network. *Semantic Web Journal*, Special Issue on The Personal and Social Semantic Web, 2012.

[27] Guido Urdaneta, Guillaume Pierre, and Maarten Van Steen. A survey of dht security techniques. *ACM Comput. Surv.*, 43(2):8:1–8:49, February 2011.

[28] Zhe Wang and Naftaly Minsky. Establishing global policies over decentralized online social networks. In *Proc. of the 9th IEEE International Workshop on Trusted Collaboration*, October 2014.

[29] Tianyin Xu, Yang Chen, Jin Zhao, and Xiaoming Fu. Cuckoo: towards decentralized, socio-aware online microblogging services and data measurements. In *Proceedings of the 2nd ACM International Workshop on Hot Topics in Planet-scale Measurement*, HotPlanet '10, pages 4:1–4:6, New York, NY, USA, 2010. ACM.

[30] Wenxuan Zhang, Constantin Serban, and Naftaly H. Minsky. Establishing global properties of multi-agent systems via local laws. In Danny Weyns, editor, *Environments for Multiagent Systems III, LNAI 4389*. Springer-Verlag, 2007.

[31] Dejin Zhao and Mary Beth Rosson. How and why people twitter: the role that micro-blogging plays in informal communication at work. In *Proceedings of the ACM 2009 international conference on Supporting group work*, GROUP '09, pages 243–252, New York, NY, USA, 2009. ACM.

10

Collaborating with executable content across space and time[*]

Mahadev Satyanarayanan[1,*], Vasanth Bala[2,**], Gloriana St. Clair[3,***], Erika Linke[3,****]

[1]School of Computer Science, Carnegie Mellon University,
[2]IBM Research,
[3]University Libraries, Carnegie Mellon University

Abstract

Executable content is of growing importance in many domains. How does one share and archive such content at Internet-scale for spatial and temporal collaboration? *Spatial collaboration* refers to the classic concept of user collaboration: two or more users who are at different Internet locations performing a task using shared context. *Temporal collaboration* refers to the archiving of context by one user and use of that context by another user, possibly many years or decades later. The term "shared context" has typically meant shared documents or a shared workspace such as a whiteboard. However, executable content forces us to think differently. Just specifying a standardized data format is not sufficient; one has to accurately reproduce *computation*. We observe that the precise encapsulation of computing state provided by a *virtual machine (VM)* may help us solve this problem. We can cope with large VM size through a streaming mechanism that demand fetches memory and disk state during execution. Based on our positive initial experience with VMs for archiving execution state, we propose the creation of *Olive*, an Internet ecosystem of curated VM image collections.

Keywords: virtual machine monitors, file systems, operating systems, open source software, archival storage

1. Introduction

Collaboration is defined as "the action of working with someone to produce or create something" [1]. *Shared context* is essential for successful collaboration. It typically takes the form of a shared workspace, document, machinery, or other tangible object. This leads to the kinds of scenarios we associate with collaboration: a group of users standing in front of a whiteboard; coauthors working on editing a document; mechanics troubleshooting an appliance; military planners studying a terrain model; and so on. The advent of the Internet has extended these scenarios to collaborators who are physically separated by considerable distances, leading to *collaboration across space*. Tools such as distributed workspaces, shared whiteboards, and collaborative authoring software, as well as control mechanisms for security and privacy have arisen from these roots.

Less explicitly recognized, but of equal impact and historical significance, is the concept of *collaboration across time*. A composer and a performer, though separated by centuries, are effectively collaborating on the creation of music. More generally, a long-dead author and a reader can collaborate on the mental transformation of the reader; these, in turn, can sometimes lead to more momentous real-world creations or transformations. Of course, there are fundamental limitations to collaboration across time. Unlike collaboration across space, where the collaborators can exert mutual influence on each other, a reader cannot reach back in time and get scientific authors' opinions on how newly available data would change their theories. [1]

The accurate preservation, easy discovery, and rapid retrieval of shared context to support collaboration over time has been the domain of the digital library community. Mechanisms such as databases, distributed storage systems, the Web, and search engines can be viewed as tools that support this effort. Underlying

[*]An early version of this work was presented in October 2011 at the 7th International Conference on Collaborative Computing: Networking, Applications and Worksharing (CollaborateCom2011).

Corresponding author. Email:* satya@cs.cmu.edu, ** vbala@us.ibm.com, *** gstclair@andrew.cmu.edu, ****el08@andrew.cmu.edu

[1]As we shall see later in this paper, emerging technology may make it possible to partly alleviate this strong asymmetry.

this effort is the fundamental assumption that shared context is in the form of *static content* such as a book or a musical score.

Today, an increasing fraction of the world's intellectual output is in the form of *executable content.* These include simulation models, tutoring systems, expert systems, data visualization tools, and so on. Even content that could be static (such as a company's product information Web page) is often dynamically generated through execution of code that customizes the content and appearance at runtime. What does it mean to preserve such content with perfect fidelity over time? There is no static object or collection of static objects that can serve as shared context to freeze and preserve. Rather, we need to *freeze and precisely reproduce the execution that dynamically produces the content.*

2. Execution Fidelity

Precise reproduction of software execution, which we call *execution fidelity,* is a complex problem in which many moving parts must all be perfectly aligned for a solution. Preserving this alignment over space and time is difficult. Many things can change: the hardware, the operating system, dynamically linked libraries, configuration and user preference specifications, geographic location, execution timing, and so on. Even a single change may hurt fidelity or completely break execution.

The need for execution fidelity is not unique to the digital library community. In the domain of commercial software, it is a problem faced by every software vendor. There is a strong desire to package software in a manner that installs and works with minimal tinkering so that the *time to value* for a customer is as short as possible. This desire to avoid extensive installation effort argues for rigid constraints on the software. At the same time, vendors wish to target the largest possible market. This argues for rich flexibility and configurability of software at installation time, to address the many unique needs and constraints of different market niches and diverse individual customers. Reconciling these contradictory goals is a difficult challenge.

Execution fidelity is also valuable when collaboration across space involves executable content. When help desk technicians assist remote customers, their ability to observe software behavior jointly in real time is likely to be more effective than having customers describe what they are seeing on their screens. Today, the most common class of tools for this purpose involves *remote desktop technology.* Examples include RDP in Windows [2] and VNC [3] in Linux, as well as Web-based services such as GoToMyPC [4].

Unfortunately, the available mechanisms for ensuring execution fidelity are weak. Most software distribution today takes the form of *install packages,* typically

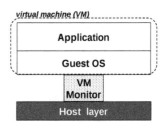

Figure 1. Basic VM Concepts

in binary form but sometimes in source form. The act of installing a package involves checking for a wide range of dependencies, discovering missing components, and ensuring that the transitive closure of dependencies involving these components is addressed. Tools can simplify and partially automate these steps. However, the process still involves considerable skill and knowledge, remains failure-prone, and typically results in a long time-to-value metric for a customer.

These limitations directly affect collaboration across time. The install packages themselves are static content, and can be archived with existing mechanisms. However, the chances of successfully installing and executing this software in the distant future are low. In addition to the software installation challenges mentioned above, there is the additional difficulty that the passage of time makes hardware and software environments obsolete. The chances of finding compatible hardware and operating system on which to even attempt an install become vanishingly small over time scales of decades. These challenges have long stymied efforts by the digital library community to archive executable content [5–8].

For collaboration across space, today's use of remote desktop technology works reasonably well but faces fundamental challenges. For highly interactive applications such as games and data visualizations, the end-to-end network latency between collaborating parties limits the perception of perfect fidelity of execution. There is growing evidence that although Internet bandwidth will continue to improve over time, there are few economic incentives to keep end-to-end latency low. As discussed elsewhere [9, 10], this limits the applicability of the remote desktop approach at Internet scale to a fairly narrow class of applications.

Is there a better way to ensure execution fidelity? Ideally, such a mechanism would simultaneously address the challenges of software distribution as well as collaboration with executable content over space and time. We present such a mechanism in the next section.

3. Virtual Machine Technology

A *virtual machine (VM)* is a computer architecture and instruction set emulator of such high accuracy that neither applications nor the operating system is able to detect its presence. In other words, emulated execution is indistinguishable from execution on genuine hardware. Since the emulated hardware is usually of the same type as the bare hardware on which emulation is performed, we are effectively cloning a physical machine into multiple VMs.

Figure 1 illustrates the key abstractions in the realization of a VM. The *guest* layer represents an unmodified legacy computing environment, including one or more applications and the operating system. The *host* layer is responsible for virtualizing the bare hardware, including devices such as disk, network, display and so on. The host layer multiplexes the concurrent execution of multiple VMs, and ensures isolation. Each VM has execution context represented in a *VM monitor (VMM)*, as shown in Figure 1.

VMs were invented by IBM in the mid-1960s as a timesharing approach that enabled concurrent, cleanly-isolated system software development on a single mainframe by multiple programmers. Since mainframe hardware of that era was expensive, VMs were a cost-effective approach to enhancing programmer productivity by providing a private "mainframe" for each developer rather than reserving dedicated time on real hardware. Accuracy of hardware emulation was paramount because the system software developed on a VM was intended for use in a mainframe operating system. That software had to work with negligible changes on the real hardware. The techniques for efficient and accurate hardware virtualization that were developed in this era have proved to be of lasting value. The accuracy of virtualization is a key reason for VMs being a potential solution to the problem of execution fidelity today.

By the early 1970s, VMs were being used for purposes well beyond those that motivated their invention. A commercial product, the VM/370 timesharing system [11], was highly successful and was in widespread use for well over a decade. Its descendants continue to be in use on IBM mainframes as z/VM today [12]. However, the emergence of the personal computer led to the eclipse of the VM as a computing abstraction by the late 1980s. Cheap PCs with a rigidly-controlled operating system (MS-DOS initially, and various versions of Windows later) displaced VMs as the most cost-effective way to deliver computing with high execution fidelity. Events have now come full circle. The emergence of cloud computing has restored lustre to the VM abstraction.[2] Large commercial investments are now being made in VM technology and VM-based systems.

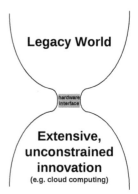

Figure 2. Legacy-compatible VM Ecosystem

Figure 2 illustrates the value proposition of the VM abstraction today. A large legacy world of software, including operating system software, represents a substantial intellectual and financial investment that has been already been made on existing computer hardware. This legacy world can be completely closed-source: there is no requirement for availability of source code, nor a requirement for recompilation or relinking. All that is needed is standard software installation, just as on real hardware. Beneath the implementation of the emulated hardware interface, there can be extensive innovation along many dimensions. This innovation is totally isolated from the idiosyncrasies of the legacy world above. In cloud computing, the freedom to innovate beneath the hardware interface allows the creation of valuable system management functionality such as server consolidation for energy savings and elastic computing for bursty server loads. More generally, it allows an enterprise to virtualize and outsource its entire data center to a remote third party such as Amazon Web Services [13].

Certain specific attributes of the VM abstraction accounts for its longevity and success. The hourglass shape in Figure 2 could depict the interface specification of any abstraction (thin waist), applications dependent on this interface (above), and implementations of this interface (below). More specifically, it could represent an execution engine such as the Java Virtual Machine (JVM) [14] or the Dalvik Virtual Machine for the Android platform [15]. While these alternatives (collectively referred to as *software virtualization*) have successful niches, they do not approach the VM abstraction (also referred to as *hardware virtualization*) in terms of longevity, widespread usage and real-world impact.

Why is hardware virtualization so much more successful? First, the interface presented by the VM abstraction is compatible with legacy operating systems and their valuable ecosystems of applications. The ability to sustain these ecosystems without code modifications is a powerful advantage of VMs. The ecosystems supported by software virtualization tend to be much smaller. For example, a JVM is only valuable in supporting applications written in specific languages

---

[2]The VMs in cloud computing are typically based on the Intel x86 architecture rather than the IBM 370 architecture, but that is a minor detail relative to the big picture.

such as Java. In contrast, a VM is language-agnostic and OS-agnostic. In fact, a JVM can be part of the ecosystem supported by a VM. Hardware virtualization can thus subsume software virtualization. Second, a VM interface is *narrow* and *stable* relative to typical software interfaces. In combination, these two attributes ensure adequate return on investments in the layer below. By definition, a narrow interface imposes less constraints on the layer below and thus provides greater freedom for innovation. The stability of a VM interface arises from the fact that the hardware it emulates itself evolves very slowly and almost always in an upward-compatible manner. In contrast, the pliability of software results in more rapid evolution and obsolescence of interfaces. Keeping up with these changes requires high maintenance effort. Pliability also leads to widening of narrow interfaces over time, because it is difficult to resist the temptation to extend an interface for the benefit of a key application. Over time, the burden of sustaining a wide interface constrains innovation below the interface.

The importance of the narrowness and stability of an interface can be seen in the contrasting fortunes of *process migration* and *VM migration*, which are essentially the same concept applied at different levels of abstraction. Process migration is an operating system capability that allows a running process to be paused, relocated to another machine, and continued there. It has been a research focus of many experimental operating systems built in the past 20 years. Examples include Demos [16], V [17], Mach [18], Sprite [19], Charlotte [20], and Condor [21]. These independent validation efforts have shown beyond reasonable doubt that process migration can indeed be implemented with acceptable efficiency. Yet, in spite of its research popularity, no operating system in widespread use today (proprietary or open source) supports process migration as a standard facility. The reason for this paradox is that a typical implementation of process migration involves such a wide interface that it is easily rendered incompatible by a modest external change such as an operating system upgrade. Long-term maintenance of machines with support for process migration involves too much effort relative to the benefits it provides. The same concept of pausing an executing entity, relocating it, and resuming execution can be applied to an entire VM rather than a single process. This is *VM migration*, a capability that is in widespread use in cloud computing systems today. Guest OS changes do not affect an implementation of VM migration. This insulation from change, embodied in the narrow and stable VM interface, is crucial to the real-world success of VM migration.

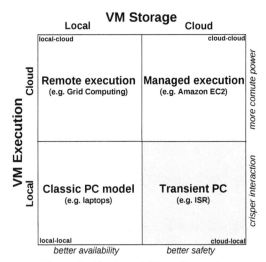

Figure 3. VM-based Cloud Computing

4. Transporting VMs across Space and Time

Modern implementations of the VM abstraction provide support for an executing VM to be *suspended*. This is conceptually similar to what happens when you close the lid of a laptop computer. An exact record of the execution state of the VM at suspend is captured and saved as files in the host file system. There are typically distinct representations of the VM's persistent state (i.e., its virtual disks) and its volatile state (i.e. memory, registers, etc.). These are referred to as a *disk image* and a *memory image* respectively, and their combination is called a *VM image*. Execution can be *resumed* from a VM image. This is equivalent to opening the lid of a suspended laptop, and seamlessly continuing work. If there is no memory image, resuming a VM is equivalent to powering up hardware, resulting in a fresh boot of the guest OS. An executable VM that is created from a VM image is called a *VM instance*. Some use cases may restrict the number of concurrent VM instances that can be created from a single VM image.

A VM image is static content that can transmitted across the Internet for sharing, or archived for later retrieval. If you have a VM image, resuming the suspended VM only requires a compatible VMM and host hardware. Everything else needed for perfect execution fidelity is contained within the VM image. The use of VMs thus transforms the difficult problem of collaborating with executable content into the more tractable problem of efficient transmission, storage and retrieval of VM images.

Separating image storage from instance execution leads to a rich design space for VM-based cloud computing. As Figure 3 shows, this design space has two dimensions. One dimension is the location of the definitive copy of the VM image (ignoring cache copies): local to the execution site, or in the cloud. The other dimension is where a VM instance executes: locally (at the edges of the Internet) or within the cloud. This results in the four quadrants depicted in Figure 3:

- The local-local quadrant is equivalent to the classic unvirtualized model of desktops and laptops today.

- The cloud-cloud quadrant corresponds to situations where both VM image storage and execution occur within the cloud. This is the model supported by public clouds such as Amazon Web Services, and is often what is meant by the term "cloud computing."

- The local-cloud quadrant corresponds to situations where a local VM image is instantiated in a remote cloud, typically for use of more powerful computing resources or for proximity to large data sets. This is essentially the metaphor of *grid computing.* Use cases in which large data sets are shared by a community of researchers using this mechanism can be viewed as a form of collaboration across space.

- The cloud-local quadrant is of particular interest to the topic of this paper and is discussed in detail below. This quadrant corresponds to a VM image archived in the cloud being instantiated and executed at an edge node of the Internet.[3] We label this quadrant *Transient PC* because it evokes the vision of a transient or disposable computing instance that is brought into existence anywhere on the Internet, used and then discarded. If its final state is valuable, that could be archived as a new image in the cloud.

The Transient PC model is well suited to supporting collaboration across time. Just as we retrieve a pdf file today and view it on a desktop, laptop or smartphone, we can envision a VM corresponding to executable content being dynamically instantiated and executed on an edge device. There are many details to get right, but in principle this approach offers better execution fidelity than any of the alternatives available today. This is because the VM contains the entire transitive closure of dependencies (including the operating system and dynamically linked libraries) along with the application of interest.

With additional machinery, the Transient PC model could also support near real-time collaboration across space between multiple users. This would consist of a VM instance executing at each user's site, along with mechanisms to propagate changes resulting from each user's interactions to the other VM instances. In effect, a collection of VM instances dispersed across the edges of the Internet are kept in sync as they interact with their users. This achieves the effect of the remote desktop approach mentioned in Section 2, but with much better execution fidelity since it is less sensitive to wide-area Internet latency. There is an extensive body of research on logging and replay of VMs that could be leveraged for this purpose [22–24]. In addition, there would need to be an appropriate model of concurrency control to ensure that the divergence of VM instances remains within acceptable bounds. The simplest concurrency control approach would be a token-passing scheme that allows at most one user at a time to be the "writer." More sophisticated models of collaboration will require more complex concurrency control approaches. For example, multi-user graphics-intensive computer gaming at Internet scale may benefit from this approach if game-specific concurrency control can be efficiently supported.

The superior execution fidelity of VMs comes at a price. A typical VM image is many gigabytes in size, possibly tens of gigabytes. In contrast, a typical pdf document is tens of kilobytes to a few megabytes in size. While storage capacity in the cloud for VM images is of some concern, a more serious concern is their efficient transmission over the Internet. Even at 100 Mbps, full transfer of a 10 GB image will take at least 800 seconds (over 13 minutes). Over the wide-area Internet, with end-to-end bandwidths approaching 10 Mbps at well-connected sites, the transfer will take over 8000 seconds (over two hours). These are clearly unacceptably long periods for a user to wait before executable content can be viewed. Ideally, the startup delay experienced by a user at a well-connected Internet site should be no more than a few seconds to tens of seconds. While Internet bandwidth will continue to improve over time, it is also likely that VM images will grow larger.

The obvious solution is to adopt the approach of *streaming* used by video sites such as YouTube. This would allow a user to begin viewing content as soon as a modest prefix has been transferred. Unfortunately, the problem is more complex than video streaming because a VM instance is unlikely to access its VM image in simple linear order. It is the complex runtime behavior of a VM instance (including user interactions, data dependencies, temporal locality and spatial locality) that determines the reference pattern to its VM image. To address this problem, we have shown how *demand-paged execution* of a VM instance can be implemented. Using this approach resume latencies of tens of seconds are achievable today at well-connected Internet sites. This work has been done in the context of the *Internet Suspend/Resume(ISR)* system [25–27]. Recently, Abe et al [28] have shown that history-based prefetching can lower the resume latency of VM-based systems on last-mile networks such as 4G wireless networks.

---

[3]The private cloud of an enterprise can be viewed as "an edge node of the Internet" for this discussion.

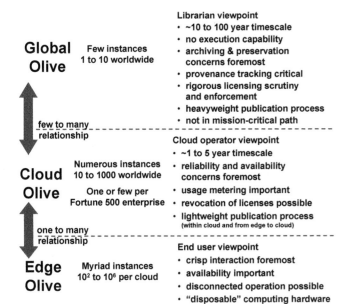

Figure 4. Olive as a Concept at Multiple Levels

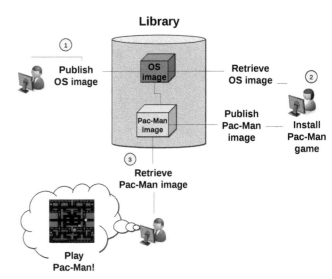

Figure 5. Extending an Olive VM Image

5. The Olive Vision

Our initial exploration with ISR suggested that VMs can indeed archive executable content. To realize the full potential of this capability we envision *Olive*, a VM-based Internet ecosystem for executable content. At the heart of Olive is open-source software for contributing VM images, curating them in Internet repositories so that licensing and intellectual property constraints are enforced, and efficiently retrieving and executing them at a cloud provider or at an edge device (i.e., the cloud-cloud and cloud-local quadrants of Figure 3).

As shown in Figure 4, Olive is a concept that applies at multiple levels of the Internet. At the global or planetary level, we envision a relatively small number of archival sites (less than 100, more likely 1–10) where VM images are curated. Olive also has a presence at the level of a public cloud provider such as Amazon Web Services, or within the private cloud of an enterprise (most likely totaling a few hundred to a few thousand clouds). At this level, VM images may be cached in their entirety from global Olive repositories. They may also have customizations that are cloud-specific or enterprise-specific. Finally, Olive's presence at any edge device on the Internet enables ubiquitous streamed execution of VM images over wired and wireless networks. For scalability, VM images may be streamed to an edge device from a cloud provider rather than directly from a global Olive repository.

The ability to customize VM images within a cloud is an important Olive capability because it helps VM image contributors to honor software licensing constraints. Executable software content created by one person almost always depends on other software content. Take for example someone who wants to contribute the popular computer game Pac-Man to a global Olive repository. This person may have the rights to contribute the Pac-Man application, but not the rights to the operating system and other software that must exist on the VM inside which Pac-Man has to run. If the contribution to Olive included those other software components, it would require negotiation of re-distribution rights on all those other components with their corresponding owners. This is not an issue with a totally open source software stack, but it can be a laborious and expensive task when proprietary software is involved. This legal hurdle and its associated litigation and business risks could discourage many from making valuable Olive contributions.

Olive could solve this problem by allowing one VM to extend another VM, thereby creating a new VM. Figure 5 illustrates one way this can work. In step 1, a person or organization that wants to contribute an operating system to Olive, does so as a VM that includes a fully installed and tested image of that operating system. A different person or organization can then retrieve this VM, start it on their own laptop, and install the Pac-Man application. The resulting VM, which includes both the operating system and the Pac-Man application, can then be published back into Olive. Olive technology will recognize that this new VM is an extension of a virtual machine that already exists in its library. It will automatically compute the delta content between the two (which is the contribution from the Pac-Man application), and store it internally. Thus, the Pac-Man contributor only contributes bits that he owns to Olive and does not violate any licensing restrictions. This process is reversed during the customization step within a cloud: the Pac-Man delta is applied to the original VM to produce a merged VM. In this context, the *dynamic VM synthesis* approach explored by Ha et al [29] is important related work.

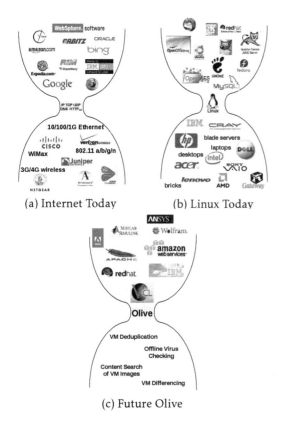

(a) Internet Today   (b) Linux Today

(c) Future Olive

Figure 6. The Power of Open Ecosystems

We envision Olive to be an ecosystem built around open standards and interfaces rather than a closed, proprietary system. The vibrant Internet and Linux ecosystems shown in Figures 6(a) and 6(b) are testimonials to the power of open standards. In both cases, a relatively small collection of open components at the waistline sustains large business investments above and below that waistline. Figures 6(c) illustrates the hypothetical Olive ecosystem of the future. At the waistline are a small set of open components such as ISR. Above are publishers of open or proprietary executable content. Below are open or proprietary tools and mechanisms. We believe that such an open ecosystem has the potential to be far more influential and viable than a proprietary ecosystem. This is especially true for an archival system that has to survive in sound operating condition over time periods of decades and (optimistically) centuries.

6. Olive and Digital Libraries

Historically across the disciplines, academic libraries have maintained the scholarly record, which fixes credit for innovation, invention, and progress. For the stone tablet, papyrus, vellum, and paper environments, successful retention has been challenging but attainable. The realm of static digital resources has proven more challenging [30], but standards and best practices have led several libraries through successful migrations of large corpuses. Libraries are also the logical stewards

for executable content as for other scholarly content. Academic libraries have universally accepted their faculty's research and publication products, which may range from cooking, to chemistry, to computing. The last now complain that they cannot fully appreciate and understand work if it is just represented by object code divorced from source code. Computer scientists need to see what a program does when it runs to be fully informed and enriched by their tradition. As Olive is realized, libraries, working with their computing colleagues, will be able to commit to the long term preservation of diverse forms of executable content. Examples include tutoring systems (such as Loop Tutor, Hypertutor, and iCarnegie), games (such as Rogue, MUDs, Doom, and Duke Nukem), databases (such as Clueset), and obsolete versions of major commercial operating systems and applications.

Trying to maintain the equipment to run these older works is not an elegant preservation solution. The Joint Information Systems Committee (JISC) in "Creative Archiving at Michigan and Leeds: Emulating the Old on the New(CAMiLEON)" looked at the feasibility and costs of using emulation for software[31]. In 2011, The Baden-Wurttemberg Functional Longterm Archiving and Access project, building on earlier work done in the European Union, announced a two year state-sponsored project to develop scalable cloud-based emulation as a service [32]. The Internet Archive is currently using JSMESS to present early productivity software, such a VisiCalc and Wordstar, on its web site while archivists at Stanford University are experimenting with Xenserver and Xenclient. None of these alternatives meets our needs for performance and long term sustainability by an open source community.

Managing the metadata around the items in the collection offers additional challenges. Dr. Jerome McDonough from the Preserving Virtual Worlds project manages metadata for the Olive project. McDonough employed OAI-ORE and METS while examining further work, such as the Carolina Digital Repository's Curator Workbench tool. We are also considering other approaches, such as Trustworthy Online Technical Environment Metadata (TOTEM) [33] and XSEAD, an NSF-supported online platform supporting networks of creativity and innovation across science, engineering, art and design [34]. We will be doing additional research in this area.

Many of the first choices of works to be archived may, of necessity, be those with less commercial value. The JSTOR database has demonstrated that rights owners can be persuaded to give permission for the use of less valuable content (journal articles over five years old). Nevertheless, intellectual property restrictions will be a significant challenge.

Another significant challenge will be sustaining the archive for academic products long term. Many models

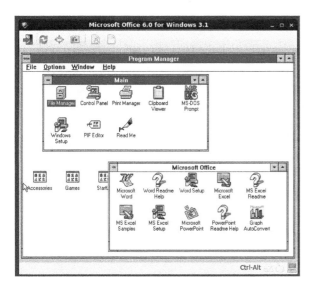

Figure 7. Microsoft Office 6.0 on Windows 3.1

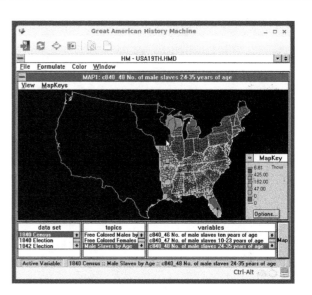

Figure 8. Great American History Machine on Windows 3.1

exist: JSTOR and HathiTrust (subscription), the dark archives Portico and LOCKSS (membership), and NIH's PubMedCentral and Bibliotheque Nationale de France's DeepArc (government funding). The Million Books Project model (multinational governments, subscription, and university computer science department and library support) has proven to be less effective [35]. The Google Books Library partnership, a commercial venture, is perhaps the most successful in the breadth of its accomplishments.

7. Olive Status

With funding from the Sloan Foundation and the Institute for Museum and Library Services, Carnegie Mellon University has created an initial proof of concept implementation of Olive. Because of software licensing constraints, this system is currently available only to small number of research collaborators. In the near future, we hope to obtain the necessary legal permissions to allow use of Olive content by a broader user community. Olive contains over 15 VMs today, and continues to grow. A summary of the collection is shown at the end of the paper (Figure 11). It includes operating systems and applications dating back to the late 1980s. For brevity, we describe only four of these VMs below.

Microsoft Office 6.0. Figure 7 shows a screenshot of this VM, containing Word, Excel and PowerPoint for Windows 3.1 from the 1993-94 time period.

Great American History Machine. This application was originally created in the late 1980s by Professor David Miller of Carnegie Mellon University. It was used by him and by many professors at other universities nationwide to teach 19th century and early 20th century American History. As the screenshot in Figure 8 shows, this educational software used census and election data to teach students important historical

concepts such as the origins of the Civil War. The Windows 3.1 version of this software was created in collaboration with the University of Maryland. Because of lack of financial resources to port the software to newer Windows platforms, it fell into disuse over time. No modern equivalent of this software exists today.

TurboTax 1997. This application for Windows 3.1 and Windows 95 was used by millions of Americans to prepare their 1997 tax returns. Figure 9 shows a screenshot of this application. Since TurboTax is updated each year to reflect the current tax laws, a suite of TurboTax VMs from consecutive years can offer unique historical value. Imagine a class in political science, public policy or economics assigning students a project based on TurboTax versions that are ten years apart. By calculating the tax returns for hypothetical families with different income profiles, students can see for themselves the impact of tax code changes over time. Such active learning can transform the abstract topic of tax law into a source of valuable real-world insights.

NCSA Mosaic. As the world's first widely-used web browser dating back to 1992-93, Mosaic has a unique historical status. This VM, whose screenshot is shown in Figure 10, is also interesting for a second reason. The version of Mosaic that it encapsulates was written for the Apple MacOS 7.5 operating system on Motorola 68040 hardware. The VM also encapsulates Basilisk II, an open source hardware emulator for Motorola 68040 on modern Intel x86 hardware running Linux. The bootable disk image of MacOS 7.5 with Mosaic is stored as a file in the virtual file system of the outer Linux guest. In spite of two levels of virtualization, performance is acceptable because modern hardware is so much faster than the original Apple hardware. Pointing the Mosaic browser at modern web sites is instructive. Since Mosaic predates web technologies such as Javascript, Cascading Style Sheets, and HTML5,

Figure 9. TurboTax 1997 on Windows 3.1

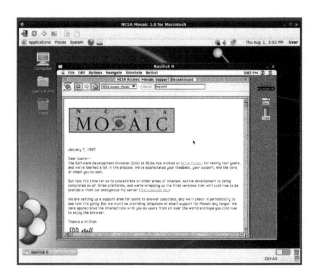

Figure 10. Mosaic Browser on MacOS 7.5

this old browser is unable to render content from modern web sites. It can, however, render static web pages from some older sites that are still on the Internet.

8. Conclusion

Rich shared context facilitates human collaboration. Face to face interaction is the gold standard for shared context, since it supports the full range of visual, aural and tactile real-time interactions involved in conveying procedural and declarative knowledge. Even in the 21st century, people travel to meetings, workshops and conferences for this highest quality of shared context.

Extending collaboration across space and time to approach this gold standard has been a human quest since the dawn of civilization. The invention of writing, and the emergence of libraries profoundly changed collaboration across time. Over centuries, this quest has led to other transformative inventions such as the printing press, telephony, the motion picture, television, the Internet, and social networks such as Facebook. Yet, in spite of these impressive advances, the shared context supported by them has always been static in nature. Today's Flickr images and YouTube videos may only bear a distant relationship to writing on clay tablets, but they both represent static content from the viewpoint of archiving. Sharing executable content has been theoretically possible since the invention of the computer. But only now have the foundational technologies for this capability matured to the point where we can build upon them.

Procedural artifacts ranging from scientific simulation models to interactive games play an increasingly important role in our lives. The ability to archive these artifacts for posterity would be an important transformative step. Imagine being able to reach back across time to execute the simulation model of a long-dead scientist on new data that you have just acquired. What do the results suggest? Would they have changed the

conclusions of that scientist? Although you aren't quite bringing the scientist back to life, you are collaborating with that person in a way that was not possible until now. As we have shown in this paper, there is now a convergence of the key technologies needed for such scenarios: VM technology, cloud computing and high bandwidth wide-area networks. From these roots, the Olive vision emerges as a natural next step for supporting collaborations across space and time.

Acknowledgements. We acknowledge the extensive contributions of Benjamin Gilbert, who has been the primary contributor to ISR since 2006. Earlier contributors to ISR include Michael Kozuch, Casey Helfrich, Dave O'Hallaron, Partho Nath, and Matt Toups. We also acknowledge the many people who contributed to the Olive vision presented here: Benjamin Gilbert, Jan Harkes, Glenn Ammons, Catherine Zhang, Mladen Vouk, Peng Ning and many other contributors at Carnegie Mellon, IBM, and North Carolina State University, as well as the participants of the Olive workshop held at IBM in April 2011. We thank Dan Ryan for his contributions to this paper, and David Baisley for providing us with the original install disks for the operating systems shown in Figure 7 through Figure 10. The creation of ISR was supported by the National Science Foundation (NSF) under grant number CNS-0509004, an IBM Open Collaborative Research grant, and Intel. The creation of Olive was supported by the Sloan foundation and the Institute for Museum and Library Services. Any opinions, findings, conclusions or recommendations expressed in this material are those of the authors and do not necessarily represent the views of their employers or the funding agencies. Internet Suspend/Resume and OpenISR are registered trademarks of Carnegie Mellon University.

References

[1] Oxford Dictionaries, http://oxforddictionaries.com. Accessed on May 2, 2014.

[2] Remote Desktop Protocol, http://en.wikipedia.org/wiki/Remote_Desktop_Protocol. Accessed on May 2, 2014.

[3] Richardson, T., Stafford-Fraser, Q., Wood, K.R. and Hopper, A. (1998) Virtual Network Computing. *IEEE Internet Computing* 2(1).

[4] GoToMyPC: Access Your Mac or PC from Anywhere, http://www.gotomypc.com/remote_access/remote_access. Accessed on May 2, 2014.

[5] Conway, P. (1996), Preservation in the Digital World, http://www.clir.org/pubs/reports/conway2/. Accessed on May 2, 2014.

[6] Conway, P. (2010) Preservation in the Age of Google: Digitization, Digital Preservation, and Dilemmas. *Library Quarterly* 80(1).

[7] Hedstrom, M., Lee, C., Olson, J. and Lampe, C. (2006) 'The Old Version Flickers More': Digital Preservation from the User's Perspective. *The American Archivist* 69: 159–187.

[8] Matthews, B., Shaon, A., Bicarreguil, J. and Jones, C. (2010) A Framework for Software Preservation. *The International Journal of Digital Curation* 5(1).

[9] Tolia, N., Andersen, D. and Satyanarayanan, M. (2006) Quantifying Interactive Experience on Thin Clients. *IEEE Computer* 39(3).

[10] Satyanarayanan, M., Bahl, V., Caceres, R. and Davies, N. (2009) The Case for VM-based Cloudlets in Mobile Computing. *IEEE Pervasive Computing* 8(4).

[11] Creasy, R. (1981) The Origin of the VM/370 Timesharing System. *IBM Journal of Research and Development* 25(5).

[12] VM (operating system), http://en.wikipedia.org/wiki/VM(operatingsystem). Accessed on May 2, 2014.

[13] Amazon Web Services, http://aws.amazon.com/. Accessed on May 2, 2014.

[14] Lindholm, T. and Yellin, F. (1999) *The Java Virtual Machine Specification (2nd Edition)* (Prentice Hall).

[15] Dalvik (software), http://en.wikipedia.org/wiki/Dalvik_%28software%29. Accessed on May 2, 2014.

[16] Powell, M. and Miller, B. (1983) Process Migration in DEMOS/MP. In *Proceedings of the 9th ACM Symposium on Operating Systems Principles* (Bretton Woods, NH).

[17] Theimer, M., Lantz, K. and Cheriton, D. (1985) Preemptable Remote Execution Facilities for the V-System. In *Proceedings of the 10th Symposium on Operating System Principles* (Orcas Island, WA).

[18] Zayas, E. (1987) Attacking the Process Migration Bottleneck. In *Proceedings of the 11th ACM Symposium on Operating System Principles* (Austin, TX).

[19] Douglis, F. and Ousterhout, J. (1991) Transparent Process Migration: Design Alternatives and the Sprite Implementation. *Software Practice and Experience* 21(8).

[20] Artsy, Y. and Finkel, R. (1989) Designing a Process Migration Facility: The Charlotte Experience. *IEEE Computer* 22(9).

[21] Zandy, V., Miller, B. and Livny, M. (1999) Process Hijacking. In *8th International Symposium on High Performance Distributed Computing* (Redondo Beach, CA).

[22] Dunlap, G.W., King, S.T., Cinar, S., Basrai, M. and Chen, P.M. (2002) ReVirt: Enabling Intrusion Analysis through Virtual-Machine Logging and Replay. In *Proceedings of the 2002 Symposium on Operating Systems Design and Implementation (OSDI)*.

[23] King, S.T., Dunlap, G.W. and Chen, P.M. (2005) Debugging operating systems with time-traveling virtual machines. In *Proceedings of the 2005 Annual USENIX Technical Conference*.

[24] Veeraraghavan, K., Lee, D., Wester, B., Ouyang, J., Chen, P.M., Flinn, J. and Narayanasamy, S. (2011) DoublePlay: Parallelizing sequential logging and replay. In *Proceedings of the 2011 International Conference on Architectural Support for Programming Languages and Operating Systems (ASPLOS)*.

[25] Internet Suspend/Resume, http://isr.cmu.edu/. Accessed on May 2, 2014.

[26] Satyanarayanan, M., Kozuch, M., Helfrich, C. and O'Hallaron, D.R. (2005) Towards Seamless Mobility on Pervasive Hardware. *Pervasive and Mobile Computing* 1(2).

[27] Satyanarayanan, M., Gilbert, B., Toups, M., Tolia, N., Surie, A., O'Hallaron, D.R., Wolbach, A. *et al.* (2007) Pervasive Personal Computing in an Internet Suspend/Resume System. *IEEE Internet Computing* 11(2).

[28] Abe, Y., Geambasu, R., Joshi, K., Lagar-Cavilla, A. and Satyanarayanan, M. (2013) vTube: Efficient Streaming of Virtual Appliances Over Last-Mile Networks. In *Proceedings of the ACM Symposium on Cloud Computing* (Santa Clara, CA).

[29] Ha, K., Pillai, P., Richter, W., Abe, Y. and Satyanarayanan, M. (2013) Just-in-time Provisioning for Cyber Foraging. In *Proceeding of the 11th Annual International Conference on Mobile Systems, Applications, and Services (MobiSys 2013)* (Taipei, Taiwan).

[30] McDonough, J. et al (2010), Preserving Virtual Worlds, http://hdl.handle.net/2142/17097. Accessed on May 2, 2014; also see 'Preserving Virtual Worlds' project website: http://pvw.illinois.edu/pvw/.

[31] CAMiLEON Project : Creative Archiving at Michigan and Leeds Emulating the Old on the New, http://www.webarchive.org.uk/ukwa/target/113954/source/alpha. Accessed on May 2, 2014.

[32] bwFLA – Emulation as a Service, http://bw-fla.uni-freiburg.de/. Accessed on May 2, 2014.

[33] TOTEM, The Trustworthy Online Technical Environment Metadata Database – TOTEM, http://keep-totem.co.uk/. Accessed on May 2, 2014.

[34] Welcome to XSEAD: A community platform for those working across disciplines., http://xsead.org. Accessed on May 2, 2014.

[35] St. Clair, G. (2010), Challenges in Sustaining the Million Book Project, a project supported by the National Science Foundation, In 'The Selected Works of Gloriana St. Clair' at http://works.bepress.com/gloriana_stclair/19.

	Timeframe	Operating System	Application	Description
1	Late 1980s to early 1990s	Microsoft MS-DOS	Preferred orientation package - Los Alamos	Texture analysis software package that provides a comprehensive treatment of material texture analysis.
2			Air Stripper Design and Costing (ASDC)	ASDC enables rapid generation and evaluation of alternative air stripper designs for removal of volatile organic compounds (VOCs) from water.
3			Amortizer Plus 3.01	Amortizer calculates loan amortization in a user-friendly, character-cell interface
4			Wanderer	Wanderer is a game similar to the old "Boulderdash" or "Repton" games, and was originally written to run under UNIX on text terminals (TVI910 and Wyse60)
5			DOOM for DOS	The original DOOM First Person Shooter game
6	Early to mid-1990s	Microsoft Windows 3.1	Microsoft Office 6.0	Microsoft Word 6.0c, Excel 5.0, and PowerPoint 4.0
7			WordPerfect 6.1	Widely used word-processing software before Microsoft Word became dominant
8			Electronic Anesthesiology Library 1991-95	A compilation in multimedia format of four journals (Anesthesiology, Anesthesia and Analgesia, British Journal of Anaesthesia, and The Canadian Journal of Anaesthesia). Includes the Knowledge Finder software for searching the journals.
9			TurboTax 1997	Tax-preparation software for tax year 1997
10			Great American History Machine	Visualization software to explore historical American census and election data from the 19th and early 20th centuries. The original version was created in the late 1980s for Carnegie Mellon University's Andrew system.
11	Mid-1990s	Apple MacIntosh 7.5	Oregon Trail 1.1	A game designed to teach school children about the realities of 19th century pioneer life on the Oregon Trail. The original pre-Mac version was conceived in 1971 and produced by the Minnesota Educational Computing Consortium (MECC) in 1974.
12			HyperCard 2.4.1	The last version of Apple's HyperCard multimedia authoring system for Macintosh.
13			NCSA Mosaic 1.0	A very early web browser that triggered world-wide awareness of the Internet
14			Netscape Navigator 1.12	One of the earliest versions of the first commercial web browser.
15	Early 2000s	Microsoft Windows XP		Basic operating system environment
16	2012	Scientific Linux 6.4		A Linux release put together by Fermilab, CERN, and various other labs and universities around the world. Its primary purpose is to reduce duplicated effort of the labs, and to have a common install base for the various experimenters.
17			ChemCollective	A collection of virtual labs, scenario-based learning activities, tutorials, and concept tests to teach and learn chemistry.

Figure 11. VM Collection in Olive as of April 2014

11

A Game Theoretic Approach for Modeling Privacy Settings of an Online Social Network

Jundong Chen*, Ankunda R. Kiremire, Matthias R. Brust, and Vir V. Phoha

Center for Secure Cyberspace, Louisiana Tech University, Ruston, LA 71270, USA

Abstract

Users of online social networks often adjust their privacy settings to control how much information on their profiles is accessible to other users of the networks. While a variety of factors have been shown to affect the privacy strategies of these users, very little work has been done in analyzing how these factors influence each other and collectively contribute towards the users' privacy strategies.

In this paper, we analyze the influence of attribute importance, benefit, risk and network topology on the users' attribute disclosure behavior by introducing a weighted evolutionary game model.

Results show that: irrespective of risk, users are more likely to reveal their most important attributes than their least important attributes; when the users' range of influence is increased, the risk factor plays a smaller role in attribute disclosure; the network topology exhibits a considerable effect on the privacy in an environment with risk.

Keywords: game theory, social network, privacy settings, network topology

1. Introduction

Online social networks provide platforms for people to share information about themselves, which facilitates the establishment and enhancement of friendships between users [20]. However, the shared information can also be exploited by identity thieves, sexual predators, stalkers, etc., and this has triggered worldwide concern about privacy issues in online social networks.

Thus, users of online social networks face a dilemma: reveal more personal information to increase their chances of finding potential new friends and identifying old friends, or reveal less information to decrease the chance of their identities being inferred by unscrupulous characters. Therefore, each user weighs both the risk and benefit to determine how many profile attributes to reveal. Additionally, the privacy settings of other users potentially affect the choice of privacy settings for a user.

Little work has been done on investigating how these factors collectively influence users' privacy settings.

Therefore, it is important to develop a model based on interaction of users that captures the influence of privacy risk and relationship-building on the level of self-disclosure.

In this paper, we propose an evolutionary game-theoretic model to study the behavior of users with regard to their privacy settings in a possible online social network. Our study conducts simulations of user behavior in a variety of network topologies, which include random, small-world, scale-free and Facebook friend networks.

The main contribution of this paper is threefold. First, our model investigates the importance of the revealed and/or hidden attributes to the users' behavior. By weighting the attributes, we consider that some attributes may have a higher impact than others in self-disclosure. As an illustration, given Alice is a user in a social network, our model investigates whether her decision to reveal important attributes (such as religion and sexual preferences) would affect other users' revelation decisions more or less than revealing her less important attributes (such as her favorite movies). Second, our model helps us to explore the users'

*Corresponding author. Email: jdc074@latech.edu

attribute disclosure behavior from different ranges of influence. For instance, how do risk and benefit affect Alice if she only discloses her attributes to her friends, as opposed to disclosing them to her friends as well as the friends of her friends? Third, our model allows us to investigate what influence the network topology has on the privacy strategy of the user. For example, if Alice decided to reveal all her attributes in a social network exhibiting small-world characteristics, would she make the same decision if the network exhibited random graph characteristics instead?

The results show that users tend to reveal their most important attributes more than their least important attributes regardless of the risk level. Important attributes are defined as the attributes which have a larger impact on the *social capital* of a user [6]. We also find that the range of influence plays a bigger role than the risk factor in users' disclosure of profile attributes. Additionally, we discover that network topologies have a higher impact on the users' attribute disclosure in the risk-included cases than they do in the risk-free cases.

The provided models and the gained results can be used to understand the influence of different factors on users' privacy choices and help users in determining how to optimize their disclosure strategies in a network while keeping the privacy risk at a low level.

The remainder of this paper is as follows. We discuss related work in the next section and specify the system model, definitions and strategies in Section 3. Our game-theoretic approach is described in Section 4, the results are presented in Section 6, and we conclude this paper with a discussion in Section 7.

2. Related work

Researchers have been studying the motivation of users to disclose their personal information in online social networks for sometime. Spiekermann et al. find that *Relationship-building* and *platform enjoyment* are the factors that motivate users' *self-disclosure* [12]. Aiello et al. show that people with higher similarity are more likely to be friends [13]. They identify similarity between users' profile attributes as an important factor in predicting the existence of a friendship between those users. It follows that if users reveal more attributes, there is an increased chance of sharing common attributes with other users and consequently becoming friends with them.

Game theory is the analysis of situations involving conflicts of interest using mathematical models [18]. Each participant is referred to as a player, and each player has a set of possible strategies they can employ to achieve their goals. Each player's utility is jointly determined by the strategies chosen by all the players in the game. Game theory is a growing field that has been applied to many areas including various

aspects of online social networks. These aspects range from modeling network formation [10], to community detection [5], and discovering influential nodes [16].

Game theory has been applied to optimizing users' data sharing in online social networks. Kamhoua et al. propose a Markov game theoretic approach to help online social network users determine their optimum data sharing policy [9]. Squicciarini et al. design a model to facilitate users' management of shared data based on Clarke-Tax mechanism [22].

Game theory has also been employed to model personal information revelation in online social networks. Squicciarini et al. [23] conduct a survey to investigate the factors that affect the behavior of personal information revelation, and then use a game theoretic model to find out the dynamics of the revelation behavior. Their results show that close friends strongly influence users' revelation decisions.

The profile attribute privacy problem is similar to the classic *stag-hunt* game [21]. The stag-hunt game models a conflict between safety and cooperation. In the game, two hunters can either jointly hunt a stag or individually hunt a hare. The highest benefit can only be achieved through cooperatively hunting a stag. In contrast, a hunter is exposed to the highest risk if he decides to hunt a stag while the other hunter decides otherwise. This game is very similar to the situation that online social network users encounter while disclosing their profile attributes. The highest benefit accrues when both users reveal all their attributes. The highest risk occurs to a user when the other user reveals less attributes because the user with more revealed attributes is vulnerable to identify inference.

The approach presented in our paper is built upon evolutionary game theory on graphs. Szabó et al. review different types of evolutionary games on different structure of graphs [24]. Antonioni et al. employ the model of evolutionary game on graphs to investigate the cooperation in social networks [1].

In previous work, we apply weighted evolutionary game theoretic model to analyze users' behavior in profile attribute disclosure in an online social network [4]. The model is employed on three different network topologies, where we show that the disclosure of profile attributes is not only influenced by attribute importance but network connectivity as well.

In this work, we extend our previous work in a variety of ways. We investigate how an increase in the influential range affects the users' privacy strategies, by considering friends-of-friends in the utility function. Furthermore, we apply our model to actual Facebook friend networks and report more comprehensive results.

3. Preliminaries

This section contains fundamental assumptions, concepts, definitions and methods used throughout the paper.

3.1. Assumptions

We assume that users with more attributes in common are more likely to be friends. This assumption is based on the *homophily principle* exhibited in social networks [15]. Additionally, we assume that all users of the network attach the same importance to the same type of attribute, e.g. all users will attach higher importance to their address attribute than to their religion attribute.

These assumptions make it possible for us to investigate the influence of local properties such as profile attributes and their importance to users on a common ground while simultaneously exploring how global network properties affect users' privacy.

3.2. Risk and identity inference

To capture the risk of identity inference, we introduce the concept of *hiding*. A User x is *hidden* by another User y if y is more distinguishable than x. This happens when User x's attributes are a subset of User y's attributes. For example, if a user John Doe reveals a set of attributes $\{Doe, 25\}$ while another user Jane Doe reveals $\{Doe, Female, 25, Chicago\}$, then Jane is more distinguishable than John. Therefore, John is hidden by Jane. This is because a third party can more easily infer the identity of Jane than John given a set of revealed profile attributes. As a result, the risk to John Doe's identity is reduced by Jane Doe.

3.3. Privacy settings

The *privacy setting* is a configuration of the user's profile information, which allows the user to enable or disable the visibility of specific profile attributes to other network users. The privacy settings of a typical social network consist of different levels of visibility for different aspects of the users' profile. The aspects include profile attributes, activity logs, and friend lists while the levels of visibility include friends, friends of friends, and public. In our model, we only consider profile attributes and two levels of visibility, i.e. friends and friends of friends.

3.4. Network topologies

We examine the behavior of our model on five network topologies, which include a random network, a small-world network, a scale-free network, and two Facebook friend networks. In these topologies, a node represents a social network user while an edge between two nodes indicates that the two users are "friends". Friends of a user represent other network users who have direct access to that user's revealed attributes.

A *random network* is a graph where an edge occurring between two nodes follows a probability distribution [28]. As in [17], random graphs have been used for modeling social networks when the node degrees follow an appropriate probability distribution. The Erdös-Rényi (ER) [7] model is one of the models that can generate such random networks. Given n nodes, and that each edge occurs between two nodes with independent probability p, the average node degree k is approximately $n \cdot p$.

In a *small-world network*, each node is connected to every other node by a relatively small number of intermediate nodes, even though most of the nodes are not directly connected to each other. Online social networks have been shown to exhibit small-world properties and can be created by using a Watts-Strogatz model [25].

A *scale-free network* is a network where node degree distribution follows a power-law, i.e. the number of nodes decreases exponentially as the node degree increases [2]. To generate the scale-free network, seed nodes are placed within the network, then new nodes are added to the existing network incrementally following the principal of preferential attachment [2].

The Facebook friend networks considered in this work are networks constructed from actual Facebook profiles. The nodes of a Facebook friend network represent all the friends of that Facebook user. An edge between two nodes indicates that the two users are friends with each other on top of being friends with the principal user. *Mathematica* provides a *SocialMediaData* function to build such a Facebook friend network for any Facebook user [14, 26, 27].

4. Our approach

We present a weighted evolutionary game to investigate the influence of attribute importance (weight) and network topology on the social network users' behavior in profile attribute disclosure.

Nowadays, there are many online social networks with a variety of designs for their privacy settings [8]. In this paper, we model a possible social network with characteristics exhibited by some of the online social networks in existence. For example, our social network and game model consists of users, each of whom owns a profile comprised of profile attributes and is allowed to select how many and which attributes to reveal to friends or *friends-of-friends* in the network. However, we do not consider a user revealing a different set of attributes to different friends, which is a feature of some social networks.

4.1. Our approach: definitions

The definition of our basic social network is as follows.

Definition 1 (Social network). We define a social network as an undirected graph $G = (N, E)$ with node set N and edge set E, where the node set $N = \{1, 2, ..., n\}$ corresponds to n users in the network.

Additionally, we consider that the connectivity pattern of the network can follow the different network types described in the previous section. These networks include random, small-world, scale-free and Facebook friend networks.

Our weighted evolutionary game is implemented on top of this possible social network. The utility of a user is a combination of both *positive utility* and *negative utility*. The positive utility is represented by the summation of the weights of the attribute pairs with each neighbor on the network. On the other hand, the negative utility is represented by the probability of the identity of a user being inferred.

A *strategy* is a set of actions that players can execute. In our approach, the strategy involves selecting which and how many attributes to disclose.

Definition 2 (Privacy settings). The vector $A_x = (a_{x,1}, a_{x,2}, ..., a_{x,m})$ denotes the profile attributes for User x in the social network, where $a_{x,i}$ is his/her i^{th} attribute. The attribute vector A_x has a corresponding weight vector $W = (w_1, w_2, ..., w_m)$. For each User x, a sign flag vector $S_x = (s_{x,1}, s_{x,2}, ..., s_{x,m})$ denotes whether specific attributes are disclosed or revealed. If attribute $a_{x,i}$ is disclosed, then $s_{x,i} = 1$, otherwise $s_{x,i} = 0$.

For example, an attribute vector for a given user Alice, is represented by $A_{Alice} = (Name, Gender, Age, ..., Hometown)$. For simplicity, we assume that all the users have the same set of profile attributes. The sign flag vector $S_{Alice} = (0, 0, 0, ..., 1)$ means that Alice decides to reveal her hometown but withholds her name, gender, and age. We use $Attr\#i$ to represent a specific attribute i.

We use the concept of *pairs* to evaluate the similarities between two users. Two users Alice and Bob are said to have a *pair* if they both reveal the same attribute, e.g. hometown. Formally, a 2-tuple $(a_{x,i}, a_{y,i})$ is called a pair if and only if $s_{x,i} = 1$ and $s_{y,i} = 1$.

Fig. 1 shows a possible profile configuration for two users x and y which exhibits r pairs. Among the m attributes, User x reveals k_x attributes while User y reveals k_y attributes. Attributes $Attr\#1, Attr\#2, ..., Attr\#r$ are revealed by both users, which constitute the r pairs. The pairs are denoted by $(a_{x,1}, a_{y,1}), (a_{x,2}, a_{y,2}), ..., (a_{x,r}, a_{y,r})$. A higher number of pairs allows for the increased possibility of common ground between users. An increase in common ground leads to an increase in the strength of their friendship

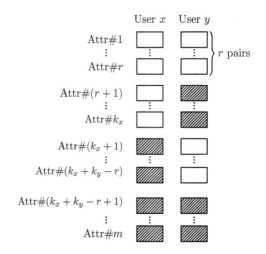

Figure 1. The figure shows a possible profile configuration for two users x and y, who disclose k_x and k_y attributes respectively out of the m possible attributes. The clear rectangles represent the disclosed attributes while the shaded rectangles represent withheld attributes.

[11]. In our case, a friendship is considered stronger if two friends reveal and share more common attributes.

We consider that the benefit and risk are affected by the users at two different levels of social closeness. The first level only includes User x's friends, and the second level also includes User x's *friends-of-friends*. We adopt *influential range* (*IR*) to represent which level of users contribute to User x's benefit and/or risk.

$$B_x(IR) = \begin{cases} \{F\}, & IR = 1, \\ \{F\} \cup \{FoF\}, & IR = 2, \end{cases} \quad (1)$$

where IR denotes influential range, F represents friend, and FoF stands for friend-of-friend. Therefore, $B_x(1)$ is the set of all the friends. $B_x(2)$ includes not just friends, but also friends-of-friends.

In our game, the utility is a combination of benefits (positive utility) and risks (negative utility). A user's positive utility is related to the amount and type of attributes that that user shares with other users in their influential range. The set of users who contribute to User x's positive utility is denoted by $B_x(IR)$.

Conversely, the risk is the probability of a user's identity being inferred. This probability is measured by the reciprocal of the number of the users who disclose the same or additional attributes, i.e. how many users in the influential range can hide that user. The set $B_x^h(IR)$ consists of users in the influential range who disclose the same attributes as x or extra attributes in addition to those disclosed by User x, and can possibly hide User x. The set $B_x^h(IR)$ determines how much risk a user is exposed to.

The combined utility (payoff) function is obtained by using Equation 2, where w_P and w_N are the weight coefficients for the positive utility $\sum_{y \in B_x(IR)} (S_x \wedge S_y) \times W^T$ and negative utility $\frac{1}{|B_x^h|}$ respectively[1].

$$u_x = w_P \cdot \sum_{y \in B_x(IR)} (S_x \wedge S_y) \times W^T - w_N \cdot \frac{1}{|B_x^h(IR)|} \quad (2)$$

We define the benefit-to-risk ratio (BRR) as $w_P : w_N$, which is the ratio of the coefficient for positive utility to the coefficient for negative utility.

4.2. Our approach: model

Our model is iterative and synchronous. First, each user in the network is assigned a random initial attribute sign flag vector. In every iteration, each user compiles a set of candidate neighbors whose privacy settings they may mimic. This set consists of the neighbors who derive a higher utility from their privacy settings than the user derives from his/her own settings. Based on the neighbors' utilities, each user decides whether to change or maintain their strategy. A user is likely to change his/her strategy if his/her neighbors derive a higher utility from their own strategies than the user derives from his/her own. If a user decides to change his/her strategy, one of the candidate neighbors is then selected as the object to mimic. The mimicking process involves a user changing one digit of their sign flag to the corresponding digit of the candidate neighbor's sign flag. This is analogous to a user Alice deciding to reveal her location attribute after seeing that her friend Bob, who has a higher utility, has a revealed location attribute. At the end of each iteration, all the users update their strategies synchronously. The procedure keeps running iteratively until there are no users who change their sign flags between two consecutive iterations. When this condition has been met, the model is said to achieve convergence.

Formally, users follow the *replicator rule* to update their strategies between two successive time steps [19]. Each node makes a decision to maintain or change its current strategy based on the utilities exhibited by its neighbors. Given u_x^t and u_y^t are the utilities of User x and User y respectively at time t, the probability of User x (at time $t + 1$) adopting the strategy of User y (at time t) is given by

$$P_{x,y}^{t+1} = \begin{cases} \frac{u_y^t - u_x^t}{d_{max}}, & u_y^t > u_x^t, \\ 0, & u_y^t \leq u_x^t. \end{cases} \quad (3)$$

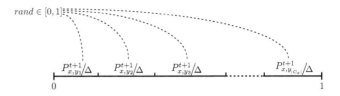

Figure 2. The figure shows the implementation of selecting one of the candidate neighbors as y^* based on the model of *balls into non-uniform bins*, where $C_x = y_1, y_2, ..., y_{|C_x|}$. The probability of selecting neighbor y_i is directly proportional to P_{x,y_i}^{t+1}

We use the largest difference d_{max} in payoff between any two users in the network to guarantee that $P_{x,y}^{t+1} \in [0, 1]$. Equation 3 implies that the probability of User x following the strategy of a neighbor (User y) is proportional to the payoff difference between users x and y, when User y's utility is higher than User x's. This probability value is evaluated for all members of the candidate neighbor set C_x.

Each user's decision to maintain or change his/her strategy depends on $P_{x,y}^{t+1}$ values for the entire candidate neighbor set C_x. The probability of User x maintaining its original strategy, as derived from [19], is given by

$$\overline{Q}_x^{t+1} = \prod_{y \in C_x} (1 - P_{x,y}^{t+1}) \quad (4)$$

Conversely, the probability of User x changing its strategy between t and $t + 1$ is given by

$$Q_x^{t+1} = 1 - \prod_{y \in C_x} (1 - P_{x,y}^{t+1}). \quad (5)$$

After evaluating all probabilities and deciding to change his/her strategy, each user selects the neighbor to mimic in the update process. A higher $P_{x,y}^{t+1}$ value for candidate y translates to a higher probability of being selected as the mimic object y^*. The implementation of selecting y^* is based on a mathematical model called *balls into non-uniform bins* [3], in which the probability[2] $P(y_i)$ of a ball falling into a certain bin is proportional to the size of the bin. In Fig. 2, the size of the each bin is exactly equal to $P_{x,y}^{t+1}/\Delta$, where $\Delta = \sum_{y \in C_x} P_{x,y}^{t+1}$. In total, there are $|C_x|$ bins. Therefore, the probability of the ball falling into ith bin is given by

$$P(y_i) = P_{x,y_i}^{t+1}/\Delta \quad (6)$$

After the mimic object is determined, the specific attribute to mimic is randomly selected from the attributes with different sign values.

The algorithm for updating the attribute sign flag is shown in Algorithm 1.

---

[1] Unless otherwise stated, we use notation $\wedge$ to represent logic AND. Notation W^T refers to the transpose of vector W.

[2] In this paper, we use y to refer to a general user, and we use y_i to refer to a specific user.

Algorithm 1: Algorithm for updating profile attribute sign flag

---

Input: Initial sign flag iSF
Output: Final sign flag fSF

1   Assign iSF for each node;
2   **do**
3   **for** *each node* **do**
4   Find the set of candidate neighbors C_x;
5   Evaluate $P_{x,y}^{t+1}$ for all members of candidate set;
6   Evaluate probability of changing strategy Q_x^{t+1};
7   Generate a random number *rand* $\in [0,1]$;
8   **if** *rand*$< Q_x^{t+1}$ **then**
9   /* *Decision is made to change strategy* */
10   Select neighbor y^* from C_x;
11   /* *Neighbor is selected using balls into non-uniform bins* */
12   Change single bit from SF_x to mimic SF_{y^*};
13   **end**
14   **end**
15   All nodes update sign flags synchronously;
16   **while** *any node changes sign flag*;
17   **return** fSF

4.3. Working case for risk–free scenario

In this subsection, we describe a working case of a risk-free scenario of our model, in which the influential range is restricted to a user's friends (neighbors). Fig. 3a shows the topology structure of the network in this example, which consists of 8 users, whose profile attributes and associated weights are shown in Fig. 3b. The profile attributes include (Name, Gender, Age,..., Hometown) with weight vector $(w_1, w_2, w_3, ..., w_7) = (0.02, 0.06, 0.10, 0.14, 0.18, 0.22, 0.28)$. Fig. 3c shows the initial sign flags for all 8 users. For example, User 5 has a sign flag $S_5 = (1100110)$ which means that only his/her name, gender, education and occupation are revealed. In the next few paragraphs, we show how User 5 may change their strategy in our model.

In the first step, every user calculates their utilities from Equation 2. This involves a comparison of the users' revealed attributes with each neighbor. User 5 has two neighbors: User 1 and User 2 with initial sign flags $S_1 = (1000110)$ and $S_2 = (0110011)$ respectively. The attributes pairs between any two users are obtained by using bit-wise AND operation between the users' sign flag vectors. The bit-wise AND operation between S_1 and S_5 is (1000110), which means that both User 1 and User 5 disclosed attributes 1, 5 and 6. The summation of the weights of attribute pairs (Equation 2) is therefore given by $w1 + w5 + w6$, which evaluates

to 0.42. Similarly, the summation of the weights of attribute pairs between S_2 and S_5 is 0.28. The positive utility for any user is obtained by summing the weighted pair sums for all his/her neighbors. In this case, the positive utility for User 5 is the sum of the weighted attribute pairs between User 5 and both User 1 and User 2. This evaluates to $0.42 + 0.28 = 0.70$. In a similar fashion, the utilities are evaluated for all the network users. Table 1 shows the positive utilities for Users 5, 1, and 2.

In the second step, each user evaluates the probability $P_{x,y}^{t+1}$ of mimicking his/her neighbors according to Equation 3. The maximum range between the utility values for the network nodes $d_{\max}$ is found to be 1.38. User 5 only has to consider User 1 and User 2 when evaluating these probability values. $P_{5,1}^1$ evaluates to 0.41 while $P_{5,2}^1$ evaluates to 0.49.

In the third step, each user decides whether to change or maintain his/her strategy by using Equation 5 which utilizes the probabilities evaluated in the step above. For User 5, Q_5^1 evaluates to 0.6991. If a randomly selected number in the range $[0,1]$ is less than Q_5^1, then User 5 decides to change his/her strategy. Otherwise, User 5 maintains his/her strategy. In our case, User 5 decides to change his/her strategy.

In the fourth step, users who decided to change their strategies select a candidate neighbor to mimic. Candidate neighbors should exhibit higher utility values than the user itself. The probability of User x selecting a specific neighbor y is directly proportional to $P_{x,y}^{t+1}$ for that neighbor. Since Users 1 and 2 both have higher utilities than User 5, they are both viable candidates for User 5 to mimic. After normalizing $P_{5,1}^1$ and $P_{5,2}^1$, the bin sizes for User 1 and User 2 are 0.46 and 0.54 respectively (cf. Equation 6 and Fig. 2). In our case, User 5 selects User 2 as the mimic object.

In the fifth step, each user who decided to change their strategy selects which attribute to reveal or withhold to resemble their mimic object. Comparing User 5 and User 2's sign flags reveals that they differ in four positions, i.e. 1, 3, 5, and 7. User 5 can mimic User 2 in one of the following ways: revealing attribute 3, revealing attribute 7, withholding attribute 1, or withholding attribute 5. In our case, User 5 decides to reveal attribute 7.

All five steps are repeated in each iteration until no single user changes his/her strategy between two successive iterations. The system is then said to have converged.

Fig. 3d shows the sign flags for all 8 users after a single iteration. Fig. 3e shows the sign flags for the whole network after convergence. In this simulation, convergence is achieved after 11 iterations.

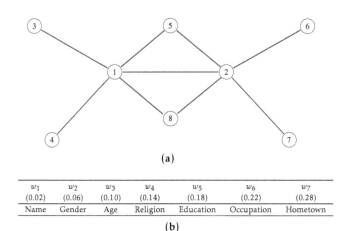

(a)

w_1	w_2	w_3	w_4	w_5	w_6	w_7
(0.02)	(0.06)	(0.10)	(0.14)	(0.18)	(0.22)	(0.28)
Name	Gender	Age	Religion	Education	Occupation	Hometown

(b)

Node	w_1	w_2	w_3	w_4	w_5	w_6	w_7
User 1	1	0	0	0	1	1	0
User 2	0	1	1	0	0	1	1
User 3	1	1	0	0	1	0	0
User 4	0	1	0	1	0	0	1
User 5	1	1	0	0	1	1	0
User 6	0	1	0	1	0	1	1
User 7	1	0	1	0	1	0	0
User 8	1	0	0	1	1	1	0

(c)

Node	w_1	w_2	w_3	w_4	w_5	w_6	w_7
User 1	1	0	0	0	1	1	0
User 2	0	1	1	0	0	1	1
User 3	1	0	0	0	1	0	0
User 4	0	1	0	1	0	0	0
User 5	1	1	0	0	1	1	1
User 6	0	1	1	0	1	1	1
User 7	1	1	1	0	1	0	0
User 8	1	0	0	1	0	1	0

(d)

Node	w_1	w_2	w_3	w_4	w_5	w_6	w_7
User 1	0	1	1	0	0	1	1
User 2	0	1	1	0	0	1	1
User 3	1	1	0	0	1	1	1
User 4	0	0	0	1	0	0	1
User 5	0	1	1	0	0	1	1
User 6	0	1	1	0	0	1	1
User 7	0	1	1	0	0	1	1
User 8	0	1	1	0	0	1	1

(e)

Figure 3. (a) A sample network consisting of 8 users connected to each other, (b) each user has a profile with 7 attributes with a weight vector $(w_1, w_2, ..., w_7) = (0.02, 0.06, 0.10, 0.14, 0.18, 0.22, 0.28)$, (c) initial sign flags for all 8 users that indicate which attributes are revealed and which attributes are withheld (a "1" indicates an attribute revealed while a "0" indicates an attribute withheld), (d) after every user compares his strategy with that of his neighbors, every user updates their strategy, (e) the illustrated system converges after 11 iterations and gives the resultant sign flags for all users.

5. Simulations settings

In this section, we describe the underlying simulation settings. The simulations deal with risk-included and risk-free cases of the weighted evolutionary game.

Table 1. THE PROCESS OF CALCULATING PAYOFF VALUE AND CHOOSING MIMIC OBJECT FROM THE CANDIDATE NEIGHBORS.

User	Neighbor	AND result	Weighted result	Positive utility	$P_{x,y}^{t+1}$
User 5	User 1	1000110	$w_1 + w_5 + w_6 = 0.42$	0.70	N/A
	User 2	0100010	$w_2 + w_6 = 0.28$		
User 1	User 2	0000010	$w_6 = 0.22$	1.26	0.41
	User 3	1000100	$w_1 + w_5 = 0.2$		
	User 4	0000000	0		
	User 5	1000110	$w_1 + w_5 + w_6 = 0.42$		
	User 8	1000110	$w_1 + w_5 + w_6 = 0.42$		
User 2	User 1	0000010	$w_6 = 0.22$	1.38	0.49
	User 5	0100010	$w_2 + w_6 = 0.28$		
	User 6	0100011	$w_2 + w_6 + w_7 = 0.56$		
	User 7	0010000	$w_3 = 0.10$		
	User 8	0000010	$w_6 = 0.22$		

Note: Maximum utility max = 1.38

Minimum utility min = 0

Maximum range between any two nodes' utilities $d_{max} = 1.38$

$(w_1, w_2, ..., w_7) = (0.02, 0.06, 0.10, 0.14, 0.18, 0.22, 0.28)$

The simulation is designed to consider user profiles with 7 attributes ($m = 7$). Each user can choose to reveal or to withhold each of these attributes. A 7-bit flag is assigned to each user, which corresponds to the attributes. For example, the flag 1000110 for User 1 means that Attributes 1, 5 and 6 are revealed while Attributes 2, 3, 4, and 7 are withheld.

We begin by randomly assigning the attribute flag to all users of the network. During each iteration, each user has two options: maintain his/her attribute flag, or change it (by revealing or withholding a single attribute).

To consider different levels of the risk, we choose 3 different benefit-to-risk ratios (*BRR*s), which are 1 : 0, 1 : 15, and 1 : 30 (cf. Table 2). While all the attributes are assigned to different weights, the weight vector for the attributes is assumed to be the same for each user of the network. Additional simulation settings are shown in Table 2. We run the simulation for each configuration 500 times. After averaging 500 simulation results, we obtain the dynamic curves in each of the considered networks, which include random, small-world, scale-free, and Facebook friend networks.

The size and average node degree for each network are all listed in Table 3.

In Fig. 4, the visualized graphs for the random, small-world, and scale-free networks are shown. The visualized graphs for the Facebook friend networks are depicted in Fig. 5. The Facebook graphs (FB1 and FB2) are obtained using the *SocialMediaData* function in *Mathematica*. Fig. 5a and Fig. 5b are from two different Facebook accounts.

6. Results

In this section, we describe the results derived from simulations of the weighted evolutionary game on a

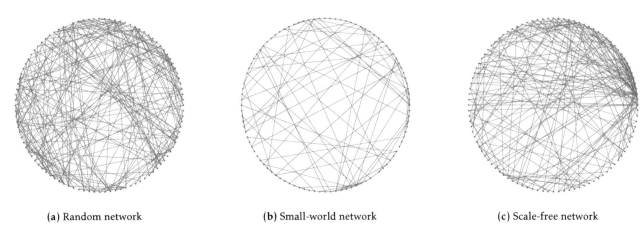

(a) Random network   (b) Small-world network   (c) Scale-free network

Figure 4. The network topologies used in the simulations. The average node degree for each network is 4, and each network includes 100 nodes.

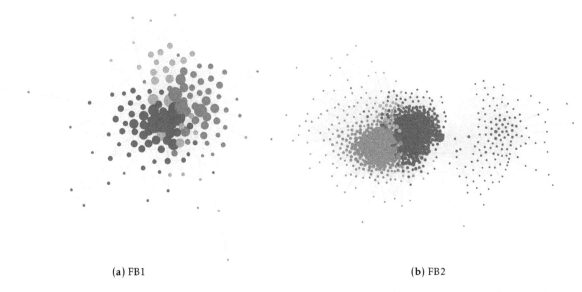

(a) FB1   (b) FB2

Figure 5. The Facebook friend networks used in the simulations. Network FB1 and FB2 are comprised of 151 and 502 nodes respectively.

Table 2. Values Assigned to Specific Parameters in order to Obtain the Presented Results

Parameter	Value
m	7
$w_P : w_N$	$1 : 0, 1 : 15, 1 : 30$
W	$(0.02, 0.06, 0.10, 0.14, 0.18, 0.22, 0.28)$

Table 3. The Properties of Networks in the Simulation

Network	Size	Average Node Degree
Random network	100	4
Small-world network	100	4
Scale-free network	100	4
FB1	151	15.0
FB2	502	49.0

random network, a small-world network, a scale-free network and two Facebook friend networks.

The attribute dynamic curves for random network, small-world network, scale-free network, FB1, and FB2 are shown in Fig. 6, Fig. 7, Fig. 8, Fig. 9, and Fig. 10 respectively. Each dynamic curve shows how the proportion of the entire population that discloses any specific attribute changes with time. Each

dynamic plot consists of 7 curves corresponding to 7 attributes, $Attr\#1$, $Attr\#2$, ..., $Attr\#7$, which are numbered according to their importance (weight), i.e. $Attr\#7$ is the most important attribute, while $Attr\#1$ is the least important attribute.

There are 6 sub-figures (Figs. a-f) in each figure. The 3 sub-figures in the left column (Figs. a, c, e) correspond to the simulation results when we consider the benefit and risk only within the users' friends. The 3 sub-figures on the right side (Figs. b, d, f) correspond to simulation results when we consider both the users' friends and friends-of-friends. The 2 sub-figures in each row have the same benefit-to-risk ratio (BRR). The top (Figs. a, b), middle(Figs. c, d) and bottom(Figs. e, f) rows correspond to BRR values of 1 : 0, 1 : 15, and 1 : 30 respectively, where (BRR = 1 : 0) represents risk-free scenario.

The first observation is a general reduction in attribute revelation with an increase in risk. Consider Fig. 6 which shows the attribute dynamics in a random network: comparing Figs. 6a, 6c, and 6e shows that increasing the risk causes less users to reveal attributes. Fig. 6a shows that over 85% of the population reveal all their attributes by 100 iterations when there is no risk. Introducing risk causes users to reveal less attributes. In fact, Fig. 6e shows that all users withhold all their attributes by 50 iterations when BRR = 1 : 30. The small-world, scale-free, and Facebook networks (cf. Figs. 7, 8, 9, and 10) all exhibit similar observations. While this observation might seem intuitive, it provides some form of vindication for our model.

The second observation is that the networks generally exhibit larger drops in attribute revelation when the range of influence is restricted to friends as opposed to when friends-of-friends are also considered. For example, Figs. 7a and 7b show almost identical levels of revelation without risk. However, increasing the risk leads to more attributes withholding in Fig. 7c and 7e than it does in Figs. 7d and 7f. This means that risk plays a more dominant role in attribute disclosure when only the friends of a user are considered.

The third observation is that increasing the users' range of influence generally results in increased levels of attribute revelation. Consider Fig. 8 which captures attribute dynamics in a scale-free network: comparing the left (Figs. 8a, 8c, 8e)and right columns (Figs. 8b, 8d, 8f) shows that maximum revelation is obtained by as early as 40 iterations for all attributes when friends-of-friends are considered (Figs. 8b, 8d, 8f). In contrast, the risk-free scenario with friends (Fig. 8a) only obtains maximum revelation for some of the attributes, while Figs. 8c and 8e do not obtain maximum revelation for any attributes at all. This observation can be attributed to the process of enlarging the influential range. Increasing the range results in an increase in the number of users who can hide any specific user which leads to a reduction in risk. Increasing the range also allows for more users who share the same attributes which leads to an increase in the user's benefit.

The next observation is related to the friends influential range (Figs. a, c, and e). Increasing the risk factor has a larger effect on attribute disclosure in the

random and small-world networks than in the scale-free and Facebook networks. Comparing Figs. 6 and 7 to Figs. 8, 9 and 10 shows that BRR = 1 : 30 causes complete attribute withholding in the random and small-world networks in contrast to partial attribute withholding in the scale-free and Facebook networks.

The final observation is related to the effect of network topology on attribute disclosure with the range of influence restricted to friends. We find that network topology plays a more considerable effect on the privacy in risk-included scenarios than in a risk-free scenario for the random, small-world, and scale-free networks. Comparing Figs. 6a, 7a and 8a shows that the networks exhibit similar performance in the risk-free environment (BRR = 1 : 0). However, comparing Figs. 6c, 7c and 8c as well as Figs. 6e, 7e and 8e shows that the performance is different for different networks. For example, Figs. 6e and 7e show complete attribute withholding while Fig. 8e shows partial attribute disclosure.

7. Conclusions

In this paper, we analyze the behavior of users in a social network regarding how they choose their privacy settings. We model a basic social network and define a game-theoretical model on top of it, in which users are able to adjust their privacy settings according to certain strategy options. In order to make the model more realistic, we include weights corresponding to the importance that users attach to certain attributes.

With the resulting weighted evolutionary game model, we aim to investigate the influence of various factors, such as attribute importance, benefit, risk and network topology, on the privacy settings employed in social networks.

The results show that the most important attributes exhibit higher levels of revelation than the least important attributes. This finding is more evident in random and scale-free networks than in small-world networks.

We also find that increasing the risk exhibits limited effect on the privacy dynamics of the network if we consider the benefit and risk from friends-of-friends. In the Facebook friend networks, which include more users and feature higher average node degree, increasing risk coefficient only slightly affect the level of attribute disclosure.

The approach presented in this paper provides an initial approach to study and understand the dynamics of privacy settings in social networks.

Acknowledgment

Jungdong Chen expresses his gratitude to Dr. Louis E. Roemer and Alberto Antonioni for their helpful discussions.

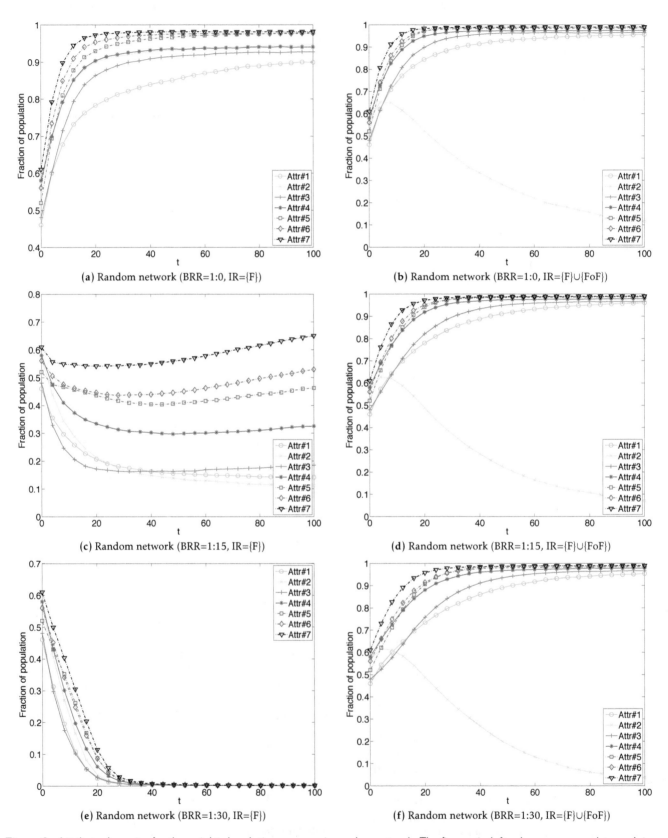

Figure 6. Attribute dynamics for the weighted evolutionary game in random network. The figures in left column correspond to applying Friends as the influential range of the utility function.

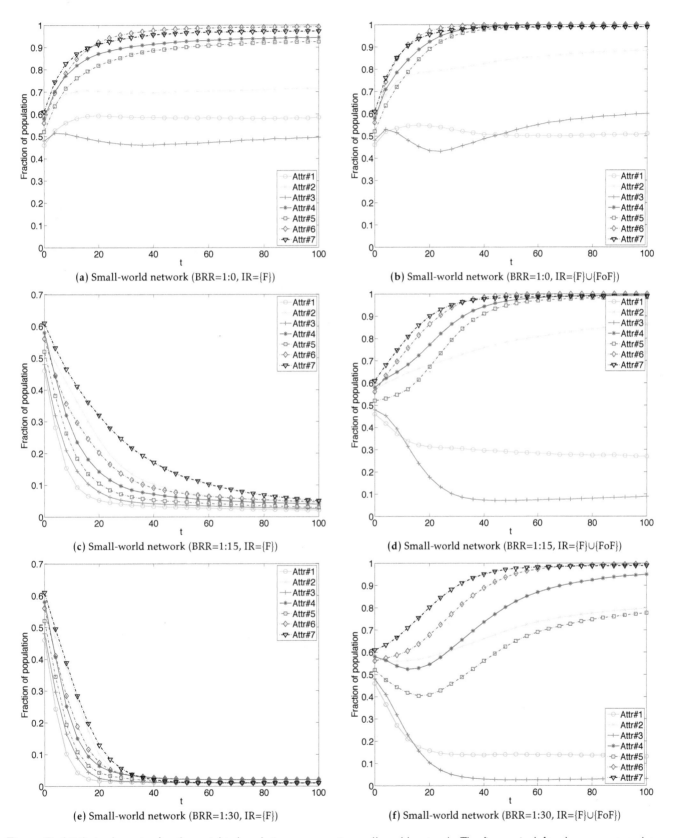

Figure 7. Attribute dynamics for the weighted evolutionary game in small-world network. The figures in left column correspond to applying Friends as the influential range of the utility function.

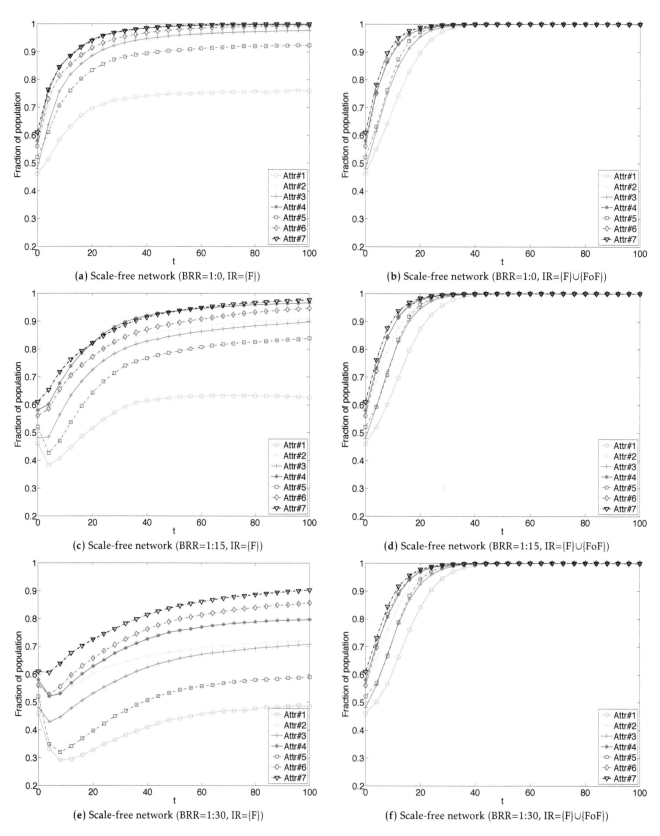

Figure 8. Attribute dynamics for the weighted evolutionary game in scale-free network. The figures in left column correspond to applying Friends as the influential range of the utility function.

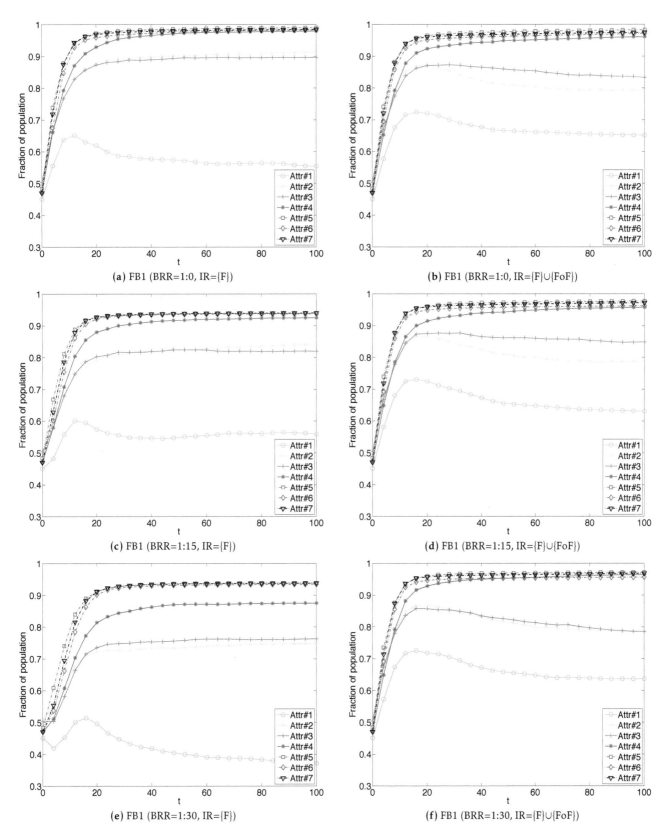

(a) FB1 (BRR=1:0, IR={F})

(b) FB1 (BRR=1:0, IR={F}∪{FoF})

(c) FB1 (BRR=1:15, IR={F})

(d) FB1 (BRR=1:15, IR={F}∪{FoF})

(e) FB1 (BRR=1:30, IR={F})

(f) FB1 (BRR=1:30, IR={F}∪{FoF})

Figure 9. Attribute dynamics for the weighted evolutionary game in FB1. The figures in left column correspond to applying Friends as the influential range of the utility function.

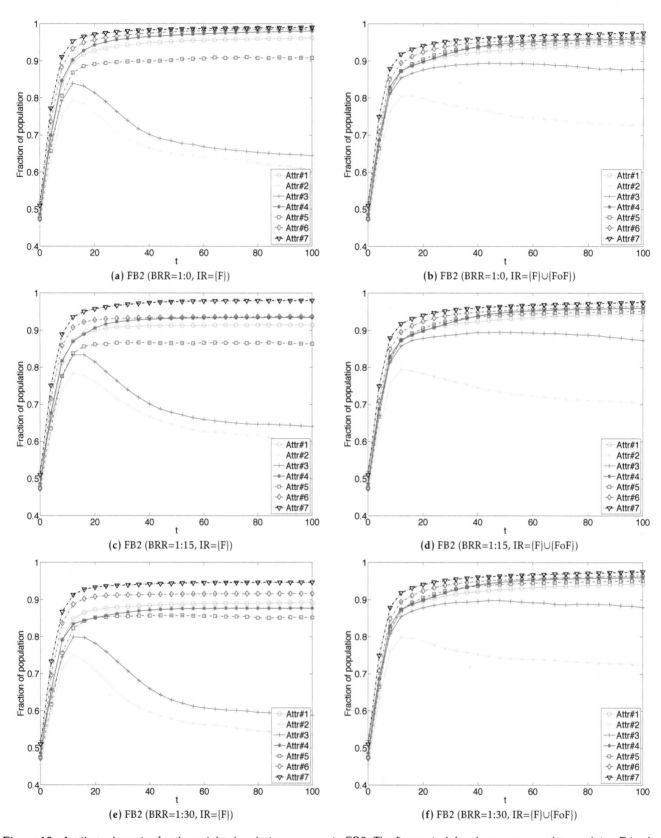

Figure 10. Attribute dynamics for the weighted evolutionary game in FB2. The figures in left column correspond to applying Friends as the influential range of the utility function.

References

[1] ANTONIONI, A. and TOMASSINI, M. (2012) Cooperation on social networks and its robustness. *Advances in Complex Systems* **15**(supp01): 1250046.

[2] BARABÁSI, A.L. and ALBERT, R. (1999) Emergence of Scaling in Random Networks. *Science* **286**(5439): 509–512.

[3] BERENBRINK, P., BRINKMANN, A., FRIEDETZKY, T. and NAGEL, L. (2010) Balls into non-uniform bins. In *2010 IEEE International Symposium on Parallel Distributed Processing (IPDPS)*: 1–10.

[4] CHEN, J., BRUST, M.R., KIREMIRE, A.R. and PHOHA, V.V. (2013) Modeling privacy settings of an online social network from a game-theoretical perspective. In *9th IEEE International Conference on Collaborative Computing: Networking, Applications and Worksharing (CollaborateCom)*: 213–220.

[5] CHEN, W., LIU, Z., SUN, X. and WANG, Y. (2011) Community detection in social networks through community formation games. In *22nd International Joint Conference on Artificial Intelligence (IJCAI)*: 2576–2581.

[6] ELLISON, N.B., STEINFIELD, C. and LAMPE, C. (2007) The benefits of facebook "friends:" social capital and college students' use of online social network sites. *Journal of Computer-Mediated Communication* **12**(4): 1143–1168.

[7] ERDÖS, P. and RENYI, A. (1960) On the evolution of random graphs. *Publ. Math. Inst. Hung. Acad. Sci* **5**: 17–61.

[8] EVANS, S. (April 24, 2013) Top 18 social networks who have joined the 100 million (and more) users club, http://sarahsfav.es/2013/04/24/socialnetworks/.

[9] KAMHOUA, C., KWIAT, K. and PARK, J. (2012) A game theoretic approach for modeling optimal data sharing on online social networks. In *9th International Conference on Electrical Engineering, Computing Science and Automatic Control (CCE)*: 1–6.

[10] KLEINBERG, J., SURI, S., TARDOS, E. and WEXLER, T. (2008) Strategic network formation with structural holes. *SIGecom Exch.* **7**(3): 11:1–11:4.

[11] KOSSINETS, G. and WATTS, D.J. (2009) Origins of Homophily in an Evolving Social Network. *American Journal of Sociology* **115**(2): 405–450.

[12] KRASNOVA, H., SPIEKERMANN, S., KOROLEVA, K. and HILDEBRAND, T. (2010) Online social networks: why we disclose. *Journal of Information Technology* **25**: 109–125.

[13] LAUW, H.W., SHAFER, J., AGRAWAL, R. and NTOULAS, A. (2010) Homophily in the digital world: A livejournal case study. *IEEE Internet Computing* **14**(2): 15–23.

[14] MATHEMATICA (2012) *SocialMediaData, Version 9.0* (Champaign, Illinois: Wolfram Research, Inc.).

[15] MCPHERSON, M., LOVIN, L.S. and COOK, J.M. (2001) Birds of a feather: Homophily in social networks. *Annual Review of Sociology* **27**(1): 415–444.

[16] NARAYANAM, R. and NARAHARI, Y. (2011) A shapley value-based approach to discover influential nodes in social networks. *IEEE Trans. Autom. Sci. Eng.* **8**(1): 130–147.

[17] NEWMAN, M.E.J., WATTS, D.J. and STROGATZ, S.H. (2002) Random graph models of social networks. *Proc. Natl. Acad. Sci. USA* **99**: 2566–2572.

[18] OSBORNE, M. (2004) *An introduction to game theory* (Oxford Univ. Press).

[19] ROCA, C.P., CUESTA, J.A. and SÁNCHEZ, A. (2009) Evolutionary game theory: Temporal and spatial effects beyond replicator dynamics. *Phys. Life Rev.* **6**(4): 208 – 249.

[20] SCOTT, C. (May 11, 2012) Facebook proposes more changes to privacy policy, http://www.pcworld.com/businesscenter/article/255518/facebook_proposes_more_changes_to_privacy_policy.html.

[21] SKYRMS, B. (2003) *The Stag Hunt and the Evolution of Social Structure* (Cambridge Univ. Press).

[22] SQUICCIARINI, A.C., SHEHAB, M. and PACI, F. (2009) Collective privacy management in social networks. In *18th International Conference on World Wide Web*: 521–530.

[23] SQUICCIARINI, A.C. and GRIFFIN, C. (2012) An informed model of personal information release in social networking sites. In *ASE/IEEE Conf. on Privacy, Security, Risk and Trust*: 636–645.

[24] SZABÓ, G. and FATH, G. (2007) Evolutionary games on graphs. *Physics Reports* **446**(4-6): 97–216.

[25] WATTS, D.J. and STROGATZ, S.H. (1998) Collective dynamics of small-world networks. *Nature* **393**(6684): 440–442.

[26] WOLFRAM, S. (August 30, 2012) Wolfram|alpha personal analytics for facebook, http://blog.wolframalpha.com/2012/08/30/wolframalpha-personal-analytics-for-facebook/.

[27] WOLFRAM, S. (November 28, 2012) Mathematica 9 is released today!, http://blog.stephenwolfram.com/2012/11/mathematica-9-is-released-today/.

[28] WONG, A.K.C. and GHAHRAMAN, D.E. (1980) Random graphs: Structural-contextual dichotomy. *IEEE Trans. Pattern Anal. Mach. Intell.* **2**(4): 341–348.

12

Effects of Cohesion-Based Feedback on the Collaborations in Global Software Development Teams

Alberto Castro-Hernández[1,*], Kathleen Swigger[1], Mirna P. Ponce-Flores[2]

[1]Computer Science and Engineering Department, University of North Texas, Denton, Texas, 76203, USA; [2]Ingeniería en Tecnologías de la Información, Universidad Politécnica de Altamira, Altamira, Tamaulipas, Mexico

Abstract

This paper describes a study that examines the effect of cohesion-based feedback on a team member's behaviors in a global software development project. Chat messages and forum posts were collected from a software development project involving students living in the US and Mexico. Half of the teams in the project received feedback in the form of a graphical representation that displayed the group's cohesion level, while the other teams received no feedback. The nature of the group interactions as well as the linguistic content of such interactions was then analyzed and compared. Results from this analysis show statistically significant differences between the feedback and non-feedback conditions. More specifically, cohesion-based feedback had a positive relation to a team's total message count, response rate, and individual cohesion score. In addition, the analysis of linguistic categories showed that the most salient categories observed were related to words about time and work. Furthermore, a comparison between feedback variables and type (i.e., positive and negative feedback) indicates that those individuals exposed to negative feedback had an increase in their communication pacing rates when exposed to positive feedback. Although the feedback system did not appear to affect individual performance, the findings suggest that the cohesion measure defined in this study positively correlated to the task cohesion construct and is also related to individual and team performance.

Keywords: Feedback, cohesion, teamwork, collaboration, global software development, virtual teams

1. Introduction

Because of the growing trend toward globalization in industries, there has been a rise in the use of global teams in organizations [1]. These types of teams generally consist of people who have diverse skills, are remotely located, operate within a global organization, and collaborate on tasks by using telecommunication technologies [2]. The reasons why global teams have flourished over the past few years is because they provide industry with many benefits such as reduced costs, access to people with different skills, a flatter organizational structure, and closer proximity to local markets [3].

On the other hand, managing global teams has its own special challenges. Dealing with cultural diversity [2] and coping with different perceptions of time and relationships [4] can have significant effects on team performance. The lack of trust within global teams is also a major problem [5], largely because of the lack of face-to-face contact [6]. Another challenge for global teams is the difficulty in establishing effective communication channels among team members. Because members of global teams generally use some type of telecommunication technology to share information and achieve their goals, members often find themselves using cumbersome software tools to manage the distributed communications [7].

Research has recently found that many of the problems found in virtual teams are often caused by a lack of cohesiveness among group members. For example, researchers report that the use of communication technologies often hinders the development of the cohesion construct [2]. Global teams have much lower cohesion levels than co-located groups, largely because they collaborate via technology rather than face-to-face. On the other hand, research suggests that the lack of group cohesiveness can be overcome through the exchange of more social communications among group members [8]. Social interactions allow team members to create stronger links, which can have the effect of increasing the levels of group cohesiveness. This particular factor appears to be extremely important because it is also seems to be linked to group performance [9].

Thus the question arises about whether one can improve the performance of global teams by providing groups with information about their overall cohesiveness levels. For example, individuals within a group might change their behavior if they receive some type of feedback about how well their team is communicating with one another. Feedback has been found to be related to performance when it is adequately provided [10]. It has also been shown to increase the engagement level among team members [11]. Therefore, it should be possible to increase cohesiveness and performance within the group by providing effective feedback about how closely team members are working together.

In this paper we describe a feedback system that is intended to show individual cohesion levels within a global software development team. Our main objective is to determine whether such displays can modify the communication behavior of team members who are participating in the project. Moreover, it is proposed that the change in the communication behaviors as a result of this feedback will have an effect on team performance. Additionally, we propose that an interaction-based measure is adequate to measure task cohesion within a team.

2. Team Cohesion Literature

Cohesion is an important emergent state that is usually defined as "a dynamic process which is reflected in the tendency for a group to stick together and remain united in the pursuit of its goals and objectives" [12]. This construct has been studied at both the individual and group levels [13] and has been linked to group performance [14]. Moreover, the strength of this relationship seems to be affected by the group's task [15].

In comparison with co-located teams, virtual teams tend to be less cohesive [5], although the performance in both types of teams is essentially the same, even when different tasks are considered. Group cohesiveness in any type of team seems to increase over time, particularly when there is a leader in the group [16]. Other elements that affect group cohesiveness include team size, degree of democratic behavior within a group, participation, and satisfaction [17].

However, strong group cohesion may not always be a positive thing for a team. For example, [17] shows that high social cohesion within a group can sometimes lead to poor performance. One explanation for this negative relationship is that a team with high social cohesion may actually lead to high levels of group conformity and a reluctance to criticize a teammate's performance.

If such a condition persists, then high social cohesion values will eventually lead to lower performance.

Although researchers use similar words to describe the cohesion construct, they generally use different techniques to measure levels of cohesiveness among groups. One highly cited work [18] describes using the Group Environment Questionnaire (GEQ) to measure different levels of cohesion within groups. In this particular study, the authors propose measuring cohesion levels across four different dimensions: Group Interaction - Task (GIT), Group Interaction - Social (GIS), Individual Attraction to the Group - Social (ATGS), and Individual Attraction to the Group - Task (ATGT). Other researches propose similar dimensions and use surveys to measure their different group cohesiveness constructs [4] [19] [20] [21].

2.1. Related Work on Cohesion Measures

In addition to measuring group cohesiveness through surveys and self-reports, researchers have also developed techniques for measuring the quantitative aspects of a team's interactions. More specifically, [22] calculates group cohesion using a Social Network Analysis technique that creates weighted links between participants based on the number of messages exchanged. Once these adjacency matrices are computed, the authors establish a group cohesion score by looking at only the links that have weights higher or equal to a pre-defined number. They argue that this particular measure is able to detect the position of the agents for a specific level of communication.

Another cohesion measure, called Linguistic Style Matching (LSM), was developed by [20]. This particular measure is based on the similarity of the use of function words between two individuals. Once all paired similarities among group members are computed, the paired values in a group are then averaged, and this number becomes the group cohesiveness score. Using this technique, the researchers found a correlation between LSM and the cohesion construct, and a limited relation between LSM and performance. This particular study tested the LSM measure using chat communications generated during a one-hour session from single gender teams. However, researchers who have applied LSM to the analysis of email messages among team members over an extended period of time were unable to duplicate the significant relationship between cohesion and performance [23].

In this paper, we use survey data and a form of LSM to measure different aspects of group cohesiveness. The survey described in the paper was developed by [8] and was based on the GEQ survey. This particular survey measures cohesiveness among work groups along three different constructs: GIT, GIS and ATGS. In this paper we report on only the GIT results. The four items related to the GIT were measured using a 9-point scale. In addition to the survey data, we used a form of LSM to measure (and display) cohesion among group members. A more detailed description of how this is incorporated into our study can be found in Section 4.4 of this paper. Related literature describing various feedback characteristics now follows.

3. Related Feedback Literature

As explained in [24], feedback can take on many different forms and uses. Thus, it is important to look at the literature on feedback to determine which characteristics are most important when developing a display that is intended to increase team interactions. Below is a description of a number of characteristics that have been suggested by researchers in the feedback literature. In our opinion, these characteristics represent some of the best formal research thinking about developing effective feedback systems.

3.1. Characteristics of Effective Feedback

[10] recommends providing feedback about how well the user is progressing toward the accomplishment of a specific task. On the other hand, [25] suggests giving users two types of feedback: *outcome* feedback that relates to how well the person is doing on the task; and *process* feedback that captures how well the individual is developing. Both types of feedback seem to be related to performance. Although the literature recommends that both outcome and process feedback should be offered, it is not always practical to display advice about a project's outcomes, particular if the feedback must be presented in real-time. Thus, providing process feedback becomes a more realistic option for a real-time system.

According to [26], feedback should be *simple* and clear. Large amounts of feedback information can often be confusing, because it may seem irrelevant to a specific task or event. According to researchers, it is especially important that automatically-generated feedback systems provide clear explanations about how the display information is calculated, and how it changes over time [24].

[27] recommends avoiding any feedback that might be construed as a *normative* comparison, because this type of information may discourage participants from pursuing the task. On the other hand, [24] argues that sharing individual information about others' performances can support adherence to social group norms.

The research literature also suggests that feedback can be displayed either *immediately* or delivered at a *later* time. If something requires a user's attention in real-time, then immediate feedback is preferred [28]. However, immediate feedback can sometimes make

individuals focus on the feedback system rather than on the task. Moreover, delayed feedback can be effective if it is provided in a timely manner, such as just before a milestone or a specific date [29]. For example, software development teams often hold a daily Scrum in order to improve the communications among team members [30]. This type of daily event provides team members with not only necessary feedback but also a routine that helps set the pace for task completion.

In a formative feedback system, the intervention usually occurs at a specific time (either immediate or delayed) [27]. The *consistency* in the timing of the feedback allows the user to remain focused on the task. However, in an automatic real-time system, the intervention is continuous, which means that the user's attention may be divided between the task and the feedback display. Thus, a real-time feedback system must somehow provide the desired information without interfering with the user's engagement in the collaborative exercise [31].

One of the obvious characteristics of an effective feedback system is a good *design*. An example of this type of exacting development process is presented in [24], which describes the process that was used to develop a feedback tool called GroupMeter. The paper highlights the different design phases and relates the reasons why particular decisions were made. In the end, the authors found that a simple, but playful, display was the best design element to use in their feedback system.

3.2. Related Work on Feedback and Groups

Given the amount of research that has examined the efficacy of providing feedback to individuals, it is not surprising to find that there are studies that have looked at the specific relationship between feedback and groups. In [11], the researchers report on using Social Network Analysis (SNA) to provide feedback concerning a team's communication activities. Teams working on a specific task were provided information about the group's centrality, reciprocity, density (cohesion) and centralization after each session of work (a total of four). The researchers found that all forms of feedback tended to increase the number of messages that were generated by group members.

Another example of a feedback system that is aimed at supporting group activities is described in [31]. This particular system was designed to provide feedback concerning a group's positivity, engagement, information exchange and participation levels. Data for these categories were obtained through the use of the Linguistic Inquiry and Word Count (LIWC) tool [32]. This particular software analyzes each word in the text, and a total count of all values is kept for a particular category. From these counts, one can determine trends in conversations and/or discussions for individuals and groups. As can be seen from the study, analyzing word usage in a group's communications can lead to a better understanding of group cohesiveness. Once the communications were analyzed, the authors provided feedback to groups through a simple text display that explained how well a group was performing on each of the four cohesion constructs. After several studies, the authors concluded that providing groups with feedback concerning their levels of engagement and information exchange had positive effects. Both types of feedback had a significant relationship to the type of words that were used during the group discussion.

Thus, the literature on feedback systems and group cohesiveness suggests that providing groups with information about their interactions can lead to changes in group behavior. However, there remain many questions about which elements of a feedback display are most effective, and what specific group behaviors are most impacted by the feedback? For example, [31] reports that students were unhappy with the immediate feedback pop-up displays, yet [28] recommends presenting feedback in a timely manner. Despite the many studies on feedback, formal research on the relationship between feedback and group cohesion is still small. In order to address this need, we present a study that looks at the effects of feedback on global software development teams.

4. Research Methodology

4.1. Teams

The students who participated in this study were drawn from two remotely-located universities; one group came from the University of North Texas (UNT) in the US, and the second group came from the Universidad Politecnica de Altamira (UPA) in Mexico. US participants were all enrolled in a Human-Computer Interface course, and the Mexican participants were enrolled in a Database design course.

Initially, 75 students participated in this project: 35 students from UNT and 40 from UPA. However, two of the Mexican students dropped the database course after the first week of the project, leaving a total of 73 participants.

Prior to the start of the project, students from both universities completed a Software Development Skill Survey in which subjects were asked to rate their competency in the different areas of software development such as Java proficiency and knowledge of database design. Responses on this survey were averaged, and an Individual Skill Level score (ISL) was assigned to each student who participated in the study. These scores were then used to place the students into the various work groups. After sorting each school's students by ISL score, 1-2 students from the top of

the list were paired with a student from the bottom of the list. Once each country' teams were assembled, a Gini index was calculated for each country-team on the two lists. (A Gini index is a measure of inequality [33] which we used to operationalize member diversity). Each university's country-team list was then sorted by their Gini index, and country-teams with similar Gini indexes were then combined into a single team. Using this procedure we were able to create 15 teams. A more detailed description of the composition of each team can be found in Section 5.

4.2. Software Development Project

Each team was asked to complete the same software development project. The assignment consisted of a redesign of an existing non-profit website. More specifically, students were asked to redesign three sections of the website (i.e., the home page, the events page, and the contribution page) and implement a database that could support the various operations that were needed to maintain the pages. The responsibilities for completing this task were divided among the two teams: UNT members developed the website front-end, whereas UPA members designed and implemented the database. Moreover, the project deliverables were further divided into four separate milestones as indicated below:

1. Team members introduced themselves to each other; exchanged information about requirements (UNT students); created an Entity-Relationship diagram for the database (UPA students). Duration: 6 days.

2. UNT members re-designed and created the new home page, and UPA members implemented the database. Duration: 8 days.

3. UNT members created remaining website modules and UPA members provided database queries. Duration: 7 days.

4. All members collaborated to finish the project. Duration: 7 days.

Members were reminded to complete their milestones on time, and checks were made to ensure that members complied with these instructions.

4.3. Collaboration Tools

Students who participated in the project were asked to communicate with one another using a project management web application based on the Redmine platform. The Redmine application platform supports several collaborative tools including chat, forums, wikis, document sharing, etc. Moreover, this particular Redmine application has been enhanced so that

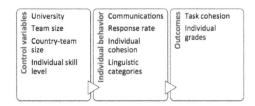

Figure 1. Control, individual behavior and outcome variables at individual level.

it records and timestamps all interactions among group members and transfers this information to a centralized database. Additional refinements were made to the Redmine tool in order to provide feedback to some groups concerning their collaborations and participation levels. A description of this special module can be found in Section 4.5.

In addition to the Redmine software, each team had access to a MySQL server, which allowed them to create and populate a database, as well as a web server, which allowed teams to publish their web pages.

4.4. Measures

In order to determine the effects of feedback on global software development teams, we examined a number of variables that capture different characteristics of a team's interactions. The list of variables are shown in Figure 1.

Control Variables. The Control variables used in this study were *University, Team size, Country-team size, Individual skill level*. Section 5 provides more details concerning each of these variables.

Individual Behaviors. The Individual Behaviors of interest to this study were: *Communications, Response rate, Individual cohesion, and the Linguistic-categories*. For example, the total number of messages generated by a group has been used as a dimension of team performance [4]. Thus, we defined a measure called *Communications* to represent the total number of messages generated by team members.

The *Response rate* measure was operationalized by counting the number of replies made to messages in the chat and forums for each individual. A *reply* was defined as either a chat message or forum post that was sent by an individual who was different from the sender of the previous chat-message or forum-post (i.e., a sequence of chat-messages or forum-posts from the same author were counted as 1).

To show how much (or how similar) teammates were responding to one another's communications, we created an *Individual cohesion* measure. This measure was calculated by summing messages between each pair

Table 1. Level of analysis of Communications, Response rate and Individual cohesion. Where C means Chat, F means Forum, NS means Non-social and S means Social

Level	Communications				Response rate			Indiv. cohesion	
Tool	C		F		C	F		C	F
Content	NS	S	NS	S	NS	S		NS	S

of individuals on a team, as follows:

$$cohesion_{ij} = 1 - \frac{abs(r_{ij} - r_{ji})}{r_{ij} + r_{ji}} \qquad (1)$$

Where r_{ij} are the replies sent from member i to member j. An *Individual's cohesion* was then obtained by averaging all the paired cohesion values, as show in equation 2.

$$cohesion_i = \frac{\sum_{j \in M, j \neq i} cohesion_{ij}}{|M| - 1} \qquad (2)$$

Where j are the teammates of i in team M. For a group-level measure, all team member's *Individual cohesion* values were averaged (see equation 3).

$$group\_cohesion = \frac{\sum_{i \in M} cohesion_i}{|M|} \qquad (3)$$

These measures were based on the similarity measure proposed in [20]. The scores on each of these measures range between 0 and 1, with a 1 representing perfect cohesion.

Communications, Response rates and *Individual cohesion* measures were also analyzed at the individual tool level [i.e., messages using either the (C)hat or (F)orum tool]. Moreover, these three measures were divided even further into those chat and forum communications that referred to Non-Social (NS) and (S)ocial[1] content (see table 1). For example, we separated the chat room messages that were non-social and identified them as *Non-social-chat-communications*. The Non-social/Social Forum messages for the Response rates and Individual Cohesion measures were not included in this study because the levels of participation of Feedback groups in the forums was too low (as reported in the next section).

The *Linguistic word category* measures were obtained by applying the sentiment analysis software (LIWC) [32]) to the group transcripts generated during this project. LIWC was utilized for this project because it looks at different linguistic features that characterize

---

[1]A message was counted as Social, if according to its LIWC Social category value, it obtained 50% or higher. Otherwise, it was counted as Non-social.

different individuals and groups. Through such a procedure, we were able to extract both an individual and a group's use of different linguistic categories.

Outcome Measures. The two Outcome measures used in this study were *Task cohesion* and *Performance*. *Task cohesion* is a measure of a team's perception of their level of commitment to complete the task. At the end of the project, *Task cohesion* scores for this project were calculated by averaging an individual's responses on a 4-item Task Cohesion survey, as described in [8]. We also calculated *Group task cohesion* scores by aggregating the individual surveys by team, as described in Section 5.4.

Performance scores were obtained by examining the individual grades assigned to students after the completion of the project. Each country team (i.e., UNT and UPA) was assessed separately by its corresponding course professor. That is, UNT students were graded by the US instructor, and UPA students were graded by the Mexican instructor. To avoid any inconsistencies between the two evaluation procedures, grades for all students were normalized by their university values. Moreover, *Team grades* were obtained by averaging students' individual grades for each group, as described in Section 5.4.

4.5. The Feedback Display

In order to determine the effect of feedback on teams, we created a special graphic that appeared in the chat module that resides within our collaborative tool. We chose the chat module for the feedback display because previous experience showed that this is the most frequently used tool for collaborations [34]. This particular module was designed to provide information about how a team was collaborating throughout the project. Following the recommendations suggested in [24], the special feedback visual was designed to consist of four elements (see Figure 2):

1. A piece of text showing the group's current cohesion level. This number is computed using the *Group cohesion* formula.

2. A piece of text showing an individual student's percentage of *Individual participation*. This number is computed as a proportion of the number of replies sent by the individual student over the total number replies sent by the team.

3. A graph that displays the group's current cohesion level. The graphic consists of a central node (in a light gray color) surrounded by other nodes (in dark gray colors), which represent the teammates of the current viewer. The central node represents the position where, ideally, all nodes should be when a team has perfect cohesion

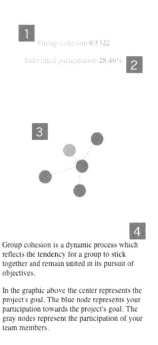

Figure 2. Cohesion-based feedback display.

(*Group cohesion* measure = 1). Edges represent the inverse *Individual cohesion* measure of a team member associated with its teammates (i.e. when an individual's cohesion measure is close to 0, its node is far from the central node). The cohesion level of current viewer of the feedback display is represented as a light blue node.

4. A text describing the above graph.

The feedback display was designed to provide students with a more focused understanding of their group's communication activities. For example, the graph shows how closely the user (represented as the blue node) and their group (represented as the dark gray nodes) relate to ideal cohesiveness (represented as the center, light gray node). While such information may discourage some students, as suggested in [24], we believed that showing teams opportunities for improvement could motivate them to move in those directions.

In addition to the graph, the display also reports on a student's individual participation rates in comparison to the total participation of the team. This information is not only helpful to the individual, but it is designed to offset any negative effects brought about by the group cohesiveness graph, since an individual can always control their own behavior, but perhaps not their team's behavior. These types of mixed reviews concerning the effects of feedback are reported in [25] and [35].

The cohesion-based feedback display was provided to eight of the fifteen teams who participated in the study. These eight teams were randomly selected and

Table 2. Control variables

University		Team size		Country-team size		Feedback	
UNT	35	4-members	8	2-members	34	No	34
UPA	38	5-members	65	3-members	39	Yes	39

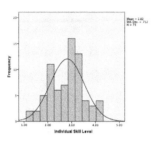

Figure 3. Individual Skill Level distribution.

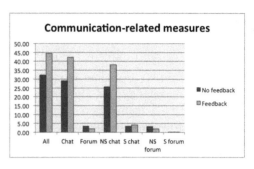

Figure 4. Comparison of Feedback and No-Feedback teams on Communication-related measures.

designated as the Feedback teams. Seven teams received no feedback through Redmine and were, therefore, designated as the No-Feedback teams. Teams assigned to the Feedback group received an email describing the information contained in the feedback display at the beginning of the project. Once the project began, the feedback displays were updated every two hours.

5. Data Analysis

A total of 2831 messages were sent during this project: 2636 chat messages, 195 forum posts and 0 wiki pages. A total of 71, out of a possible 73, *Task Cohesion* surveys were received, with an internal consistency of 0.807 (Cronbach's alpha).

The total number of participants for each of the control variables is listed in Table 2. Moreover, Figure 3 reports the overall distribution levels of student scores on the Individual Skill Level survey. The mean for subjects completing the Individual Skill Level survey was 2.82 ($SD = 0.712$).

Unless otherwise specified, the following correlations that are reported were controlled by *University, Team size, Country-team size* and *Individual skill level*. In addition, the presence or absence of *Feedback* was operationalized with a dummy variable (1 or 0).

5.1. Feedback Effect on Individual Behaviors

We anticipated that overall *Communications* would be higher in Feedback teams than in No-Feedback teams. The results from a partial correlation analysis show a marginal and positive relationship between Feedback and *Communications* ($r = 0.187^2$, $p = 0.062^3$). When the

communication variables were analyzed at the tool-level (i.e., Chat and Forum communications), we found a positive correlation ($r = 0.206$, $p < 0.05$) between Feedback teams and Chat communications. The correlation between Feedback and Forum communications, however, was negative ($r = -0.204$, $p < 0.05$). Feedback seems to have affected the total number of Communications as well as the Chat communications generated by Feedback teams. The negative relationship between Feedback and Forum communications can be explained by the fact that Feedback teams had a much greater preference for the Chat tool as opposed to the Forum tool. Since our Feedback graphic was displayed within the Chat tool module, it seems reasonable to assume that the Feedback teams were more likely to keep returning to the Chat tool for their group information rather than use the Forum tool.

When *Chat and Forum Communications* were analyzed at the linguistic level, we found that there were no correlations between Feedback and *Social-Chat-Communications* or between Feedback and *Social-Forum-Communications*. On the other hand, there was a significant relationship between Feedback teams and *Non-social-Chat-Communications* ($r = 0.214$, $p < 0.05$), and between No-feedback teams and *Non-social-Forum-Communications* ($r = -0.196$, $p = 0.053$). As [2] reports, the low level of social communication is expected in virtual teams, since they tend to have weaker social cohesiveness than face-to-face groups. However, both Feedback and No-Feedback groups seem to use non-social messages to communicate about the task. A more graphic illustration of the relationships that we found can be seen in Figure 4, which shows a comparison of the means of Feedback and No-Feedback groups on all the communication-related measures.

It was also hypothesized that the feedback display would affect a team's *Response rates*. Results of partial correlations between Feedback and the different response-rate measures indicate that Feedback was significantly and positively related to overall *Response Rates* ($r = 0.262$, $p < 0.05$), *Chat-Response-Rates* ($r = 0.296$, $p < 0.01$), and *Non-social-Chat-Response-Rates*

---

[2] r measures the strength and direction of a linear relationship
[3] p-value is defined as the probability of obtaining a result equal to the proposed hypothesis

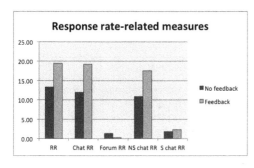

Figure 5. Comparison of Feedback and No-Feedback teams on Response Rate (RR) –related measures.

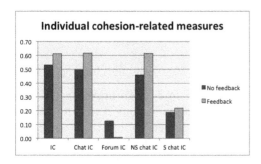

Figure 6. Comparison of Feedback and No-Feedback teams on Individual Cohesion (IC) –related measures.

($r = 0.306$, $p < 0.01$). As anticipated, feedback teams had fewer responses within the forums, and so the relationship between Feedback and *Forum-Response-Rates* was negative ($r = -0.298$, $p < 0.01$). Lastly, there was no correlation between Feedback teams and *Social-Chat-Response-Rates* ($r = 0.105$, $p = 0.194$). Again, the mean comparisons of Feedback and No-Feedback teams on each of the Response-Rate measures can be seen in Figure 5.

Results also indicate that Feedback teams were much more cohesive than Non-Feedback teams. A partial correlation analysis of Feedback teams and *Individual Cohesion* rates indicate that individuals in Feedback teams were significantly more cohesive than individuals in No-Feedback teams ($r = 0.183$, $p = 0.066$). This higher cohesiveness extended to all chat communications ($r = 0.260$, $p < 0.05$), and to those chat communications related to non-social messages ($r = 0.330$, $p < 0.01$). Not surprising, *Forum-Individual-Cohesion* was negatively correlated with Feedback teams ($r = -0.369$, $p < 0.01$), and *Social-Chat-Individual-Cohesion* was not correlated with Feedback ($r = 0.014$, $p = 0.455$). The mean comparisons between Feedback and No-Feedback teams on the Individual Cohesion measures are presented in Figure 6.

To further understand the effects of feedback on global software teams, we examined the content of the messages that were sent between team members. As noted earlier, we used the LIWC software to determine the frequency of different *Linguistic categories* within Feedback and No-Feedback teams. Correlations between the different word categories and Feedback teams are presented in Table 3. As the table shows, there were significant correlations between nine word categories and Feedback teams.

Interestingly, the words used most frequently in this project were related to the *inclusive* category. This category contains words such as *add*, *and*, *we* [36]. Moreover, the single word that was most frequently used in this category was the *we* word – 396 times in Feedback teams, and 260 times in No-Feedback teams. The heavy use of the *we* word suggests that groups in both Feedback and No-Feedback were starting to act (and think) as a team. Also, the use of *we* has been shown to have a relationship to hard work in organizations [37].

Conjunction words were also used quite frequently within the global teams. This category shares a number of words with the *inclusive* word-type such as *and*, *with*, *together*. There was a high correlation between both categories ($r = 0.945$, $p < 0.001$). This word category is related to narrative thinking, which is a trait often associated with people who have good social skills.

The *Time* category contains words such as *today*, *tomorrow*, *now*, *yesterday*, *date*. Thus, the substantial use of these types of words suggests that Feedback teams were very aware of schedules and the passing of time, which was probably related to the group's efforts to complete the task.

The *Work* and *Achievement* categories have a number of words in common such as *accomplish*, *work*, *success*, *team*. As a result of these shared words, it is not surprising that there was a strong correlation between these two categories ($r = 0.854, p < 0.001$).

The *Assent* category includes words such as *agree*, *ok*, *yes*, *yeah*, *haha*, *cool*. The high correlation between Feedback teams and the *assent* category suggests that members within Feedback teams had similar opinions, and they tended to agree with one another more than members in Non-Feedback teams. However, frequent agreement has also been associated with passivity, as reported in [38].

Categories of *leisure* and *home* were also strongly related to Feedback teams. Words related to these two categories generally indicate that the group is engaged in non-work related communications. The presence of words from these two categories suggests that members within Feedback teams were more likely to share social or personal information with one another than those members in No-Feedback teams.

Table 3. LIWC categories with significant differences. *p<0.1, **p<0.05

Word category	Mean	Correlation with Feedback
Inclusive	27.48	0.202*
Conjunctions	26.64	0.215*
Time	20.76	0.298**
Adverbs	17.57	0.201*
Work	14.74	0.214*
Achieve	10.58	0.206*
Assent	5.33	0.273**
Leisure	4.74	0.246**
Home	2.00	0.242**

Table 4. Correlations between communication- and response-rate- measures and Individual grades. *$p < 0.01$, **$p < 0.001$

Individual grades		
	Communications	Response rate
All	0.345*	0.336*
Chat	0.337*	0.350*
Forum	0.122	-0.124
Social chat	0.363*	0.464**
Non-social chat	0.319*	0.003*
Social forum	0.148	
Non-social forum	0.107	

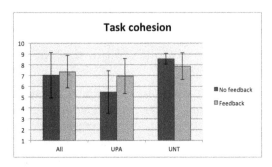

Figure 7. Comparison of Feedback and No-Feedback teams on Task Cohesion values.

5.2. Effects on Outcome Variables

We also analyzed the relationships between Feedback and the two outcome variables of *Task cohesion* and *Individual grades*. Results showed that Feedback had a positive correlation with *Task cohesion*, but it was not significant (r = 0.118, p = 0.110). Overall mean values on the Task Cohesion survey were much higher for Feedback groups than No-Feedback groups (mean difference = 0.3295). Moreover, a Levene's Test of the data revealed that there was a significant difference between the variances of Task Cohesion values of No-Feedback teams and Feedback teams ($p < 0.05$) (see Figure 7, column All). Given this high variance, we analyzed the *Task Cohesion* responses by university and feedback type and found that the UNT students assigned to the No-Feedback teams had much higher perceived values of task cohesion than UPA students in No-Feedback teams, while the differences between the Task cohesion scores in the two universities was much lower in Feedback teams. Therefore, this result suggests that task cohesion's perception was shaped by the feedback display.

It was suspected that students who received feedback would also receive higher grades on their global software development projects. However, a partial correlation analysis found that *Individual Grades* were unrelated to Feedback ($r = 0.026, p = 0.415$), and that

the variance between the Feedback and No-Feedback groups was not significant.

5.3. Effects of Other Measures on Outcome Variables

Since this study found significant relationships between Feedback and the various Communication and Response rate variables (see Section II), we anticipated that there might be similar correlations between the communication and response-rate measures and our outcomes measures (i.e., Task Cohesion and Performance). Partial correlations (controlled by *University, Team size, Country-team size, Individual Skill Level* and *Feedback*) between the *Communication* variables and *Task cohesion*, and between the *Response rate* measures and *Task cohesion* produced no significant relationships. However, as indicated in Table 4, all *Communication* and *Response rate* variables (except forum communications) had a positive and significant relationship to *Individual grades*. While individual communication behaviors do not appear to affect how an individual "feels" about their group and the task, they do seem to affect how well an individual "performs" the task.

The *Individual cohesion* measures used in this study capture the response rate similarity between an individual and his/her teammates. As such, it was assumed that there would be strong correlations between the Individual cohesion measures and the Task cohesion construct. Thus, we calculated partial correlations between *Individual cohesion* and *Task cohesion*, while controlling for *University, Team size, Country-team size, Individual Skill Level* and *Feedback*. Results indicate that *Individual cohesion* rates (except forum and social chat cohesion levels) were strongly related to a group's perception of how well they were committed to completing the task. Evidence for this relationship is strongest among individual cohesion and chat cohesion levels, particularly as they pertain to non-social activities (see Table 5).

We also related the *Individual cohesion* measures to individual grades while controlling for *University, Team size, Country-team size, Individual Skill Level* and

Table 5. Correlations between Individual cohesion measures and Task cohesion. $^*p < 0.1$, $^{**}p < 0.05$

Task cohesion	
Individual Cohesion	0.214*
Chat Individual Cohesion	0.215*
Forum Individual Cohesion	0.005
Social chat Individual Cohesion	0.135
Non-social chat Individual Cohesion	0.265**

Table 6. Correlations between Individual cohesion measures and Individual grades. $^*p < 0.001$

Individual grades	
Individual Cohesion	0.412*
Chat Individual Cohesion	0.432*
Forum Individual Cohesion	-0.079
Social chat Individual Cohesion	0.468*
Non-social chat Individual Cohesion	0.426*

Feedback (see Table 6). Correlations show that all of the *Individual cohesion* measures predict individual performance, except forum messages.

The relationships between the *Individual cohesion* measures and *Task Cohesion* supports the notion that a group's perception of how well they are doing on a task is shaped by a person's response activities [8]. In addition, the strong positive relation between the cohesion measures and *Individual grades* demonstrates the link between response levels within a group and individual performance.

5.4. Group Cohesion and Outcome Variables

Since the results showed that students who had more interactions with their teammates not only performed better but also had better perceptions of their team's ability to accomplish the task, it was anticipated that a group-level analyses of these variables would achieve similar results. Prior to running the analysis, however, it was necessary to determine how to aggregate the data and, at the same time, adjust for the large variation between UNT and UPA responses on the Task Cohesion survey. Techniques suggested by [39] indicate that the variance problem can be overcome by treating each country team separately. Therefore, we aggregated Task cohesion, Individual cohesion, Chat-Individual-Cohesion, Non-social-Chat-Individual-Cohesion and Individual grades for each team at each university and labeled these new variables as *Group Task Cohesion, Group Cohesion, Group Chat-Cohesion, Group Non-social-Chat-Cohesion* and *Team Grade*, respectively.

Correlations, as shown in Table 7, were controlled by *Team size, Country-team size, Feedback* and average of *Individual Skill Level*. Results show that only *Group*

Table 7. Correlations between Group Cohesion, Chat Group Cohesion, Work-Chat Group Cohesion, Group Task Cohesion and Team Grades. $^*p < 0.1$, $^{**}p < 0.05$, $^{***}p < 0.01$

	Group Task Cohesion	Team Grades
Group Cohesion	-0.181	0.425**
Chat Group Cohesion	-0.087	0.466***
Non-social Chat Group Cohesion	0.307*	0.587***

Non-social-Chat-Cohesion predicts *Group Task Cohesion*. On the other hand, all group cohesion measures were significantly correlated with *Team grades*.

It is important to note that *Group Task Cohesion* and *Team grades* were not correlated ($r = 0.168, p = 0.187$). A possible explanation for this result is that student responses on the Task Cohesion surveys represent an individual's perceptions of the "global" team, whereas Team grades represent student performance at the university level. While teams may have perceived that the global team was capable of completing the task, a specific country team may not have performed as well as other teams within the same country.

6. Feedback effects on pacing

Our previous results showed that the feedback display had an effect on the number of communications generated by members who received feedback information. Since the feedback system showed a number of different types of information, it was important to determine which one provoked the change of behavior in participants' communications. In addition, it is also important to determine whether there was a difference between the effects of positive versus negative feedback.

6.1. Pacing definition

The feedback effect on participants' communications was defined as the *average pacing* and was computed by taking the average time between the next three messages that were sent by a user who had just received a specific type of feedback (see Figure 8). It was assumed that every time a user sent a chat message, he or she also had been exposed to the feedback information. *Pacing* was defined as the number of seconds between any two chat messages sent by a user. This calculation was based on [40], which assessed the effects of positive and negative feedback on the quality of future post in online news communities.

6.2. Feedback information

We identified four specific variables presented to the participants in the feedback system: 1) *Group cohesion* was a numerical value between 0 and 1; 2) *Individual*

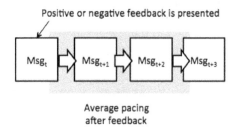

Figure 8. Feedback effect on pacing.

Table 8. Descriptive statistics for feedback variables.

Feedback variable	Mean	Std. Dev.	Min	Max
Group cohesion	0.3729	0.1728	0	0.8474
Individual participation	0.3100	0.1392	0	0.9999
Individual cohesion	0.2899	0.1956	0	0.9999
Position	2.98	1.39	1	5

participation was a numerical value between 0 and 100; 3) *Individual cohesion* was a numerical value between 0 and 1, presented graphically to the user as the proximity of a user's node to the center (ideal cohesion); 4) *Position* was the visual comparison of a member to the rest of the team, and defined as a value between 1 (closest to the center) and 5 (farthest to the center).

Only data from teams with 5 members was used in this analysis, so that the *Position* values would be comparable. In total, we obtained 1193 user's *average pacing* values, after being exposed to a specific combination of feedback variables. The descriptive values for each feedback variable is shown in Table 8.

6.3. Positive and negative feedback

Every feedback variable was converted to a binary label: positive or negative.

Group cohesion was labeled as positive when its value was higher or equal than 0.5; otherwise, negative.

Based on their descriptive values, *Individual participation* was labeled as positive when its value was higher or equal to 0.4; negative, when its value was lower or equal to 0.2; otherwise, it was not used in the analysis.

Similarly, *Individual cohesion* was labeled as positive when its value was higher or equal to 0.4; negative, when its value was lower or equal to 0.2; otherwise, it was not used in the analysis. We decided to separate positive and negative feedback by 0.20, since this variable measures a graphical perception that may be affected by Weber's law [41] (i.e., very small changes may not have been perceptible).

Position was labeled as positive when its value was higher or equal to 4; negative, when its value was lower or equal to 2; otherwise, it was not used in the analysis.

Table 9. Instance distribution in feedback variables.

Feedback variable	Positive	Negative
Group cohesion	43	195
Individual participation	96	142
Individual cohesion	128	110
Position	78	160

Table 10. Linear model for estimating average pacing by feedback variables and their interactions, controlled by university, skill and country–team size. GC means Group cohesion; IP means Individual participation; IC means individual cohesion; P means Position. $^*p<0.05$.

Variable	Mean square	F	Sig.
Intercept	3.E+10	3.024	0.083
University	1.0E+9	0.094	0.759
Skill	2.E+10	2.202	0.139
Country-team size	3.2E+10	0.030	0.863
Group cohesion	5.E+10	4.573	**0.034***
Individual participation	3.2+9	0.296	0.587
Position	2.4E+9	0.218	0.641
Individual cohesion	6.E+10	5.350	**0.022***
GC+IP	.	.	.
GC+P	.	.	.
GC+IC	.	.	.
IP+P	6.5E+9	0.603	0.438
IP+IC	2.1E+9	0.194 + 0.660	
P+IC	3.2E+9	0.299	0.585
GC+IP+P	.	.	.
GC+IP+IC	.	.	.
GC+P+IC	.	.	.
IP+P+IC	.	.	.
GC+IP+P+IC	.	.	.

As a result, we kept 238 instances for this analysis. Their distribution is shown in Table 9.

6.4. Effects on future pacing

An univariate linear model was developed, using the binary feedback variables and their interactions. It was also controlled by *university*, *skill level* and *contry-team size*. For its construction, we used the SPSS's General Linear Model tool.

As shown in Table 10, *Group cohesion* and *Individual cohesion* variables have a significant pacing effect when comparing positive and negative feedback.

Table 11 shows a comparison of students' future pacing behavior after a user receives specific feedback. Based on these results, we observed that people who received *negative group-cohesion feedback* had higher pacing values than people who received *positive group-cohesion feedback*. Similarly, people who received *negative individual-cohesion feedback* had higher pacing

Table 11. Pacing mean comparison between positive and negative feedback on Group cohesion and Individual cohesion variables

Feedback variable	Type	Mean	Std. Dev.	Time
Group cohesion	Negative	55042.012	10351.0	15:17
	Positive	101896.06	19274.4	28:18
Individual cohesion	Negative	54593.049	13681.2	15:09
	Positive	79030.238	11072.6	21:57

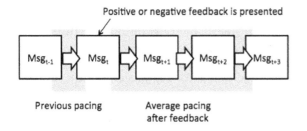

Positive or negative feedback is presented

Previous pacing   Average pacing
                         after feedback

Figure 9. Comparison of previous pacing to future average pacing.

values than people who received *positive individual-cohesion feedback*.

Therefore, it seems that construct-based feedback (*Group cohesion* and *Individual cohesion*) increases communication, specifically when negative feedback is provided.

On the other hand, it seems that the information about a subject's relationship to other members of the team (i.e., *Position*) was not important enough to modify pacing behavior consistently; which is contrary to the research suggested by [24]. Possibly, the existence of other, more informative feedback information may have interfered with this particular effect.

In addition, it seems that the measure-based individual feedback (*Individual participation*) had no effect on communication pacing. Again, it is possible, that other feedback elements were more useful to the student then this display element.

6.5. Change in previous pacing

It is clear that in the previous results the pacing of people who received negative feedback was higher when they received positive feedback. However, it is possible that both positive and negative feedback can have an effect on the previous user's pacing patterns. Thus, we decided to compare each of our data *average pacing* values to its related previous pacing values (see Figure 9).

As shown in Table 12, none of the obtained results is significant. Probably, the effect of increasing or decreasing previous pacing is more apparent in the communication data collected immediately after the

Table 12. Differences in pacing after feedback exposure.

Feedback variable	Type	Difference	Sig.	Pacing
Group cohesion	Negative	-2377.23	0.46	Decrease
	Positive	-1212.94	0.89	Decrease
Individual cohesion	Negative	-7723.63	0.19	Decrease
	Positive	5634.14	0.39	Increase

Table 13. Differences in pacing after feedback exposure by milestone. GC means Group cohesion; IC means Individual cohesion. $^*p < 0.05$.

Milestone	Feedback	Type	Difference	Sig.	Pacing
I	GC	**Negative**	6282.98	**0.02°**	**Increase**
		Positive	-45.01	0.93	Decrease
	IC	**Negative**	22201.14	**0.00°**	**Increase**
		Positive	-589.77	0.89	Decrease
II	GC	Negative	2466.89	0.54	Increase
		Positive	-6418.87	0.62	Decrease
	IC	Negative	6798.28	0.13	Increase
		Positive	-11467.07	0.37	Decrease
III	GC	Negative	-8986.91	0.37	Decrease
		Positive	6601.05	0.54	Increase
	IC	Negative	5119.67	0.77	Increase
		Positive	5746.81	0.57	Increase
IV	GC	Negative	331.66	0.91	Increase
		Positive	2534.24	0.81	Increase
	IC	Negative	1260.78	0.77	Increase
		Positive	4672.11	0.87	Increase

subject receives feedback as opposed to data collected much later in the project. Therefore, we computed the same difference by splitting the data into the project's milestones.

Table 13 shows an increase in pacing when receiving *negative feedback* in *Group cohesion* and *Individual cohesion* during the period of milestone I. However, this effect is not present during any of the other milestones. On the other hand, *positive feedback* seems not to have affected the pacing patterns of students in any period.

7. Conclusion

Research on group dynamics has long established the relationship between a group's cohesiveness and team performance [42]. While earlier studies focused on investigations of group cohesion within face-to-face teams, more recent research has shifted toward analyses of the cohesion construct within technology-supported teams that are distributed in different cities and even countries [4]. Due to time pressures, geographical constraints, or organizational structures, global virtual teams do not always have the opportunity to come together and establish a sense of group cohesiveness. Therefore, it seems appropriate to explore ways in which distributed technology can be used to provide feedback to global teams that will help them establish group cohesiveness.

In this study we examined the relationships between cohesion-based feedback and group behaviors and outcomes. A cohesion-based feedback module was developed and inserted into a distributed collaborative software system. This cohesion-based feedback module provided a graphic display of a group's response rate similarities. The cohesion-based feedback display was then tested on students from the US and Mexico who were collaborating on a global software development project. Half of the teams received the feedback throughout the project, and half the teams received no feedback. Data obtained from the groups' communication activities, Task Cohesion surveys, and individual/group grades were then analyzed and compared. Results indicate that students in the Feedback teams had significantly more overall communications, higher response rates, and more similar response behaviors (as measured by the Individual Cohesion variable) than No-Feedback teams. These Feedback effects could be seen in all types of chat messages, particularly those labeled non-social text messages.

Feedback was also found to affect the linguistic characteristics of a group. For example, Feedback teams were more likely to use words related to the work, time, and achievement categories than No-Feedback teams. At the same time, Feedback teams were more apt to use words linked to personal categories such as leisure and home as opposed to No-Feedback teams. Thus, while Feedback teams seemed more focused on the task, they also seemed more willing to engage in personal communications.

An analysis of the effects of Feedback on our outcome measures (i.e., Task Cohesion and Performance), however, was not significant. Students who viewed the feedback module, did not score higher on the Task Cohesion survey, nor did they receive higher grades on the projects. This result seems to suggest that increasing interaction among team members does not necessarily lead to better performance. Perhaps a more robust feedback system that included a link to different performance measures would result in improved group performance.

Although the study found no relationship between feedback and the outcome measures, it did find relationships between some of our indirect measures and the outcome variables. While we found no significant relationship between either Communications and Task cohesion or between Response Rates and Task cohesion, both Communications and Response Rates affected Individual grades. We also looked for relationships between our cohesion-based measures and Task cohesion and Individual grades and found that ALL the cohesion-based measures (except forum cohesion) were positively correlated to Task cohesion and Individual grades. The relationship was highest for cohesion-based scores that were related to non-social chat messages. This result suggests that the cohesion-based measure is an accurate predictor of both task cohesion and performance; thus reinforcing the notion that effective team collaborations will lead to more effective team performance and a more positive perception of group members.

In addition, the individual cohesion-based measures were aggregated to the group level to determine whether there were any relationships between the group-cohesion measures and the outcome variables. The large variation between UNT and UPA responses on the Task Cohesion survey indicated that the group-level measures could be combined at only the country (i.e., university) level. Analysis of the University-level variables indicated that only the *Group Non-social-Chat-Cohesion* scores were significantly correlated with Task Cohesion, although all the Group-Cohesion scores were significantly related to *Team Grades*. Although these findings differ from the Individual cohesion results, they tend to confirm the relationship between the cohesion measure and performance. The relationship between a group's overall response similarity and task cohesion remains an open question. There is also some question about how instructors evaluate team projects and how this might affect the results reported in studies of this type.

An analysis of the feedback variables and types (positive and negative), showed that participants had a higher pacing rate when sending chat messages after they were exposed to negative feedback; specifically, to *Group cohesion* feedback and *Individual cohesion* feedback. This suggests that *Position* within the team and *Individual participation* does not seem to have an effect on a team member's behavior. This also indicates that construct-based feedback can be useful to modify behavior either as a numerical (*Group cohesion*) or graphical representation (*Individual cohesion*). A further analysis of pacing behavior for each milestone showed that pacing changed significantly during the project's first time period, particularly for students who were provided negative feedback. However, the rest of the time periods showed no significant changes in pacing behavior. Possibly, negative feedback has the most effect on student's pacing behavior when presented during the early part of the project. This pacing effect then gradually becomes a more consistent behavior (i.e., less difference) during subsequent stages of the project.

Although the results presented in this study occurred within an academic setting, we believe that many of the characteristics of the project are similar to real-world environments [43, 44]. For example, many industry-related group projects must cope with rational task distributions, shared milestones, collaborative environments with team-specific information, and distributed leadership. The presence of these characteristics in a team will, surely, affect the cohesiveness within a group. The cohesion measure described in this study, as well as the feedback display, could potentially help groups better understand what type of communication and feedback is most effective.

Finding a feedback display that will affect group performance has always been a concern for researchers in human-computer interactions. This study examines the effects of a cohesion-based display on group behaviors. The display was intended to provide group members with a clear vision of not only how their group was interacting, but also how they, as individuals, were contributing to the group, and how this contribution was being measured. A clear understanding among team members of how their group is interacting appears to facilitate a group's communications, response levels, and individual cohesion scores. While our feedback module did not appear to significantly affect outcome measures, the cohesion-based measure that was used in the feedback display appears to be a good predictor of both Task Cohesion and Performance.

Acknowledgment

The first author gratefully acknowledges financial support from a CONACYT scholarship and from the Support for Graduate Studies Program of SEP. This material was also based upon work supported by the National Science Foundation under Grant No. 0705638.

References

[1] HERBSLEB, J.D. and MOITRA, D. (2001) Global software development. *Software, IEEE* 18(2): 16–20.

[2] POWELL, A., PICCOLI, G. and IVES, B. (2004) Virtual teams: a review of current literature and directions for future research. *ACM Sigmis Database* 35(1): 6–36.

[3] AGERFALK, P.J., FITZGERALD, B., OLSSON, H.H. and CONCHÃZIR, E.Ã. (2008) Benefits of global software development: the known and unknown. In *Making Globally Distributed Software Development a Success Story* (Springer), 1–9.

[4] SWIGGER, K., NUR APLASLAN, F., LOPEZ, V., BRAZILE, R., DAFOULAS, G. and SERCE, F.C. (2009) Structural factors that affect global software development learning team performance. In *Proceedings of the Special Interest Group on Management Information System's 47th Annual Conference on Computer Personnel Research*, SIGMIS CPR '09 (New York, NY, USA: ACM): 187–196. doi:10.1145/1542130.1542167.

[5] FURUMO, K. and PEARSON, J. (2006) An empirical investigation of how trust, cohesion, and performance vary in virtual and face-to-face teams. In *Proceedings of the 39th Annual Hawaii International Conference on System Sciences, 2006. HICSS '06*, 1: 26c–26c. doi:10.1109/HICSS.2006.51.

[6] MCDONOUGH, E.F., KAHNB, K.B. and BARCZAKA, G. (2001) An investigation of the use of global, virtual, and colocated new product development teams. *Journal of Product Innovation Management* 18(2): 110–120.

[7] TOWNSEND, A.M., DEMARIE, S.M. and HENDRICKSON, A.R. (1998) Virtual teams: Technology and the workplace of the future. *The Academy of Management Executive* 12(3): 17–29.

[8] CARLESS, S.A. and PAOLA, C.D. (2000) The measurement of cohesion in work teams. *Small Group Research* 31(1): 71–88. doi:10.1177/104649640003100104.

[9] GOODMAN, P., RAVLIN, E. and SCHMINKE, M. (1987) Understanding groups in organizations. *Tepper School of Business* .

[10] KLUGER, A.N. and DENISI, A. (1996) The effects of feedback interventions on performance: A historical review, a meta-analysis, and a preliminary feedback intervention theory. *Psychological Bulletin* 119(2): 254–284. doi:10.1037/0033-2909.119.2.254.

[11] GAMBERINI, L., MARTINO, F., SPAGNOLLI, A., BAÃŹ, R. and FERRON, M. (2011) âĂIJyour team cohesion is lowâĂİ: A systematic study of the effects of social network feedback on mediated activity. In HUTCHISON, D., KANADE, T., KITTLER, J., KLEINBERG, J.M., MATTERN, F., MITCHELL, J.C., NAOR, M. *et al.* [eds.] *Online Communities and Social Computing* (Berlin, Heidelberg: Springer Berlin Heidelberg), 6778, 172–181.

[12] CARRON, A.V. (1982) Cohesiveness in sport groups: Interpretations and considerations. *Journal of Sport psychology* .

[13] GULLY, S.M., DEVINE, D.J. and WHITNEY, D.J. (1995) A meta-analysis of cohesion and performance effects of level of analysis and task interdependence. *Small Group Research* 26(4): 497–520.

[14] WEBBER, S.S. and DONAHUE, L.M. (2001) Impact of highly and less job-related diversity on work group cohesion and performance: A meta-analysis. *Journal of management* 27(2): 141–162.

[15] KOZLOWSKI, S.W. and ILGEN, D.R. (2006) Enhancing the effectiveness of work groups and teams. *Psychological Science in the Public Interest* 7(3): 77–124. doi:10.1111/j.1529-1006.2006.00030.x.

[16] SCHWANDA, V.L., BARRON, K., LIEN, J., SCHROEDER, G., VERNON, A. and HANCOCK, J.T. (2011) Temporal patterns of cohesiveness in virtual groups. In *Proceedings of the ACM 2011 Conference on Computer Supported Cooperative Work*, CSCW '11 (New York, NY, USA: ACM): 709–712. doi:10.1145/1958824.1958951.

[17] ROVIO, E., ESKOLA, J., KOZUB, S.A., DUDA, J.L. and LINTUNEN, T. (2009) Can high group cohesion be harmful? a case study of a junior ice-hockey team. *Small Group Research* 40(4): 421–435. doi:10.1177/1046496409334359.

[18] CARRON, A.V., WIDMEYER, W. and BRAWLEY, L.R. (1985) The development of an instrument to assess cohesion in sport teams: The group environment questionnaire. *Journal of sport psychology* .

[19] SALISBURY, W.D., CARTE, T.A. and CHIDAMBARAM, L. (2006) Cohesion in virtual teams: Validating the perceived cohesion scale in a distributed setting. *SIGMIS Database* 37(2-3): 147–155.

doi:10.1145/1161345.1161362.

[20] GONZALES, A.L., HANCOCK, J.T. and PENNEBAKER, J.W. (2010) Language style matching as a predictor of social dynamics in small groups. *Communication Research* **37**(1): 3–19. doi:10.1177/0093650209351468.

[21] CARRINGTON, P.J., SCOTT, J. and WASSERMAN, S. (2005) *Models and methods in social network analysis*, **28** (Cambridge university press).

[22] REFFAY, C. and CHANIER, T. (2003) How social network analysis can help to measure cohesion in collaborative distance-learning. In WASSON, B., LUDVIGSEN, S. and HOPPE, U. [eds.] *Designing for Change in Networked Learning Environments*, no. 2 in Computer-Supported Collaborative Learning (Springer Netherlands), 343–352.

[23] MUNSON, S.A., KERVIN, K. and ROBERT JR, L.P. (2014) Monitoring email to indicate project team performance and mutual attraction .

[24] LESHED, G., PEREZ, D., HANCOCK, J.T., COSLEY, D., BIRNHOLTZ, J., LEE, S., MCLEOD, P.L. *et al.* (2009) Visualizing real-time language-based feedback on teamwork behavior in computer-mediated groups. In *Proceedings of the SIGCHI Conference on Human Factors in Computing Systems* (ACM): 537–546.

[25] EARLEY, P.C., NORTHCRAFT, G.B., LEE, C. and LITUCHY, T.R. (1990) Impact of process and outcome feedback on the relation of goal setting to task performance. *Academy of Management Journal* **33**(1): 87–105. doi:10.2307/256353.

[26] KULHAVY, R.W. (1977) Feedback in written instruction. *Review of Educational Research* **47**(2): 211–232. doi:10.3102/00346543047002211.

[27] SHUTE, V.J. (2008) Focus on formative feedback. *Review of Educational Research* **78**(1): 153–189. doi:10.3102/0034654307313795.

[28] MASON, B.J. and BRUNING, R. (2001) Providing feedback in computer-based instruction: What the research tells us. *Retrieved February* **15**: 2007.

[29] SCHARFF, C. and VERMA, R. (2010) Scrum to support mobile application development projects in a just-in-time learning context. In *Proceedings of the 2010 ICSE Workshop on Cooperative and Human Aspects of Software Engineering*, CHASE '10 (New York, NY, USA: ACM): 25–31. doi:10.1145/1833310.1833315.

[30] SCHARFF, C. (2011) Guiding global software development projects using scrum and agile with quality assurance. In *2011 24th IEEE-CS Conference on Software Engineering Education and Training (CSEE T)*: 274–283.

doi:10.1109/CSEET.2011.5876097.

[31] TAUSCZIK, Y.R. and PENNEBAKER, J.W. (2013) Improving teamwork using real-time language feedback .

[32] PENNEBAKER, J.W., FRANCIS, M.E. and BOOTH, R.J. (2001) Linguistic inquiry and word count: LIWC 2001. *Mahway: Lawrence Erlbaum Associates* .

[33] OGWANG, T. (2000) A convenient method of computing the gini index and its standard error. *Oxford Bulletin of Economics and Statistics* **62**(1): 123–129.

[34] SERĂĞE, F.C., SWIGGER, K., ALPASLAN, F.N., BRAZILE, R., DAFOULAS, G. and LOPEZ, V. (2011) Online collaboration: Collaborative behavior patterns and factors affecting globally distributed team performance. *Computers in Human Behavior* **27**(1): 490–503. doi:10.1016/j.chb.2010.09.017.

[35] TAUSCZIK, Y.R. (2012) Changing group dynamics through computerized language feedback .

[36] PENNEBAKER, J.W., CHUNG, C.K., IRELAND, M., GONZALES, A. and BOOTH, R.J. (2007) The development and psychometric properties of LIWC2007. *Austin, TX, LIWC. Net* .

[37] PENNEBAKER, J. (2013) *The Secret Life of Pronouns: What Our Words Say About Us* (Bloomsbury USA).

[38] LESHED, G. (2009) *Automated language-based feedback for teamwork behaviors*. Ph.D. thesis, Cornell University.

[39] LEBRETON, J.M. and SENTER, J.L. (2007) Answers to 20 questions about interrater reliability and interrater agreement. *Organizational Research Methods* .

[40] CHENG, J., DANESCU-NICULESCU-MIZIL, C. and LESKOVEC, J. (2014) How community feedback shapes user behavior. In *Eighth International AAAI Conference on Weblogs and Social Media*.

[41] WEBER, E.H. (1996) *EH Weber on the tactile senses* (Psychology Press).

[42] MATHIEU, J., MAYNARD, M.T., RAPP, T. and GILSON, L. (2008) Team effectiveness 1997-2007: A review of recent advancements and a glimpse into the future. *Journal of Management* **34**(3): 410–476. doi:10.1177/0149206308316061.

[43] BATTIN, R., CROCKER, R., KREIDLER, J. and SUBRAMANIAN, K. (2001) Leveraging resources in global software development. *IEEE Software* **18**(2): 70–77. doi:10.1109/52.914750.

[44] EBERT, C. and DE NEVE, P. (2001) Surviving global software development. *IEEE Software* **18**(2): 62–69. doi:10.1109/52.914748.

13

Reconciling Schema Matching Networks Through Crowdsourcing

Nguyen Quoc Viet Hung[1], Nguyen Thanh Tam[1], Zoltán Miklós[2], Karl Aberer[1]

[1]École Polytechnique Fédérale de Lausanne
[2]Université de Rennes 1

Abstract

Schema matching is the process of establishing correspondences between the attributes of database schemas for data integration purposes. Although several automatic schema matching tools have been developed, their results are often incomplete or erroneous. To obtain a correct set of correspondences, usually human effort is required to validate the generated correspondences. This validation process is often costly, as it is performed by highly skilled experts. Our paper analyzes how to leverage crowdsourcing techniques to validate the generated correspondences by a large group of non-experts.

In our work we assume that one needs to establish attribute correspondences not only between two schemas but in a network. We also assume that the matching is realized in a pairwise fashion, in the presence of consistency expectations about the network of attribute correspondences. We demonstrate that formulating these expectations in the form of integrity constraints can improve the process of reconciliation. As in the case of crowdsourcing the user's input is unreliable, we need specific aggregation techniques to obtain good quality. We demonstrate that consistency constraints can not only improve the quality of aggregated answers, but they also enable us to more reliably estimate the quality answers of individual workers and detect spammers. Moreover, these constraints also enable to minimize the necessary human effort needed, for the same expected quality of results.

Keywords: data integration, schema matching, crowdsourcing, worker assessment, user effort

1. Introduction

More and more online services enable users to upload and share structured data, including Google Fusion Tables [1], Freebase [2], and Factual [3]. These services primarily offer easy visualization of uploaded data as well as tools to embed the visualization to blogs or Web pages. As fragmentation of data in different sources is a common phenomenon, it is essential to create the interlinks between them [4]. An example is the often quoted coffee consumption data found in Google Fusion Tables, which is distributed among different tables that represent a specific region [1]. Extraction of information over all regions requires means to query and aggregate across multiple tables, thereby raising the need of interconnecting schemas to achieve an integrated view of the data. The number of publicly available datasets grows rapidly, making the integration more and more challenging.

In all of the above contexts one needs to integrate data that is stored using different schemas and the interactions between the datasets (or schemas) form a network. Designing a mediated schema for the entire network of schemas might be impractical, especially if the number of schemas that are involved in a network changes, as this might require modifications also in the mediated schema. For this reason we study schema matching techniques that construct the attribute correspondences in a pairwise fashion between the schemas of the network. In this case, we need to ensure that the created correspondences are globally (and not only pairwise) consistent in the network, since these natural consistency conditions are important for the applications.

Since automatic schema matching tools rely on heuristic techniques [5, 6], their result is inherently uncertain. In practice, data integration tasks frequently include a post-matching reconciliation, in which correspondences are reviewed and validated by a human expert. This post-matching reconciliation phase is often the most costly part of schema matching (or even data integration), because of the involvement of expensive experts. In our previous work [7] we demonstrated that the network-level integrity constraints can be exploited to reduce this effort.

In the current paper we analyze how to realize this task through crowdsourcing, where not a single expert but a group of non-experts reconcile the network of attribute correspondences. In this way we leverageing the "wisdom of the crowd" to assert correspondences. Crowdsourcing is a promising approach to reduce the costs of involvement of human experts. While one could potentially reduce the costs, we need to adopt specific techniques to deal with the quality problems that might be present in the user input. This paper is a largely extended version of our own paper [8], where we already demonstrate the use of crowdsourcing techniques for schema matching reconciliation. In this paper, we consolidate this approach by showing that the integrity constraints can be also useful for assessing workers, towards improving the reconciliation quality.

Our contributions and the outline of this paper can be summarized as follows.

- Section 2: We provide an overview of our crowd-sourcing framework, including the elements of a matching network, reconciliation through crowd-sourcing, the probabilistic model for integrity constraints. We also present a system where our techniques and algorithms can be realized that we also used to evaluate our techniques.

- Section 3: We provide a probabilistic model for combining the answers from multiple crowd workers. This model enables to compute for each candidate correspondence the probability whether it is true.

- Section 4: We show how to evaluate and control the worker quality. On the one hand, we would like to take into account that crowd workers have wide-ranging levels of expertise, thus the quality of their responses can also vary. On the other hand we would like to detect spammers, who exploit the platform to obtain payments for completing tasks without a proper engagement. In particular, we propose mechanisms to detect an individual spammer and groups of spammers, since these malicious workers lower the accuracy of the aggregated results.

- Section 5: We design an aggregation mechanism to instantiate the final decision for each corre-spondence using the computed probabilities. In particular, we study how to aggregate answers in the presence of matching network constraints. Our theoretical and empirical results show that by harnessing the network constraints, the worker effort can be lowered considerably.

- Section 6: We run the experiments on real datasets to show the effectiveness of leveraging integrity constraints in worker assessment and answer aggregation.

The remaining sections are structured as follows. Section 7 summarizes related work, before Section 8 concludes the paper.

2. Overview

This section starts with a motivating example of a network of schemas. Although the involved schemas are simple, they are sufficient to demonstrate certain problems that arise, when we attempt to interconnect their attributes. Next, we explain the elements of a matching network and our techniques for using crowdsourcing to validate the correspondences in this network. Then, we proceed with a formulation of integrity constraints in our probabilistic model. Finally, we describe our framework for obtaining aggregate values for attribute correspondences from potentially unreliable crowd answers.

2.1. Motivating Example

Let us consider a scenario with online services, where three video content providers Eoverl, BBC, and DVDizzy have their own websites to publicize their offers. Consumers can find the products they want by searching information on the sites (e.g. title, release date). Now the three providers would like to incorporate their websites to broaden the marketplace. Similar product information is stored in their different databases, whose simplified schemas are illustrated in Figure 1. A matching network is created by establishing pairwise matchings between the three schemas in order to facilitate integration scenarios (e.g. support search queries) between the three databases. The figure shows five correspondences c_1, c_2, c_3, c_4, and c_5 which were generated by an automatic matching tool for pairs of schemas. As the involved attribute names are rather similar (date, screenDate, releaseDate, and productionDate), automatic schema matching tools (schema matchers) often fail to output the correct attribute matches.

Problematic correspondences are typically elimi-nated by reconciliation based on human input: a given correspondence is asserted whether it shall be dis-regarded or accepted [9]. Since a large-scale match-ing network has a lot of correspondences, reconciling through human experts could be expensive, in fact this is usually the most costly phase of schema matching, as it involves human efforts. One can hope to reduce this cost by using a crowdsourcing platform, where a group of non-experts can execute this task. If we let execute the reconciliation task by crowd workers, we need to take attention to various issues. In particular, we need to cope with incorrect user input that might

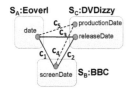

Figure 1. A matching network of real–world schemas

even come from malicious users (for example, from those who just want to obtain the financial compensation for the task without providing useful input). While asking more questions, thus increasing the tasks assigned to the crowd, could improve the quality of the (aggregated) results, this would at the same time increase the financial costs, that we would minimize. As we will demonstrate the use of network-level integrity constraints can help both with quality improvements and also with cost reduction: these constraints can on the one hand help to reduce the number of necessary questions we need to ask, this it can reduce the overall cost of work, and at the same time, integrity constraints can largely contribute to detect quality problems with use input.

We illustrate these effect in Figure 1. We can see that if we approve both c_3, c_5, the two attributes productionDate and releaseDate are equivalent, which is intuitively incorrect. Regarding the malicious worker problem, we can approach as follows. The workers who approve both these correspondences should be penalized by decreasing their reliability. Based on this evidence, we can assess the reliability of workers and, for instance, filter the low-quality workers out of the pool. Regarding the cost minimization problem, we can approach as follows. We can see that if c_3 is approved by all workers, there is no need to validate c_5 since c_5 and c_3 cannot be true at the same time. This leads to a smaller number of necessary questions; and thus, reduces the monetary cost for paying the workers.

In the following we introduce the schema matching network model [7] that we we will use in our work.

2.2. Matching Networks and Reconciliation through Crowdsourcing

We model a *schema* as a finite set of attributes $s = \{a_1, ..., a_k\}$. Let $S = \{s_1, ..., s_n\}$ be a set of schemas of a data integration task. Each schema is built of unique attributes (by using unique identifiers), i.e. $s_i \cap s_j = \emptyset$ for all $1 \leq i, j \leq n$ and $i \neq j$. Further, $A_S = \bigcup_i s_i$ is the set of attributes in S. The *interaction graph* G_S represents which schemas need to be matched in the network, i.e. the vertices in $V(G_S)$ are labelled by the schemas from S and there is an edge between two vertices, if the corresponding schemas need to be matched.

An *attribute correspondence* between a pair of schemas $s_1, s_2 \in S$ is an attribute pair (a, b), such that $a \in$

s_1 and $b \in s_2$. The set of *candidate correspondences* $C_{i,j}$ for a pair of schemas $s_i, s_j \in S$ is a set of attribute correspondences which is typically the outcome of schema matchers [10]. The set of candidate correspondences C for an interaction graph G_S consists of all candidate correspondences for pairs of schemas corresponding to its edges, i.e. $C = \bigcup_{(s_i, s_j) \in E(G_S)} C_{i,j}$. Although more complex models for correspondences have been proposed, cf., [11], we focus on correspondences modelled as attribute pairs since this model is followed by the majority of schema matchers [5, 6].

Based on the above notions, we define a network of schemas to be a triple $N = \langle S, G_S, C \rangle$, where S is a set of schemas (of unique attributes), G_S is an interaction graph, Γ is a set of constraints, and C is a set of candidate correspondences. Since the results of automatic matchers are inherently uncertain, the set of candidate correspondences C of N does not often provide a satisfactory result for a data integration task. Instead, we are interested in finding the ground truth – the set of all correspondences that are correct. However, the ground truth is hidden and could not be known before-hand. We denote X_c as a random variable of the existence of a correspondence c in the ground truth. X_c being equal to *true/false* indicates that c exists/not exists in ground truth. We try to estimate the value of X_c with the help of crowd workers.

Reconciliation of a network of schemas $N = \langle S, G_S, C \rangle$ through crowdsourcing is an incremental process, where a set of workers $W = \{w_1, ..., w_k\}$ provide input to the answer matrix $[M_{ij}]_{|C| \times |W|}$. Each element M_{ij} is the validation of worker w_j on the correspondence $c_i \in C$. Domain values of M_{ij} are $\{true, false, null\}$, where *true/false/null* indicates c_i is approved/disapproved/not validated yet. These validation results correspond to simple validation tasks that are proposed to workers. Note that we might ask the same question from several workers, while each worker receives a particular question only once. Since crowd workers have wide-ranging levels of expertise, they provide different answers for a correspondence. To aggregate the worker's answers, we compute for each correspondence c the probability $Pr(X_c = true)$ that c exists in ground truth. The set of all these probabilities of candidate correspondences is denoted as $P = \{Pr(X_c = true) \mid c \in C\}$. Summing up the above notions, we denote the state of the crowdsourced matching network as a tuple $\langle N, W, M, P \rangle$, where N is the network of schemas, W is the worker pool, M is the answer matrix, and P is the probability set.

2.3. Integrity Constraints

We can express natural expectations that one has w.r.t. the entire network in the form of consistency constraints as follows. Given a network of schemas $N = \langle S, G_S, C \rangle$, let us denote $\Gamma = \{\gamma_1, \ldots, \gamma_n\}$ be a finite set of constraints that are used to represent the expected consistency conditions on N. We say that a set of correspondences $C' \in C$ violating a constraint $\gamma \in \Gamma$ is a constraint violation. In practice, we are not interested in all possible violations, but the minimal ones: We say that a violation is minimal w.r.t. γ, if none of its proper subsets is violating γ.

In [7], we relied on Answer Set Programming formalism to express the integrity constraints. In this paper, we provide a different formulation for the same constraints, using probabilities. The advantage of this formulation is that the constraints can be softened and parametrized based on particular scenarios. We do not impose assumptions on the definition of integrity constraints. For illustration, we rely on the examples of the one-to-one constraint and cycle constraint as defined in [7].

Generalized 1-1 constraint. Each attribute of one schema should be matched to at most one attribute of any other schema. For example in Figure 1, the set $\{c_3, c_5\}$ violates the 1-1 constraint. However there are some exceptions where this constraint does not hold, such as the attribute *name* of a schema might be a concatenation of the attributes *firstname* and *lastname* of another schema. To capture this observation, we provide a relaxed version of the constraint using probability theory:

$$Pr(\gamma_{1-1}|X_{c_0}, X_{c_1}, \ldots, X_{c_k}) = \begin{cases} 1 & \text{If } m \leq 1 \\ \Delta \in [0,1] & \text{If } m > 1 \end{cases}$$

(1)

where $\{c_0, c_1, \ldots, c_k\}$ is a set of correspondences that share a common source attribute and m is the number of X_{c_i} assigned as *true*. When $\Delta = 0$, there is no constraint exception (the constraint is hard). The constraint can be softened by adjusting the Δ value.

Cycle constraint. If multiple schemas are matched in a cycle, the matched attributes should form a closed cycle. For example in Figure 1, the set $\{c_1, c_2, c_5\}$ violates the *cycle constraint*. Formally, following the notion of cyclic mappings in [12], we formulate the conditional probability of a cycle as follows:

$$Pr(\gamma_{\circlearrowright}|X_{c_0}, X_{c_1}, \ldots, X_{c_k}) = \begin{cases} 1 & \text{If } m = k + 1 \\ 0 & \text{If } m = k \\ \Delta \in [0,1] & \text{If } m < k \end{cases}$$

(2)

where $c_0, c_1, \ldots, c_k$ forms a sequence of correspondences that starts and ends at the same attribute; and m is the number of X_{c_i} assigned as *true* and Δ is the probability of compensating errors along the cycle (i.e., two or more incorrect assignment resulting in a correct reformation).

Learning Constraint Parameter. Under our probabilistic model, each constraint $\gamma \in \Gamma$ is associated with a parameter Δ, as illustrated with the one-to-one constraint and cycle constraint above. In practice, the parameter Δ is often specified by the application expert or administrator. However, as crowdsourcing is an incremental process, in this work we propose an adaptive learning method to adjust Δ based on the worker answers obtained so far.

More precisely, we use the following heuristic to learn the parameter Δ for each constraint γ. The idea is that the more violations the workers make, the more the associated constraints should be hardened; and vice-versa. Initally, we set $\Delta = 0.5$ since the integrity constraints do not affect the correctness of validated correspondences. Then periodically (e.g. after obtaining other 20 answers from the crowd), we compute the set of constraint violations, for each worker, on the set of correspondences he approved. Denote $V = \{v_1, \ldots, v_n\}$ as the union set of all constraint violations (note that two different violations can be of the same constraint). For each violation $v_i \in V$, we count the percentage of workers who made this violation. Then for each constraint γ involved in V, we set its new parameter Δ to the average value of the percentages of its violations.

2.4. Crowdsourcing Framework

Figure 2 presents the overall reconciliation process through crowdsourcing and the global architecture of our platform. The reconciliation process starts with a set of candidate correspondences that are generated by schema matchers. Based on these candidate correspondences, we initialize a network of candidate correspondences. We employ workers from the crowd to answer validation questions, i.e. for each correspondence, we automatically generate a crowd task where we ask a worker to validate the correspondence. The crowd workers then provide their input.

During the process, the workers are continuously evaluated by the component *Worker Assessment*. Since the workers might provide different answers for the same question, we need to estimate the probability that a given correspondence is true. *Probability Computation* component is responsible for these calculations. The component *Answer Aggregation* aggregates the workers answers into a single decision. In the end, the output of our framework is an aggregated matching, which consist of the correspondences, their aggregated values and the associated error rates.

Following this general structure, crowdsourcing for schema matching network requires the realization of the following components.

Probability Computation. Given a crowdsourced matching network, this component computes the

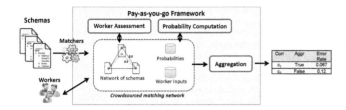

Figure 2. Architecture of the crowdsourced reconciliation framework

probability of each correspondence whether it should be correct, based on the worker inputs obtained so far. More precisely, it computes the probability $Pr(X_c = true)$ of each correspondence $c \in C$. Then, the resulting probabilities can be used for the other components since any worker input is implicitly incorporated in the probabilities. The probability computation is described in Section 3.

Worker Assessment. This component is responsible for evaluating worker reliability based on their answers. In this paper, we tackle the problem of detecting low-quality workers. As soon as the spammers workers are detected, we can remove them out of the worker pool and exclude their answers from the aggregation procedures. This can also save the monetary cost and improve the quality of the aggregated matching. Our worker assessment techniques are described in Section 4.

Answer Aggregation. Given a matching network at the end of a reconciliation process through crowdsourcing, the answer aggregation component will decide the final value of the validated correspondences. More precisely, it decides whether a given correspondence should exist in the final matching and provides an (estimated) error rate of this decision. The details of this component is described in Section 5.

3. Probability Computation

In this Section we discuss the the techniques we used to compute $Pr(X_c)$, the probability that a given correspondence c is true. There are several techniques proposed in the literature to compute this probability [13]. In this paper, we use the expectation-maximization (EM) algorithm, which aggregates all answers of workers and estimates their reliability simultaneously. The reason behind this choice is that the EM model is quite effective for labelling tasks and robust to noisy workers [14].

In the following, we provide a formulation of the Expectation-Maximization (EM) algorithm, which is inspired from [15–17]. The EM algorithm takes as input an answer matrix $[M_{ij}]_{n \times m}$ (n correspondences and m workers) and returns a tuple $\langle P, V \rangle$. V is a vector in

which each element v_j is the (estimated) quality of the worker w_j. P is a vector in which each element p_i is the (estimated) probability of correctness for each correspondence c_i. The algorithm alternates between two steps: Expectation step (E-step) and Maximization step (M-step) until it reaches a convergence state where the estimated values of v_j and p_i are stable. In the k-th E-step, it takes the calculated worker quality V^{k-1} estimated in the previous step to calculate the probability of correctness for the correspondences P^k in this step according to the following equation:

$$p_i^k = \sum_{t=1}^{m} v_t^{k-1} \times f(M_{it}) \times \mathbb{1}_{M_{it}=true} \qquad (3)$$

where f is a function that estimates the correctness of the answers given by the workers and $\mathbb{1}_{cond} = 1$ if $cond$ is true and 0 otherwise. In practice, we can estimate the value of f by the probability of correctness for the answer M_{ij} calculated in the previous step. After this step, for each correspondence, the correct answer can be estimated by selecting the one with the highest probability. For correspondences that have been validated from workers, we take the provided answers as the correct values. We denote the estimated correct values at step k as $G^k = \{g_1, g_2, ..., g_n\}$ where g_i is the correct answer for correspondence c_i.

Since the estimated correct values change after each E-step, we need to update the estimated quality of the workers to reflect these changes. In the k-th M-step, we re-estimate the quality of the workers by computing the loss value L_i^k for each worker. This loss value measures how deviating the answers provided by a worker to the estimated correct values:

$$L_j^k = \sum_{i=1}^{n} v_j \times h(M_{ij}, g_i) \qquad (4)$$

where h is a function that measure the distance between two values. Based on the loss value of each worker, we can re-estimate its quality based on the intuition that the higher the loss value, the lower the quality of the worker.

In the end, the probabilities of possible aggregations of each correspondence c_i are:

$$\begin{cases} Pr(X_{c_i} = true) = p_i \\ Pr(X_{c_i} = false) = 1 - p_i \end{cases} \qquad (5)$$

4. Worker Assessment

The potentially low quality of results obtained from crowd workers is a major problem for crowdsourcing applications. While a large group of crowd workers from diverse background can perform challenging tasks, individual workers are typically not experts on any particular domain thus their responses cannot be trusted. A common way to cope with this situation is to ask the same question multiple times and aggregate the results. There is however often a big difference in the expected quality of answers from different workers. A possible way is to cope with this situation is to assess the quality of the workers and use this assessment when aggregating the answers.

Besides the quality problems that exists with honest crowd workers with varying response quality, there is another problem that can largely influence the quality of results obtained from the crowd. As the workers are paid upon completion of a task, there is a group of workers who just would like to obtain the offered money, by giving random answers to the questions (or by providing answers that are identical to a honest worker). This group is often referred as spammers. In this section we propose techniques to detect spammers.

Spammers exist very frequently in online communities, especially at crowdsourcing platforms. Several experiments [18, 19] have showed that the proportion of spammers at popular crowdsourcing platforms could be up to 40%. In this way they can significantly increase the cost (since they need to be paid) and at the same time decrease the accuracy of final aggregated results, thus a mechanism to detect and eliminate the spammer's responses is desirable for any crowdsourcing application.

In the following, we first show our methods for detecting an individual spammer. Then we demonstrate how to extend these methods to detect a group of spammers.

4.1. Detecting Individual Spammers

There is a simple simple technique for detecting spammers: one needs to prepare a test set where one knows the answers to the questions. If we ask these test questions then we can estimate their performance and consider these estimations as result quality. The workers who fail to answers correctly a specified minimal number of questions are regarded as spammers. This schema has however several disadvantages: since the spammers already know they are tested, they can work honestly to bypass the test. As the test questions are injected implicitly into the question set, we have to pay the workers for the extra questions.

We propose a constraint-based detection mechanism, that is applicable in our context, where we do not need to add test questions. Spammers validate the correspondences randomly thus their input can create constraint violations. We define a *violation rate* (VR) for each worker, calculated by:

$$VR(w_i) = \frac{\mu(C_i)}{\mu(C)} \qquad (6)$$

where $C_i = \{c_j \in C \mid M_{ij} = true\}$ is the set of correspondences approved by worker w_i and C is the original set of candidate correspondences. The higher value of VR a worker has, the higher chance that he is a spammer. For the detection, we define a filtering threshold α and regard all workers with $VR > \alpha$ as spammers. In the experiments, we vary this threshold and study its effect.

The $\mu(.)$ function measures the amount of violations for a set of correspondences and is formulated as follows. Given a set of correspondences $C' \in C$, we can obtain a set of violations $Vio_{C'} = \{v_1, \ldots, v_m\}$ following the definition of integrity constraints in Section 2.3. Also due to this definition, each violation v_i is associated with the constraint parameter Δ_i that reflects the chance that the constraint of this violation is incorrect. In other words, $1 - \Delta_i$ reflects the chance that the violation v_i is correct. Formally, we have:

$$\mu(C') = \sum_{v_i \in Vio_{C'}} (1 - \Delta_i) \qquad (7)$$

The value domain of $\mu(.)$ is $[0, |Vio_{C'}|]$. Note that if all the integrity constraints are hard constraints (i.e. $\Delta_i = 0, \forall i$), the function $\mu(.)$ becomes the counting function for the number of violations (i.e. $\mu(.) = |Vio_{C'}|$).

The advantage of our detection scheme is that it can be used at any time during the crowdsourcing process to remove the spammers out of the worker pool. The spammers do not know before-hand they are being tested; and thus, avoiding any preparation from them. Moreover, it does not take any extra cost for either paying workers for the test questions or designing the test.

4.2. Detecting Spammer Groups

One of the major problems in crowdsourcing systems is the existence of imitating groups (or spammer groups). Such groups arise in the following way: a user created multiple clone accounts, executes the tasks at his main account and he gives the same answers to questions at all of his clone accounts in order to obtain more money for completed tasks. In the presence of imitating groups, the final aggregated decision would be compromised since false answers may be duplicated and dominate the result. For example, consider five workers w_1, w_2, w_3, w_4, w_5 validating a correspondence whose correct answer is *yes*. Assume w_3, w_4 and w_5 is an imitating group. The answers of five workers are $\{yes, yes, no, no, no\}$ respectively. Without knowing this imitating group, the aggregated answer is *no* (w.r.t. majority voting). Whereas, if we can detect this group and eliminate w_4 and w_5, the aggregated answer is *yes* (w.r.t majority voting). This example shows that the imitating groups are indeed dangerous and we need to design a detection mechanism for this specific scenario.

However, detecting imitating groups is challenging since it is often hard to know whether a worker shares the same answers with another by imitating or by accidence. A naive method to detect the imitation is using the number of correct answers and incorrect answers that two given workers share with each other. The idea is that two workers who share more incorrect answers have a higher chance of belonging to an imitating group. However, this method is not applicable in our setting since the ground truth is unknown (i.e. cannot know for sure an answer is correct or not).

In this section, we propose a detection mechanism based on constraint violations. The idea is that the answers of two workers having the same violations would have high chances of being incorrect since each violation must have at least one incorrect answer. Thus the more violations the two workers share, the high chance these workers belong to an imitating group.

Problem Formulation. Given two workers $w_1, w_2 \in W$ whose answers are all identical, we would like to detect whether these two workers belong to an imitating group (denoted as $w_1 \sim w_2$) or not (denoted as $w_1 \perp w_2$). Denote $V = \{v_1, \ldots, v_k\}$ as the set of identical violations between w_1 and w_2 (assuming that the violations are disjoint). Let $D = \cup_{v_i \in V} v_i$ be the union set of all correspondences in these violations. Denote k_t and k_f as the number of common correct and incorrect answers between the two workers respectively; i.e. $|D| = k_t + k_f$.

To solve the detection problem, we approach by using the probability theory. More precisely, we aim to compute the probability that w_1 and w_2 belong to an imitating group given their common violations:

$$Pr(w_1 \sim w_2|D) =$$

$$\frac{Pr(D|w_1 \sim w_2) \cdot \alpha}{Pr(D|w_1 \sim w_2) \cdot \alpha + Pr(D|w_1 \perp w_2) \cdot (1 - \alpha)} \quad (8)$$

where $\alpha = Pr(w_1 \sim w_2) = 1 - Pr(w_1 \perp w_2)$ $(0 < \alpha < 1)$ is the a-priori probability that there exists an imitating group in the crowd. Now we need to compute the two probabilities $Pr(D|w_1 \sim w_2)$ and $Pr(D|w_1 \perp w_2)$. To this end, we denote r $(0 \leq r \leq 1)$ as the probability that an independently provided answer is true.

We first consider the case where w_1 and w_2 do not belong to an imitating group. Since each correspondence either exists or does not exist in ground truth, the probability that w_1 and w_2 provide the same correct answer for a correspondence $c \in D$ is:

$$Pr(c \text{ is correct}|w_1 \perp w_2) = r \cdot r = r^2$$

And the probability that w_1 and w_2 provide the same incorrect answer for a correspondence $c \in D$ is:

$$Pr(c \text{ is incorrect}|w_1 \perp w_2) = (1 - r) \cdot (1 - r) = (1 - r)^2$$

As a result, the conditional probability of observing D is:

$$Pr(D|w_1 \perp w_2) = r^{2k_t}(1 - r)^{2k_f} \quad (9)$$

Similarly, we consider the case where w_1 and w_2 belong to an imitating group. The probability that w_1 and w_2 provide the same correct answer for a correspondence $c \in D$ is:

$$Pr(c \text{ is correct}|w_1 \sim w_2) = r$$

And the probability that w_1 and w_2 provide the same incorrect answer for a correspondence $c \in D$ is:

$$Pr(c \text{ is incorrect}|w_1 \sim w_2) = (1 - r)$$

Consequently, the conditional probability of observing D is:

$$Pr(D|w_1 \sim w_2) = r^{k_t}(1 - r)^{k_f} \quad (10)$$

Put it altogether, we have a concrete calculation of eq. (8) as follows.

$$Pr(w_1 \sim w_2|D) = \left(1 + (\frac{1 - \alpha}{\alpha})r^{k_t}(1 - r)^{k_f}\right)^{-1} \quad (11)$$

This equation captures several intuitions we expect in practice. For example, when the number of common false answers increases (k_f increases), the probability that two workers are dependent increases. This is because two independent workers rarely give all the same incorrect answers. Moreover, it should be noted that our method works better when the two given workers have more common questions.

Boundary Computation. Since the ground truth is unknown, we cannot compute the exact value of r, k_f, and k_t. However, this computation is unnecessary if we can bound the probability in eq. (11). For this purpose, we have two propositions as follows.

Proposition 1. $\forall \alpha \in [0, 1], k_t \in \mathbb{N}, k_f \in \mathbb{N}$. We have:

$$Pr(w_1 \sim w_2|D) \geq \left(1 + \frac{1 - \alpha}{\alpha} \frac{k_f^{k_f} k_t^{k_t}}{(k_f + k_t)^{k_f + k_t}}\right)^{-1} \quad (12)$$

Proof. The proof is given in the appendix. □

Proposition 2. $\forall \alpha \in [0, 1]$, we have:

$$Pr(w_1 \sim w_2|D) \geq \left(1 + \frac{1 - \alpha}{\alpha} \frac{|V|^{|V|}(|D| - |V|)^{|D| - |V|}}{(|D|)^{|D|}}\right)^{-1} \quad (13)$$

Proof. The proof is given in the appendix. □

Example 1. Consider two workers w_1 and w_2 who share three violations $V = \{v_1, v_2, v_3\}$, where each violation is joint and contains three correspondences ($|D| = 9$). A crowdsourcing system is vulnerable when there are enough imitating groups in the crowd. Thus, let us assume that $\alpha > 0.3$ (i.e. the probability that any two workers in the crowd belong to an imitating group is greater than 0.3). Then following the inequality in eq. (13) and having the function $\frac{1-x}{x}$ being monotonically decreasing with $x \in [0, 1]$, we have:

$$Pr(w_1 \sim w_2 | D) \geq \left(1 + \frac{1 - 0.3}{0.3} \frac{3^3 6^6}{9^9}\right)^{-1} \approx 0.9925$$

In other words, we can conclude that these two workers belong to an imitating group with a probability greater than 0.99.

5. Answer Aggregation

As we explained, we demand to validate a given attribute correspondence from several crowd workers. In this section we explain how we aggregate the possibly different responses to a single value such that the (expected) quality of the aggregated value meets a predefined standard. In fact, we first estimate the error rate of any given aggregated value using our probabilistic models and then we show how to minimize the financial costs of obtaining a a set of correspondences of a given quality with the help of the integrity constraints.

5.1. Deriving Aggregated Value and Error Rate

We will derive the aggregated value of a correspondence based on the probability $Pr(X_c)$ that is the probability of a given correspondence is *true*. We compute these probabilities, as we explained in Section 3. We compute the aggregation decision $g_\pi(c)$ for each correspondence $c \in C$ that is a pair $g_\pi(c) = \langle a_c, e_c \rangle$, where a_c is the aggregated value (*true* or *false*) and e_c is the error rate. The aggregation decision is obtained as follows:

$$g_\pi(c) = \begin{cases} \langle true, 1 - Pr(X_c = true)\rangle, \text{if } Pr(X_c = true) \geq 0.5 \\ \langle false, 1 - Pr(X_c = false)\rangle, \text{otherwise} \end{cases}$$

(14)

The aggregated value in the aggregation decision thus corresponds to the value that has a higher probability (and lower error rate). The error rate is the probability of making wrong decision.

We would like to reduce this error rate, for each correspondence. We could achieve a lower error rate if we ask more questions, however asking more questions induces higher costs as well. Instead, we will try to lower the error rate given a limited budget of money with the help of the integrity constraints that we explain in the next section.

5.2. Leveraging Constraints to Reduce the Error Rate

For several crowdsourcing tasks, one could achieve a lower error rate through asking more questions [20, 21]. This is, in fact, a trade-off between the costs and the accuracy [22].

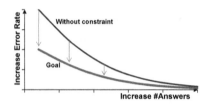

Figure 3. Optimization goal

Figure 3 depicts this situation: higher number of answers correspond to lower error rates. We would like to lower this error-rate curve as much as possible. If we can achieve the same error rate, with a lower number of answers then we can reduce the number of questions that is needed to achieve a given error rate. To achieve this goal, we leverage the network-level consistency constraints. In the following, we will show how to exploit these constraints and how can we aggregate the worker's responses in the presence of the constraints. These aggregation techniques require more complex probability estimations than those we presented in Section 3. While we present the precise definitions, we do not detail here how to compute these probabilities efficiently. We mention that there exists methods that enable to compute the required probabilities fast enough, such that our methods can be used in real application contexts.

Aggregating with Constraints. We extend here the definitions of Section 5.1, and include the effects of the integrity constraints to the calculation of aggregation decision. We will show that by using constraints, we need fewer answers to obtain an aggregated result with the same error rate. In other words, given the same set of answers on a certain correspondence, the error rate of aggregation with constraints is lower than those without constraints (i.e. Section 5.1).

Given the aggregation $g_\pi(c)$ of a correspondence c, we compute the justified aggregation $g_\pi^\gamma(c)$ when taking into account the integrity constraint γ. The aggregation $g_\pi^\gamma(c)$ is obtained similarly to equation 14, but we use here the conditional prbability $Pr(X_c|\gamma)$ instead of $Pr(X_c)$. Formally,

$$g_\pi^\gamma(c) = \begin{cases} \langle true, 1 - Pr(X_c = true|\gamma)\rangle, \text{If } Pr(X_c = true|\gamma) \geq 0.5 \\ \langle false, 1 - Pr(X_c = false|\gamma)\rangle, \text{Otherwise} \end{cases}$$

(15)

In the following, we describe how to obtain the conditional probabilities $Pr(X_c|\gamma)$ in the case of 1-1 constraint and the cycle constraint. Then, we show why the use of constraints can reduce the error rate. We leave the investigation of other types of constraints as an interesting future work.

Aggregating with 1-1 Constraint. Our approach is based on the intuition illustrated in Figure 4(A), depicting two correspondences c_1 and c_2 with the same source attribute. After receiving the answer set from workers and applying the probabilistic model (section 5.1), we obtained the probability $Pr(X_{c_1} = true) = 0.8$ and $Pr(X_{c_2} = false) = 0.5$. When considering c_2 independently, it is hard to conclude c_2 being approved or disapproved. However, when taking into account c_1 and 1-1 constraint, c_2 tends to be disapproved since c_1 and c_2 cannot be *true* at the same time. Indeed, following probability theory, the conditional probability $Pr(X_{c_2} = false|\gamma_{1-1}) \approx 0.83 > Pr(X_{c_2} = false)$.

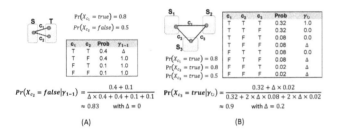

Figure 4. Compute conditional probability with (A) 1-1 constraint and (B) cycle constraint

Computing conditional probability. Given the same set of correspondences $\{c_0, c_1, \ldots, c_k\}$ above, let us denote p_i as $Pr(X_{c_i} = true)$ for short. Without loss of generality, we consider c_0 to be the favorite correspondence whose probability p_0 is obtained from the worker answers. Using the Bayesian theorem and equation 1, the conditional probability of correspondence c_0 with 1-1 constraint γ_{1-1} is computed as:

$$Pr(X_{c_0} = true|\gamma_{1-1}) = \frac{Pr(\gamma_{1-1}|X_{c_0} = true) \cdot Pr(X_{c_0} = true)}{Pr(\gamma_{1-1})}$$
$$= \frac{(x + \Delta(1-x)) \times p_0}{y + \Delta(1-y)} \quad (16)$$

where
$$x = \prod_{i=1}^{k} (1 - p_i)$$
$$y = \prod_{i=0}^{k} (1 - p_i) + \sum_{i=0}^{k} [p_i \prod_{j=0, j\neq i}^{k} (1 - p_j)]$$

x can be interpreted as the probability of the case where all other correspondences except c being disapproved. y can be interpreted as the probability of the case where all correspondences being disapproved or only one of them being disapproved. The precise derivation of equation 16 is given in the appendix.

Theorem 1. The conditional probability of a correspondence c being false with 1-1 constraint is less than or

equal to the probability of c being false without constraint. Formally, $Pr(X_c = false|\gamma_{1-1}) \geq Pr(X_c = false)$.

Proof. The proof can be found in the appendix. □

From this theorem, we can conclude that the error rate is reduced only when the aggregated value is *false*. From equation 14 and 15, the error rate with 1-1 constraint (i.e. $1 - Pr(X_c = false|\gamma_{1-1})$) is less than or equal to the one without constraint (i.e. $1 - Pr(X_c = false)$). In other words, the 1-1 constraint supports reducing the error rate when the aggregated value is *false*.

Aggregating with Cycle Constraint. To motivate our definitions we present a small matching network. Figure 4(B) depicts an example of cycle constraint for three correspondences c_1, c_2, c_3. After receiving the set of answers from workers and applying probabilistic model (section 5.1), we obtained the probability $Pr(X_{c_1} = true) = Pr(X_{c_2} = true) = 0.8$ and $Pr(X_{c_3} = true) = 0.5$. When considering c_3 independently, it is hard to conclude c_3 being *true* or *false*. However, when taking into account c_1, c_2 under the cycle constraint, c_3 tends to be *true* since the cycle created by c_1, c_2, c_3 shows an interoperability. Therefore, following probability theory, the conditional probability $Pr(X_{c_3} = true|\gamma_{1-1}) \approx 0.9 > Pr(X_{c_3} = true)$.

Computing conditional probability. Given a closed cycle along $c_0, c_1, \ldots, c_k$, let denote the constraint on this circle as $\gamma_{\circlearrowleft}$ and p_i as $Pr(X_{c_i} = true)$ for short. Without loss of generality, we consider c_0 to be the favorite correspondence whose probability p_0 is obtained by the answers of workers in the crowdsourcing process. Following the Bayesian theorem and equation 2, the conditional probability of correspondence c_0 with circle constraint is computed as:

$$Pr(X_{c_0} = true|\gamma_{\circlearrowleft}) = \frac{Pr(\gamma_{\circlearrowleft}|X_{c_0} = true) \times Pr(X_{c_0} = true)}{Pr(\gamma_{\circlearrowleft})}$$
$$= \frac{(\prod_{i=1}^{k} (p_i) + \Delta(1-x)) \times p_o}{\prod_{i=0}^{k} (p_i) + \Delta(1-y)} \quad (17)$$

where
$$x = \prod_{i=1}^{k} (p_i) + \sum_{i=1}^{k} [(1 - p_i) \prod_{j=1, j\neq i}^{k} p_j]$$
$$y = \prod_{i=0}^{k} (p_i) + \sum_{i=0}^{k} [(1 - p_i) \prod_{j=0, j\neq i}^{k} p_j]$$

x can be interpreted as the probability of the case where only one correspondence among $c_1, \ldots, c_k$ except c_0 is disapproved. y can be interpreted as the probability of the case where only one correspondence among $c_0, c_1, \ldots, c_k$ is disapproved. The detail derivation of equation 17 is given in the appendix.

Theorem 2. Given a correspondence c together with other correspondences $c_1, \ldots, c_k$ creating a closed cycle

$\gamma_{\circlearrowleft} = \{c_0, c_1, \ldots, c_k\}$, the conditional probability $Pr(X_c = true|\gamma_{\circlearrowleft})$ is greater than or equal to the probability $Pr(X_c = true)$, $Pr(X_c = true|\gamma_{\circlearrowleft}) \geq Pr(X_c = true)$ if $\frac{1}{\Delta} \geq \sum_{i=1}^{k} \frac{1-p_i}{p_i}$.

Proof. The proof can be found in the appendix. □

Note that the condition of Δ is often satisfied since Δ closed to 0 and p_i closed to 1. From this theorem, we conclude that the error rate is reduced only when the aggregated value is *true*. With an appropriately chosen Δ, in equation 14 and 15, the error rate with cycle constraint (i.e. $1 - Pr(X_c = true|\gamma_{\circlearrowleft})$) is less than or equal to the one without constraint (i.e. $1 - Pr(X_c = true)$). In other words, circle constraint supports reducing the error rate when the aggregated value is *true*.

Aggregating with Multiple Constraints. In general settings, we could have a finite set of constraints $\Gamma = \{\gamma_1, \ldots, \gamma_n\}$. Let denote the aggregation with a constraint $\gamma_i \in \Gamma$ is $g_\pi^{\gamma_i}(c) = \langle a_c^i, e_c^i \rangle$, whereas the aggregation without any constraint is simply written as $g_\pi(c) = \langle a_c, e_c \rangle$. Since the constraints are different, not only could the aggregated value a_c^i be different ($a_c^i \neq a_c^j$) but also the error rate e_c^i could be different ($e_c^i \neq e_c^j$). In order to reach a single decision, the challenge then becomes how to define the multiple-constraint aggregation $g_\pi^\Gamma(c)$ as a combination of single-constraint aggregations $g_\pi^{\gamma_i}(c)$.

Since the role of constraints is to support reducing the error rate and the aggregation $g_\pi(c)$ is the base decision, we compute the multiple-constraint aggregation as $g_\pi^\Gamma(c) = \langle a_c, e_c^\Gamma \rangle$, where $e^\Gamma = min(\{e_c^i|a_c^i = a_c\} \cup e_c)$. We take the minimum of error rates in order to emphasize the importance of integrity constraints, which is the focus of this work. Therefore, the error rate of the final aggregated value is reduced by harnessing constraints. For the experiments with real datasets described in the next section, we will show that this aggregation reduces half of worker efforts while preserving the quality of aggregated results.

6. Experiments

The main goal of the following comprehensive experimental evaluation is to demonstrate the usage of crowdsourcing and integrity constraints in reconciling schema matching results in a matching network. To verify the effectiveness of our proposed methods, four experiments are performed: (i) evaluations on detecting spammers, (ii) relationship between the error rate and the matching accuracy, (iii) effects of spammer ratio on termination of crowdsourcing process, and (iv) evaluations on answer aggregation. We proceed to report the results on the real datasets using both real workers and simulated workers. The results highlight that the presented approach supports reconciling

schema matching by effectively using crowdsourcing harnessing integrity constraints.

6.1. Experimental Settings

Datasets. We have used many real-world datasets spanning various application domains, from Web forms to business schemas observed in data marketplaces.

- *Business Partner (BP):* The set comprises database schemas that model business partners in enterprise systems.

- *PurchaseOrder (PO):* We extracted purchase order e-business schemas from various resources.

- *University Application Form (UAF):* We extracted schemas from Web interfaces of American university application forms.

- *WebForm:* The schemas for this dataset have been automatically extracted from Web forms using OntoBuilder [23].

These datasets are publicly available [24] and descriptive statistics for the schemas are given in Table 1. In the experiments, the topology of schema matching network is a complete graph (i.e., all graph nodes are interconnected with all other nodes). To generate candidate correspondences, we used two well-known schema matchers (with default parameters), COMA++ [25, 26] and AMC [27]. All experiments ran on an Intel Core i7 system (2.8GHz, 4GB RAM).

Table 1. Datasets   **Table 2.** Constraint violations

Dataset	#Schemas	#Attributes (Min/Max)
BP	3	80/106
PO	10	35/408
UAF	15	65/228
WebForm	89	10/120

Dataset	# Violations per matcher COMA	AMC
BP	252	244
PO	10078	11320
UAF	40436	41256
WebForm	6032	6367

Integrity Constraints. For demonstration purposes, we consider the two integrity constraints, the one-to-one constraint and the cycle constraint, cf., Section 2.1. Table 2 lists the number of constraint violations among the candidate correspondences generated by the matchers. Rather independent of the applied schema matcher, we observe a large number of violations. Hence, there is a clear need for an efficient and effective crowdsourcing framework. All constraint violations are detected before-hand in the experiments.

Crowd Simulation. Since workers have wide-ranging levels of expertise, using real crowdsourcing services cannot cover all scenarios. We also develop a simulation engine that generates simulated workers to show the effectiveness of our approach in different settings.

In our simulation, we assume that the ground truth is known in advance (i.e. the ground truth is known for the experimenter, but not for the (simulated) crowd worker). Many previous studies [18, 28] characterized different types of crowd workers to reflect their expertise. Based on the classification in [18], we simulate 5 worker types as depicted in Figure 5. (1) *Experts:* who have deep knowledge about specific domains and answer questions with very high reliability. (2) *Normal workers:* who have general knowledge to give correct answers, but with few occasional mistakes. (3) *Sloppy workers:* who have very little knowledge and thus often give wrong answers, but unintentionally. (4) *Uniform spammers:* who intentionally give the same answer for all their own questions. (5) *Random spammers:* who carelessly give the random answer for any question. To model these types of workers, we use two parameters: *sensitivity—* the proportion of actual positives that are correctly identified—and *specificity*—the proportion of negatives that are correctly identified. Following the statistical result in [28], we set randomly the sensitivity and specificity of each type of workers as follows. For experts, the range is [0.9, 1]. For normal workers, it falls into [0.6, 0.9]. For sloppy workers, the range [0.1, 0.4] is selected. For random spammers, it varies from 0.4 to 0.6. Especially for uniform spammers, there are two regions: (i) *sensitivity* $\in [0.8, 1]$, *specificity* $\in [0, 0.2]$ and (ii) *sensitivity* $\in [0, 0.2]$, *specificity* $\in [0.8, 1]$.

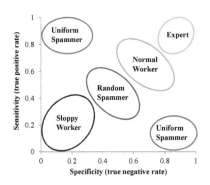

Figure 5. Characterization of worker types

Evaluation metrics. We rely on the following evaluation measures.

- *Matching Precision & Matching Recall:* To measure the quality of matching results, we rely on an exact matching G (which contains correct correspondences validated before-hand). Formally, the precision and recall of a set of correspondences V are $MPrec(V)=(|V \cap G|)/|V|$ and $MRec(V)=(|V \cap G|)/|G|$, where G is the exact matching (i.e. ground truth) given by the dataset provider.

- *Detecting Precision & Detecting Recall:* To measure the quality of spammer detection techniques, we define precision and recall of their detection results. Given W_S as the set of spammers in the crowd and W_D as the set of detected spammers, we have: $DPrec=(|W_D \cap W_S|)/|W_D|$ and $DRec=(|W_D \cap W_S|)/|W_S|$.

6.2. Evaluations on detecting spammers

In this set of experiments, we would like to evaluate the effectiveness of our worker assessment methods, including spammer detection and imitating group detection.

Detecting Spammers. In this experiment, we study our proposed method of detecting spammers as described in Section 4.1. To do so, we create a population of 100 simulated workers, among which 20% are experts, 35% are normal workers, 45% are sloppy workers. Such a worker expertise distribution has been observed at real-world crowdsourcing services [18]. In our experiments we vary gradually the ratio of spammers.

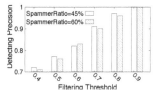 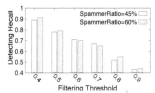

Figure 6. Effects of Spammer Ratio on Precision   **Figure 7.** Effects of Spammer Ratio on Recall

Figure 6 and 7 depict the results, that we have obtained as an average over 100 runs of our simulation. The X-axis is the filtering threshold α (that is the threshold value above which we consider a worker a spammer), varying from 0.4 to 0.9. The Y-axes is the detecting precision and detecting recall. We experimented with a spammer ratio of 45% and of 60% (while keeping the distribution of non-spammers, i.e. expert, normal and sloppy workers unchanged).

An interesting finding is that there is a tradeoff between detecting precision and detecting recall. When we raise the filtering threshold, the detecting precision increases while the detecting recall decreases. This is because other workers might also give the answers that create violations. Therefore, on the one hand, if the filtering threshold is too low, the detection mechanism could return both spammers and non-spammers, leading to low precision but high recall. On the other hand, if the filtering threshold is too high, the detection could not return all spammers, leading to high precision but low recall.

Another noticeable observation is that the detecting precision and recall are not affected by the ratio of spammers in the crowd. More precisely, the average difference of precision and recall between the two settings (SpammerRatio=60% and SpammerRatio=45%) are 0.01 and 0.02, respectively. This is reasonable since our detection mechanism calculates the violation rate for each worker independently.

Detecting Imitating Groups. In this experiment, we study our proposed method for detecting imitating groups as described in Section 4.2. To this end, we create a population of 100 simulated workers, in which there are 20% experts, 35% are normal workers, 45% are sloppy workers. To simulate the imitating groups, we modify this worker population as follows. Denote r_g is a pre-defined imitating ratio in the crowd. A copier (who imitates answers from other workers) is simulated by randomly choosing one of $1 - r_g$ independent workers and copying one or many his answers. Two workers are called belonging to an imitating group if one copies from another (one independent and one copier) or both of them copy from a same worker (two copiers).

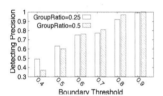

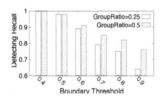

Figure 8. Effects of Imitating Group Ratio on Precision

Figure 9. Effects of Imitating Group Ratio on Recall

Figure 8 and 9 illustrate the results. There are 100 correspondences given to workers for validation. The X-axis is boundary threshold, varying from 0.4 to 0.9. For each pair of workers, if the imitating probability between them (eq. (13)) is greater than the boundary threshold, they are detected as belonging to an imitating group. The Y-axes is the detecting precision and detecting recall based on the detected workers. In our simulation experiments we used imitating ratio r_g of 25% and of 50%.

An interesting finding is that there is also a trade-off between detecting precision and detecting recall. Similar to the previous experiment, increasing the boundary threshold would increase the precision but lowering the recall. This is because a worker who does not imitate might still give some answers similar to the others (by accidence or the answers are the common ground themselves).

Another noticeable observation is that the detecting precision and recall are sensitive to the imitating ratio. More precisely, the difference between the two cases ($r_g = 25\%$ and $r_g = 50\%$) are considerable (0.3 for precision and 0.5 for recall). This can be explained by the fact that an imitating group might contain many workers. As the size of imitating groups is larger, the belonging worker is more likely to be detected by one

or many other workers in the same group (the detection considers every pair of workers). In other words, more true-positive cases are detected as the group ratio is larger, leading to higher precision and recall.

6.3. Relationship between Error Rate and Matching Accuracy

In order to assess the matching accuracy, we borrow the *precision* metric from information retrieval, which is the ratio of (*true*) correspondences existing in ground truth among all correspondences whose aggregated value is *true*. However, the ground truth is not known in general. Therefore, we use an indirect metric—error rate—to estimate the matching quality. We expect that the lower error rate, the higher quality of matching results.

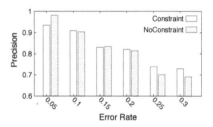

Figure 10. Relationship between error rate and precision

The following empirical results aim to validate this hypothesis. We conduct the experiment on all real datasets with the population of 100 simulated workers as above (20% experts, 35% normal workers, 45% spammers). Since the purpose of this experiment is to study the relationship between error rate and matching accuracy only, we do not consider spammers and imitating groups in the crowd.

Figure 10 depicts the resulting relationship of the error rate and precision, which is averaged over all datasets. In that, we vary error threshold ϵ from 0.05 to 0.3, meaning that the questions are posted to workers until the error rate of aggregated value is less than the given threshold ϵ. The precision is plotted as a function of ϵ. We aggregate the worker answers by two strategies: without constraint and with constraint. Here we consider both 1-1 constraint and cycle constraint as hard constraints, thus $\Delta = 0$.

The key observation is that when the error rate is decreased, the precision approaches to 1. Reversely, when the error rate is increased, the precision is reduced but greater than $1 - \epsilon$. Another interesting finding is that when the error rate is decreased, the value distribution of precision in case of with and without constraint is quite similar. This indicates that our method of updating the error rate is relevant.

In summary, the error rate is a good indicator of the quality of aggregated results. Since the ground truth is hidden, our goal was to verify if the error rate is a useful metric for matching quality. The result indicated that there was no significant difference between the two metrics. In terms of precision, the quality value is always around $1 - \epsilon$. In other words, the error threshold ϵ can be used to control the real matching quality.

6.4. Evaluations on Answer Aggregation

In Section 5.2, we already saw the benefit of using constraints in reducing error rate. In other words, with given requirement of low error, the constraints help to reduce the *expected cost* of crowd validation (i.e. the number of questions that need to be asked the workers). In this set of experiments, we will study the effects of harnessing such constraints on real datasets (BP, PO, WebForm, etc.).

We will analyze the effectiveness of constraints in three different settings: (i) effects of worker population, (ii) effects of spammers, and (iii) effects of imitating groups. All the settings have a common process as follows. Given an error threshold ($\epsilon = 0.1$), we iteratively post questions to workers and aggregate the worker answers (with and without constraints) until the error rate is less than ϵ. After the process ends, we instantiate an aggregated matching that consists of correspondences aggregated as correct (i.e. exists in ground truth). The reported numbers are averaged over all datasets.

Effects of Worker Reliability. We create a population of 100 simulated workers with 55% normal workers and 45% spammers. We use the detection method in Section 4.1 to detect the spammers and remove their answers from the answer set (we choose the filtering threshold = 0.6 as it balances the accuracy trade-off as in Section 6.2). The results are presented in Figure 11. The Y-axes is the expected cost, the matching precision and the matching recall of the aggregated matching. The X-axis is the reliability (denoted as r) of normal workers in the population, varying from 0.6 to 0.8. The reliability of a worker is $r = \frac{2 sensitivity \times specificity}{sensitivity + specificity}$, where *sensitivity* and *specificity* of a worker are already described in the experimental setting.

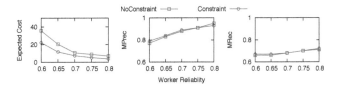

Figure 11. Effects of worker reliability on answer aggregation

A significant observation in the results is that for all values of error threshold and worker reliability, the expected cost of the aggregation with constraints

is definitely smaller (approximately a half) than the case without constraints. For example, with worker reliability is $r = 0.6$, the expected number of questions is reduced from 35 (without constraints) to 22 (with constraints). This concludes the fact that the constraints help to reduce the error rate, and subsequently reduce the expected cost.

Another key finding in Figure 11 is that both the matching precision and matching recall improve when the worker reliability increases. This implies that our detection method works well and the aggregated matching does not affected by spammers. Moreover, it is worth noting that the differences in MPrec and MRec between using constraints and not using constraints are not significant, since both cases are computed for the same error threshold ($\epsilon = 0.1$).

Effects of Spammers. We use the same worker population like the above experiment, except that we fix the reliability of normal workers to 0.75. Similar to the spammer detection experiment in Section 6.2, we increase the spammer ratio from 45% to 60% to study its effect on the expected cost and matching quality. The results are presented in Figure 12. The X-axis is the ratio of spammers in the crowd. The Y-axes are the expected cost, matching precision, and matching recall.

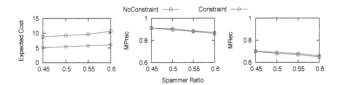

Figure 12. Effects of spammers on answer aggregation

An interesting finding is that when the spammer ratio increases, the expected cost only slightly increases. Moreover, the *Constraint* case always has a lower cost than the *NoConstraint* case. This supports the fact that our detection method is effective and insensitive to the spammer ratio. Although there are many spammers (who often give incorrect answers which increase the error rate) in crowd, most of them are detected and prevented from increasing the expected cost.

Another highlighted observation is that both the matching precision and matching recall only slightly decrease when the spammer ratio increases. This is reasonable and can be explained the same as above: our detection method is not significantly affected by the number of spammers.

Effects of Imitating Groups. We use the same worker population like the above experiment, in which we also fix the reliability of normal workers to 0.75. Similar to the imitating group detection experiment in Section 6.2, we increase the imitating ratio to study its effects on the expected cost and matching quality. The results are showed in Figure 13. The X-axis is the ratio of workers belonging to imitating groups in the crowd, varying from 30% to 60%. The Y-axes are the expected cost, matching precision, and matching recall.

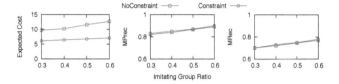

Figure 13. Effects of imitating groups on answer aggregation

A key finding is that when the number of imitating groups increases, the expected cost slightly decreases. This can be explained by the experimental result in Section 6.2: the detection is more effective when the size of imitating groups increases. This leads to early filtering of incorrect answers; and thus, reduce the error rate (or equivalently reduce the expected cost). It is worth noting that the *Constraint* case still has a lower cost than the *NoConstraint* case. This concludes the fact that the both cases are not affected by imitating groups since most of these groups are always detected.

Another interesting observation is that the matching precision and matching recall slightly increase when the imitating ratio increases. This is straightforward to understand. The more malicious workers are likely to be removed, the higher chances that we get a better aggregated matching.

Moreover, it is worth nothing that the matching precision and matching recall in all the three experimental settings have a similar trend since we do not add new correspondences in the validation process.

7. Related Work

We now review salient work in schema matching and crowdsourcing areas that are related to our research.

7.1. Schema matching

Database schema matching is an active research field. The developments of this area have been summarized in two surveys [6, 29]. Existing works on schema matching focused mainly on improving quality parameters of matchers, such as precision or recall of the generated matchings. Recently, however, ones started to realize that the extent to what precision and recall can be improved may be limited for general-purpose matching algorithms. Instead of designing new algorithms, there has been a shift towards matching combination and tuning methods. These works include YAM [30], systematic matching ensemble selection [31] or automatic tuning of the matcher parameters [32].

While there is a large body of works on schema matching, the post-matching reconciliation process (that is central to our work) has received little attention in the literature. Recently, there are some works [33–36] using pay-as-you-go integration method that establishes the initial matching and then incrementally improves matching quality. While the systems in [33, 34] rely on one user only, the framework in [35, 37] relies on multiple users.

7.2. Schema matching network

The idea of exploiting the presence of a large set of schemas to improve the matchings has been studied before. Holistic matching [38] attempted to exploit statistical co-occurrences of attributes in different schemas and use them to derive complex correspondence. Whereas, corpus-based matching [39] attempted to use a 'corpus' of schemas to augment the evidences that improve existing matchings and exploit constraints between attributes by applying statistical techniques. Network level constraints, in particular the circle constraints, were originally considered in [12, 40] in which they studied the establishment of semantic interoperability in a large-scale P2P network. There are several applications based on schema matching networks in particular and schema matching in general, including schema reuse [41], web search [42], and Deep Web [43].

In this paper, we study contextual information and integrity constraints (e.g., 1-1 and circle constraints) on top of the schema matching network. A somewhat related concept of alignment space was introduced in Euzenat [44]. The authors consider a network of ontologies and alignments between them, which is similar to our setting, however unlike us, they do not consider network-aware consistency conditions. The alignment space is mainly used for designing similarity-measures.

7.3. Crowdsourcing

In recent years, crowdsourcing has become a promising methodology to overcome human-intensive computational tasks. Its benefits vary from unlimited labor resources of user community to cost-effective business models. The book [13] summarized problems and challenges in crowdsourcing as well as promising research directions for the future. A wide range of crowdsourcing platforms, which allows users to work together in a large-scale online community, have been developed such as Amazon Mechanical Turk and CloudCrowd.

On top of these platforms, there are also many crowdsourcing applications that have been built for specific domains. For example, in [22], the crowdsourcing is employed to validate the search results of automated image search on mobile devices. In [45], the authors leveraged the user CAPTCHAs inputs in web forms to recognize difficult words that cannot solved precisely by optical character recognition (OCR) programs.

Similar to our work, the authors of [46] also make use of crowdsourcing to validate the correspondences and reduce their uncertainty. However, they only focus on a pair-wise matching and using entropy-based decision strategy to maximize the uncertainty reduction at a single validation step. Whereas, our work leverages integrity constraints on top of a schema matching network to reduce the overall validation effort.

Regarding the utilization of constraints, there are some previous works such as [47, 48]. In [47], the constraints were used to define the tasks for collaborative planning systems whereas in [48], the constraints were used to check worker quality by quantifying the consistency of worker answers. In our work, the constraints are used to provide evidences for detecting malicious workers and adjust the error rate for reducing worker efforts.

Deutch et al. [49] also use integrity constraints, in particular database key constraints to identify problems with the data that is collected through crowdsourcing. They also propose repair mechanisms for the cases where the user input violates the constraints.

8. Conclusions and Future Work

We have presented our techniques to reconcile a schema matching network through crowdsourcing. The algorithms take the correspondences generated by automatic schema matchers as input and they generate validation questions. The crowd workers respond to these questions by indicating whether a particular attribute correspondence should be accepted or rejects. We can express various natural expectations about the network in the form of integrity constraints. We demonstrated that these constraints can be exploited in various ways: they enable to improve the worker assessment methods, they can be used to reduce the necessary validation efforts. Moreover they are also usful for spam detection. We demonstrated these desirable properties through our experiments on real datasets, with the help of a simulated crowd population.

Our work opens up several future research directions. First, one can extend our notion of schema matching network and consider representing other integrity constraints (e.g., functional dependencies or domain-specific constraints). Second, one can devise more applications which could be transformed into the schema matching network. While our work focuses on schema matching, our techniques, especially the constraint-based aggregation method, can be applied to other tasks such as entity resolution, business process matching, or Web service discovery.

Acknowledgement. This research has received funding from the NisB project - European Union's Seventh Framework Programme (grant agreement number 256955) and the PlanetData project - Network of Excellence (grant agreement number 257641). The work of Zoltán Miklós was partially supported by the project Aresos, financed by CNRS through the mastodons programme. The authors thank for anonymous referees for their helpful suggestions.

References

[1] Gonzalez, H., Halevy, A.Y., Jensen, C.S., Langen, A., Madhavan, J., Shapley, R., Shen, W. et al. (2010) Google fusion tables: web-centered data management and collaboration. In *SIGMOD*: 1061–1066.

[2] Bollacker, K., Evans, C., Paritosh, P., Sturge, T. and Taylor, J. (2008) Freebase: a collaboratively created graph database for structuring human knowledge. In *SIGMOD*: 1247–1250.

[3] http://www.factual.com.

[4] Das Sarma, A., Fang, L., Gupta, N., Halevy, A., Lee, H., Wu, F., Xin, R. et al. (2012) Finding related tables. In *SIGMOD*: 817–828.

[5] Bernstein, P., Madhavan, J. and Rahm, E. (2011) Generic Schema Matching, Ten Years Later. In *VLDB*.

[6] Rahm, E. and Bernstein, P.A. (2001) A Survey of Approaches to Automatic Schema Matching. *JVLDB* : 334–350.

[7] Nguyen, Q.V.H., Wijaya, T.K., Miklos, Z., Aberer, K., Levy, E., Shafran, V., Gal, A. et al. (2013) Minimizing Human Effort in Reconciling Match Networks. In *ER*.

[8] Nguyen, Q.V.H., Nguyen, T.T., Miklós, Z. and Aberer, K. (2013) On leveraging crowdsourcing techniques for schema matching networks. In *DASFAA*: 139–154.

[9] Belhajjame, K., Paton, N.W., Fernandes, A.A.A., Hedeler, C. and Embury, S.M. (2011) User feedback as a first class citizen in information integration systems. In *CIDR*: 175–183.

[10] Gal, A. (2011) *Uncertain Schema Matching* (Morgan & Claypool).

[11] Gal, A., Sagi, T., Weidlich, M., Levy, E., Shafran, V., Miklós, Z. and Hung, N. (2012) Making sense of top-k matchings: A unified match graph for schema matching. In *IIWeb*.

[12] Cudré-Mauroux, P., Aberer, K. and Feher, A. (2006) Probabilistic message passing in peer data management systems. In *ICDE*: 41.

[13] von Ahn, L. (2009) Human computation. In *Design Automation Conference*: 418 –419.

[14] Quoc Viet Hung, N., Tam, N., Tran, L. and Aberer, K. (2013) An evaluation of aggregation techniques in crowdsourcing. In *WISE*: 1–15.

[15] Dawid, A.P. and Skene, A.M. (1979) Maximum likelihood estimation of observer error-rates using the EM algorithm. *J. R. Stat. Soc.* : 20–28.

[16] Gao, N., Webber, W. and Oard, D. (2014) Reducing reliance on relevance judgments for system comparison by using expectation-maximization. In *Advances in Information Retrieval*, 1–12.

[17] Hosseini, M., Cox, I.J., Milić-Frayling, N., Kazai, G. and Vinay, V. (2012) On aggregating labels from multiple

crowd workers to infer relevance of documents. In *Advances in information retrieval*, 182–194.

[18] VUURENS, J., DE VRIES, A. and EICKHOFF, C. (2011) How much spam can you take? an analysis of crowdsourcing results to increase accuracy. In *CIR*.

[19] DIFALLAH, D.E., DEMARTINI, G. and CUDRE-MAUROUX, P. (2012) Mechanical cheat: Spamming schemes and adversarial techniques on crowdsourcing platforms. In *CrowdSearch*.

[20] IPEIROTIS, P.G., PROVOST, F. and WANG, J. (2010) Quality management on amazon mechanical turk. In *HCOMP*: 64–67.

[21] PARAMESWARAN, A.G., GARCIA-MOLINA, H., PARK, H., POLYZOTIS, N., RAMESH, A. and WIDOM, J. (2012) Crowdscreen: algorithms for filtering data with humans. In *SIGMOD*: 361–372.

[22] YAN, T. and KUMAR, V. (2010) CrowdSearch: exploiting crowds for accurate real-time image search on mobile phones. *8th international conference on Mobile* : 77–90.

[23] ROITMAN, H. and GAL, A. (2006) Ontobuilder: fully automatic extraction and consolidation of ontologies from web sources using sequence semantics. In *ICSNW*: 573–576.

[24] http://lsirwww.epfl.ch/schema_matching.

[25] Do, H.H. and RAHM, E. (2002) COMA - A System for Flexible Combination of Schema Matching Approaches. In *VLDB*: 610–621.

[26] AUMUELLER, D., Do, H.H., MASSMANN, S. and RAHM, E. (2005) Schema and ontology matching with coma++. In *SIGMOD*: 906–908.

[27] PEUKERT, E., EBERIUS, J. and RAHM, E. (2011) AMC - A framework for modelling and comparing matching systems as matching processes. In *ICDE*: 1304–1307.

[28] KAZAI, G., KAMPS, J. and MILIC-FRAYLING, N. (2011) Worker types and personality traits in crowdsourcing relevance labels. In *CIKM*: 1941–1944.

[29] BERNSTEIN, P.A., MADHAVAN, J. and RAHM, E. (2011) Generic Schema Matching, Ten Years Later. *PVLDB* : 695–701.

[30] DUCHATEAU, F., COLETTA, R., BELLAHSENE, Z. and MILLER, R.J. (2009) (not) yet another matcher. In *CIKM*: 1537–1540.

[31] GAL, A. and SAGI, T. (2010) Tuning the ensemble selection process of schema matchers. *JIS* : 845–859.

[32] LEE, Y., SAYYADIAN, M., DOAN, A. and ROSENTHAL, A.S. (2007) eTuner: tuning schema matching software using synthetic scenarios. *JVLDB* : 97–122.

[33] JEFFERY, S.R., FRANKLIN, M.J. and HALEVY, A.Y. (2008) Pay-as-you-go user feedback for dataspace systems. In *SIGMOD*: 847–860.

[34] QI, Y., CANDAN, K.S. and SAPINO, M.L. (2007) Ficsr: feedback-based inconsistency resolution and query processing on misaligned data sources. In *SIGMOD*: 151–162.

[35] McCANN, R., SHEN, W. and DOAN, A. (2008) Matching Schemas in Online Communities: A Web 2.0 Approach. In *ICDE*: 110–119.

[36] NGUYEN, Q.V.H., NGUYEN, T.T., MIKLÓS, Z., ABERER, K., GAL, A. and WEIDLICH, M. (2014) Pay-as-you-go reconciliation in schema matching networks. In *ICDE*: 220–231.

[37] NGUYEN, H.Q.V., LUONG, X.H., MIKLÓS, Z., QUAN, T.T. and ABERER, K. (2013) Collaborative schema matching reconciliation. In *CoopIS*: 222–240.

[38] SU, W., WANG, J. and LOCHOVSKY, F. (2006) Holistic schema matching for web query interfaces. In *EDBT*: 77–94.

[39] MADHAVAN, J., BERNSTEIN, P.A., DOAN, A. and HALEVY, A. (2005) Corpus-based schema matching. In *ICDE*: 57–68.

[40] ABERER, K., CUDRÉ-MAUROUX, P. and HAUSWIRTH, M. (2003) Start making sense: The Chatty Web approach for global semantic agreements. *JWS* : 89–114.

[41] HUNG, N.Q.V., TAM, N.T., ABERER, K. *et al.* (2014) Privacy-preserving schema reuse. In *DASFAA*: 234–250.

[42] HE, H., MENG, W., YU, C. and WU, Z. (2004) Automatic integration of web search interfaces with wise-integrator. *JVLDB* : 256–273.

[43] WU, W., YU, C., DOAN, A. and MENG, W. (2004) An interactive clustering-based approach to integrating source query interfaces on the deep web. In *SIGMOD*: 95–106.

[44] DAVID, J., EUZENAT, J. and SVÁB-ZAMAZAL, O. (2010) Ontology similarity in the alignment space. In *International Semantic Web Conference (1)*: 129–144.

[45] VON AHN, L., MAURER, B., McMILLEN, C., ABRAHAM, D. and BLUM, M. (2008) recaptcha: Human-based character recognition via web security measures. *Science* : 1465–1468.

[46] ZHANG, C.J., CHEN, L., JAGADISH, H.V. and CAO, C.C. (2013) Reducing uncertainty of schema matching via crowdsourcing. In *PVLDB*: 757–768.

[47] ZHANG, H., LAW, E., MILLER, R., GAJOS, K., PARKES, D. and HORVITZ, E. (2012) Human computation tasks with global constraints. In *CHI*: 217–226.

[48] CHEN, K.T., WU, C.C., CHANG, Y.C. and LEI, C.L. (2009) A crowdsourceable qoe evaluation framework for multimedia content. In *MM*: 491–500.

[49] DEUTCH, D., GREENSHPAN, O., KOSTENKO, B. and MILO, T. (2012) Declarative platform for data sourcing games. In *Proceedings of the 21st International Conference on World Wide Web*, WWW '12: 779–788.

Appendix

Sketch proof for proposition 1: Based on Cauchy's inequality, we have:

$$\left(\frac{k_f}{k_t}\right)^{k_t} r^{k_t}(1-r)^{k_f} \leq \left(\frac{k_t \frac{k_f^r}{k_t} + k_f(1-r)}{k_f + k_t}\right)^{k_f+k_t} \leq \frac{k_t^{k_f+k_t}}{(k_f+k_t)^{k_f+k_t}}$$

Hence,

$$r^{k_t}(1-r)^{k_f} \leq \frac{k_f^{k_f} k_t^{k_t}}{(k_f+k_t)^{k_f+k_t}}$$

Using this inequality with eq. (11) completes the proof.

Sketch proof for proposition 2: Let n and m be two positive integers with $0 < m < n$. Given $x \in [m, n-m]$, it can be easily seen that $f(x) = x^x(n-x)^{n-x}$ is a convex function. Thus, w we have:

$$x^x(n-x)^{n-x} \leq max(f(m), f(n-m)) = m^m(n-m)^{n-m}$$

We will apply this inequality with $m = |V|$, $n = |D|$, and $x = k_f$. By definition, we have $k_t + k_f = |D|$. Moreover, we have the fact that each violation has at least one correct correspondence and one incorrect correspondence; i.e. $m \leq k_f, k_t \leq n$. As a result, we have:

$$\frac{k_f^{k_f} k_t^{k_t}}{(k_f + k_t)^{k_f + k_t}} = \frac{k_f^{k_f}(|D| - k_f)^{|D| - k_f}}{(|D|)^{|D|}} \leq \frac{|V|^{|V|}(|D| - |V|)^{|D| - |V|}}{|D|^{|D|}}$$

Using this inequality with eq. (12) completes the proof.

Computing the conditional probability $Pr(X_{c_0}|\gamma_{1-1})$: According to Bayes theorem, $Pr(X_{c_0}|\gamma_{1-1}) = \frac{Pr(\gamma_{1-1}|X_{c_0}) \times Pr(X_{c_0})}{Pr(\gamma_{1-1})}$. Now we need to compute $Pr(\gamma_{1-1})$ and $Pr(\gamma_{1-1}|X_{c_0})$. Let denote $p_i = Pr(X_{c_i} = true)$, for short. In order to compute $Pr(\gamma_{1-1})$, we do following steps: (1) express $Pr(\gamma_{1-1})$ as the sum from the full joint of $\gamma_{1-1}, c_0, c_1, \ldots, c_k$, (2) express the joint as a product of conditionals. Formally, we have:

$$
\begin{aligned}
Pr(\gamma_{1-1}) &= \sum_{c_0, c_1, \ldots, c_k} Pr(\gamma_{1-1}, X_{c_0}, X_{c_1}, \ldots, X_{c_k}) \\
&= \sum Pr(\gamma_{1-1}|X_{c_0}, X_{c_1}, \ldots, X_{c_k}) \times Pr(X_{c_0}, X_{c_1}, \ldots, Xc_k) \\
&= 1 \times Pr(X_{c_0}, X_{c_1}, \ldots, X_{c_k}|m(X_{c_0}, X_{c_1}, \ldots, X_{c_k}) \leq 1) \\
&\quad + \Delta \times Pr(X_{c_0}, X_{c_1}, \ldots, X_{c_k}|m(X_{c_0}, X_{c_1}, \ldots, X_{c_k}) > 1) \\
&= y + \Delta \times (1 - y)
\end{aligned}
$$

where $m()$ counts the number of X_{c_i} assigned as *true*

$$y = \prod_{i=0}^{n}(1 - p_i) + \sum_{i=0}^{n}[p_i \prod_{j=0, j \neq i}^{n}(1 - p_j)]$$

Similar to computing $Pr(\gamma_{1-1})$, we also express $Pr(\gamma_{1-1}|X_{c_0})$ as the sum from the full joint of $\gamma_{1-1}, c_1, \ldots, c_k$ and then express the joint as a product of conditionals. After these steps, we have $Pr(\gamma_{1-1}|X_{c_0} = true) = x + \Delta \times (1 - x)$, where $x = \prod_{i=1}^{k}(1 - p_i)$. After having $Pr(\gamma_{1-1})$ and $Pr(\gamma_{1-1}|X_{c_0})$, we can compute $Pr(X_{c_0}|\gamma_{1-1})$ as in equation 16.

Computing the conditional probability $Pr(X_{c_0}|\gamma_\circlearrowleft)$: According to Bayes theorem, $Pr(X_{c_0}|\gamma_\circlearrowleft) = \frac{Pr(\gamma_\circlearrowleft|X_{c_0}) \times Pr(X_{c_0})}{Pr(\gamma_\circlearrowleft)}$. In order to compute $Pr(\gamma_\circlearrowleft|X_{c_0})$ and $Pr(\gamma_\circlearrowleft)$, we also express $Pr(\gamma_\circlearrowleft|X_{c_0})$ as the sum from the full joint of $\gamma_{1-1}, c_0, c_1, \ldots, c_k$ and then express the joint as a product of conditionals. After some transformations, we can obtain equation 17.

Sketch proof for theorem 1: From equation 16, we can obtain $y = x + \sum_{i=1}^{k}[p_i \prod_{j=0, j \neq i}^{k}(1 - p_j)]$. Since $\sum_{i=1}^{k}[p_i \prod_{j=0, j \neq i}^{k}(1 - p_j)] \geq 0$ and $\Delta \leq 1$, we have $x + \Delta(1 - x) \leq y + \Delta(1 - y)$. Following this inequality and equation 16, we conclude $Pr(X_c = true|\gamma_{1-1}) \leq Pr(X_c = true)$.

Sketch proof for theorem 2: After some transformations, we can derive that $Pr(X_c = true|\gamma_\circlearrowleft) \geq Pr(X_c = true)$ is equivalent to $(1 - p_0) \prod_{1}^{k} p_i \geq \Delta(x - y)$. Moreover, we have $x - y = (1 - p_0) \sum_{i=1}^{k}[(1 - p_i) \prod_{j=1, j \neq i}^{k} p_j]$. Therefore, we conclude $Pr(X_c = true|\gamma_\circlearrowleft) \geq Pr(X_c = false)$ if $\frac{1}{\Delta} \geq \sum_{i=1}^{k} \frac{1 - p_i}{p_i}$.

14

MOSDEN: A Scalable Mobile Collaborative Platform for Opportunistic Sensing Applications

Prem Prakash Jayaraman[*1], Charith Perera[1], Dimitrios Georgakopoulos[2] and Arkady Zaslavsky[†1]

[1]CSIRO Computational Informatics, Canberra, Australia 2601
[2]School of Computer Science and Information Technology, RMIT University, GPO Box 2476, Melbourne VIC 3001

Abstract

Mobile smartphones along with embedded sensors have become an efficient enabler for various mobile applications including opportunistic sensing. The hi-tech advances in smartphones are opening up a world of possibilities. This paper proposes a mobile collaborative platform called MOSDEN that enables and supports *opportunistic sensing* at run time. MOSDEN captures and shares sensor data across multiple apps, smartphones and users. MOSDEN supports the emerging trend of separating sensors from application-specific processing, storing and sharing. MOSDEN promotes reuse and re-purposing of sensor data hence reducing the efforts in developing novel *opportunistic sensing* applications. MOSDEN has been implemented on Android-based smartphones and tablets. Experimental evaluations validate the scalability and energy efficiency of MOSDEN and its suitability towards real world applications. The results of evaluation and lessons learned are presented and discussed in this paper.

Keywords: opportunistic sensing, crowdsensing, mobile middleware, mobile data analytics

1. Introduction

Today mobile phones have become a ubiquitous computing and communication device in people's lives [1]. The mobile device market is growing at a frantic pace and it won't be long before it outnumbers the human population. It is predicted that mobile phones combined with tablets will exceed the human population by 2017 [2]. Current generation smartphones are equipped with plethora of features such as rich set of sensors (e.g. ambient light sensor, accelerometer, gyroscope, digital compass, GPS, microphone and camera) to enable on-the-move sensing and technologies such as NFC, Bluetooth, WiFi that enable them to communicate and interact with external sensors available in the environment. Smartphones have the potential to generate an unprecedented amount of data [3] that can revolutionise many sectors of economy, including business, healthcare, social networks, environmental monitoring and transportation.

Mobile opportunistic sensing is one such new wave of innovative application popularly called collaborative community sensing or crowdsensing [4, 5]. Mobile Opportunistic sensing is an autonomous collaborative sensing approach that takes advantage of a population of users to measure large-scale phenomenon which cannot be measured using a user. Mobile opportunistic sensing applications require minimal user involvement (e.g. continuous computation of user activity passively i.e. in the background). Opportunistic sensing applications [6] thrive on the widespread availability of smartphones and the diverse sets of data generated by these devices. Date captured from an individual smartphone user can be used to infer the user's current context and activity. On the other hand, by fusing data from a multitude of smartphone user population, high level context information such as crowd activity within a given environment [6] can be inferred. In either form, the data generated by the smartphones is valuable and offers unique opportunities to develop novel and innovative applications.

To date most efforts to develop opportunistic sensing/crowdsensing[1] applications have focused on building monolithic mobile applications that are built

---

*Corresponding author
Email: {prem.jayaraman, charith.perera, arkady.zaslavsky}@csiro.au
dimitrios.georgakopoulos@rmit.edu.au
†Prof. Zaslavsky is an International Adjunct Professor at StPetersburg National Research University of IT, Mechanics and Optics, Russia

[1]In this paper, we use the terms *opportunistic sensing* and *crowdsensing* synonymously.

for specific requirements [7]. These application silos have very little capability for extensions and sharing of sensed data with a community of users often making the data available only within the application's context [4]. However, to realise the greater vision of mobile collaborative opportunistic sensing we need a common extensible platform that facilitates easy development and deployment of collaborative opportunistic sensing applications on-demand.

The key challenge here is to develop a platform that is autonomous, scalable, interoperable and supports efficient sensor data capturing, processing, storage and sharing. The autonomous ability of the system enables self-management and independent operations during device disconnections and off-line modes. We strongly believe that providing an easy-to-use, scalable platform to develop and deploy collaborative mobile opportunistic sensing applications will be significant. To this end, we propose a collaborative mobile sensing platform namely Mobile Sensor Data Engine (MOSDEN). MOSDEN is capable of functioning on multitude of resource-constrained devices (e.g. Raspberry Pi[2]) including smartphones. MOSDEN is a scalable platform that enables collaborative processing of sensor data. The MOSDEN platform follows component-based design philosophy allowing users/developers to implement custom data analytic algorithms (e.g. data mining algorithms [8]) and models to suit application requirements. Further, MOSDEN incorporates local processing, storage and sharing as a means to accomplish data reduction for Big Data applications. By limiting the continuous transmission of data to a centralised server which is typical of most mobile opportunistic sensing application, MOSDEN reduces bandwidth and power consumption. The key contributions of this paper are summarised as follows:

- We propose MOSDEN, a scalable, easy-to-use, interoperable platform that facilitates the development of collaborative mobile opportunistic sensing applications

- We demonstrate the ease of development and deployment of a opportunistic sensing application using the MOSDEN platform

- We experimentally evaluate and validate the scalability, performance and energy-efficiency of MOSDEN under varying collaborative opportunistic sensing workloads

The rest of the paper is organised as follows. Section II discusses related work. Section III considers a motivation scenario. Section IV presents the proposed MOSDEN platform architecture. Section V discusses MOSDEN implementation and Section VI presents MOSDEN platform evaluations and results. Section VI concludes the paper with indicators to future work.

2. Related Work

Numerous real and successful mobile opportunistic sensing applications have emerged in recent times such as WAYZ[3] for real-time traffic/navigation information and Wazer2[4] for real-time, location-based citizen journalism, context-aware open-mobile miner (CAROMM)[6] among others. Mobile opportunistic sensing applications [9, 10] thrive on the data obtained from heterogeneous sets of smart phones owned and operated by humans. Until recently mobile sensing application such as activity recognition (*personal sensing*), where people's activity (e.g. walking, talking, sitting) is classified and monitored, required specialised mobile devices [11, 12]. This has significantly changed with advent of smartphones equipped with on-board sensing capabilities. More recently, research efforts have focused on development of activity recognition, context-aware [13] and data mining models for smartphones [8, 14, 15] that leverage on smartphone's processing and on-board sensing capabilities.

Recent efforts to build opportunistic sensing application have focused on building monolithic mobile applications that are built with specific purpose and requirements. The MetroSense [16] project at Dartmouth is an example of one such opportunistic sensing system. The project aims in developing classification techniques, privacy approaches and sensing paradigms for mobile phones. The CenceMe [17] project under the MetroSense umbrella is a personal sensing system that enable members of social networks to share their presence. The CenceMe application incorporates mobile analytics by capturing user activity (e.g., sitting, walking, meeting friends), disposition (e.g., happy, sad, doing OK), habits (e.g., at the gym, coffee shop today, at work) and surroundings (e.g., noisy, hot, bright, high ozone) to determine presence. The CenceMe system comprises two parts, the phone software and back-end software. The phone software is implemented on a Nokia N95 running Symbian operating system. The phone software is developed in Java Micro Edition (JME) which interfaces with Symbian C++ modules controlling the hardware.

MineFleet [8] is a distributed vehicle performance data mining system designed for commercial fleets. In MineFleet, dedicated patented custom built hardware devices are used on fleet trucks to continuously process data generated by the truck. MineFleet system comprises an on-board data stream mining module

---

[2]http://www.raspberrypi.org/

[3]http://www.wayz.com/
[4]https://www.wazer2.co.il/

that performs extensive processing of data using various statistical and data stream mining algorithms. This data stored locally is transmitted to an external MineFleet Server for further processing when network connectivity is available.

Crowdsourcing data analytics system (CDAS) [18] is a crowd sourcing framework in which, the participants are part of a distributed crowdsourced system. The CDAS system enables deployment of crowdsourcing applications that require human involvement for simple verification tasks using Amazon Mechanical Turk (AMT). E.g. users in the system would be sent a picture for identification by a centralised task distributor. Humans users participating in the crowdsourcing application respond with appropriate answers. The results from human workers are combined to compute the final result. The CDAS system incorporates complex analytics that enables it to disseminate jobs, obtain results and compare results obtained from different workers to determine the correct one. GeoCrowd [19] is another crowdsourcing system that employs spatial characteristics to estimate task assignments among user populations. Mobile edge capture and analysis middleware for social sensing applications (MECA) [20] is another middleware for efficient data collection from mobile devices in a efficient, flexible and scalable manner. MECA provides a platform by which different applications can use data generated from diverse mobile data sources (sensors). The proposed MECA architecture has three layers comprising data layer (mobile data sources âĂŞ mobile phones), edge layer (base stations that select and instruct a device or group of devices to collect data and process data), phenomena/application layer (the back-end that determines the edge nodes to process application request).

Applications like Waze[5], MetroSense [16] and Mine-Fleet [8] are built around specific data handling models (e.g. GPS for Waze, Microphone for MetroSense and Data mining algorithms for object monitoring) and application requirements reducing its re-usability. On the other hand, frameworks like CDAS[18], GeoCrowd [19] and MECA [20] offload processing to centralised servers increasing bandwidth usage and making them less suitable for working in off-line modes. Moreover, in these frameworks, the smartphones are viewed as mere data collection or user response collection devices lacking capabilities to implement localised data analytics. On contrast, the proposed MOSDEN platform is developed with the design goal of 1) re-usability, 2) ease of use, 3) ease of development/deployment, 4) scalability, 5) easy interface to access both on-board and external sensors, 6) support for on-board complex

data analytics and 7) distributed mobile data sharing. The MOSDEN platform provides the application developer with implementation options i.e. choice of using processing on the smartphone and/or processing at the server. It also provides extensions to implement mobile distributed load-balancing that can determine on-demand the best location to process data. We note, discussions on load-balancing and task allocation to different collaborative MOSDEN smartphone devices are outside the scope of this paper. The MOSDEN platform promotes a distributed collaborative sensing infrastructure where each MOSDEN instance running on a smartphone is self-managed. In our previous work [21] we proposed the architecture of MOSDEN supported by evaluations focusing on system performance. In this paper, we further analyse and present evaluation results of MOSDEN's scalability performance and energy-efficiency under varying workloads typical of collaborative opportunistic sensing applications. Specifically, we have critically evaluated the energy efficiency of MOSDEN platform when performing operations like continuous sensing and sensing/sending. We also evaluate MOSDEN's query processing efficiency when answering to distributed queries from multiple MOSDEN instances in a collaborative experimental setup.

3. Opportunistic Sensing Scenario

In this section we present a motivating scenario that explains the need for a scalable, collaborative, mobile sensing platform like MOSDEN. The scenario under consideration is an environmental monitoring application (e.g. noise pollution) in smart cities as depicted in Fig. 1.

In step (1), a remote-server (cloud-based) registers the interest for data within user communities. In the example depicted in Fig. 1, the user communities are grouped based on location. In step (2), the data captured and processed on the smartphones are made available to the remote-server. In step (3), the opportunistic sensing application obtains data from the remote-server for further processing and visualisation. The above scenario is a typical case for many opportunistic sensing applications that require data from diverse user communities. The same approach is applied to another opportunistic sensing application that computes air pollution within the environment. To accomplish this requirement, the smartphone will also have to rely on external sensors that are part of a smart city infrastructure to obtain air pollution data.

Using a monolithic approach may results in developing a niche class of applications built for a single purpose. Such an application may not be scalable/adaptable to work in other scenarios which is a major obstacle. E.g. the algorithm required to process

---

[5]http://www.wayz.com/

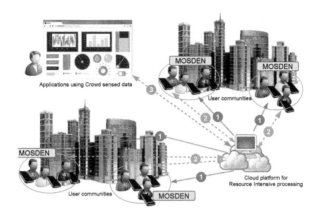

Figure 1. Environmental Monitoring – Mobile Opportunistic Sensing Scenario

noise data is different to air pollution computation. Moreover, such an opportunistic sensing application is hard-wired making it extremely difficult to make changes to different parts of the code. E.g. adding new interface to communicate with external sensors to collect air pollution data.

To achieve the level of extensibility and scalability to support a range of different opportunistic sensing application requirements, the opportunistic sensing platform needs to follow the design principle of separating the sensor capturing operation and application specific processing. This will in turn promote on-demand application composition. Further, the platform needs to support real-time data collection, processing and storage, ability to incorporate application specific data analytic algorithms/models, energy-efficient operation and autonomous functions i.e. ability to work with minimal user interaction and with support for off-line modes. The proposed MOSDEN platform supports the above mentioned features natively.

4. MObile Sensor Data ENgine (MOSDEN): A collaborative mobile opportunistic sensing platform

We propose MOSDEN, a crowdsensing platform built around the following design principles:

- Separation of data collection, processing and storage to application specific logic

- A distributed collaborative crowdsensing application deployment with relative ease

- Support for autonomous functioning i.e. ability to self-manage as a part of the distributed architecture

- A component-based system that supports access to internal and external sensor and implementation of domain specific models and algorithms

These design principles address the obstacles mentioned in Section 3. The proposed MOSDEN platform overcomes the key barriers of developing and deploying scalable collaborative mobile opportunistic sensing applications.

Architecture. MOSDEN platform follows the design principle of Global Sensor Network (GSN) [22]. GSN is a sensor network middleware developed to run on high-powered computing devices (e.g. servers and cloud resources). GSN presents a unified middleware approach that facilitates acquisition, processing and storage of sensor data. We reuse the concept of virtual sensors proposed by GSN. A virtual sensor is a abstraction of the underlying data source (e.g. wireless sensor network). Since, GSN was not developed for resource constrained environment, we made significant enhancement to GSN when designing and implementing MOSDEN described in the following section. MOSDEN follows a component-based architecture allowing extensibility without modifying the existing codebase. The architecture of the proposed MOSDEN platform is presented in Fig. 2 followed by description of each component.

Plugin: In MOSDEN, we introduce the concept of Plugins. In GSN, a developer had to implement wrappers to accommodate new sensor data sources into the system. To accommodate a new wrapper, the system had to be recompiled and redeployed. This approach is not very practical especially for real-time applications. Hence, we introduced a plugin-based approach to overcomes this challenge. The Plugins are independent applications that communicates with MOSDEN. MOSDEN uses a discovery mechanism specific to the implementation platform to discover the list of plugins installed in the system. E.g. in case of android operating system, a plugin discovery services provides a list of registered plugins and their description. The key function of the plugin is to describe how to interface with a sensor that needs to be connected with MOSDEN.

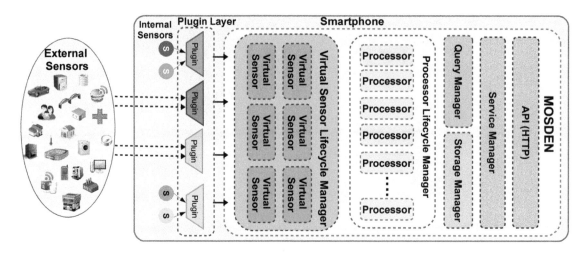

Figure 2. MOSDEN Platform Architecture

We have developed a plugin descriptor that opportunistic sensing application developer can use to implement plugins to interface with new sensors. A conceptual description of the plugin is shown in XML format in Fig. 3.

Virtual Sensor: The virtual sensor is an abstraction of the underlying data source from which data is obtained. The virtual sensor can perform stream level operation e.g. fuse data from multiple sensor sources (on-board, external sensors connected to the mobile device and remote MOSDEN instances). The virtual sensor can be used to specify configurations to capture data from distributed MOSDEN instances. In such situations, the query and service manager at the remote MOSDEN instance is responsible for processing the query. The virtual sensor file dynamically links the sensor plugins with MOSDEN platform via an XML configuration file. The virtual sensor lifecycle manager is responsible to manage the instantiation, updation and removal of virtual sensor resources.

Processors: The processor classes are used to implement application specific data analytics models and algorithms. For example, a Fast Fourier Transform (FFT) algorithm to compute the decibel level from microphone recordings or a data mining algorithm to perform high speed data stream clustering and classification [8].

Storage Manager: The function of the storage manage is to store the data acquired from the virtual sensor and processor workflow. The storage manager uses a data collection window to delete old data. This function of the data collection windows is very similar to sliding window protocol. The virtual sensor configuration file is used to configure the data collection window size during application deployment. The window size can be modified during runtime.

Query Manager: The query manager is responsible to resolve and answer queries from external entities. An external entity can be another MOSDEN instance, a user or an application querying for data collected by the smartphone. The query manager employs a queuing mechanism to resolve incoming queries. The local storage and query processing functionality of MOSDEN is a key enabler of off-line mode operations.

Service Manager: The service manager is responsible to manage subscriptions to data from external entities. The service manager registers subscription request and depending on the mode of data delivery (e.g. persistent/non-persistent) will deliver available data to the requested external source when possible. The service manager is responsible to handle data connections with external data sources. The service manager is specifically designed to manage the working of MOSDEN in resource constrained environments where frequent disconnection occurs.

API Manager: The application programmable interfaces (APIs) provides a standard way to subscribe and access data to/from MOSDEN instances. The API requests are received and processed over HTTP. Request received via the API are passed to the service manager for further processing and management.

Each MOSDEN instance running on the mobile smartphones can run with minimal user interaction. It can received and register a data capture

```
<DataFields>
  <DataField>
    <name> accelerationX_axis_incl_gravity </name>
    <type> double </type>
    <description> Acceleration force along the X axis
    (including gravity)measures in m/s2.
      </description>
  </DataField>
  <DataField>
    <name> accelerationY_axis_incl_gravity </name>
    <type> double </type>
    <description> Acceleration force along the Y axis
    (including gravity)measures in m/s2.
      </description>
  </DataField>
  <DataField>
    <name> accelerationZ_axis_incl_gravity </name>
    <type> double </type>
    <description> Acceleration force along the Z axis
    (including gravity)measures in m/s2.
      </description>
  </DataField>
</DataFields>
```

Figure 3. A Conceptual Description of MOSDEN Plugin

request/processing from a remote-server (e.g. cloud-based). MOSDEN then works in the background processing the request by collecting, processing and storing the requested data locally. When the processed data is required by the application running at the remote-server, it can query the specific MOSDEN instance running on user smartphone for the data. MOSDEN realises a true distributed collaborative system architecture as it has the ability to function independent of the remote-server.

As depicted in the architecture, each individual MOSDEN instance is self contained and managed and is capable of working in mobile environments that encounter frequent disconnections. The use of APIs to communicate between instances encourages collaborative workload sharing and processing. The plugin based approach increases re-usability and promotes interoperability allowing MOSDEN to communicate with any sensors both internal and external. This remove the burden on opportunistic sensing developer. Further, the use of a component-based architecture and a workflow style processing allows system developers to implement and integrate domain specific data analytics algorithms with relative ease. Moreover, the MOSDEN platform enables the development of mobile opportunistic sensing applications that can scale from an individual user to a community. E.g. an individual personal fitness monitoring application to a group activity recognition application involving a community of users can be developed and deployed using the MOSDEN platform.

5. Implementing a Collaborative opportunistic sensing Application using MOSDEN

In Section 3 we presented an environmental monitoring scenario to determine the noise pollution level using the data obtained from a community of user. Using

the information obtained from the user communities, a opportunistic sensing application running on a remote-server (e.g. cloud) can further analyse and visualise the noise pollution level of a smart city. Each user community in this scenario is grouped by their locations.

In this section we present a detailed description of the noise pollution opportunistic sensing proof-of-concept application implemented using MOSDEN platform. Fig. 4 presents the overview of the application implemented on MOSDEN platform. In the scenario depicted in 4, in step (1) MOSDEN instances running on the smartphone registers with the cloud GSN instance (clients are aware of server's IP address during configuration process). Once registration is complete in step (2) the cloud GSN instance registers its interest to receive noise data from MOSDEN running on the smartphones. When data is available, MOSDEN on the smartphones stream the data to the cloud GSN. The data transfer process could employ push or pull techniques over a persistent or non-persistent connection depending on application requirement. In this specific example we implemented a pull-based approach where GSN running on the remote-server will specifically query each MOSDEN instance running on the smartphones.

The MOSDEN reference architecture presented in Fig. 2 has been implemented using the Android[6] SDK platform. We deployed the noise pollution application developed on the MOSDEN platform on a set of smartphone and tablet devices that simulate a user community. To compute the noise decibel

---

[6]http://www.android.com/

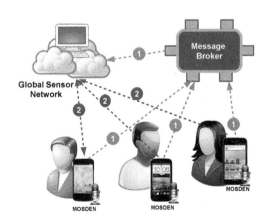

Figure 4. Implementation of Opportunistic Sensing Application using MOSDEN

Figure 5. MOSDEN screenshots: (a) List of sensors connected the MOSDEN; (b) List of virtual sensors currently running on the MOSDEN and their details; (c) Map that shows sensor locations; and (d) Interface for data fusing and filtering

level, we implemented a modified version of the processing class from Audalyzer open source project[7]. The microphone sensor on the smartphones was used to obtain raw sound recordings. Code to interface with the microphone sensor was already available as a part of the MOSDEN platform via plugins (we have developed plugins for on-board sensors and few selected external sensors e.g. waspmotes - http://www.libelium.com/products/waspmote/). For our proof-of-concept implementation, we implemented GSN in the cloud that queries data from individual MOSDEN instances running on user mobile devices. A MOSDEN instance once deployed on the smartphone/tablet registers itself with the GSN in the cloud. As we stated earlier, the design of MOSDEN makes it easily extensible to suit any opportunistic sensing application requirements. To validate this, we implemented the registration process via a message broker as depicted in Fig. 4. Along with the registration, each MOSDEN instances also updates the cloud GSN instance with a list of available sensors. We note, MOSDEN API extends support to any form of registration. It is the responsibility of the opportunistic sensing application developer to choose the most appropriate registration process best suited to the application.

MOSDEN's API enables it to query data from any other MOSDEN instances. Hence, it is to be noted that the GSN running in the cloud instance could be replaced by another smartphone running MOSDEN. In such a scenario, the MOSDEN instance is also responsible to query data from other smartphones, performs further data analytics on collected data and perform visualisation. The analytics and visual

Table 1. LOC to develop a Noise Pollution Monitoring Application

Component	Lines of Code
Virtual Sensor (MOSDEN)	30 Lines
Plugin Wrapper (MOSDEN)	190 Lines
Plugin Application: Capture Microphone data (External)	75 lines
Data Analytics: Decibel Computation FFT (External)	194 Lines

components required to accomplish the previously states functions can be easily integrated with MOSDEN as individual components. Screenshots of the MOSDEN implementation on Android smartphone and GSN in the cloud are illustrated in Fig. 5 and 6. We note, the default version of GSN with no enhancements was used to demonstrated the proof-of-concept implementation. Fig. 6b depicts the noise graph computed from 3 MOSDEN users. In this example, we have plotted the noise data individually. To demonstrate the ease of deploying complex opportunistic sensing applications using MOSDEN, Table 1 presents the total lines of code that was required to develop the previously mentioned noise pollution monitoring application. We note, the configuration files required by MOSDEN to implement a new application are Virtual Sensor and Plugin Wrapper. The plugin application to capture microphone data and data analytics component are application specific implementations external to MOSDEN code and would change depending on application complexity. In the current implementation, the plugin application is a standard android sensor service implementation.

---

[7]https://code.google.com/p/moonblink/

(a). GSN Sensor Registration Screenshot

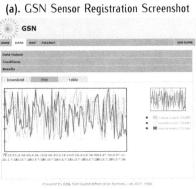

(b). GSN Noise Plot Screenshot

Figure 6. Opportunistic Sensing Noise Pollution Application Screenshots

Benefits of MOSDEN Design. The proposed MOSDEN model is architected to support scalable, efficient data sharing and collaboration between multiple application and users while reducing the burden on application developers and end users. The scalable architecture can easily be orchestrated for opportunistic sensing applications that range from an individual to a community of users. It facilitates easy sharing of data among large community of users which is a vital requirement for opportunistic sensing applications.

By separating the data collection, storage and sharing from domain-specific application logic, our platform allows developers to focus on application development rather than understanding the complexities of the underlying mobile platform. In fact, our model hides the complexities involved in accessing, processing, storing and sharing the sensor data on mobile devices by providing standardised interfaces that makes the platform reusable and easy to develop new application. This we believe will is critical and will significantly reduce the time to develop new innovative opportunistic sensing applications. Since, MOSDEN is designed as a component-based architecture, it provides easy interfaces to implement application specific data analytic models and algorithms.

Further, our model works in the background with minimal user interaction reducing the burden on smartphone users. By providing support for processing and storage on the device, we also reduce frequent transmission to a centralised server as compared to current opportunistic sensing frameworks. The potential reduction in data transmission has the following benefits: 1) saves energy on users' mobile device; 2) reduces network load by avoiding long-running data transmissions and 3) reduces data transmission costs by limiting continuous data transmissions.

The benefits of MOSDEN Design can also be articulated from a Big Data perspective. Evidence from Big Data applications like Phenonet[23] indicate, only 0.1% of the data collected for scientific plant experiments (from 1 million data points) represent golden data points. A typical Big Data approach introduces the challenges of capturing, storing filtering and analysing such volumes of data streams in remote cloud servers. Such an approach is both time and resourcing consuming. An alternative approach that we propose is to leverage on MOSDEN-like architecture leveraging on distributed local data analytics, storage, retrieval on-demand and off-line functioning capability for the following benefits: 1) Data reduction: data filtering near the data capturing location using local data analytics e.g. using statistical approaches to filter unwanted and erroneous data; 2) Relevant Data stream Selection: ability to selectively choose relevant data sources and query these sources for data depending on application needs. This will again reduce transfer and processing of large amounts of data to a remote-location; 3) Better real-time access to data on-demand and 4) Reduction in resource and bandwidth consumption due to collaborative distributed data analytics, storage and querying.

To validate the performance of the proposed MOSDEN platform to support scalable,energy and resource efficient data sharing and collaboration, in the next section we present MOSDEN platform evaluations. To this end, we evaluate MOSDEN under extreme loads typical of collaboratively opportunistic sensing application scenarios.

6. Evaluation of MOSDEN Platform

In this section, we present the details of our experimental test-beds and evaluation methodology. Further, we discuss the results and present the lessons learnt from experimental evaluations. The overall objective of the experimental evaluations is to examine the scalability, resource consumption, performance and energy consumption of MOSDEN platform in collaborative environments. Scalability of MOSDEN under collaborative application scenarios is tested by experimenting MOSDEN's ability to handle growing amount of sensing and querying tasks in a capable manner.

6.1. Experimentation Testbed and Setup

For the evaluation of the proof of concept implementations, we used four mobile devices and a laptop. From here onwards we refer them as D1, D2, D3, D4, and D5 respectively. The technical specifications of the devices are as follows.

- **Devices (D1 & D4):** Google Nexus 4 mobile phone, Qualcomm Snapdragon S4 Pro CPU, 2 GB RAM, 16GB storage, Android 4.2.2 (Jelly Bean)

- **Devices (D2 & D3):** Google Nexus 7 tablet, NVIDIA Tegra 3 quad-core processor, 1 GB RAM, 16GB storage, Android 4.2.2 (Jelly Bean)

- **Device (D5):** ASUS Ultrabook Intel(R) Core i5-2557M 1.70GHz CPU and 4GB RAM (Windows 7 operating system)

For experimentation, we devised two setups as illustrated in Fig. 7 and evaluated the proposed framework in each setup independently. For ease of illustration, in each setup, the parent node performs the operations of the remote-server including issuing queries to fetch data and process and store obtained data while child nodes perform client operations including data capturing, local analytics, storage and query processing. The proposed MOSDEN platform can be deployed in either roles i.e. remote-server or client depending on application requirements. In our setup depicted in Fig. 7a, the MOSDEN platform on the mobile device (D1, D2, D3) assumes the role client while in Fig. 7b, the MOSDEN platform on the mobile device (D1, D2, D3, D4) assumes the role of both remote-server and client. The laptop computer (D5) in Fig. 7b is configured to run GSN engine [22]. The MOSDEN architecture promotes a distributed collaborative system with connection between MOSDEN instances (client and server) maintained and managed independently as peers. The term "client" and "server" is used to specify the temporary role of the mobile devices during experiments i.e. server is responsible to answer to user queries while clients only collect data. For example, in setup 2, the mobile device (D1) running MOSDEN can also perform local sensing and respond to requests from other MOSDEN instances transforming this setup into a hierarchical peer-to-peer architecture. At any time using minimal configurations, MOSDEN on mobile devices can perform the role of both client and server making the collection of MOSDEN's devices peers. We aim to extend out experiments in future for peer-to-peer scenarios. It is to be noted, the use of client server terminology does not limit MOSDEN platform to only

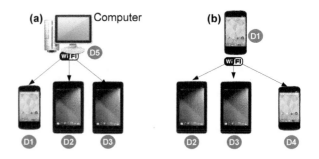

Figure 7. Experimental Testbed has been configured in two different ways: (a) Setup 1: Three mobile devices are connected to a laptop and (b) Setup 2: three mobile devices are connected to another mobile device.

client server setup, rather is used for ease of illustration. Further, for evaluations purposes, we chose a setup with 4 devices in different configurations. Experimental evaluations show that MOSDEN can scale to n number of devices when working in either client or server modes.

The maximum number of sensors was set to 13 and kept fixed throughout the experiments[8]. In all the evaluations, CPU usage (consumption) is measured in units of jiffies[9]. Sampling rate for all the sensors connected to MOSDEN is one second.

In Fig. 7(a) and (b), a query in the form of a *request* is sent from the server to MOSDEN client instances. Depending on the number of sensors queried on MOSDEN instances, the number of requests increase. We use the term 'MOSDEN client' to refer to mobile devices where MOSDEN act as a client such as D1, D2 and D3 in setup 1 in Fig. 7(a) and D2, D3 and D4 in setup 2 in Fig. 7(b)). We use the term 'MOSDEN server' to refer to a mobile device where MOSDEN performs the role of a server such as D1 in setup 2 in Fig. 7(b)).

6.2. Experimental Results and Discussion

In this section, we will present discussions of each experiment we conducted in detail.

CPU and Memory Consumption Experiment. In this experiment, we evaluate the CPU and memory usage of MOSDEN platform functioning as client and server in setups (a) and (b) illustrated in Fig. 7. To experimentally evaluate MOSDEN client's resource consumption, we conducted two experiments. In the first experiments, we computed the total CPU and

---

[8]All the sensors available on the given device has been used (e.g. In D1: accelerometer, microphone, light, orientation, proximity, gyroscope, magnetic, pressure).

[9]In computing, a jiffy is the duration of one tick of the system timer interrupt. It is not an absolute time interval unit, since its duration depends on the clock interrupt frequency of the particular hardware platform

memory consumption when performing sensing (on-board sensors), processing and local storage (henceforth we use the term *sensing* to represent the 3 operations). In the second experiment, we also include resource consumption incurred due to data transmission over Wi-Fi For MOSDEN server (D1 in Fig. 7)(b)), the experiment only considered the resources consumed to process queries from distributed MOSDEN client instances (D1, D2 and D3 in Fig. 7)(a)).

For the query processing experiment, we used two data transmission methods between the MOSDEN client and server namely *restful streaming* and *push-based streaming*. Restful streaming is designed to have a persistent connection between the client and the server. On the other hand, the push-based approach makes a new connection every time to transmit data. Both these techniques can be used to perform communication between two (or more) distributed GSN or MOSDEN instances (i.e. GSN ↔ GSN, MOSDEN ↔ MOSDEN, GSN ↔ MOSDEN). The two approaches have their own strengths and weakness. The former is good for clients running MOSDEN that have a reliable data connection. The latter is useful for clients that need to work in off-line modes. The MOSDEN platform supports both the operations and the application developer has the choice to choose the best approach that satisfies the application requirements. The resource consumption experiment outcome of MOSDEN client is presented in Fig. 8, 9, 10 and 11. The resource consumption experiment outcomes of MOSDEN server is presented in Fig. 12 and 13.

Fig. 8 and 9 presents the CPU and memory consumption of MOSDEN client when performing sensing operation. We computed the memory and CPU consumption of the two devices independently due to the difference in their memory and processing capabilities. The memory allocation to MOSDEN is entirely managed by the Android operating system depending on available memory. As its can noted, MOSDEN has very little memory and CPU footprint for continuous operation even when the number

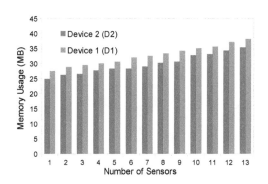

Figure 9. Comparison of Memory Usage by MOSDEN Client - Sensing

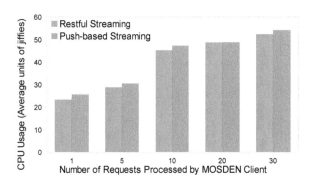

Figure 10. Comparison of CPU Usage by MOSDEN Client - Sensing + Sending

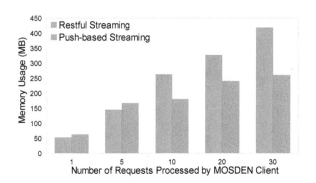

Figure 11. Comparison of Memory Usage by MOSDEN Client - Sensing + Sending

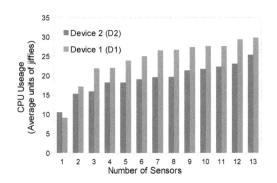

Figure 8. Comparison of CPU Usage by MOSDEN Client - Sensing

of sensors connected increase to 13. This clearly validates the scalability of MOSDEN client to work under collaborative sensing application consuming significantly less resources. Fig. 10 and 11 illustrates the difference in CPU and memory usage of MOSDEN client during sensing and sending operations. The experiments observes the variation in CPU and memory consumption when the number of requests increases. According to Fig. 10, it is evident that restful streaming is marginally better than push-based streaming from CPU consumption perceptive. On contrast, restful streaming consumes more memory than push-based streaming as depicted in Fig. 11. One reason for such a

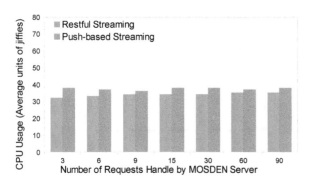

Figure 12. Comparison of CPU Usage by MOSDEN Server

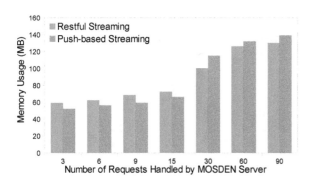

Figure 13. Comparison of Memory Usage by MOSDEN Server

outcome could be attributed to the overheads involved in maintaining a persistent network connections. In both the cases, the MOSDEN client performed well to handle data capture, processing, storage and querying operations. Further, as it can be noted from the result in Fig. 10, the memory consumption increases to 400MB when MOSDEN is processing data concurrently from 30 sensors. The device used for this experiment was the Nexus 7 tablet (D2) with an available memory of 1 GB (average among most current day smartphones and tablets). As android manages memory allocation and the tablet was only running the device monitoring application, MOSDEN was allocated more memory as needed. When there is contention from other applications, the memory allocation to MOSDEN might decrease. Under such circumstances, MOSDEN will still perform significantly well which is further justified by the query response latency experiments presented later. Moreover, newer devices such as Google Nexus 5 and Samsung Galaxy S5 have over 3GB of on-board memory which will significantly increase the performance of MOSDEN.

In Fig. 12 and 13, we compare the performance of restful streaming and push-based streaming techniques in terms of CPU and memory usage by the mobile device (D1) functioning as MOSDEN Server (Fig. 7(b)). The experiments compute the difference in CPU and memory usage by MOSDEN server when the number of requests increases. According to Fig. 12

restful streaming is better than push-based in terms of CPU usage while as indicated in Fig. 13 push based streaming is slightly better that restful streaming in terms of memory consumption. This is due to the fact, push-based makes connection on-demand hence requiring more CPU and less memory while restful maintains a constant connection consuming less CPU and more memory (connection maintenance overhead). Further, it is important to note that both techniques maintain the same amount of CPU consumption over time despite the increase in requests it handles. Additionally, MOSDEN server consumes significantly less amount of memory in comparison to MOSDEN client. One reason is that MOSDEN client performs sensing, processing and local storage activities in addition to sending data to the server. In contrast, MOSDEN server performs query processing task only (from clients). As we mentioned earlier, when the number of requests handled by MOSDEN increases (give that no other tasks are performed), restful streaming technique performs better in term of both CPU consumption and memory consumption.

Storage Requirements Experiment. In this experiment we examine how storage requirements vary when number of sensors handled by the MOSDEN client increases. For this experiment, we used Setup 1 in 7. All the sensors on-board the client mobile device (i.e. accelerometer, microphone, light, orientation, proximity, gyroscope, magnetic, pressure) are used as sensor sources. Sampling rate for sensors are configured as one second. The D1 (Setup 1) has been configured to receive data request from the server in an one second interval. The experiment was conducted for three hours. The exact storage requirements depend on multiple factors such as number of active sensors sending data, number of data items generated by the sensor[10], sampling rate, and history size [24]. We used external sensor to increase the number of sensors connected to MOSDEN during the experiment in order to examine the behaviour of MOSDEN from a storage requirement perceptive. The results of the experiment is presented in Fig. 14.

According to the outcome shown in Fig. 14, storage requirements are linear i.e. the increase in storage changes at a constant rate depending on the history-size. History-size defines how much data record needs to be stored at a given time. Large history sizes can be used for summarising purposes or archival purposes. However, the amount of storage in easily predictable due to history size, because MOSDEN always deletes old items in order to accommodate new data items. In MOSDEN, storage can be easily controlled by changing

---

[10]E.g. accelerometer generates 3 data items i.e. x, y, and z while temperature sensor generate one data item

the history-size. Specially, for real time reasoning history can be set to one. Considering all the above factor, it is fair to conclude that modern mobile devices have the storage capacity to store sensor data collected over long period of time.

Query Processing Experiment. In this section, we present results of MOSDEN servers' query processing efficiency evaluation. To measure query performance, we evaluate how the round trip time[11] is impacted when the number of requests handled MOSDEN server (D1 in Fig. 7(b)) increases. Both restful streaming and push-based streaming techniques are evaluated separately. As a comparison, we compute the round-trip time in processing a request by GSN server (D5 in Fig. 7(a)). Further, we also evaluate and compare the amount of time (average) it takes to process a single request[12]. This is different from round trip time and is calculated as denoted in Equation 1. The results of the experiments are presented in Fig. 15 and 16.

$$= \frac{\textit{Average time to process single request}}{\textit{Total number of Round Trips Completed}} \quad (1)$$

According to Fig. 15, it is clearly evident that resource constrained device such as mobile phones take more time to perform computations. As a result delay time is comparatively high when the server node is a mobile device in contrast to a computer-based processing node. Further it has been observed that (also we predicted in earlier section), push-based technique has much larger delay time due to additional overheads involved in connection setup and

---

[11]The round-trip time is the time taken for the server MOSDEN instance to request a data item from a given virtual sensor on a client MOSDEN instance. The total time is computed as the interval elapsed between server request and client response.

[12]Time taken to process a single request is the time interval elapsed between two subsequent requests made by the server to any client irrespective of the virtual sensor

tear down For laptop-based server instances, the reason for having much less round trip time when handling 90 requests (3 clients * 30 queries each) is due to the availability of more computational resources. However, when resource constrained devices play the role of a server node, the CPU and memory resources are limited hence resulting in greater round trip times. Fig. 16 also shows the impact of increased overheads when using a push-based streaming technique. It is important to note that, even though, the average round trip time is higher as observed in Fig. 15 (e.g. 20 seconds when handling 90 requests) when restful steaming techniques is used, the amount of time taken to make subsequent requests by the server is mush less (e.g. less than a second when handling 90 requests) as observed in Fig. 16. This outcomes is further validated by results of the following experiment.

In Fig. 17 and 18, we presents results of the experiments (Fig. 7-Setup 2) that examine how each request was processed. We compared the performance using both restful streaming and push-based streaming. In this experiment, we configured MOSDEN server to make 30 requests to each of the three distributed client MOSDEN instances. We conducted the experiment for a fixed interval of time. Later, we calculated using Equation 2, the number of round-trips completed by each request and plotted them as a percentage. We denote the total number of round-trip requests

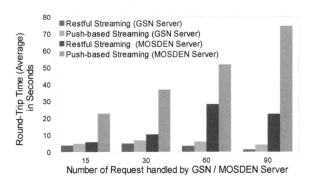

Figure 15. Comparison of Round-trip Times

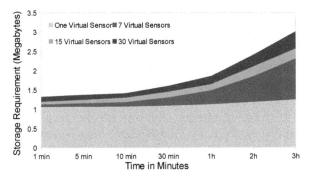

Figure 14. Storage Requirement of MOSDEN client

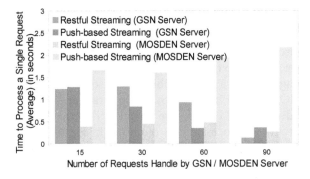

Figure 16. Comparison of Data Retrieval and Processing Ability

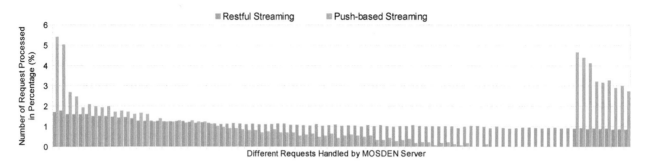

Figure 17. Comparison of Requests Processing Variation

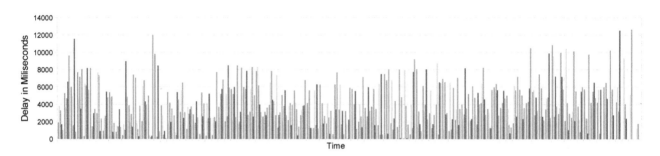

Figure 18. Variation of round-trip time (delay / latency) over a period of time where seven requests are being processed

completed for a virtual sensors S as S_i where i is the virtual sensor identifier. The x-axis in Fig. 17 represents i.

$$= \left(\frac{\textit{Number of round-trips completed by each request}}{\text{Total number of Round Trips Completed } \sum_{i=1}^{n} S_i} \right) \times 100 \quad (2)$$

According to Fig. 17, restful streaming technique allows each request to have fair amount of computational resources but push-based streaming does not. The main reason is attributed to the fact that restful streaming maintains a persistent connection between the client and server. When devices use push-based streaming, more computational resources are required to handle the connection setup and tear down Specially, when the number of requests that needs to be handled increases significantly, it places significant overheads on round-trip times for the push-based streaming approach as shown in Fig. 17. Due to restricted resources, under extremely high loads, in push-based streaming, there is a fair possibility that some requests made MOSDEN server to MOSDEN clients may not get executed at all. In Fig. 18, we visually illustrate how delay occurs in processing 90 requests (in Fig. 17, we only show 7 requests due to space limitation). Each request is shown in a different colour. Different requests (a combination of both restful and push based streaming queries were employed to compute the round-trip

time) have different round-trip times depending on how processing capabilities and priorities of both server and client devices. This clearly shows the significance of the variation observed in previous experimental outcomes. Some requests (at some point of time) take only 6 milliseconds whereas some other requests take 12 seconds to complete a round trip.

Energy Consumption Experiment. This experiment evaluates the energy consumption of MOSDEN platform while functioning as both client and server. Energy consumption is vital consideration for any mobile device application. For this experiment, the MOSDEN client was tested with a 13 sensors including a combination of on-board sensors (accelerometer, gravity, gyroscope, linear acceleration, ambient temperature, light, pressure, relative humidity, magnetic field, orientation, proximity) and additional data source generators. We used the experimental setup depicted in Fig. 7(b). For the MOSDEN client, energy consumption for sensing only and sensing + sending operations were measured. The MOSDEN server was responsible to request data from 3 distributed clients and process the response instantaneously. Each MOSDEN client was issued 30 queries by the MOSDEN server. This resulted in MOSDEN server processing 90 queries in total (30 x 3). For this experiment, we chose the restful data streaming approach as a persistent data connection involves longer usage of Wi-Fi connection. During the experiment continuous requests with sampling rate of 1 second were made by MOSDEN server. The experimental outcomes are presented in Fig. 19, 20 and 21.

According to the results in Fig. 19, 20 and 21 it can be concluded that MOSDEN functions energy-efficiently under extreme loads (MOSDEN client sensing and processing 30 requests while MOSDEN server processing 90 requests). The experimental outcome clearly validates and supports this inference. We note, the average energy consumption by MOSDEN client over a 30 minute time window for 13 virtual sensors and MOSDEN server processing 90 requests was $\approx$ 40J. It is to be noted, in our energy consumption experiment we did not consider LCD consumption as this is entirely dependent on user's usage pattern. Further, we controlled the amount of data transmitted during experimentation by increasing and decreasing the number of queries sent to MOSDEN instance. Changes to the size of sensed data did not impact the energy consumption significantly.

Discussion. Overall MOSDEN performs extremely well in both server and client roles in collaborative environments. MOSDEN (as a server) was able to handle 90 requests (i.e. 180 sub requests including 90 requests/90 responses) where each request has a sampling rate of one second. This resulted in

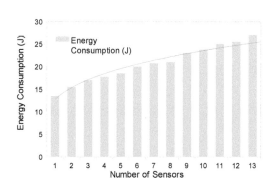

Figure 19. Energy Consumption - MOSDEN Client (Sensing)

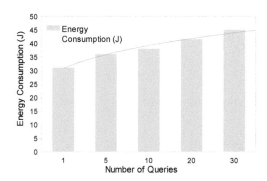

Figure 20. Energy Consumption - MOSDEN Client (Sensing + Sending)

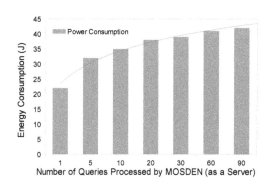

Figure 21. Energy Consumption - MOSDEN Server

a MOSDEN server (running on a mobile device) processing 5400 data points (90 requests * 60 seconds) every minute from distributed clients. Similarly, a MOSDEN client was stress tested with up to 13 virtual sensors which included a combination of on-board sensors and additional data source generators. Hence, the MOSDEN clients was processing 1800 data points (30 queries on 13 sensors * 60 seconds) every minute. It is to be noted, that for evaluation purposes and to test the energy efficiency, resource consumption, performance and scalability of MOSDEN, we conducted experiments on MOSDEN server and client under extreme loads. Such processing is intensive and rare in real-world applications. However, our experiments showed that MOSDEN can withstand such intensive loads proving to be a scalable, performance oriented and energy efficient platform for deploying large-scale opportunistic sensing applications. Under such extensive loads, considering the battery rating of Google Nexus 7 (16Wh), the MOSDEN server and MOSDEN client (sensing + sending) in continuous processing mode with 1 second sampling rate can last $\approx$ 20 hours while the MOSDEN client in sensing only mode can last $\approx$ 35 hours. If MOSDEN is configured to collect data from 10 different sensors and handle 30 requests (typical of real-world situations), it can perform real-time sensing with delay of 0.4 - 1.5 seconds.

7. Conclusion and Future Work

A mobile opportunistic sensing application development framework must scale from an individual user to user communities (tens of thousands of users). In this paper, we proposed MOSDEN, a collaborative mobile platform to develop and deploy opportunistic sensing applications. MOSDEN differs from existing opportunistic sensing platforms by separating the sensing, collection and storage from application specific processing. This unique feature of MOSDEN renders it an easy-to-use, reusable framework for developing novel opportunistic sensing applications. We proposed the architecture of the MOSDEN framework. We then demonstrated its ease of use and minimal development effort requirement by developing a proof-of-concept noise pollution application. We validated MOSDEN's performance, energy efficiency, resources consumption and scalability when working in distributed collaborative environments by extensive evaluations under extreme loads resolving and answering queries from external sources (MOSDEN instances and GSN in the cloud). Overall MOSDEN is extremely energy and resource efficient and performs exceedingly well under high degrees of load in collaborative environments validating its suitability to develop large-scale opportunistic sensing applications.

Our next step is to explore protocols for dynamic discovery, load balancing and task allocation among MOSDEN sensing and processing resources in a typical mobile ad-hoc network scenario. The aim of the extension is to dynamically distribute a collective task to a set of MOSDEN clients and servers autonomously to achieve a common goal.

Acknowledgements. Part of this work has been carried out in the scope of the ICT OpenIoT Project which is co-funded by the European Commission under seventh framework program, contract number FP7-ICT-2011-7-287305-OpenIoT. The authors acknowledge help and support from CSIRO Sensors and Sensor Networks Transformational Capability Platform (SSN TCP).

References

[1] LANE, N., MILUZZO, E., LU, H., PEEBLES, D., CHOUDHURY, T. and CAMPBELL, A. (2010) A survey of mobile phone sensing. *Communications Magazine, IEEE* **48**(9): 140–150.

[2] LILLY, P., Mobile devices to outnumber global population by 2017. URL http://tinyurl.com/pbodtus[Accessedon:2013-08-06].

[3] EAGLE, N. (2011) *Mobile Phones as Social Sensors* (Oxford University Press). URL http://realitymining.com/pdfs/handbook.05.pdf.

[4] GANTI, R., YE, F. and LEI, H. (2011) Mobile crowdsensing: current state and future challenges. *Communications Magazine, IEEE* **49**(11): 32–39.

[5] LE, V.D., SCHOLTEN, H. and HAVINGA, P. (2012) Towards opportunistic data dissemination in mobile phone sensor networks. In *Eleventh International Conference on Networks, ICN 2012* (France: International Academy, Research and Industry Association (IARIA)): 139–146.

[6] SHERCHAN, W., JAYARAMAN, P., KRISHNASWAMY, S., ZASLAVSKY, A., LOKE, S. and SINHA, A. (2012) Using on-the-move mining for mobile crowdsensing. In *Mobile Data Management (MDM), 2012 IEEE 13th International Conference on*: 115–124.

[7] BROUWERS, N. and LANGENDOEN, K. (2012) Pogo, a middleware for mobile phone sensing. In *Proceedings of the 13th International Middleware Conference*, Middleware '12 (New York, NY, USA: Springer-Verlag New York, Inc.): 21–40.

[8] KARGUPTA, H., SARKAR, K. and GILLIGAN, M. (2010) Minefleet: an overview of a widely adopted distributed vehicle performance data mining system. In *Proceedings of the 16th ACM SIGKDD international conference on Knowledge discovery and data mining*, KDD '10 (New York, NY, USA: ACM): 37–46.

[9] ZASLAVSKY, A., PERERA, C. and GEORGAKOPOULOS, D. (2012) Sensing as a service and big data. In *International Conference on Advances in Cloud Computing (ACC-2012)* (Bangalore, India): 21–29.

[10] PERERA, C., ZASLAVSKY, A., CHRISTEN, P. and GEORGAKOPOULOS, D. (2014) Sensing as a service model for smart cities supported by internet of things. *Transactions on Emerging Telecommunications Technologies (ETT)* : n/a–n/a.

[11] CHOUDHURY, T., CONSOLVO, S., HARRISON, B., HIGHTOWER, J., LaMARCA, A., LEGRAND, L., RAHIMI, A. *et al.* (2008) The mobile sensing platform: An embedded activity recognition system. *Pervasive Computing, IEEE* **7**(2): 32–41.

[12] STARNER, T. (1999) *Wearable computing and contextual awarenes*. Ph.D. thesis, Massachusetts Institute of Technology. Dept. of Architecture. Program in Media Arts and Sciences. URL http://hdl.handle.net/1721.1/9543.

[13] PERERA, C., ZASLAVSKY, A., CHRISTEN, P. and GEORGAKOPOULOS, D. (2013) Context aware computing for the internet of things: A survey. *Communications Surveys Tutorials, IEEE* **xx**: x–x.

[14] GOMES, J., KRISHNASWAMY, S., GABER, M., SOUSA, P. and MENASALVAS, E. (2012) Mobile activity recognition using ubiquitous data stream mining. In CUZZOCREA, A. and DAYAL, U. [eds.] *Data Warehousing and Knowledge Discovery* (Springer Berlin Heidelberg), *Lecture Notes in Computer Science* **7448**, 130–141.

[15] RAENTO, M., OULASVIRTA, A., PETIT, R. and TOIVONEN, H. (2005) Contextphone: a prototyping platform for context-aware mobile applications. *Pervasive Computing, IEEE* **4**(2): 51–59.

[16] Metrosense. URL http://metrosense.cs.dartmouth.edu/[Accessedon:2013-08-06].

[17] MILUZZO, E., LANE, N.D., EISENMAN, S.B. and CAMPBELL, A.T. (2007) Cenceme: injecting sensing presence into social networking applications. In *Proceedings of the 2nd European conference on Smart sensing and context*, EuroSSC'07 (Berlin, Heidelberg: Springer-Verlag): 1–28.

[18] LIU, X., LU, M., OOI, B.C., SHEN, Y., WU, S. and ZHANG, M. (2012) Cdas: a crowdsourcing data analytics system. *Proc. VLDB Endow.* **5**(10): 1040–1051.

[19] KAZEMI, L. and SHAHABI, C. (2012) Geocrowd: Enabling query answering with spatial crowdsourcing. In *Proceedings of the 20th International Conference on Advances in Geographic Information Systems*, SIGSPATIAL '12 (New York, NY, USA: ACM): 189–198. doi:10.1145/2424321.2424346, URL http://doi.acm.org/10.1145/2424321.2424346.

[20] YE, F., GANTI, R., DIMAGHANI, R., GRUENEBERG, K. and CALO, S. (2012) Meca: mobile edge capture and analysis middleware for social sensing applications. In *Proceedings of the 21st international conference companion on World Wide Web*: 699Ú702.

[21] JAYARAMAN, P.P., PERERA, C., GEORGAKOPOULOS, D. and ZASLAVSKY, A. (October, 2013) Efficient opportunistic sensing using mobile collaborative platform mosden. In *9th IEEE International Conference on Collaborative Computing: Networking, Applications and Worksharing (COLLABORATECOM)* (Austin, Texas, United States).

[22] GSN TEAM (2011), Global sensor networks project. URL http://sourceforge.net/apps/trac/gsn/ [Accessedon:2011-12-16].

[23] Phenonet: wireless sensors in agriculture. URL http://www.csiro.au/Outcomes/ICT-and-Services/National-Challenges/Wireless-sensors-in-agriculture.aspx.

[24] ABERER, K., HAUSWIRTH, M. and SALEHI, A. (2007) Infrastructure for data processing in large-scale interconnected sensor networks. In *International Conference on Mobile Data Management*: 198–205.

Achieving Security Assurance with Assertion-based Application Construction

Carlos E. Rubio-Medrano[1], Gail-Joon Ahn[1,*], Karsten Sohr[2]

[1]Arizona State University, 699 S. Mill Avenue, Tempe, Arizona, 85282, USA
[2]Universität Bremen, Am Fallturm 1, 28359 Bremen, Germany

Abstract

Modern software applications are commonly built by leveraging pre-fabricated modules, e.g. *application programming interfaces* (APIs), which are essential to implement the desired functionalities of software applications, helping reduce the overall development costs and time. When APIs deal with security-related functionality, it is critical to ensure they comply with their design requirements since otherwise unexpected flaws and vulnerabilities may consequently occur. Often, such APIs may lack sufficient specification details, or may implement a *semantically*-different version of a desired security model to enforce, thus possibly complicating the runtime enforcement of security properties and making it harder to minimize the existence of serious vulnerabilities. This paper proposes a novel approach to address such a critical challenge by leveraging the notion of software *assertions*. We focus on security requirements in role-based access control models and show how proper verification at the source-code level can be performed with our proposed approach as well as with automated *state-of-the-art* assertion-based techniques.

Keywords: security assurance, software specification, software assertions, role-based access control, API, SDK

1. Introduction

In recent years, there has been an increasing interest in using *heterogeneous* pre-fabricated software modules, e.g. *application programming interfaces* (APIs) and *software development kits* (SDKs), in order to not only reduce the overall development costs and time in producing high-quality applications, but also minimize the number of incorrect behaviors (*bugs*) observed in the final product. However, recent literature has shown that such modules often lack the proper specification details (in the form of formal or informal documentation) that are essential to guide how a module should be used correctly for implementing security-related functionality [2] [3]. Common pitfalls include missing code assumptions or prerequisites, as well as the lack of foundation on a standardized, well-defined security model that serves as a common reference to help developers understand and correctly implement security-related code. Such a problem may potentially become the source of serious security vulnerabilities, as developers may not be fully aware of the omissions and flaws they may introduce into their applications by failing to implement a security model in a proper way. In order to solve this problem, we propose an assertion-based approach to capture security requirements of security models and create well-defined representations of those requirements. This way, the security features could be effectively understood by all participants in the software development process, in such a way that they can leverage these features when implementing security-related functionalities for multi-module applications, at the same time they engage in a highly-collaborative environment. These *assertion-based* security specifications would be used in conjunction with existing *state-of-the-art* methodologies and tools to verify security properties at the source-code level. In this paper, we choose the well-known *role-based access control* (RBAC) [4] as the security model to enforce access control

★A preliminary version of this paper appeared in the Proceedings of the 2014 IEEE International Conference on Collaborative Computing: Networking, Applications and Worksharing (CollaborateCom) [1].
*Corresponding author. Email: gahn@asu.edu

requirements over an application that is in turn composed of several heterogeneous modules. Concretely, we show how the semantic variations, the lack of proper specification, and the absence of proper verification techniques can lead to the existence of non-trivial access control vulnerabilities in mission-critical applications such as banking applications. Moreover, we provide a well-defined description of RBAC based on the standard provided by the *American National Standards Institute* (ANSI) [5]. We model this reference description by using *assertions* which are later used to provide access control constraints. To inject assertions as part of the documentation devised for software modules, we also adopt *design by contract* (DBC) [6] paradigm. For such a purpose, we leverage the *Java Modeling Language* (JML) [7], a DBC-like specification language for Java, to serve as a vehicle for a*proof-of-concept* implementation of our approach. Also, we utilize existing tools to verify a set of security properties, thus providing a way to locate and possibly correct potential security vulnerabilities in software applications.

This paper is organized as follows: we start by providing some background on the topics addressed in this paper in Section 2. Next, we examine the general problem, as well as the problem instance addressed in this work in Section 3. We then present our approach in Section 4, and a case study depicting three Java-based software applications and our experimental results in Section 5. In Section 6, we provide some discussion on the benefits and shortcomings of our approach as well as some related work. Finally, Section 7 presents directives for our future developments and concludes the paper.

2. Background

Software assertions are commonly described as formal constraints intended to describe the *behavior* of a software system, e.g., what it is expected to do at runtime, and are commonly written as annotations in the system's source code [8]. Using assertions, developers can specify what conditions are expected to be valid before and after a certain portion of code gets executed, e.g. the range of values that the parameter of a given function is allowed to take. *Design by contract* (DBC) [6] is a software development methodology based on assertions and the assumption that the developers and the prospective users (clients) of a given software module establish a *contract* between each other in order for the module to be used correctly. Commonly, such a contract is defined in terms of assertions in the form of *pre* and *post* conditions, among other related constructs. Before using a DBC-based software module *M*, clients must make sure that *M*'s preconditions hold. In a similar fashion, developers must guarantee that *M*'s postconditions hold once it has finished

```
 1  public interface Account{
 2
 3    //@ public instance model double balance;
 4
 5    //@ public invariant balance > 0.0;
 6
 7    /*@ public normal_behavior
 8      @   requires amt > 0.0;
 9      @   assignable balance;
10      @   ensures balance == (\old(balance) - amt);
11      @*/
12    public void withdraw(double amt)
13                        throws SecurityException;
14
15  }
```

Figure 1. An Excerpt of a JML-annotated Banking Application.

execution, assuming its corresponding preconditions were satisfied beforehand. The *Java Modeling Language* (JML) [7], is a *behavioral interface specification language* (BISL) for Java, with a rich support for DBC contracts. Using JML, the behavior of Java modules can be specified using pre- and postconditions, as well as class *invariants*, which are commonly expressed in the form of assertions, and are added to Java source code as the form of comment such as //@ or /*@...@*/. Fig. 1 shows an excerpt of a Java interface named Account, which belongs to a banking application and has been annotated with JML specifications.

The contract for the withdraw method (shown in lines 7-11) makes use of the *model* field balance. In JML, it is possible to define model fields, methods and classes [9], which differ from their regular (*concrete*) counterparts in the sense they are used for specification purposes only, in an effort to better describe a given JML contract in a higher level of abstraction, without worrying about how it is implemented at the source code level. The model field balance, shown in line 3, is used to provide an abstract representation of the amount of money held by the bank account represented by interface Account. Following JML rules, a given class implementing interface Account will be required to provide a suitable implementation for it. The preconditions of method withdraw (defined by means of the requires keyword) require the value of the method parameter amt to be greater than zero, as shown in the assertion depicted in line 8. Postconditions for the same method, which are in turn defined by the ensures keyword, guarantee that the new value of model field balance will be equal to its previous value before the method was executed (as denoted by the \old keyword) minus the value of the method parameter amt. The set of memory locations, e.g. instance variables, that are allowed to be modified by the withdraw method is specified by means of the assignable clause (line 9). Line 5 depicts an assertion representing an *invariant*: the value of model field balance must be always greater than zero, before and after each method of interface Account executes. Finally, specification contracts that are expected to terminate *normally*, that is, without *diverging* nor throwing exceptions at runtime, are defined by means of the normal_behavior keyword (line 7). Conversely, contracts that allow a method to throw a runtime exception are specified by means of the exceptional_behavior keyword. A summary of the JML features exercised in this paper can be found in [7] and [9].

In recent years, the *American National Institute of Standards* (ANSI) released a standard document that provides well-defined descriptions of the main components and functions that define RBAC [5], and it is mostly based on the well-known Z specification language [10]. In addition, a dedicated profile [11] has been introduced to provide support for expressing RBAC policies by taking both the aforementioned ANSI RBAC standard as a reference foundation as well as the well-known *eXtensible Access Control Markup Language* (XACML), which is a standard language for supporting the distributed definition, storage and enforcement of rich access control policies [12]. Fig. 2 shows an excerpt of an RBAC policy that has been written in the RBAC XACML profile: roles are encoded using so-called *role policy set* (RPS) files (Fig. 2 (a)), which include the name of the role (*teller*, lines 4-13) as well as a reference to a *permission policy set* (PPS) file that includes the set of access rights (permissions) authorized for such a role (lines 16-18), and is in turn shown in Fig. 2 (b). In the RBAC XACML profile, permissions are encoded as XACML rules and role hierarchies are established by allowing a PPS file *P* to reference other PPS files containing the permissions that are assigned to roles that happen to be *junior* to the roles whose RPS files reference *P*. For instance, Fig. 2 (b) (lines 16-18) references the PPS file defined for role *employee* (not shown in Fig. 2 (a)), which happens to be a junior role to *teller*.

3. Problem Description

As mentioned earlier, recent literature includes examples showing that *mission-critical* applications, e.g., banking mobile applications, have suffered from serious security vulnerabilities derived from an incorrect use of their supporting security APIs at the source-code level [2, 3]. Among the possible causes of this problem, insufficient software specifications, including the definition of prerequisites and hidden assumptions, as well as the existence of multiple *semantic* variations of a given security model, e.g., the lack of foundation on a standardized, well-defined model serving as a reference, are cited as common sources of incorrect implementations. Moreover, the problem gets aggravated by the lack of effective software verification procedures at the source-code level, which could affect the chances of identifying and potentially correcting security vulnerabilities exhibited by applications before deployment

to a production system. In this paper, we address an instance of this problem by choosing RBAC as the security model to enforce access control requirements in a software application that is in turn composed of several modules. In addition, each of these modules may implement a different version of RBAC whose semantics may or may not strictly adhere to an existing RBAC reference model such as the ANSI RBAC [5]. We therefore aim to verify that such *heterogeneous* modules, when used to build a target application, correctly enforce a well-defined and consistent *high-level* RBAC policy, despite the differences they may exhibit with respect to their inner workings related to RBAC features, which could eventually result in security vulnerabilities.

As an illustrative example, Fig. 3 (a) and Fig. 3 (b) show a Java-based example where a high-level RBAC policy is enforced at runtime by placing authorization checks before performing security-sensitive operations. In both instances, a policy depicts a role *manager* as a senior role to *teller*, and allows for users, who are assigned to roles that happen to be senior to *manager*, to execute both the *transfer* and *withdraw* operations, whereas users holding *teller* role are allowed to execute the *withdraw* operation only, as shown in Fig. 2. Moreover, Fig. 3 (a) shows a Java class BankAccount, which implements the interface Account described in Fig. 1 and leverages the Spring Framework API [13] for implementing an authorization check (lines 7-16). Similarly, Fig. 3 (b) shows another class DebitBankAccount depicting an authorization check using the Apache Shiro API [14] (lines 7-11). In such a setting, it is desirable to evaluate the correct enforcement of the aforementioned RBAC policy as follows: first, the authorization checks depicted in both examples must correctly specify the roles that are allowed to execute each of the security-sensitive operations. For instance, the authorization check depicted in Fig. 3 (a) incorrectly allows for another role *agent* to also execute the withdraw method, which in turn represents a potential security vulnerability. Second, the role *hierarchy* depicted in the high-level policy must be correctly implemented at the source-code level by leveraging both APIs. As roles that happen to be senior to role *manager* should be allowed to execute both the transfer and withdraw methods, the role hierarchy must be correctly implemented by placing accurate authorization checks within the source code. In addition, the role hierarchy must be also defined correctly in the supporting API configuration files. as an incorrect implementation, e.g. missing role names within the XML files defined for the Spring API, may prevent users with the role *manager* from executing the transfer method. A more serious problem may be originated if users with the role *teller* are allowed to execute the transfer method. Finally, if users with the role *manager* are allowed

```
1  <PolicySet PolicySetId="RPS:teller:role" ...>
2   <Target>
3    <Subjects>
4     <Subject>
5      <SubjectMatch MatchId="...:string-equal">
6       <AttributeValue DataType="...#string">
7        teller
8       </AttributeValue>
9       <SubjectAttributeDesignator
10        AttributeId="...:attributes:role"
11        DataType="....#string"/>
12      </SubjectMatch>
13     </Subject>
14    </Subjects>
15   </Target>
16  <PolicySetIdReference>
17   PPS:teller:role
18  </PolicySetIdReference>
19  </PolicySet>
```

(a) An excerpt of a RPS File.

```
1  <PolicySet PolicySetId="PPS:teller:role" ...>
2  <Policy PolicyId="Permissions:for:teller" ...>
3  <Rule RuleId="withdraw:permission" Effect="Permit">
4   <Resource>
5    <AttributeValue DataType="...#string">
6     BankAccount
7    </AttributeValue>
8   </Resource>
9   <Action>
10    <AttributeValue DataType="...#string">
11     public void withdraw(double amt)
12    </AttributeValue>
13   </Action>
14  </Rule>
15  </Policy>
16  <PolicySetIdReference>
17   PPS:employee:role
18  </PolicySetIdReference>
19  </PolicySet>
```

(b) An Excerpt of a PPS File.

Figure 2. A Sample Policy Using the RBACXACMIProfile

```
1  import org.springframework.security.core.*;
2  public class BankAccount implements Account{
3
4   public void withdraw(double amt)
5                    throws SecurityException{
6
7    Iterator iter = SecurityContextHolder
8                   .getAuthorities().iterator();
9
10   while(iter.hasNext()){
11    GrantedAuthority auth = iter.next();
12    if (!auth.getAuthority().equals("teller") ||
13        !auth.getAuthority().equals("agent")){
14     throw new SecurityException("Access Denied");
15    }
16   }
17   this.balance -= amt;
18  }
19 }
```

(a) Spring FrameworkAPI.

```
1  import org.apache.shiro.*;
2  public class DebitBankAccount{
3
4   public void transfer(double amt, BankAccount acc)
5                    throws SecurityException{
6
7    if(!SecurityUtils.getSubject().hasRole("manager")){
8
9     throw new SecurityException("Access Denied");
10
11   }
12
13   acc.withdraw(amt);
14   this.balance += amt;
15
16  }
17
18
19 }
```

(b) ApacheShiro API.

Figure 3. Enforcing an RBAC Policy by Leveraging *Heterogeneous* Security Modules.

to execute the transfer method, but are disallowed from executing the withdraw method (Fig. 3 (b)) by incorrectly configuring the Spring API depicted in Fig. 3 (a), a given object of class DebitBankAccount may be left in an *inconsistent* state, thus also creating a serious security problem.

4. Our Approach: Assertion-based Construction

In order to provide a solution to the problem described in Section 3, we propose an approach that combines the concepts of specification modeling and software assertions for describing security features at the source-code level. These so-called *assertion-based security models* are intended to provide compact, well-defined and consistent descriptions that may serve as a common reference for implementing security-related functionality. Our approach strives to fill in the gap between high-level descriptions

of security features, which are mostly abstract and implementation-agnostic, and supporting descriptions focused at the source-code level, which are intended to cope with both security-related and behavioral-based specifications, such as the ones described in Section 2. As it will be described in Section 6, previous work has also explored the use of software assertions and DBC-like contracts for specifying access control policies. However, our approach is intended to leverage the *modeling* capabilities offered by software specification languages using a well-defined reference description of a security model as a source, in such a way that it not only allows for the correct communication, enforcement and verification of security-related functionality, but it also becomes independent of any supporting APIs used at the source-code level, thus potentially allowing for its deployment over applications composed of several heterogeneous modules. Fig. 4 depicts our proposed approach: an assertion-based security model is intended to be enforced over a target application that is in turn composed of two modules leveraging security APIs and two modules whose security-related functionality has been implemented from scratch. This way, the semantic differences exhibited by such modules, as shown in Section 3, can be effectively mitigated. Moreover, by leveraging state-of-the-art methodologies based on assertions, effective automated verification of security properties at the source-code level becomes feasible, thus providing a means for discovering and possibly correcting potential security vulnerabilities.

To address the problem instance discussed in this paper, we leverage the JML *modeling* capabilities, e.g. model classes [9], to describe the ANSI RBAC standard described in Section 2. Later on, these model classes are used to create assertion-based constraints, which are in turn incorporated into the DBC contracts devised for each module in an application. This way, a high-level RBAC policy can be specified at the source-code level by translating it into assertion-based constraints included in DBC contracts. Following our running example, Fig. 5 shows an excerpt of a model class JMLRBACRole, which depicts the role component and some of its related functionalities as devised in the ANSI RBAC standard, e.g. role hierarchies. Such a model class is leveraged in Fig. 7 to augment the JML-based contract depicted in Fig. 1 with security-related assertions restricting the execution of the withdraw method to users who activate a role senior to *teller*. We start by defining a model variable role, of type JMLRBACRole (line 5), which is later used for defining access control constraints in the two specification cases depicted in Fig. 7: the first specification case, depicted in lines 9-14, allows one to properly execute the withdraw method, e.g. deducting from the balance of a given account, only if the object stored in the role variable represents a role senior to *teller*[1]. The second specification case, shown in lines 16-20, allows for the withdraw method to throw a runtime exception if the aforementioned constraint is found to be false. In addition, such a specification case also prevents any modification to the *state* (e.g. private fields) of a given object of type BankAccount from taking place.

Fig. 6 depicts our approach: a high-level RBAC policy, which is encoded by means of the dedicated RBAC profile provided by XACML [11], is translated into a series of DBC contracts. Later on, such contracts, along with the source code for a given software application, are fed into JML-based automated tools for verification purposes. Since such an application may be in turn

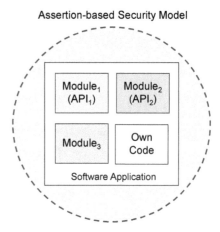

Assertion-based Security Model

Figure 4. Deploying Assertion-based Security Models over a Multi-module Application.

```
 1  package edu.asu.sefcom.ac.rbac;
 2  public class JMLRBACRole
 3                    extends JMLRBACAbstractRole{
 4
 5   public boolean isSeniorRoleOf(
 6           JMLRBACAbstractRole role){
 7
 8    if(this.equals(role)){ return true; }
 9
10    return getAllJuniorRoles().contains(role);
11   }
12  }
```

Figure 5. An Excerpt of a JML *Model* Class Depicting an ANSI RBAC *Role* Component.

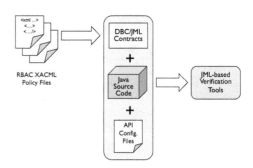

Figure 6. A Framework for Assertion-based Security Assurance.

composed of heterogeneous modules and each of them possibly represents a different API for implementing security-related functionality, e.g. enforcing an RBAC policy, the configuration files for such APIs must be also taken into account when leveraging automated tools for verification, as described in Section 3. In order to automate the creation of DBC contracts such as the ones depicted in Fig. 7, we designed an automated tool that translates RBAC policies encoded in the RBAC XACML profile into JML-based specifications, thus relieving policy designers and software architects from crafting

---

[1] Following the ANSI RBAC standard, a given role is always *senior* to itself.

```
1  //@ model import edu.asu.sefcom.ac.rbac.*;
2  public interface Account{
3
4   //@ public instance model double balance;
5   //@ public instance model JMLRBACRole role;
6
7   //@ public invariant balance > 0.0;
8
9   /*@ public normal_behavior
10  @   requires amt > 0.0;
11  @   assignable balance;
12  @   ensures role.isSeniorRoleOf(
13  @   new JMLRBACRole("teller"))  ==>
14  @   (balance == \old(balance) - amt);
15  @ also
16  @ public exceptional_behavior
17  @   requires !role.isSeniorRoleOf(
18  @   new JMLRBACRole("teller"));
19  @   assignable \nothing;
20  @   signals_only SecurityException;
21  @*/
22  public void withdraw(double amt)
23                      throws SecurityException;
24
25 }
```

Figure 7. Enhancing a DBC contract with Access Control Assertions.

```
1  import org.springframework.security.core.*;
2  public class BankAccount implements Account{
3
4   //@ public represents role <- mapRole();
5
6   /*@ public pure model JMLRBACRole mapRole(){
7   @
8   @   JMLRBACRole newRole = new JMLRBACRole("");
9   @   RBACMonitor monitor  = new RBACMonitor();
10  @
11  @   Iterator iter = SecurityContextHolder
12  @                   .getAuthorities().iterator();
13  @
14  @   while(iter.hasNext()){
15  @     GrantedAuthority auth = iter.next();
16  @     if (auth.getAuthority().equals("teller")){
17  @       newRole = new JMLRBACRole("teller");
18  @     }
19  @   }
20  @
21  @   return newRole;
22  @ }
23  @*/
24  ...
25 }
```

Figure 8. An Excerpt Showing a JML *Abstraction* Function.

such contracts manually and eliminating a potential source for errors.

Algorithm P shows a procedure for translating a set of XACML files into a set of data structures depicting an ANSI RBAC policy. The algorithm takes as an input the set of RPS and PPS XACML files as introduced in Section 2 and produces the set R of roles, the set P of permissions, the permission assignment $PA \subseteq R \times P$ relation involving the last two, and the $RH \subseteq R \times R$ relation depicting a role hierarchy between the roles included in R. The algorithm starts by initializing the sets/relations to be returned as a result as well as two auxiliary data structures: REF and $ROLE\text{-}DICT$

(lines 1-3). Entries in the REF relation store the file references within PPS files that are used to establish a role hierarchy. As an example, an entry of the form ($PPS:teller:role, PPS:employee:role$) will be added to REF when the policy reference shown in Fig. 2(b) (lines 16-18)) is processed. Conversely, the $ROLE\text{-}DICT$ relation is introduced to keep a map between the names of the PPS files being referenced in the REF relation and the actual role names depicted in their corresponding RPS files. As an example, an entry of the form ($PPS:teller:role, teller$) will added to $ROLE\text{-}DICT$ when processing the RPS and PPS files belonging to the *teller* role depicted in Fig. 2. The first phase of Algorithm P continues by retrieving the pair of RPS and PPS files depicting both the role declaration as well as the set of permissions that are assigned to such role. First, the RPS file is retrieved and the name for a role r is extracted. Such a name is then used to populate the R set as well as to introduce an initial entry of the form (r, r) to the RH relation indicating that each role is always *senior* or *junior* to itself (lines 5-7). Next, the PPS file corresponding to role r is retrieved, an entry to the $ROLE\text{-}DICT$ relation is added, and each of the permissions included in such PPS file is parsed to populate the PA relation (lines 8-14). The first phase ends by processing each of the file references included in the PPS file and adding corresponding entries into the REF relation as discussed before. The second phase of Algorithm P (lines 18-20) focuses on *expanding* the RH relation by adding an entry for each pair of roles in R that are in a senior-junior role relationship. We model such calculation as a *graph reachability* problem assuming RH to be a *directed* graph. With this in mind, implement a *depth-first search* (DFS) algorithm over all roles in R: each entry in the REF relation is retrieved, the role name corresponding to the file acting as the senior role is obtained from $ROLE\text{-}DICT$ and the auxiliary Algorithm *expandRH* is called. Such a algorithm takes an initial role r as an input and populates the RH relation by recursively obtaining all entries in REF and $ROLE\text{-}DICT$ that belong to roles that happen to be junior to a given role r. The runtime performance of the first phase of Algoritm P can be regarded to be $O(|RPS| + |PPS|) \approx O(|R| + |P|)$ in the best case, which occurs when every permission in P is assigned to only one role in R. When several permissions in P are assigned to several different roles in R then the performance turns out to be $O(|R| + |R| * |P|) \approx O(|R| * |P|)$. In a similar fashion, performance of the second phase can be analyzed as follows: since the DFS algorithm is known to run in $O(E)$ for a graph having V nodes and E edges, our implementation may then run on $O(V * E) \approx O(|R| * |P|)$ in the best case when $V = R$ and $E = P$, which occurs when every permission in P is assigned to only one role in R. In the case when the same permission is assigned to different roles in R, the running time may be regarded as $O(V * E) \approx O(|R| * (|R| * |P|))$ for $V = R$ and $E = R \times P$.

Taking as an input the data structures produced by Algorithm P, Algorithm $\overline{\upsilon}$ produces DBC contracts written in a subset of the JML syntax defined in [15], like the one shown in Fig. 7, by leveraging a *template* in the form of an *abstract syntax tree* (AST), which is shown in Fig. 9. The algorithm starts by exploring the *PA* relation to obtain the entry depicting the *junior-most* role being assigned to every permission in P (lines 2-6). For such a purpose, line 4 of Algorithm $\overline{\upsilon}$ queries the *RH* structure to determine if there exists a *seniority* relationship between two nodes r_i and r_j ($i \neq j$) in R. Such queries can be potentially answered in constant time ($O(1)$), as it suffices to locate the entry (r_i, r_j) in *RH*, due to the *expansion* procedure conducted by the second phase of Algorithm P. Finally, the algorithm produces a DBC/JML contract for each of the *junior-most* entries obtained in the previous step (lines 7-13). An alternative approach would include eluding the aforementioned *expansion* procedure carried on by Algorithm P and leaving any further algorithms, e.g., Algorithm $\overline{\upsilon}$, with the duty of determining if a role happens to be senior to another one. Such an alternative approach may be beneficial in the case when only a few permissions in P happen to be assigned to more than one role in R, in such a way that the seniority relation between those roles may need to be determined when calculating the *junior-most* role only for such few permissions. In Algorithm $\overline{\upsilon}$, since we potentially explore the entries in the *PA* relation twice, and such a relation may be of size $|R| * |P|$ in the worst case, the runtime performance can be regarded as $O(2* |R| * |P|) \approx O(|R| * |P|)$. We present an analysis of the correctness of our approach in Appendix A.

As described in Section 1, we aim to support the verification of security properties in mission-critical applications. For such a purpose, we leverage an approach based on automated *unit testing* [16] by adopting JET [16]: a dedicated tool tailored for providing automated runtime testing of Java modules with JML-based assertions, e.g. classes. Using JET, testers can verify the correctness of a Java module by checking the implementation of each method against their corresponding JML specifications. In addition, we also support the detection of potential security vulnerabilities by means of static techniques by leveraging the ESC/Java2 tool [7], which is based on a theorem prover and internally builds *verification conditions* (VCs) from the source code being analyzed, and its corresponding JML-based specifications, which the theorem prover then attempts to prove, thus allowing for the automated analysis of

---

Algorithm P : Parsing RBAC XACML Files.

Data: Sets *RPS* and *PPS* of RBAC XACML files
Result: Sets R of roles, P of permissions, and the *PA* and *RH* relations

1 Initialize R and P to empty sets;
2 Initialize *PA* and *RH* to empty relations;
3 Initialize ROLE-DICT and REF to empty relations;
4 **for** *each file rps in RPS* **do**
5   r = Get role name from *rps*;
6     $R = R \cup r$;
7     $RH = RH \cup (r,r)$;
8   *ref-pps* = Get name of permissions file referenced by r;
9     $ROLE\text{-}DICT = ROLE\text{-}DICT \cup (ref\text{-}pps, r)$;
10   *pps* = Get file from *PPS* using *ref-pps*;
11   **for** *each permission p in pps* **do**
12   **if** $p \notin P$ **then**
13          $P = P \cup p$;
14       $PA = PA \cup (r, p)$;
15   *JUNIOR-PPS* = Get names of files referenced by *pps*;
16   **for** *each junior-pps-name in JUNIOR-PPS* **do**
17       $REF = REF \cup (ref\text{-}pps, junior\text{-}pps\text{-}name)$;
18 **for** *each (senior-ref, junior-ref) in REF* **do**
19   *(senior-ref, role)* = Get from *ROLE-DICT* using *senior-ref*;
20    $RH = expandRH(role, senior\text{-}ref, RH, REF, ROLE\text{-}DICT)$;
21 **return** R, P, *PA* and *RH*;

Algorithm *expandRH* : Constructing the *RH* of an RBAC Policy.

Data: A role $r \in R$, a String *key* depicting a file name, the *RH*, *REF* and *ROLE-DICT* relations
Result: The *RH* relation

1 Initialize *JM* and *C* to empty sets;
2 ENTRIES = Get entries from *REF* using *key*;
3 **for** *each (senior-ref, junior-ref) in ENTRIES* **do**
4   *(junior-ref, junior-role)* = Get from *ROLE-DICT*;
5   **if** *(role, junior-role)* $\notin RH$ **then**
6        $RH = RH \cup (role, junior\text{-}role)$;
7     $RH = expandRH(role, junior\text{-}ref, RH, REF, ROLE\text{-}DICT)$;
8 **return** *RH*;

---

whole code modules without running the applications. In particular, ESC/Java2 uses *modular reasoning* [17], which is regarded as an effective technique when used in combination with static checking since code sections can be analyzed and their JML-based specifications can

Algorithm $\widetilde{v}$: Transforming an RBAC Policy to DBC/JML Contracts.

Data: The *PA* and *RH* relations depicting an ANSI RBAC Policy

Result: A Set *C* of DBC/JML Contracts

1 Initialize *JM* and *C* to empty sets;
2 **for** *each (r,p) in PA* **do**
3   *(r',p)* = Get entry from *JM* using *p*;
4   **if** *(r', p) ≠ null and (r',r) ∈ RH* **then**
5   *JM = JM \ (r'p)* ;
6   *JM = JM ∪ (r,p)*;
7 **for** *each (r,p) in JM* **do**
8   Create *signature* from *p*;
9   Get *contract* from *C* using *signature*;
10   **if** *contract is null* **then**
11   *contract* = Create using AST and *signature*;
12   *C = C ∪ contract*;
13   Add *r* to roles in *contract*;
14 **return** *C*;

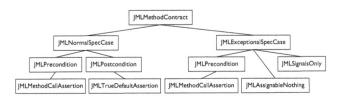

Figure 9. A Sample AST template for Producing JML Syntax.

be proved by inspecting the specification contracts of the methods they call within their method *bodies*.

Later, in Section 5, we present our findings on leveraging both techniques in a set of case studies depicting mission-critical Java applications. In order to support the verification process just described, proper constructs are needed to map the modeling features included in DBC contracts (as depicted in Fig. 7) and the implementation source code of each heterogeneous module. For such a purpose, we leverage the features offered by the JML *abstraction* functions [9], which allow for JML model features to be properly *mapped* to source-code level constructs, thus providing a way to verify that each heterogeneous module implements a given high-level policy correctly. As an example, Fig. 8 shows an excerpt where a JML model method is used to map the source code implementing security features as provided by the Spring Framework API with the model features depicted in Fig. 7.

In general, the correct enforcement of a security model may involve the following cases: first, a high-level security policy, which is based on a well-defined security model definition, should be correctly defined and all policy conflicts must have been resolved, e.g.

Table 1. Distribution of Responsibilities for Enforcing an Assertion-based Security Model In a Collaborative Setting.

Actor	Description of Tasks
Security Domain Experts	Develop an assertion-based security model by using a precise definitio as a reference, e.g. using the ANSI RBAC standard. (See Fig. 5).
Policy Administrators	Instantiate the security model to be enforced e.g. specificatio of an RBAC policy based on the ANSI RBAC standard. (See Fig. 2).
Software Architects	Incorporate the security policy into DBC constructs by specifying assertion-based constraints (See Fig. 7).
Code Developers	Correctly implement the DBC specifications define by software architects (including security checks). Provide a mapping between the security model and the security APIs used for implementation purposes (See Fig. 8).
Code Testers	Verify both the functional and the security related aspects of a given software application based on their DBC specification (See Section 5).

evaluating a given RBAC policy by using techniques such as the ones discussed in [18]. Second, access to all protected resources within a given application, e.g. the withdraw operation depicted in Fig. 7, is *guarded* by an authorization check (adhering to the well-known *principle of complete mediation*). Following our example, authorization checks should depict the RBAC constructs defined in the overall policy, e.g. checking for the correct roles and/or permissions before executing any sensitive operation. Third, supporting components for the security model features are implemented correctly, e.g. RBAC role hierarchies. Finally, we also require that the detection of runtime policy violations is implemented properly, e.g. exception handling and data consistency. With this in mind, for the problem instance addressed in this paper, we make the following assumptions: first, the ANSI RBAC model is well-understood by all participants in the software development process, e.g. policy designers, software architects and developers. Second, the assertion-based specification of the security model is correct: in other words, it has been verified beforehand. Third, any supporting RBAC modules, including security APIs and SDKs, have been implemented correctly, even though their semantics with respect to RBAC may differ, as addressed in Section 3.

Finally, our approach is intended to be carried out by the different participants in the software development process, in such a way that the process of constructing vulnerability-free software becomes a collaborative responsibility shared by all involved actors, obviously including the source-code level developers. Table 1 shows a summary of the tasks devised for each participant.

5. Case Study

In order to provide a *proof-of-concept* implementation of our approach, we developed a reference description of the security model under study by using a set of JML model classes based on the case illustrated in Fig. 5. Such a reference model contains 960 lines of code grouped in 17 Java classes, including 1,383 lines of JML specifications depicting the functionality desired for RBAC as described in the ANSI RBAC standard. For our case study, we leveraged a pair of open-source Java applications: OSCAR EMR [19], which is a rich web-based software platform tailored for handling *electronic medical records* (EMR). It consists of approximately 35,000 lines of code organized into 110 classes and 35 packages. In addition, we also leveraged JMoney [20], a financial application consisting of 7,500 lines of code grouped into 45 classes. Moreover, we developed a banking application depicting the running examples shown in this paper. Such an application leverages the Apache Shiro and Spring Framework Security APIs, as well as our own RBAC monitor developed for implementing security-related functionality. It consists of 36 classes and contains 1,550 lines of code as well as 1,450 lines of JML specifications, which utilize our JML model classes in DBC contracts, as shown in Fig. 7.

In addition, we performed an evaluation over the automated translation tool described in Section 4 that takes as an input a set of XACML files depicting an ANSI RBAC policy and produces a set of DBC contracts in the JML language. Such a tool consists of 6,246 lines of code grouped in 25 classes in Java, and implements the Algorithms labeled as P, $\overline{v}$ and *expandRH*, also shown in Section 4 as well as the AST structure shown in Fig. 9. In order to evaluate the effectiveness of the tool we designed an experiment tailored to measure the overall processing time in milliseconds taken by the tool to process XACML-based policies and produce their corresponding DBC/JML contracts. In such experiments, we varied the policy *size* by varying the number of roles included in the policy as well as the number of permissions being assigned to each role. In addition, we controlled the number of different role hierarchies depicted by each policy as well as the number of permissions that were simultaneously assigned to the same role. Fig. 10 shows the results of our experimental approach when allowing the tool to process synthetically-created policies to produce DBC/JML contracts such as the one shown in Fig. 7. We produced 4 different policies varying the number of roles from 5 to 20, as well as the number of permissions

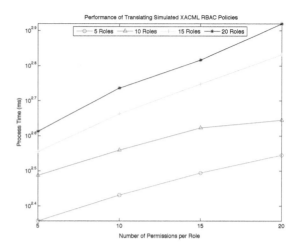

Figure 10. Runtime performance of our Translation Tool.

included on each role. All roles in the policy belonged to the same role hierarchy and the same permission was allowed to be assigned to at most two roles. As expected, the execution time depicted by our tool remains linear as the size of the policy given as an input is varied.

As described in Section 4, our approach is intended to identify inconsistencies in the implementation of security models that can eventually become security vulnerabilities. In the context of the security model addressed in this paper, an incorrect implementation of an RBAC policy may end up introducing non-trivial vulnerabilities to applications. Based on the description of RBAC depicted by the ANSI RBAC standard, inconsistencies on the implementation of RBAC policies can be described as follows: first, an incorrect mapping between access rights (permissions) and sensitive operations performed by applications. Sensitive operations should be properly *guarded* by permissions, in such a way that the execution of such operations is only allowed when the requesting entity is found to be granted the permissions devised for them. Failing to identify such sensitive operations as well as the need to secure them by properly requesting for the permissions, may also result in non-trivial security vulnerabilities. Following our running example, the transfer operation featured in Fig. 3(b) must be identified as security-sensitive and being guarded by a permission to be assigned only to users holding the *manager* role. Second, failures in the assignment of permissions to roles may exist. As an example, incorrect assignment of a given permission P to a role R may allow R and roles that happen to be senior to it to execute the unintended operations *guarded* by P. On the other hand, unintended removal of P from the list of permissions devised for R will deprive such a role and all other roles senior to it from exercising P and its related operations, possibly causing an *availability* problem by restricting the number of operations that such roles can execute in the context of a given application. Third, there may be failures in the implementation of role hierarchies. As an example, the introduction or removal of a role or a set of roles at a given *level* of the hierarchy may produce vulnerabilities: introduction of an unintended role R in a given hierarchy may allow for R to unintentionally *inherit* the permissions assigned to all roles that happen to be junior to R, and it may also allow for senior roles to R to obtaining the permissions assigned to R. Conversely, removal of a role R in a given hierarchy may deprive roles senior to R from obtaining the permissions assigned to it, which can yield vulnerabilities such as the state inconsistency problem described at the end of Section 3. In the context of applications composed of heterogeneous modules, the aforementioned inconsistencies can be potentially introduced either in the source code of the application itself, or by incorrect configuration of policy files. As an example, failures in the implementation of authorization checks, as the ones depicted in Fig. 3, can be regarded as a common source of potential inconsistencies at the source code level. In addition, state-of-the-art security APIs, as the ones depicted throughout this paper, leverage text files for configuring security features. With respect to RBAC, our featured APIs provide configuration files depicting the assignment of permissions to roles. In summary, an incorrect configuration of those files may also introduce security vulnerabilities.

With this in mind, we modeled implementation inconsistencies of the RBAC security model by leveraging an approach inspired by *mutation testing* [21]: we inserted variations (also known as *mutants*) in both the source code and the API configuration files of the applications considered in our study. As an example, Fig. 11 shows different mutants introduced to the RBAC policy shown in Table 2: first, the original policy is modified to add an unintended permission (*transfer*, (*t*)) to a role *employee* (Fig. 11 (a)). Such a modification creates a potential security vulnerability as it allows *employee*, and all other roles senior to it, e.g. *agent* and *teller*, to execute an operation that was originally intended only for a role *manager*. A configuration file depicting such modification is shown in Fig. 12 (lines 14, 19, 23). Similarly, Fig. 11 (b) shows a permission (*deposit*, (*d*)) being removed from the *employee* role. Such a modification produces an inconvenience to such a role and all other roles that happen to be senior to it, as execution of the deposit operation will be denied at runtime. Fig. 11 (c) shows another example where the original role hierarchy of the RBAC policy is modified to introduce an unintended role (*supervisor*, (*S*)). This way, the newly-introduced role creates a pair of security vulnerabilities: first, it inherits the permissions from all junior roles in the hierarchy, thus allowing for the execution of unintended operations. Fig. 13 shows an

Table 2. A Sample RBAC Policy for Evaluation Purposes.

Role	Junior Roles	Allowed Operations
Employee	-	deposit
Teller	Employee	withdraw, deposit
Agent	Employee	close, deposit
Manager	Teller, Agent	transfer, withdraw, deposit, close

example depicting such modification (lines 6,7). Second, it also allows for a senior role in the hierarchy to obtain an extra permission (*audit*, (*a*)), thus possibly allowing them to perform unintended operations as well. Fig. 13 shows an excerpt of an XML configuration file depicting the role hierarchy modification shown in Fig. 11 (c) (lines 6-8). Finally, Fig. 11 (d) shows a case when a role is removed from a role hierarchy: *teller* is left aside by removing the relationships with both the *manager* (senior) and the *employee* (junior) roles. It exposes an inappropriate permission revocation not only to users holding the role *teller* as it is prevented from getting the permissions of its junior roles (e.g. *deposit*, (*d*)), but also to senior roles since revocation prevented them from getting the permissions assigned to *teller* (e.g., *withdraw*, (*w*)) including all other permissions that could be obtained from junior roles to *teller*.

In the rest of this section, we describe the experimental procedure we have conducted on the sampled software applications by leveraging existing assertion-based tools to detect (*kill*) mutant-based inconsistencies in the implementation of RBAC policies like the ones described above, in an effort to show the suitability of our approach for the effective verification of security properties. In particular, we present the results when applying both the dynamic and the static approach to the aforementioned case-study applications. Later, in Section 6, we highlight some shortcomings we have identified in this experimental process, and propose some alternative solutions.

5.1. Applying Dynamic Analysis Techniques to Assertion-based Verificatio

As described in previous sections, we aim to support the verification of security properties by leveraging an approach based on automated *unit* testing [16] as well as the JML specifications depicting our assertion-based models that were introduced in Section 4. For such a purpose, we adopted JET [16], which is a dedicated tool tailored for providing automated runtime testing of Java modules with JML-based assertions, e.g. classes. Using JET, testers can verify the correctness of a Java module by checking the implementation of each method against their corresponding JML specifications. As an example, the contract of a given method M is used as a *test oracle*, by first translating it into

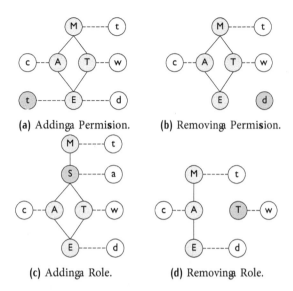

(a) Adding a Permision. (b) Removing a Permision.

(c) Adding a Role. (d) Removing a Role.

Figure 11. Introducing *Mutants* in the RBAC Policy shown in Table 2: roles are labeled using their uppercase initial. Permisions are shown using lowercase initials and dotted lines. E.g., in Fig. 11 (a), role *Manager* is shown as a colored circle labeled as *M*. Permision *transfer* is shown as a white circle labeled as *t*. The assignment of permision *transfer* to the role *Manager* is shown as a dotted line.

runtime assertion checking (RAC) code. Then, proper values (of either primitive or reference data types) are *randomly* created for each of *M*'s formal parameters, and compared for compliance against the RAC code created for *M*'s precondition. If such a precondition is satisfied, a *valid* test case is said to be created [2], and *M*'s body is executed. If any exception not devised for *M* is thrown, the test case is regarded as *failed*. Otherwise, the RAC code for *M*'s postcondition is executed. If such a postcondition is satisfied, the test is regarded as a *success*, otherwise, it is regarded as *failed* as well. Many different test cases can be created for *M*, as soon as different combinations of values for *M*'s parameters are created by JET.

Following the automated testing approach just described, we conducted a set of experiments to measure the effectiveness of our assertion-based models, along with our enhanced DBC contracts, in detecting the mutations introduced into the applications tested in our case study. Such experiments were carried out on a PC equipped with an Intel Core Duo CPU running at 3.00 GHZ, with 4 GB of RAM, running Microsoft Windows 7 64-Bit Enterprise Edition. First, we measured the impact of our approach in the average execution time of the applications. In order to provide a mapping between the modeling features included in JML contracts (as depicted in Fig. 7) and the implementation code of each heterogeneous module, we leveraged the

---

[2] Otherwise, the test case is said to be *meaningless*, so it is discarded.

```
1  public static Ini getStaticIni(){
2  Ini ini = new Ini();
3  ini.addSection("roles");
4  ini.setSectionProperty("roles",
5                          "manager",
6                          "p:deposit, "  +
7                          "p:withdraw, "  +
8                          "p:close, "  +
9                          "p:transfer" );
10 ini.setSectionProperty("roles",
11                         "agent",
12                         "p:close, "  +
13                         "p:deposit"  +
14                         "p:transfer");
15 ini.setSectionProperty("roles",
16                         "teller",
17                         "p:deposit, "  +
18                         "p:withdraw"  +
19                         "p:transfer");
20 ini.setSectionProperty("roles",
21                         "employee",
22                         "p:deposit "  +
23                         "p:transfer");
24 return ini;
25 }
```

Figure 12. Introducing *mutants* in an Apache Shiro configuration.

```
1  <?xml ...>
2  <beans:bean id="roleHierarchy" ...>
3    <beans:property name="hierarchy">
4      <beans:value>
5        manager    > supervisor
6        supervisor > teller
7        supervisor > agent
8        teller     > employee
9        agent      > employee
10     </beans:value>
11 ...
```

Figure 13. Introducing *Mutants* in Spring Framework.

features offered by the JML *abstraction* functions [9]: we enhanced our supporting tool described in Section 4 to also produce abstraction functions for the referred Spring Framework and Apache Shiro APIs. We then executed a sample trace of the Java methods exposed by our three applications and calculated the average execution time over 1,000 repetitions. Such a trace was created to contain representative operations for each application, e.g. the trace created for the OSCAR EMR application that contains Java methods used to update a patient's personal data as well as information about medical appointments and prescriptions.

As shown in Table 3, the introduction of RAC code has a moderate impact on the performance, which is mostly due to the overhead introduced by the RAC code generated to process both the JML contracts as well as the abstraction functions. We then recorded the results obtained by our tool while attempting to detect (*kill*) the mutants introduced in both the configuration of the Security APIs as well as the authorization checks guarding each of the Java methods contained in our sample traces, following the approach depicted in Fig. 11. Table 3 shows a report on the number of generated test cases, including the number of

Table 3. ExperimentalData UsingJET.

	Banking	JMoney	OSCAR
Total methods	46	136	125
Analysis time per method/s	4.56	17.32	15.4
Total analysis time/s	209.76	2355	1925
Runtime overhead/s	0.97	2.34	1.78
Generated test cases	1000	1000	1000
Meaningful test cases	150	250	225

Table 4. ExperimentalData Using ESC/Java2.

	Banking	JMoney	OSCAR
Analysis time per method/s	0.43	2.07	0.5
Total analysis time/s	19.66	281.41	63.00

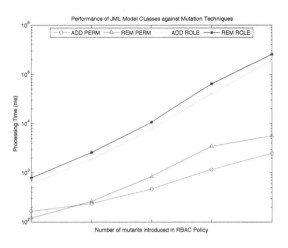

Figure 14. Runtime performance of our Verificatio Approach.

meaningful ones produced by the tool. [3] Our *meaningful* test cases were able to *kill* all the mutants inserted into our case study applications.

In an additional experiment, we compared the time taken by our JML model classes to detect each of the mutant generation techniques depicted in Fig. 11. Once again, we used a trace of Java methods depicting the main functionality for each application, and used the automated mutant-generation tool described before to generate different variations to an original RBAC policy. The results, as shown in Fig. 14, show that adding/removing a role to a given hierarchy is the most costly mutation to be detected by the RAC code through processing our assertion-based JML classes. This is mostly due to the way how role hierarchies are implemented in our JML classes, by using a series of java.util.ArrayList objects to store references to each senior/junior role in a given hierarchy, and allowing for such references to be inspected recursively when determining if there is a seniority relationship between two given roles.

5.2. ApplyingStatic Analysis Techniquesto Assertion-based Verificatio

As mentioned in previous sections, we also leverage the ESC/Java2 tool for providing verification guarantees based on static analysis techniques and our proposed approach. However, despite the support provided for JML-based constructs by such a tool, some challenges must be addressed: first, in order to prove the correctness of a certain source code C against its corresponding JML contracts, the tool additionally requires that the JML specifications of

each library called within C are available, including the specifications of additional libraries the original ones may eventually call later on. In some cases, such a requirement may notoriously increase the amount of VCs that need to be proved by the tool, so the verification process becomes prohibitively expensive, resulting in the *specification-creep* problem [17]. Second, an additional problem arises from the lack of support offered by the current tool for advanced JML concepts, such as the JML model classes introduced in Section 4 and the JML abstraction functions depicted in in Fig. 8, as the internally-produced VCs are too complex for the tool to handle, which limits the applicability of our assertion-based models.

Subsequently, we present an approach that addresses these challenges while still providing verification guarantees for our assertion-based approach. First, we addressed the specification-creep problem. In particular, as described in Section 4, we assumed the Security APIs leveraged within our case study have been implemented correctly and previously verified elsewhere. Therefore, there is no need to include their corresponding source code in our verification process. Based on this observation, we provided *specification stubs* for the leveraged Security APIs whose JML-based annotations are trivially satisfied. Fig. 15 shows the translated JML specifications for the method hasRole of class Subject, which implements an authorization check in the Apache Shiro API, as shown in Fig. 3 (b). One can see that a trivial method body has been provided; for the task of static checking a Shiro module only the contract and not the specification of hasRole is needed by ESC/Java2. The process of providing specification stubs can be carried out by security domain experts (see Table 1) for the Security APIs and must only be revised when new API versions are released.

Second, as mentioned before, the JML model classes, which are a core part of the approach shown in

---

[3] In JET, a test case T for a given method M is said to be *meaningful* if the tool is able to randomly create values for M's formal parameters in such a way that M's preconditions involving such parameters are satisfied. Otherwise T is said to be *meaningless*.

```
1  public class Subject{
2
3  /*@ public normal_behavior
4    @  requires  true;
5    @  ensures \result == true || \result == false;
6    @ also
7    @ public exceptional_behavior
8    @  requires  false;
9    @  assignable \nothing;
10   @  ensures true;
11   @*/
12   public /*@ pure @*/ boolean hasRole(String r){
13     return true;
14   }
15 }
```

Figure 15. Specification Stubs for the ApacheShiro API.

```
1  public interface Account{
2
3  /*@ public normal_behavior
4    @  requires amt > 0.0;
5    @  assignable balance;
6    @  ensures
7    @    (SecurityUtils.getSubject()
8    @                   .hasRole("teller") ||
9    @     SecurityUtils.getSubject()
10   @                   .hasRole("manager"))
11   @    ==> ...
12   @*/
13 public void withdraw(double amt)
14                      throws SecurityException;
15 }
```

Figure 16. Translating Model JML Classes.

Section 4, are beyond the current capabilities of ESC/-Java2. To overcome this limitation, we provided JML specifications that do not employ the JML model classes and use low-level JML concepts instead. Table 5 shows the implementation-independent model classes and their corresponding low-level specifications for each framework. As an example, the aforementioned hasRole and getAuthority methods are directly called rather than using JML model classes: the role hierarchy depicted in Table 2 and Fig. 7, which checks that the current user is granted a role senior to *teller* (e.g. *manager*), can be translated into the JML contracts shown in Fig. 16 (lines 7-10): the references to the model class JMLRBACRole have been substituted for the has-Role method of class Subject provided by the Apache Shiro API, and are integrated together by using the operator || in JML, applied to all relevant senior roles (e.g., the *manager* role in line 10). We call this technique *unrolling* the role hierarchy. It is also supported by the JML-based translation tool described in Section 4 by automatically translating XACML policies to JML specifications suitable for ESC/Java2 and inserting them into the corresponding source code. This step relieves the software architect (see Table 1) from manually providing JML contracts, which is an error-prone process. Software architects can now leverage an automated tool for this purpose.

In addition, web-based Java software frameworks, e.g. Spring Framework, provide support for declarative access control in addition to programmatic access control (e.g. by using authorization checks). Declarative authorization allows a developer to define role-based restrictions on access to certain protected resources such as a given Java method (see also Section 3). As an example, in the Spring Framework we can define access restrictions in an XML configuration file as follows:

```
<sec:protect method="BankAccount.withdraw"
              access="teller"/>
```

In the dynamic analysis approach described before, such declarative rules are implicitly considered because the Spring framework enforces this role assignment under the hood. However, in a static approach, we must also include such configuration files to obtain a complete picture about the access control features implemented in the web application. Otherwise, we would produce false positives because ESC/Java2 would falsely report that an authorization check is missing although it has been defined in the XML configuration file (and not in the code). To implement this additional feature, we parse the XML configuration files to retrieve the access control statements and insert their corresponding JML assume statements in the body of the referenced Java methods—the JML assume statement lets ESC/Java2 unconditionally assume a constraint without checking it [17]. For instance, the XML configuration shown above can be translated into the following specification that is to be inserted in the implementation body of the withdraw method of class BankAccount (Fig. 8):

```
//@ assume GrantedAuthority.getAuthorities()
//@                        .contains("teller");
```

After the preparing steps, we applied our analysis technique to the applications under our case study, by following the mutation-based approach described before. All mutants were automatically detected by ESC/Java2 even if they were hidden within the many methods of the real-world case studies JMoney (125 methods) and OSCAR EMR (136 methods). As an example, in the following authorization check included in the JMoney application

```
if(!currentUser.hasRole("accountant"))
   throw new SecurityException("Permission denied!");
```

a user with the *acountant* role is permitted to execute the method. If the user, however, has assumed a role senior to *accountant* (e.g. *owner*), a security exception is thrown, since the Apache Shiro library call has-Role provides no native support for implementing role hierarchies, which must be in turn encoded into a series of nested hasRole calls listing all the roles that are authorized to execute a given method.

We used a conventional Lenovo Thinkpad T510 laptop (Intel Core i7-620M Processor, 2.66GHz, 8 GB

Table 5. Mapping between the JML RBAC and Security-API-based specifications

	JMLRBACRole.equals(new JMLRBACRole(r))	JMLRBACRole.isSeniorOf(new JMLRBACRole(r))
Spring Framework	GrantedAuthority.getAuthorities().contains(r)	GrantedAuthority.getAuthorities().contains(r) ||...|| GrantedAuthority.getAuthorities().contains(mostSeniorRole)
Apache Shiro	Subject.hasRole(r)	Subject.hasRole(r) ||...|| Subject.hasRole(mostSeniorRole)
RBAC Monitor	RBACMonitor.hasRole(r)	RBACMonitor.hasRole(r) ||...|| RBACMonitor.hasRole(mostSeniorRole)

RAM) for our experiments with the static analysis technique, in an effort to provide increased RAM capabilities to the theorem prover serving as a back-end for ESC/Java2. The runtime of the three applications under our case study is given in Table 4, which confirmed that the preparation steps enabled us to use ESC/Java2 efficiently. Specifically, we avoided the expensive analysis of container classes, e.g. `java.util.Collection`, by applying the aforementioned *specification stub* technique. For example, the method `getAuthorities()`.`contains()` uses a container class of the Java type `Collection` and by leveraging the stub technique we succeeded in eliminating this problem.

6. Discussion and Related Work

In order for the approach presented in Section 4 to properly detect implementation flaws at the source-code level, a correct and sound translation from such a model into our assertion-based constructs is needed. With this in mind, a formal proof must include the following: first, only the access rights depicted in the original policy must be present in their JML-based counterpart, that is, no potential security vulnerabilities are introduced by adding extra access rights in the resulting specifications. Second, all access rights included in the original policy must be present in the translated specifications, that is, no *inconveniences*, e.g. preventing a legitimate access from taking place, are introduced by missing access rights included in the original policy. We present an sketch of such a proof in Appendix A.

The experimental results depicted in Section 5.1 and 5.2 support our claim that our approach can effectively expose the set of security vulnerabilities caused by the incorrect source-code level implementations of security models. In our approach, we have selected Java for our *proof-of-concept* implementation due to its extensive use in practice. Moreover, we have also chosen JML as the specification language for defining our assertion-based security models due to its enhanced tool support as well as its language design paradigm, which supports rich behavioral specifications. At the same time it strives to handle the complexity of using complex specification constructs, in such a way that it becomes suitable for average developers to use [7] (see Table 1).

We believe that our approach can be extended to other programming languages/development platforms.

For instance, Spec# [22] provides rich DBC-based specifications for the C# language, depicting an approach similar to JML. Moreover, our approach can be also applied to other Java-based frameworks such as JEE [23] or Android [24], which may help implement authorization checks for guarding access to its core system services.

Despite our success, some issues still remain in the verification process. In particular, ESC/Java2 may produce *false positives* (in case the built-in theorem prover cannot prove a VC) and *false negatives* (e.g., restrictions on loop unrolling). To deal with this situation, a possible solution may consider a runtime testing approach, like the one we have described using the JET tool, for all methods raising warnings by ESC/-Java2, thus showing a way in which both techniques can be used to provide stronger guarantees for the verification. Second, as shown in Table 3, the number of *meaningful* test cases produced by the JET tool is considerably less than the number of test cases created, which may affect the test coverage provided by the tool and could allow for potential security vulnerabilities to remain hidden during the verification process. This is mostly due to the limitations on the automated testing technique [16]. A possible solution would adopt a static approach for those methods whose test coverage is found to be below a given threshold. Finally, we have found that extended static checking is valuable when analyzing applications with respect to checking the implementation of an assertion-based access control model. In particular, we supported different concepts depicted in our model, which are in turn based on the ANSI RBAC standard, such as role hierarchies.

Furthermore, extended static checking represents a promising approach as there is no need to provide dedicated test cases nor implement a complete *running* system, as software modules can be tested in isolation by using modular reasoning techniques. Although ESC/Java2 is quite mature as a research prototype, some shortcomings still exist with respect to its current tools and development kits. As there are currently ongoing efforts for building a new extended static checker for Java within the OpenJML initiative[4], we hope this approach can be applied to larger case studies in industrial contexts, supporting advanced

---
[4]http://jmlspecs.sourceforge.net/

JML concepts, such as *model* features, as well as complex data structures. This newer extended static checker is expected to leverage more powerful backend SMT solvers such as Yices [25]. At the time of this writing, however, this tool does not completely support advanced JML specifications, which we use in our analysis and which are well-supported by ESC/-Java2. For example, heavyweight JML specifications, i.e. specifiations that contain normal and exceptional behavior, are not correctly implemented by OpenJML's extended static checker as our early experiments have shown. However, we use heavyweight specifications as the basis for our assertations (for example see Fig. 7).

Our work is related to other efforts in software security: Architectural risk analysis [26] attempts to identify security flaws on the level of the software architecture and hence is unrelated to the source-code level addressed in this approach. Language-based security approaches in the sense of Jif [27] allow software to be verified against information flow policies rather than supporting specific security requirements for different Security APIs. In addition, formal verification of RBAC properties has been already discussed in the literature [18]. These approaches are mostly focused on verifying the correctness of RBAC models without addressing their corresponding verification against an implementation at the source-code level.

The work closely related to ours involves the use of DBC, which was explored by Dragoni, et al. [28]. In addition, Belhaouari et al. introduced an approach to the verification of RBAC properties based on DBC [29]. Both approaches, while using DBC for checking RBAC properties, do not include the use of reference models to better aid the specification of DBC constraints in the security context. Moreover, no support is provided as API-independent constructs, such as the JML model capabilities discussed in our approach.

Other works that apply a DBC approach based on JML in the security context are presented by Lloyd et al. (biometric authentication system) [30], Cataño et al. [31] (smart card system), and Mustafa et al. [32] (Android system services). These works, however, do not cover applications consisting of heterogeneous modules and do not use the combination of dynamic and static analysis technique for assertion-based verification.

7. Conclusions and Future Work

In this paper, we have addressed the problem originated by the existence of security vulnerabilities in software applications. We have shown how such vulnerabilities, which may exist due to the lack of proper specification and verification of security checks at the source-code level, can be tackled by using well-defined reference models with the help of software assertions, thus providing a reference for the correct enforcement of security properties over applications composed of heterogeneous modules such as APIs and SDKs. Future work would include the introduction of assertion-based models to better accommodate other relevant security paradigms, e.g., the correct usage of cryptography APIs. We also plan to refine our proposed RBAC model introduced in Section 4 by introducing an automated translation from the specifications depicted in the ANSI RBAC standard, which are written in the Z specification language, to our supporting assertion-based language JML. In addition, we plan to refine the translation Algorithms shown in Section 4, in such a way their runtime efficiency can be considerably improved.

Appendix A. Analyzing the Correctness of our Proposed Approach

In this appendix, we present an analysis of the correctness of our approach as presented in Section 4. Recall from Fig. 4, our approach is based on the translation of ANSI RBAC security policies expressed in the well-known XACML policy language into DBC contracts written in the JML specification language. Then, such contracts, along with the source code of the software modules and any other supporting configuration files are fed into JML-based tools for automated verification. With this in mind, an analysis for correctness may need to take into account the following: first, the correct implementation of our proposed JML-based Model Classes, which depict the ANSI RBAC standard, must be verified. As mentioned in Section 2, such a standard contains functional specifications written in the Z language that unambiguously describe the inner components of RBAC as well as the interactions between them. We have provided a manual translation of those Z-based specifications into the JML language, in such a way the implementation of our referred model classes can be guided by them. Since we have proposed in this paper to use of JML-tools for verification purposes, a natural step will include to use such tools for verifying the correct implementation of our model classes, in an approach similar to the one we have described in Section 5. We plan to carry on such process as a part of future work, which may also focus on providing an automated translation of Z-based specifications into JML, in such a way any errors or redundancies introduced by our manual translation effort can be detected and resolved. Second, the correlation between our approach, the ANSI RBAC standard, and the semantics of the JML language needs to be explored. Concretely, a rigorous analysis involving the semantics of DBC contracts written in JML must be carried on to guarantee that a given RBAC policy is correctly enforced at runtime by a software module. For such a purpose, the work of Bruns [33] may serve as a reference for a formal description of the semantics of the JML language. We plan to work on such challenging endeavor in the future as well. Finally, in the remainder of this section, we focus on showing the correctness the translation of an ANSI RBAC policy into DBC/JML contracts. As mentioned before, our approach is mostly concerned with verifying that a given policy P is correctly enforced by a set of heterogeneous modules that are used to build up a software application S. More concretely, our approach must guarantee that every role in P can potentially *exercise* in S only the permissions that were originally intended in the aforementioned policy P. With this in mind, we base our correctness claims by showing that the set of permissions that a given role in P can exercise at runtime, namely *effective* runtime permissions, are the same in both the original policy P as well as in the produced DBC/JML contracts that are later used for software verification as described in this paper.

A.1. Basics

As described in Section 4, an ANSI RBAC XACML Policy can be parsed into the following: a set R of roles, a set P of permissions, the permission assignment relation ($PA \subseteq R \times P$) and the role hierarchy $RH \subseteq R \times R$ where $(r_i, r_j) \in RH$ if and only if r_i is senior to role r_j. In addition, a role r_i is always senior to itself, e.g., $(r_i, r_i) \in RH$. For simplicity, and without loss of generality, let us assume only a single permission exists for executing each method in a given Java module. As an example, given our sample policy depicted in Table 2, we have: R = {Manager, Agent, Teller, Employee}, P = {Transfer, Withdraw, Deposit, Close}, PA = {(Manager, Transfer), (Manager, Withdraw), (Teller, Withdraw), (Agent, Close), (Employee, Deposit)}, RH = {(Manager, Manager), (Agent, Agent,) (Teller, Teller), (Employee, Employee), (Manager, Agent), (Manager, Teller), (Manager, Employee), (Agent, Employee), (Teller, Employee)}. Finally, the set of DBC/JML contracts can be modeled as a relation $C \subseteq R \times M$ when R is the set of roles as described before and M is the set of Java methods included in a given application being the subject of a verification process. For each role name enlisted in a given contract, an entry in C is produced. As an example, the contract shown in Fig. 7 can be modeled as an entry of the form (Teller, *withdraw(double)*).

A.2. AuxiliaryAlgorithms

In order to support our analysis, we introduce two auxiliary algorithms: first, Algorithm $\mathcal{R}$ takes a set of DBC/JML contracts and produces the PA' relation obtained from the roles and permissions enlisted in the contracts provided as an input, thus potentially

---

Algorithm $\mathcal{R}$: Reconstructing an ANSI RBAC policy from DBC/JML Contracts.

Data: A Set C of DBC/JML Contracts
Result: the PA' relation depicting an ANSI RBAC Policy

1 Initialize PA' to an empty relation;
2 **for** *each $(r, m) \in C$* **do**
3   p = Get permission from m;
4   **if** *$(r, p) \notin PA'$* **then**
5         $PA' = PA' \cup (r, p)$;
6 **return** PA';

Algorithm EP : Obtaining the set of effective runtime permissions of a role in an ANSI RBAC Policy.

Data: A role $r \in R$, the PA and RH relations
Result: the set EP of effective runtime permissions

1 Initialize EP to the empty set;
2 **for** *each $(r', p) \in PA$* **do**
3   **if** *$(r, r') \in RH$* **then**
4         $EP = EP \cup p$;
5 **return** EP;

---

reversing the transformation procedure carried on by our proposed Algorithm $\mathcal{T}$. Second, Algorithm EP calculates the set of effective runtime permissions for a given role r in the set of roles R belonging to an ANSI RBAC policy whose PA and RH relations are provided as an input. Recall that following the ANSI RBAC standard, the set of effective permissions that are available to a given role r are those defined in the PA relation of the policy plus all other permissions that are also assigned to roles that happen to be *junior* to it. As an example, executing Algorithm EP on the role *Manager* defined in the policy described in Table 2 will lead to the following permissions: {Transfer, Withdraw, Deposit, Close}.

A.3. Correctnes Analysis

We start our analysis by showing that the set of produced DBC/JML contracts contains no extra permissions other than the ones defined in the original ANSI RBAC XACML policy. This way, we guarantee that no security *vulnerabilities* are introduced by our translation procedure into the generated set of DBC/JML contracts by allowing a given role to execute at runtime a permission not intended in the original policy. We formalize such requirement in the following:

Lemma 1. All effective runtime permissions present in the produced DBC/JML contracts are included in the original ANSI RBAC XACML policy. Formally, given an

XACML RBAC policy encoded as (R, P, PA, RH), $\forall r \in R$, $\nexists\, p \in P$ s.t. $p \notin EP\,(r, PA, RH) \land p \in EP\,(r, \mathcal{R}\,(\overline{\mathfrak{b}}\,(PA, RH)))$, RH).

Proof. Let us assume $\exists\, p \in P$ s.t. $p \notin EP\,(r, PA, RH) \land p \in EP\,(r, \mathcal{R}\,(\overline{\mathfrak{b}}\,(PA, RH)))$, RH) for some $r \in R$. In order to have $p \in EP\,(r, \mathcal{R}\,(\overline{\mathfrak{b}}\,(PA, RH))), RH)$, following Algorithm EP (lines 2-4), there must be $(r', m) \in C$ for some $(r, r') \in RH$ and $m = p$ (Algorithm $\mathcal{R}$, lines 2-5). Moreover, since $(r', m) \in C$, then, following Algorithm $\overline{\mathfrak{b}}$ (lines 7-13), there must be $(r', p) \in JM$ such that $m = p$. If $(r', p) \in JM$, then $(r', p) \in PA$ since $JM \subseteq PA$, following Algorithm $\overline{\mathfrak{b}}$ (lines 2-6). If $(r', p) \in PA$ and $(r, r') \in RH$, then $p \in EP$ (r, PA, RH), which contradicts our assumption that $p \notin EP\,(r, PA, RH)$. $\square$

A.4. Soundnes Analysis

In addition, we must also show that all the permissions included in the original ANSI RBAC policy are also included in the set of DBC/JML contracts. This way, we also guarantee that no security *vulnerabilities* are introduced into the produced contracts by missing to include one or more permissions included in the original policy. As described at the end of Section 3, failing to execute a permission originally included in a given policy may be the source of non-trivial vulnerabilities by leaving applications in an *inconsistent* state. We formalize this requirement as follows:

Lemma 2. All effective permissions included in the original RBAC XACML policy are included in the produced DBC/JML contracts. Formally, given an XACML RBAC policy encoded as (R, P, PA, RH), $\forall r \in R$, $\nexists\, p \in P$ s.t. $p \in EP\,(r, PA, RH) \land p \notin EP\,(r, \mathcal{R}\,(\overline{\mathfrak{b}}\,(PA, RH)))$, RH).

Proof. Let us assume $\exists\, p \in P$ s.t. $p \in EP\,(r, PA, RH) \land p \notin EP\,(r, \mathcal{R}\,(\overline{\mathfrak{b}}\,(PA, RH))), RH)$ for some $r \in R$. If $p \in EP\,(r, PA, RH)$ then $(r', p) \in PA$ for some $(r, r') \in RH$ following Algorithm EP lines 2-4. If $(r', p) \in PA$, then $(r', p) \in JM$ following Algorithm $\overline{\mathfrak{b}}$ (lines 2-6). Moreover, since $(r', p) \in JM$, then, following Algorithm $\overline{\mathfrak{b}}$ (lines 9-11), there must be $(r', m) \in S$ such that $m = p$. Since $(r', m) \in S$, then $(r', p) \in PA'$ following Algorithm $\mathcal{R}$ (lines 2-5). Subsequently, if $(r', p) \in PA'$, then $p \in EP\,(r, \mathcal{R}\,(\overline{\mathfrak{b}}\,(PA, RH))), RH)$ following Algorithm EP (lines 3-4). This contradicts our assumption that $p \notin EP\,(r, \mathcal{R}\,(\overline{\mathfrak{b}}\,(PA, RH))), RH)$. $\square$

A.5. Final Remarks

Finally, following the topics discussed in the beginning of this Appendix, we formalize the correctness claims of our translation approach by means of the following:

Theorem 1. The set of effective runtime permissions of each role listed the original XACML RBAC policy and the set of effective runtime permissions from the same role obtained from the translated DBC/JML contracts are the same. Formally, given an XACML RBAC policy encoded as (R, P, PA, RH), $\forall r \in R$, $EP\,(r, PA, RH) \equiv EP\,(r, \mathcal{R}\,(\overline{\mathfrak{b}}\,(PA, RH))), RH)$.

Proof. The theorem follows from Lemma 1 and Lemma 2, as those two cases are sufficient to show that the set of effective runtime permissions from the original ANSI RBAC XACML policy and the ones from the DBC/JML are the same. $\square$

Acknowledgement. The work of Carlos Rubio-Medrano and Gail-Joon Ahn was partially supported by a grant from the US Department of Energy (DE-SC0004308). The work of Karsten Sohr was supported by the German Federal Ministry of Education and Research (BMBF) under the grant 16KIS0074.

References

[1] RUBIO-MEDRANO, C.E. and AHN, G.J. (2014) Achieving security assurance with assertion-based application construction. In *Proc. of the 10th Int'l Conf. on Collaborative Computing: Networking, Applications and Worksharing (Collaboratecom)* (IEEE): 520–530.

[2] GEORGIEV, M., IYENGAR, S., JANA, S., ANUBHAI, R., BONEH, D. and SHMATIKOV, V. (2012) The most dangerous code in the world: validating SSL certificates in non-browser software. In *Proc. of the ACM Conf. on Computer and comm. security*: 38–49.

[3] FAHL, S., HARBACH, M., MUDERS, T., BAUMGÄRTNER, L., FREISLEBEN, B. and SMITH, M. (2012) Why eve and mallory love Android: an analysis of Android SSL (in)security. In *Proc. of the ACM Conf. on Computer and communications security*: 50–61.

[4] SANDHU, R.S., COYNE, E.J., FEINSTEIN, H.L. and YOUMAN, C.E. (1996) Role-Based Access Control Models. *IEEE Computer* **29**(2): 38–47.

[5] AMERICAN NATIONAL STANDARDS INSTITUTE INC. (2004), Role Based Access Control. ANSI-INCITS 359-2004.

[6] HOARE, C.A.R. (1969) An axiomatic basis for computer programming. *Communications of the ACM* **12**(10): 576–580.

[7] BURDY, L., CHEON, Y., COK, D., ERNST, M., KINIRY, J., LEAVENS, G.T., LEINO, K. *et al.* (2003) An overview of JML tools and applications. In *Proc. 8th Int'l Workshop on Formal Methods for Industrial Critical Systems (FMICS 03)*: 73–89.

[8] ROSENBLUM, D.S. (1995) A practical approach to programming with assertions. *IEEE Trans. Softw. Eng.* **21**(1): 19–31.

[9] CHEON, Y., LEAVENS, G., SITARAMAN, M. and EDWARDS, S. (2005) Model variables: cleanly supporting abstraction in design by contract: Research articles. *Softw. Pract. Exper.* **35**(6): 583–599.

[10] SPIVEY, J.M. (1989) *The Z notation: a reference manual* (Upper Saddle River, USA: Prentice-Hall, Inc.).

[11] OASIS (2014), XACML v3.0 Core and Hierarchical Role Based Access Control (RBAC) Profile Version

1.0. http://docs.oasis-open.org/xacml/3.0/xacml-3.0-rbac-v1-spec-cd-03-en.html.

[12] OASIS (2014), eXtensible Access Control Markup Language (XACML) TC. https://www.oasis-open.org/committees/xacml/.

[13] Pivotal, Inc. (2013), Spring security 3.1.2. http://static.springsource.org/spring-security/site/index.html.

[14] The Apache Software Foundation (2013), Apache shiro 1.2.1. http://shiro.apache.org/.

[15] G. T. Leavens and E. Poll and C. Clifton and Y. Cheon and C. Ruby and D. Cok and J. Kiniry (2004), JML Reference Manual. http://www.eecs.ucf.edu/~leavens/JML/jmlrefman/jmlrefman_toc.html.

[16] Cheon, Y. (2007) Automated random testing to detect specification-code inconsistencies. In *Proc. of the 2007 Int'l Conf. on Software Engineering Theory and Practice* (Orlando, Florida, U.S.A.).

[17] Flanagan, C., Leino, K.R.M., Lillibridge, M., Nelson, G., Saxe, J.B. and Stata, R. (2002) Extended static checking for Java. In *Proc. of the ACM SIGPLAN Conf. on Prog. language design and implementation*: 234–245.

[18] Hu, H. and Ahn, G.J. (2008) Enabling verification and conformance testing for access control model. In *Proc. of the 13th ACM Symp. on Access Control Models and Technologies*: 195–204.

[19] OSCAR EMR (2014), OSCAR Electronic Medical Records System. http://oscar-emr.com/.

[20] J. Gyger and N.l Westbury (2014), JMoney Financial System. http://jmoney.sourceforge.net/.

[21] Jia, Y. and Harman, M. (2011) An analysis and survey of the development of mutation testing. *IEEE Transactions on Software Engineering* 37(5): 649 –678.

[22] Barnett, M., Leino, R. and Schulte, W. (2005) The spec# programming system: An overview. In *Proc. of the 2004 Int'l Conf. on Construction and Analysis of Safe, Secure, and Interoperable Smart Devices* (Berlin: Springer-Verlag): 49–69.

[23] Oracle Inc. (2014), Java Platform Enterprise Edition. http://www.oracle.com/technetwork/java/javaee/overview/index.html.

[24] Google Inc. (2014), Android. http://www.android.com.

[25] Dutertre, B. and de Moura, L. (2006) A fast linear-arithmetic solver for dpll(t). In *Proc. of the 18th Int'l Conf. on Computer Aided Verification*, CAV'06 (Berlin: Springer): 81–94.

[26] McGraw, G. (2006) *Software Security: Building Security In* (Addison-Wesley).

[27] Sabelfeld, A. and Myers, A.C. (2003) Language-based information-flow security. *IEEE J. Selected Areas in Communications* 21(1): 5–19.

[28] Dragoni, N., Massacci, F., Naliuka, K. and Siahaan, I. (2007) Security-by-contract: Toward a semantics for digital signatures on mobile code. In *Public Key Infrastructure* (Springer Berlin), *LNCS* **4582**, 297–312.

[29] Belhaouari, H., Konopacki, P., Laleau, R. and Frappier, M. (2012) A design by contract approach to verify access control policies. In *17th Int'l Conf. on Engineering of Complex Computer Systems (ICECCS)*: 263 –272.

[30] Lloyd, J. and Jürjens, J. (2009) Security analysis of a biometric authentication system using UMLsec and JML. In *MoDELS* (Springer), *Lecture Notes in Computer Science* **5795**: 77–91.

[31] Cataño, N. and Huisman, M. (2002) Formal specification of Gemplus's electronic purse case study. In *FME 2002* (Springer), **LNCS 2391**: 272–289.

[32] Mustafa, T. and Sohr, K. (2014) Understanding the implemented access control policy of android system services with slicing and extended static checking. *International Journal of Information Security* : 1–20doi:10.1007/s10207-014-0260-y, URL http://dx.doi.org/10.1007/s10207-014-0260-y.

[33] Bruns, D. (2010) Formal semantics for the java modeling language. In *Informatiktage* (GI), *LNI* **S-9**: 15–18.

16

Optimistic Scheduling: facilitating the collaboration by prioritizing the individual needs

Salvatore F. Pileggi[1]

[1]INRIA & UPMC-LIP6, Paris, France.

Abstract

The collaboration among people is one of the key factors for the optimization of many processes and activities. The efficiency and the effectiveness of the collaboration has an intrinsic value which significantly affects performances and outcomes, at a quantitative and a qualitative level both. Open communities, as well as spontaneous or predefined virtual organizations, are demanding for a more solid and consistent support for activity scheduling and managing in a context of flexibility and respect of individual needs. This paper proposes a privacy-friendly model that can be materialized in concrete tools and applications to support virtual organizations in the scheduling and management of the most valuable resource: the time. The model is formally defined and, than, analysed and evaluated by simulations as the function of complex user behaviours. Finally, an implementation of the basic prototype aimed at a large scale deployment is described.

1. Introduction

The collaboration among people is one of the key factors for most processes and activities. The efficiency and the effectiveness of the collaboration has an intrinsic value which significantly affects performances and outcomes, at a quantitative and a qualitative level both [1]. Common but significant examples are easy to find from trivial observations of the real world: researchers, for instance, can have excellent individual skills, expertise and motivation; but it is the convergence of their experience and ability that allows to reach the best results; it is easy to detect like addressing a competitive business implies a pragmatic approach that takes into account multiple perspectives and contributions from different members of specialized heterogeneous teams; it is evident in sport competition at any level: explicitly in team sports, as well as implicitly in individual ones, where top-level (and not only) athletes are supported in the background by specialized teams. The obvious conclusion is that individuals are (or can be) good but, together, they are better. Therefore, a team is much more than people working together.

For a long time the optimization of human resource has been investigated, especially inside specific context aimed at the maximization of the productivity. Classic models commonly applied by companies in the real world have evolved at a theoretical level to integrate a more flexible philosophy (e.g.[2]). More recently some of those models are being considered in practice, as many companies are progressively leaving from classic schemas to evolve towards novel approaches where individual needs and effectiveness converge, under the realistic assumption that personal and collective development come together. It is the case of the "flextime", in which employees can choose when they work, subject to achieving total daily, weekly or monthly hours and to the necessary work being done. More recently, successful and powerful companies have experimented cutting-edge solutions aimed at the empowerment of workers that should fortify the relationship with the company. As an example, Netflix is proposing a model that assumes an unlimited number of holiday days that employees can take at their best convenience as long as the planned work is performed and main goals achieved.

In this paper we uniquely address the problem of the activity scheduling as a response to the needs of new emerging organizational models. Indeed, open

*Email: flavio.pileggi@lip6.fr
Web-page: http://www.flaviopileggi.net

communities, as well as spontaneous or predefined virtual organizations (VOs) [30], are demanding for a more solid and consistent support for activity scheduling and managing in a context of flexibility and respect of individual needs.

This paper proposes a privacy-friendly model called *optimistic scheduling* due to the implicit positivity that drives interactions among people in the paradigm. It can be materialized in concrete tools and applications to support virtual organizations in the scheduling and management of their most valuable resource: the time.

However, simple observations in everyday life clearly show unpredictable human behaviour, even in simple and well-known situations. Therefore, the model is first formally defined and, than, analysed and evaluated by simulations as the function of complex user behaviours. As demonstrated, the human factor has a critical impact on the model performance.

Finally, an implementation of the basic prototype aimed at a large scale deployment is proposed. An empirical overview of collaborative tools demonstrate as the simplest approaches (e.g.[3]) usually reach the best results, meaning products are well accepted by users and indeed they are usable in practice.

The introductory part of the document is aimed at the contextualization of this work and follows with an overview of the latest tools on the market, with a deep description of the reference use cases and, finally, with a brief explanation of the methodological aspects. The second section describes *Optimistic Scheduling* that is analysed and discussed in the third section. Then, in the section 4, an implementation of a basic tool inspired by the model for a large scale deployment is described. As usual, the paper ends with a section about conclusions and future works.

This paper is an extended version of [16], recently presented at *CollaborateCom 2015*. The original paper focuses exclusively on the model and on its behavioural analysis. This extended version definitely addresses a wider scope, integrating the original contribution with an extended discussion, a short overview of the related work, as well as details about the current implementations and applications on a large scale.

1.1. Related Work

Cloud and mobile technology [17] has enabled a massive development of applications and tools that users can get and run through commercial ecosystems (e.g. Apple, Google, Microsoft). The impressive number of apps currently available on the most common marketplaces makes the normal "state of the art" of popular applications (including shared calendars and similar tools) hard to be proposed. Also a simple survey looks definitely far away from an exhaustive analysis.

From a quick overview of commercial solutions, the most novel tools on the market offers features that current reference tools (e.g. Google Calendar) are missing. That is the case of *Kalendi* [4] which includes features to add attachments to event invites, to schedule individual SMS reminders, to publish calendars online and to set up unlimited calendars to share across groups. *UpTo* [5] proposes a calendar model which provides a kind of "new dimension", providing the ability to discover important events ahead of time and plan accordingly. The key idea is to get a more complete view of everything coming up that matters to users but without the clutter. This calendar has two layers: the front layer is the existing calendar and the back layer includes calendars the user follows based on likes and interests. *Teamweek* [6] is designed according to a model that should efficiently support those who are collaborating on time-sensitive projects, which require a step-by-step approach. Many other examples could be reported. A full overview is out of the scope of this paper.

Summarizing, the most dominating trends appear in coherence with the current technological climate [18] that pushes towards a progressive socialization of tools and applications. The main limitation of those products look the base model itself: shared activities are always scheduled with a kind of implicit high priority established a priori and somehow passively "pushed" to individuals. The model proposed in this paper works with a completely opposite logic and pretends to push the cooperation or collaboration among people by priorizing individual needs. Even though it can appear like a contradiction, we are pretty confident that this approach can suit the requirements of emerging organizational models, as well as the philosophy of many professionals and cutting-edge organizational models.

1.2. Beyond the state of the art: overcoming a simple use case

The primary scope of this work is to provide a privacy-friendly model for effective and efficient time sharing.

With the support of current digital tools, the dynamic scheduling of a shared event is commonly done according to two different main models:

- *Scheduling by invitation.* The organizer sends an explicit invitation to all the expected participants by using some shared channel (e.g. email, message, sms, social network). Due to the extensive use of emails and messaging in both private and professional life, this is evidently the simplest and, indeed, the most used method. But this model is very vulnerable in fact. First of all, considering a group of peers, the event cannot be considered as committed if confirmations are not received from all the group members. If at least one of the expected participants rejects the invitation, in theory the organizer needs to restart the process sending a new invitation. Furthermore, a missed notification from at least one member of the group can generate misunderstandings (not received? Not seen? Not interested? Unable to respond?), requires further actions from the organizer (e.g. reminders) and can lead to a situation of potential deadlock. A different organization of the group (e.g. assuming a leader or people that are requested but not strictly needed) can mitigate the impact of those situations but, in general, the synchronization schema among users is pretty poor even considering the support of specific tools.

- *Scheduling by poll.* It is the most common alternative to the method previously described. The organizer proposes a set of possible slots and participants are asked to give their preferences in order to reach an agreement. Having a poll of possible chooses reduces significantly the vulnerability of the model as the organizer, always assuming a group of peers in which everyone is requested to join the scheduled event, has to set up a new poll only if there is no agreement on any of the proposed slots. On the other hand, a lack of response from some member proposes the same problems described above. This method is commonly supported by specific tools (such as the very famous *Doodle* [7]) to minimize human efforts. The poll allows to simultaneously reason on a set of possibilities instead of on just one but, at the same time, can be quite uncomfortable and inefficient: waiting for the result of the poll, people are blocking a part of their time according to the preferences in the poll.

Last but not the least, both models present a further common weakness: what if a group member changes his plans after a commitment? In general, under the assumptions mentioned above, the process should start over. In practice there is no support provided by existing tools.

1.3. Methodology and Approach

The model proposed in the paper has been designed combining practical needs and requirements (e.g. usability and privacy preserving) with a research-oriented approach aimed at complex studies in the field of social science [8] (e.g. human behaviour [9]) and other domains (e.g. organizational models

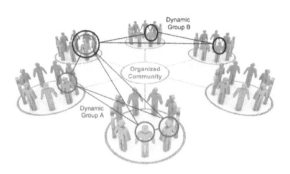

Figure 1. Virtual Organizations as a reference model.

[31]). The key methodological idea assumes scientists and application designers as the main actors of a feedback process that produces concrete tools on one side and valuable data for analysis and improvements/refinements on the other side.

One of the key factor that affects the whole understanding of this work and that determines clear design decisions at the time to materialize the model in a concrete tool is the *Reference Community Model* (fig. 1). Indeed, proposing a completely generic approach is hard and could result non-effective or ambiguous. On the other hand, abstractions could provide a simplified view of complex realities with a consequent and fundamental lack of realism. In the context of this work, the community is understood as a whole, meaning that users can interact among them at a global level. However, the ideal application domain assumes a *virtual organization* model where existing and relatively static real groups (e.g. companies, institutions, teams, group friends) can be integrated with dynamic groups that can often change in the time (such as in cooperative projects) or that are defined on the fly as a function of concrete tasks or activities.

It is also assumed that users inside groups are peers. Even though implicitly maintaining some of the typical roles (such as the "organizer" or "moderator" of a shared activity), that is not always realistic considering that real groups are often organized according to some structure or hierarchy. Moreover, it is assumed that a shared activity inside a dynamic group requires the participation of all the members of the group. This ideal case could not suit virtual organizations that propose some kind of internal priority among members, as well as other common concepts such as "optional" or "not mandatory".

Finally, the philosophy of the model assumes that individual preferences have a priority over groups. The scope is to facilitate the cooperation and to optimize the use of the time. Limiting or conditioning individual behaviours would mean re-proposing common approaches.

2. Efficient and effective time sharing inside Virtual Organizations

This section proposes the description of *Optimistic Scheduling*. This model can be materialized in concrete tools and applications designed according to its philosophy.

At the time t, each community member has his own calendar TS_P. It is considered like a private asset as no-one else in the community has access or visibility to it. Each user i performs on his private calendar a kind of preliminary filtering as he sets a priori the slots that can be used for some personal activity ts_P or shared activity ts_S, defining his personal space K_i. A simple example of preliminary filtering is represented by a work calendar that only includes normal work hours and that doesn't include leaves or other kind of absences known a priori.

The whole space K of slots is given merging users' spaces according to eq.1.

$$K = \bigcup_i K_i \quad \forall i \qquad (1)$$

On that filtered calendar, a user i can schedule personal activities (eq.2) for any available slot $k \in K_i$.

$$TS_P^i(t) = \sum_k ts_P^i(k, t) \qquad (2)$$

According to the same logic, a user can try to schedule a shared event (eq.3) involving other persons (group).

$$TS_S^i(t) = \sum_g \sum_k ts_S^g(k, t), \quad i \in g \qquad (3)$$

The full activity set TS for a community member is given by merging his personal activities (TS_P) and shared activities (TS_S) as in eq.4.

$$TS^i(t) = TS_P^i(t) \cup TS_S^i(t) \qquad (4)$$

The whole potentially shared time can be at least equal to K assuming people have no personal activities scheduled (eq.5).

$$\bigcup_i TS^i(t) = O(K) \quad \Rightarrow \quad TS_P^i(t) = \emptyset, \quad \forall i \qquad (5)$$

As previously mentioned, users can only see their own calendars. In order to get an effective guide to schedule shared events, any user can access, for any defined group he joins, a shared structure FTS obtained by merging the personal calendars and returning the anonymized complementary set according to eq.6.

$$FTS^g(t) = K - \bigcup_i TS^i(t), \quad i \in g \qquad (6)$$

That structure shows (fig.2a) the slots that can be potentially used, inside a considered group, to schedule

a shared event. This simple operation allows users to automatically understand the availability of a certain group in the respect of the privacy of its members. Assuming a significant size for a group, inferring information is not easy in practice, so the privacy is completely preserved.

By using those structures, whichever member in a group can schedule a shared activity for a dynamic or static group with a very good chance to be successful (fig.2b).

The semantic described implicitly defines the main global invariant (a logical assertion that is held to always be true during a certain phase of execution of a program [10]) for applications working according to this model: if a time slot ts is used by a member i of the group g for a private purpose, then that slot cannot be used for a shared activity inside any group i is member of (eq.7).

$$\exists ts_P^i(k_a, t) \quad \Rightarrow \quad \nexists ts_S^{i \in g}(k_a, t), \quad k_a \in K \quad \forall t \qquad (7)$$

The model scales to a multi-group environment (fig.2c) providing an individual-specific view of each group in a privacy-friendly context.

As already mentioned, users preferences have a priority on group activities according to a logic that wants to push co-operation/collaboration without adding barriers or constraints. Consequently, users can still schedule their own activities also for slots that are already used as a shared resource. In this case the invariant defined by the eq.7 is not respected any more, determining a non-valid state for the system that, coherently with the assumptions, reacts (fig.3) cancelling the shared event and notifying the interested group about. An extensive discussion about this strong condition, as well as about its implications on performance and possible variants are discussed later in the paper.

3. Model Analysis

As activities involve people, the validation and evaluation of the model have to take into account the human factor. Simple empirical observations show how unpredictable people can be, even in well know and straightforward situations.

The most significant issue for the analysis and the full understanding of the model is the definition of simple but realistic behaviours under the assumption that people are or can be unpredictable. Indeed, the simple fact that different personalities act in a different way in a given context often reduces the standardization or categorization of the human behaviour just to an academic exercise.

In this study we assume a simple and uniform behaviour at the time to schedule shared activities,

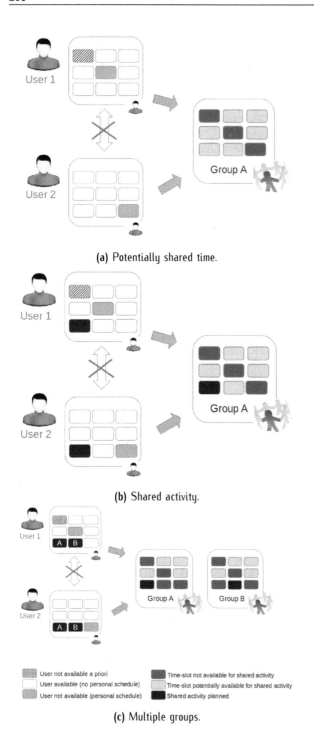

(a) Potentially shared time.

(b) Shared activity.

(c) Multiple groups.

Figure 2. Overview of the model behaviour.

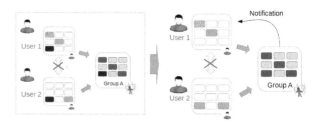

Figure 3. Cancelling a shared activity as a reaction to a global invariant violation.

is submitted; else there is the possibility to don't submit the request or to look for another slot. Concerning the personal activities management, there are three different possible behaviours, defined as in the follow:

- *Constructive.* The user is cooperative and, therefore, acts according to a logic that facilitates the successful scheduling of group initiatives. A constructive user schedules his activities only in slots not currently used for shared events and uses shared slots only if there is no other choice.

- *Disruptive.* This is the opposite of the previous as he schedules his personal activities prioritizing the slots currently occupied by shared events. This behaviour causes the continuous re-organization of the already scheduled shared events. It is not necessarily reproducing a malicious user, as it could also simulate an involuntary noise caused by random circumstances or periodic conflicts on schedules.

- *Random/Independent.* Between the two extremes (constructive and disruptive) there is a wide range of behaviours, including an independent user that acts according to a pseudo-random logic that doesn't take into account groups: an independent user schedules independently his activities without taking care if the target slot is currently used for some shared activity or not.

The metric to evaluate the model performance (eq.8) is directly proportional to the number of shared activities successfully scheduled and inversely proportional to the number of shared events cancelled upon request of users.

$$\alpha(t) = \frac{1 + \sum_i TS_S^i(t)}{\sum_i TS_S^i(t) + \sum_i TS_S^i(t)_{|cancelled}} \quad (8)$$

The simulations are assuming a *sliding window* to reproduce the logic time (fig.4): users have a view of a finite number of slots m and, at the generic time t, they can only schedule between the slot $t+1$ and the slot $t+m$. As a simulation of the time, the logic transition from t to $t+1$ implies the slot t no more available (past) and a new free slot $t+m+1$ available.

which are periodically scheduled according to a regular pattern. But we assume more than one possible behaviour to manage personal activities, affecting indirectly the shared ones.

The synthetic actor that emulates the users uses a linear logic to schedule a shared event: the activity is planned and associated with a well determined time slot; if the slot is available for shared activities, then it

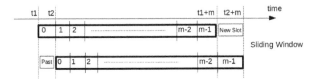

Figure 4. Sliding Window.

Furthermore, for the experiments proposed in this work, the qualitative behaviour previously described is integrated with a quantitative profile as in eq.9: the number of scheduled events tends to increase in the time. In other words, users averagely schedule a higher number of events than the number of events they cancel.

$$\frac{d}{dt} TS^i(t) > 0, \quad \forall i \qquad (9)$$

For simplicity we are assuming atomic slots that don't overlap each others (eq.10).

$$ts^i_{P/S}(k_1, t) \cap ts^i_{P/S}(k_2, t) = \emptyset, \quad \forall k_1, k_2 \in K \quad \forall i \qquad (10)$$

The simulations performed assume a sliding window of 12 weeks to schedule activities and members averagely available 35 hours (slots) per week. This is the reproduction of a common calendar. The calendar is assumed to be empty when the simulation starts, so there is a transitory period. The members schedule averagely an activity per day and the 25% of the planned activities are shared. The simulation ends when the system is saturated (no more possibility to schedule events due to the quantitative behaviour) or when the system has reached stationary/stable conditions.

The simulation results are showed in fig.5. The chart at the top represents the decreasing of performance when the group size increases and assumes independent behaviours (as previously defined). That is a very good approximation of the performance inside a virtual organization where users are not explicitly acting according to the model but in a kind of "neutral" mode. The chart in the middle proposes the same statistics assuming a cooperative behaviour. This emulates a community that acts according to the model. Performances are evidently higher than the previous and decrease only as a function of the natural saturation of the system determined by the quantitative behaviour (fig.9). The chart at the bottom provides an overview of the potential impact of disruptive behaviours on the whole performance. As showed, if one or more members is acting according to a disruptive behaviour, then performances quickly decrease and the system tends after a very short time to the instability.

Disruptive behaviours are part of the real life and have to be taken into account at the time of designing real tools. They are easy to detect in common mechanisms such as invitation and polls due to the explicit character of the interactions. On the contrary, disruptive behaviours are hidden in a privacy-friendly context.

At a model level, the global invariants (eq.7) can be relaxed to mitigate the effect of disruptive behaviours. This approach introduces at least one significant and critical trade-off between functionality and privacy/simplicity. Indeed, as showed in fig.6, assuming that a slot inside a group can be used simultaneously for a personal and a shared activity protects the system from disruptive behaviours, as well as it support role-based and hierarchical virtual organizations. But it also introduces a complexity and ambiguities in the understanding and the management of the system state. Considering anonymous non-availabilities, the organizer cannot know who is missed, so the further steps of the activity planning could be negatively affected. On the other hand, concessions about privacy could invalidate most premises and, consequently, modify significantly the whole model focus. In any case, integrating a complex state that assumes the simultaneous use of shared slots limits tools autonomy and, in general, applications could miss their aimed simplicity.

4. Applications and Implementations

Optimistic Scheduling has a generic focus and, consequently, can be used to approach specific problems related to the activity scheduling in the context of different application domains.

This section proposes the description of a generic purpose tool for activity scheduling and a brief discussion on the potential applications of the model in e-Education [19][27], as en example of target domain.

4.1. A generic purpose tool supporting deployment on a large scale

Tools and applications designed according to this model can be understood like systems working at a low scale (such as a corporative tool), as well as like services working at a global scale (e.g.[32]). This implementation focuses on large scale deployments.

To assure a scalable and fault-tolerant environment, the application is implemented upon replicated databases. More concretely, a noSQL [11] philosophy, assuming key-value interface, is adopted and data structures are CRDTs [10][12] to support a partition-tolerant [13] deployment on a large scale in a context of eventual consistency [14][15].

The design of the application can follow two main common approaches for distributed systems:

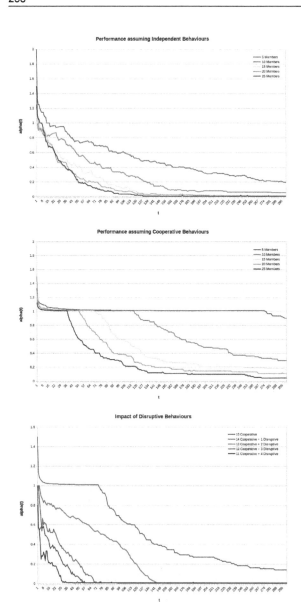

Figure 5. Simulation outcomes.

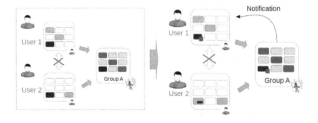

Figure 6. Relaxing global invariants.

- *Computation in the cloud* [20] which is commonly defined as a type of Internet-based computing, where different services, such as servers, storage and applications, are delivered through the Internet.(fig.7, top).

- *Computation at the edge* (e.g. [21]) that pushes the frontier of computing applications, data, and services away from centralized nodes to the logical extremes of a network (fig.7, bottom). It enables analytics and knowledge generation to occur at the source of the data. This approach requires leveraging resources that may not be continuously connected to a network such as laptops, smart-phones, tablets and sensors.

This implementation is in fact a fully distributed application composed of local agents without any central coordination that assumes data in the cloud and computation at the edge. The *consensus* to assure the system converging to a correct state is defined as part of the application logic. The weak consistency model allows off-line activity and eventual synchronization once online.

The application distinguishes between:

- *State* of the system, which is a correct state according to the application logic.

- *Meta-state* of the system, that is a kind of pseudo-state that can evolve to different states as the function of the application logic (fig. 6). A meta-state is a situation of conflict that is not preserving the application invariants.

Concerning the data model, there are two main possibilities in terms of data structure to use:

- *Sets of data*. Data is modelled on a pure key-value interface. Each group is associated with an unique identifier that is also the identifier of the corresponding data set. Each element of the set includes a prefix of the time slot, the anonymized user identifier and an informative part. This representation is simple and explicitly allows both the representation of states and meta-states of the system.

- *Maps of data*. Using maps, keys do not contain all the information but points to an object. A different map is defined for each group and keys are the time slots. Therefore, the information is the combination of the key and the object. The main advantage of maps is the explicit representation of the last state for each slot, due to the effective concurrency on the keys. On the other hand it requires to maintain the history of the updates to assure the convergence and, therefore, the correct implementation of the application logic.

For this implementation, sets are preferred as they are a simpler solution.

Fairness is not completely assured, as the causality of events is not guaranteed [24]. Indeed, actions happening almost simultaneously can generate conflicts that,

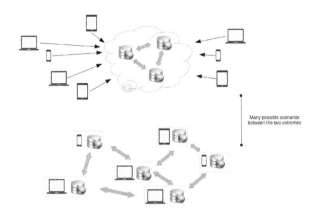

Figure 7. Computation in the Cloud (top) and computation at the edges (bottom) assuming replicated databases.

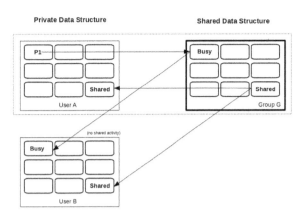

Figure 8. Maintaining consistent states by comparing private and shared data structures.

according to a fair approach, should be solved giving priority to actions generated before. Typical situations of conflict happen when users try to use simultaneously the same free slot (fig.9). However, assuming a low latency, the lack of fairness has a very minor impact on real cases.

The implementation directly follows the model logic, as the mechanism for the detection and the resolution of inconsistent states is developed by comparing the user private information structure (in the cache) with the shared structures in the cloud (fig.8). The conflict resolution is model-driven, giving a priority to the personal scheduling (fig.9, on the top). In case of conflict between two shared activities (by two different users in the same group) that are targeting the same free slot (fig.9, down), the conflict resolution is solved according to a *last-write-wins* philosophy that, as mentioned, is not reflecting a fair approach in this case.

Future evolutions of the system will include advanced features for the management of the meta-states according to different philosophies and VOs classes (e.g. role-based).

4.2. Applications in e-Education

Team-work is a rather important aspect also in e-learning [22], where moderation [23], supervision and any other activities that explicitly require the synchronization of people are affected by problems of dynamic scheduling.

For instance, last trends include advanced features in e-Learning programs that move from the relatively simple personalization of processes [25] to their socialization [26]. Indeed, dynamic groups [33] can be established for people with similar needs, lacks or marks in order to push the co-operation among them in most advanced e-Education systems.

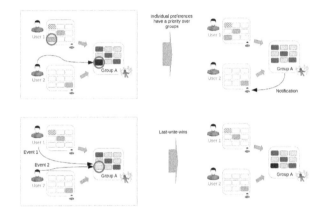

Figure 9. Conflicts resolution.

Prioritizing individual needs could be one of the key issues for the effectiveness and efficiency of the e-learning approaches involving groups of people.

Furthermore, the potential automaton of the activity scheduling in a privacy-friendly context would be useful and easy to integrate in many advanced systems (e.g. [29]) that are already addressing security and privacy issues [28].

5. Conclusions and Future Work

Optimistic Scheduling is designed from empirical observations assuming realistic conditions. It has been analysed considering unpredictable human behaviours inside virtual organizations and require a cooperative attitude to achieve high performances.

The flexibility of the model suggests a family of interesting tools for generic or specific purpose communities in a wide range of application domains.

The basic prototype is implemented according to a large scale philosophy and can be easily extended or integrated with further advanced features, as well as it can be particularized to address specific environments, requirements and purposes.

Acknowledgements

This research has been partially funded by the EU Project *SyncFree* (grant agreement number 609551).

References

[1] J. A. Wagner, "Studies of individualism-collectivism: Effects on cooperation in groups," *Academy of Management journal*, vol. 38, no. 1, pp. 152–173, 1995.

[2] G. R. Jones and J. M. George, "The experience and evolution of trust: Implications for cooperation and teamwork," *Academy of management review*, vol. 23, no. 3, pp. 531–546, 1998.

[3] M. Raman, "Wiki technology as a" free" collaborative tool within an organizational setting," *Information systems management*, vol. 23, no. 4, pp. 59–66, 2006.

[4] "Kalendi," https://www.kalendi.com/, accessed: 2015-06-05.

[5] "Upto," http://upto.com/, accessed: 2015-06-05.

[6] "Teamweek," https://teamweek.com/, accessed: 2015-06-05.

[7] "Doodle," http://doodle.com/, accessed: 2015-06-05.

[8] R. Conte, N. Gilbert, G. Bonelli, C. Cioffi-Revilla, G. Deffuant, J. Kertesz, V. Loreto, S. Moat, J.-P. Nadal, A. Sanchez *et al.*, "Manifesto of computational social science," *The European Physical Journal Special Topics*, vol. 214, no. 1, pp. 325–346, 2012.

[9] B. Schmidt, *The modelling of human behaviour.* Society for Computer Simulation International, 2000.

[10] M. Shapiro, N. Preguiça, C. Baquero, and M. Zawirski, "Conflict-free replicated data types," in *Stabilization, Safety, and Security of Distributed Systems.* Springer, 2011, pp. 386–400.

[11] J. Pokorny, "Nosql databases: a step to database scalability in web environment," *International Journal of Web Information Systems*, vol. 9, no. 1, pp. 69–82, 2013.

[12] S. Burckhardt, A. Gotsman, H. Yang, and M. Zawirski, "Replicated data types: specification, verification, optimality," in *ACM SIGPLAN Notices*, vol. 49, no. 1. ACM, 2014, pp. 271–284.

[13] D. J. Abadi, "Consistency tradeoffs in modern distributed database system design: Cap is only part of the story," *Computer*, no. 2, pp. 37–42, 2012.

[14] A. Bieniusa, M. Zawirski, N. Preguiça, M. Shapiro, C. Baquero, V. Balegas, and S. Duarte, "Brief announcement: Semantics of eventually consistent replicated sets," in *Distributed Computing.* Springer, 2012, pp. 441–442.

[15] W. Vogels, "Eventually consistent," *Communications of the ACM*, vol. 52, no. 1, pp. 40–44, 2009.

[16] S.F. Pileggi, "A privacy-friendly model for an efficient and effective activity scheduling inside dynamic virtual organizations," in *11th EAI International Conference on Collaborative Computing: Networking, Applications and Worksharing (CollaborateCom 2015).* Wuhan, China, 10-11 November, 2015.

[17] H.T. Dinh, C. Lee, D. Niyato, and P. Wang, "A survey of mobile cloud computing: architecture, applications, and approaches," *Wireless communications and mobile computing*, vol. 13, no. 18, pp. 1587–1611, 2013.

[18] S.F. Pileggi, C. Fernandez-Llatas, and V. Traver, "When the social meets the semantic: Social semantic Web or Web 2.5," *Future Internet*, vol. 4, no. 3, pp. 852–864, 2012.

[19] A.T. Bates, "*Technology, e-learning and distance education,*" Routledge, 2005.

[20] M. Michael at al., "A view of cloud computing," *Communications of the ACM*, vol. 53, no. 4, 50–58, 2010.

[21] M. Rabinovich, Z. Xiao, and A. Aggarwal, "Computing on the edge: A platform for replicating internet applications," *Web content caching and distribution*, pg.57–77, Springer, 2004.

[22] E. Williams, R. Duray, and V. Reddy, "Teamwork orientation, group cohesiveness, and student learning: A study of the use of teams in online distance education," *Journal of Management Education*, vo. 30, no. 4, 592–616, 2006.

[23] G. Salmon, "*E-moderating: The key to teaching and learning online,*" Psychology Press, 2004.

[24] W. Vogels, "Eventually consistent, " *Communications of the ACM*, vo. 52, no. 1, 40–44, 2009.

[25] M.K. Khrib, M. Jemn, and O. Nasraoui, "Automatic recommendations for e-learning personalization based on web usage mining techniques and information retrieval, " *Eighth IEEE International Conference on Advanced Learning Technologies*, 2008.

[26] J. Dron, and T. Anderson, "Collectives, networks and groups in social software for e-Learning, "*World conference on e-learning in corporate, government, healthcare, and higher education*, vo. 2007, no. 1, 2460–2467, 2007.

[27] S. Guri-Rosenblit, "Distance Education' and 'E-learning: Not the same thing, "*Higher education*, vo. 49, no. 4, 467–493, 2005.

[28] B. Jerman-Blažič, and T. Klobučar, "Privacy provision in e-learning standardized systems: status and improvements, " *Computer standards & interfaces*, vo. 27, no. 6, 561–578, 2005.

[29] B. Dong, Q. Zheng, J. Yang, H. Li, and M. Qiao, "An e-learning ecosystem based on cloud computing infrastructure, "*Ninth IEEE International Conference on Advanced Learning Technologies*, 2009.

[30] L. Camarinha-Matos, and H. Afsarmanesh, "*Brief historical perspective for virtual organizations*, "Springer, 2005.

[31] D. Ancona, and D. Caldwell, "Bridging the boundary: External activity and performance in organizational teams, "*Administrative science quarterly*, 634–665, 1992.

[32] B. Zhao, L. Huang, J. Stribling, S. Rhea, A. Joseph, and J. Kubiatowicz, "Tapestry: A resilient global-scale overlay for service deployment, " *IEEE Journal on Selected Areas in Communications*, vo. 22, no. 1, 41–53, 2004.

[33] K. Franceschi, R. Lee, S. Zanakis, and D. Hinds, "Engaging group e-learning in virtual worlds, "*Journal of Management Information Systems*, vo. 26, no. 1, 73–100, 2009.

Permissions

The contributors of this book come from diverse backgrounds, making this book a truly international effort. This book will bring forth new frontiers with its revolutionizing research information and detailed analysis of the nascent developments around the world.

We would like to thank all the contributing authors for lending their expertise to make the book truly unique. They have played a crucial role in the development of this book. Without their invaluable contributions this book wouldn't have been possible. They have made vital efforts to compile up to date information on the varied aspects of this subject to make this book a valuable addition to the collection of many professionals and students.

This book was conceptualized with the vision of imparting up-to-date information and advanced data in this field. To ensure the same, a matchless editorial board was set up. Every individual on the board went through rigorous rounds of assessment to prove their worth. After which they invested a large part of their time researching and compiling the most relevant data for our readers.

The editorial board has been involved in producing this book since its inception. They have spent rigorous hours researching and exploring the diverse topics which have resulted in the successful publishing of this book. They have passed on their knowledge of decades through this book. To expedite this challenging task, the publisher supported the team at every step. A small team of assistant editors was also appointed to further simplify the editing procedure and attain best results for the readers.

Apart from the editorial board, the designing team has also invested a significant amount of their time in understanding the subject and creating the most relevant covers. They scrutinized every image to scout for the most suitable representation of the subject and create an appropriate cover for the book.

The publishing team has been an ardent support to the editorial, designing and production team. Their endless efforts to recruit the best for this project, has resulted in the accomplishment of this book. They are a veteran in the field of academics and their pool of knowledge is as vast as their experience in printing. Their expertise and guidance has proved useful at every step. Their uncompromising quality standards have made this book an exceptional effort. Their encouragement from time to time has been an inspiration for everyone.

The publisher and the editorial board hope that this book will prove to be a valuable piece of knowledge for researchers, students, practitioners and scholars across the globe.

List of Contributors

De Wang, Danesh Irani and Calton Pu
College of Computing, Georgia Institute of Technology, Atlanta, Georgia 30332-0765

Yu-Ru Lin
School of Information Sciences, University of Pittsburgh, Pittsburgh, PA 15260, USA

Drew Margolin
Department of Communication, Cornell University, Ithaca, NY 14850, USA

David Lazer
Political Science Department, Northeastern University, Boston, MA 02115, USA

Lakshmish Ramaswamy, Raga Sowmya Tummalapenta, Deepika Sethi and Kang Li
Computer Science Department, The University of Georgia, Athens, GA 30602, USA

Calton Pu
College of Computing, Georgia Institute of Technology, Atlanta, GA 30332, USA

Keith B. Frikken
Miami University, Oxford

Shumiao Wang and Mikhail J. Atallah
Purdue University, West Lafayette

Davide Alberto Albertini, Barbara Carminati and Elena Ferrari
DISTA, Università degli Studi dell'Insubria, Via Mazzini 5, Varese, Italy

Ingo Zinnikus, Xiaoqi Cao, Matthias Klusch, Christopher Krauss, Andreas Nonnengart, Torsten Spieldenner, Stefan Warwas and Philipp Slusallek
German Research Center for Artificial Intelligence GmbH, Stuhlsatzenhausweg 3, 66123 Saarbrücken, Germany

Sergiy Byelozyorov
Saarland University, Campus E1 1, 66123 Saarbrücken, Germany

Xiwei Wang
Department of Computer Science, Northeastern Illinois University, Chicago, Illinois 60625, USA

Jun Zhang
Department of Computer Science, University of Kentucky, Lexington, Kentucky 40506-0633, USA

Ruxin Dai
Department of Computer Science and Information Systems, University of Wisconsin River Falls, River Falls, Wisconsin 54022, USA

Pierre St Juste, Kyuho Jeong, Heungsik Eom and Renato Figueiredo
Advanced Computing and Information Systems Lab

Corey Baker
Wireless and Mobile Systems Lab Electrical and Computer Engineering, University of Florida, Gainesville, FL, 32611, USA

Zhe Wang and Naftaly H. Minsky
Rutgers University, Department of Computer Science

Mahadev Satyanarayanan
School of Computer Science, Carnegie Mellon University,

Vasanth Bala
IBM Research

Gloriana St. Clair and Erika Linke
University Libraries, Carnegie Mellon University

Jundong Chen, Ankunda R. Kiremire, Matthias R. Brust and Vir V. Phoha
Center for Secure Cyberspace, Louisiana Tech University, Ruston, LA 71270, USA

Alberto Castro-Hernández and Kathleen Swigger
Computer Science and Engineering Department, University of North Texas, Denton, Texas, 76203, USA

Mirna P. Ponce-Flores
Ingeniería en Tecnologías de la Información, Universidad Politécnica de Altamira, Altamira, Tamaulipas, Mexico

Nguyen Quoc Viet Hung, Nguyen Thanh Tam and Karl Aberer
École Polytechnique Fédérale de Lausanne

Zoltán Miklós
Université de Rennes

Prem Prakash Jayaraman, Charith Perera and Arkady Zaslavsky
CSIRO Computational Informatics, Canberra, Australia 2601

Dimitrios Georgakopoulos
School of Computer Science and Information Technology, RMIT University, GPO Box 2476, Melbourne VIC 3001

Carlos E. Rubio-Medrano and Gail-Joon Ahn
Arizona State University, 699 S. Mill Avenue, Tempe, Arizona, 85282, USA

Karsten Sohr
Universität Bremen, Am Fallturm 1, 28359 Bremen, Germany

Salvatore F. Pileggi
INRIA & UPMC-LIP6, Paris, France

Index

Printed in the USA
CPSIA information can be obtained
at www.ICGtesting.com
JSHW051431221024
72173JS00006B/1430